Londonderry
LONDONDERRY   ANTRIM

NORTHERN
IRELAND

TYRONE

BELFAST •

DOWN

ARMAGH

MONAGHAN

AVAN

Dundalk
LOUTH

MIDLANDS

EATH   MEATH

DUBLIN

KILDARE

OIS

WICKLOW

CARLOW

OUTHEAST
IRELAND

ILKENNY   WEXFORD

aterford   Wexford •

NORTHERN IRELAND
Pages 254–285

DUBLIN CITY CENTRE

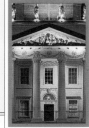

**NORTH OF
THE LIFFEY**
Pages 84–93

LIFFEY

SOUTHEAST
DUBLIN

D0964112

SOUTHWEST DUBLIN
Pages 72–83

SOUTHEAST DUBLIN
Pages 56–71

THE MIDLANDS
Pages 236–253

SOUTHEAST IRELAND
Pages 124–151

EYEWITNESS TRAVEL

IRELAND

EYEWITNESS TRAVEL

IRELAND

MAIN CONTRIBUTORS:
LISA GERARD-SHARP AND TIM PERRY

LONDON, NEW YORK,
MELBOURNE, MUNICH AND DELHI
www.dk.com

PROJECT EDITOR Ferdie McDonald
ART EDITOR Lisa Kosky
EDITORS Maggie Crowley, Simon Farbrother, Emily Hatchwell,
Seán O'Connell, Jane Simmonds
DESIGNERS Joy FitzSimmons, Jaki Grosvenor,
Katie Peacock, Jan Richter
RESEARCHERS John Breslin, Andrea Holmes
PICTURE RESEARCHERS Sue Mennell, Christine Rista
DTP DESIGNERS Samantha Borland, Adam Moore

CONTRIBUTORS
Una Carlin, Polly Phillimore, Susan Poole, Martin Walters

PHOTOGRAPHERS
Joe Cornish, Tim Daly, Alan Williams

ILLUSTRATORS
Draughtsman Maps, Maltings Partnership, Robbie Polley

Reproduced by Colourscan, Singapore
Printed and bound in China by Toppan Printing Co. (Shenzhen Ltd)

First American edition 1995
07 08 09 10 9 8 7 6 5 4 3 2 1
Published in the United States by DK Publishing,
Inc., 375 Hudson Street, New York, New York 10014

**Reprinted with revisions 1997, 1999, 2000, 2001,
2002, 2003, 2004, 2006, 2007**

Copyright © 1995, 2007 Dorling Kindersley Limited, London
A Penguin Company

ALL RIGHTS RESERVED UNDER INTERNATIONAL AND PAN-AMERICAN COPYRIGHT
CONVENTIONS. NO PART OF THIS PUBLICATION MAY BE REPRODUCED, STORED IN
A RETRIEVAL SYSTEM, OR TRANSMITTED IN ANY FORM OR BY ANY MEANS,
ELECTRONIC, MECHANICAL, PHOTOCOPYING, RECORDING OR OTHERWISE
WITHOUT THE PRIOR WRITTEN PERMISSION OF THE COPYRIGHT OWNER.

Published in Great Britain by Dorling Kindersley Limited.

ISSN 1542-1554
ISBN 978-0-75661-544-4

FLOORS ARE REFERRED TO THROUGHOUT IN ACCORDANCE WITH EUROPEAN USAGE,
I.E., THE "FIRST FLOOR" IS THE FLOOR ABOVE GROUND LEVEL.

Front cover main image: Inishmore, Aran Islands

**The information in this DK Eyewitness Travel Guide
is checked regularly.**
Every effort has been made to ensure that this book is as up-to-date as
possible at the time of going to press. Some details, however, such as
telephone numbers, opening hours, prices, gallery hanging
arrangements and travel information, are liable to change. The
publishers cannot accept responsibility for any consequences arising from
the use of this book, nor for any material on third-party websites, and
cannot guarantee that any website address in this book will be a
suitable source of travel information. We value the views and
suggestions of our readers highly. Please write to:
Publisher, DK Eyewitness Travel Guides,
Dorling Kindersley, 80 Strand, London, Great Britain WC2R 0RL.

CONTENTS

An evangelical symbol from the
Book of Kells *(see p64)*

INTRODUCING
IRELAND

DUBLIN AREA
BY AREA

Georgian doorway in Fitzwilliam
Square, Dublin *(see p68)*

Grazing cows at Spanish Point near Mizen Head *(see p167)*

TRAVELLERS' NEEDS

SURVIVAL GUIDE

Façade of a pub in Dingle *(see p157)*

IRELAND REGION BY REGION

Detail of the Chorus Gate at
Powerscourt *(see pp134–5)*

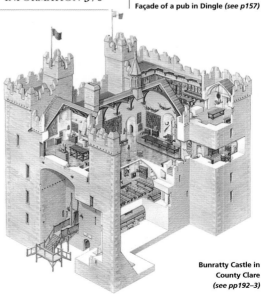

Bunratty Castle in
County Clare
(see pp192–3)

HOW TO USE THIS GUIDE

This guide helps you to get the most from your visit to Ireland. It provides both expert recommendations and detailed practical information. *Introducing Ireland* maps the country and sets it in its historical and cultural context. The seven regional chapters, plus *Dublin Area by Area*, contain descriptions of all the important sights, with maps, pictures and illustrations. Restaurant and hotel recommendations can be found in *Travellers' Needs*. The *Survival Guide* has tips on everything from the telephone system to transport both in the Republic and in Northern Ireland.

DUBLIN AREA BY AREA

Central Dublin is divided into three sightseeing areas. Each has its own chapter, which opens with a list of the sights described. A fourth chapter, *Further Afield*, covers the suburbs and County Dublin. Sights are numbered and plotted on an *Area Map*. The descriptions of each sight follow the map's numerical order, making sights easy to locate within the chapter.

Sights at a Glance lists the chapter's sights by category: Churches, Museums and Galleries, Historic Buildings, Parks and Gardens.

2 Street-by-Street Map
This gives a bird's-eye view of the key area in each chapter.

A suggested route for a walk is shown in red.

All pages relating to Dublin have red thumb tabs.

A locator map shows where you are in relation to other areas of the city centre.

1 Area Map
For easy reference, the sights are numbered and located on a map. Sights in the city centre are also shown on the Dublin Street Finder *on pages 118–19.*

Stars indicate the sights that no visitor should miss.

3 Detailed information
The sights in Dublin are described individually with addresses, telephone numbers and information on opening hours and admission charges.

Story boxes highlight noteworthy features of the sights.

1 Introduction
The landscape, history and character of each region is described here, showing how the area has developed over the centuries and what it offers to the visitor today.

IRELAND REGION BY REGION
Apart from Dublin, Ireland has been divided into seven regions, each of which has a separate chapter. The most interesting towns and places to visit in each area have been numbered on a *Regional Map*.

Each region of Ireland can be quickly identified by its colour coding, shown on the inside front cover.

2 Regional Map
This shows the road network and gives an illustrated overview of the whole region. All interesting places to visit are numbered and there are also useful tips on getting around the region by car and train.

Getting Around gives tips on travel within the region.

3 Detailed information
All the important towns and other places to visit are described individually. They are listed in order, following the numbering on the Regional Map. Within each town or city, there is detailed information on important buildings and other sights.

The Visitors' Checklist provides all the practical information you will need to plan your visit to all the top sights.

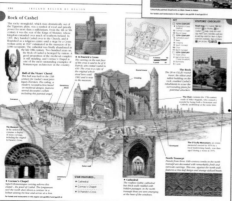

4 Ireland's top sights
These are given two or more full pages. Historic buildings are dissected to reveal their interiors. The most interesting towns or city centres are shown in a bird's-eye view, with sights picked out and described.

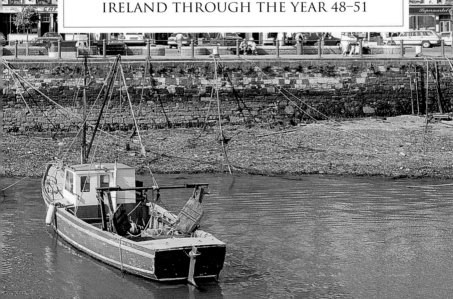

INTRODUCING IRELAND

DISCOVERING IRELAND

Ireland's popularity as a tourist destination is ensured by its profound cultural heritage, breathtaking scenery and famously easy-going lifestyle. Much of the joy of travelling around Ireland is the warmth of the people; their welcome rarely

Bust of St Patrick

feels forced. Celtic ruins, medieva forts and stately homes dot the landscape, giving the island a certain majesty. The chapters in this guide have been divided into eight colour-coded regions, each incorporating counties of the Republic or Northern Ireland.

DUBLIN

- **Historic Trinity College**
- **Celtic treasures at the National Museum**
- **Superb theatre & pubs**

Newly cosmopolitan Dublin, with most of its attractions within easy walking distance, has much to offer the visitor. **Trinity College**, founded in 1592 by Queen Elizabeth I, allows access to its spectacular Old Library, which houses the medieval Book of Kells *(see pp62–4)*. The **National Museum** *(see pp66–7)*, just a few blocks from the college, offers a fascinating insight into Ireland's past, while the **National Gallery** *(see pp70–71)* presents excellent exhibitions – particularly in the stunning Millennium Wing.

Theatre in Dublin is top notch with plays by the Irish greats staged at venues such as the **Abbey** *(see p88)*, which was founded by WB Yeats.

The lively district of **Temple Bar** *(see p78)* offers a flavour of traditional Irish "crack", with a host of busy bars and

The vivid greens surrounding the Killarney Lakes, County Kerry

restaurants. Keep in mind however that this city is far more expensive than anywhere else in the country.

SOUTHEAST IRELAND

- **Powerscourt**
- **Wicklow Mountains**
- **Fine beaches**

The "sunny southeast" is one of the most popular holiday regions in the country, with summer weather more reliable than elsewhere in Ireland. The port town **Rosslare** *(see p151)* boasts a fine 9.5-km (6-mile) beach and an excellent golf course nearby.

Located at the foot of the Great Sugar Loaf Mountain, the extensive grounds at **Powerscourt** *(see pp134–5)* are among the most beautiful in the country, with the stately Italian Garden cascading down landscaped terraces.

Glendalough *(see pp140–41)* in the Wicklow Mountains features the atmospheric ruins of a once flourishing monastic settlement established by St Kevin during the 6th century.

CORK & KERRY

- **Cork and the Blarney Stone**
- **Colourful fishing villages**
- **Lakes of Killarney**

This region, one of the country's most picturesque, has a long indented coastline which blends with the highest peaks in Ireland. Hundreds of miles of walking and cycling routes crisscross the area, including the celebrated **Ring of Kerry** *(see pp164–5)* which encircles the Iveragh Peninsula. The clear **Lakes of Killarney** *(see pp162–3)* are nestled into the lush hills of central Kerry and are one of the area's most popular holiday destinations.

Cork is a small, pretty city of riverside quays and winding alleys, enlivened by an exciting cultural buzz *(see pp174–7)*. Nearby, at the ruins of **Blarney Castle** *(see p171)*, visitors queue to kiss the Blarney Stone, said to bless them with the gift of the gab. To the east of Cork, the **Old Midleton Distillery** *(see p179)* offers tours and tastings that no whiskey drinker should miss.

Crossing the River Liffey over Ha'penny Bridge, Dublin

THE LOWER SHANNON

- **The rugged Burren**
- **Majestic Cliffs of Moher**
- **Early Christian settlements**

The River Shannon runs through the region, dominated by barren limestone and wet marshy land, before empty-ing into the sea. Few trees grow on the vast **Burren**, an atmospheric and otherworldly landscape *(see pp186–8)*. The sudden 200-m (650-ft) drop of the **Cliffs of Moher**, shrouded in mist and battered by Atlantic gales, is one of the most dramatic stretches of coastline in the country *(see p184)*. Built on a strategic hill-ock, the 5th-century **Rock of Cashel** was first a stronghold of the Munster kings and later of the Church *(see pp196–7)*.

Poulnabrone Dolmen, perched on the limestone plateau of the Burren

THE WEST OF IRELAND

- **Unspoilt Aran Islands**
- **Connemara National Park**
- **Galway's infectious charm**

The West of Ireland is a region of contradictions, with farming areas, rugged coast-lines and cosmopolitan towns. The Irish language (Gaelic) is still spoken in many areas and the region is a haven for traditional music and dancing. The **Aran Islands** *(see pp214–15)* offer a chance to experience unspoilt Ireland; island life has changed little in the last hundred years. **Connemara National Park** *(see p208)* encompasses four of the Twelve Bens, which rise high above the surround-ing heathland. This dazzling

Brightly painted shop fronts in the centre of Galway, West of Ireland

landscape provides habitats for peregrin falcons and semi-wild Connemara ponies.

Lively **Galway** is Ireland's fastest growing city, yet it somehow manages to retain much of its medieval charm *(see pp210–11)*.

NORTHWEST IRELAND

- **Deserted beaches and rugged coasts**
- **Prehistoric Celtic sites**

Perched at the furthest reaches of the island, the northwest has remained isolated from events, retaining a large popu-lation of Gaelic speakers. The dramatic landscape includes the breathtaking cliffs of **Slieve League**, best visited at sunset when they are streaked with red *(see p229)*. The large herd of deer is reason enough to visit **Glenveagh National Park and Castle** *(see pp216–17)*, but there's also the stunning Lough Veagh and, just outside the park, the eerily forbidding valley, Poisoned Glen.

THE MIDLANDS

- **Newgrange's ancient grave**
- **Ruins of Clonmacnoise**

The pastures of the Midlands are the cradle of Irish civiliza-tion. Pre-dating the Celts, the mysterious passage graves of **Newgrange** were built around 3200 BC *(see pp246–7)*. The once thriving monastery of **Clonmacnoise** is now in ghostly ruins *(see pp250–51)*.

Elegant **Birr** *(see p253)* com-prises a Georgian layout and beautifully restored houses.

NORTHERN IRELAND

- **Giant's Causeway**
- **Magnificent lakeland**
- **Belfast's exciting nightlife**

For many years, Northern Ireland has been associated with sectarian conflict. Finally visitors are rediscovering the region, which encapsulates the **Mountains of Mourne** *(see p284)* and Ireland's biggest lake, **Lough Neagh** *(see p274)*.

Belfast *(see pp276–9)* is a fascinating city, where the political loyalties of its citizens are preserved in the murals of West Belfast. The Cathedral Quarter is a cultural hotspot, with culinary and architectural gems adorning its streets.

The **Giant's Causeway** *(see pp262–3)*, a volcanic forma-tion of basalt columns, is an unusual sight, which adds to the rugged beauty of the **Causeway Coast** *(see p261)*.

The crumbling remains of Dunluce Castle in Northern Ireland

Putting Ireland on the Map

The island of Ireland covers an area of 84,430 sq km (32,598 sq miles). Lying in the Atlantic Ocean to the northwest of mainland Europe, it is separated from Great Britain by the Irish Sea. The Republic of Ireland takes up 85 per cent of the island, with a population of 3.9 milllion. Northern Ireland, part of the United Kingdom, has 1.7 million people. Dublin is the capital of the Republic and has good international communications.

Europe

Most visitors to Ireland come through Dublin, either by air or on the ferry to Dun Laoghaire or Dublin Port. The main ferry routes are from Wales, Scotland and France. There are also international flights to Shannon, Belfast and Cork airports. Flights from European capitals are usually non-stop to Dublin, but there is a greater choice of routes and airlines via Great Britain.

0 kilometres   100

0 miles   50

KEY

✈	Airport
⛴	Ferry port
⛴	Fast ferry port
═	Motorway
═	Major road
─	Railway line

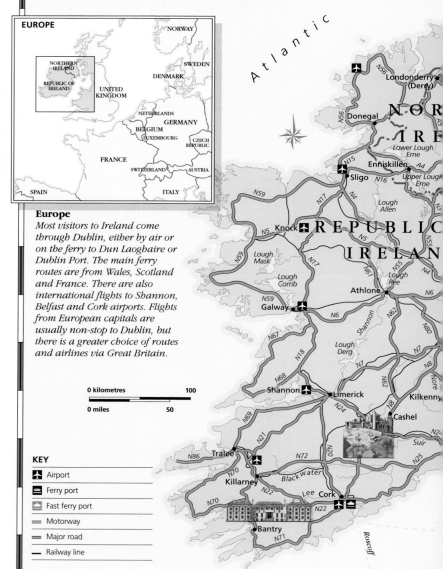

GREATER DUBLIN

Swords

Malahide

N3

N2

Dublin Airport

N1

Finglas

M50

Glasnevin

Royal Canal

Marino

Howth

Liffey

N4

Lucan

Kilmainham

Dublin

Grand Canal

Clondalkin

N7

Ballsbridge

Dublin Bay

Rathmines

Dundrum

Blackrock

N81

N11

Dun Laoghaire

0 km 5

0 miles 5

Greater Dublin

Nearly one third of the Republic's population lives in Dublin. The city centre has become very congested in recent years, but access to the ports and airport is still relatively easy.

Islay

SCOTLAND

A83

A82

Glasgow

North Channel

Arran

Campbeltown

Troon

A77

Ballycastle

Coleraine

A37

A6

A29

A26

A2

Cairnryan

A36

Larne

A75

Stranraer

ERN

A26

AND

A1

M1

Lough Neagh

Belfast

ENGLAND

A44

A3

A1

A2

magh

N2

Isle of Man

A595

A65

Newry

Douglas

Dundalk

M6

Heysham

OF

Irish Sea

Fleetwood

M62

Manchester

Boyne

N3

M1

Liverpool

M62

M56

DUBLIN

N7

Mostyn

M6

Dun Laoghaire

Holyhead

A5

A55

A5

M54

Liffey

N11

N9

A487

A470

Severn

Carlow

Slaney

N80

Cherbourg

M50

N25

St George's Channel

Wexford

aterford

Roslare

WALES

A487

Fishguard

M4

M5

A40

A477

Pembroke

Swansea

M4

CARDIFF

Bristol

Roscoff/Cherbourg

Bristol Channel

M5

A PORTRAIT OF IRELAND

Many visitors see Ireland as a lush green island, full of thatched cottages, pubs, music, wit and poetry. Like all stereotypes, this image of the country has a basis in truth and the tourist industry helps sustain it. The political and economic reality is, of course, rather less ideal, but the relaxed good humour of the people still makes Ireland a most welcoming place to visit.

Ireland, at least for the time being, is a divided island. History and religion created two hostile communities in North and South. The IRA ceasefire of 1997 and the subsequent Good Friday Agreement brought new hope, however. John Hume of the SDLP and David Trimble of the Ulster Unionist Party were jointly awarded the Nobel prize for peace for their work in the peace process, and the inaugural meeting of the Northern Ireland Assembly took place on 1 July 1998.

Ireland has had more than its fair share of wars and disasters, culminating in the Great Famine of 1845–8, since when poverty and emigration have been part of the Irish way of life. More people of Irish descent live in the USA than in Ireland itself. Suffering and martyrdom in the cause of independence also play an important part in the Irish consciousness. The heroine of WB Yeats's play *Cathleen ni Houlihan* inspires young men to lay down their lives for Ireland. Her image appeared on the first banknote issued by the newly created Irish Free State in 1922.

Cathleen ni Houlihan, personification of Ireland

Yet, the Irish retain their easy-going attitude to life, with a young, highly educated population working hard to make its way in today's European Union. In the Republic, over 50 per cent of the population is under 30.

Façade of Trinity College, Dublin, the Republic's most prestigious university

◁ Thatching a traditional cottage in Adare, County Limerick

Young first communicant in County Kerry

Despite its high birth rate, rural Ireland is sparsely populated. The Industrial Revolution of the 19th century barely touched the South and for much of the 20th century the Republic seemed an old-fashioned place, poorer than almost all its fellow members of the European Union.

ECONOMIC DEVELOPMENT

In recent years, tax breaks and low inflation have attracted more foreign investment to the Republic and many multinationals, especially computing and chemical companies, have subsidiaries here. Ireland joined the single European currency on 1 January 1999, and the Republic's economy continues to grow while unemployment is falling. Another important industry is tourism. The South receives over 3 million visitors a year and visitors to the North are now steadily increasing.

Traditionally, Northern Ireland had far more industry than the South, but during the 25 years of the Troubles, old heavy

Traditional Irish dancing

industries, such as shipbuilding, declined and new investors were scared away. However, the election of members to the new Northern Ireland Assembly in June 1998 ushered in a new political and economic era for the North. For both parts of Ireland, geography is still a barrier to prosperity. Located on the periphery of Europe, the island is isolated from its main markets and thus saddled with high transport costs. Fortunately, subsidies from the EU have helped improve the infrastructure in the Republic.

RELIGION AND POLITICS

The influence of Catholicism is strong. In the Republic, the Church runs most schools, along with some hospitals and social services. Irish Catholicism runs the gamut from missionary zeal to simple piety. According to some

Pavement artist on O'Connell Street, Dublin

estimates, over 90 per cent of the population goes to Mass. Religion plays an important role in the politics of the Republic and moral conservatism is evident in attitudes to divorce, contraception, abortion and homosexuality.

The election of liberal lawyer Mary Robinson as President in 1990, the first woman to hold the post, was seen as a sign of more enlightened times by many people, an attitude reinforced by the election of Mary McAleese as her successor in 1998. A new political climate has favoured the quiet spread of feminism

Traditional farming: a field of haystacks overlooking Clew Bay, County Mayo

and challenged the old paternalism of Irish politics, not only in social issues but also in helping break down the clannish cronyism of the traditional parties Fianna Fáil and Fine Gael.

LANGUAGE AND CULTURE

Ireland was a Gaelic-speaking nation until the 16th century, since when the language has declined. Today, however, the Republic is officially bilingual. Knowledge of Irish is a requirement for university entrance and a career in the public sector, although only 11 per cent of the population speaks Gaelic fluently.

Irish culture, on the other hand, is in no danger of being eroded. The people have a genuine love of old folk legends and epic poetry and songs. Festivals, whether dedicated to St Patrick or James Joyce, pubs or oysters, salmon or sailing, are an important part of community life. Music is a national passion - from the rock of U2 and the Cranberries to the folk music of Clannad, the Chieftains and Mary Black.

Connemara pony show

Another national passion is horse racing. Ireland's breeders and trainers are masters of their trade and enjoy astonishing international success for such a small country. Other sports are followed with equal intensity, as witnessed during the 1994 football World Cup. Drinking also plays an important part in Irish culture: social life centres on the pub and the "crack" (convivial chat) to be enjoyed there. With smoking now banned in pubs in the Republic, many wonder whether pubs and the life surrounding them will collapse. Given the attachment to Guinness, gossip and music, this is extremely unlikely.

Matt Molloy's pub in Westport, County Mayo

The Landscape and Wildlife of Ireland

The landscape is one of the Ireland's greatest attractions. It varies from bogs and lakes in the central lowlands to mountains and rocky islands in the west. Between these two extremes, the island has abundant lush, green pastureland, the result of plentiful rainfall, but little natural woodland. Parts of the far west, where the land is farmed by traditional methods, are havens for threatened wildlife, including the corncrake, which needs undisturbed hayfields in which to nest.

Corncrake

THE FAUNA OF IRELAND

Natterjack toad

Many animals (including snakes) did not make it to Ireland before the Irish Sea rose after the Ice Age. Other surprising absentees are the mole, weasel and common toad (the natterjack, however, can be seen). The wood mouse is the only small native rodent, but the once common red squirrel has now been virtually taken over by the grey.

ROCKY COASTS

The Dingle Peninsula *(see pp158–9)* is part of a series of rocky promontories and inlets created when sea levels rose at the end of the Ice Age. Cliffs and islands offer many sites for sea birds, with some enormous colonies, such as the gannets of Little Skellig *(pp164–5)*. The chough still breeds on cliffs in the extreme west. Elsewhere in Europe, this rare species of crow is declining in numbers.

Chough

Thrift *grows in cushion-like clumps, producing its papery pink flowerheads from spring right through to autumn.*

Sea campion *is a low-growing plant. Its large white flowers brighten up many a cliff top and seaside shingle bank.*

LAKES, RIVERS AND WETLANDS

This watery landscape around Lough Oughter is typical of the lakelands of the River Erne *(pp270–71)*. Rainfall is high throughout the year, which results in many wetlands, especially along the Shannon *(p185)* and the Erne. The elegant great crested grebe breeds mainly on the larger lakes in the north.

Great crested grebe

Water lobelia *grows in the shallows of stony lakes. Its leaves remain below the water, while the pale lilac flowers are borne on leafless stems above the surface.*

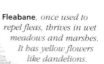

Fleabane, *once used to repel fleas, thrives in wet meadows and marshes. It has yellow flowers like dandelions.*

Red deer *have been introduced into many areas, notably the hills of Connemara.*

Grey seals *are a common sight in the waters off the Atlantic coast, feeding on fish and occasionally on sea birds.*

Pine martens, *though mainly nocturnal, may be spotted in daytime during the*

Otters *are more likely to be seen in the shallow seas off rocky coasts than in rivers and lakes, though they live in both habitats.*

MOUNTAIN AND BLANKET BOG

Wheatear

As well as the raised bogs of the central lowlands *(p252)*, much of Ireland's mountainous ground, particularly in the west, is covered by blanket bog such as that seen here in Connemara *(pp206–209)*. On drier upland sites this grades into heather moor and poor grassland. The wheatear, which inhabits rocky scree and heathland, is a restless bird with an unmistakable white rump. It flits about, dipping and bobbing in pursuit of flies.

Bog myrtle *is an aromatic shrub, locally common in Ireland's bogs. Its leaves can be used to flavour drinks.*

Bogbean, *a plant found in fens and wet bogland, has attractive white flowers splashed with pink. Its leaves were once used as a cure for boils.*

PASTURELAND

Rook

Rolling pastureland with grazing livestock, as seen here in the foothills of the Wicklow Mountains *(pp138–9)*, is a very common sight throughout Ireland. The traditional farming methods employed in many parts of the island (particularly in the west) are of great benefit to wildlife. Rooks, for example, which feed on worms and insect larvae found in pasture, are very common.

Meadow vetchling *uses its tendrils to clamber up grasses and other plants. It has clusters of pretty pale yellow flowers.*

Marsh thistle *is a common flower of wet meadows and damp woodland. It is a tall species with small, purple flowerheads.*

Architecture in Ireland

Window of an Irish cottage

Ireland's turbulent history has done incalculable damage to its architectural heritage. Cromwell's forces, in particular, destroyed scores of castles, monasteries and towns in their three-year campaign against the Irish in the mid-17th century. However, many fascinating buildings and sites remain, with Iron Age forts being the earliest surviving settlements. Christianity in Ireland gave rise to monasteries, churches and round towers; conflict between Anglo-Norman barons and Irish chieftains created castles and tower houses. The later landlord class built luxurious country mansions, while their labourers had to make do with basic, one-roomed cottages.

LOCATOR MAP

☐ Iron Age forts

☐ Round towers

☐ Tower houses

☐ Georgian country houses

IRON AGE FORTS

Thatched hut   **Entrance**   **Souterrain**

Ring forts (raths) *were Iron Age farmsteads enclosed by an earth bank, a timber fence and a ditch to protect against cattle-raiders. Inside, people lived in huts with a souterrain (underground passage) for storage and refuge. Some were in use as late as the 17th century, but all you can usually see today are low circular mounds. In the west, stone was used for cahers (stone ring forts) and promontory forts (semi-circular forts built on cliff tops using the sea as a natural defence).*

ROUND TOWER

Lookout window   **Conical roof**

Round towers, *often over 30m (100 ft) tall, were built between the 10th and 12th centuries on monastic sites. They were bell towers, used as places of refuge and to store valuable manuscripts. The entrance, which could be as high as 4 m (13 ft) above ground, was reached by a ladder that was hauled up from the inside. Other moveable ladders connected the tower's wooden floors.*

Wooden floor

Moveable ladder

TOWER HOUSES

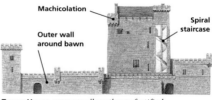

Machicolation

Spiral staircase

Outer wall around bawn

Tower House *were small castles or fortified residences built between the 15th and 17th centuries. The tall square house was often surrounded by a stone wall forming a bawn (enclosure), used for defence and as a cattle pen. Machicolations (projecting parapets from which to drop missiles) were sited at the top of the house.*

COTTAGE

One-roomed cottages, *thatched or slate-roofed, are still a common feature of the Irish landscape. Built of local stone with small windows to retain heat, the cottages were inhabited by farm workers or smallholders.*

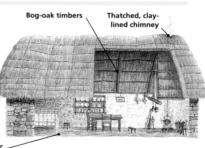

Bog-oak timbers   **Thatched, clay-lined chimney**

Clay floor

IRON AGE FORTS

① Staigue Fort *p164*
② Dún Aonghasa *p214*
③ Craggaunowen *p190*
④ Grianán of Ailigh *pp226–7*
⑤ Hill of Tara *p248*

ROUND TOWERS

⑥ Kilmacduagh *p212*
⑦ Ardmore *p145*
⑧ Clonmacnoise *pp250–51*
⑨ Devenish Island *p271*
⑩ Kilkenny *p144*
⑪ Glendalough *pp140–41*

TOWER HOUSES

⑫ Aughnanure Castle *p209*
⑬ Thoor Ballylee *pp212–13*
⑭ Knappogue Castle *p189*
⑮ Blarney Castle *p171*
⑯ Donegal Castle *p230*

GEORGIAN COUNTRY HOUSES

⑰ Strokestown Park House *pp218–19*
⑱ Castle Coole *p272*
⑲ Emo Court *p253*
⑳ Russborough House *pp132–3*
㉑ Castletown House *pp130–31*

The well-preserved round tower at Ardmore

GEORGIAN COUNTRY HOUSES

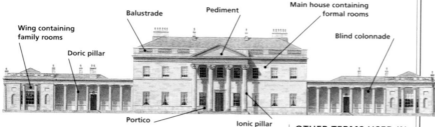

Wing containing family rooms

Doric pillar

Balustrade

Pediment

Main house containing formal rooms

Blind colonnade

Portico

Ionic pillar

Between the 1720s and 1800, *prosperous landlords commissioned palatial country mansions in the Palladian and Neo-Classical styles popular in England over that period. Castle Coole (above) has a Palladian layout, with the main house in the centre and a colonnade on either side leading to a small pavilion. The Neo-Classical influence can be seen in the unadorned façade and the Doric columns of the colonnades. Noted architects of Irish country houses include Richard Castle (1690–1751) and James Wyatt (1746–1813).*

STUCCO

Stucco (decorative relief plasterwork), popular in the 18th century, is found in many Georgian country houses as well as town houses and public buildings. The Italian Francini brothers were particularly sought after for their intricate stuccowork (notably at Castletown and Russborough) as was Irish craftsman Michael Stapleton (Trinity College, Dublin and Dublin Writers Museum).

Trompe l'oeil detail at Emo Court

Ceiling at Dublin Writers Museum

Stucco portrait at Castletown House

Stuccowork at Russborough House

OTHER TERMS USED IN THIS GUIDE

Beehive hut: Circular stone building with a domed roof created by corbelling (laying a series of stones so that each projects beyond the one below).

Cashel: Stone ring fort.

Crannog: Defensive, partly artificial island on a lake. Huts were often built on crannogs (*see p33*).

Curtain wall: Outer wall of a castle, usually incorporating towers at intervals.

Hiberno-Romanesque: Style of church architecture with rounded arches highly decorated with geometric designs and human and animal forms. Also called Irish-Romanesque.

Motte and bailey: Raised mound (motte) topped with a wooden tower, surrounded by a heavily fenced space (bailey). Built by the Normans in the 12th century, they were quickly erected in time of battle.

Tympanum: Decorated space over a door or window.

Literary Ireland

For a land the size of Ireland to have produced four Nobel prizewinners in Shaw, Yeats, Beckett and Séamus Heaney is a considerable feat. Yet it is not easy to speak of an "Irish literary tradition" as the concept embraces rural and urban experiences, Protestant and Catholic traditions and the Gaelic and English languages. Irish fiction today, as in the past, is characterized by a sense of community and history, a love of storytelling and a zest for language.

A first edition of *Ulysses*

WB Yeats – Ireland's most famous poet

The Blasket Islands, which provided inspiration for several writers

Wilde, who entered Oxford University in 1874 and later became the darling of London society with plays such as *The Importance of Being Earnest*. George Bernard Shaw *(see p100)*, writer of *St Joan* and *Pygmalion*, also made London his home. This dramatist, critic, socialist and pacifist continued to write until well into the 20th century.

GAELIC LITERATURE

Irish literature proclaims itself the oldest vernacular literature in Western Europe, dating back to early monastic times when Celtic folklore and sagas such as the epics of Cúchulainn *(see p26)* were written down for the first time. The disappearance of Gaelic literature followed the demise, in the 17th century, of the Irish aristocracy for whom it was written. Gaelic literature has had several revivals. Peig Sayers is famous for her accounts of the harsh life on the Blasket Islands *(see p158)* in the early 20th century.

Novelist Maria Edgeworth

ANGLO-IRISH LITERATURE

The collapse of Gaelic culture and the Protestant Ascendancy led to English being the dominant language. Most literature was based around the privileged classes.

An early Anglo-Irish writer was satirist Jonathan Swift *(see p82)*, author of *Gulliver's Travels*, who was born in Dublin in 1667 of English parents. Anglo-Irish literature was strong in drama, the entertainment of the cultured classes, and owed little to Irish settings or sensibilities. By the 1700s, Ireland was producing an inordinate number of leading playwrights, many of whom were more at home in London. These included Oliver Goldsmith, remembered for his comedy *She Stoops to Conquer*, and Richard Brinsley Sheridan, whose plays include *The School for Scandal*. Near the end of the century, Maria Edgeworth set a precedent with novels such as *Castle Rackrent*, based on the class divide in Irish society.

The 19th century saw an exodus to England of Irish playwrights, including Oscar

Playwright George Bernard Shaw

20TH-CENTURY WRITERS

In 1898, WB Yeats and Lady Gregory founded Dublin's Abbey Theatre *(see p88)*. Its opening, in 1904, heralded the Irish Revival, which focused on national and local themes. Playwright John Millington Synge drew inspiration from a love of the Aran Islands and Irish folklore, but the "immoral language" of his *Playboy of the Western World* caused a riot when first performed at the Abbey Theatre. Along with contemporaries, like Sean O'Casey and WB Yeats, Synge influenced subsequent generations of Irish writers, including novelist Seán O'Faolain, humorous writer and columnist Flann O'Brien, and hard-drinking, quarrelsome playwright Brendan Behan. The literary revival also produced many notable poets in the mid-20th century such as the gifted Patrick Kavanagh and Belfast-born Louis MacNeice, often considered to be one of the finest poets of his generation.

The writer Brendan Behan enjoying the company in a Dublin pub

Caricature of protesters at Dublin's Abbey Theatre in 1907

THREE LITERARY GIANTS

From the mass of talent to emerge in Irish literature, three figures stand out as visionaries in their fields. WB Yeats *(see p233)* spent half his life outside Ireland but is forever linked to its rural west. A writer of wistful, melancholic poetry, he was at the forefront of the Irish Revival, helping forge a new national cultural identity. James Joyce *(see p90)* was another trailblazer of Irish literature – his complex narrative and stream of consciousness techniques influenced the development of the modern novel. *Ulysses* describes a day in the life of Joyce's beloved Dublin and shaped the work of generations of writers. Bloomsday, which is named after one of the novel's characters, Leopold Bloom, is still celebrated annually in the city. The last of the three literary giants, novelist and playwright Samuel Beckett *(see p62)*, was another of Dublin's sons, though he later emigrated to France. His themes of alienation, despair, and the futility of human existence pervade his best-known plays, *Waiting for Godot* and *Endgame*.

The poet Patrick Kavanagh celebrating Bloomsday

CONTEMPORARY WRITERS

Ireland's proud literary tradition is today upheld by a stream of talented writers from both North and South. Among the finest are Cork-born William Trevor, regarded as a master of the short story, and Brian Moore, whose stories of personal and political disillusionment are often based in his native Belfast. Similarly, Dubliner Roddy Doyle mines his working-class origins in novels such as *The Snapper* and *Paddy Clarke Ha Ha Ha*. Other established Irish writers are Brian Friel and Edna O'Brien. Out of Ireland's contemporary poets, the Ulster-born writers Séamus Heaney and Derek Mahon are considered among the most outstanding.

IRELAND IN THE MOVIES

Ireland has long been fertile ground for the world's film makers, and its people have been the subjects of major films, notably *The Crying Game* (1992), *In the Name of the Father* (1994) and *Michael Collins* (1996). Another popular film was *The Commitments* (1991). Filmed on location in and around Dublin with an all-Irish cast, it was based on a novel by Roddy Doyle. More recently, parts of Co Wexford doubled as the beach heads of Normandy in Steven Spielberg's World War II epic *Saving Private Ryan* (1997).

Cast of *The Commitments*, written by Roddy Doyle

The Music of Ireland

An Irish jig

Ireland is the only country in the world to have a musical instrument – the harp – as its national emblem. In this land, famous for its love of music, modern forms such as country-and-western and rock flourish, but it is traditional music that captures the essence of the country. Whether you are listening to Gaelic love songs that date back to medieval times or 17th- and 18th-century folk songs with their English and Scottish influences, the music is unmistakably Irish. Dance is an equally important aspect of Irish traditional music, and some of the most popular airs are derived from centuries-old reels, jigs and hornpipes. Nowadays these are mainly performed at *fleadhs* (festivals) and *ceilís* (dances).

Turlough O'Carolan *(1670– 1738) is the most famous Irish harper. The blind musician travelled the country playing his songs to both rich and poor. Many of O'Carolan's melodies, such as* The Lamentation of Owen O'Neill, *still survive.*

Piano accordion

The *bodhrán* is a hand-held goatskin drum that is usually played with a small stick. It is particularly effective when accompanying the flute.

Flute

John F McCormack *(1884–1945) was an Irish tenor who toured America to great acclaim during the early part of the 20th century. His best-loved recordings were arias by Mozart. Another popular tenor was Derry-born Josef Locke. A singer of popular ballads in the 1940s and '50s, he was the subject of the 1992 film* Hear My Song.

Two-row button accordion

THE CURRENT MUSIC SCENE

Mary Black

Ireland today is a melting pot of musical styles. The resurgence of Irish traditional music has produced many highly respected musicians, such as the pipe-players Liam Ó Floin and Paddy Keenan from Dublin, while groups like the Chieftains and the Fureys have gained worldwide fame by melding old with new. Ireland is also firmly placed on the rock'n'roll map, thanks to singers such as Van Morrison in the 1970s and later bands like Thin Lizzy and the Boomtown Rats. The most famous rock band to come out of Ireland is Dublin's U2 who, in the 1980s, became one of the world's most popular groups. Other international successes include singers Enya, Mary Black and Sinéad O'Connor; and, more recently, bands like the Cranberries and the Corrs.

Bono of U2

Traditional Irish dancing *is currently enjoying renewed popularity. From the 17th century the social focus in rural areas was the village dance held every Sunday. From these gatherings, Irish dancing became popular.*

LIVE TRADITIONAL MUSIC

Wherever you go in Ireland, you won't be far from a pub with live music. For the Irish traditional musician, there are few set rules – the improvisational nature of the music means that no two performances of any piece are ever likely to be the same.

Violins, or fiddles, can either be tucked under the chin or held against the upper arm, shoulder or chest.

The New National Song—

ERIN Remember 1916

Copyright date 3rd 1913

PRICE 2 NET

Published by
QUINN & COMPANY,
13 UPPER ABBEY ST.,
DUBLIN.

Irish folk songs, *such as this one about the 1916 Easter Rising, tend to have a patriotic theme. But some of the most powerful songs have been written not just about the national struggle, but also about hardship, emigration and the longing for the homeland.*

TRADITIONAL INSTRUMENTS

There is no set line-up in traditional Irish bands. The fiddle is probably the most common instrument used. Like the music, some instruments have Celtic origins – the uillean pipes are related to the bagpipes played in Scotland and Brittany today.

The melodeon *is a basic version of the button accordion. Both these instruments are better suited to Irish music than the piano accordion.*

The uillean pipes *are similar to bagpipes and are generally considered to be one of the main instruments in Irish traditional music.*

The harp *has been played in Ireland since the 10th century. In recent years, there has been a keen revival of harp playing in Irish traditional music.*

The banjo *comes from the Deep South of the US and adds a new dimension to the sound of traditional bands.*

Tin whistle

Flute

The flute and tin whistle *are among the most common instruments used in traditional Irish music. The latter is often called the penny whistle.*

The violin *is called a fiddle by most musicians. The style of playing and sound produced varies from region to region.*

Ireland's Celtic Heritage

Stone carving on Boa Island

Ireland's rich tradition of storytelling embraces a folk heritage that abounds with myths and superstitions. Some stories have been in written form since the 8th century, but most originated over 2,000 years ago when druids passed on stories orally from one generation to the next. Like the Gaelic language itself, many of Ireland's legends have links with those of ancient Celtic races throughout Europe. As well as the heroic deeds and fearless warriors of mythology, Irish folklore is also rich in tales of fairies, leprechauns, banshees and other supernatural beings.

The formidable Queen Maeve of Connaught

Part of the 2,300-year-old Gundestrup Cauldron unearthed in Denmark, which depicts Cúchulainn's triumph in the Cattle Raid of Cooley

CUCHULAINN

The most famous warrior in Irish mythology is Cúchulainn. At the age of seven, going by the name of Setanta, he killed the savage hound of Culainn the Smith by slaying it with a hurling stick (one of the first times the sport of hurling is mentioned in folklore). Culainn was upset at the loss so Setanta volunteered to guard the house,

earning himself the new name of Cúchulainn, meaning the hound of Culainn.

Before he went into battle, Cúchulainn swelled to magnificent proportions, turned different colours and one of his eyes grew huge. His greatest victory was in the "Cattle Raid of Cooley" when Queen Maeve of Connaught sent her troops to capture the coveted prize bull of Ulster. Cúchulainn learned of the plot and defeated them

single-handedly. However, Queen Maeve took revenge on Cúchulainn by using sorcerers to lure him to his death. Today, in Dublin's GPO (see p89), a statue of Cúchulainn commemorates the heroes of the 1916 Easter Rising.

FINN MACCOOL

The warrior Finn MacCool is the most famous leader of the Fianna, an elite band of troops chosen for their strength and valour and who defended Ireland from foreign forces. Finn was not only strong and bold but also possessed the powers of a seer, and could obtain great wisdom by putting his thumb in his mouth and sucking on it. When they were not at war, the Fianna spent their time hunting. Finn had a hound called Bran which stood almost as high as himself and is said to be the original ancestor of the breed known today as the Irish wolfhound. Many of the

FAIRIES, LEPRECHAUNS AND BANSHEES

The diminutive figure of the leprechaun

The existence of spirits, and in particular the "little people", plays a large part in Irish folklore. Centuries ago, it was believed that fairies lived under mounds of earth, or "fairy raths", and that touching one of these tiny figures brought bad luck. The most famous of the "little people" is the leprechaun. Legend has it that if you caught one of these, he would lead you to a crock of gold, but take your eyes off him and he would vanish into thin air. The banshee was a female spirit whose wailing presence outside a house was said to signal the imminent death of someone within.

A banshee with long flowing hair

Fianna possessed supernatural powers and often ventured into the life beyond, known as the Otherworld. Among these was Finn's son Ossian who was not only a formidable warrior, like his father, but was also renowned as a wise and knowledgeable poet. Through time, Finn has come to be commonly portrayed as a giant. Legend has it that he constructed the Giant's Causeway in County Antrim *(see pp262–3)*.

A 19th-century engraving of Finn MacCool dressed for battle

THE CHILDREN OF LIR

One of the saddest tales in Irish folklore involves King Lir, who so adored his four children that their stepmother was driven wild with jealousy. One day she took the children to a lake and cast a spell on them, turning them into white swans confined to the waters of Ireland for 900 years. However, as soon as she had done the deed, she became racked with guilt and bestowed upon them the gift of exquisite song. The

The children of King Lir being turned into white swans

king then decreed that no swan in Ireland should be killed – an act which is still illegal today. The end of the children's 900-year ordeal coincided with the coming of Christianity. They regained human form but were wizened and weak. They died soon afterwards, but not before being baptized.

SAINT BRENDAN

Brendan the Navigator, like many other 6th-century monks, travelled widely. It is known that although he lived in western Ireland he visited Wales, Scotland and France. It is likely, though, that his most famous journey is fictitious. This story tells of a shipload of monks who, after seven years of all kinds of strange encounters designed to test their faith, found the Land of Promise. It is essentially a Christian retelling of the common tales of the Celtic Otherworld. The Feast of St Brendan on 16 May is celebrated in Kerry by the climbing of Mount Brandon.

Engraving showing St Brendan and his monks encountering a siren

ORIGINS OF IRISH PLACE NAMES

The names of many of Ireland's cities, towns and villages today are largely based on ancient Gaelic terms for prominent local landmarks, some of which no longer exist. Here are just a few elements of the place names the traveller may come across.

The fort on the Rock of Cashel that gives the town its name

Ar, ard – *high, height*
Ass, ess – *waterfall*
A, ah, ath – *ford*
Bal, bally – *town*
Beg – *small*
Ben – *peak, mountain*
Carrick, carrig – *rock*
Cashel – *stone fort*
Crock, knock – *hill*
Curra, curragh – *marsh*
Darry, derry – *oak tree*
Dun – *castle*
Eden – *hill brow*
Innis, inch – *island*
Inver – *river mouth*
Isk, iska – *water*
Glas, glass – *green*
Glen, glyn – *valley*
Kil, kill – *church*
Lough – *lake, sea inlet*
Mona, mone – *peat bog*
Mor – *great, large*
Mullen, mullin – *mill*
Rath, raha – *ring fort*
Slieve – *mountain*
Toom – *burial ground*
Tul, tulagh – *small hill*

St Canice's Cathedral in Kilkenny (the town's name means "church of Canice")

The Sporting Year

All major international team sports are played in Ireland, but the most popular games are the two uniquely native ones of Gaelic football and hurling. Most of the big games, plus soccer and rugby internationals, are sold out well in advance. However, if you can't get a ticket you'll find plenty of company with whom to watch the event in pubs. Horse racing, with over 240 days of racing a year, attracts fanatical support. For those keen on participatory sports, there are also Ireland's famous fishing waters and golf courses *(see pp362–7).*

The North West 200 *is the fastest motorcycle race in the world over public roads – held near Portstewart* (see p260).

Round-Ireland Yacht Race – held every two years

Four-day national hunt racing festival at

The Irish Grand National *is a gruelling steeplechase run at Fairyhouse in County Meath.*

January	February	March	April	May	June

Irish Champion Hurdle, run at Leopardstown, County Dublin

The International Rally of the Lakes is a prestigious car rally around the Lakes of Killarney *(see pp162–3).*

Start of the salmon fishing season

The Six Nations Rugby Tournament, *between Ireland, Scotland, Wales, England, France and Italy, runs until April. Ireland play their home games at Lansdowne Road, Dublin.*

KEY TO SEASONS

- Hurling
- Gaelic football
- Flat racing
- National Hunt racing
- Rugby
- Association football
- Salmon fishing
- Equestrianism

Irish Football League Cup – Northern Ireland's final

The Irish Derby, *Ireland's premier flat race, attracts many of Europe's best three-year-olds to The Curragh (see p129).*

The All-Ireland Football Final *is held at Croke Park in Dublin. The top two counties play for this Gaelic football championship. More people watch the game than any other event in Ireland.*

Cork Week *is a biennial regatta, organized by Royal Cork Yacht Club, where crews and boats of all classes meet and compete.*

Galway Race Week is one of Ireland's premier festival meetings and a popular social event.

Greyhound Derby, run at Shelbourne Park, Dublin

Football Association of Ireland Cup – the Republic's football final

The Dublin Marathon *is Ireland's foremost marathon event. It attracts a huge field including top-class athletes from around the world.*

Millstreet Indoor International showjumping event

July	August	September	October	November	December

The Dublin Horse Show *is Ireland's premier horse show and a major event in the social calendar.*

All-Ireland Hurling Final at Croke Park, Dublin

The Irish Open Golf Championship *is held at a different course each year and attracts a world-class field to courses such as Ballybunion in County Kerry.*

THE GAELIC ATHLETIC ASSOCIATION

The GAA was founded in 1884 to promote indigenous Irish sport. Today, despite heavy competition from soccer, the most popular sport in Ireland remains Gaelic football. Its rules are somewhere between rugby and soccer, though it predates both games. In it, the ball can be carried and points scored over the goalpost. Another intriguing GAA game is hurling, a fast and physical field sport played with sticks and said to have originated in ancient Celtic times. Both games are played at parish and county level on a wholly amateur basis. The season ends with the All-Ireland finals, which draw large and passionate crowds to Dublin.

Camogie, a version of hurling played by women

THE HISTORY OF IRELAND

Ireland's relative isolation has cut it off from several of the major events of European history. Roman legions, for example, never invaded and the country's early history is shrouded in myths of warring Gods and heroic High Kings. Nevertheless, the bellicose Celtic tribes were quick to embrace Christianity after the arrival of St Patrick on the island in AD 432.

Until the Viking invasions of the 9th century, Ireland enjoyed an era of relative peace. Huge monasteries like Clonmacnoise and Glendalough were founded, where scholarship and art flourished. The Vikings failed to gain control of the island, but in 1169 the Anglo-Normans did. Many Irish chiefs submitted to Henry II of England, who declared himself Lord of Ireland. He left in 1172, and his knights shared out large baronies between themselves.

Matters changed when Henry VIII broke with the Catholic church in 1532. Ireland became a battleground between native Irish Catholics and the forces of the English Crown. Where the Irish were defeated, their lands were confiscated and granted to Protestants from England and Scotland. England's conquest was completed with the victory of William of Orange over James II at the Battle of the Boyne in 1690. Repressive Penal Laws were put into place, but opposition to English rule continued.

The Famine of 1845 to 1848 was one of the bleakest periods in Irish history. Two million people died or emigrated, and many who stayed were evicted by English landlords. A campaign for Home Rule gathered strength, but it was 1920 before the Government of Ireland Act divided the island. The South became the Irish Free State, gaining full independence in 1937, while the North became part of the UK. In the 1970s, 1980s and much of the 1990s, Northern Ireland was a battleground, with both Loyalist and Republican paramilitary groups waging bombing campaigns. In 1998, the Good Friday Agreement was signed, paving the way for a new Northern Ireland Assembly and hopes of peace.

South Cross, Clonmacnoise

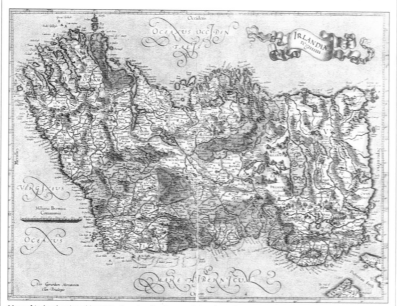

Map of Ireland, printed in 1592, showing the four traditional provinces

◁ *The Feast of St Kevin amid the Ruins of Glendalough* by Joseph Peacock (1813)

Prehistoric Ireland

Until about 9,500 years ago Ireland was uninhabited. The first people, who may have crossed by a land bridge from Scotland, were hunter-gatherers and left few traces of permanent settlement. The 4th millennium BC saw the arrival of Neolithic farmers and herdsmen who built stone field walls and monumental tombs such as Newgrange.

Early Bronze Age stone axe-head

Metalworking was brought from Europe around 2000 BC by the Bronze Age Beaker people, who also introduced new pottery skills. The Iron Age reached Ireland in the 3rd century BC along with the Celts, who migrated from Central Europe, via France and Britain, and soon established themselves as the dominant culture.

IRELAND C.8000 BC

☐ *Former coastline*

☐ *Present-day coastline*

The terminal discs were worn on the shoulders.

GLENINSHEEN GORGET

Many remarkable pieces of gold jewellery were created in the late Bronze Age. This gold collar dates from about 700 BC. The Iron Age Celts produced similarly fine metalwork and ornaments.

Three strands of ropework

Dolmens or Portal Tombs

These striking megalithic tombs date from around 2000 BC. Legananny Dolmen in the Mountains of Mourne (see p284) is a fine example.

Wooden Idol

This Iron Age fetish would have played a role in pagan fertility rites.

Celtic Stone Idol

This mysterious three-faced head was found in County Cavan. In Celtic religion the number three has always had a special significance.

Bronze Bridle Bit

Celtic chiefs rode into battle on two-horse chariots with beautifully decorated harnesses.

TIMELINE

8000 BC	6000	4000	2000	1000
c. 7500 BC First inhabitants of Ireland *Extinct giant deer or "Irish Elk"*		**5000–3000** Ireland covered by dense woodland dominated by oak and elm	**2500** Building of Newgrange passage tomb *(see pp246–7)*	**1500** Major advances in metalworking, especially gold
6000 Date of huts excavated at Mount Sandel, Co London-derry; oldest known dwellings in Europe		**3700** Neolithic farmers reach Ireland; they clear woods to plant cereals	**2050** Beaker people (so-called for their delicate pottery vessels) reach Ireland at the beginning of Bronze Age	

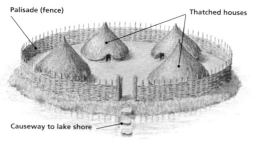

Palisade (fence) Thatched houses

Causeway to lake shore

Reconstruction of a Crannog

Originating in the Bronze Age, crannogs were artificial islands built in lakes. At first used for fishing, they soon developed into well-protected homesteads. Some remained in use up to the 17th century.

The raised bands on the collar were created by repoussé work, pushed through from the back. The delicate rope motifs were added from the front with a knife.

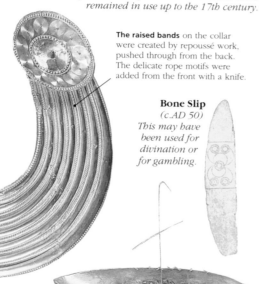

Bone Slip
(c.AD 50)
This may have been used for divination or for gambling.

Gold Boat
Part of a hoard of gold objects found at Broighter, County Londonderry, the boat (1st century AD) was made as a votive offering.

WHERE TO SEE PREHISTORIC IRELAND

Prehistoric sites range from individual tombs such as Newgrange, Browne's Hill Dolmen (*see p141*) or Ossian's Grave to whole settlements, as at Céide Fields (*p204*) and Lough Gur (*p194*). The largest Stone Age cemetery is at Carrowmore (*p234*). Good reconstructions of prehistoric structures can be seen at Craggaunowen (*p190*) and the Ulster History Park (*p269*). The National Museum in Dublin (*pp66–7*) houses the finest collection of artifacts, including wonderful gold objects from the Bronze Age.

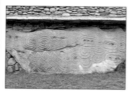

Newgrange (pp246–7) *is Ireland's finest restored Neolithic tomb. At the entrance lie huge spiral-patterned boulders*

Ossian's Grave *is a court grave, the earliest kind of Neolithic tomb (p267). An open court stood before the burial mound*

600 First wave of Celtic invaders	500 Intertribal warfare; chieftains vie for title of *Ard Rí* (High King)	AD 80 Roman general Agricola considers invasion of Ireland from Britain		367 Roman Britain attacked by Irish, Picts and Saxons
50	500	250	AD 1	AD 250

Bronze goad decorated with birds

250 Second wave of Celts, who bring La Tène style of pottery

Bronze sword hilt imported from southern France

c. 150 Greek geographer Ptolemy draws up map and account of Ireland

Celtic Christianity

Celtic Ireland was divided into as many as 100 chiefdoms, though these often owed allegiance to kings of larger provinces such as Munster or Connaught. At times, there was also a titular High King based at Tara *(see p248)*. Ireland became Christian in the 5th century AD, heralding a golden age of scholarship centred on the new monasteries, while missionaries such as St Columba travelled abroad. At the end of the 8th century, Celtic Ireland was shattered by the arrival of the Vikings.

Monk illuminating a manuscript

IRELAND IN 1000
- Viking settlements
- Traditional Irish provinces

Ogham Stone
The earliest Irish script, Ogham, dates from about AD 300. The notches correspond to Roman letters, like a form of Morse code.

CELTIC MONASTERY
Monasteries were large centres of population. This reconstruction shows Glendalough *(see pp140–41)* in about 1100. The tall round tower served as a lookout for Viking raiders.

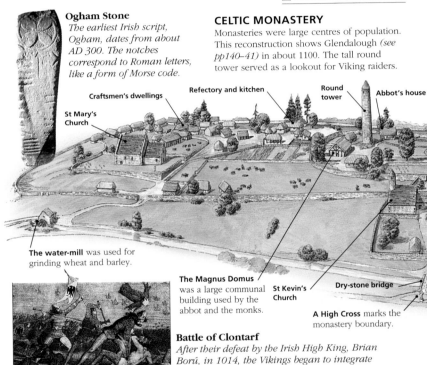

Refectory and kitchen

Round tower

Abbot's house

Craftsmen's dwellings

St Mary's Church

The water-mill was used for grinding wheat and barley.

The Magnus Domus was a large communal building used by the abbot and the monks.

St Kevin's Church

Dry-stone bridge

A High Cross marks the monastery boundary.

Battle of Clontarf
After their defeat by the Irish High King, Brian Ború, in 1014, the Vikings began to integrate more fully with the native population. Brian Ború himself was killed in the battle.

TIMELINE

430 Pope sends first Christian missionary, Palladius

455 St Patrick founds church at Armagh

St Patrick

563 St Columba (Colmcille), the first Irish missionary, founds monastery on Iona in the Hebrides

664 Synod of Whitby decides that Irish Church should conform with Rome over date of Easter

400	500	600	700

432 Start of St Patrick's mission to Ireland

c. 550 Beginning of golden age of Celtic monasticism

615 St Columbanus dies in Italy after founding many new monasteries on the Continent

c.690 *Book of Durrow (see p63)* completed

Viking Raids and Settlements

The first longships reached Ireland in 795. Though notorious for pillaging monasteries, the Vikings introduced new farming methods and coinage. They also founded walled cities such as Dublin, Waterford and Limerick.

Garryduff Gold Bird

Irish metalwork in the early Christian era was of very high quality. This gold ornament, possibly a wren, dates from around the 7th century AD.

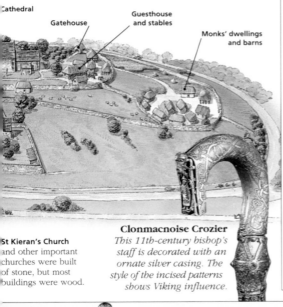

Cathedral

Gatehouse

Guesthouse and stables

Monks' dwellings and barns

St Kieran's Church and other important churches were built of stone, but most buildings were wood.

Clonmacnoise Crozier

This 11th-century bishop's staff is decorated with an ornate silver casing. The style of the incised patterns shows Viking influence.

WHERE TO SEE EARLY CHRISTIAN IRELAND

Important early monastic sites besides Glendalough include Clonmacnoise and Devenish Island. Churches from this period can also be seen at Gallarus *(see p157)*, Clonfert *(p213)* and the Rock of Cashel *(pp196–7)*, while High Crosses *(p243)* and round towers *(p20)* survive all over Ireland. Dublin's National Museum *(pp66–7)* has the best collection of ecclesiastical (and Viking) artifacts and Trinity College *(pp62–4)* houses the finest illuminated manuscripts.

Devenish Island has a fine 12th-century round tower and enjoys a peaceful setting on Lower Lough Erne (p271).

Clonmacnoise (pp250–51) lies on the eaast bank of the Shannon. This Romanesque doorway is part of the ruined Nuns' Church.

Viking silver brooch

795 First Viking invasion of coastal monasteries

967 Irish warriors sack Limerick and begin military campaign against Viking overlords

999 Sitric Silkenbeard, the Viking king of Dublin, surrenders to BrianBorú

1166 Dermot McMurrough, King of Leinster, flees overseas

1134 Cormac's Chapel is built at Cashel *(see pp196–7)*

800	900	1000	1100

841 A large Viking fleet spends the winter at Dublin

1014 High King BrianBorú of Munster defeats joint army of Vikings and the King of Leinster at Clontarf

1142 Ireland's first Cistercian house founded at Mellifont *(see p245)*

807 Work starts on Kells monastery *(see p241)*

Viking coin

Anglo-Norman Ireland

Anglo-Norman nobles, led by Richard de Clare (nicknamed Strongbow), were invited to Ireland by the King of Leinster in 1169. They took control of the major towns and Henry II of England proclaimed himself overlord of Ireland. In succeeding centuries, however, English power declined and the Crown controlled just a small area around Dublin known as the Pale *(see p132)*. Many of the Anglo-Norman barons living outside the Pale opposed English rule just as strongly as did the native Irish clans.

13th-century gold brooch

IRELAND IN 1488

☐ *Extent of the Pale*

CARRICKFERGUS CASTLE

The first Anglo-Norman forts were wooden structures, but they soon started to build massive stone castles. Carrickfergus *(see p275)* was begun in the 1180s and by 1250 had acquired a keep and a gatehouse.

Marriage of Strongbow
The King of Leinster gave his daughter to Strongbow for helping him regain his lands. Daniel Maclise's painting (1854) emphasizes Anglo-Norman power over the Irish.

Norman Weapons
These bows and arrows, unearthed at Waterford, may be relics of Strongbow's assault on the city in 1170.

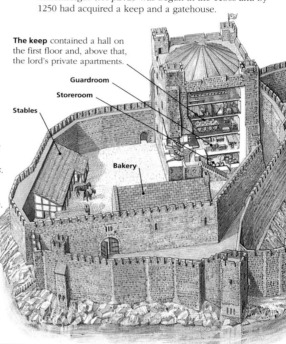

The keep contained a hall on the first floor and, above that, the lord's private apartments.

Guardroom

Storeroom

Stables

Bakery

TIMELINE

1172 Pope affirms King Henry II of England's lordship over Ireland

1177 John de Courcy's forces invade Ulster

Dermot McMurrough, King of Leinster, who invited Strongbow to come to his aid

1318 Bruce killed in battle

1315 Scots invade Ireland; Edward Bruce crowned king

1200 | **1250** | **1300**

1169 Strongbow's Anglo-Normans arrive at invitation of exiled King of Leinster, Dermot McMurrough

1224 Dominican order enters Ireland and constructs friaries

1260 Powerful Irish chieftain Brian O'Neill killed at the Battle of Down

1297 First Irish Parliament meets in Dublin

Richard II's Fleet Returning to England in 1399
Richard made two trips to Ireland – in 1394 and 1399. On the first he defeated Art McMurrough, King of Leinster, and other Irish chiefs, but the second was inconclusive.

WHERE TO SEE ANGLO-NORMAN IRELAND

The strength of Norman fortifications is best seen in the castles at Carrickfergus, Limerick (*see p191*) and Trim (*p248*) and in Waterford's city walls. Gothic cathedrals that survive include Dublin's Christ Church (*pp80–81*) and St Patrick's (*pp82–3*) and St Canice's (*p144*) in Kilkenny. There are impressive ruins of medieval Cistercian abbeys at Jerpoint and Boyle (*p219*).

Kitchen

The gatehouse was the last addition made in the 15th century. The two towers have arrow loops for longbowmen.

Drawbridge

Chapel

The Hall was where the lord of the castle held public court and decided cases brought before him.

Éamonn Burke
The 14th-century Lord of Mayo was a typically independent chieftain of Anglo-Norman descent.

Jerpoint Abbey (p145) *has a well-preserved 15th-century cloister decorated with carvings of curiously elongated figures.*

Waterford's *Anglo-Norman city walls include this sturdy watchtower (pp146–7).*

Great Charter Roll of Waterford (1372) showing portraits of the mayors of four medieval cities

1394 King Richard II lands with army to reassert control; returns five years later but with inconclusive results

1471 8th Earl of Kildare made Lord Deputy of Ireland

1496 Kildare regains Lord Deputy position

1491 Kildare supports Perkin Warbeck, pretender to the English throne

1350	1400	1450

1366 Statutes of Kilkenny forbid marriage between Anglo-Normans and Irish

1348 The Black Death: one third of population killed in three years

English force (left) confront Irish horsemen on Richard II's return expedition

1487 Kildare crowns Lambert Simnel, Edward VI in Dublin

1494 Lord Deputy Edward Poynings forbids Irish Parliament to meet without royal consent

Protestant Conquest

England's break with the Catholic Church, the dissolution of the monasteries and Henry VIII's assumption of the title King of Ireland incensed both the old Anglo-Norman dynasties and resurgent Irish clans such as the O'Neills. Resistance to foreign

Hugh O'Neill, Earl of Tyrone

rule was fierce and it took over 150 years of war to establish the English Protestant ascendancy. Tudor and Stuart monarchs adopted a policy of military persuasion, then Plantation. Oliver Cromwell was even more forceful. Irish hopes were raised when the Catholic James II ascended to the English throne, but he was deposed and fled to Ireland, where he was defeated by William of Orange (William III) in 1690.

IRELAND IN 1625

Main areas of Plantation in the reign of James I

The first relief ship to reach Londonderry was the *Phoenix*. For three months English ships had been prevented from sailing up the Foyle by a wooden barricade across the river.

James II's army on the east bank of the Foyle attacks the ship.

Battle of the Boyne
This tapestry, from the Bank of Ireland (see p60), shows William of Orange leading his troops against the army of James II in 1690. His victory is still celebrated by Orangemen in Northern Ireland.

Silken Thomas Fitzgerald
Silken Thomas, head of the powerful Kildares, renounced his allegiance to Henry VIII in 1534. He was hanged along with his five uncles in 1537.

The artist's depiction of 17th-century weapons and uniforms is far from accurate.

TIMELINE

Henry VIII

1541 Henry VIII declared King of Ireland by Irish Parliament

Sir Thomas Lee, an officer in Elizabeth I's army, dressed in Irish fashion

1585 Ireland is mapped and divided into 32 counties

1592 Trinity College, Dublin founded

1500	1525	1550	1575	160(

1534 Silken Thomas rebels against Henry VIII

1557 Mary I orders first plantations in Offaly and Laois

1582 Desmond rebellion in Munster

1504 8th Earl of Kildare becomes master of Ireland after victory at Knocktoe

1539 Henry VIII dissolves monasteries

1588 Spanish Armada wrecked off west coast

The Siege of Drogheda
Between 1649 and 1652 Cromwell's army avenged attacks on Protestant settlers with ruthless efficiency. Here Cromwell himself directs the gunners bombarding Drogheda.

PLANTATION IRELAND

James I realized that force alone could not stabilize Ireland. The Plantation programme uprooted the native Irish and gave their land to Protestant settlers from England and Scotland. London livery companies organized many of the new settlements. The policy created loyal garrisons who supported the Crown.

Bellaghy *in County Londonderry was settled by the Vintners Company. This map of the neatly planned town dates from 1622.*

The Walls of Derry have never been breached by any attacker and many of the original 17th-century gates and bastions that withstood the siege of 1689 are still in place *(see pp258–9).*

St George's flag

Ship Quay

Protestants emerge from the besieged city to greet the English relieving force and to engage the enemy.

Loftus Cup
Adam Loftus, Chancellor of Ireland, used his position to enrich his family. In 1593 he had the Great Seal of Ireland melted down and made into this silver-gilt cup.

THE RELIEF OF DERRY *(1689)*

Some 20,000 Protestants were besieged for 105 days in Londonderry by James II's forces. Thousands died from starvation, until relief finally came from English warships. This 18th-century painting by William Sadler II gives a rather fanciful picture of the ending of the siege.

1607 Flight of the Earls: old Irish leaders flee to the Continent; Plantation of Ulster	**1632** Important Irish history, *The Annals of the Four Masters,* written by four Franciscan friars from Donegal	*Protestant apprentice boys closing the gates of Derry before the siege of 1689*		**1690** William of Orange defeats James II at Battle of the Boyne; James's army surrenders the following year in Limerick
1625		**1650**	**1675**	**1700**
1603 Earl of Tyrone ends nine years of war by signing the Treaty of Mellifont		**1649** Cromwell lands in Dublin; razes Drogheda and Wexford; Catholic landowners transplanted to far west	**1688** James II, deposed Catholic king of England, flees to Ireland and raises army	**1695** Penal code severely reduces rights of Roman Catholics
1641 Armed rebellion in Ulster opposes Plantation				**1689** Siege of Derry

Georgian Ireland

The Protestant ascendancy was a period of great prosperity for the landed gentry, who built grand country houses and furnished them luxuriously. Catholics, meanwhile, were denied even the right to buy land. Towards the end of the century, radicals, influenced by events in America and France, started to demand independence from the English Crown. Prime Minister Henry Grattan tried a parliamentary route; Wolfe Tone and the United Irishmen opted for armed insurrection. Both approaches ultimately failed.

Lacquer cabinet in Castletown House

IRELAND IN 1703

□ Counties where Protestants owned over 75 per cent of land

The Irish House of Commons
This painting shows Irish leader Henry Grattan addressing the house (see p60). The "Grattan Parliament" lasted from 1782 to 1800, but was then abolished by the Act of Union.

State Bedroom

The saloon, the Casino's main room, was used for formal entertaining. It has a magnificent parquet floor.

Stone lions by Edward Smyth (1749–1812)

The basement contains the servants' hall, the kitchen, pantry and wine cellar.

Surveyors
The 18th century saw work begin on ambitious projects such as the Grand Canal, new roads and Dublin's network of wide streets and squares.

TIMELINE

Janathan Swift (1667–1745)

1724 Swift attacks Ireland's penal code in *A Modest Proposal*

1731 Royal Dublin Society founded to encourage agriculture, art and crafts

1738 Death of Ireland's most famous harper, Turlough O'Carolan *(see p24)*

| 1710 | 1720 | 1730 | 1740 | 1750 |

1713 Jonathan Swift appointed Dean of St Patrick's Cathedral *(see p82)*

1731 First issue of the *Belfast Newsletter*, the world's oldest continually running newspaper

1742 First performance of Handel's *Messiah* given in Dublin

1751 Dublin's Rotunda Lying-In Hospital is first maternity hospital in the British Isles

Linen Bleaching
Ulster's linen industry flourished thanks to the expertise of Huguenot weavers from France. The woven cloth was spread out in fields or on river banks to bleach it (see p268).

WHERE TO SEE GEORGIAN IRELAND
Dublin preserves many fine Georgian terraces and public buildings such as the Custom House *(see p88)* and the Four Courts *(p93)*. Around Dublin, the grand houses at Castletown *(pp130–31)*, Russborough and Powerscourt *(pp134–5)* are fascinating reminders of the lifestyle of the gentry. Other 18th-century country seats open to the public include Emo Court, Westport House *(pp204–05)* and Castle Coole *(p272)*.

The Classical urns on the roof conceal chimneys.

The china closet was originally designed as a bedroom.

Emo Court's *façade, with its plain Ionic portico, is by James Gandon, architect of many of Dublin's public buildings (p253).*

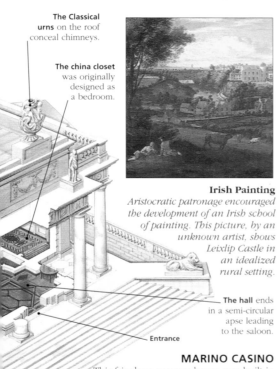

Irish Painting
Aristocratic patronage encouraged the development of an Irish school of painting. This picture, by an unknown artist, shows Leixlip Castle in an idealized rural setting.

The hall ends in a semi-circular apse leading to the saloon.

Entrance

MARINO CASINO
This frivolous summer house was built in the 1760s for the first Earl of Charlemont on his estate just north of Dublin *(see p100)*. Palladian architecture of this kind was popular among the Irish aristocracy, who followed 18th-century English fashions.

Russborough House (p132) *was built in 1741 by Richard Castle. Elegant niches with Classical busts flank the grand fireplace in the entrance hall*

GUINNESS

Guinness Brewery Gate

1782 Parliament gains greater degree of independence from Westminster

The Irish Volunteers, a local militia which pressed Parliament for reform

1798 Rebellion of Wolfe Tone's United Irishmen quashed

1760	1770	1780	1790

Custom House

1759 Arthur Guinness buys the St James's Gate Brewery in Dublin

1791 James Gandon's Custom House built in Dublin

1793 Limited emancipation for Irish Catholics

1795 Orange Order formed by Ulster Protestants

Famine and Emigration

Ration card from Famine period

The history of 19th-century Ireland is dominated by the Great Famine of 1845–8, which was caused by the total failure of the potato crop. Although Irish grain was still being exported to England, around one million people died from hunger or disease, with even more fleeing to North America. By 1900, the pre-famine population of eight million had fallen by half. Rural hardship fuelled a campaign for tenants' rights which evolved into demands for independence from Britain. Great strides towards "Home Rule" were made in Parliament by the charismatic politician Charles Stewart Parnell.

IRELAND IN 1851

Areas where population fell by over 25% during the Famine

The ships that brought the Irish to America were overcrowded and fever-ridden, and known as "coffin ships".

Daniel O'Connell
Known as "The Liberator", O'Connell organized peaceful "monster rallies" of up to a million people in pursuit of Catholic emancipation. He was elected MP for Clare in 1828.

Castle Clinton was used for processing new arrivals to New York prior to the construction of the huge depot on Ellis Island.

The Boycotting of Landlords
In 1880, troops guarded the crops of Captain Boycott, the first notable victim of a campaign to ostracize landlords guilty of evicting tenants. His name later passed into the English language.

TIMELINE

Charles Bianconi's coach service, 1836

1815 First coach service begins in Ireland

1817 Royal Canal is completed

1838 Father Mathew founds temperance crusade – five million Irish take abstinence pledge and whiskey production is reduced by half

1845 Start of Great Famine which lasts for four years

1800	1810	1820	1830	1840

1803 Uprising, led by Robert Emmet, is crushed after feared Napoleonic invasion of England fails to materialize

1800 Act of Union: Ireland legally becomes part of Britain

1828 After a five-year campaign by Daniel O'Connell, Catholic Emancipation Act is passed, giving a limited number of Catholics the right to vote

Father Mathew

Eviction of Irish Farmers
In the late 1870s, agricultural prices plummeted. Starving tenant farmers fell into arrears and were mercilessly evicted. Their plight spawned the Land League, which lobbied successfully for reform.

THE IRISH ABROAD

One result of the Famine was the growth of a strong Irish community in the USA. From the lowest rung of American society, the immigrants rose up the social scale and became rich by Irish Catholic standards. They sent money to causes back home, and as a well-organized lobby group put pressure on the American government to influence British policies in Ireland. A more militant group, Clan na Gael, sent veterans of the American Civil War to fight in the Fenian risings of 1865 and 1867.

New Yorkers *stage a huge St Patrick's Day parade, 17 March 1870.*

The Irish were widely perceived as illiterate peasants in the USA and often met with a hostile reception.

IMMIGRANTS ARRIVE IN NEW YORK

The Irish who survived the journey to America landed at Castle Garden in New York, seen here in a painting by Samuel Waugh (1855). Although mainly country people, most new arrivals settled in Manhattan, often enduring horrific living conditions.

Charles Stewart Parnell
A campaigner for the Land League and Home Rule, Parnell saw his political career ruined in 1890, when he was cited as co-respondent in a divorce case.

1853 Dublin Exhibition is opened by Queen Victoria

Dublin Exhibition

1877 Parnell becomes leader of the new Home Rule Party

1884 Founding of Gaelic Athletic Association, first group to promote Irish traditions

1892 Second Home Rule Bill is defeated

1850	1860	1870	1880	1890

1867 Irish-Americans return home to fight in a rising led by the Irish Republican Brotherhood, also known as the Fenians

1881 Parnell is jailed in Kilmainham Gaol, Dublin

1886 British PM Gladstone sponsors first Home Rule Bill but is defeated by Parliament

1848 Failure of the Young Ireland Uprising – a spontaneous response to insurrections elsewhere in Europe

1879–82 Land War, led by Michael Davitt's Land League, campaigns for the reform of tenancy laws

War and Independence

Irish Free State stamp of 1922

Plans for Irish home rule were shelved because of World War I; however, the abortive Easter Rising of 1916 inspired new support for the Republican cause. In 1919 an unofficial Irish Parliament was established and a war began against the "occupying" British forces. The Anglo-Irish Treaty of 1921 divided the island in two, granting independence to the Irish Free State, while Northern Ireland remained in the United Kingdom. There followed a civil war between pro-Treaty and anti-Treaty factions in the South.

IRELAND IN 1922

Northern Ireland

Irish Free State

The Unionist Party
Leader of the campaign against Home Rule was Dublin barrister Edward Carson. In 1913 the Ulster Volunteer Force was formed to demand that six counties in Ulster remain part of the UK.

The 1916 Service Medal, issued to all who fought in the Easter Rising, depicts, on one side, the mythical Irish warrior Cúchulainn.

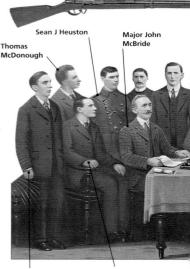

Thomas McDonough

Sean J Heuston

Major John McBride

William Pearse

Patrick Pearse, a poet, read the Proclamation of the Republic from the steps of the GPO on Easter Monday.

The Black and Tans
Named for their makeshift uniforms, these British troops – mostly demobbed World War I soldiers – carried out savage reprisals against the Irish in 1920–21.

TIMELINE

The Titanic

1904 Dublin's Abbey Theatre opens

1905 Sinn Féin (We Ourselves) party founded

1912 Belfast-built *Titanic* sinks on her maiden voyage

1912 Edward Carson rallies Ulster Protestants; solemn covenant to defeat Home Rule signed by 471,414 people

1913 General strike in Dublin

Despatch bag carried by Constance Markievicz during Easter Rising

1916 Easter Rising quashed

1918 Sinn Féin wins 73 seats at Westminster; Constance Markievicz elected first woman MP

1919 First meeting of independent parliament (*Dáil Éireann*)

1920 Government of Ireland Act proposes partition of the island

1921 Anglo-Irish Treaty signed; de Valera resigns; southern Ireland plunged into civil war

1905	1910	1915	1920

The General Post Office, Easter 1916
*What was supposed to be a national uprising
was confined to 2,500 armed insurgents in
Dublin. They managed to hold the GPO and
other public buildings for five days.*

This Mauser rifle, smuggled in
from Germany in 1914, was
used by rebels in the Rising.

Tom Clarke

James Connolly

Joseph
Plunkett

Mementos
of the Rising
at Dublin's
Kilmainham
Gaol *(see
p97)* include
this crucifix made
by a British soldier
from rifle bullets.

LEADERS OF THE 1916 RISING
This collage portrait shows 14 leaders of the Easter
Rising, who were all court-martialled and shot at
Kilmainham Gaol. The brutality of their executions
(the badly injured James Connolly was tied to a
chair before being shot) changed public opinion of
the Rising and guaranteed their status as martyrs.

EAMON DE VALERA
(1882–1975)
After escaping execution for his part in
the Easter Rising, American-born de
Valera went on to dominate Irish politics
for almost 60 years. The opposition of
his party, Sinn Féin, to the Anglo-Irish
Treaty of 1921 plunged the new Irish
Free State into civil war. After forming
a new party, Fianna
Fáil, he became
Prime Minister
(Taoiseach) in
1932. De Valera
remained in
office until
1948, with
further terms
in the 1950s.
Between 1959
and 1973 he was
President of Ireland.

Election Poster
*Cumann na nGaedheal, the
pro-Treaty party in the Civil
War, won the Free State's
first general election in 1923.
It merged with other parties
in 1933 to form Fine Gael.*

1922 Irish Free State
inaugurated; Michael
Collins shot dead in
ambush in Co Cork

*Michael Collins (1890–1922),
hero of the War of Independence,
became chairman of the Irish
Free State and Commander-
in-Chief of the Army*

1932 Fianna Fáil sweeps to
victory in general election,
and de Valera begins
16-year term as *Taoiseach*
(Prime Minister)

1936 IRA proscribed by
Free State Government

1939 Éire declares
neutrality during
World War II

1925	1930	1935

1923 WB
Yeats wins
Nobel prize
for Literature

1926 De Valera quits
Sinn Féin; sets up
Fianna Fáil (Soldiers
of Destiny) party

1925 GB Shaw also
receives Nobel prize

1929 Work starts
on River Shannon
hydro-electric
power scheme

1933 Fine Gael
(United Ireland)
party formed to
oppose Fianna Fáil

1937 New
constitution
declares complete
independence
from Britain;
country's name
changes to Éire

Modern Ireland

Since joining the European Economic Community (now called the European Union) in 1973, the Irish Republic has done much to modernize its traditional rural-based economy. There have been social changes too, and laws prohibiting abortion and divorce have slowly been relaxed. Meanwhile, Northern Ireland has lived through more than 25 years of bombings and shootings. But recent peace agreements have brought new hope to the province, especially since the inauguration in 1998 of the new Northern Ireland Assembly.

Mary Robinson, Ireland's first woman President

1972 Bloody Sunday – British soldiers shoot dead 13 demonstrators in Derry. Northern Ireland Parliament is suspended and direct rule from Westminster imposed

1976 Organizers of the Ulster Peace Movement, Mairead Corrigan and Betty Williams, are awarded the Nobel Peace Prize in Oslo

1969 Violent clashes between the police and demonstrators in Belfast and Derry. British troops sent to restore order

1956 IRA launches a terrorism campaign along the border with Northern Ireland which lasts until 1962

1967 Northern Ireland Civil Rights Association is set up to fight discrimination against Catholics

NORTHERN IRELAND			
1945	1955	1965	1975
REPUBLIC OF IRELAND			

1949 New government under John A Costello. Country changes name from Éire to Republic of Ireland and leaves British Commonwealth

1959 Eamon de Valera resigns as *Taoiseach* (Prime Minister) and is later elected President

1973 The Republic joins the European Economic Community. Membership has given the country access to much needed development grants

1955 Republic of Ireland joins United Nations

1963 John F Kennedy, the first American President of Irish Catholic descent, visits Ireland. He is pictured here with President Eamon de Valera

1969 Samuel Beckett, seen here rehearsing one of his own plays, is awarded the Nobel prize for literature, but does not go to Stockholm to receive it

1947 Statue of Queen Victoria is removed from the courtyard in front of the Irish Parliament in Dublin

1981 Hunger-striker Bobbie Sands dies in Maze Prison

1994 IRA and Unionist cease-fires. Gerry Adams, Sinn Féin leader, allowed to speak on British radio and television

1985 Barry McGuigan beats the Panamanian, Eusebio Pedroza, for world featherweight boxing title

1986 Bitter Loyalist opposition follows the previous year's signing by the British and Irish governments of the Anglo-Irish Agreement

1995 For the first time in 25 years, there are no troops on daylight patrols in Northern Ireland

1998 The Good Friday Agreement sets out proposed framework for self-government in Northern Ireland

2001 David Trimble resigns as first minister, but is later re-elected. The beginning of a tortuous period of suspended talks and return to Westminster's direct rule

1987 IRA bomb explodes during Enniskillen's Remembrance Day parade, killing 11 people

2002 Sinn Féin's offices at Stormont are raided in an alleged intelligence-gathering operation

2005 The IRA announces an end to its armed campaign, saying it will follow an exclusively democratic path

		NORTHERN IRELAND
1985	1995	2005
		REPUBLIC OF IRELAND

1982 Rising debt and unemployment lead to economic crisis and instability. Three elections are held in two years

1994 Republic of Ireland football team reaches quarterfinals of World Cup in the USA. Here, Ray Houghton is congratulated on scoring the winning goal against Italy

1991 Mary Robinson becomes first female President of the Republic, succeeded by Mary McAleese in 1998

1988 Dublin's millennium is celebrated, boosting the city's image

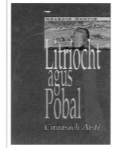

2005 Foreign ministers of the European Union unanimously agree to make Irish an official language of the EU

2002 The single European currency, the euro, replaces Irish punt notes and coins. Initially, the euro was introduced in 1999 for banking purposes

1979 Pope John Paul II visits Ireland and celebrates Mass in Dublin's Phoenix Park, in front of more than a million people

1987 Dubliner Steven Roche wins the Tour de France, Giro d'Italia and World Championship in one incredible season

IRELAND THROUGH THE YEAR

Popular months for visiting Ireland are July and August, though Belfast tends to close down in July for the marching season. June and September can be pleasant but never count on the weather, for Ireland's lush beauty is the product of a wet climate. Most tourist sights are open from Easter to September but have restricted opening hours or close in the low season. During spring and summer, festivals are held in

honour of everything from food to religion. A common thread is music, and few festivities are complete without musical accompaniment. Ireland is at its best when it has something to celebrate, so is an inspired choice for Christmas and New Year. Look out for the word *fleadh* (festival) on your travels but remember, too, that the Irish are a spontaneous people: festivities can spring from the air, or from a tune on a fiddle.

Ladies' Day at Dublin Horse Show

Dublin's annual parade to celebrate St Patrick's Day (17 March)

SPRING

St Patrick's Day is often said to mark the beginning of the tourist season. Later, the spring bank holiday weekend in May, when accommodation is in short supply, is celebrated with music in most places. After the quiet winter months, festivals and events start to become more common.

MARCH

St Patrick's Day *(17 Mar)*. Parades and pilgrimages held at Downpatrick, Armagh, Dublin, Cork, Limerick and many other places.
Jameson International Dublin Film Festival *(Feb)*. International film festival.
Horse Ploughing Match and Heavy Horse Show, Ballycastle *(17 Mar, see p266)*. This popular annual competition is more than 100 years old.

A St Patrick's Day float advertising Guinness

APRIL

Feis Ceoil, Dublin *(end Mar or early Apr)*. A classical music festival held at many different venues throughout the city.
Pan Celtic Festival, Tralee *(mid-Apr, see p156)*. A lively celebration of Celtic culture, with music, dance and song.
Cork Choral Festival *(late Apr–May, see pp174–5)*.

MAY

Belfast Civic Festival and Lord Mayor's Show *(mid-May, see pp276–9)*. Street parade with bands and floats.
Royal Ulster Agriculture Society Show, Belfast *(mid-May)*. A three-day show with diverse events ranging from sheep-shearing competitions to fashion shows.
"A Taste of Baltimore" Shellfish Festival *(end May, see p170)*.
Fleadh Nua, Ennis, *end May, see p189)*. Four days of traditional Irish music, songs and dance.

SUMMER

For the visitor, summer represents the height of the festive calendar. This is the busiest time of year for organized events, from music and arts festivals to lively local race meetings, summer schools and matchmaking festivals. Book accommodation if your plans include a popular festival.

Beach races at Laytown (June)

JUNE

Laytown Beach Races, Co Meath *(late May or early Jun)*. Horse races on the sand.
County Wicklow Garden Festival *(May–Jun)*. Held at private and public gardens around the county, including Powerscourt *(see pp134–5)*.
National Country Fair, Birr Castle Demesne, Co Offaly *(early Jun, see p253)*. One of Ireland's most popular country fairs.
Women's Mini Marathon, Dublin City *(early Jun)*.
Bloomsday, Dublin *(16 Jun)*. Lectures, pub talks, readings, dramatizations and walks to celebrate James Joyce's greatest novel, *Ulysses*.

AVERAGE DAILY HOURS OF SUNSHINE

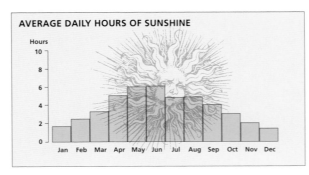

Hours

10
8
6
4
2
0

Jan Feb Mar Apr May Jun Jul Aug Sep Oct Nov Dec

Sunshine Chart
The chart gives figures for Dublin, though conditions are similar around the country. The Southeast enjoys more sunshine hours than any other part of Ireland, while Northern Ireland receives marginally fewer hours of sun than the Republic.

Scurlogstown Olympiad Celtic Festival, Trim *(mid-Jun, see p248)*. Traditional Irish music, dance, fair and selection of a festival queen.

Music in Great Irish Houses *(first two weeks)*. Classical music recitals in grand settings at various venues.

Castle Ward Opera, Strangford *(all month, see p284)*. Opera festival in the grounds of 18th-century stately home.

County Wexford Strawberry Fair, Enniscorthy *(end Jun–early Jul, see p149)*. Includes a craft fair, music, street theatre and, of course, strawberries.

JULY

Battle of the Boyne Day *(12 Jul, see p244)*. Members of the Orange Order march in towns across Northern Ireland to celebrate the Protestants' landmark victory over King James II's Catholic army in 1690.

Galway Arts Festival *(third & fourth weeks, see pp210–11)*. Processions, concerts, street theatre, children's shows and many other events in the medieval city centre. Followed

Traditional sailing craft in the Cruinniú na mBád at Kinvarra (August)

immediately by Galway's popular five-day race meeting.

Mary from Dungloe International Festival, Dungloe *(last week, see p228)*. Dancing, music and selection of "Mary", the beauty queen.

Lughnasa Fair, Carrickfergus Castle *(end Jul, see p275)*. A popular medieval-style fair.

Ballyshannon International Folk Festival *(end Jul or early Aug, see p231)*. Three days of traditional Irish music.

O'Carolan Harp and Traditional Music Festival, Keadue, Co Roscommon *(end Jul or early Aug)*. Traditional music and dance celebrations.

AUGUST

Stradbally Steam-engine Rally, Co Laois *(early Aug)*. Many types of steam-engine join this rally.

Orangemen parading on Battle of the Boyne Day

Letterkenny Folk Festival, Co Donegal *(early Aug, see p227)*. A week of celebration.

Dublin Horse Show *(first or second week)*. A premier showjumping competition and social event.

Puck Fair, Killorglin, Co Kerry *(mid–Aug, see p165)*. A wild goat is crowned "king" at this two-day-long traditional festival.

Blessing of the Sea *(second or third Sunday)*. Held in seaside towns all over Ireland.

Oul' Lammas Fair, Ballycastle *(mid-end Aug, see p266)*. A popular fair that is particularly famous for its edible seaweed.

Kilkenny Arts Week *(middle of the month, see pp142–3)*. A major arts festival including poetry, film and crafts.

Rose of Tralee Festival, *(end Aug, see p156)*. Bands, processions, dancing and selection of the "Rose".

Cruinniú na mBád, Kinvarra *(end Aug, see pp211–12)*. Various types of traditional sailing craft take part in this "gathering of the boats".

Steam-engine at Stradbally Rally (August)

AVERAGE MONTHLY RAINFALL

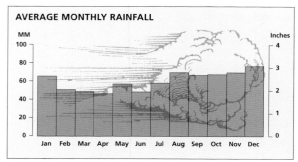

Rainfall Chart
Ireland is one of the wettest countries in Europe, with rainfall distributed evenly through the year – the figures displayed here are for Dublin. The West has the heaviest annual rainfall, while the Southeast receives marginally less rain than other regions.

Galway Oyster Festival (September)

AUTUMN

Oysters and opera are the two big events in autumn. There are also festivals devoted to jazz, film and music. The October bank holiday weekend is celebrated with music in many towns; though it is low season, it can be difficult to find accommodation.

SEPTEMBER

Heritage Week *(early Sep)*. Special events countrywide.
All-Ireland Hurling Final, Croke Park, Dublin *(first or second Sunday, see p29)*.

Lisdoonvarna Matchmaking Festival *(all month and first week of Oct, see p188)*. Singles gather for traditional music and dance.
Waterford International Festival of Light Opera *(mid-Sep –early Oct, see p359)*. Musicals and operettas at the Theatre Royal.
All-Ireland Football Final, Croke Park, Dublin *(3rd Sunday, see p29)*. Gaelic football final.
Galway Oyster Festival *(end Sep, see pp210–11)*. Oyster tastings at different venues.

OCTOBER

Octoberfest, Londonderry *(all month, see pp258–9)*. Dance, poetry, film, comedy, theatre and music.
Cork Film Festival *(early Oct, see pp174–5)*. Irish and international films.
Kinsale International Festival of Fine Food *(early Oct, see pp172–3)*. Superb food served

All-Ireland Hurling at Croke Park, Dublin

in restaurants hotels and pubs of Kinsale.
Ballinasloe Fair, Co Galway *(first week)*. One of Europe's oldest horse fairs, staged amid lively street entertainment.
Dublin Theatre Festival *(first two weeks)*. Features works by both Irish and foreign playwrights.
Wexford Opera Festival *(last two weeks in Oct, see p359)*. A festival of lesser known operas.
Hallowe'en (Shamhana) *(31 Oct)*. An occasion celebrated all over the country.
Cork Jazz Festival *(end Oct, see pp174–5)*. An extremely popular festival, with music throughout the city.

Horse and trap at Lisdoonvarna fair

NOVEMBER

Sligo International Choral Festival *(early Nov, see p234)*. Choirs from around the world in concert and competition.
Belfast Festival at Queen's, Queen's University *(end Oct to early Nov, see pp276–9)*. Arts festival featuring drama, ballet, cinema and all types of music from classical to jazz.
Éigse Sliabh Rua, Slieverue, Co Kilkenny *(mid Nov)*. Festival of local history and music with special guests and interesting talks.

Traditional horse fair at Ballinasloe in County Galway (October)

AVERAGE MONTHLY TEMPERATURE

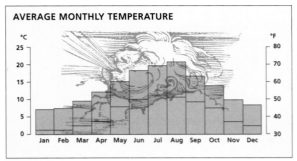

Temperature Chart
This chart gives the average minimum and maximum temperatures for the city of Dublin. Winter is mild throughout Ireland, except in the high mountain ranges, while the warmest summer temperatures are in the Southeast.

WINTER

Although a quiet time for festivals, there's a range of entertainment including musical and theatrical events. Christmas is the busiest social period and there are plenty of informal celebrations. There is also a wide choice of National Hunt race meetings *(see p28)*.

DECEMBER

Pantomime Season *(Dec–Jan)*. Traditional pantomime performed at many theatres throughout Ireland.
Leopardstown Races *(26 Dec, see p129)*. The biggest meeting held on this traditional day for racing. There are other fixtures at Limerick and Down Royal.
St Stephen's Day *(26 Dec)*. Catholic boys traditionally dress up as Wren boys (chimney sweeps with blackened faces) and sing hymns to raise money for charitable causes.

Young boys dressed up as Wren boys on St Stephen's Day

JANUARY

Salmon and Sea Trout Season *(1 Jan–end Sep, see pp362–3)*. Season begins for one of Ireland's most popular pastimes.

FEBRUARY

Dublin Film Festival *(end Feb–early Mar)*. International films at various venues.
Belfast Music Festival *(end Feb–mid-Mar)*. Young people take part in music (and speech and drama) competitions.
Six Nations Rugby Tournament, Lansdowne Road, Dublin *(varying Saturdays Feb–Apr, see p28)*.

PUBLIC HOLIDAYS

New Year's Day (1 Jan)
St Patrick's Day (17 Mar)
Good Friday
Easter Monday
May Day (first Mon in May)
Spring Bank Holiday (Northern Ireland: last Mon in May)
June Bank Holiday (Republic: first Mon in Jun)
Battle of the Boyne Day (Northern Ireland: 12 Jul)
August Bank Holiday (first Mon in Aug).
Summer Bank Holiday (Northern Ireland: last Mon in Aug)
October Bank Holiday (last Mon in Oct)
Christmas Day (25 Dec)
St Stephen's Day (Republic: 26 Dec)
Boxing Day (Northern Ireland: 26 Dec)

Glendalough *(see pp140–41)* in the snow

DUBLIN AREA BY AREA

Dublin at a Glance

Ireland's capital has a wealth of attractions, most within walking distance of each other. For the purpose of this guide, central Dublin has been divided into three sections: *Southeast Dublin*, heart of the modern city and home to the prestigious Trinity College; *Southwest Dublin*, site of the old city around Dublin Castle; and *North of the Liffey*, the area around the imposing O'Connell Street. The map references given for sights in the city refer to the *Dublin Street Finder* on pages 118–119.

Christ Church Cathedral
was built by Dublin's Anglo-Norman conquerors between 1172 and 1220. It stands on high ground above the River Liffey. Much of the cathedral's present appearance is due to restoration carried out in the 1870s. (See pp80–81.)

NORTH OF THE LIFFEY
Pages 84–93

LIFFE

SOUTHWEST DUBLIN
Pages 72–83

Dublin Castle *stands in the heart of old Dublin. St Patrick's Hall is part of the suite of luxury State Apartments housed on the upper floors on the south side of the castle. Today, these rooms are used for functions of national importance such as presidential inaugurations.* (See pp76–7.)

St Patrick's Cathedral
has a spectacular choir featuring banners and stalls decorated with the insignia of the Knights of St Patrick. The cathedral also holds Ireland's largest and most powerful organ, as well as memorials to Dean Jonathan Swift and prominent Anglo-Irish families. (See pp82–3.)

O'Connell Street, *Dublin's busiest thoroughfare, has a fine mix of architectural styles and a grand central mall punctuated with statues of famous Irish citizens and the 120-m (394-ft) Monument of Light spire. Just off O'Connell Street, on Moore Street, is a lively market. (See pp88–9.)*

The Custom House, *a classic Georgian public building by James Gandon, was built between 1781 and 1791. The sculpted heads on the keystones are personifications of the rivers of Ireland; the one shown above represents the River Foyle. (See p88.)*

Trinity College *is home to the Old Library which contains priceless illuminated manuscripts. These include the* Book of Durrow *which dates from the middle of the 7th century. (See pp62–4.)*

SOUTHEAST
DUBLIN
Pages 56–71

0 metres 400

0 yards 400

The National Gallery *was opened in 1864. Housed on two floors, it holds an eclectic collection, particularly strong on Irish and Italian works. The gallery's most prized painting is Caravaggio's* The Taking of Christ. *The new Millennium Wing has over 500 works on display (See pp70–71.)*

The National Museum *has an impressive collection of artifacts dating from the Stone Age to the 20th century. The Ardagh Chalice (c.AD 800) is one of the many Celtic Christian treasures on display. (See pp66–7.)*

SOUTHEAST DUBLIN

Despite its location close to the old walled city, this part of Dublin remained virtually undeveloped until the founding of Trinity College in 1592. Even then, it was almost a hundred years before the ancient common land further south was enclosed to create St Stephen's Green, a spacious city park.

Georgian doorknocker in Merrion Square

The mid-18th century saw the beginning of a construction boom in the area. During this time, magnificent public buildings such as the Old Library at Trinity College, Leinster House and the Bank of Ireland were built. However, the most conspicuous reminders of Georgian Dublin are the beautiful squares and terraces around

Merrion Square. Many of these buildings still have their original features, including doorknockers, fanlights and wrought-iron balconies.

Today, Southeast Dublin is very much the tourist heart of the city: few visitors can resist the lively atmosphere and attractive shops of Grafton Street. The area is also home to much of Ireland's cultural heritage. The National Gallery has a good collection of Irish and European paintings while the National Museum has superb displays of Irish Bronze Age gold and early Christian treasures. Nearby, the fascinating Natural History Museum has preserved its wonderful Victorian interior.

SIGHTS AT A GLANCE

Museums, Libraries and Galleries
National Gallery pp70–71 ⓫
National Library ❽
National Museum pp64–5 ❼
Natural History Museum ❿
Royal Hibernian Academy ⓭

Historic Buildings
Bank of Ireland ❶
Leinster House ❾
Mansion House ❺
Trinity College pp62–3 ❷

Historic Streets
Fitzwilliam Square ⓮
Grafton Street ❸
Merrion Square ⓬

Churches
St Ann's Church ❻

Parks and Gardens
St Stephen's Green ❹

KEY

- ▨ Street-by-Street *See pp58–9*
- 🚆 Railway station
- Ⓓ DART station
- 🚊 Luas stop
- ℹ Tourist information

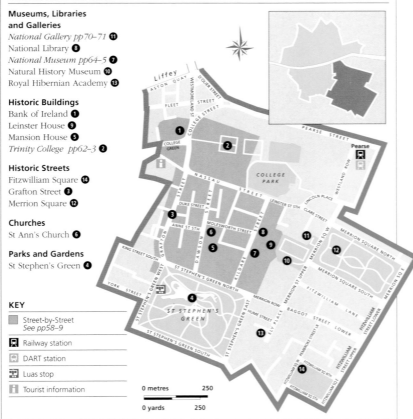

0 metres   250
0 yards   250

◁ **Marble bust of Jonathan Swift in the Old Library, Trinity College**

Street-by-Street: Southeast Dublin

The area around College Green, dominated by the façades
of the Bank of Ireland and Trinity College, is very much
the heart of Dublin. The alleys and malls cutting across
busy pedestrianized Grafton Street boast many of
Dublin's better shops, hotels and restaurants. Just off
Kildare Street are the Irish Parliament, the National
Library and the National Museum. To escape the city
bustle many head for sanctuary in St Stephen's Green,
which is overlooked by fine Georgian buildings.

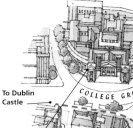

To Dublin
Castle

COLLEGE GRE

Grafton Street
*Brown Thomas department store is one of the
main attractions on this pedestrianized street,
alive with buskers and pavement artists* **3**

Bank of Ireland
*This grand Georgian
building was origi-
nally built as the
Irish Parliament* **1**

**Statue of Molly
Malone (1988)**

St Ann's Church
*The striking façade
of the 18th-century
church was
added in 1868.
The interior
features lovely
stained-glass
windows* **6**

Mansion House
*This has been the official
residence of Dublin's Lord
Mayor since 1715* **5**

Fusiliers' Arch (1907)

★ St Stephen's Green
*The relaxing city park is surrounded by many
grand buildings. In summer, lunch-time
concerts attract tourists and workers alike* **4**

For hotels and restaurants in this region see pp294–8 and pp324–8

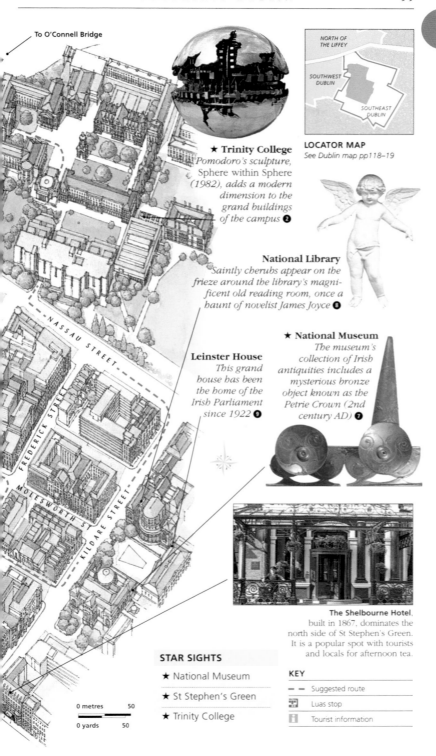

To O'Connell Bridge

LOCATOR MAP
See Dublin map pp118–19

NORTH OF
THE LIFFEY

SOUTHWEST
DUBLIN

SOUTHEAST
DUBLIN

★ **Trinity College**
Pomodoro's sculpture,
Sphere within Sphere
(1982), adds a modern
dimension to the
grand buildings
of the campus ❷

National Library
Saintly cherubs appear on the
frieze around the library's magni-
ficent old reading room, once a
haunt of novelist James Joyce ❽

★ **National Museum**
The museum's
collection of Irish
antiquities includes a
mysterious bronze
object known as the
Petrie Crown (2nd
century AD) ❼

Leinster House
This grand
house has been
the home of the
Irish Parliament
since 1922 ❾

NASSAU STREET

FREDERICK STREET

MOLESWORTH ST.

KILDARE STREET

The Shelbourne Hotel,
built in 1867, dominates the
north side of St Stephen's Green.
It is a popular spot with tourists
and locals for afternoon tea.

STAR SIGHTS

★ National Museum

★ St Stephen's Green

★ Trinity College

0 metres   50

0 yards   50

KEY

- - Suggested route

🚊 Luas stop

ℹ Tourist information

Original chamber of the Irish House of Lords at the Bank of Ireland

Bank of Ireland ❶

2 College Green. **Map** D3. **Tel** 671 2261. ◯ 9:30am–4pm Tue–Fri, 11am–4pm Sat. ⬤ Mon & public hols. **House of Lords** 🗹 10:30am, 11:30am & 1:45pm Tue or by appt.

The prestigious offices of the Bank of Ireland began life as the first purpose-built parliament house in Europe. The original central section was started by Irish architect Edward Lovett Pearce and completed in 1739 after his death. Sadly, Pearce's masterpiece, the great octagonal chamber of the House of Commons (see p40), was removed at the behest of the British government in 1802. The House of Lords, however, remains gloriously intact, especially its coffered ceiling and oak panelling. There are also huge tapestries of the Battle of the Boyne and the Siege of Londonderry, and a splendid 1,233-piece crystal chandelier dating from 1788.

The east portico was added by architect James Gandon in 1785. Further additions to the building were made around 1797.

Bronze statue of Molly Malone at the bottom of Grafton Street

After the dissolution of the Irish Parliament in 1800, the Bank of Ireland bought the building. The present structure was then completed in 1808 with the transformation of the former lobby of the House of Commons into a magnificent cash office and the addition of a curving screen wall and the Foster Place annexe.

At the front of the bank on College Green – common grazing land in the 17th century – is a statue (1879) by John Foley of Henry Grattan (see p40), the most formidable leader of the old parliament.

Trinity College ❷

See pp62–3.

Grafton Street ❸

Map D4.

The spine of Dublin's most popular and stylish shopping district (see pp104–107) runs south from Trinity College to the glass St Stephen's Green Shopping Centre. At the junction with Nassau Street is a statue by Jean Rynhart of Molly Malone (1988), the celebrated street trader from the traditional song "Molly Malone". This busy pedestrianized strip, characterized by energetic buskers and talented

street theatre artists, boasts Brown Thomas, one of Dublin's finest department stores (see p104). In addition, there are plenty of recognisable high street retailers to tempt shoppers, including Monsoon, HMV and Oasis. There are also many excellent jewellers in Grafton Street. Number 78 stands on the site of Samuel Whyte's school, whose illustrious roll included Robert Emmet (see p77), leader of the 1803 Rebellion, and the Duke of Wellington.

Hidden along many of the side streets are quaint, traditional Irish pubs, catering to the weary shopper's need for a refreshment break.

St Stephen's Green ❹

Map D5. ◯ daylight hours. **Newman House** 85–86 St Stephen's Green. **Tel** 716 7422. ◯ Jun–Aug: 11am–5pm; Sept–May: by appointment. ⬤ public hols. 🗹 🗹 obligatory.

Royal College of Surgeons, which overlooks St Stephen's Green

Originally one of three ancient commons in the old city, St Stephen's Green was enclosed in 1664. The 9-ha (22-acre) green was laid out in its present form in 1880, using a grant given by Lord Ardilaun, a member of the Guinness family. Landscaped with flowerbeds, trees, a fountain and a lake, the green is dotted with memorials to eminent Dubliners, including Ardilaun himself. There is a bust of James Joyce (see p90), and a memorial by Henry Moore (1967) dedicated to WB Yeats (see pp232–3). At

Dubliners relaxing by the lake in St Stephen's Green

the Merrion Row corner stands a massive monument (1967) by Edward Delaney to 18th-century nationalist leader Wolfe Tone – it is known locally as "Tonehenge". The 1887 bandstand is still the focal point for free daytime concerts in summer.

The imposing Royal College of Surgeons stands on the west side. Built in 1806, it was commandeered by rebel troops under Countess Constance Markievicz in the 1916 Rising *(see pp44–5)* and its columns still bear the marks of bullets from the fighting.

The busiest side of the Green is the north, known during the 19th century as the Beaux' Walk and still home to several gentlemen's clubs. The most prominent building is the venerable Shelbourne Hotel. Dating back to 1867, its entrance is adorned by statues of Nubian princesses and attendant slaves. It is well worth popping in for a look at the chandeliered foyer and for afternoon tea in the Lord Mayor's Lounge.

Situated on the south side is Newman House, home of the Catholic University of Ireland (now part of University College). Opened in 1854, its first rector was English theo-logian John Henry Newman. Famous past pupils include Patrick Pearse, a leader of the 1916 Rising, former Taoiseach Eamon de Valera *(see p45)* and author James Joyce. Tours reveal some of the best

Georgian interior decor to survive in the city. The walls and ceilings of the Apollo Room and Saloon at No. 85 are festooned with intricate Baroque stuccowork (1739) by the Swiss brothers Paolo and Filippo Francini. The Bishops' Room at No. 86 is decorated with heavy 19th-century furniture.

The small University Church (1856) next door has a colourful, richly marbled Byzantine interior. Also on the south side of St Stephen's Green is Iveagh House, a town house once owned by the Guinness family and now the Depar-tment of Foreign Affairs.

Mansion House ❺

Dawson St. **Map** E4. ◯ *to the public.*

Set back from Dawson Street by a neat cobbled forecourt, the Mansion House is an attractive Queen Anne-style building. It was built in 1710 for the aristocrat Joshua Dawson, after whom the street is named. The Dublin Corpor-ation bought it from him five years later as the official residence of the city's Lord Mayor. The Round Room adjacent to the main building was built in 1821 for the visit of King George IV. The Dáil Éireann *(see p65)*, which adopted the Declaration of Independence, first met here on 21 January 1919.

St Ann's Church ❻

Dawson St. **Map** E4. **Tel** 676 7727. ◯ *10am–4pm Mon–Fri (also for Sun services at 8am, 10:45am & 6:30pm).*

Founded in 1707, St Ann's striking Romanesque façade was added in 1868. Inside are colourful stained-glass win-dows, dating from the mid-19th century. The church has a long tradition of charity work: in 1723 Lord Newton left a be-quest to buy bread for the poor. The original shelf for the bread still stands next to the altar.

Famous past parishioners include Wolfe Tone *(see p41)*, who was married here in 1785, Douglas Hyde *(see p45)* and Bram Stoker (1847–1912), author of *Dracula*.

Detail of window depicting Faith, Hope and Charity, St Ann's Church

Trinity College ②

Trinity College coat of arms

Trinity College was founded in 1592 by Queen Elizabeth I on the site of an Augustinian monastery. Originally a Protestant college, it only began to take Catholics in numbers after 1970, when the Catholic Church relaxed its opposition to their attending. Among Trinity's many famous students were playwrights Oliver Goldsmith and Samuel Beckett, and political writer Edmund Burke. The college's lawns and cobbled quads provide a pleasant haven in the heart of the city. The major attractions are the Old Library and the *Book of Kells*, housed in the Treasury.

★ **Campanile**
The 30-m (98-ft) bell tower was built in 1853 by Sir Charles Lanyon, architect of Queen's University, Belfast (see p278).

Reclining Connected Forms (1969) by Henry Moore

Chapel *(1798)*
This was the first university chapel in the Republic to accept all denominations. The painted window above the altar is from 1867.

Dining Hall (1761)

Parliament Square

statue of Edmund Burke (1868) by John Foley

Main entrance

SAMUEL BECKETT (1906–89)

Nobel prizewinner Samuel Beckett was born at Foxrock, south of Dublin. In 1923 he entered Trinity, and later graduated with a first in modern languages and a gold medal. He was also a keen member of the college cricket team. Forsaking Ireland, Beckett moved to France in the early 1930s. Many of his major works such as *Waiting for Godot* (1951) were written first in French, and later translated, by Beckett, into English.

Statue of Oliver Goldsmith (1864) by John Foley

Provost's House (c. 1760)

Examination Hall
Completed in 1791 to a design by Sir William Chambers, the hall features a gilded oak chandelier and ornate ceilings by Michael Stapleton.

Library Square
The red-brick building (known as the Rubrics) on the east side of Library Square was built around 1700 and is the oldest surviving part of the college.

VISITORS' CHECKLIST

College Green. **Map** D3. *Tel* 608 1724. 🚉 DART to Pearse Street. 🚌 10, 14, 15, 46 & many other routes. **Old Library and Treasury** ⬜ 9:30am–5pm Mon–Sat, 9:30am (noon in winter)–4:30pm Sun & some public hols (last adm: 30 min before closing). ● 10 days at Christmas. ♿ 🚫 ♿ 🎥 by arrangement. Chapel ⬜ by appt. **Douglas Hyde Gallery** ⬜ for exhibitions. **www**.tcd.ie/library

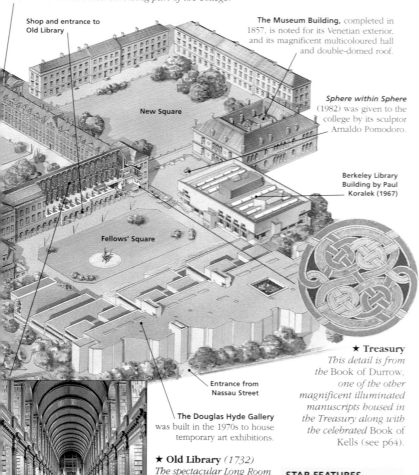

Shop and entrance to Old Library

The Museum Building, completed in 1857, is noted for its Venetian exterior, and its magnificent multicoloured hall and double-domed roof.

New Square

Sphere within Sphere
(1982) was given to the college by its sculptor Arnaldo Pomodoro.

Berkeley Library Building by Paul Koralek (1967)

Fellows' Square

★ **Treasury**
This detail is from the Book of Durrow, one of the other magnificent illuminated manuscripts housed in the Treasury along with the celebrated Book of Kells *(see p64).*

Entrance from Nassau Street

The Douglas Hyde Gallery was built in the 1970s to house temporary art exhibitions.

★ **Old Library** *(1732)*
The spectacular Long Room measures 64 m (210 ft) from end to end. It houses 200,000 antiquarian texts, marble busts of scholars and the oldest surviving harp in Ireland.

STAR FEATURES

★ Campanile

★ Old Library

★ Treasury

The Book of Kells

The most richly decorated of Ireland's medieval illuminated manuscripts, the *Book of Kells* may have been the work of monks from Iona, who fled to Kells *(see p241)* in AD 806 after a Viking raid. The book, which was moved to Trinity College *(see pp62–3)* in the 17th century, contains the four gospels in Latin. The scribes who copied the texts also embellished their calligraphy with intricate interlacing spirals as well as human figures and animals. Some of the dyes used were imported from as far as the Middle East.

Pair of moths

Stylized angel

The Greek letter "X"

The symbols *of the four evangelists are used as decoration throughout the book. The figure of the man symbolizes St Matthew.*

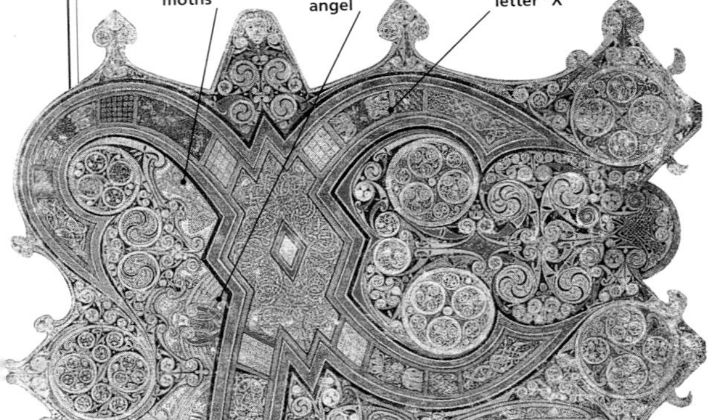

The letter that looks like a "P" is a Greek "R".

The letter "I"

Interlacing motifs

A full-page portrait *of St Matthew, shown standing barefoot in front of a throne, precedes the opening words of his gospel.*

Cat watching rats

MONOGRAM PAGE

This, the most elaborate page of the book, contains the first three words of St Matthew's account of the birth of Christ. The first word "XRI" is an abbreviation of "Christi".

Rats eating bread could be a reference to sinners taking Holy Communion. The symbolism of the animals and people decorating the manuscript is often hard to interpret.

The text *is in a beautifully rounded Celtic script with brightly ornamented initial letters. Animal and human forms are often used to decorate the end of a line.*

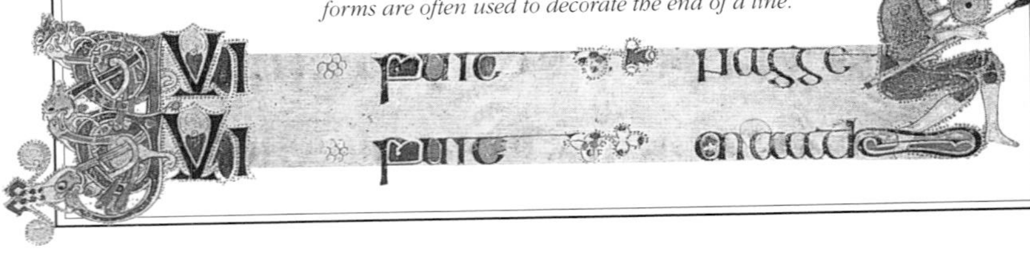

The magnificent domed Reading Room on the first floor of the National Library

National Museum ❼

See pp66–7.

National Library ❽

Kildare St. **Map** E4. **Tel** 603 0200.
◷ 10am–9pm Mon–Wed, 10am–
5pm Thu & Fri, 10am–1pm Sat.
● public hols. **www**.nli.ie

Designed by Sir Thomas Deane, the National Library was opened in 1890. It was built to house the collection of the Royal Dublin Society, which was formed in 1731 to promote the arts and sciences and improve conditions for the poor. The Library contains first editions of every major Irish writer and a copy of almost every book ever published in Ireland. The list of distinguished Irish writers is well known and all are represented here. There is a huge collection of old maps, papers, and manuscripts by such names as playwright George Bernard Shaw and politician and liberator Daniel O'Connell (see p42).

The first-floor Reading Room (where Joyce sited the literary debate in Ulysses) has well-worn desks and green-shaded lamps. Simply ask an attendant for a visitor's pass. There is also a small genealogy exhibit; a more extensive display,

along with details on how to trace family trees, can be found at the Heraldic Museum in the Genealogical Office a few doors down at Nos. 2 and 3 Kildare Street.

Leinster House ❾

Kildare St. **Map** E4. **Tel** 618 3000. ◷ groups by appt; foreign visitors to book through their own embassy. ✆ phone for details. **www**.oireachtas.ie

This stately mansion houses the Dáil and the Seanad – the two chambers of the Irish Parliament. It was originally

built for the Duke of Leinster in 1745. Designed by German-born architect Richard Castle, the Kildare Street façade resembles that of a large town house. However, the rear, looking on to Merrion Square, has the air of a country estate complete with sweeping lawns. The Royal Dublin Society bought the building in 1815. The government obtained a part of it in 1922 for parliamentary use and bought the entire building two years later.

Phone ahead to arrange a tour of the rooms, including the Seanad chamber with its heavily ornamented ceiling.

THE IRISH PARLIAMENT

The Irish Free State, forerunner of the Republic of Ireland, was inaugurated in 1922 (see p44), although an unofficial Irish parliament, the Dáil, had already been in existence since 1919. Today, parliament is made up of two houses: the Dáil (House of Representatives) and Seanad Éireann (the Senate). The Prime Minister is the Taoiseach and the deputy, the Tánaiste. The Dáil's 166 representatives – Teachta Dála, known as TDs – are elected by proportional representation. The 60-strong Seanad is appointed by various individuals and authorities, including the Taoiseach and the University of Dublin.

Opening of the first parliament of the Irish Free State in 1922

National Museum ❼

The National Museum of Ireland (Archaeology and History) was built in the 1880s to the design of Sir Thomas Deane. Its domed rotunda features marble pillars and a mosaic floor. The Treasury houses priceless items such as the Broighter gold boat *(see p33)*, while *Ór – Ireland's Gold*, an exhibition of Ireland's Bronze Age gold, has jewellery such as the Glensheen Gorget *(see pp32–3)*. Many collections have moved to the annexe of the museum at Collins Barracks *(see p92)*.

Egyptian Mummy
This mummy of the lady Tentdinebu is thought to date back to c.945–716 BC. Covered in brilliant colours, it is part of the stunning Egyptian collection.

★ **Ór – Ireland's Gold**
This is one of the most extensive collections of Bronze Age gold in Western Europe. This gold lunula (c.1800 BC) is one of many pieces of fine jewellery in the exhibition.

KEY TO FLOORPLAN

- ☐ The Road to Independence
- ☐ Ór – Ireland's Gold
- ☐ The Treasury
- ☐ Prehistoric Ireland
- ☐ Medieval Ireland
- ☐ Viking Ireland
- ☐ Ancient Egypt
- ☐ Temporary exhibition space
- ☐ Non-exhibition space

Flag from 1916 Rising
The Road to Independence *exhibition covers historical events between 1900 and 1921. This flag flew over Dublin's GPO during the Easter Rising (see p89).*

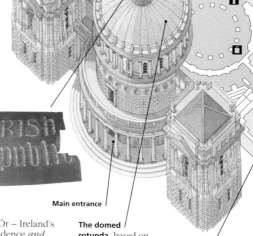

Main entrance

GALLERY GUIDE

The ground floor holds The Treasury, Ór – Ireland's Gold exhibition, The Road to Independence and the Prehistoric Ireland display. On the first floor is the Medieval Ireland exhibition, which illustrates many aspects of life in later medieval Ireland. Also on the first floor are artifacts from Ancient Egypt and from the Viking settlement of Dublin.

The domed rotunda, based on the design of the Altes Museum in Berlin, makes an impressive entrance hall.

The Treasury houses masterpieces of Irish crafts such as the Ardagh Chalice *(see p55).*

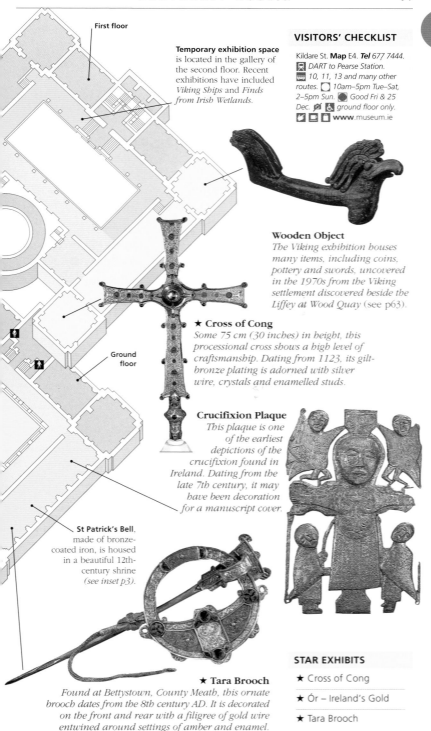

First floor

Temporary exhibition space is located in the gallery of the second floor. Recent exhibitions have included *Viking Ships* and *Finds from Irish Wetlands*.

VISITORS' CHECKLIST

Kildare St. **Map** E4. **Tel** 677 7444.
DART to Pearse Station.
10, 11, 13 and many other routes. 10am–5pm Tue–Sat, 2–5pm Sun. Good Fri & 25 Dec. ground floor only.
www.museum.ie

Wooden Object
The Viking exhibition houses many items, including coins, pottery and swords, uncovered in the 1970s from the Viking settlement discovered beside the Liffey at Wood Quay (see p63).

★ Cross of Cong
Some 75 cm (30 inches) in height, this processional cross shows a high level of craftsmanship. Dating from 1123, its gilt-bronze plating is adorned with silver wire, crystals and enamelled studs.

Ground floor

Crucifixion Plaque
This plaque is one of the earliest depictions of the crucifixion found in Ireland. Dating from the late 7th century, it may have been decoration for a manuscript cover.

St Patrick's Bell, made of bronze-coated iron, is housed in a beautiful 12th-century shrine (see inset p3).

★ Tara Brooch
Found at Bettystown, County Meath, this ornate brooch dates from the 8th century AD. It is decorated on the front and rear with a filigree of gold wire entwined around settings of amber and enamel.

STAR EXHIBITS

★ Cross of Cong

★ Ór – Ireland's Gold

★ Tara Brooch

Natural History Museum ❿

Merrion St. **Map** E4. **Tel** *677 7444.*
⬜ *10am–5pm Tue–Sat, 2–5pm Sun.*
⬛ *Mon, Good Fri & Dec 25.* ♿
ground floor only. **www**.museum.ie

Known affectionately as the "Dead Zoo", this museum is crammed with antique glass cabinets containing stuffed animals from around the world. The museum was opened to the public in 1857 with an inaugural lecture by Dr David Livingstone. The building has barely altered since Victorian times, and is now practically a museum piece itself.

The Irish room on the ground floor holds exhibits on Irish wildlife. Inside the front door are three huge skeletons of the extinct giant deer, better known as the "Irish elk". Also on this floor are shelves stacked with jars of bizarre creatures such as octopuses, leeches and worms preserved in embalming fluid.

The upper gallery houses the noted Blaschka Collection of glass models of marine life, and a display of buffalo and deer trophies. Suspended from the ceiling are the skeletons of a fin whale, found at Bantry Bay *(see p167)* in 1862, and a humpback whale, which was found stranded at Inishcrone in County Sligo in 1893.

Lawn and front entrance of the Natural History Museum

National Gallery ⓫

See pp70–71.

Georgian town houses overlooking Merrion Square gardens

Merrion Square ⓬

Map F4.

Merrion Square is one of Dublin's largest and grandest Georgian squares. Covering about 5 ha (12 acres, the square was laid out by John Ensor around 1762.

On the west side are the impressive façades of the Natural History Museum, the National Gallery and the front garden of Leinster House *(see p65)*. However, this august triumvirate does not compare with the lovely Georgian town houses on the other three sides of the square. Many have brightly painted doors with original features such as wrought-iron balconies, ornate doorknockers and fanlights. The oldest and finest houses are on the north side.

Many of the houses – now predominantly used as office space – have plaques detailing the rich and famous who once lived in them. These include Catholic emancipation leader Daniel O'Connell *(see p42)*, who lived at No. 58 and poet WB Yeats *(see pp232–3)*, who lived at No. 82. The playwright Oscar Wilde *(see p22)* spent his childhood at No. 1.

The attractive central park features colourful flower and shrub beds. In the 1840s it served a grim function as an emergency soup kitchen, feeding the hungry during the Great Famine *(see p219)*. On the northwest side of the park stands the restored Rutland Fountain. It was originally erected in 1791 for the sole use of Dublin's poor.

Just off the square, at No. 24 Merrion Street Upper, is the birthplace of the Duke of Wellington, who, when teased about his Irish background, said, "Being born in a stable does not make one a horse."

Royal Hibernian Academy ⓭

15 Ely Place. **Map** E5. **Tel** *661 2558.*
⬜ *11am–5pm Tue, Wed, Fri & Sat, 11am–9pm Thu, 2–5pm Sun.*
⬛ *Mon, public & Christmas hols.* ♿
www.royalhibernianacademy.com

The academy is one of the largest exhibition spaces in the city. It puts on touring exhibitions and mounts shows of painting, sculpture and other work by Ireland's best young art and design students. This modern building does, however, look out of place at the end of Ely Place, an attractive Georgian cul-de-sac.

Fitzwilliam Square ⓮

Map E5. **No. 29 Fitzwilliam St Lower**
Tel *702 6165.* ⬜ *10am–5pm Tue–Sat, 1–5pm Sun.* ⬛ *Mon & 3 weeks at Christmas.* 🎫 📷
www.esb.ie/numbertwentynine

Dating from 1825, this was one of the last Georgian squares to be laid out in central Dublin. Much smaller than Merrion Square, it is a popular location for medical practices.

In the 1960s, more than 20 town houses on Fitzwilliam Street Lower were torn down to make way for the headquarters of the Electricity Supply Board. The company has since tried to appease public indignation by renovating No. 29 as a Georgian showpiece home.

Dublin's Georgian Terraces

Doorknocker, Merrion Square

The 18th century was Dublin's Age of Elegance, a time of relative prosperity when the Irish gentry, keen not to appear as the poor relations of Britain, set about remodelling Dublin into one of the most elegant cities in Europe. Terraced town houses were built, forming handsome new streets and squares. During the 19th century the city's wealth declined, forcing some middle-class families to divide their homes into tenements. Many of Dublin's once grand streets slowly deteriorated. A century later the property boom of the 1960s threatened to rip out what was left of Georgian Dublin. Fortunately, much has survived and some of the city's finest architecture can be seen in Merrion Square and Fitzwilliam Square.

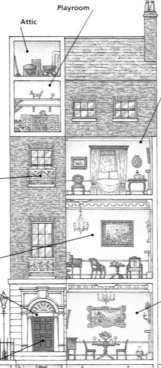

Playroom

Attic

The bedrooms were usually on the second floor, while the upper floors contained the servants' quarters and children's rooms.

Wrought-iron balconies *gave added prestige to the Georgian house. Those still in place today are mostly later Victorian additions.*

Lavish stuccowork *was an important way of showing an owner's wealth during the 18th century.*

The drawing room was always on the first floor. The high ceiling was decorated with the finest plasterwork.

The dining room was normally on the ground floor.

Architrave

The kitchen contained a huge cooking range which was fired by either coal or wood. The adjoining pantry was used to store the household's groceries.

The doorway *was usually crowned with a segmented fanlight. The principal decoration on the door itself was a heavy brass knocker.*

GEORGIAN TERRACED HOUSE

While Georgian streetscapes may appear uniform, closer inspection reveals a diversity of styles in terms of details such as fanlights, architraves and balconies. The hallways usually had stone floors and, facing the hall door, a staircase rising to the upper floors. Many of the town houses did not have gardens – the railed-off parks in the centre of the squares were reserved for residents only and served as such.

National Gallery ⓫

This purpose-built gallery was opened to the public in 1864. It houses many excellent exhibits, largely due to generous bequests, such as the Milltown collection of works of art from Russborough House *(see p132)*. Playwright George Bernard Shaw was also a benefactor, leaving a third of his estate to the gallery. A new wing has been added to the gallery, which now has more than 700 works on display. Although the emphasis is on Irish landscape art and portraits, the major schools of European painting are well represented with works by Goya, El Greco, Vermeer, Titian and Monet.

The Houseless Wanderer by John Foley

★ **Pierrot**
This Cubist-style work, by Spanish-born artist Juan Gris, is one of many variations he painted on the theme of Pierrot and Harlequin. This particular one dates from 1921.

GALLERY GUIDE
The main entrance is through the lofty Millennium Wing on Clare Street. Irish and British collections are housed on level 1, with the National Portrait Gallery on the mezzanine level. The European schools are located on level 2, with changing special exhibitions installed in the adjacent Millennium Wing.

Mezzanine level

★ **For the Road**
The Yeats Museum houses works by Jack B Yeats (1871–1957) and his family. This mysterious painting reflects the artist's obsession with the Sligo countryside.

STAR PAINTINGS

★ The Taking of Christ by Caravaggio

★ Pierrot by Juan Gris

★ For the Road by Jack Yeats

The Shaw Room is an elegant hall, lined with full-length portraits, dating from the 17th century onwards, and lit by magnificent Waterford Crystal chandeliers.

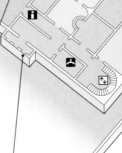

Merrion Square entrance

★ **The Taking of Christ**
Rediscovered in a Dublin Jesuit house in 1990, this 1602 composition by Caravaggio has enhanced the gallery's reputation.

VISITORS' CHECKLIST

Clare Street, Merrion Square West. Map E4. **Tel** 661 5133. DART to Pearse. 5, 7, 45, 48A. 9:30am–5:30pm Mon–Wed, Fri & Sat, 9:30am–8:30pm Thu, noon–5:30pm Sun. Good Fri, 24–26 Dec. for special exhibitions. www.nationalgallery.ie

The Millennium Wing, a new airy entrance court, has provided the gallery with space to showcase major travelling shows.

Level 2

Judith with the Head of Holofernes
This monochrome image by Andrea Mantegna (c. 1431–1506) depicts the decapitation of an Assyrian chief.

Level 1

The Sick Call
Painted in a Pre-Raphaelite style by Matthew James Lawless, this 1863 canvas evokes the suffering of the Irish population in the years following the Famine.

Entrance level

Main entrance
(Clare Street)

KEY TO FLOORPLAN

- Irish School
- British School
- Portraiture
- European Sculpture and Decorative Arts
- Print Room
- Italian School
- French School
- Spanish School
- Northern European Schools
- Baroque
- Temporary exhibitions
- Non-exhibition space

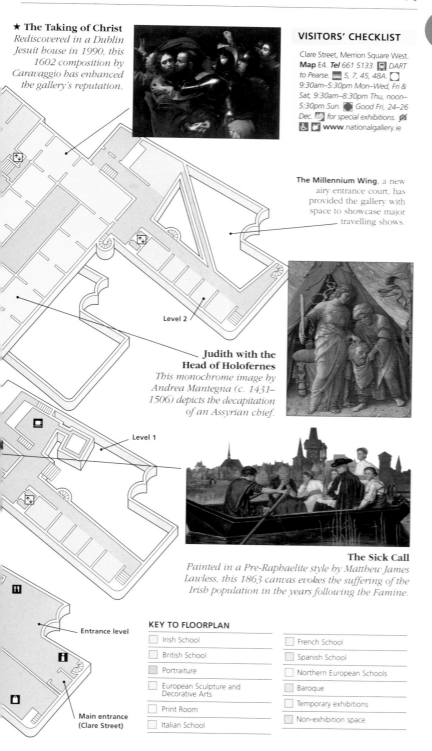

SOUTHWEST DUBLIN

The area around Dublin Castle was first settled in prehistoric times, and it was from here that the city grew. Dublin gets its name from the dark pool *(Dubh Linn)* which formed at the confluence of the Liffey and the Poddle, a river which once ran through the site of Dublin Castle. It is now channelled underground and trickles out into the Liffey by Grattan Bridge. Archaeological excavations behind Wood Quay, on the banks of the Liffey, reveal that the Vikings established a trading settlement here around 841.

Following Strongbow's invasion of 1170, a medieval city began to emerge; the Anglo-Normans built strong defensive walls around the castle.

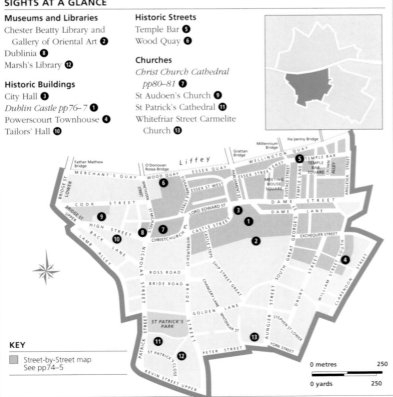

Memorial to Turlough O'Carolan in St Patrick's Cathedral

A small reconstructed section of these old city walls can be seen at St Audoen's Church. More conspicuous reminders of the Anglo-Normans are provided by the grand medieval Christ Church Cathedral and Ireland's largest church, St Patrick's Cathedral. When the city expanded to the north and east during the Georgian era, the narrow cobbled streets of Temple Bar became a quarter of skilled craftsmen and merchants. Today this area is considered to be the trendiest part of town, and is home to a variety of "alternative" shops and cafés. The Powerscourt Townhouse, an elegant 18th-century mansion, has been converted into one of the city's best shopping centres.

SIGHTS AT A GLANCE

Museums and Libraries
Chester Beatty Library and Gallery of Oriental Art ❷
Dublinia ❽
Marsh's Library ⓬

Historic Buildings
City Hall ❸
Dublin Castle pp76–7 ❶
Powerscourt Townhouse ❹
Tailors' Hall ❿

Historic Streets
Temple Bar ❺
Wood Quay ❻

Churches
Christ Church Cathedral pp80–81 ❼
St Audoen's Church ❾
St Patrick's Cathedral ⓫
Whitefriar Street Carmelite Church ⓭

KEY

Street-by-Street map See pp74–5

0 metres   250
0 yards   250

◁ **Temple Bar, a centre for the arts and a popular meeting spot for young Dubliners**

Street-by-Street: Southwest Dublin

Despite its wealth of ancient buildings, such as
Dublin Castle and Christ Church Cathedral,
this part of Dublin lacks the sleek appeal of
the neighbouring streets around Grafton
Street. In recent years, however,
redevelopment has helped to rejuvenate the
area, especially around Temple Bar, where
the attractive cobbled streets are lined with
interesting shops, galleries and cafés.

Sunlight Chambers
were built in 1900 for
the Lever Brothers
company. The
delightful terracotta
decoration on the
façade advertises
their main business
of soap manufacturing.

Wood Quay
*This is where the Vikings
established their first
permanent settlement in
Ireland around 841* ❻

★ Christ Church Cathedral
*Huge family monuments
including that of the
19th Earl of Kildare
can be found in
Ireland's oldest cath-
edral, which also has a
fascinating crypt* ❼

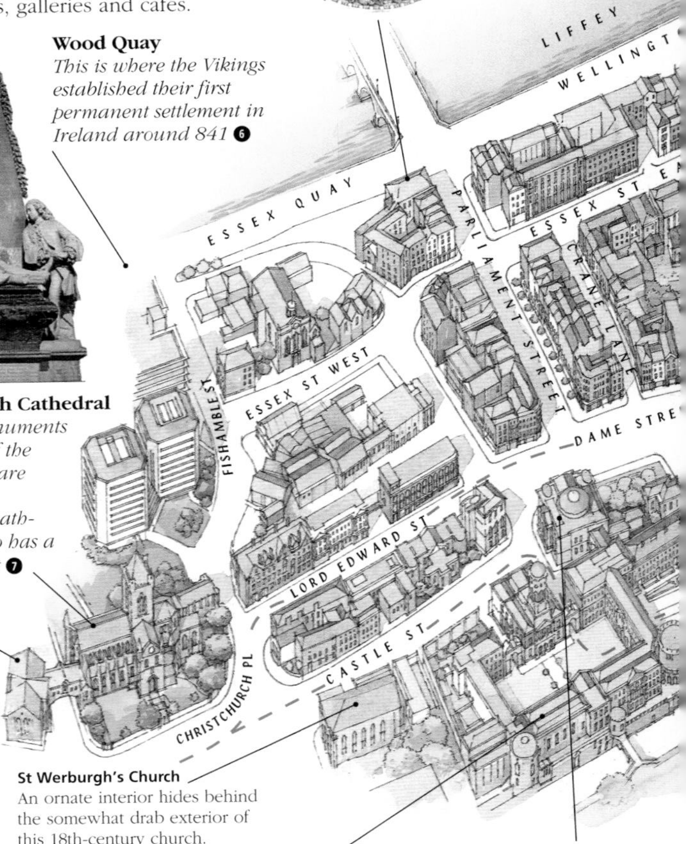

St Werburgh's Church
An ornate interior hides behind
the somewhat drab exterior of
this 18th-century church.

Dublinia
*Medieval Dublin is
the subject of this
interactive museum,
located in the
former Synod Hall
of the Church of
Ireland. It is linked
to Christ Church by
a bridge* ❽

City Hall
*Originally built as the
Royal Exchange in
1779, the city's muni-
cipal headquarters is
fronted by a huge
Corinthian portico* ❸

★ Dublin Castle
*The Drawing Room, with its
Waterford crystal chandelier, is
part of a suite of luxurious rooms
built in the 18th century for the
Viceroys of Ireland* ❶

For hotels and restaurants in this region see pp294–8 and pp324–8

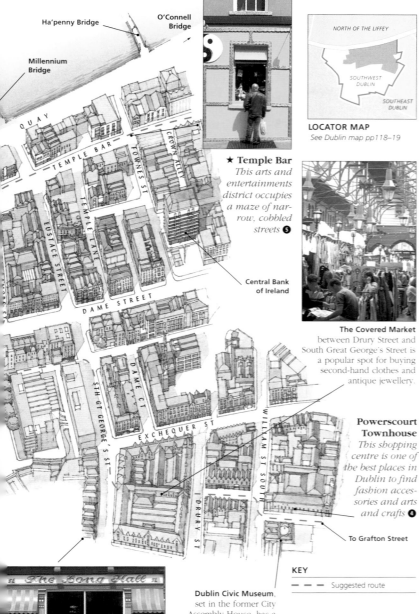

Ha'penny Bridge

O'Connell Bridge

Millennium Bridge

QUAY

TEMPLE BAR

TOWNES ST

CROWN ALLEY

TEMPLE LANE

EUSTACE STREET

DAME STREET

DAME CT

STH GT GEORGE'S ST

DRURY CT

EXCHEQUER ST

WILLIAM ST SOUTH

DRURY ST

★ Temple Bar
This arts and entertainments district occupies a maze of narrow, cobbled streets ❺

Central Bank of Ireland

NORTH OF THE LIFFEY

SOUTHWEST DUBLIN

SOUTHEAST DUBLIN

LOCATOR MAP
See Dublin map pp118–19

The Covered Market
between Drury Street and South Great George's Street is a popular spot for buying second-hand clothes and antique jewellery.

Powerscourt Townhouse
This shopping centre is one of the best places in Dublin to find fashion accessories and arts and crafts ❹

To Grafton Street

KEY

— — — Suggested route

Dublin Civic Museum, set in the former City Assembly House, has a wide range of displays covering the history of Dublin from pre-Viking times until the 1960s.

STAR SIGHTS

★ Christ Church Cathedral

★ Dublin Castle

★ Temple Bar

The Long Hall is a magnificent, old-fashioned pub. Behind the narrow room's long bar stands a bewildering array of antique clocks.

0 metres 50

0 yards 50

Dublin Castle ❶

St Patrick by Edward Smyth

For seven centuries Dublin Castle was a symbol of English rule, ever since the Anglo-Normans built a fortress here in the 13th century. All that remains of the original structure is the Record Tower and the butt of the Powder Tower. Following a fire in 1684, the Surveyor-General, Sir William Robinson, laid down the plans for the Upper and Lower Castle Yards in their present form. On the first floor of the south side of the Upper Yard are the luxury State Apartments, including St Patrick's Hall. These rooms, with Killybegs carpets and chandeliers of Waterford glass, served as home to the British-appointed Viceroys of Ireland.

Figure of Justice
Facing the Upper Yard above the main entrance from Cork Hill, this statue aroused much cynicism among Dubliners, who felt she was turning her back on the city.

★ **Throne Room**
Built in 1740, this room contains a throne said to have been presented by William of Orange after his victory at the Battle of the Boyne (see p244).

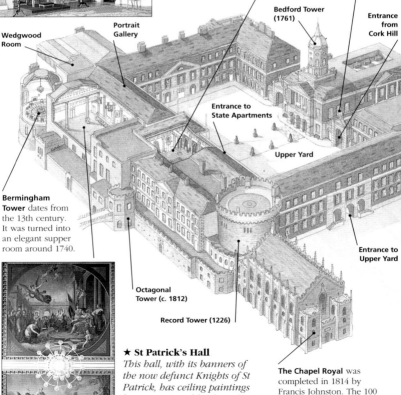

Wedgwood Room

Portrait Gallery

Bedford Tower (1761)

Entrance from Cork Hill

Entrance to State Apartments

Upper Yard

Bermingham Tower dates from the 13th century. It was turned into an elegant supper room around 1740.

Entrance to Upper Yard

Octagonal Tower (c. 1812)

Record Tower (1226)

★ **St Patrick's Hall**
This hall, with its banners of the now defunct Knights of St Patrick, has ceiling paintings by Vincenzo Valdré (1778), symbolizing the relationship between Britain and Ireland.

The Chapel Royal was completed in 1814 by Francis Johnston. The 100 heads on the exterior of this Neo-Gothic church were carved by Edward Smyth.

VISITORS' CHECKLIST

Off Dame St. **Map** C3. *Tel* 677
7129. 🚌 49, 56A, 77, 77A, 123.
State Apartments ⬭ 10am–
4:45pm Mon–Fri, 2–4:45pm Sat,
Sun & public hols. ● Good Fri,
25–26 Dec, 1 Jan and for State
functions. 📷 🎫 obligatory.
www.dublincastle.ie

ROBERT EMMET

Robert Emmet (1778–1803),
leader of the abortive 1803
rebellion, is remembered
as a heroic champion of
Irish liberty. His plan was
to capture Dublin Castle as
a signal for the country to
rise up against the Act of
Union (*see p42*). Emmet
was caught and publicly
hanged, but the defiant,
patriotic speech he made
from the dock helped to
inspire future generations
of Irish freedom fighters.

Government
offices

ver Yard

Dame Street

STAR FEATURES

★ St Patrick's Hall

★ Throne Room

Manuscript (1874) from the Holy Koran written by calligrapher
Ahmad Shaikh in Kashmir, Chester Beatty Library

Chester Beatty Library and Gallery of Oriental Art ❷

Clock Tower Building, Dublin Castle.
Tel 407 0750. ⬭ 10am–5pm Mon–
Fri (Tue–Fri Oct–Apr), 11am–5pm Sat,
1pm–5pm Sun. ● Good Fri, 24–26
Dec & public holidays. 🚻 ♿ 🛗
www.cbl.ie

This world-renowned collection was named European
Museum of the Year in 2002.
It was bequeathed to Ireland
by the American mining mag-
nate and art collector Sir
Alfred Chester Beatty, who
died in 1968. This generous
act no doubt led to his
selection as Ireland's first
honorary citizen in 1957.

During his lifetime, Beatty
accumulated almost 300 copies
of the Koran, representing the
works of master calligraphers.
Also on display are 6,000-year-
old Babylonian stone tablets,
Greek papyri and biblical
material written in Coptic, the
ancient language of Egypt.

Treasures from the Far East
include a collection of Chinese
jade books – each leaf is made
from thinly cut jade, engraved
with Chinese characters which
are then filled with gold.
Burmese and Siamese art is
represented by the collection
of 18th- and 19th-century
Parabaiks, books of folk tales
with colourful illustrations on
mulberry leaf paper. The
Japanese collection includes
paintings, woodblock prints
and books and scrolls from

the 16th to 18th centuries.
One of the most beautiful
manuscripts in the western
European collection is the
Coëtivy Book of Hours, an
illuminated 15th-century
French prayer book.

City Hall ❸

Cork Hill, Dame St. **Map** C3. *Tel* 222
2204. ⬭ 10am–5:15pm Mon–Sat,
2pm–5pm Sun and public holidays. ●
Good Fri, 24–26 Dec. 🎫 ♿ 🛗 🎥

Designed by Thomas Cooley,
this imposing Corinthian-
style building was erected
between 1769 and 1779 as the
Royal Exchange. It was taken
over by Dublin Corporation
in 1852 as a meeting place for
the city council – a role it
keeps to this day.

The building has recently
been restored to its original
condition and a permanent
exhibition on the city's history,
Dublin City Hall – The Story
of the Capital, is housed on
the lower ground floor.

City Hall from Parliament Street

Interior of Powerscourt Townhouse Shopping Centre

Powerscourt Townhouse ❹

South William St. **Map** D4. **Tel** 671 7000. ◯ 10am–6pm Mon–Fri (8pm Thu), 9am–6pm Sat, noon–6pm Sun. See also **Shopping in Ireland** pp352–5. www.powerscourtcentre.com

Completed in 1774 by Robert Mack, this grand mansion was built as the city home of Viscount Powerscourt, who also had a country estate at Enniskerry (see pp134–5). Granite from the Powerscourt estate was used in its construction. Today the building houses one of Dublin's best shopping centres. Inside it still features the original grand mahogany staircase, and detailed plasterwork by Michael Stapleton.

The building became a drapery warehouse in the 1830s, and major restoration during

the 1960s turned it into a centre of specialist galleries, antique shops, jewellery stalls, cafés and other shop units. The enclosed central courtyard, topped by a glass dome, is a popular meeting place with Dubliners. The centre can also be reached from Grafton Street down the Johnson Court alley.

Temple Bar ❺

Map C3. **Temple Bar Information Tel** 677 2255 **Entertainment in Dublin** p114. **Project** 39 East Essex Street. **Tel** 679 6622. **Irish Film Institute** 6 Eustace Street. **Tel** 679 5744. 🎬 Diversions, (May–Sep). www.temple-bar.ie

Some of Dublin's best night spots, restaurants and unusual shops line these narrow, cobbled streets running between the Bank of Ireland (see p60) and Christ Church Cathedral. In the 18th century the area was home to many insalubrious characters – Fownes Street was noted for its brothels. It was also the birthplace of parliamentarian Henry Grattan (see p40). Skilled craftsmen and artisans, such as clockmakers and printers, lived and worked around Temple Bar until postwar industrialization led to a decline in the area's fortunes.

In the 1970s, the CIE (the national transport authority) bought up parcels of land in this area to build a major bus depot. Before building, the CIE rented out, on cheap leases, some of the old retail and warehouse premises to young artists and to record, clothing and book shops. The area developed an "alternative" identity and when the development plans were scrapped the artists and retailers stayed on. Described by some cynics as the city's "officially designated arts zone", Temple Bar today is an exciting place with bars, restaurants, shops and several galleries. Stylish residential and commercial development is contributing further to the area's appeal.

Highlights include the **Project**, a highly respected venue for avant garde performance art; and the **Irish Film Institute**, which shows art house and independent films, and has a popular restaurant/bar and shop.

Nearby Meeting House Square is one of the venues for Diversions, a summer programme of free outdoor concerts, theatre and film screenings. The National Photographic Archive and

A pub in Temple Bar

Gallery of Photography are also on the square and there is an excellent organic food market here on Saturdays, where you can sample oysters, salmon, cheese and other local produce.

Wood Quay ❻

Map B3.

Named after the timber supports used to reclaim the land, Wood Quay has undergone excavations revealing the remains of one of the earliest Viking villages in Ireland (see p79). It is hoped that part of the excavated area will eventually be open to public view.

Viking artifacts can be seen at the Dublinia exhibition (see p79) and at the National Museum (see pp66–7).

Strolling through the streets of Temple Bar

For hotels and restaurants in this region see pp294–8 and pp324–8

Former Synod Hall, now home to the Dublinia exhibition

Christ Church Cathedral **7**

See pp80–81.

Dublinia **8**

St Michael's Hill. **Map** B3. *Tel 679 4611.* ◯ *Apr–Sep: 10am–5pm daily; Oct–Mar: 11am–4pm Mon–Fri, 10am–4pm Sat, Sun & public hols.* ● *23–26 Dec, 17 Mar.* 🖼 *charge to enter Christ Church Cathedral via bridge.* 🚻 **www**.dublinia.ie

Managed by the non-profit-making Medieval Trust, the Dublinia exhibition covers the formative period of Dublin's history from the arrival of the Anglo-Normans in 1170 to the closure of the monasteries in the 1540s *(see p38).*

The exhibition is housed in the Neo-Gothic Synod Hall, which, up until 1983, was home to the ruling body of the Church of Ireland. The building and the hump-backed bridge linking it to Christ Church Cathedral date from the 1870s. Before Dublinia was established in 1993, the Synod Hall was used as a nightclub.

The exhibition is entered via the basement where visitors walk through life-size reconstructions of the Medieval City. These depict major events in Dublin's history, such as the Black Death and the rebellion of Silken Thomas *(see p38).* The ground floor houses a large scale model of Dublin in around 1500, a display of artifacts from the Wood Quay excavation, and reconstructions including the inside of a late medieval merchant's kitchen. There are also information panels on the themes of trade, merchants and religion. A multi-screen presentation on Dublin's medieval history can be seen in the dark-wood panelled Great Hall on the first floor.

The 60-m (200-ft) high St Michael's Tower offers one of the best vantage points for views across the city.

St Audoen's Church **9**

High St, Cornmarket. **Map** B3. *Tel 677 0088.* ◯ *Jun–Sep.* 🖼 🚻

Tower of St Audoen's Church

Designated a national monument and open for visitors throughout the summer months, St Audoen's is the earliest surviving medieval church in Dublin.

The 15th-century nave remains intact and the three bells date from 1423. The church stands in an attractive churchyard with well-maintained lawns and shrubs. To the rear, steps lead down to St Audoen's Arch, the only remaining gateway of the old city. Flanking the gate are restored sections of the 13th-century city walls.

Next door stands St Audoen's Roman Catholic Church, which was built in the 1840s. The two Pacific clam shells by the front door hold holy water.

THE VIKINGS IN DUBLIN

Viking raiders arrived in Ireland in the late 8th century and founded Dublin in 841. They built a fort where the River Poddle met the Liffey at a black pool (Dubh Linn), on the site of Dublin Castle. They also established a settlement along the banks of the Liffey at Wood Quay *(see p78).* Much of their trade was based on silver, slaves and piracy.

Following their defeat by Brian Ború at the Battle of Clontarf in 1014 *(see p34),* the Vikings integrated fully with the local Irish, adopting Christian beliefs. After Strongbow's Anglo-Norman invasion in 1170 *(see p36),* the flourishing Hiberno-Viking trading community declined, and many were banished to a separate colony called Oxmanstown, just north of the river.

Artist's impression of a Viking ship in Dublin Bay

Christ Church Cathedral ❼

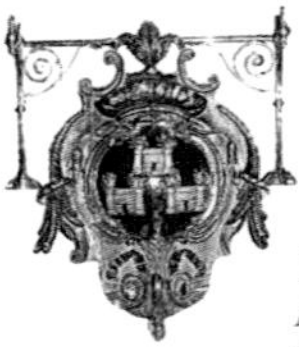

Arms on Lord Mayor's pew

Christ Church Cathedral was established by the Hiberno-Norse king of Dublin, Sitric "Silkbeard", and the first bishop of Dublin, Dunan. It was rebuilt by the Anglo-Norman archbishop, John Cumin in 1186. It is the cathedral for the Church of Ireland (Anglican) diocese of Dublin and Glendalough. By the 19th century it was in a bad state of repair, but was completely remodelled by architect George Street in the 1870s. The vast 12th-century crypt was restored in 2000.

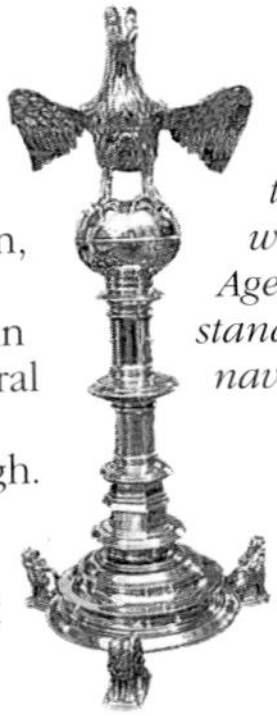

★ **Medieval Lectern**
This beautiful brass lectern in the north transept, was hand-wrought during the Middle Ages. A matching lectern stands on the north side of the nave, in front of the pulpit.

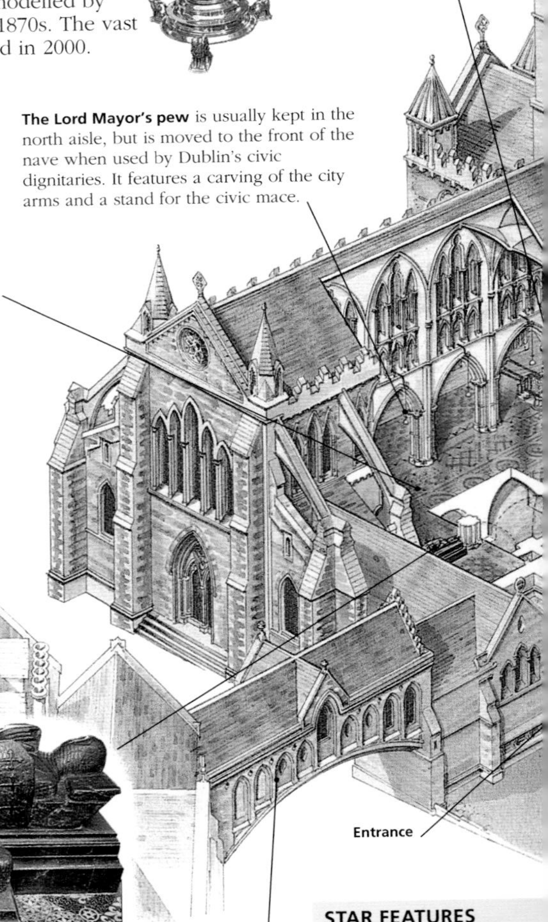

The Lord Mayor's pew is usually kept in the north aisle, but is moved to the front of the nave when used by Dublin's civic dignitaries. It features a carving of the city arms and a stand for the civic mace.

Great Nave
The 25-m (68-ft) high nave has some fine early Gothic arches. On the north side, the original 13th-century wall leans out by as much as 50 cm (18 in) due to the weight of the roof.

★ **Strongbow Monument**
The large effigy in chain armour is probably not Strongbow. However, his remains are buried in the cathedral and the curious half-figure may be part of his original tomb.

The bridge to the Synod Hall was added when the cathedral was being rebuilt in the 1870s.

Entrance

STAR FEATURES

★ Crypt

★ Medieval Lectern

★ Strongbow Monument

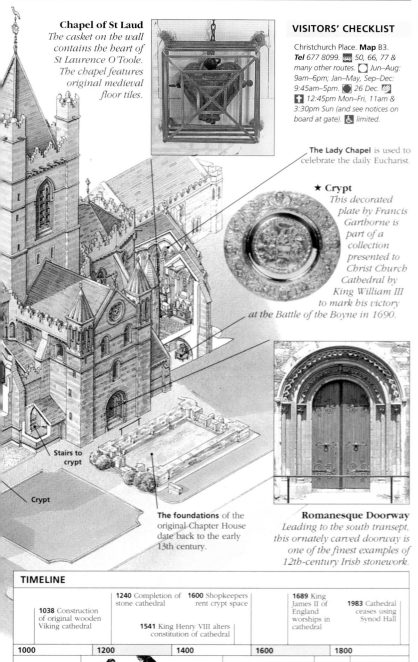

Chapel of St Laud
The casket on the wall contains the heart of St Laurence O'Toole. The chapel features original medieval floor tiles.

VISITORS' CHECKLIST

Christchurch Place. **Map** B3.
Tel 677 8099. 🚌 50, 66, 77 &
many other routes. ◯ Jun–Aug:
9am–6pm; Jan–May, Sep–Dec:
9:45am–5pm. ● 26 Dec. 📷
✝ 12:45pm Mon–Fri, 11am &
3:30pm Sun (and see notices on
board at gate). ♿ limited.

The Lady Chapel is used to celebrate the daily Eucharist.

★ Crypt
This decorated plate by Francis Garthorne is part of a collection presented to Christ Church Cathedral by King William III to mark his victory at the Battle of the Boyne in 1690.

Stairs to crypt

Crypt

The foundations of the original Chapter House date back to the early 13th century.

Romanesque Doorway
Leading to the south transept, this ornately carved doorway is one of the finest examples of 12th-century Irish stonework.

TIMELINE

1000	1200	1400	1600	1800
1038 Construction of original wooden Viking cathedral	**1240** Completion of stone cathedral	**1600** Shopkeepers rent crypt space	**1689** King James II of England worships in cathedral	**1983** Cathedral ceases using Synod Hall
		1541 King Henry VIII alters constitution of cathedral		
1186 The first Anglo-Norman archbishop, John Cumin, begins work on the new cathedral.		*Meeting between Lambert Simnel and the Earl of Kildare (see p37)*	**1742** Choir participates in first performance of Handel's *Messiah* **1487** Coronation of 10-year-old Lambert Simnel as King of England	**1871** Major rebuilding of the cathedral begins, including Synod Hall and bridge

Tailors' Hall ❿

Back Lane. **Map** B4. **Tel** 454 1786.
⬤ to the public. www.antaisce.org

Dublin's only surviving guildhall preserves a delightful corner of old Dublin in an otherwise busy redevelopment zone. Built in 1706, it stands behind a limestone arch in a quiet cobbled yard. The building is the oldest guildhall in Ireland and was used by various trade groups including hosiers, saddlers and barber-surgeons as well as tailors. It also hosted many political meetings – Wolfe Tone addressed a public United Irishmen rally here before the 1798 rebellion (see p41). The building closed in the early 1960s due to neglect, but a successful appeal by Desmond Guinness saw it refurbished. It is now the home of An Taisce (the Irish National Trust).

Façade of Tailors' Hall, home of the Irish National Trust

St Patrick's Cathedral with Minot's Tower and spire

St Patrick's Cathedral ⓫

St Patrick's Close. **Map** B4. **Tel** 475 4817. ☐ Mar–Oct: 9am–6pm Mon–Fri, 9am–6pm Sat & Sun; Nov–Feb: 9am–6pm Mon–Fri, 10am–3pm Sun. ✚ 12am & 3:15pm Sun. Tours are not admitted during services. 🌐 www.stpatrickscathedral.ie

Ireland's largest church was founded beside a sacred well where St Patrick is said to have baptized converts around AD 450. A stone slab bearing a Celtic cross and covering the well was unearthed over a century ago. It is now preserved in the west end of the cathedral's nave. The original building was just a wooden chapel and remained so until 1192 when Archbishop John Comyn rebuilt the cathedral in stone. Over the centuries, St Patrick's came to be seen as the people's church, while the older Christ Church Cathedral (see pp80–81) nearby was more associated with the British establishment. In the mid-17th century, Huguenot refugees from France arrived in Dublin, and were given the Lady Chapel by the Dean and Chapter as their place of worship. The chapel was separated from the rest of the cathedral and used by the Huguenots until the late 18th century. Today St Patrick's Cathedral is the Protestant Church of Ireland's national cathedral.

Much of the present building dates back to work completed between 1254 and 1270. The cathedral suffered over the centuries from desecration, fire and neglect but, thanks to the generosity of Sir Benjamin Guinness, it underwent extensive restoration during the 1860s. The building is 91 m (300 ft) long; at the western end is a 43-m (141-ft) tower, restored by Archbishop Minot in 1370 and now known as Minot's Tower. The spire was added in the 18th century.

The interior is dotted with busts, brasses and monuments. A leaflet available at the front desk helps identify them. The largest, most colourful and elaborate tomb was dedicated to the Boyle family in the 17th century. Erected by Richard Boyle, Earl of Cork, in memory of his second wife Katherine, it is decorated with painted figures of his family,

JONATHAN SWIFT (1667–1745)

Jonathan Swift was born in Dublin and educated at Trinity College (see pp62–3). He left for England in 1689, but returned in 1694 when his political career failed. Back in Ireland he began a life in the church, becoming Dean of St Patrick's in 1713. In addition to his clerical duties, Swift was a prolific political commentator – his best-known work, *Gulliver's Travels*, contains a bitter satire on Anglo-Irish relations. Swift's personal life, particularly his friendship with two younger women, Ester Johnson, better known as Stella, and Hester Vanhomrigh, attracted criticism. In his final years, Swift suffered from Ménière's disease – an illness of the ear which led many to believe him insane.

including his wife's parents. Other famous citizens remembered in the church include the harpist Turlough O'Carolan (1670–1738) *(see p24)* and Douglas Hyde (1860–1949), the first President of Ireland.

Many visitors come to see the memorials associated with Jonathan Swift, the satirical writer and Dean of St Patrick's. In the north transept is "Swift's Corner", containing various memorabilia such as an altar table and a bookcase holding his death mask and various pamphlets. A self-penned epitaph can be found on the wall on the southwest side of the nave. A few steps away, two brass plates mark his grave and that of his beloved Stella, who died in 1728.

At the west end of the nave is an old door with a hole in it – a relic from a feud which took place between the Lords Kildare and Ormonde in 1492. The latter took refuge in the Chapter House, but a truce was soon made and a hole was cut in the door by Lord Kildare so that the two could shake hands in friendship.

Marsh's Library 🄑

St Patrick's Close. **Map** B4. ***Tel*** 454 3511. ▢ *10am–1pm & 2–5pm Mon & Wed–Fri, 10:30am–1pm Sat.* ● *Tue & Sun, 10 days at Christmas & public hols.* ▣ www.marshlibrary.ie

The oldest public library in Ireland was built in 1701 for Archbishop Narcissus Marsh, a Dean of St Patrick's Cathedral. It was designed by Sir William Robinson, architect of much of Dublin Castle *(see pp 76– 7)* and the Royal Hospital Kilmainham *(see p97)*.

Inside, the bookcases are topped by a mitre and feature carved gables with lettering in gold leaf. To the rear of the library are wired alcoves (or "cages") where readers were locked in with rare books. The collection, from the 16th, 17th and early 18th centuries, includes irreplaceable volumes, such as Bishop Bedell's 1685 translation of the Old Testament into Irish and Clarendon's *History of the Rebellion*, with anti-Scottish margin notes by Jonathan Swift.

Statue of Virgin and Child in Whitefriar Street Carmelite Church

Whitefriar Street Carmelite Church 🄓

56 Aungier St. **Map** C4. ***Tel*** 475 8821. ▢ *8am–6:30pm Mon & Wed–Fri, 8am–9pm Tue, 8am–7pm Sat, 8am–7:30pm Sun, 9:30am–1pm public hols.* www.carmelites.ie

Designed by George Papworth, this Catholic church was built in 1827. It stands alongside the site of a Medieval Carmelite foundation of which nothing remains.

In contrast to the two Church of Ireland cathedrals, St Patrick's and Christ Church, which are usually full of tourists, this church is frequented by city worshippers. Every day they come to light candles to various saints, including St Valentine – the patron saint of lovers. His remains, previously buried in the cemetery of St Hippolytus in Rome, were offered to the church as a gift from Pope Gregory XVI in 1836. Today they rest beneath the commemorative statue of St Valentine, which stands in the northeast corner of the church beside the high altar.

Nearby is a Flemish oak statue of the Virgin and Child, dating from the late 15th or early 16th century. It may have belonged to St Mary's Abbey *(see p93)* and is believed to be the only wooden statue of its kind to escape destruction when Ireland's monasteries were sacked at the time of the Reformation *(see p38)*.

Carved monument (1632) to the Boyle family in St Patrick's Cathedral

NORTH OF THE LIFFEY

Dublin's northside was the last part of the city to be developed during the 18th century. The city authorities envisioned an area of wide, leafy avenues, but the reality of today's heavy traffic has rather spoiled their original plans. Nonetheless, O'Connell Street, lined with fine statues and monuments, is an impressive thoroughfare. This is where Dubliners come to shop and some of the adjacent streets, particularly Moore Street, have a colourful parade of stalls and street vendors offering cut-price tobacco.

Some public buildings, such as James Gandon's glorious Custom House and majestic Four Courts, together with the

Statue of James Joyce on Earl Street North

historic General Post Office *(see p89)*, add grace to the area. The Rotunda Hospital, Europe's first purpose-built maternity hospital, is another fine building. Dublin's two most celebrated theatres, the Abbey and the Gate, act as a cultural magnet, as do the Dublin Writers Museum and the James Joyce Cultural Centre, two museums dedicated to writers who lived in the city.

Some of the city's finest Georgian streetscapes are found in the north of the city. Many have been neglected for decades, but thankfully some areas, most notably North Great George's Street, are undergoing restoration.

SIGHTS AT A GLANCE

Museums and Galleries
Dublin Writers Museum **9**
Hugh Lane Municipal Gallery of Modern Art **10**
Old Jameson's Distillery **13**
James Joyce Cultural Centre **5**

Historic Buildings
Custom House **1**
Four Courts **15**
King's Inns **11**
Rotunda Hospital **7**

Historic Streets and Bridges
Ha'penny Bridge **17**
O'Connell Street **3**
Smithfield **12**

Theatres
Abbey Theatre **2**
Gate Theatre **6**

Churches
St Mary's Abbey **16**
St Mary's Pro-Cathedral **4**
St Michan's Church **14**

Parks and Gardens
Garden of Remembrance **8**

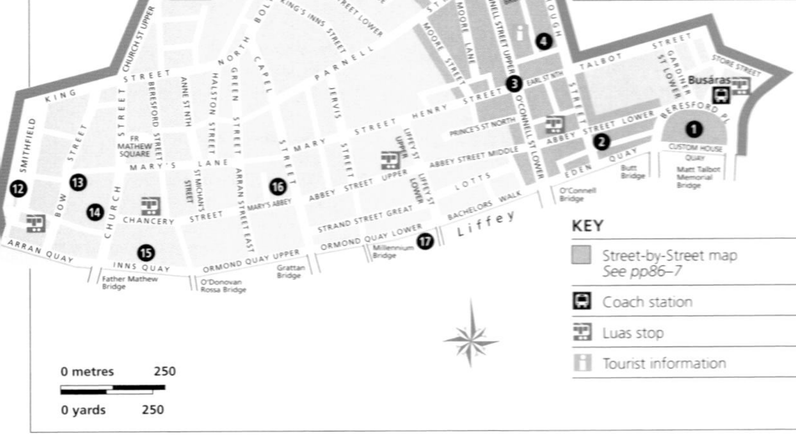

KEY

Street-by-Street map
See pp86–7

Coach station

Luas stop

Tourist information

0 metres   250
0 yards   250

◁ **Portico of the Custom House, illuminated at night**

Street-by-Street: Around O'Connell Street

Detail of pavement mosaic, Moore Street

Throughout the Georgian era, O'Connell Street was very much the fashionable part of Dublin to live in. However, the 1916 Easter Rising destroyed many of the fine buildings along the street, including much of the General Post Office – only its original façade still stands. Today, this main thoroughfare is lined with shops and businesses. Other attractions nearby include St Mary's Pro-Cathedral and James Gandon's Custom House, overlooking the Liffey.

James Joyce Cultural Centre
This well-restored Georgian town house contains a small Joyce museum ❺

Parnell Monument (1911)

Gate Theatre
Founded in 1928, the Gate is renowned for its productions of contemporary drama ❻

Rotunda Hospital
Housed in the Rotunda Hospital is a chapel built in the 1750s to the design of Richard Cassels. It features lovely stained-glass windows, fluted columns, panelling and intricate iron balustrades ❼

Moore Street Market is the busiest of the streets off O'Connell. Be prepared for the shrill cries of the stall holders offering an enormous variety of fresh fruit, vegetables and cut flowers.

The Monument of Light, an elegant stainless steel spire, rises to 120 m (394 ft).

The General Post Office, the grandest building on O'Connell Street, was the centre of the 1916 Rising.

James Larkin Statue (1981)

KEY

—	Suggested route
🚊	Luas stop
ℹ	Tourist information

0 metres   50

0 yards   50

STAR SIGHTS

★ Custom House

★ O'Connell Street

St Mary's Pro-Cathedral
*Built around 1825, this is
Dublin's main place of
worship for Catholics. The
plaster relief above the
altar in the sanctuary
depicts The Ascension* ❹

LOCATOR MAP
See Dublin map pp118–19

The statue of James Joyce (1990), by
Marjorie Fitzgibbon, commemorates one
of Ireland's most famous novelists. Born in
Dublin in 1882, he catalogued the people
and streets of Dublin in *Dubliners* and in
his most celebrated work, *Ulysses*.

Abbey Theatre
*Ireland's national
theatre is known
throughout the world
for its productions by
Irish playwrights,
such as Sean O'Casey
and JM Synge* ❷

★ O'Connell Street
*This monument to Daniel
O'Connell by John Foley took
19 years to complete from the
laying of its foundation
stone in 1864* ❸

ARL STREET NORTH

MARLBOROUGH ST

SACKVILLE PL

ABBEY STREET LR

EDEN QUAY

CUSTOM HOUSE QUAY

Butt Bridge

LIFFEY

O'Connell
Bridge

To Trinity College

★ Custom House
*This grotesque head, by
Edward Smyth, symbolizes
the River Liffey. It is one of
14 carved keystones that
adorn the building* ❶

Illuminated façade of the Custom House reflected in the Liffey

Custom House ❶

Custom House Quay. **Map** E2 *Tel*
888 2538. ⬜ *10am–12:30pm*
Mon–Fri (Nov–Mar: Wed–Fri), 2–5pm
Sat–Sun. ♿ *on weekdays only.*
www.visitdublin.com

This majestic building was
designed as the Custom
House by the English architect
James Gandon. However, just
nine years after its completion,
the 1800 Act of Union *(see p42)*
transferred the customs and
excise business to London,
rendering the building
practically obsolete. In 1921,
supporters of Sinn Féin celebrated their election victory
by setting light to what they
saw as a symbol of British
imperialism. The fire blazed
for five days causing extensive
damage. Reconstruction took
place in 1926, although further
deterioration meant that the
building was not completely
restored until 1991, when it reopened as government offices.
The main façade is made up
of pavilions at each end with
a Doric portico in its centre.
The arms of Ireland crown the
two pavilions and a series of
14 allegorical heads, by Dublin
sculptor Edward Smyth, form
the keystones of arches and
entrances. These heads depict
Ireland's main rivers and the
Atlantic Ocean. Topping the
central copper dome is a
statue of Commerce, while the
north façade is decorated with
figures representing Europe,
Africa, America and Asia.
The best view of the building
is from the south of the Liffey
beyond Matt Talbot Bridge.

Abbey Theatre ❷

Lower Abbey St. **Map** E2. *Tel* 878
7222. ⬜ *for performances only.* **Box
office** ⬜ *10:30am–7pm Mon–Sat. See
also* **Entertainment in Dublin** *p108.*
www.abbeytheatre.ie

Logo of the Abbey Theatre

Founded in 1898 with WB
Yeats and Lady Gregory as co-
directors, the Abbey staged its
first play in 1904. The early
years of this much lauded
national theatre witnessed
works by WB Yeats, JM Synge
and Sean O'Casey. Many were
controversial: nationalist sensi-
tivities were severely tested in
1926 during the premiere of
O'Casey's *The Plough and the*
Stars when the flag of the Irish
Free State appeared on stage
in a scene which featured a
pub frequented by prostitutes.
  While presenting the work
of eminent foreign authors
from time to time, the prime
objective of the Abbey &
Peacock Theatres is to
provide a performance space
for Irish dramatic writing.
Some of the most acclaimed
performances have been Brian
Friel's *Dancing at Lughnasa*
and *Translations*, Patrick
Kavanagh's *Tarry Flynn*, Dion
Boucicault's *The Colleen*
Bawn and Hugh Leonard's
Love in the Title.

O'Connell Street ❸

Map D1–D2.

O'Connell Street is very
different from the original
plans of Irish aristocrat Luke
Gardiner. When he bought
the land in the mid-18th
century, Gardiner envisioned
a grand residential parade
with an elegant mall running
along its centre. Such plans
were short-lived. The construction of Carlisle (now
O'Connell) Bridge in 1790
transformed the street into the
city's main north-south route.
Also, several buildings were
destroyed during the 1916
Easter Rising and the Irish
Civil War. Since the 1960s

many of the old buildings
have been replaced by the
plate glass and neon of fast
food joints, amusement
arcades and chain stores.

A few venerable buildings
remain, such as the General
Post Office (1818), Gresham
Hotel (1817), Clery's department store (1822) and the
Royal Dublin Hotel, part of
which occupies the street's
only original town house.

A walk down the central
mall is the most enjoyable
way to see the street's mix of
architectural styles and take a
close look at the series of
monuments lining the route.
At the south end
stands a massive
monument to Daniel
O'Connell *(see p42)*,
unveiled in 1882. The
street, which throughout
the 19th century had
been called Sackville
Street, was renamed
after O'Connell in 1922.
Higher up, almost facing
the General Post Office,
is an animated statue of
James Larkin (1867–
1943), leader of the
Dublin general strike
in 1913. The next
statue is of Father
Theobald Mathew
(1790–1856), founder of the
Pioneer Total Abstinence

South end of O'Connell Street with monument to Daniel O'Connell

**Statue of James
Larkin (1981) in
O'Connell Street**

Movement. At the north end of
the street is the obelisk-shaped
monument to
Charles Stewart
Parnell (1846–
91), who was leader
of the Home Rule
Party and known as the
"uncrowned King of
Ireland" *(see p43)*. A
new addition to
O'Connell Street is the
Monument of Light,
erected on the site where
Nelson's column used
to be. It is a stainless
steel, conical spire
which tapers from a
3-metre diameter base
to a 10 cm pointed tip of
optical glass at a height of 120
metres (394 ft).

St Mary's Pro-Cathedral ❶

Marlborough St. **Map** D2. *Tel 874
5441.* ☐ *7:30am–6:45pm Mon–Fri
(7:15pm Sat), 9am–1:45pm & 5:30pm–
–7:45pm Sun.* **www**.procathedral.ie

Dedicated in 1825 before
Catholic emancipation *(see
p42)*, St Mary's backstreet site
was the best the city's Anglo-
Irish leaders would allow a
Catholic cathedral.

The façade is based on a
Greek temple. Doric columns
support a pediment with
statues of St Mary, St Patrick
and St Laurence O'Toole, 12th-
century Archbishop of Dublin
and patron saint of the city.
Inside, one striking feature is
the intricately carved high altar.

St Mary's has a great musical
tradition and is home to the
famous Palestrina Choir, with
which the great tenor John
McCormack *(see p24)* began
his career in 1904. The choir
still sings on Sundays at 11am.

THE GENERAL POST OFFICE (GPO)

Irish Life magazine cover showing the 1916 Easter Rising

Built in 1818 halfway along
O'Connell Street, the GPO
became a symbol of the
1916 Irish Rising. Members
of the Irish Volunteers and
Irish Citizen Army seized the
building on Easter Monday,
and Patrick Pearse *(see p44)*
read out the Proclamation of
the Irish Republic from its
steps. The rebels remained
inside for a week, but shelling
from the British eventually
forced them out. At first,
many Irish people viewed
the Rising unfavourably.
However, as WB Yeats wrote,
matters "changed utterly"
and a "terrible beauty born" when, during the
following weeks, 14 of the leaders were caught and shot at
Kilmainham Gaol *(see p97)*. Inside the building is a sculpture
of the mythical Irish warrior Cúchulainn *(see p26)*, dedicated
to those who died for their part in the Easter Rising.

Austere Neo-Classical interior
of St Mary's Pro-Cathedral

James Joyce Cultural Centre ❺

35 North Great George's St. **Map** D1.
Tel 878 8547. ◯ 9:30am–3:30pm
Mon–Fri, 12:30–5pm Sun. ● 1 Jan,
Good Fri & 23–31 Dec. ♿
www.jamesjoyce.ie

This agreeable stop on the literary tourist trail is primarily a meeting place for Joyce enthusiasts, but is also worth visiting for its Georgian interior. The centre is in a 1784 town house which was built for the Earl of Kenmare. Michael Stapleton, one of the greatest stuccoers of his time, contributed to the plasterwork, of which the friezes are particularly noteworthy.

The main literary display is an absorbing set of biographies of around 50 characters from Joyce's novel *Ulysses*, who were based on real Dublin people. Professor Dennis J Maginni, a peripheral character in *Ulysses*, ran a dancing school from this town house. Leopold and Molly Bloom, the central characters of *Ulysses*, lived a short walk away at No. 7 Eccles Street. The centre also organizes walking tours of Joyce's Dublin, so a visit is a must for all Joycean zealots.

At the top of the road, on Great Denmark Street, is the Jesuit-run Belvedere College attended by Joyce between 1893 and 1898. He recalls his unhappy schooldays there in *A Portrait of the Artist as a Young Man*. The college's interior contains some of Stapleton's best and most colourful plasterwork (1785).

JAMES JOYCE (1882–1941)

Born in Dublin, Joyce spent most of his adult life in Europe. He used the city of Dublin as the setting for all his major works including *Dubliners*, *A Portrait of the Artist as a Young Man* and *Ulysses*. Joyce claimed that if the city was ever destroyed it could be re-created through the pages of *Ulysses*. However, the Irish branded the book pornographic and banned it until the 1960s.

Gate Theatre ❻

1 Cavendish Row. **Map** D1.
◯ for performances only. **Box office**
Tel 874 4045. ◯ 10am–7pm Mon–
Sat. See also **Entertainment in**
Dublin pp108. **www**.gate-theatre.ie

Entrance to the Gate Theatre

Renowned for its staging of contemporary international drama in Dublin, the Gate Theatre was founded in 1928 by Hilton Edwards and Mícheál Mac Liammóir. The latter is now best remembered for *The Importance of Being Oscar*, his long-running one-man show about the writer Oscar Wilde (see p22). An early success was Denis Johnston's *The Old Lady Says No*, so-called because of the margin notes made on one of his scripts by Lady Gregory, founding director of the Abbey Theatre (see p88). Although still noted for staging new plays, the Gate's current output often includes classic Irish plays. Among the young talent to get their first break here were James Mason and a teenage Orson Welles.

Rotunda Hospital ❼

Parnell Square West. **Map** D1.
Tel 873 0700.

Standing in the middle of Parnell Square is Europe's first purpose-built maternity hospital. Founded in 1745 by Dr Bartholomew Mosse, the design of the hospital is similar to that of Leinster House (see p65). German-born architect Richard Cassels designed both.

At the east end of the hospital is the Rotunda, after which the hospital is named. It was built in 1764 by John Ensor as Assembly Rooms to host fundraising functions and concerts. Franz Liszt gave a concert here in 1843.

On the first floor is a chapel featuring striking stained-glass windows and exuberant Rococo plasterwork and ceiling (1755) by the stuccoer Bartholomew Cramillion.

Across the road from the hospital is Conway's Pub. Opened in 1745, it is a popular retreat for expectant fathers.

Stained-glass Venetian window (c.1863) in Rotunda Hospital's chapel

For hotels and restaurants in this region see pp294–8 and pp324–8

Garden of Remembrance ❽

Parnell Square. **Map** C1.
☐ *dawn–dusk daily.*

At the northern end of Parnell Square is a small, peaceful park, dedicated to the men and women who have died in the pursuit of Irish freedom. The Garden of Remembrance marks the spot where several leaders of the 1916 Easter Rising were held overnight before being taken to Kilmainham Gaol *(see p97),* and was also where the Irish Volunteers movement was formed in 1913.

Designed by Daithí Hanly, the garden was opened by President Eamon de Valera *(see p45)* in 1966, to mark the 50th anniversary of the Easter Rising. In the centre of the garden's well-kept lawns is a cruciform pool. A mosaic on the floor of the pool depicts abandoned, broken swords, spears and shields, symbolizing peace. The focal point at one end of the garden is a large bronze sculpture by Oisín Kelly (1971) of the legendary *Children of Lir,* who were changed into swans by their stepmother *(see p27).*

Children of Lir in the Garden of Remembrance

Gallery of Writers at Dublin Writers Museum

Dublin Writers Museum ❾

18 Parnell Sq North. **Map** C1. *Tel* 872 2077. ☐ *10am–5pm Mon–Sat; (Jun–Aug: 10am–6pm Mon–Fri) 11am–5pm Sun & public hols (last adm: 45 min before closing.)* ● *25 & 26 Dec.* 🖳 www.writersmuseum.com

Opened in 1991, the museum occupies a tasteful 18th-century town house. There are displays relating to Irish literature in all its forms from 300 years ago to the present day. The exhibits include paintings, manuscripts, letters, rare editions and mementoes of many of Ireland's finest authors. There are a number of temporary exhibits and a sumptuously decorated Gallery of Writers upstairs. The museum also hosts frequent poetry readings and lectures. A good café and a specialist bookstore, providing an out-of-print search service, add to the relaxed, friendly ambience.

Hugh Lane Municipal Gallery of Modern Art ❿

Charlemont House, Parnell Square North. **Map** C1. *Tel* 222 5550. ☐ *9:30am–6pm Tue–Wed (Apr–Sep 8pm Thu), 9:30am–5pm Thu, Fri & Sat, 11am–5pm Sun.* ● *23–25 Dec & public hols.* www.hughlane.ie

Art collector Sir Hugh Lane donated his collection of Impressionist paintings to the Dublin Corporation in 1905, but the lack of a suitable location for them prompted Lane to begin transferring his gift to the National Gallery in London. The Corporation then proposed Charlemont House and Lane relented. However, before Lane's revised will could be witnessed, he died on board the *Lusitania (see p178).* This led to a 50-year dispute which has been resolved by the Corporation and the National Gallery swapping the collection every five years.

Besides the Lane bequest of paintings by Degas, Courbet and Monet, the gallery has an extensive collection of modern Irish paintings and a sculpture hall with work by Rodin and others. An exciting new addition is a bequest by John Edwards of the contents of Francis Bacon's London studio. A new extension will double the exhibition space by 2006.

Beach Scene (c.1876) by Edgar Degas, Hugh Lane Municipal Gallery

Detail of wood carving (c.1724) at St Michan's Church

King's Inns 🕦

Henrietta St/Constitution Hill.
Map B1. 🌑 *to the public.*

This classically proportioned public building was founded in 1795 as a place of residence and study for barristers. To build it, James Gandon chose to seal off the end of Henrietta Street, which at the time was one of Dublin's most fashionable addresses. Francis Johnston added the graceful cupola in 1816, and the building was finally completed in 1817.
Inside is a fine Dining Hall, and the Registry of Deeds (formerly the Prerogative Court). The west façade has two doorways flanked by Classical caryatids carved by Edward Smyth. The male figure, with book and quill, represents the law.
Sadly, much of the area around Constitution Hill is less attractive than it was in Georgian times. However, the gardens, which are open to the public, are still pleasing.

Caryatid, King's Inns

Smithfield 🕬

Map A2.

Laid out in the mid-17th century as a marketplace, Smithfield used to be one of Dublin's oldest residential areas. However, the two and a half acre space received a £3.5 million makeover with a

well-designed pedestrian cobbled plaza. It is used as a venue for outdoor civic events and is lit by tall gas lighting masts. The traditional horse fair is still held here on the first Sunday of the month and is well worth seeing.

Old Jameson's Distillery 🕬

Bow St. **Map** A2. **Tel** 807 2355.
🕙 9am–6pm daily (last tour: 5:15pm).
⬤ Good Friday, 25 & 26 Dec. 📷
📹 🍽 🏪 www.irishwhiskey.ie

Proof of recent investment in the emerging Smithfield area is this large exhibition in a restored part of John Jameson's distillery, which produced whiskey from 1780 until 1971. A visit here starts with a video and further whiskey-related facts are then explained on a 40-minute tour. This takes you around displays set out as a working distillery, with different rooms devoted to the various stages of production.
The tour guides show how the Irish process differs from that of Scotch whisky: here the barley is dried with clean air, while in Scotland it is smoked over peat. The claim is that the Irish product is a smoother, less smoky tipple. After the tour, visitors can test this in the bar.

Sampling different brands at Old Jameson's Distillery

St Michan's Church 🕮

Church St. **Map** B3. **Tel** 872 4154.
🕙 mid-Mar–Oct: 10am–12:45pm & 2–4:45pm Mon–Fri, 10am–12:45pm Sat; Nov–mid-Mar: 12:30–3:30pm Mon–Fri, 10am–12:45pm Sat. 📷 📹
🏪 ♿ limited.

Largely rebuilt in 1686 on the site of an 11th-century Hiberno-Viking church, the dull façade of St Michan's hides a more exciting interior. Deep in its vaults lie a number of bodies preserved because of the dry atmosphere created by the church's magnesian limestone walls. Their wooden caskets, however, have cracked open, revealing the intact bodies, complete with skin and strands of hair. Among those thought to have been mummified in this way are the brothers Henry and John Sheares, leaders of the 1798 rebellion (see p41), who were executed that year.
Other less gory attractions include the magnificent wood carving of fruits and violins and other instruments above the choir. There is also an organ (1724) on which Handel is said to have played. It is thought that the churchyard contains the unmarked grave of United Irishman Robert Emmet (see p77), leader of the abortive 1803 Rising.

Four Courts 🕯

Inns Quay. **Map** B3. **Tel** 872 5555.
🕙 9:30am–12:30pm, 2–4:30pm Mon–Fri (when courts in session).

Completed in 1796 by James Gandon, this majestic public building overlooks the River Liffey. It was virtually gutted

120 years later during the Irish Civil War (see pp44–5) when government forces bombarded anti-Treaty rebels into submission. The adjacent Public Records Office, with its irreplaceable collection of historical and legal documents dating back to the 12th century, was destroyed by fire.

By 1932, the main buildings were sympathetically restored using Gandon's original design. An imposing copper-covered lantern dome rises above the six-columned Corinthian portico, which is crowned with the figures of Moses, Justice, Mercy, Wisdom and Authority. This central section is flanked by two wings containing the four original courts: Common Pleas, Chancery, Exchequer and King's Bench. You can walk into the central waiting hall under the grand dome; an information panel to the right of the entrance gives details about the building's history.

St Mary's Abbey ⑯

Meetinghouse Lane. **Map** C2.
Tel 872 1490. ⬡ mid-Jun–mid-Sep.
🖳 www.heritageireland.ie

Founded by Benedictines in 1139, but transferred to the Cistercian order just eight years later, this was one of the largest and most important monasteries in medieval Ireland. As well as controlling extensive estates, including

The Ha'penny Bridge looking from Temple Bar to Liffey Street

whole villages, mills and fisheries, the abbey acted as state treasury and meeting place for the Council of Ireland. It was during a council meeting in St Mary's that "Silken Thomas" Fitzgerald (see p38) renounced his allegiance to Henry VIII and marched out to raise the short-lived rebellion of 1534. The monastery was dissolved in 1539 and during the 17th century the site served as a quarry. Stone from St Mary's was used in the construction of Essex Bridge (replaced by Grattan Bridge in 1874), just to the south of the abbey.

All that remains of the abbey today is the vaulted chamber of the Chapter House. This contains a historical display and a model of how the entire complex would have looked 800 years ago.

Ha'penny Bridge ⑰

Map D3.

Linking the Temple Bar area (see p78) and Liffey Street, this high-arched cast-iron footbridge is used by thousands of people every day. It was built by John Windsor, an ironworker from Shropshire, England. One of Dublin's most photographed sights, it was originally named the Wellington Bridge. It is now officially called the Liffey Bridge, but is also known as the Metal Bridge. Opened in 1816, the bridge got its better known nickname from the halfpenny toll that was levied on it up until 1919. A recent restoration, which included the installation of period lanterns, has made the bridge even more attractive.

James Gandon's Four Courts overlooking the River Liffey

FURTHER AFIELD

There are many interesting sights just outside the city centre. The best part of a day can be spent exploring the western suburbs taking in the Museum of Modern Art housed in the splendid Royal Kilmainham Hospital and the eerie Kilmainham Gaol. Phoenix Park, Europe's largest city park, is a good place for a stroll and also has a zoo. Further north are the National Botanic Gardens, with over 20,000 plant species from around the world. Nearby is Marino Casino, one of Ireland's finest examples of Palladian architecture.

Candelabra at Malahide Castle

The magnificent coastline with its stunning views of Dublin Bay is easily reached by the DART rail network. It encompasses the towering promontory of Howth, while the highlights of the southern stretch are around Dalkey village and Killiney Bay. One of many Martello towers built as defences along this coast is known as the James Joyce Tower and houses a collection of Joyce memorabilia. To the northeast, a bit further from the city centre, is Malahide Castle, former home of the Talbot family.

SIGHTS AT A GLANCE

Museums and Galleries
Collins Barracks **9**
Guinness Storehouse **4**
Irish Museum of Modern Art/
   Royal Hospital Kilmainham **3**
James Joyce Tower **13**

Kilmainham Gaol **2**
Shaw's Birthplace **6**
Waterways Visitors' Centre **8**

Parks and Gardens
National Botanic Gardens **5**
Phoenix Park **1**

Historic Buildings
Malahide Castle **10**
Marino Casino **7**

Towns and Villages
Dalkey **14**
Dun Laoghaire **12**
Howth **11**
Killiney **15**

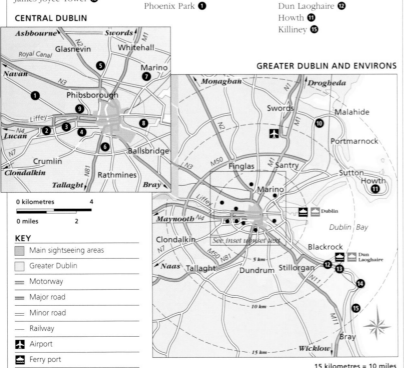

CENTRAL DUBLIN

GREATER DUBLIN AND ENVIRONS

0 kilometres — 4
0 miles — 2

KEY
- Main sightseeing areas
- Greater Dublin
- Motorway
- Major road
- Minor road
- Railway
- Airport
- Ferry port
- Fast ferry port

15 kilometres = 10 miles

◁ **Martello tower at Howth Head**

Phoenix Park ❶

Park Gate, Conyngham Rd, Dublin 8.
🚌 *10, 25, 26, 37, 38, 39 & many
other routes.* ⏰ *7am–11pm daily.*
Phoenix Park Visitor Centre *Tel*
677 0095. ⏰ *Jun–mid Mar:
10am–5pm Sat &Sun; mid Mar–end
Mar: 10am–5:30pm daily; Apr–Sep:
10am–6pm daily; Oct: 10am–5:30pm
daily; Nov–Dec: 10am–5pm.* 🎦 📷
🍴 ♿ *ground floor only.* **Zoo** *Tel*
474 8900. ⏰ *Mar–Sep:
9:30am–6pm Mon–Sat, 10:30am–
6pm Sun; Oct–Feb: 9:30am–dusk
Mon–Sat, 10:30am–dusk Sun.* 🎦 🍴
♿ 📷 www.heritageireland.ie

Just to the west of the city
centre, ringed by an 11-km (7-
mile) wall, is Europe's largest
enclosed city park. The name
"Phoenix" is said to be a corruption of the Gaelic *Fionn
Uisce*, or "clear water". The

Phoenix Column is crowned
by a statue of the mythical
bird. Phoenix Park originated
in 1662, when the Duke of
Ormonde turned the land into
a deer park. In 1745 it was
landscaped and opened to
the public.

Near Park Gate is the lakeside **People's Garden** – the
only part of the park which
has been cultivated. A little
further on are the **Zoological
Gardens**, established in 1830,
making them the third oldest
zoo in the world. The zoo is
renowned for the successful
breeding of lions, including
the one that appears at the
beginning of MGM movies.
The African Plains savannah
houses the larger residents.

In addition to the Phoenix
Column, the park has two
other conspicuous monuments.

The **Wellington
Testimonial**, a 63-m
(206-ft) obelisk, was
begun in 1817 and
completed in 1861. Its
bronze bas-reliefs were
made from captured
French cannons. The

**Pope John Paul II celebrating Mass
in Phoenix Park in 1979**

27-m (90-ft) steel **Papal Cross**
marks the spot where the
pope celebrated Mass in front
of one million people in 1979.
Buildings within the park
include two 18th-century
houses: **Áras an Uachtaráin**,
the Irish President's official
residence, for which 525
tickets are issued every
Saturday for a free guided tour,
and Deerfield, home of the US
Ambassador. **Ashtown Castle** is
a restored 17th-century tower
house, now home to the
Phoenix Park Visitor Centre.

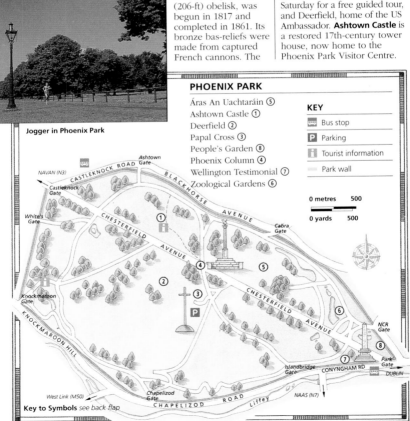

Jogger in Phoenix Park

PHOENIX PARK

Áras An Uachtaráin ⑤
Ashtown Castle ①
Deerfield ②
Papal Cross ③
People's Garden ⑧
Phoenix Column ④
Wellington Testimonial ⑦
Zoological Gardens ⑥

KEY

🚌	Bus stop
🅿	Parking
ℹ	Tourist information
▬	Park wall

0 metres   500
0 yards   500

Key to Symbols *see back flap*

Restored central hall at Kilmainham Gaol

Kilmainham Gaol ❷

Inchicore Rd, Kilmainham, Dublin 8.
Tel 453 5984. 🚌 51B, 51C, 78A, 79,
79A. ◻ Apr–Sep: 9:30am–5pm
daily; Oct–Mar: 9:30am–4pm Mon–
Sat, 10am–5pm Sun (last adm: 1 hr
15 mins before closing). ⬤ 25 & 26
Dec. 📷 📁 ◻ ◻

A long tree-lined avenue
runs from the Royal Hospital
Kilmainham to the grim, grey
bulk of Kilmainham Gaol. The
building opened in 1796, but
was restored in the 1960s.
During its 130 years as a
prison, it housed many of
those involved in the fight for
Irish independence, including
Robert Emmet *(see p77)* and
Charles Stewart Parnell *(p43)*.
The last prisoner held was
Eamon de Valera *(p45)*, who
was released on 16 July, 1924.
    Tours start in the chapel,
where Joseph Plunkett married
Grace Gifford just a few hours
before he faced the firing
squad for his part in the 1916
Rising *(see pp44–5)*. The tours
end in the prison yard where
Plunkett's badly wounded
colleague James Connolly, unable to stand up, was strapped

into a chair before being shot.
You also pass the dank cells
of those involved in the 1798,
1803, 1848 and 1867 uprisings,
as well as the punishment
cells and hanging room.
Exhibits in the central hall
include personal mementos
of some of the former inmates
and depictions of various
events which took place in
the Gaol until it closed in 1924.
    The *Asgard*, an arms-running
ship previously exhibited
in the courtyard, has been
removed from display.

Irish Museum of Modern Art – Royal Hospital Kilmainham ❸

Military Road, Kilmainham, Dublin 8.
Tel 612 9900. 🚆 Heuston Station. 🚌
26, 51, 51B, 78A, 79, 90, 123. **Irish
Museum of Modern Art** ◻ 10am–
5:30pm Tue–Sat, 10:30am– 5:30pm
Wed, noon–5:30pm Sun (last adm:
5:15pm). ⬤ Good Fri & 24–26 Dec.
📷 📁 ◻ ♿ limited. **www**.imma.ie

Ireland's finest surviving 17th-
century building was laid out
in 1680, styled on Les Invalides
in Paris. It was built by Sir
William Robinson as a home
for 300 wounded soldiers – a
role it kept until 1927. When
it was completed, people were
so impressed by its Classical
symmetry that it was suggested it would be better used as
a campus for Trinity College.
The Baroque chapel has fine
carvings and intricate stained
glass. The plaster ceiling is a
replica of the original, which
fell in 1902. The Formal
Gardens, restored using many
of the 17th-century designs,
are now open to the public.
    In 1991, the hospital's former
residential quarters became the
Irish Museum of Modern Art.
The collection includes a
cross-section of Irish and
international modern and
contemporary art. Works are
displayed on a rotating basis
and include group and solo
shows, retrospectives and
special visiting exhibitions. A
recent addition is the separate,
multi-screen film theatre.

The Royal Hospital Kilmainham

Drinking Guinness at a local pub

Guinness Storehouse ❹

St James's Gate, Dublin 8.
Tel 408 4800. 🚌 78A, 51B, 123.
⬤ 9:30am–5pm (8pm Jul & Aug)
daily. ⬤ Good Fri, 24–26 Dec, 1 Jan.
🅿 ♿ 🏠 🍴
www.guinness-storehouse.com

The Guinness storehouse is a new development based in St James's Gate Brewery, the original house of Guinness, now completely remodelled. This 1904 listed building covers nearly four acres of floor space over six floors built around a huge pint glass atrium. The first impression the visitor has is of walking into a large glass pint with light spilling down from above and a copy of the original lease signed by Arthur Guinness enshrined on the floor. The Ingredients section is next where visitors can touch, smell and feel the ingredients through interactive displays. The tour continues into an authentic Georgian anteroom to 'meet' Arthur Guinness and see him at work. The Brewing Process is a noisy, steamy and 'hoppy' area giving the impression of brewing all around with full explanation of the process. The historical development of Guinness cooperage is accompanied by video footage of the craft. Models and displays tell the story of Guinness transportation, the appeal of Guinness worldwide, and their popular advertising campaigns. The tour ends with a generous tasting of draught Guinness in the traditional Brewery Bar and the rooftop Gravity Bar.

The Brewing of Guinness

Label from a Guinness bottle

Guinness is a black beer, known as "stout", renowned for its distinctive malty flavour and smooth creamy head. From its humble beginnings over 200 years ago, the Guinness brewery site at St James's Gate now sprawls across 26 ha (65 acres). It is the largest brewery in Europe and exports beers to more than 120 countries throughout the world. Other famous brands owned by Guinness include Harp Lager and Smithwick's Ale.

HOW GUINNESS IS MADE

The four main ingredients used to brew Guinness are barley, hops, yeast and water which, contrary to popular belief, comes from the Wicklow Mountains rather than the River Liffey.

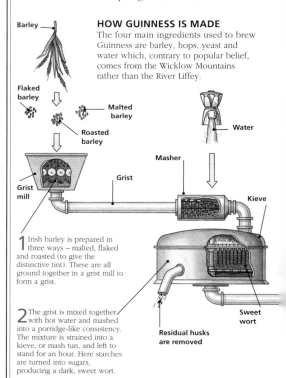

Barley

Flaked barley

Malted barley

Roasted barley

Water

Masher

Grist

Grist mill

Kieve

1 Irish barley is prepared in three ways – malted, flaked and roasted (to give the distinctive tint). These are all ground together in a grist mill to form a grist.

2 The grist is mixed together with hot water and mashed into a porridge-like consistency. The mixture is strained into a kieve, or mash tun, and left to stand for an hour. Here starches are turned into sugars, producing a dark, sweet wort.

Residual husks are removed

Sweet wort

Guinness advertising *has become almost as famous as the product itself. Since 1929, when the first advertisement announced that "Guinness is Good for You", poster and television advertising campaigns have employed many amusing images of both animals and people.*

ARTHUR GUINNESS

Arthur Guinness

In December 1759, 34-year-old Arthur Guinness signed a 9,000-year lease at an annual rent of £45 to take over St James's Gate Brewery, which had lain vacant for almost ten years. At the time the brewing industry in Dublin was at a low ebb – the standard of ale was much criticized and in rural Ireland beer was virtually unknown, as whiskey, gin and poteen were the more favoured drinks. Furthermore, Irish beer was under threat from imports. Guinness started brewing ale, but was also aware of a black ale called porter, produced in London. This new beer was so called because of its popularity with porters at Billingsgate and Covent Garden markets. Guinness decided to stop making ales and develop his own recipe for porter (the word "stout" was not used until the 1920s). So successful was the switch that he made his first export shipment in 1769.

Engraving (c.1794) of a satisfied customer

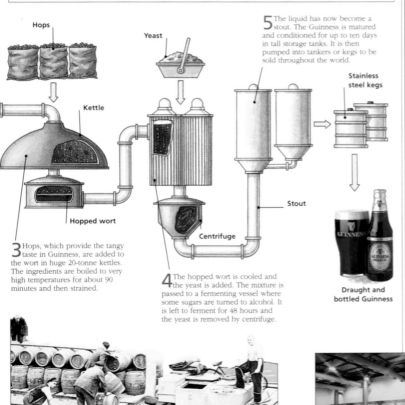

Hops

Yeast

5 The liquid has now become a stout. The Guinness is matured and conditioned for up to ten days in tall storage tanks. It is then pumped into tankers or kegs to be sold throughout the world.

Stainless steel kegs

Kettle

Hopped wort

Stout

Centrifuge

3 Hops, which provide the tangy taste in Guinness, are added to the wort in huge 20-tonne kettles. The ingredients are boiled to very high temperatures for about 90 minutes and then strained.

4 The hopped wort is cooled and the yeast is added. The mixture is passed to a fermenting vessel where some sugars are turned to alcohol. It is left to ferment for 48 hours and the yeast is removed by centrifuge.

Draught and bottled Guinness

The Guinness brewery *has relied heavily on water transport since its first export was shipped to England in 1769. The barges, which up until 1961 made the short trip with their cargo up the Liffey to Dublin Port, were a familiar sight on the river. Once at port, the stout would be loaded on to huge tanker ships for worldwide distribution.*

Steel kettles used in modern-day brewing

Giant water lilies in the Lily House, National Botanic Gardens

National Botanic Gardens ❺

Botanic Ave, Glasnevin, Dublin 9. *Tel 857 0909*. 🚌 *13, 19, 19A, 83, 134*. ⭕ *Apr–Oct: 9am–6pm daily; Nov–Mar: 10am–4:30pm daily*. ⭘ *25 Dec*. 🔲 🍴 ♿ 📷 *free on Sun 2:30pm, groups on request*.
Glasnevin Cemetery Finglas Rd. *Tel 830 1133*. 🚌 *40A, 40B from Parnell Street*. ⭕ *8am–4:30pm daily*.

Opened in 1795, the National Botanic Gardens are Ireland's foremost centre of botany and horticulture. They still possess an old-world feel, thanks to the beautiful cast-iron Palm House and other curvilinear glasshouses. These were built between 1843 and 1869 by Richard Turner, the architect who was also responsible for the Palm House at Kew Gardens, London, and the glasshouses at Belfast's Botanic Gardens *(see p278)*.
The 20-ha (49-acre) park contains over 20,000 different plant species. Particularly attractive are the colourful old-fashioned Victorian carpet bedding, the rich collections of cacti and orchids, renowned rose garden, and 30-m (100-ft) high redwood tree. The gardens back on to the

huge Glasnevin or Prospect Cemetery where many of Ireland's political figures are buried, including Charles Stewart Parnell *(see p43)* and Daniel O'Connell *(see p42)*.

Shaw's Birthplace ❻

33 Synge St, Dublin 8. *Tel 475 0854*. 🚌 *16, 19, 122*. ⭕ *May–Sep: 10am–1pm & 2–5pm Mon–Fri (closed Wed), 2–5pm Sat, Sun & public hols*. 🎫 📷 **www**.visitdublin.com

Kitchen at Shaw's Birthplace

Playwright and Nobel prize-winner George Bernard Shaw was born in this house on 26 July 1856. In 1876 he followed his mother to London. She had left four years earlier with her daughters, fed up with her husband's drinking habits. It was in London that Shaw

met his wife Charlotte Payne-Townsend. He stayed in England until his death in 1950.
Inside the house visitors can see the young Shaw's bedroom and the kitchen where the author remembered he drank "much tea out of brown delft left to 'draw' on the hob until it was pure tannin". Although there is little on Shaw's productive years, the home gives a fair idea of the lifestyle of a Victorian middle-class family.

Marino Casino ❼

Cherrymount Crescent. *Tel 833 1618*. 🚆 *DART to Clontarf*. 🚌 *20A, 20B, 27, 42, 42C, 123*. ⭕ *Apr–Oct 10am–5pm daily (Jun–Sep: 6pm); Nov–Mar: noon–4pm Sat & Sun (Apr: 5pm)*. 🎫 📷 *obligatory (last tour 45 min before closing)*. **www**.heritageireland.ie

This delightful little villa *(see pp40–41)*, designed by Sir William Chambers in the 1760s for Lord Charlemont, now sits incongruously next to a busy road and a housing estate. Originally built as a summer house for the Marino Estate, the villa survives although the main house was pulled down in 1921. The Casino is acknowledged to be one of the finest examples of Neo-Classical architecture in Ireland. Some

Carved stone lion at Marino Casino

innovative features were used in its construction, including chimneys disguised as urns and hollow columns that accommodate drains. Outside, four carved stone lions, thought to be by English sculptor Joseph Wilton, stand guard at each of the corners.
The building's squat, compact exterior conceals 16 rooms built on three floors around a central staircase. The ground floor comprises a spacious hall and a saloon, with beautiful silk hangings, elaborate flooring and a coffered ceiling. On the first floor is the ostentatious State Room.

Waterways Visitors' Centre **8**

Grand Canal Quay, Dublin 2. *Tel* 677 7510. 🚉 DART to Grand Canal Dock. 🚌 2, 3. ◯ Jun–Sep: 9:30am–5:30pm daily; Oct–May: 12:30pm–5pm Wed–Sun (last adm 45 mins before closing). ● 25 Dec. ♿ 📷 on request.

Fifteen minutes' walk from Trinity College this building overlooks the Grand Canal Basin. Audiovisual displays and models illustrate Ireland's inland waterways and the wildlife found on and around them. One of the most interesting displays focuses on their construction: in the 18th century, canals were often called "navigations" and the men who built them were "navigators", a term shortened to "navvies".

DUBLIN'S CANALS

The affluent Georgian era witnessed the building of the Grand and Royal canals linking Dublin with the River Shannon and the west coast. These two canals became the main arteries of trade and public transport in Ireland from the 1760s until the coming of the railways, which took much of the passenger business, almost a century later. However, the canals continued to carry freight until after World War II, finally closing to commercial traffic in 1960. Today the canals are well maintained and used mainly for pleasure-boating, cruising and fishing.

Late 18th-century engraving of passenger ferry passing Harcourt Lock on the Grand Canal, taken from a painting by James Barralet

Stretch of the Grand Canal near Waterways Visitors' Centre

National Museum at Collins Barracks **9**

Benburb St, Dublin 7. *Tel* 677 7444. 🚌 25, 25A, 66, 67, 90. ◯ 10am–5pm Tue–Sat, 2–5pm Sun. ● Good Fri, 25 Dec. 📷 ♿ 🚫

Close to Phoenix Park and just across the Liffey from the Guinness Brewery stands the wonderful decorative arts and history annexe of the National Museum *(see pp66–7)*. Its setting in this historic building is an inspired move. The massive complex was commissioned by King William III in 1700, just ten years after victory at the Battle of the Boyne, and was the largest barracks in his domain, with accommodation for over 5,000 people. It was in use

right up to the 1990s. Originally known as Dublin Barracks, the prefix was changed to "Royal" in 1803. After Irish independence the barracks was finally named for Michael Collins, the first commander-in-chief of the Irish Army.

The large central courtyard, measured at one hundred marching paces, is an object lesson in simplicity. In marked contrast to the grey institutional exterior, the museum's interior presents the exhibits in an innovative way that makes use of the latest technology.

Furniture, silver and scientific instrument collections form the bulk of items on show in the South Block. In the West Block, however, visitors get an insight into the

history, work and development of the National Museum. The Out of Storage exhibit brings together a wide array of artifacts from around the world, complemented by banks of interactive multimedia computers. One of the highlights of the museum is the Curator's Choice section where 25 unusual exhibits – such as, for instance, an early hurling stick and ball – are displayed with a story line that explains their cultural significance.

There is also a large hall set aside for temporary displays. Expansion plans incorporate the entire barracks and include the building of a new wing.

An 18th-century, gilded wooden chair on display at Collins Barracks

The oak-beamed Great Hall at Malahide Castle

Malahide Castle ⑩

Malahide, Co Dublin. 🚂 *and DART to Malahide.* 🚌 *42 from Beresford Place, near Busáras.* **Tel** *846 2184.* 🕐 *Apr–Sep: 10am–5pm Mon–Sat, 10am–6pm Sun & public hols; Oct–Mar: 10am–5pm Mon–Sat, 11am–5pm Sun & public hols (check for lunchtime closures in winter).* 📷 🎫 *obligatory (last tours 4:30pm).* **Fry Model Railway** 🕐 *Apr–Sep: 10am–1pm 2–6pm Mon–Sat, 2–6pm Sun & public hols; Oct: 10am–1pm 2–5pm Sat, 2–5pm Sun.* ⚫ *Nov–Mar.* 📷 ♿

Near the seaside dormitory town of Malahide stands a huge castle set in 100 ha (250 acres) of grounds. The castle's core dates from the 14th century but later additions, such as its rounded towers, have given it a classic fairy-tale appearance. The building served as a stately home for the Talbot family until 1973. They were staunch supporters of James II: on the day of the Battle of the Boyne in 1690 *(see p244)*, 14 members of the family breakfasted here; none came back for supper.

Guided tours take you round the castle's collection of 18th-century Irish furniture, the oak-beamed Great Hall and the impressively carved Oak Room. Part of the Portrait Collection, on loan from the National Gallery *(see pp70–71)*, can be seen here. It includes portraits of the Talbot family and other figures such as Wolfe Tone *(see p41)*.

In the old corn store is the Fry Model Railway, started in the 1920s by Cyril Fry, a local railway engineer. The 240 sq m (2,500 sq ft) exhibit contains models of Irish trains, miniatures of stations, streets and local landmarks such as the River Liffey and Howth Head.

Howth ⑪

Co Dublin. 🚂 *DART.* **Howth Castle grounds** 🕐 *8am–sunset daily.*

The commercial fishing town of Howth marks the northern limit of Dublin Bay. Howth Head, a huge rocky mass, has lovely views of the bay. A footpath runs around the tip of Howth Head, which is known as the "Nose". Nearby is Baily Lighthouse (1814). Sadly, much of this area – some of Ireland's prime real estate – has suffered from building development.

To the west of the town is Howth Castle, which dates back to Norman times. Its grounds are particularly beautiful in May and June when the rhododendrons and azaleas are in full bloom. The National Transport Museum in the grounds is worth a visit.

Ireland's Eye, an islet and bird sanctuary where puffins nest, can be reached by a short boat trip from Howth.

Dun Laoghaire ⑫

Co Dublin. 🚂 *DART.* **National Maritime Museum** **Tel** *280 0969.* 🕐 *May–Sep: 1–5pm Tue–Sun.* **Comhaltas Ceoltóirí Éireann** **Tel** *280 0295.* 🎵 *music Wed, Fri & Sat nights, céilí Fri*

Ireland's major passenger ferry port and yachting centre, with its brightly painted villas, parks and palm

Baily Lighthouse on the southeastern tip of Howth Head

Yachts anchored in Dun Laoghaire harbour

trees, can sometimes exude a decidedly continental feel. Many visitors head straight out of Dun Laoghaire (pronounced Dunleary) but the town offers some magnificent walks around the harbour and to the lighthouse along the east pier. The villages of Sandycove and Dalkey can be reached via "The Metals" footpath which runs alongside the railway line.

In the 1837 Mariners' Church is the National Maritime Museum. Exhibits include a longboat used by French officers during Wolfe Tone's unsuccessful invasion at Bantry in 1796 (see pp168–9).

Up the road in Monkstown's Belgrave Square is the Comhaltas Ceoltóirí Éireann, Ireland's main centre for traditional music and dance, with music sessions and céilís (dances).

Guitar at James Joyce Tower

hundred years later James Joyce (see p90) stayed here for a week as the guest of Oliver St John Gogarty, poet and model for the *Ulysses* character Buck Mulligan. Gogarty rented the tower for a mere £8 per year. Inside the squat 12-m (40-ft) tower's granite walls is a small museum with some of Joyce's correspondence, personal belongings, such as his guitar, cigar case and walking stick, and his death mask. There are also photographs and first editions of his works, including a de luxe edition (1935) of *Ulysses* illustrated by Henri Matisse. The roof, originally a gun platform but later used as a sunbathing deck by Gogarty, affords marvellous views of Dublin Bay. Below the tower is Forty Foot Pool, traditionally an all-male nude bathing spot, but now open to all.

James Joyce Tower 🔟

Sandycove, Co Dublin. **Tel** 280 9265. DART to Sandycove. 59. 10am–5pm Mon–Sat, 2–6pm Sun & public hols. 1–2pm weekdays.

Standing on a rocky promontory above the village of Sandycove is this Martello tower. It is one of 15 defensive towers erected between Dublin and Bray in 1804 to withstand a threatened invasion by Napoleon. One

Dalkey 🔟

Co Dublin. DART.

Dalkey was once known as the "Town of Seven Castles", but only two of these now remain. They are both on the main street of this attractive village whose tight, winding roads and charming villas give it a Mediterranean feel.

A little way offshore is tiny Dalkey Island, a rocky bird sanctuary with a Martello tower and a medieval Benedictine church, both now in a poor state of repair. In summer the island can be reached by a boat ride from

Killiney 🔟

Co Dublin. DART to Dalkey or Killiney.

South of Dalkey, the coastal road climbs uphill before tumbling down into the village of Killiney. The route offers one of the most scenic vistas on this stretch of the east coast, with views often compared to those across the Bay of Naples. Howth Head is clearly visible to the north, with Bray Head (see p133) and the foothills of the Wicklow Mountains (see pp138–9) to the south. There is another exhilarating view from the top of Killiney Hill Park, off Victoria Road – well worth tackling the short steep trail for. Down below is the popular pebbly beach, Killiney Strand.

Shopfronts on the main street of Dalkey

SHOPPING IN DUBLIN

Dublin has two main shopping thoroughfares, each on either side of the River Liffey. On the north side, the area around Henry Street is where swanky department stores and small specialty shops beckon. The south side, especially trendy Grafton Street with its upmarket boutiques and shops, is reputed for its glamour and style. Yet, despite the wide choice of internationally known brands and retail chains found through-

Sign from a specialty food shop

out the city, the spirit of Dublin shines in the cheerful cacophony of its street markets, many of which stock a cornucopia of highly original Irish crafts and gifts. Dublin is also a haven for those searching for bargains and second-hand deals on everything from books and CDs to clothes and trinkets. There is something for everyone in this lively city, and the following pages will tell you where to start looking.

WHERE TO SHOP

Temple Bar has become a staple tourist destination. While the area is usually frequented by revellers at night, the area is a treasure trove of funky craft, design and souvenir outlets during the day.

Those who prefer a more relaxed and upmarket shopping experience should head for the the Old City. To the west of Temple Bar, between Parliment and Fishamble Streets, it is home to sleek high-end designer stores and cosmopolitan cafés, and is a good alternative to the often frenetic pace of Temple Bar.

Dublin's rapid development has contributed to the growth of bustling markets in areas that, until recently, were little more than wastelands. The first of these areas is the strip known as the Docklands, running along the shores of the Liffey, particularly on the north side, east of Custom House. New shops, restaurants

and markets are opening up regularly in the area.

Around Liffey Street, new apartment blocks have been built, leading to the regeneration of several old shopping areas. In contrast to just a few years back, Capel Street is now a thriving location, as is the impressive new Bloom's Lane at the Millennium Bridge.

WHEN TO SHOP

Shopping hours are generally from 9am to 6pm, Monday to Saturday. Some department stores open from noon to 6pm on Sundays. Many shops stay open until 9pm on Thursdays.

HOW TO PAY

Major credit cards such as Visa and Mastercard are accepted in almost all outlets. Sales tax or VAT is usually 21 per cent, which non-EU visitors can redeem at airports and ports. Redemption forms are available at points of purchase.

Brown Thomas department store

DEPARTMENT STORES

The best known department stores in Dublin are **Arnott's** and the newly refurbished **Roches Stores**, both on Henry Street. One of Dublin's oldest shops, **Clery's** on O'Connell Street, stocks everything from Irish-made gifts and clothing to internationally recognized branded goods. Prominent Irish retailer **Brown Thomas** is known for its upmarket style.

A branch of the British department store Debenhams is found in the Jervis Centre. There are also numerous Marks & Spencer shops, including branches on Grafton Street and Mary Street.

SHOPPING CENTRES

There are four main shopping centres in Dublin – three on the the south side and one on the north. South of the Liffey, you will find **Stephen's Green Centre** and the **Powerscourt**

Shoppers on busy Grafton Street

The colourful George's Street Arcade

Centre. Stephen's Green Centre is one of the largest enclosed shopping areas, with scores of shops under its roof. These include many craft and gift stores, clothing outlets and an abundance of restaurants.

In an enclosed four-storey Georgian courtyard, the Powerscourt Centre is more upmarket and plush. It is home to many fine boutiques, restaurants and lovely antique shops. Also on the south side of the city is the new **Dundrum Centre**.

On the north side of the river is the relatively new **Jervis Centre**, which houses many British chain stores as well as a number of Irish retailers.

MARKETS

On Dublin's north side, just off Henry Street, the famous and still-evolving Moore Street Market hosts a daily fruit and vegetable bazaar, replete with very vocal street vendors. The area has recently become a hive of ethnic shops, where you can source anything from Iranian dance music CDs to tinned bok choi.

The wonderful **Temple Bar Food Market**, where you will find a wide range of organically produced items, is held every Saturday. A particularly popular stall sells delicious fresh oysters and wine by the glass – a great stop-off point for the weary shopper.

Quirky, quaint and unique, **George's Street Arcade** is open seven days a week and has many second-hand shops. It

is a good place for records, books, Irish memorabilia and bric-à-brac, as well as funky clothing and accessories.

SOUVENIRS AND GIFTS

The most popular destination for souvenirs in Dublin is unsurprisingly found at the home of Ireland's most popular drink – the **Guinness Storehouse** *(see pp 98–9)*. The interactive tours of the storehouse are best rounded off with a visit to the gift shop, where a multitude of Guinness branded souvenirs and clothing can be bought.

Finely crafted pottery

Nassau Street has a concentration of fine tourist gift shops, such as **Heraldic Artists**, which assists visitors in tracing their ancestry. **Knobs and Knockers** specializes in a wide range of door accessories. For a more varied range of gifts on the same street, drop in to the **Kilkenny Shop**. This store stocks uniquely Irish ceramic wares, the famous Waterford crystal and many other handcrafted products.

Across the road, the gift shop at Trinity College sells university memorabilia and mementos of the *Book of Kells*, as well as many other souvenirs.

Rather less upmarket, **Carroll's Irish Gift Stores**, a chain of souvenir and clothing

outlets, are difficult to miss while traversing the city. They stock a surfeit of kitschy leprechauns and other such amusing odds and ends.

FOOD AND WINE

Connoisseurs of fine wines and whiskies have many choices in Dublin. **Claudio's**, where the proprietor often attends to visitors personally, is one of the city's best fine wine shops. **Cabot & Co** boasts one of the largest selections of wine, as well as cellaring facilities. The **Celtic Whiskey Shop** stocks a variety of Irish and Scotch whiskies, and the staff are very knowledgeable.

A number of gourmet food retailers add culinary character to the city. **Sheridan's Cheesemongers** specializes in Irish farmhouse cheeses but stocks a wide array of other cheeses and foods too. **La Maison des Gourmets**, a café and bakery with a French flavour, serves patisserie and delicatessen treats. **Butler's Irish Chocolate** tempts with gift boxes of exquisite handmade chocolates. For those craving freshly caught Irish salmon, **Sawer's Fishmongers** on Chatham Street is a good bet. Dublin's growing multiculturalism has led to the proliferation of an impressive range of ethnic food stores in the city.

Sheridan's Cheesemongers' tempting display

FASHION

Although there are many elegant boutiques in Dublin, the most fashionable among them are clustered close to Dublin's "Fifth Avenue" – the smart Grafton Street area. **Costume**, with its wide range of Irish and international designer labels, is a popular destination for women's *haute couture*. Shoe aficionados will find that **Le Cherche Midi** stocks some 3very enticing ladies' footwear.

Bargain hunters should head for the Temple Bar Old City fashion market, where many outlets sell uniquely Irish designs at reduced prices.

For classic menswear, **Louis Copeland** is Dublin's most famous tailor, with branches on both sides of the city. For traditional clothing, stop at the Kilkenny Shop *(see p105)* or **Kevin & Howlin**. Both stock tweeds, Arans and other typically Irish clothing.

BOOKS

Given its rich literary heritage, it is not surprising that there are a number of specialist and interesting bookstores peppering Dublin's streets. **The Winding Stair**, with its own café, is a popular shop. **Books Upstairs**, next to Trinity College, has a good selection of Irish titles. Antiquarian bookseller, **Cathach Books**, is Dublin's specialist provider of old Irish titles. The shop stocks an impressive selection of first editions and rarities.

Shoppers looking to buy, sell or exchange used books should make their way to **Chapters**, which has one of the largest second-hand sections in the city.

MUSIC

The most concentrated area for record shops is in Temple Bar, where small stores stock everything from obscure electronica to indie and reggae. **City Discs** caters to independent rock and metal tastes, with both new and second-hand music. Fans of such music also converge at **Borderline Records** and **Purple Moon** nearby. For the best techno, R&B and

house on vinyl and CD, pay a visit to **Big Brother Records** or **Selectah Records** just above it. Alternative titles and a wide variety of second-hand records can also be found at **Freebird Records**, a long established music retailer on Eden Quay.

Most record shops in Dublin stock traditional Irish music, but **Celtic Note** on Nassau Street has one of the largest selections. The staff will gladly make recommendations. **McCullough Piggot** on the South side, and **Waltons** on the North are best for sheet music and traditional Irish instruments including uillean pipes and *bodhráns*.

ANTIQUES

One of Dublin's oldest antique retailers, **Oman Antique Galleries** specializes in quality Georgian, Victorian and Edwardian furniture. **Clifford Antiques** offers both original and reproduction antique furniture, as well as decorative fireplaces. Its collection of bronze fountains and figures is unrivalled in the city. The eclectic collection by **Christy Bird** includes an array of salvaged and recycled furniture and pub fittings.

The Powerscourt Centre is also home to many antique dealers. Of these, **Delphi** is a specialist in Victorian and Edwardian period jewellery, and also stocks beautifully fragile Belleek porcelain antiques. **Windsor Antiques** is the best for antique watches, cuff links, brooches, diamond rings and other jewellery. For silver antiques, including Irish and English portrait miniatures from the 18th to the 20th century, visit **The Silver Shop**.

For antique maps and prints, the Grafton Street area is a good hunting ground with the **Neptune Gallery** and **Antique Prints** nearby.

Located in one the oldest areas of the city and near the historical Coombe, Francis Street offers a mish-mash of antique stores. Old clocks, second-hand furniture and loads of bric-à-brac line the streets, inviting visitors into shops that are almost antiques themselves.

Outside the city centre, **Beaufield Mews** specializes in porcelain and early 20th-century pictures, while **Q Antiques** in Dun Laoghaire stocks an interesting range of period lighting and furniture.

Those who wish to further explore vintage Irish treasures should consult the website and local listings for the **Antiques Fairs** that are held in the city at different times and locations throughout the year.

GALLERIES

The abundance of galleries and artists' workshops in Dublin make it a favourite destination of art lovers and collectors. Many galleries are located on Dawson Street, which runs parallel to Grafton Street. The prestigious **Apollo Gallery** flaunts a trendy pop sensibility and exhibits works by many of Ireland's best-known artists.

On Westland Row, the **Oisín Gallery** sells the work of some of Ireland's best young artists in its split-level exhibition space. Visitors may also visit **Whyte's Auction Rooms** to bid on international and Irish art. The catalogues are published online and can be consulted for those seriously interested in investigating Irish painting.

On Sundays, an outdoor art market is held at Merrion Square close to the museum quarter. Works of vastly varying quality are hung from the square's perimeter black railing, and in good weather, the colourful, impromptu exhibition makes for very enjoyable browsing.

The Temple Bar area is also home to many of the city's galleries, including the **Temple Bar Gallery and Studios**. It is one of the more modish, cutting-edge venues, housing the eclectic work of more than 30 Irish artists working in several mediums. Nearby, in the heart of Dublin's Left Bank, is the **Original Print Gallery** and the **Gallery of Photography**, which stocks an impressive collection of glossy art books. Despite its association with partying and drunken misconduct, the area is still deserving of its "cultural quarter" status.

DIRECTORY

DEPARTMENT STORES

Arnott's
12 Henry St.
Map D2. **Tel** 01 805 0400.

Brown Thomas
88–95 Grafton St.
Map D4.
Tel 01 605 6666.

Clery's
18–27 Lower O'Connell St.
Map D2. **Tel** 01 878 6000.

Roches Stores
54–62 Henry St.
Map D2. **Tel** 01 873 0044.

SHOPPING CENTRES

Jervis Centre
125 Upper Abbey St.
Map C2.
Tel 01 878 1323.

Powerscourt Centre
59 South William.
Map D4.
Tel 01 679 4144.

Stephen's Green Centre
St Stephen's Green West.
Map D4.
Tel 01 478 0888.

Dundrum Centre
Dundrum.
Tel 01 299 1700.

MARKETS

George's Street Market Arcade
George's St. **Map** C4.

Temple Bar Food Market
Meeting House Sq,
Temple Bar. **Map** D3.

SOUVENIRS AND GIFTS

Carroll's Irish Gift Stores
57 Upper O'Connell St.
Map A3. **Tel** 01 873 5709.

Guinness Storehouse
St. James's Gate. **Map** A3.
Tel 01 408 4800.

Heraldic Artists
3 Nassau St. **Map** A3.
Tel 01 679 7020.

Kilkenny Shop
6–10 Nassau Street.
Map E4. **Tel** 01 677 7066.

Knobs and Knockers
19 Nassau St. **Map** A3.
Tel 01 671 0288.

FOOD AND WINE

Butler's Irish Chocolate
24 Wicklow St. **Map** D4.
Tel 01 6710591.

Cabot & Co.
Valentia House, Custom
House Sq, IFSC. **Map** F2.
Tel 01 636 0616.

Celtic Whiskey Shop
27–28 Dawson St.
Map D4. **Tel** 01 675 9744.

Claudio's
29 George's Street Arcade,
Drury St. **Map** D4.
Tel 01 671 5917.

La Maison des Gourmets
15 Castle St. **Map** D4.
Tel 01 672 7258.

Sawer's Fishmongers
3 Chatham St. **Map** D4.
Tel 01 677 7643.

Sheridan's Cheesemongers
11 South Anne St.
Map D4. **Tel** 01 679 3143.

FASHION

Costume
10 Castle Market. **Map** D4.
Tel 01 679 4188.

Le Cherche Midi
23 Drury St. **Map** D4.
Tel 01 675 3974

Louis Copeland
39–41 Capel St. **Map** C2.
Tel 01 872 1600.

Kevin & Howlin
31 Nassau St. **Map** E4.
Tel 01 677 0257.

BOOKS

Books Upstairs
36 College Green.
Map D3.
Tel 01 679 6687.

Cathach Books
10 Duke St. **Map** D4.
Tel 01 671 8676.

Chapters
108/109 Middle Abbey St.
Map D2. **Tel** 01 872 3297.

The Winding Stair
40 Ormond Quay Lower.
Map C3. **Tel** 01 873 3292.

MUSIC

Big Brother Records
4 Crow St, Temple Bar.
Map C3. **Tel** 01 672 9355.

Borderline Records
17 Temple Bar. **Map** C3.
Tel 01 679 9097

Celtic Note
14/15 Nassau St. **Map** E4.
Tel 01 670 4157.

City Discs
The Granary, Temple Lane.
Map C3.
Tel 01 633 0066.

Freebird Records
1 Eden Quay. **Map** D2.
Tel 01 873 1250.

McCullough Piggot
25 Suffolk St.
Map D3.
Tel 01 677 3138.

Purple Moon
7 Crow St, Temple Bar.
Tel 01 671 9347.

Selectah Records
4 Crow St, Temple Bar.
Map C3.
Tel 01 616 7020.

Waltons
2–5 North Frederick St.
Map D1.
Tel 01 874 7805.

ANTIQUES

Antiques Fairs
www.antiquefairsireland.com

Antique Prints
16 South Anne St.
Map D4. **Tel** 01 671 9523.

Beaufield Mews
Woodlands Ave, Stillorgan,
Co Dublin. **Road map** D4.
Tel 01 2880375.

Christy Bird
32 S Richmond St.
Tel 01 475 4049.

Clifford Antiques
7/8 Parnell St. **Map** D1.
Tel 01 872 6062.

Delphi
Powerscourt Centre.
Map D4.
Tel 01 679 0331.

Neptune Gallery
41 S William's. **Map** D4.
Tel 01 671 5021.

Oman Antique Galleries
20/21 S William St.
Map D4.
Tel 01 616 8991.

Q Antiques
76 York Rd,
Dun Laoghaire, Co Dublin.
Road map D4.
Tel 01 280 2895.

The Silver Shop
Powerscourt Centre.
Map D4.
Tel 01 679 4147.

Windsor Antiques
23D Powerscourt Centre.
Map D4.
Tel 01 670 3001.

GALLERIES

Apollo Gallery
15–18 W Essex St,
Temple Bar. **Map** C3.
Tel 01 671 2609.

Gallery of Photography
Meeting House Sq,
Temple Bar. **Map** C3.
Tel 01 671 4654.

Oisin Gallery
44 Westland Row.
Map F3.
Tel 01 661 1315.

Original Print Gallery
4 Temple Bar.
Map D3.
Tel 01 677 3657.

Temple Bar Gallery and Studios
5–9 Temple Bar.
Map D3.
Tel 01 671 0073.

Whyte's Auction Rooms
38 Molesworth St.
Map D2.
Tel 01 676 2888.
www.whytes.ie

ENTERTAINMENT IN DUBLIN

Although Dublin is well served by theatres, cinemas, nightclubs and rock venues, what sets the city apart from other European capitals is its pubs. Lively banter, impromptu music sessions and great Guinness are the essential ingredients for an enjoyable night in any of the dozens of atmospheric hostelries here.

Olympia Theatre façade

One of the most popular entertainment districts is the rejuvenated Temple Bar area. Along this narrow network of cobbled streets, you can find everything from traditional music in grand old pubs to the latest dance tracks in a post-industrial setting. The many pubs and venues around this area make the city centre south of the Liffey the place to be at night. The north side does, however, boast the two most illustrious theatres, the largest cinemas and the 7,000-seater Point Theatre, a converted 19th-century rail terminal beside the docks. It is now the venue for all major rock concerts and stage musicals, as well as a number of classical music performances.

Buskers playing near Grafton Street in southeast Dublin

ENTERTAINMENT LISTINGS

Listings for clubs, cinemas, theatre and other entertainment can be found in most newspapers, such as the *Irish Times* and the *Tribune*, particularly on weekends. *Hot Press*, a national bimonthly newspaper covering both rock and traditional music, has comprehensive listings for Dublin. The *Event Guide* and *In Dublin* are free sheets available at pubs, cafés, restaurants and record shops. They are published fortnightly and are particularly strong on music and nightclubs.

BOOKING TICKETS

Tickets for many events are available on the night, but it is usually safer to book in advance. All the major venues take credit card payment over the telephone. **Ticketmaster** accepts phone bookings by credit card only for many of the major shows and events in and around Dublin, while **HMV** and **Dublin Tourism** (Suffolk Street) sell tickets for most of the top theatres and major rock gigs.

THEATRE

Although Dublin only has a limited number of theatres, there is almost always something worth seeing. Most theatres are closed on Sunday. Ireland's national theatre, the **Abbey** *(see p88)*, is the most popular venue, concentrating on major new productions as well as revivals of works by Irish playwrights such as Brendan Behan, Sean O'Casey, JM Synge and WB Yeats. The smaller Peacock Theatre downstairs features experimental works. Also on the north side is the **Gate Theatre** *(see p90)*, founded in 1929 as a rival to the Abbey, and noted for its interpretations of well-known international plays.

The main venue south of the Liffey, the **Gaiety Theatre**, stages a mainstream mix of plays, emphasizing the work of Irish playwrights. Some of the best fringe theatre and modern dance in Dublin can be seen at the **Project Arts Centre** in Temple Bar and the **City Arts Centre**, which sometimes holds midnight performances. **Andrew's Lane Theatre** provides a forum for new writers and directors. The **Olympia Theatre** has the feel of a Victorian music hall. It specializes in comedy and popular drama, and occasionally stages rock and Irish music concerts.

Every October, the **Dublin Theatre Festival** takes over all the city venues with mainstream, fringe and international plays.

Record shop and ticket office in Crown Alley, Temple Bar

Crowds enjoying the Temple Bar Blues Festival

CINEMA

The city's cinemas had a boost in the 1990s with the success of Dublin-based films such as *My Left Foot* (1989). Huge growth in the country's movie production industry followed, and hits like *Dancing at Lughnasa* (1998) and *Intermission* (2004) keep Ireland in the spotlight.

The **Irish Film Institute** opened its doors in 1992 and is a most welcome addition to the city's entertainment scene. Showcasing mostly foreign and independent films, along with a programme of lectures, it boasts two screens, as well as a bar and restaurant. **Screen**, close to Trinity College, has a repertoire of art house films.

The large first-run cinemas are all located on the north side. They usually offer tickets at reduced prices for afternoon screenings, and show late-night films on the weekend. The summer-long **Diversions** festival in Temple Bar includes open-air screenings, mainly in Meeting House Square. Tickets are available from Temple Bar Properties.

CLASSICAL MUSIC, OPERA AND DANCE

Dublin may not have the range of classical concerts of other European capitals, but it has a great venue in the **National Concert Hall**. In the 1980s,

The listings magazine *In Dublin*

this 19th-century exhibition hall was redesigned, and is where the National Symphony Orchestra plays most Friday evenings. The programme also includes opera, jazz, chamber music, dance and some traditional music.

The **Hugh Lane Municipal Gallery of Modern Art** *(see p91)* has regular Sunday lunch-time concerts. Other venues include the **Royal Hospital Kilmainham** *(see p97)*, **Bank of Ireland Arts Centre** and the **Royal Dublin Society (RDS)**. International opera is staged in the **Point Theatre**. The Dublin Grand Opera Society performs every April and November at the Gaiety Theatre.

ROCK, JAZZ, BLUES AND COUNTRY

Dublin has had a thriving rock scene ever since local band Thin Lizzy made it big in the early 1970s. U2's success acted as a further catalyst for local bands, and each night there's usually an interesting gig somewhere in the city. **Whelan's** is probably the most popular live venue. Since 1989,

many famous names have performed on its stage. Temple Bar venue, **The Mezz**, hosts live music most nights of the week. Set on two floors, this place is always packed with students. Get there early if you want to find a good seat by the stage.

Eamonn Doran's in Temple Bar is another favourite for rock fans (and pizza lovers). Located in the same building is Di Fontaine's pizzeria, partly owned by Huey Morgan of the rock group, Fun Lovin' Criminals. Eamonn Doran's is a suitably grungy environment for visitors looking for an authentic Dublin rock experience. Also partly owned by the Fun Lovin' Criminals' frontman is **The Voodoo Lounge**. This dark venue's live performances are fast gaining a reputation among rock fans.

The upstairs room at the likeable **International Bar** caters mostly to acoustic acts and singer-songwriters, while the **Ha'penny Bridge Inn** has folk and blues on Friday and Saturday nights.

Big names play at either the **Point Theatre** or, in summer, at the local sports stadia. The **Olympia**, a Victorian theatre, hosts memorable concerts in extraordinary surroundings. Outside Dublin, **Slane Castle** hosts a big rock event every summer *(see p245)*.

The **Temple Bar Music Centre** and **The Sugar Club** offer jazz, salsa, Latin and blues all year, with the Heineken Green Energy Festival, a highlight in May. Country music is popular in Ireland, and plays at several Dublin pubs. Check entertainment listings for details.

Live rock band performing at the Sugar Club

TRADITIONAL MUSIC AND DANCE

To many Irish people, the standard of music in a pub is just as important as the quality of the Guinness. Central Dublin has a host of pubs reverberating to the sound of *bodhráns*, fiddles and uilleann pipes. One of the most famous is **O'Donoghue's**, where the legendary Dubliners started out in the early 1960s. The **Cobblestone** and the **Auld Dubliner** are also renowned venues. Established acts play at venues such as **Mother Redcap's Tavern**, which is a fun place occupying an old factory. **Castle Inn** stages Irish cabaret (May–October) featuring dancing, singing and music.

PUBS AND BARS

Dublin's pubs are a slice of living history. These are the places where some of the best-known scenes in Irish literature have been set, where rebellious politicians have met, and where world-famous music acts have made their debuts. Today, it's the singing, dancing, talk and laughter that make a pub tour of Dublin an absolute must.

There are nearly 1,000 pubs inside the city limits. Among the best of the traditional bars are **Neary's**, popular with actors and featuring a gorgeous marble bar, the atmospheric **Long Hall**, and the friendly and chic **Stag's Head** dating from 1770.

Cosy snugs, where drinkers could lock themselves away for private conversation, were an important feature of 19th-century bars. A few remain, notably at the tiny, journalists' haunt of **Doheny & Nesbitt** and intimate **Kehoe's**.

The **Brazen Head** claims to be the city's oldest pub, dating back to 1198. The present pub, built in the 1750s, is lined with old photographs and dark wood panelling, and showcases traditional music sessions nightly. Every pub prides itself on the quality of its Guinness, though most locals acknowledge that **Mulligan's**, founded in 1782, serves the best pint in the city.

The **Grave Diggers** is situated on the northern outskirts of the city in Phibsborough. Located next to a graveyard, this bar has more character than most, and it's worth the taxi ride just to see what a Dublin bar would have looked like hundreds of years ago. On summer weekends, the green outside fills with lazy drinkers enjoying pints and swapping stories.

Grogan's bar, on William Street, is frequented by many of Dublin's bohemian characters. Part bar, part art gallery, it exhibits an array of paintings by local artists.

Café en Seine is influenced by a *belle époque* Parisian bar. Its interior is huge and cavernous, and the decor rich and alluring. At weekends, this bar heaves with Dublin's movers and shakers. Situated next door is **Ron Black's**, one of Dublin's more style-conscious bars, usually frequented by members of the film industry. Lofty ceilings, dark panelled walls and off-white furnishings set the mood for relaxed networking or enjoyable people-watching.

Grand Central is one of the very few bars on the city's main thoroughfare, O'Connell Street. Housed in a former bank, many of the original features have been retained.

Rush, a small chic bar, has a strictly pop-music policy and is populated by a trendy young crowd. **The Welcome Inn** is a journey back to the 1970s; low formica tables and vinyl stools complement the antiquated wallpaper. The young crowd can be rambunctious, depending on who has programmed the jukebox.

Dice Bar is a pseudo-dive bar with a dark interior of clashing blacks and reds. The music policy is a combination of rare rock 'n' roll and blues records.

Urban and cosmopolitan, **The Globe** is as popular during the day for coffee as it is at night. The crowd is a cool mix of musicians and city hipsters. Not unlike the Globe, but with a modern twist, **4 Dame Lane** is a slickly designed bar. At night it fills with a young crowd that loves the eclectic music. Two flaming torches mark the entrance.

Part of the sleek Morgan Hotel in Temple Bar, the beautifully designed **Morgan Bar** prides itself on serving outstanding cocktails. **The Market Bar**, a relative newcomer to the scene, is fast becoming one of the city's favourite gastro-pubs. Set in an old factory, high ceilings and red-brick walls lend this place a certain retro-industrial charm. Superb food is served throughout the day.

Small, comfy **Peter's Pub** has a reputation for quality pints and is considered by many to be the quintessential Dublin boozer.

GUINNESS TIME

A Guinness advertisement at a Dublin pub

A traditional Irish music session in O'Donoghue's

Traditional façade of Doheny & Nesbitt

A LITERARY PUB CRAWL

Pubs with strong literary associations abound in Dublin, particularly around Grafton Street. **McDaid's**, an old pub with an Art Deco interior, still retains some of its bohemian air from the time when writers such as Patrick Kavanagh and Brendan Behan were regulars.

Davy Byrne's has a plusher decor than it did when Leopold Bloom dropped in for a gorgonzola and mustard sandwich in *Ulysses*, but it is still well worth paying a visit. These pubs, and others frequented by Ireland's most famous authors and playwrights, are featured on the excellent **Dublin Literary Pub Crawl**. The two-and-a-half-hour tours, which are led by actors, start with a beer in **The Duke**, and are by far the most entertaining way to get a real feel for the city's booze-fuelled literary heritage. Tours take place daily in summer, but are usually held only at weekends in winter.

NIGHTCLUBS

Dublin's clubs are continually revamping and relaunching, and variety remains the key in clubland, with plenty of massive superclubs and more intimate, laidback venues. The scene is somewhat curtailed, however, by the city's licensing laws. A nightclub licence allows a club to remain open until 2:30am – early by many major cities' standards. So Dublin clubbers start their night early, often beginning at a pub.

The **POD** complex houses four spaces, providing some of Dublin's most diverse offerings. **Crawdaddy** features live acts ranging from local hip-hop groups to international reggae stars. Next door is the ultra trendy **Lobby Bar**, featuring soul music and avantgarde design. Next to it is the original POD, where a trendy mix of cutting-edge sounds and attractive clubbers combine to produce an exclusive atmosphere. Upstairs, **Red Box** is the largest space and attracts a younger crowd; the music policy is varied and depends upon the night.

Club M is another multi-level nightclub with an impressive light and sound system. It attracts dedicated club aficionados and weekend revellers.

Spirit is a unique clubbing experience. Like its sister club in New York, this club is divided into three areas – Mind, Body and Soul. Spirit also houses a therapy centre where jaded clubbers can relax with holistic treatments such as *reiki* and Indian head massage. A nightly show features dancing and other performances. Cocktails and glamour abound at luxurious **Traffic**, which also has a New York sister. Located next door to Spirit, it attracts house music fans. Dress to impress as these clubbers are always wearing their best.

For those looking for laid-back sophistication, **Joy's** is technically a wine bar and has a licence to stay open late.

Viperoom, named after the famous Hollywood club, usually has a pianist to provide an intimate soundtrack. For those with more energy to burn, a dance floor is located in the basement.

Located in a magnificently restored Georgian town house, **Spy** is one of the most comfortable nightclubs in town. The door policy is strict at this popular spot, so arriving early and dressing up are essential if you want to dance to cutting-edge music or sink into a dangerously comfortable couch.

Zanzibar covers several floors and features exotic Moorish decor. At the weekend, the young clubbers crowd at the bar and dance to chart music. **Isaac Butt's** is a little more intimate, with varied live music and DJs seven nights a week. There's a youth hostel just around the corner and entry is free, so this club tends to be popular with backpackers.

Ri-Ra, Irish for uproar, is at the cutting edge of R&B and dance music, and is one of Dublin's longest running nightclubs. An annexe to the ever popular Globe, Ri-Ra is packed with serious night owls, intent on dancing and having a ball, every night of the week.

Play at the Gaiety opens its doors after Friday and Saturday night theatre performances. Live bands play Latin, reggae, jazz, soul or salsa. **The Boom Boom Room** promotes the kind of music that is often overlooked by regular clubs – live jazz, electronica and avantgarde. Full of young, restless bohemians and musical connoisseurs, the Boom Boom Room is a style-shaping force in the city's club scene.

Touted as Dublin's most prestigious night club, **Lillie's Bordello** has a luxurious, decadent atmosphere. The legendary VIP room has long been a favourite of Dublin's rich and famous, and regulars often rub shoulders with the entertainment elite.

The **PLU Bar** is another exclusive haunt where many media types hang out. The club is a warren of VIP rooms and boasts Bono as a lifetime member (he occasionally drops by with the rest of U2 in tow). **Renards**, the not-so-VIP section, usually plays chart music, but hosts live jazz on Sundays.

DIRECTORY

BOOKING AGENTS

Dublin Tourism
Tourism Centre,
Suffolk St, Dublin 2.
Tel 1800 230330.

HMV
18 Henry St.
Map D2
65 Grafton St.
Map D4.
www.hmv.co.uk

Ticketmaster
Tel 0818 719300.
www.ticketmaster.ie

THEATRE

Abbey Theatre
Abbey St Lower.
Map E2.
Tel 01 878 7222.
www.abbeytheatre.ie

Andrew's Lane Theatre
9–11 St Andrew's Lane.
Map D3.
Tel 01 679 5720.
www.andrewslane.com

City Arts Centre
23–25 Moss St.
Map E2.
Tel 01 639 4608.
www.cityartscentre.ie

Dublin Theatre Festival
44 Essex St East.
Map C3.
Tel 01 677 8439.
www.dublintheatre
festival.com

Focus Theatre
6 Pembroke Place.
Map E5.
Tel 01 676 3071.

Gaiety Theatre
King St South.
Map D4.
Tel 01 677 1717.
www.gaietytheatre.com

Gate Theatre
Cavendish Row.
Map D1.
Tel 01 874 4045.
www.gate-theatre.ie

Olympia Theatre
Dame St.
Map C3.
Tel 01 677 1020.

Project Art Centre
39 East Essex St.
Map C3.
Tel 01 881 9613.
www.project.ie

CINEMA

Diversions
Meeting House Sq.
Map C3.
Tel 01 677 2255.
www.templebar.ie

Irish Film Institute
6 Eustace St,
Temple Bar.
Map C3.
Tel 01 679 5744.
www.ifi.ie

Screen
D'Olier St.
Map D3.
Tel 01 672 5500.

Cineworld Cinemas
Parnell St.
Map C2.
Tel 01 872 8444.
www.ugc.ie

CLASSICAL MUSIC, OPERA AND DANCE

Bank of Ireland Arts Centre
Bank of Ireland Arts
Centre, Foster Place,
College Green.
Map D3.
Tel 01 671 1488.
www.bankofireland.ie

Hugh Lane Municipal Gallery of Modern Art
Charlemont House,
Parnell Sq North.
Map C1.
Tel 01 222 5550.
www.hughlane.ie

National Concert Hall
Earlsfort Terrace.
Map D5.
Tel 01 417 0000.
www.nch.ie

Point Theatre
East Link Bridge,
North Wall Quay.
Map D1.
Tel 01 836 3633.
www.thepoint.ie

Royal Dublin Society (RDS)
Ballsbridge.
Tel 01 668 0866.
www.rds.ie

Royal Hospital Kilmainham
Military Lane,
Kilmainham, Dublin 18.
Tel 01 612 9900.
www.modernart.ie

ROCK, JAZZ, BLUES AND COUNTRY

Eamonn Doran's
Crown Alley,
Temple Bar, Dublin 2.
Map D3.
Tel 01 6799114.

Ha'penny Bridge Inn
Wellington Quay.
Map C3.
Tel 01 677 0616.

International Bar
23 Wicklow St.
Map D3.
Tel 01 677 9250.

The Mezz
Eustace St,
Temple Bar, Dublin 2.
Map C3.
Tel 01 670 7655.

Slane Castle
Slane, Co Meath.
Tel 01 988 4400.
www.slanecastle.ie

The Sugar Club
8 Lower Leeson St.
Map E5.
Tel 01 678 7188.
www.thesugarclub.com

Temple Bar Music Centre
Curved St, Temple Bar.
Map E4.
Tel 01 670 9202.
www.tbmc.ie

The Voodoo Lounge
Arran Quay, Dublin 7.
Map A3.
Tel 01 8736013.

Whelan's
25 Wexford St.
Map E4 C5.
Tel 01 478 0766.
www.whelanslive.com

TRADITIONAL MUSIC AND DANCE

Auld Dubliner
Auld Dubliner, 24–25
Temple Bar.
Map D3.
Tel 01 677 0527.

Castle Inn
5–7 Lord Edward St.
Map C3.
Tel 01 478 0663.

Cobblestone
77 King St North.
Map A2.
Tel 01 872 1799.

The Temple Bar
48 Temple Bar. Dublin 2
Map C3.
Tel 01 672 5287.

Mother Redcap's Tavern
Back Lane, Christchurch.
Map B4.
Tel 01 453 3960.

O'Donoghue's
15 Merrion Row.
Map E5.
Tel 01 660 7194.
www.odonoghues.ie

DIRECTORY

PUBS AND BARS

4 Dame Lane
4 Dame Lane,
Dublin 2.
Map C3.
Tel 01 679 0291.

Brazen Head
20 Bridge St Lower.
Map A3.
Tel 01 679 5186.
www.brazenhead.com

Café en Seine
40 Dawson St,
Dublin 2.
Map D4.
Tel 01 677 4567.
www.capitalbars.com

Davy Byrne's
21 Duke St.
Map D4.
Tel 01 677 5217.
www.davybyrnes.com

Dice Bar
79 Queen St,
Dublin 7.
Map A2.
Tel 01 872 8622.

Doheny & Nesbitt
5 Lower Baggot St.
Map E5.
Tel 01 676 2945.
www.dohenyandnesbitt.
com

**Dublin Literary
Pub Crawl**
37 Exchequer St.
Map D3.
Tel 01 670 5602.
www.dublinpubcrawl.
com

The Duke
9 Duke St.
Map D4.
Tel 01 679 9553.

The Globe
11 S Great George's St,
Dublin 2.
Map C4.
Tel 01 671 1220.
www.globe.ie

Grand Central
Abbey St / O'Connell St,
Dublin 1.
Map D2.
Tel 01 872 8662.

The Grave Diggers
Prospect Sq, Glasnevin,
Dublin 9.
Map D1.

Grogan's
15 S William St,
Dublin 2.
Map D4.
Tel 01 677 9320.

Kehoe's
9 S Anne St.
Map D4.
Tel 01 677 8312.

Long Hall
51 S Great George's St.
Map C4.
Tel 01 475 1590.

The Market Bar
14a Fade St,
Dublin 2.
Map D4.
Tel 01 613 9094.
www.pod.ie

McDaid's
3 Harry St,
off Grafton St.
Map D4.
Tel 01 679 4395.

The Morgan Bar
The Morgan Hotel,
10 Fleet St,
Dublin 2.
Map D3.
Tel 01 643 7000.
www.themorgan.com

Mulligan's
8 Poolbeg St.
Map E3.
Tel 01 677 5582.
www.mulligans.ie

Neary's
1 Chatham St.
Map D4.
Tel 01 677 8596.

Peter's Pub
Johnson's Place,
Dublin 2.
Map D4.
Tel 01 677 8588.

Ron Black's
38 Dawson St,
Dublin 2.
Map D4.
Tel 01 670 3702.

Rush
65 S William St,
Dublin 2.
Map D4.
Tel 01 671 9542.

Stag's Head
1 Dame Court,
off Dame Lane.
Map D3.
Tel 01 679 3701.

The Welcome Inn
13 Parnell St,
Dublin 1.
Map D1.
Tel 01 874 3227.

NIGHTCLUBS

**The Boom Boom
Room**
70 Parnell St,
above Patrick Conway's,
Dublin 7.
Map D1.
Tel 01 873 2687. www.
theboomboomroom.tv

Club M
Blooms Hotel,
Temple Bar.
Map D3.
Tel 01 6715622.
www.clubm.ie

Crawdaddy
Harcourt St.
Map D5.
Tel 01 4780225.
www.crawdaddy.ie

Isaac Butt's
Store St, Dublin 1.
Map E2.
Tel 01 855 5021.
www.theisaacbutt.com

Joy's
Baggot St, Dublin 2.
Map F5.
Tel 01 676 6729.

Lillie's Bordello
Adam Court,
off Grafton St.
Map E4 D4.
Tel 01 679 9204.
www.lilliesbordello.ie

Play at the Gaiety
S King St, Dublin 2.
Map D4.
Tel 01 677 1717.
www.gaietytheatre.com

Renards
S Frederick St, Dublin 2.
Tel 01 677 5876.
www.renards.ie

**POD, Lobby Bar,
Red Box**
Harcourt St. **Map** D5.
Tel 01 4780166.
www.pod.ie

Ri-Ra
South Great George's St,
Dublin 2.
Map E3.
Tel 01 671 1220.
www.rira.ie

Spirit
Abbey St, Dublin 1.
Map C2.
Tel 01 877 9999.
www.spiritdublin.com

Spy
South William St.
Map D4.
Tel 01 677 0014.
www.spydublin.com

Traffic
Abbey St, Dublin 1.
Map C2.
Tel 01 873 4800.

Viper Room
Aston Quay, Dublin 2.
Map D3.
Tel 01 672 5566.

Zanzibar
Ormond Quay, Dublin 1.
Map C3.
Tel 01 878 7212.
www.capitalbars.com

Dublin's Best: Entertainment

It's easy to pack a lot into a night out in Dublin. Most of the best nightspots are situated close to each other and, in the Temple Bar area alone, there are plenty of exciting haunts to try out. The city offers something to suit every taste and pocket: choose from world-class theatre, excellent concert venues, designer café-bars and lively or laid-back clubs hosting nights of traditional, country, jazz or rock music. Even when there is no specific event that appeals, you can simply enjoy Dublin's inexhaustible supply of great traditional pubs.

Gate Theatre
The Gate puts on both foreign plays and Irish classics such as Sean O'Casey's Juno and the Paycock. *(See p90.)*

NORTH OF
THE LIFFEY

Stag's Head
This gorgeous Victorian pub has a long, mahogany bar and has retained its original mirrors and stained glass. Located down an out-of-the-way alley, this atmospheric pub is well worth seeking out. (See p110.)

SOUTHWEST
DUBLIN

0 metres 500
0 yards 500

THE TEMPLE BAR AREA

It will take more than a couple of evenings to explore fully all that these narrow streets have to offer. Many of Dublin's best mid-priced restaurants are here, while modern bars sit next to traditional pubs hosting fiddle sessions. There are also theatres and the Irish Film Centre. Later, clubs play music ranging from country to the latest dance sounds.

HA'PENNY BRIDGE
MILLENNIUM BRIDGE
LIFFEY
WELLINGTON QUAY
THE GARAGE BAR
PROJECT
ESSEX STREET EAST
THE AULD DUBLINER
TEMPLE BAR
THE BAD ASS CAFÉ
CROWN ALLEY
BAD BOBS
SYCAMORE ST
MEETING HOUSE SQUARE
TEMPLE LANE
FOWNES STREET
CROW ST
COPE STREET
Irish Film Centre
OLYMPIA
DAME STREET

0 metres 100
0 yards 100

Queuing for a concert in Temple Bar

Street theatre events take place throughout the summer in Temple Bar. This actor is portraying George Bernard Shaw in a typical street performance.

Abbey Theatre
Despite recurring financial problems, Ireland's prestigious national theatre still manages to stage compelling new drama, such as Dancing at Lughnasa *by Brian Friel. (See p88.)*

Point Theatre
Once a Victorian railway terminus, this is now the country's top live music arena. Major acts, including Van Morrison (above) and Luciano Pavarotti, have appeared here and it's also a popular venue for hit musicals. (See p109.)

McDaid's
Playwright Brendan Behan (see p23) downed many a pint in this pub, which dates from 1779. Though firmly on the tourist trail, McDaid's retains its bohemian charm, and bars upstairs and downstairs provide space for a leisurely drink. (See p113.)

SOUTHEAST DUBLIN

National Concert Hall
The National Symphony Orchestra performs most Friday evenings. A combination of dance, chamber music and other performance arts makes up a full programme of events. From May to July, inexpensive Tuesday lunch-time concerts are held. (See p109.)

Street Finder Index

KEY TO THE STREET FINDER

- Major sight
- Place of interest
- Railway station
- DART station
- Luas stop
- Main bus stop

- Coach station
- Taxi rank
- Main car park
- Tourist information office
- Hospital with casualty unit
- Police station

- Church
- Post office
- Railway line
- Pedestrian street

0 metres	200	
0 yards	200	**1:11,500**

KEY TO STREET FINDER ABBREVIATIONS

Ave	Avenue	**E**	East	**Pde**	Parade	**Sth**	South
Br	Bridge	**La**	Lane	**Pl**	Place	**Tce**	Terrace
Cl	Close	**Lr**	Lower	**Rd**	Road	**Up**	Upper
Ct	Court	**Nth**	North	**St**	Street/Saint	**W**	West

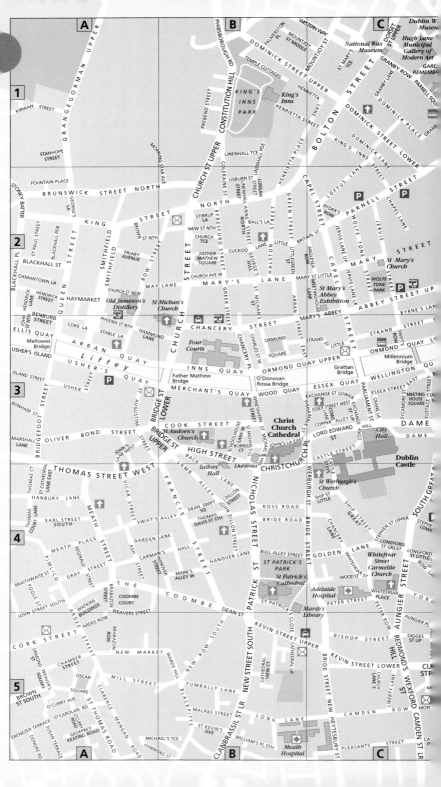

IRELAND REGION BY REGION

Ireland at a Glance

The lure of Ireland's much-vaunted Atlantic shores, from the wild coastline of Cork and Kerry to the remote peninsulas of the Northwest, is strong. However, to neglect the interior would be to miss out on Ireland's equally characteristic landscapes of lush valleys, dark peatlands and unruffled loughs. Most regions are rich in historic sights: from world-famous Neolithic sites in the Midlands to imposing Norman castles in the North and Palladian mansions in the Southeast.

Yeats Country *is a charming part of County Sligo closely associated with WB Yeats. The poet was born here and is buried within sight of Ben Bulben's ridge.* (See pp232–3.)

NORTHWEST IRELAND
(See pp220–35)

THE WEST OF IRELAND
(See pp200–219)

Connemara National Park *in County Galway boasts stunning landscapes in which mountains and lakes are combined with a dramatic Atlantic coastline. The extensive blanket bogs and moorland are rich in wildlife and unusual plants.* (See p208.)

Bunratty Castle
(See pp192–3)

The Rock of Cashel, *a fortified medieval abbey, perches on a limestone outcrop in the heart of County Tipperary. It boasts some of Ireland's finest Romanesque sculpture.* (See pp196–7.)

THE LOWER SHANNON
(See pp180–99)

CORK AND KERRY
(See pp152–79)

Bantry House
(See pp168–9)

The Lakes of Killarney, *flanked by the lush, wooded slopes of some of the country's highest mountains, are the principal attraction in the southwest of Ireland.* (See pp162–3)

The Giant's Causeway, *where ancient lava flows have been eroded to reveal columns of unnatural regularity, is Northern Ireland's most curious sight. According to local mythology, the rocks were placed here by a giant called Finn MacCool to enable him to walk across the sea to Scotland.* (See pp262–3.)

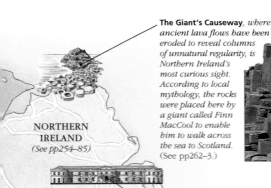

NORTHERN IRELAND
(See pp254–85)

Mount Stewart House, *a 19th-century mansion, is most renowned for its magnificent gardens. These were created as recently as the 1920s, but a colourful array of exotic plants has thrived in the warm microclimate enjoyed in this part of County Down.* (See pp282–3.)

Newgrange
(See pp246–7)

THE MIDLANDS
(See pp236–53)

SOUTHEAST IRELAND
(See pp124–51)

Powerscourt *is a large estate in superb countryside on the edge of the Wicklow Mountains. Its grounds rank among the last great formal gardens of Europe. Originally planted in the 1730s, they were restored and embellished in the 19th century.* (See pp134–5.)

| 0 kilometres | 50 |
| 0 miles | 25 |

Kilkenny Castle *was for centuries the stronghold of the Butler dynasty, which controlled much of southeast Ireland in the Middle Ages. The vast Norman fortress was remodelled during the Victorian period and still dominates Kilkenny – one of the country's most historic and pleasant towns.* (See pp142–3.)

SOUTHEAST IRELAND

KILDARE · WICKLOW · CARLOW · KILKENNY WATERFORD · WEXFORD

Blessed with the warmest climate in Ireland, the Southeast has always presented an attractive prospect for settlers. Landscapes of gently rolling hills have been tamed by centuries of cultivation, with lush farmland, imposing medieval castles and great houses enhancing the region's atmosphere of prosperity.

The Southeast's proximity to Britain meant that it was often the first port of call for foreign invaders. Viking raiders arrived here in the 9th century and founded some of Ireland's earliest towns, including Waterford and Wexford. They were followed in 1169 by the Anglo-Normans *(see pp36–7)*, who shaped the region's subsequent development.

Given its strategic importance, the Southeast was heavily protected, mostly by Anglo-Norman lords loyal to the English Crown. Remains of impressive castles attest to the power of the Fitzgeralds of Kildare and the Butlers of Kilkenny, who between them virtually controlled the Southeast throughout the Middle Ages. English influence was stronger here than in any other part of the island. From the 18th century, wealthy Anglo-Irish families were drawn to what they saw as a stable zone, and felt confident enough to build fine mansions like the Palladian masterpieces of Russborough and Castletown. English rule was not universally accepted, however. The Wicklow Mountains became a popular refuge for opponents to the Crown, including the rebels who fled the town of Enniscorthy after a bloody battle during the uprising against the English in 1798 *(see p41)*.

This mountainous region is still the only real wilderness in the Southeast, in contrast to the flat grasslands that spread across Kildare to the west. To the east, sandy beaches stretch almost unbroken along the shore between Dublin and Rosslare in Wexford.

Traditional thatched cottages in Dunmore East, County Waterford

◁ Staircase hall with ornate 18th-century stuccowork in Castletown House, County Kildare

Exploring Southeast Ireland

The southeast has something for everyone, from busy seaside resorts to quaint canalside villages, Norman abbeys and bird sanctuaries. The Wicklow Mountains, the location of several major sights such as the monastic complex of Glendalough and the magnificent gardens of Powerscourt, provide perfect touring and walking territory. Further south, the most scenic routes cut through the valleys of the Slaney, Barrow and Nore rivers, flanked by historic ports such as New Ross, from where you can explore local waterways by boat. Along the south coast, which is more varied than the region's eastern shore, beaches are interspersed with rocky headlands, and quiet coastal villages provide good alternative bases to the busy towns of Waterford and Wexford. Further inland, the best places to stay include Lismore and Kilkenny, which is one of the finest historic towns in Ireland.

Graiguenamanagh, on the Barrow north of New Ross

SIGHTS AT A GLANCE

Enfield
Kilcock
CASTLETOWN HOUSE ❶ 🏛
Dublin
Clane
ROBERTSTOWN ❷
Naas
Dalkey
Killiney
Killiney Bay
POWERSCOURT
🏛 ❼
❽ BRAY
RUSSBOROUGH HOUSE
❾ KILLRUDDERY HOUSE
Liffey ❻
❿ MILITARY ROAD
DARE
Mullaghcleevaun 848m
Hollywood
Roundwood
Ballitore
⓫
❶❷ MOUNT USHER GARDENS
GLENDALOUGH ⓭
Lugnaquillia Mt. 926m
Rathdrum
Wicklow
Baltinglass
WICKLOW
⓮ AVONDALE HOUSE
Castledermot
Rathvilly
Aughrim
BROWNE'S HILL ⓯ DOLMEN
Woodenbridge
Tullow
Tinahely
Ferrybank
Ballon
Shillelagh
Arklow
Carnew
Gorey
Bunclody
Courtown
Ferns
Kiltealy
Ballycanew
Kilnamanagh
ENNISCORTHY ㉔
Castleellis
WEXFORD
Clonroche
Blackwater
NEW ROSS
Wexford Bay
IRISH NATIONAL HERITAGE PARK
Wexford Wildfowl Reserve
Ballynabola
㉕ ㉖ WEXFORD
JOHNSTOWN CASTLE ㉗ ㉙ ROSSLARE
Wellington Bridge
🚢 Rosslare Harbour
Bridgetown
Fethard
Churchtown
MORE *Ballyteige Bay*
Kilmore Quay
㉘
SALTEE ISLANDS 🍴

A 19th-century winged horse at Powerscourt

GETTING AROUND

Routes N11, N9 and N7 fan out from Dublin, serving Wexford, Waterford and Kildare respectively. Rail lines follow a similar course: the eastern coastal towns are served by the Dublin Rosslare railway, and there are good train services to Kildare and Kilkenny. You will need a car to explore the south coast; the Passage East–Ballyhack ferry is a useful shortcut between Waterford and Wexford.

KEY

═══	Motorway
═══	Major road
───	Secondary road
═══	Minor road
───	Scenic route
─•─	Main railway
───	Minor railway
───	County border
△	Summit

The seaside resort of Bray on the east coast

Castletown House ❶

See pp130–31.

Robertstown ❷

Road map D4. Co Kildare. 240

Ten locks west along the Grand Canal from Dublin, Robertstown is a characteristic 19th-century canalside village, with warehouses and cottages flanking the waterfront. Freight barges plied the route until about 1960, but pleasure boats have since replaced them. Visitors can take barge cruises from the quay and the Grand Canal Company's Hotel, built in 1801 for canal passengers, is now used for banquets.

Near Sallins, about 8 km (5 miles) east of Robertstown, the canal is carried over the River Liffey along the **Leinster Aqueduct**, an impressive structure built in 1783.

The Grand Canal Company's Hotel in Robertstown

Bog of Allen Nature Centre ❸

Road map D4. Lullymore, Co Kildare. **Tel** 045 860133. to Newbridge. to Allenwood. 9:30am–5:30pm Mon–Fri. ltd. www.ipcc.ie

Anyone interested in the natural history of Irish bogs should visit The Nature Centre. Housed in an old farmhouse at Lullymore, 9 km (6 miles) northeast of Rathangan, Peatland World lies at the heart of the Bog of Allen, a vast expanse of raised bogland *(see p252)* that extends across the counties of Offaly, Laois and Kildare. An exhibition of flora, fauna and archaeological finds explores the history and ecology of the bog, while guided walks across the peatlands introduce visitors to the bog's delicate ecosystem.

Stacking peat for use as fuel

Monasterevin ❹

Road map D4. Co Kildare. 2,200.

This Georgian market town lies west of Kildare, where the Grand Canal crosses the River Barrow. Waterborne trade brought prosperity to Monasterevin in the 18th century, but the locks now see little traffic. However, you can still admire the aqueduct, which is a superb example of canal engineering.

Moore Abbey, next to the church, was built in the 18th century on the site of a monastic foundation, but the grand Gothic mansion owes much to Victorian remodelling. Once the ancestral seat of the Earls of Drogheda, in the 1920s Moore Abbey became the home of the celebrated tenor, John McCormack *(see p24)*. It is now a hospital.

Kildare ❺

Road map D4. Co Kildare. 4,200. *Market House (Jun–Sep: 045 522696)* Thu.

The charming and tidy town of Kildare is dominated by **St Brigid's Cathedral**, which commemorates the saint who founded a religious community on this site in 480. Unusually, monks and nuns lived here under the same roof, but this was not the only unorthodox practice associated with the community. Curious pagan rituals, including the burning of a perpetual fire, continued until the 16th century. The fire pit is still visible, as is the highest round tower that can be climbed in Ireland, which was probably built in the 12th

St Brigid's Cathedral and roofless round tower in Kildare town

Japanese Gardens at Tully near Kildare

century and has a Romanesque doorway. The cathedral was rebuilt in the Victorian era, but the restorers largely adhered to the 13th-century design.

🔒 **St Brigid's Cathedral**
Market Square. ⬭ *May–Sep: daily.*
Donation. ♿

Environs
Kildare lies at the heart of racing country: the Curragh racecourse is nearby, stables are scattered all around and bloodstock sales take place at Kill, northeast of town.

The **National Stud** is a semi-state-run bloodstock farm at Tully, just south of Kildare. It was founded in 1900 by an eccentric Anglo-Irish colonel called William Hall-Walker. He sold his foals on the basis of their astrological charts, and put skylights in the stables to allow the horses to be "touched" by sunlight and moonbeams. Hall-Walker received the title Lord Wavertree in reward for bequeathing the farm to the British Crown in 1915.

Visitors can explore the 400-ha (1,000-acre) grounds and watch the horses being exercised. Mares are generally kept in a separate paddock from the stallions. Breeding stallions wait in the covering shed: each one is expected to cover 100 mares per season. There is a special foaling unit where the mare and foal can remain undisturbed after the birth.

The farm has its own forge and saddlery, and also a Horse Museum. Housed in an old stable block, this illustrates the importance of horses in Irish life. Exhibits include the frail skeleton of Arkle, a famous champion steeple-chaser in the 1960s.

Sharing the same estate as the National Stud are the **Japanese Gardens** and **St Fiachra's Garden**. The Japanese Gardens were laid out in 1906–10 by Japanese landscape gardener Tassa Eida, with the help of his son Minoru and 40 assistants. The impressive array of trees and shrubs includes maple, bonsai, mulberry, magnolia, sacred bamboo and cherry. The gardens take the form of an allegorical journey through life, beginning with the Gate of Oblivion and leading to the Gateway of Eternity, a contemplative Zen rock garden.

St Fiachra's Garden covers 1.6 ha (4 acres) of woodland, wetland, lakes and islands, and features a Waterford Crystal Garden within the monastic cells.

🌿 **National Stud and Japanese and St Fiachra's Gardens**
Tully. *Tel 045 521617.* ⬭ mid-Feb–mid-Nov: 9:30am–6pm daily (last admission 60 mins before closing). 📷 ♿ 🎥 *National Stud only.* ⬭ 🌐 www.irish-national-stud.ie

---

HORSE RACING IN IRELAND

Ireland has a strong racing culture and, thanks to its non-elitist image, the sport is enjoyed by all. Much of the thoroughbred industry centres around the Curragh, a grassy plain in County Kildare stretching unfenced for more than 2,000 ha (5,000 acres). This area is home to many of the country's studs and training yards, and every morning horses are put through their paces on the gallops. Most of the major flat races, including the Irish Derby, take place at the Curragh racecourse just east of Kildare. Other fixtures are held at nearby Punchestown – most famously the steeplechase festival in April/May – and at Leopardstown, which also hosts major National Hunt races *(see pp28–9)*.

Finishing straight at the Curragh racecourse

Castletown House ❶

Built in 1722–32 for William Conolly, Speaker of the Irish Parliament, the façade of Castletown was the work of Florentine architect Alessandro Galilei and gave Ireland its first taste of Palladianism. The magnificent interiors date from the second half of the 18th century. They were commissioned by Lady Louisa Lennox, wife of William Conolly's great-nephew, Tom, who lived here from 1759. Castletown remained in the family until 1965, when it was taken over by the Irish Georgian Society. The state now owns the house and it is open to the public.

Conolly crest on an armchair

★ Long Gallery
The heavy ceiling sections and friezes date from the 1720s and the walls were decorated in the Pompeian manner in the 1770s.

Green Drawing Room

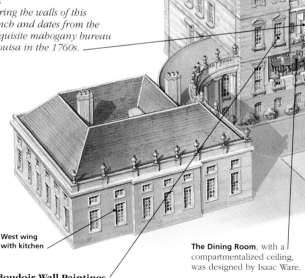

Red Drawing Room
The red damask covering the walls of this room is probably French and dates from the 19th century. This exquisite mahogany bureau was made for Lady Louisa in the 1760s.

West wing with kitchen

The Dining Room, with a compartmentalized ceiling, was designed by Isaac Ware.

Boudoir Wall Paintings
The boudoir's decorative panels, moved here from the Long Gallery, were inspired by the Raphael Loggia in the Vatican.

★ **Print Room**
In this, the only intact 18th-century print room in Ireland, Lady Louisa indulged her taste for Italian engravings. It was fashionable at that time for ladies to paste prints directly on to the wall and frame them with elaborate festoons.

VISITORS' CHECKLIST

Road map D4. Celbridge, Co Kildare. *Tel 01 628 8252.* 67, 67A from Dublin. *Easter Day–Sep: 10am–6pm Mon–Fri, 1–6pm Sat, Sun & public hols; Oct: 10am–5pm Mon–Fri, 1–5pm Sun & public hols.* obligatory. **Summer concerts.**

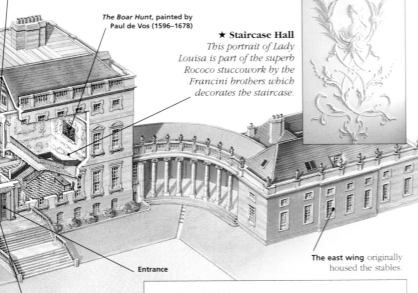

The Boar Hunt, painted by Paul de Vos (1596–1678)

★ **Staircase Hall**
This portrait of Lady Louisa is part of the superb Rococo stuccowork by the Francini brothers which decorates the staircase.

The east wing originally housed the stables.

Entrance

The Entrance Hall is an austere Neo-Classical room. Its most decorative feature is the delicate carving on the pilasters of the upper gallery.

STAR FEATURES

★ Long Gallery

★ Print Room

★ Staircase Hall

CONOLLY'S FOLLY

This folly, which lies just beyond the grounds of Castletown House, provides the focus of the view from the Long Gallery. Speaker Conolly's widow, Katherine, commissioned it in 1740 as a memorial to her late husband, and to provide employment after a harsh winter. The unusual structure of superimposed arches crowned by an obelisk is from designs by Richard Cassels, architect of Russborough House *(see p132).*

Saloon in Russborough House with original fireplace and stuccowork

Russborough House ⑥

Road map D4. Blessington, Co Wicklow. **Tel** 045 865239. 🚌 65 from Dublin. ◯ May–Sep: 10am–5pm daily; Apr & Oct: 10am–5pm Sun & public hols. 📷 🎫 obligatory. ♿ 🏠 🛍️

This Palladian mansion, built in the 1740s for Joseph Leeson, Earl of Milltown, is one of Ireland's finest houses. Its architect, Richard Cassels, also designed Powerscourt House (see pp134–5) and is credited with introducing the Palladian style to Ireland.

Unlike many grand estates in the Pale, Russborough has survived magnificently, both inside and out. The house claims the longest frontage in Ireland, with a façade adorned by heraldic lions and curved colonnades. The interior is even more impressive. Many rooms feature superb stucco decoration, which was done largely by the Italian Francini brothers, who also worked on Castletown House (see pp130–31). The best examples are found in the music room, saloon and library, which are embellished with exuberant foliage and cherubs. Around the main staircase, a riot of Rococo plasterwork

Vernet seascape in the drawing room

depicts a hunt, with hounds clasping garlands of flowers. The stucco mouldings in the drawing room were designed especially to enclose marine scenes by the French artist, Joseph Vernet (1714–89). The paintings were sold in 1926, but were tracked down more than 40 years afterwards and returned to the house.

Russborough has many other treasures, including finely worked fireplaces of Italian marble, imposing mahogany doorways and priceless collections of silver, porcelain and Gobelin tapestries.

Such riches aside, one of the principal reasons to visit Russborough is to see the **Beit Art Collection**, famous for its Flemish, Dutch and Spanish Old Master paintings. Sir Alfred Beit, who bought the house in 1952, inherited the pictures from his uncle – also named Alfred Beit and co-founder of the de Beers diamond mining empire in South Africa. In 1974, 1986 and 2000 several masterpieces were stolen from the house. Most were later retrieved. More disappeared in another robbery in 2001, all of which were recovered. Only a selection of paintings is on view in the house at any one time, while others are on

---

THE HISTORY OF THE PALE

The term "Pale" refers to an area around Dublin which marked the limits of English influence from Norman to Tudor times. The frontier fluctuated, but at its largest the Pale stretched from Dundalk in County Louth to Waterford town. Gaelic chieftains outside the area could keep their lands provided they agreed to bring up their heirs within the Pale.

The Palesmen supported their rulers' interests and considered themselves the upholders of English values. This widened the gap between the Gaelic majority and the Anglo-Irish, a foretaste of England's doomed involvement in the country. Long after its fortifications were dismantled, the idea of the Pale lived on as a state of mind. The expression "beyond the pale" survives as a definition of those outside the bounds of civilized society.

An 18th-century family enjoying the privileged lifestyle typical within the Pale

---

Tourist road train on the beachfront esplanade at Bray

permanent loan to the National Gallery in Dublin *(see pp70–71)*.

Russborough enjoys a fine position near the village of **Blessington**, with a good view across to the Wicklow Mountains. The house lies amid wooded parkland rather than elaborate flower gardens. As Alfred Beit said of Irish Palladianism, "Fine architecture standing in a green sward was considered enough."

Environs
The **Poulaphouca Reservoir**, which was formed by the damming of the River Liffey, extends south from Blessington. The placid lake is popular with watersports enthusiasts, while other visitors come simply to enjoy the lovely mountain views.

Powerscourt **7**

See pp134–5.

Bray **8**

Road map D4. Co Wicklow. 🏯 *33,000.* 🚆 *DART.* 🚌 🛈 *Old Court House, Main St (01 286 7128).* **www**.bray.ie

Once a refined Victorian resort, Bray is nowadays a brash holiday town, with amusement arcades and fish and chip shops lining the sea-front. Its beach attracts large crowds in summer, including many young families. A more peaceful alternative is nearby

Bray Head, where there is scope for bracing cliffside walks. Bray also makes a good base from which to explore Powerscourt Gardens, the Wicklow Mountains and the coastal villages of Killiney and Dalkey *(see p103)*.

Killruddery House and Gardens **9**

Road map D4. Bray, Co Wicklow. **Tel** *0404 46024.* ⬜ *May–Sep: 1pm–5pm daily.* 📷 ♿ *limited.* **www**.killruddery.com

Killruddery House lies just to the south of Bray, in the shadow of Little Sugar Loaf Mountain. Built in 1651, it has been the family seat of the Earls of Meath ever since, although the original mansion was remodelled in an Eliza-bethan Revival style in the early 19th century. The house

contains some good carving and stuccowork, but the real charm of Killruddery lies in the 17th-century formal gardens, regarded as the finest French Classical gardens in the country. They were laid out in the 1680s by a French gardener named Bonet, who also worked at Versailles.

The gardens, planted with great precision, feature rom-antic parterres, a whole array of different hedges and many fine trees and shrubs, both native and foreign. The sylvan theatre, a small enclosure surrounded by a bay hedge, is the only known example of its kind in Ireland.

The Long Ponds, a pair of canals which extend 165 m (542 ft), were once used to stock fish. Beyond, a pool enclosed by two circular hedges leads to a Victorian arrangement of paths flanked by statues and hedges of yew, beech, lime and hornbeam.

View across the Long Ponds to Killruddery House

Powerscourt 🌀

The gardens at Powerscourt are probably the finest in Ireland, both for their design and their dramatic setting at the foot of Great Sugar Loaf Mountain. The house and grounds were commissioned in the 1730s by Richard Wingfield, the 1st Viscount Powerscourt. New ornamental gardens were completed in 1858–75 by the 7th Viscount, who added gates, urns and statues collected during his travels in Europe. The house was gutted by an accidental fire in 1974, but the ground floor has been beautifully renovated and now accommodates an upmarket shopping centre with an excellent restaurant and café.

Laocoön statue on upper terrace

Bamberg Gate
Made in Vienna in the 1770s, this gilded wrought-iron gate was brought to Powerscourt by the 7th Viscount from Bamberg Church in Bavaria.

The Walled Gardens include a formal arrangement of clipped laurel trees but are also used for growing plants for Powerscourt's gardens.

The Pets' Cemetery contains the graves of Wingfield family dogs, cats and even horses and cattle.

Statue of Laocoön

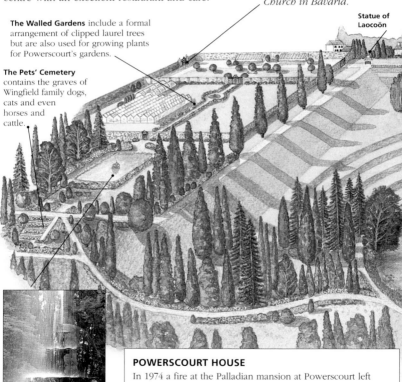

Dolphin Pond
This pool, designed as a fish pond in the 18th century, is enclosed by exotic conifers in a lovely secluded garden.

POWERSCOURT HOUSE

In 1974 a fire at the Palladian mansion at Powerscourt left the fine building a burnt-out shell. In recent years the Slazenger family, who now own the estate, have restored the ground floor and the ballroom upstairs.

Originally built in 1731 on the site of a Norman castle, the house was designed by Richard Cassels, who was also the architect of Russborough House *(see p132).*

Powerscourt ablaze in 1974

★ The Perron
Leading down to Triton Lake is the Perron, a beautiful Italianate stairway added in 1874. Beside the lake, it is guarded by two statues of Pegasus – the mythical winged horse and emblem of the Wingfield family.

VISITORS' CHECKLIST

Road map D4. Enniskerry, Co Wicklow. *Tel* 01 204 6000.
185 from Bray DART station.
9:30am–5:30pm (dusk Oct–Mar) daily. 25 & 26 Dec.
www.powerscourt.ie

Pebble Mosaic
Many tonnes of pebbles were gathered from nearby Bray beach to build the Perron and to make this mosaic on the terrace.

The Italian Garden is laid out on terraces which were first cut into the steep hillside in the 1730s.

The Pepper Pot Tower was built in 1911.

★ Triton Lake
Made for the first garden, the lake takes its name from its central fountain, which is modelled on a 17th-century work by Bernini in Rome.

★ Japanese Gardens
These enchanting Edwardian gardens, created out of bogland, contain Chinese conifers and bamboo trees.

STAR FEATURES

★ Japanese Gardens

★ The Perron

★ Triton Lake

Powerscourt Gardens with Great Sugar Loaf Mountain beyond ▷

A Tour of the Military Road ⓾

Rare red squirrel

The British built the Military Road through the heart of the Wicklow Mountains during a campaign to flush out Irish rebels after an uprising in 1798 *(see p149)*. Now known as the R115, this road takes you through the emptiest and most rugged landscapes of County Wicklow. Fine countryside, in which deer and other wildlife flourish, is characteristic of the whole of this tour.

Powerscourt Waterfall ⑨
The River Dargle cascades 130 m (425 ft) over a granite escarpment to form Ireland's highest waterfall.

Glencree ①
The former British barracks in Glencree are among several found along the Military Road.

Sally Gap ②
This remote pass is surrounded by a vast expanse of blanket bog dotted with pools and streams.

Glenmacnass ③
After Sally Gap, the road drops into a deep glen where a waterfall spills dramatically over rocks.

Glendalough ④
This ancient lakeside monastery *(see pp140–41)*, enclosed by wooded slopes, is the prime historical sight in the Wicklow Mountains.

Great Sugar Loaf ⑧
The granite cone of Great Sugar Loaf Mountain can be climbed in under an hour from the car park on its southern side.

Lough Tay ⑦
Stark, rocky slopes plunge down to the dark waters of Lough Tay. Though it lies within a Guinness-owned estate, the lake is accessible to walkers.

Roundwood ⑥
The highest village in Ireland at 238 m (780 ft) above sea level, Roundwood enjoys a fine setting. Its main street is lined with pubs, cafés and craft shops.

TIPS FOR DRIVERS

Length: 96 km (60 miles).
Stopping-off points: There are several pubs and cafés in Enniskerry (including Poppies, an old-fashioned tearoom), and also in Roundwood, but this area is better for picnics. There are several marked picnic spots south of Enniskerry. (see also pp387–9.)

0 kilometers   5

0 miles   5

KEY

━━━ Tour route

╌╌╌ Other roads

☆ Viewpoint

Vale of Clara ⑤
This picturesque wooded valley follows the River Avonmore. It contains the tiny village of Clara, which consists of two houses, a church and a school.

Wicklow Mountains ⓫

Road map D4. 🚌 to Rathdrum & Wicklow. 🚌 to Enniskerry, Wicklow, Glendalough, Rathdrum & Avoca. 🛈 Rialto House, Fitzwilliam Square, Wicklow (0404 69117). **www**.eastcoastmidlands.ie

Standing amid the rugged wilderness of the Wicklow Mountains, it can be hard to believe that Dublin is under an hour's drive away. The inaccessibility of the mountains meant that they once provided a safe hideout for opponents of English rule. When much of the Southeast was obedient to the English Crown, within an area known as the Pale *(see p132)*, warlords such as the O'Tooles ruled in the Wicklow Mountains. Rebels who took part in the 1798 uprising *(see p41)* sought refuge here too. One of their leaders, Michael Dwyer, remained at liberty in the hills around Sally Gap until 1803.

The building of the **Military Road**, started in 1800, made the area more accessible, but the mountains are still thinly populated. There is little traffic to disturb enjoyment of the beautiful rock-strewn glens, lush forest and bogland where heather gives a purple sheen to the land. Turf-cutting is still a thriving cottage industry, and you often see peat stacked up by the road. Numerous walking trails weave through these landscapes. Among them is the **Wicklow Way**, which extends 132 km (82 miles) from Marlay Park in Dublin to Clonegal in County Carlow. It is marked but not always easy to follow, so do not set out without a decent map. Although no peak exceeds 915 m (3,000 ft), the Wicklow Mountains can be dangerous in bad weather.

Hiking apart, there is plenty to see and do in this region. A good starting point for exploring the northern area is the picture-postcard estate village of **Enniskerry**. In summer, it is busy with tourists who come to visit the gardens at Powerscourt *(see pp134–5)*. From Laragh, to the south, you can reach Glendalough *(see pp140–41)* and the **Vale of Avoca**, where cherry trees are laden with blossom in the spring. The beauty of this gentle valley was captured in the poetry of Thomas Moore (1779–1852):

"There is not in the wide world a valley so sweet as that vale in whose bosom the bright waters meet" – a reference to the confluence of the Avonbeg and Avonmore rivers, the so-called **Meeting of the Waters** beyond Avondale House *(see p141)*. Nestled among wooded

Road sign in the Wicklow Mountains

Mount Usher Gardens, on the banks of the River Vartry

hills at the heart of the valley is the hamlet of Avoca, where the **Avoca Handweavers** produce colourful tweeds in the oldest hand-weaving mill in Ireland, in operation since 1723.

Further north, towards the coast near Ashford, the River Vartry rushes through the deep chasm of the **Devil's Glen**. On entering the valley, the river falls 30 m (100 ft) into a pool known as the Devil's Punchbowl. There are good walks around here, with fine views of the coast.

🏠 **Avoca Handweavers**
Avoca. **Tel** 0402 35105. ◯ daily. ● 25 & 26 Dec. 🍴 🏠 www.avoca.ie

Mount Usher Gardens ⓬

Road map D4. Ashford, Co Wicklow. **Tel** 0404 40205. 🚌 to Ashford. ◯ Mar–Oct: 10:30am–6pm daily. 🍴 🏠 ◻ ♿ limited. 🎧 call to book. **www**.mount-usher-gardens.com

Set beside the River Vartry just east of Ashford are the Mount Usher Gardens. They were designed in 1868 by a Dubliner, Edward Walpole, who imbued them with his strong sense of romanticism.

The gardens contain many rare shrubs and trees, from Chinese conifers and bamboos to Mexican pines and pampas grass. The Maple Walk is glorious in autumn. The river provides the main focus, and amid the exotic vegetation you can glimpse herons.

Colourful moorland around Sally Gap in the Wicklow Mountains

Glendalough ⑬

Road map D4. Co Wicklow. 🚌 *St Kevin's Bus from Dublin.* **Ruins** ⬭ *daily.* 🎫 *in summer.* **Visitors' Centre Tel** *0404 45325/45352.* ⬭ *daily.* ⬤ *24–27 Dec.* ♿ 👫

The steep, wooded slopes of Glendalough, the "valley of the two lakes", harbour one of Ireland's most atmospheric monastic sites. Established by St Kevin in the 6th century, the settlement was sacked time and again by the Vikings but nevertheless flourished for over 600 years. Decline set in only after English forces partially razed the site in 1398, though it functioned as a monastic centre until the Dissolution of the Monasteries in 1539 *(see p38)*. Pilgrims kept on coming to Glendalough even after that, particularly on St Kevin's feast day, 3 June, which was often a riotous event *(see p30)*.

The age of the buildings is uncertain, but most date from the 8th to 12th centuries. Many were restored during the 1870s.

View along the Upper Lake at Glendalough

The main group of ruins lies east of the Lower Lake, but other buildings associated with St Kevin are by the Upper Lake. Here, where the scenery is much wilder, you are better able to enjoy the tranquillity of Glendalough and to escape the crowds which inevitably descend on the site. Try to arrive as early as possible in the day, particularly during the peak tourist season. You enter the monastery through the double stone arch of the **Gatehouse**, the only surviving example in Ireland of a gateway into a monastic enclosure.

A short walk leads to a graveyard with a **Round Tower** in one corner. Reaching 30 m (91 ft) in height, this is one of the finest of its kind in the country. Its cap was rebuilt in the 1870s using stones found inside the tower. The roofless **Cathedral** nearby dates mainly from the 12th century and is

St Kevin's Kitchen

the valley's largest ruin. At the centre of the churchyard stands the tiny **Priests' House**, whose name derives from the fact that it was a burial place for local clergy. The worn carving of a robed figure above the door is possibly of St Kevin, flanked by two disciples. East of here, **St Kevin's Cross** dates from the 8th century and is one of the best preserved of Glendalough's various High Crosses. Made of granite, the cross may once have marked the boundary of the monastic cemetery. Below, nestled in the lush valley, a minuscule oratory with a steeply pitched stone roof is a charming sight. Erected in the 11th century or even earlier, it is popularly known as **St Kevin's Kitchen**; this is perhaps because its belfry, thought to be a later addition, resembles a chimney. One of the earliest churches at Glendalough, **St Mary's**, lies across a field to the west.

Remains of the Gatehouse, the original entrance to Glendalough

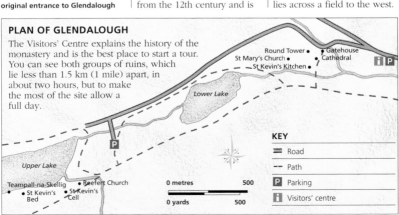

PLAN OF GLENDALOUGH

The Visitors' Centre explains the history of the monastery and is the best place to start a tour. You can see both groups of ruins, which lie less than 1.5 km (1 mile) apart, in about two hours, but to make the most of the site allow a full day.

Round Tower •
St Mary's Church •
St Kevin's Kitchen •

Gatehouse •
Cathedral

ℹ️ P

Lower Lake

Upper Lake

Teampall-na-Skellig •
• St Kevin's Bed

• Reefert Church
St Kevin's Cell

0 metres   500

0 yards   500

KEY

▬ Road

-- Path

P Parking

ℹ️ Visitors' centre

Round tower at Glendalough

ST KEVIN AT GLENDALOUGH

St Kevin was born in 498, a descendant of the royal house of Leinster. He rejected his life of privilege, however, choosing to live instead as a hermit in a cave at Glendalough. He later founded a monastery here, and went on to create a notable centre of learning devoted to the care of the sick and the copying and illumination of manuscripts. St Kevin attracted many disciples to Glendalough during his lifetime, but the monastery became more celebrated as a place of pilgrimage after his death in around 618.

Colourful legends about the saint make up for the dearth of facts about him. That he lived to the age of 120 is just one of the stories told about him. Another tale claims that one day, when St Kevin was at prayer, a blackbird laid an egg in one of his outstretched hands. The saint remained in the same position until it was hatched.

Some traces of Romanesque moulding are visible outside the east window. Following the path along the south bank of the river, you reach the Upper Lake. This is the site of more monastic ruins and is also the chief starting point for walks through the valley and to a number of abandoned lead and zinc mines.

Situated in a grove not far from the Poulanass waterfall are the ruins of the **Reefert Church**, a simple Romanesque building. Its unusual name is a corruption of *Righ Fearta*, meaning "burial place of the kings"; the church may mark the site of an ancient cemetery. Near here, on a rocky spur overlooking the Upper Lake, stands **St Kevin's Cell**, the ruins of a beehive-shaped structure which is thought to have been the hermit's home.

There are two sites on the south side of the lake which cannot be reached on foot but are visible from the opposite shore. **Teampall-na-Skellig**, or the "church on the rock", was supposedly built on the site of the first church that St Kevin founded at Glendalough. To the east of it, carved into the cliff, is **St Kevin's Bed**. This small cave, in reality little more than a rocky ledge, may have been used as a tomb in the Bronze Age, but it is more famous as St Kevin's favourite retreat. It was from here that the saint allegedly rejected the advances of a naked woman by tossing her into the lake.

Avondale House ⑭

Road map D4. Co Wicklow. *Tel 0404 46111.* 🚌 🚉 *to Rathdrum.* **House** ⬜ *mid-Mar–Oct: 11am–6pm (Nov–Feb 5pm) daily.* ⬤ *Good Fri & 23–28 Dec; Mar–Apr, Sep–Oct: Mon.* 🎟 🍴 🛍 🛗 *ltd.* **Grounds** ⬜ *daily.* www.coillte.ie

Lying just south of Rathdrum, Avondale House is the birthplace of the 19th-century politician and patriot, Charles Stewart Parnell (*see p43*). The Georgian mansion is now a museum dedicated to Parnell and the fight for Home Rule.

The grounds are open to the public. Known as **Avondale Forest Park**, they include an impressive arboretum first planted in the 18th century and much added to since 1900. There are some lovely walks through the woods, with pleasant views along the River Avonmore.

Browne's Hill Dolmen ⑮

Road map D4. Co Carlow. 🚌 🚉 *to Carlow.* ⬜ *daily.*

In a field 3 km (2 miles) east of Carlow, along the R726, stands a dolmen boasting the biggest capstone in Ireland. Weighing a reputed 100 tonnes, this massive stone is embedded in the earth at one end and supported at the other by three much smaller stones. Dating back to 2000 BC, Browne's Hill Dolmen is thought to mark the tomb of a local chieftain. A path leads to it from the road.

Browne's Hill Dolmen, famous for its enormous capstone

Street-by-Street: Kilkenny ⑯

Kilkenny coat of arms

Kilkenny is undoubtedly Ireland's loveliest inland city. It rose to prominence in the 13th century and became the medieval capital of Ireland. The Anglo-Norman Butler family came to power in the 1390s and held sway over the city for 500 years. Their power has gone but their legacy is visible in the city's historic buildings, many of which have been restored. Kilkenny is proud of its heritage and every August hosts the Republic's top arts festival.

To Irishtown, St Canice's Cathedral

Grace's Castle was built in 1210 and later converted into a jail. Remodelled in the 18th century, it has functioned as a courthouse ever since.

PARLIAMENT STREET

ST KIERAN'S STREET

HIGH STREET

Narrow alleyways, known locally as "slips", are part of Kilkenny's medieval heritage. Several slips survive, and these are currently undergoing restoration.

Marble City Bar

Tholsel (City Hall)

★ Rothe House
This fine Tudor merchant's house, built around two court-yards, is fronted by arcades once typical of Kilkenny's main streets. A small museum inside the house contains a display of local archaeological artifacts and a costume collection.

Butter Slip
The alley is named after the butter stalls that once lined this small market place.

View of the High Street
The 18th-century Tholsel, with its distinctive clock tower and arcade, is the main landmark on the High Street. Its elegant Georgian chamber is used by city councillors to this day.

STAR SIGHTS
★ Kilkenny Castle

★ Rothe House

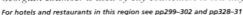

Kyteler's Inn

This medieval coaching inn (see p346) is named after Dame Alice Kyteler, a 14th-century witch who once lived in the building. Like most of the pubs in the city, Kyteler's Inn sells Smithwick's beer, which has been brewed in Kilkenny since 1710.

VISITORS' CHECKLIST

Road map C4. Co Kilkenny. 🚌 20,000. 🚉 Dublin Rd (056 772 2024). 🚌 Rose Inn St (056 776 4933). 🚹 Shee Almshouse, Rose Inn St (056 775 1500). **Rothe House Tel** 056 772 2893. 🕐 Apr–Oct: 10:30am–5pm Mon–Sat, 3–5pm Sun; Nov–Mar: 1–5pm Mon–Sat. 🌐

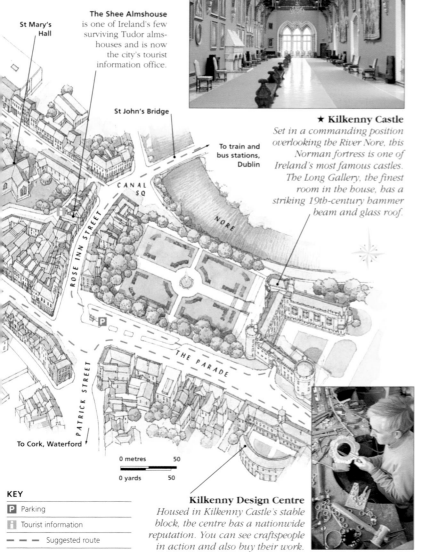

St Mary's Hall

The Shee Almshouse is one of Ireland's few surviving Tudor alms-houses and is now the city's tourist information office.

St John's Bridge

To train and bus stations, **Dublin**

★ **Kilkenny Castle**

Set in a commanding position overlooking the River Nore, this Norman fortress is one of Ireland's most famous castles. The Long Gallery, the finest room in the house, has a striking 19th-century hammer beam and glass roof.

CANAL SQ

NORE

ROSE INN STREET

THE PARADE

PATRICK STREET

To Cork, Waterford

| 0 metres | 50 |
| 0 yards | 50 |

KEY

🅿 Parking

🚹 Tourist information

– – – Suggested route

Kilkenny Design Centre

Housed in Kilkenny Castle's stable block, the centre has a nationwide reputation. You can see craftspeople in action and also buy their work.

Exploring Kilkenny

In a lovely spot beside a kink in the River Nore, Kilkenny is of great architectural interest, with much use made of the distinctive local black limestone, known as Kilkenny marble. A tour of the town also reveals many unexpected treasures: a Georgian façade often seems to conceal a Tudor chimney, a Classical interior or some other surprise.

The survival of the Irishtown district, now dominated by St Canice's Cathedral, recalls past segregation in Kilkenny. The area once known as Englishtown still boasts the city's grandest public buildings.

As a brewery city, Kilkenny is a paradise for keen drinkers. Not counting the popular private drinking clubs, there are about 80 official pubs.

North side of Kilkenny Castle showing Victorian crenellations

Sign of the Marble City Bar on Kilkenny's High Street

♣ Kilkenny Castle

The Parade. **Tel** 056 772 1450.
◯ daily. ● Good Fri & 10 days at Christmas. 🎫 🖭 📷 obligatory. ♿ limited. Queues are likely during the summer. **www**.heritageireland.ie
Built in the 1190s, Kilkenny Castle was occupied right up until 1935. The powerful Butler family (see p142) lived in it from the late 14th century, but because of the exorbitant running costs, their descendants eventually donated Kilkenny Castle to the nation in 1967. With its drum towers and

solid walls, the castle retains its medieval form, but has undergone many alterations. The Victorian changes made in Gothic Revival style have had the most enduring impact, and are even more impressive since recent restoration work.

High spots of a tour include the library, the wood-panelled dining room and the Chinese bedroom.

Best of all, however, is the Long Gallery, built in the 1820s to house the Butler art collection. Its elaborate painted ceiling has a strong Pre-Raphaelite feel, with many of the motifs inspired by the *Book of Kells (see p64)*.

The castle grounds have shrunk over the centuries, but the French Classical gardens remain, with terraces opening onto a woodland walk and pleasant rolling parkland.

♙ St Canice's Cathedral

Irishtown. **Tel** 056 776 4971 ◯
daily. 🎫 📷 ♿
The hilltop cathedral, flanked by a round tower, was built in the 13th century in an Early English Gothic style. It was

Tomb of 2nd Marquess of Ormonde in St Canice's Cathedral

sacked by Cromwell's forces in 1650, but has survived as one of Ireland's medieval treasures. Walls of the local Kilkenny limestone and pillars of pale limestone combine to create an interior of simple grandeur. An array of splendid 16th-century tombs includes the beautiful effigies of the Butler family in the south transept. It is worth climbing the tower for a fine view over Kilkenny.

♙ Black Abbey

Abbey St. **Tel** 056 772 1279.
◯ daily. ♿
Lying just west of Parliament Street, this Dominican abbey was founded in 1225. Part of it was turned into a courthouse in the 16th century, but is once again a working monastery. The church has a fine vaulted undercroft, distinctive stonework, some beautiful stained-glass windows, and a 14th-century alabaster statue of the holy trinity.

Environs

Just north of the town lies **Dunmore Cave**, a limestone cavern with an impressive series of chambers, noted for its steep descent and curious rock formations.

Bennettsbridge, on the Nore 8 km (5 miles) south of Kilkenny, is famous for its ceramics. The Nicholas Mosse Pottery (see p357) specializes in colourful earthenware made from the local clay.

🏚 Dunmore Cave

Ballyfoyle. **Tel** 056 776 7726.
◯ Mar–Oct: daily; Nov–Feb: Sat, Sun & public hols. 🎫 📷 obligatory. **www**.heritageireland.ie

Jerpoint Abbey ⑰

Road map D5. Thomastown, Co Kilkenny. *Tel 056 772 4623.* 🚌 🚌 to Thomastown. ⬜ Mar–May & mid-Sep–Oct: 10am–5pm (Nov 4pm) daily; Jun–mid-Sep: 9:30am–6pm daily; Dec: by appt only. 🔲 🔲 🔲

On the banks of the Little Arrigle just south of Thomastown, Jerpoint Abbey is one of the finest Cistercian ruins in Ireland. Founded in 1160, the fortified medieval complex rivalled Duiske Abbey *(see p149)* in prestige. Jerpoint flourished until the Dissolution of the Monasteries *(see pp38–9)*, when it passed to the Earl of Ormonde.

The 15th-century cloisters have not survived as well as some earlier parts of the abbey. Despite this, they are the highlight of Jerpoint, with their amusing sculptures of knights, courtly ladies, bishops and dragons. The church itself is well preserved. The Irish-Romanesque transepts date back to the earliest period of the Abbey's development and contain several 16th-century tombs decorated with exquisite stylized carvings. The north side of the nave has a rich array of decorated Romanesque capitals and throughout the abbey are tombs and effigies of early bishops and patrons. The battlemented crossing tower was added during the 1400s.

Stylized carving of saints on 16th-century tomb in Jerpoint Abbey

Burne-Jones window in St Carthage's Cathedral, Lismore

Lismore ⑱

Road map C5. Co Waterford. 👥 1,200. 🚌 ℹ️ Lismore Heritage Centre (058 54975). ⬛ craft shop. **www.discoverlismore.com**

This genteel riverside town is dwarfed by **Lismore Castle**, perched above the River Blackwater. Built in 1185 but remodelled in the 19th century, the castle is the Irish seat of the Duke of Devonshire and is closed to the public. However, you can visit the sumptuous gardens, which include a lovely riverside walk. **Lismore Heritage Centre** tells the story of St Carthage, who founded a monastic centre here in the 7th century. The town has two cathedrals dedicated to him. The Protestant **Cathedral of St Carthage** is the more interesting. It dates from 1633 but incorporates older elements and was later altered to suit the Neo-Gothic tastes of the Victorians. It has fine Gothic vaulting, and a stained-glass window by the Pre-Raphaelite artist, Sir Edward Burne-Jones.

♛**Lismore Castle Gardens** *Tel* 058 54424. ⬜ Apr, May, 1–28 Sep: 1:45–4:45pm daily; Jun–Aug: 11am–4:45pm daily. 🔲

Environs
From Lismore you can follow a picturesque route through the **Blackwater Valley** *(see p177)*. This runs from Cappoquin, in an idyllic woodland setting east of Lismore, to the estuary at Youghal *(see p179)*.

Ardmore ⑲

Road map C5. Co Waterford. 👥 450. 🚌 ℹ️ Jun–Sep: Beach Car Park (024 94444).

Ardmore is a popular seaside resort with a splendid beach, lively pubs, good cliff walks and some interesting architecture. The hill beside the village is the site of a monastery established in the 5th century by St Declan, the first missionary to bring Christianity to this area.

Most of the buildings, including the ruined **St Declan's Cathedral**, date from the 12th century. The cathedral's west wall has fine Romanesque sculptures, arranged in a series of arcades. The scenes include The Archangel Michael Weighing Souls in the upper row, and below this The Adoration of the Magi and The Judgment of Solomon.

The adjacent round tower is one of the best preserved examples in Ireland, and rises to a height of 30 m (98 ft). An oratory nearby is said to mark the site of St Declan's grave.

St Declan's Cathedral at Ardmore, with its near-perfect round tower

Waterford ⑳

Waterford city coat of arms

Waterford, Ireland's oldest city, was founded by Vikings in 914. Set in a commanding position by the estuary of the River Suir, it became southeast Ireland's main seaport. From the 18th century, the city's prosperity was consolidated by local industries, including the glassworks for which Waterford is famous. The strong commercial tradition persists today and Waterford's port is still one of Ireland's busiest. In the last few years, following extensive archaeological excavations in the city centre, a new heart and atmosphere has been put into the old city with the creation of pedestrian precincts in the historic quarter and along the quays.

Reginald's Tower on the quayside

Cathedral Close, looking towards Lady Lane in the heart of the city

Exploring Waterford

The extensive remains of the city walls clearly define the area originally fortified by the Vikings. The best-preserved section runs northwest from the **Watch Tower** on Castle Street, although Reginald's Tower, overlooking the river, is the largest structure in the old defences. In The Reginald Bar you can see the arches through which boats sailed forth down the river; these sallyports are one of several Viking sections of the largely Norman fortifications.

Although Waterford retains its medieval layout, most of the city's finest buildings are Georgian. Some of the best examples can be seen on the Mall, which runs southwest from Reginald's Tower, and in the lovely Cathedral Square. The latter takes its name from **Christchurch Cathedral**, which

was built in the 1770s to a design by John Roberts, a local architect who contributed much to the city's Georgian heritage. It is fronted by a fine Corinthian colonnade. A grim 15th-century effigy of a rotting corpse is an unexpected sight inside. Heading down towards the river, you pass the 13th-century ruins of **Grey Friars**, often known as the French Church after it became a Huguenot chapel in 1693.

West along the waterfront, a Victorian clock tower stands at the top of Barronstrand Street. Rising above the busy shops is **Holy Trinity Cathedral**, which has a rich Neo-Classical interior. George's Street, which runs west from here, is dotted with period houses and cosy pubs. It leads to O'Connell Street, whose partially restored warehouses contrast with the shabbier buildings on the quay. In the summer, you can enjoy another view of the waterfront by taking a cruise on the river.

♨ Reginald's Tower

The Quay. **Tel** 051 304220. ◯ Easter–Oct: daily; Nov–Easter: Wed–Sun. ▨

The Vikings built a fort on this site in 914 but it was the Anglo-Normans who, in 1185, built the stone structure seen today. With impregnable walls 3 m (10 ft) thick, the tower is said to be the first Irish building to use mortar, a primitive concoction of blood, lime, fur and mud. It is the oldest civic urban building in Ireland.

🏛 Waterford Museum of Treasures

The Granary, Merchants Quay. **Tel** 051 304500. ◯ Jun–Aug: 9:30am–9pm; Apr, May, Sep: 9:30am–6pm; Oct–Mar: 10am–5pm. ● 1 Jan. ▨ ♿ 🍴 📷 ℹ **www**.waterfordtreasures.com

This multi-award-winning interactive museum tells the story of Waterford from its Viking foundation to the late 19th century.

View of the city of Waterford across the River Suir

Waterford Crystal Factory

Kilbarry. **Tel** 051 332500. ☐ Mar–Oct:
8:30am–6pm daily; Nov–Feb: 9am–5pm
Mon–Fri. ☐ 17 Dec. 🖼 &
📷 Last tour 2 hrs before close.
www.waterfordvisitorcentre.com

A visit to the Waterford Crystal
Factory, just 2.5 km (1.5 miles)
south of the city, is highly
recommended to observe the
process of crystal-making.

The original glass factory
was founded in 1783 by two
brothers, George and William

**Craftsman engraving a vase at
the Waterford Crystal Factory**

Penrose, who chose Waterford
because of its port. For many
decades their crystal enjoyed
an unrivalled reputation, but
draconian taxes caused the
firm to close in 1851. A new
factory was opened in 1947,
however, and master blowers
and engravers were brought
from the Continent to train local
apprentices. Competition from
Tipperary and Galway Crystal
had an effect in the early
1990s, but sales have revived
in recent years.

Visitors can follow all stages
of production, observing the
process by which sand, lead
and potash are transformed
by fire into sparkling crystal.
The main difference between
ordinary glass and crystal is
the latter's high lead content,
30 per cent in Waterford's
case. The glass-blowers
require great skill to create
walls of the right thickness to
take the heavy incisions
typical of Waterford Crystal.
The factory's other main hallmark is the Waterford
signature, which is engraved
on the base of each piece.

In the showroom, a crystal
chandelier lights up a table
laden with pottery and glass.

VISITORS' CHECKLIST

Road map D5. Co Waterford.
🏠 44,000. ✈ 10 km (6 miles) S.
🚉 Plunkett Station, The Bridge
(051 873401). 🚌 The Quay (051
879000). 🛈 The Granary,
Merchant's Quay (051 875823). 🚏
(051 421723): Jun–Aug. 🚢 Fri.
🎭 Int Festival of Light Opera (Sep).

**Ballyhack port, across Waterford
Harbour from Passage East**

Environs

The small port of **Passage East**,
12 km (7 miles) east of
Waterford, witnessed the landing
of the Normans in 1170 (see
p36), but little has happened
since. A car ferry links the village
to Ballyhack in County Wexford,
providing a scenic shortcut
across Waterford Harbour as well
as an excellent entry point to the
Hook Peninsula (see p148).

WATERFORD
CITY CENTRE

Christchurch Cathedral ④
Clock Tower ①
Holy Trinity Cathedral ②
Reginald's Tower ⑥
Watch Tower ③
Waterford Museum of
Treasures ⑤

0 metres   200

0 yards   200

Key to Symbols see back flap

Dunmore East ㉑

Road map D5. Co Waterford.
🏠 *1,500*. 🚌

The appeal of Dunmore East, Waterford's most charming fishing village, lies chiefly in its red sandstone cliffs and bustling harbour. Paths run along the foot of the cliffs, but for the best views take the road that winds uphill from the beach, past tidy cottages and the ivy-clad Ship Inn to the Haven Hotel. A gate nearby leads to delightful gardens overlooking the fishing boats below. Climbing further, up steps cut into the rock, you are rewarded by views of the cliffs and noisy kittiwake colonies.

Busy fishing harbour at Dunmore East

Hook Peninsula ㉒

Road map D5. Co. Wexford.
🚌 *to Duncannon*. 🚢 *from Passage East to Ballyhack (051 382480)*.
ℹ️ *Fethard-on-Sea (051 397502)*.
www.thehook-wexford.com

This tapering headland of gentle landscapes scattered with ancient ruins and quiet villages is perfect for a circular tour. The "Ring of Hook" route begins south of New Ross at **Dunbrody Abbey**, the ruins of a 12th-century Cistercian church, but **Ballyhack** is another good place to start. Once a fortified crossing point into County Waterford, the town still has a ferry service to neighbouring Passage East *(see p147)*. **Ballyhack Castle**, built by the Knights Templar in about 1450, contains a small museum. About 4 km (2.5

miles) beyond is the small resort of **Duncannon**, with a broad sandy beach and a star-shaped fort, which was built in 1588 in expectation of an attack by the Spanish Armada.

The coast road continues south to **Hook Head**. Here is Europe's oldest working lighthouse, dating from 1172 and now with its own visitor centre. Paths skirt the coast famous for its fossils, seals and a variety of seabirds.

Just 2 km (1.5 miles) east is the village of **Slade**. A ruined 15th-century tower house, **Slade Castle**, presides over the harbour where fishing boats cluster around the slipways. The road proceeds along the rugged coastline, past the resort of Fethard-on-Sea and Saltmills to the dramatic ruin of **Tintern Abbey**. This 13th-century Cistercian foundation was built by William Marshall, Earl of Pembroke, in fulfilment of a vow made when his boat was caught in a storm off the coast nearby. Fields lead to an old stone bridge and views over **Bannow Bay**, where it is

thought the Normans made their first landing in 1169.

🏰 **Dunbrody Abbey**
Campile. **Tel** *051 388603*.
⭕ *Apr–Sep: daily.* 📷 🅿️ 🚻 🏪 🛒

♟️ **Ballyhack Castle**
Ballyhack. **Tel** *051 389468*.
⭕ *Jun–Sep: daily.*

🏰 **Tintern Abbey**
Tel *051 562 650*.
📷 *May–Oct: daily.* 🅿️ 🛒

Norman lighthouse at Hook Head, on the tip of the Hook Peninsula

New Ross ㉓

Road map D5. Co Wexford. 🏠 *6,000*.
🚌 ℹ️ *mid-Jun–Aug: The Quay (051 421857)*. 🛒 *Tue*. **Galley Cruising Restaurants** *The Quay (051 421723)*.

Lying on the banks of the River Barrow, New Ross is one of the oldest towns in the county. Its importance, now as in the past, stems from its status as a port. In summer there is much activity on the river, with cruises plying the Barrow, Nore and Suir rivers. Traditional shopfronts line the streets, which rise steeply

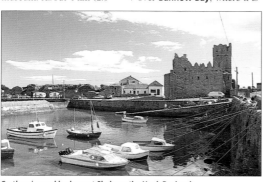
Castle ruins and harbour at Slade on the Hook Peninsula

For hotels and restaurants in this region see pp299–302 and pp328–31

from the quayside. The **Tholsel**, now the town hall but originally a tollhouse, was occupied by the British during the 1798 rebellion *(see pp40–41)*. Opposite, a monument to a Wexford pikeman commemorates the bravery of the Irish rebels who faced the British cannons.

Nearby is **St Mary's** which, when founded in the 13th century, was the largest parish church in Ireland. A modern church occupies the site, but the original (now roofless) south transept remains, as do many medieval tombstones.

View over Enniscorthy and St Aidan's cathedral from Vinegar Hill

Environs

A popular trip up the meandering Barrow goes 16 km (10 miles) north to **Graiguenamanagh**. The main attraction of this market town is **Duiske Abbey**, the largest Cistercian church in Ireland. Founded in 1207, it has been extensively restored and now acts as the parish church. The most striking features include a Romanesque door in the south transept, the great oak roof and traces of a medieval pavement below floor level. There is also a cross-legged statue of the Knight of Duiske, which is one of the finest medieval effigies in Ireland. Outside are two 9th-century granite High Crosses.

Trips along the Nore take you to **Inistioge**. Lying in a deep, wooded valley, this is an idyllic village, with neat 18th-century houses, a square planted with lime trees and a ten-arched bridge spanning the Nore. On a rock above the river stands a ruined Norman fort, a popular place for picnics.

From Inistioge you can walk along the river or up to **Woodstock House Demesne**, a national park. Among the beech woods stands an 18th-century mansion, currently undergoing restoration.

On a hill 12 km (7.5 miles) south of New Ross, a large area of woodland is enclosed within the **John F Kennedy Park and Arboretum**. Founded in 1968, near the late president's ancestral home in Dunganstown (now **The Kennedy Homestead**), the 400-acre park boasts more than 4,500 types of tree and provides splendid panoramic views. There are marked paths and nature trails.

⚓ **Duiske Abbey**
Graiguenamanagh, Co Kilkenny.
Tel *059 972 4238.* ◯ *daily.* ♿

🌿 **John F Kennedy Park and Arboretum**
New Ross, Co Wexford. ***Tel*** *051 388171.* ◯ *daily.* ⬤ *Good Fri & 25 Dec.* 🅿 ♿ 🚻 *May–Dec.*
www.heritageireland.ie

Enniscorthy ㉔

Road map D5. Co Wexford.
🏘 *5,000.* 🚉 🚌 ℹ *The 1798 visitor centre (054 37596)*

The streets of Enniscorthy, on the banks of the River Slaney, are full of character and redolent of the town's turbulent past. In 1798, Enniscorthy witnessed the last stand of the Wexford pikemen, when a fierce battle was fought against a British force of 20,000 on nearby **Vinegar Hill**. The events of that year are told both at the County Museum inside the imposing **Enniscorthy Castle**, and at the multimedia **National 1798 Visitor Centre**. Enniscorthy's other main sight is the Neo-Gothic **St Aidan's Cathedral**, designed in the 1840s by AWN Pugin (1812–52), better known for his work on London's Houses of Parliament.

Granaries, mills and potteries overlook the Slaney, including Carley's Bridge, founded in 1654 and still operational. Enniscorthy's historic pubs are another attraction. They include the Antique Tavern *(see p346)*, which is hung with pikes used during the Battle of Vinegar Hill in 1798.

⚓ **Enniscorthy Castle**
Castle Hill. ***Tel*** *054 35926.* ◯ *daily (Oct–Dec: pm only).* 🅿 ♿ *limited.*

🏛 **National 1798 Visitor Centre**
Millpark Road. ***Tel*** *054 37596.* ◯ *daily.* 🅿 🚻 🛍
www.1798centre.com

The inland port of New Ross seen from the west bank of the River Barrow

View across the harbour to Wexford town

Irish National Heritage Park 25

Road map D5. Ferrycarrig, Co Wexford. 🚌 *from Wexford in summer.* **Tel** 053 20733. ☐ *Jan–Dec: 9:30am–6:30pm.* ● *week at Christmas.* 🅿 🗲 *Mar–Oct.* 🖼 🍴 🕭 **www**.inhp.com

Built on former marshland near Ferrycarrig, north of Wexford, the Irish National Heritage Park is a bold open-air museum. Trails lead through woods to replicas of homesteads, places of worship and burial sites, providing a fascinating lesson on the country's ancient history *(see pp32–3)*.

Highlights include the Viking boatyard, complete with raiding ship, and a 7th-century horizontal watermill.

Wexford 26

Road map D5. Co Wexford. 🏚 17,000. 🚌 🚆 🛈 *Crescent Quay (053 23111).* **www**.southeastireland.com

Wexford's name derives from *Waesfjord*, a Norse word meaning "estuary of the mud flats". It thrived as a port for centuries but the silting of the harbour in the Victorian era put an end to most sea traffic. Wexford's quays, from where ships once sailed to Bristol, Tenby and Liverpool, are now used mainly by a fleet of humble mussel dredgers.

Wexford is a vibrant place, packed with fine pubs and

boasting a varied arts scene. The town's singular style is often linked to its linguistic heritage. The *yola* dialect, which was spoken by early settlers, survives in the local pronunciation of certain words.

Wexford retains few traces of its past, but the Viking fish-bone street pattern still exists, with narrow alleys fanning off the meandering Main Street. Keyser's Lane, linking South Main Street with The Crescent, is a tiny tunnel-like Viking alley which once led to the Norse water-front. The Normans were responsible for Wexford's town walls, remnants of which include one of the original gateways. Behind it lies **Selskar Abbey**, the ruin of a 12th-century Augustinian monastery. King Henry II is said to have done penance here for the murder of Thomas à Becket in 1170.

Sign of a popular Wexford pub

Wexford also has several handsome buildings dating from a later period, including the 18th-century market house, known as the **Cornmarket**, on Main Street. The nearby square, the **Bull Ring**, is notable only for its history: it was used for bull-baiting in Norman times and was the scene of a cruel massacre by Cromwell's men in 1649.

Wexford Opera Festival, held in October, is the leading operatic event in the country. Aficionados praise it for its intimate atmosphere – both during performances and afterwards, when artists and audience mingle together in the pubs: the Centenary

Stores off Main Street is a favourite, though the Sky and the Ground, on South Main Street, is better for traditional music.

Environs
Skirting the shore just east of the town is the **Wexford Wildfowl Reserve**. It covers 100 ha (250 acres) of reclaimed land and is noted in particular for its geese: over a third of the world's entire population of Greenland white-fronted geese winter here between October and April.

The mudflats also attract large numbers of swans and waders, and provide a rich hunting ground for birds of prey. The birds can be viewed from a number of hides and an observation tower. Another way to enjoy the region's wildlife is to take a boat trip up the Slaney River to **Raven Point** to see the seal colony.

🦆 **Wexford Wildfowl Reserve**
Wexford. **Tel** 053 23129. ☐ *daily.* 🗲 *at weekends*

Boat Trips
Wexford Harbour. **Tel** 053 71626 or 086 860 8328.

Johnstown Castle 27

Road map D5. Co Wexford. **Tel** 053 42888. 🚌 🚆 *to Wexford.* **Gardens** ☐ *daily.* ● *24 & 25 Dec.* 🖼

Façade of Johnstown Castle

Johnstown Castle, a splendid Gothic Revival mansion, lies amid gardens and woodland 6 km (4 miles) southwest of Wexford. In state hands since 1945, the castle is closed for refurbishment. However, it is

Vast crescent of sand and shingle beach at Rosslare

possible to visit the **Irish Agriculture Museum**, housed in the castle's farm buildings. Reconstructions illustrate traditional trades and there is an exhibition on the Famine.

The real glory of Johnstown Castle are the grounds, from the sunken Italian garden to the ornamental lakes. Azaleas and camellias flourish alongside an array of trees including Japanese cedars and redwoods.

Hidden among the dense woods west of the house lurk the ruins of **Rathlannon Castle**, a medieval tower house.

🏛 **Irish Agriculture Museum**
Johnstown Castle. *Tel 053 42888.*
⭘ *Apr, May & Sep–Nov: 9am–12:30pm & 1:30–5pm Mon–Fri, 2–5pm Sat, Sun & public hols; Jun–Aug: 9am–5pm Mon–Fri, 11am–5pm Sat, Sun & public hols; Nov–Mar: 9am–12:30pm & 1:30–5pm Mon–Fri.* 🖼 🖥 🛓 *limited.*

Saltee Islands ㉘

Road map D5. Co Wexford. 🚌 *from Wexford to Kilmore Quay: Wed & Sat.* 🚢 *from Kilmore Quay: Apr–Sep (weather permitting). Tel 053 29637.*

These islands off the south coast of Wexford are a haven for sea birds. Great and Little Saltee together form Ireland's largest bird sanctuary, nurturing an impressive array of birds, from gannets and gulls to puffins and Manx shearwaters. Great Saltee particularly is famous for its colonies of cormorants. It also

has more than 1,000 pairs of guillemots and is a popular stopping-off place for spring and autumn migrations. A bird-monitoring and research programme is in progress, and a close watch is also kept on the colony of grey seals.

The two uninhabited islands are privately owned, but visitors are welcome. Boat trips are run in fine weather from **Kilmore Quay**. These leave in late morning and return mid-afternoon.

Kilmore Quay is a fishing village built on Precambrian gneiss rock – the oldest rock in Ireland. Pretty thatched cottages nestle above a fine sandy beach and the harbour, where a moored lightship houses a **Maritime Museum**. The boat's original fittings are just as interesting as the exhibits.

🏛 **Guillemot Maritime Museum**
Kilmore Quay. *Tel 053 29655.*
⭘ *May & Sep: Sat–Sun; Jun–Aug: daily.* 🖼 📷 🖥

Rosslare ㉙

Road map D5. Co Wexford. 🏠 *1,200.* 🚍 🚌 🛈 *(053 23111)* ⭘ *May–Sep.* www.southeastireland.com

Rosslare replaced Wexford as the area's main port after the decline of the original Viking city harbour. The port is so active today that people tend to associate the name Rosslare more with the ferry terminal for France and Wales than with the town lying 8 km (5 miles) further north.

Rosslare town is one of the sunniest spots in Ireland and draws many holidaymakers. It boasts a fine beach stretching for 9.5 km (6 miles), lively pubs and an excellent golf course fringed by sand dunes. There are good walks north to Rosslare Point.

Environs
At Tagoat, 6 km (4 miles) south of Rosslare, **Yola Farmstead Folk Park** is a recreated traditional 18th-century village, with thatched roofs and a windmill.

🏛 **Yola Farmstead Folk Park**
Tagoat. *Tel 053 32611.* ⭘ *Mar, Apr & Nov: Mon–Fri; May–Oct: daily.* 🖼 📷 🖥 🛓

Colony of gannets nesting on the cliffs of Great Saltee Island

CORK AND KERRY

CORK · KERRY

Magnificent scenery has attracted visitors to this region since Victorian times. Rocky headlands jut out into the Atlantic and colourful fishing villages nestle in the shelter of the bays. County Kerry offers dramatic landscapes and a wealth of pre-historic and early Christian sites, whereas County Cork's gentle charm has enticed many a casual visitor into becoming a permanent resident.

Killarney and its romantic lakes are a powerful magnet for tourists, and so are Cork's attractive coastal towns and villages. Yet the region remains remarkably unspoiled, with a friendly atmosphere and authentic culture still alive in Irish-speaking pockets. There is also a long tradition of arts and crafts in the area.

This corner of Ireland used to be the main point of contact with the Continent. In the 17th century, in response to the threat of invasions from France and Spain, the English built a line of forts along the Cork coast, including the massive Charles Fort at Kinsale.

In the 19th century, the city of Cork was an important departure point for people fleeing from the Famine *(see p219)*, with Cobh the main port for emigrants to the New World. Cork's importance as a port has diminished, but it is still the Republic's second city with a lively cultural scene.

Poverty and temperament helped foster a powerful Republican spirit in the southwest. The region saw much guerrilla action in the War of Independence and the subsequent Civil War. In 1920, the centre of Cork city was burned in an uncontrolled act of reprisal by the notorious Black and Tans *(see pp44–5)*.

Kerry is known as "the Kingdom" on account of its tradition of independence and disregard for Dublin rule. The Irish recognize a distinctive Kerry character, with a boisterous sense of living life to the full. They also make Kerrymen the butt of countless jokes.

As well as the friendliest people in Ireland, the region has some of the finest scenery. Cork has lush valleys and a beautiful coast while Kerry is wilder and more mountainous. The islands off the Kerry coast appear bleak and inhospitable, but many were once inhabited. Remote, rocky Skellig Michael, for example, was the site of a 6th-century Christian monastery.

Puffins on the island of Skellig Michael off the coast of Kerry

◁ Beach at Barley Cove near Mizen Head, County Cork

Exploring Cork and Kerry

Killarney is a popular base with tourists for exploring Cork and Kerry, especially for touring the Ring of Kerry and the archaeological remains of the Dingle Peninsula. Despite the changeable weather, the region attracts many visitors who come to see its dramatic scenery and lush vegetation. As you pass through quiet fishing villages and genteel towns, such as Kenmare, you will always encounter a friendly welcome from the locals. For the adventurous there are plenty of opportunities to go riding, hiking or cycling. Cork city offers a more cosmopolitan atmosphere, with its art galleries and craft shops.

CARRIGAFOYLE CASTLE ①
Limeri
Ballybunnion
Tarb
Ballylongfo
R553
Ballyduff
Athe
Listowel
Feale
Cashen
N69
Abbeyfeale
Ballyheige
R556
Banna Strand
K
ARDFERT CATHEDRAL ②
Ardfert
R551
TRALEE ③
Glanaruddery Mountains
Bros
Brandon Bay
Tralee Bay
Fenit
N21
Castleisla
Brandon Peak 953m
Castlegregory
Ballydes
Camp
N22
R57
GALLARUS ORATORY ⑤
Slieve Mish Mountains
N70
Farranfore
Ballyferriter
Anascaul
KERRY
Dunquin ⑥
DINGLE ④
Castlemaine
DINGLE PENINSULA
Killorglin
KILLARNEY ⑦
Rath
Great Blasket Island
Dingle Bay
Glenbeigh
Laune
LAKES OF KILLARNEY ⑧
N72
RING OF KERRY
Macgillycuddy's Reeks
Carrantuohil 1038m
Muckross House
Cahirciveen
Coomacarrea 772m
N71
Mangerton Moun 838m
VALENTIA ISLAND ⑨
Knightstown
Iny
Derreendarragh
Kilgarva
Portmagee
Sneem
N70
KENMARE ⑫
Ballir
Ballinskelligs
Waterville
Killabunane
Ballinskelligs Bay
Kenmare Bay
Lauragh
Caha Mountains
THE SKELLIGS ⑩
Scariff Island
Ardgroom
R574
Glengarriff
GARINISH ISLAND ⑭
Eyeries
R571
Adrigole
Bantry
⑯
BANTRY HOUSE ⑮
Ballydonegan
BEARA PENINSULA ⑬
Castletownbere
Bear Island
BANTRY BAY
Durrus
Dursey Island
N71
The Bull
Kilcrohane
Ballydehob
Skibbere
Dunmanus Bay
R591
R592
R5
Toormore
MIZEN HEAD ⑰
Crookhaven
BALTI ⑱
Barley Cove
Roaringwater Bay
Sherkin Is
Clear Island

Kissing the Blarney Stone at Blarney Castle near Cork

GETTING AROUND

To explore the region a car is essential. The N22 connects Cork, Killarney and Tralee while the N71 follows the coastline via Clonakilty, Bantry and on to Killarney. In the more remote parts the road signs may only be written in Irish. Killarney is the base for organized coach tours of the area. The train service from Cork to Dublin is efficient, and trains also connect Killarney with Dublin and Cork, but you may have to change trains en route. Buses run throughout the region, but services to the smaller sights may be infrequent.

Cattle grazing near Ardfert Cathedral

SIGHTS AT A GLANCE

Ardfert Cathedral ②
Baltimore ⑱
Bantry Bay ⑯
Bantry House pp168–9 ⑮
Beara Peninsula ⑬
Blarney Castle ㉓
Carrigafoyle Castle ①
Clonakilty ⑳
Cobh ㉗
Cork pp174–7 ㉕
Dingle ④
Drombeg Stone Circle ⑲

Gallarus Oratory ⑤
Garinish Island ⑭
Kenmare ⑫
Killarney ⑦
Kinsale pp172–3 ㉔
Lakes of Killarney pp162–3 ⑧
Mizen Head ⑰
Old Midleton Distillery ㉘
River Blackwater ㉖
River Lee ㉒
The Skelligs ⑩
Timoleague Abbey ㉑
Tralee ③
Valentia Island ⑨
Youghal ㉙

Tours
Dingle Peninsula ⑥
Ring of Kerry ⑪

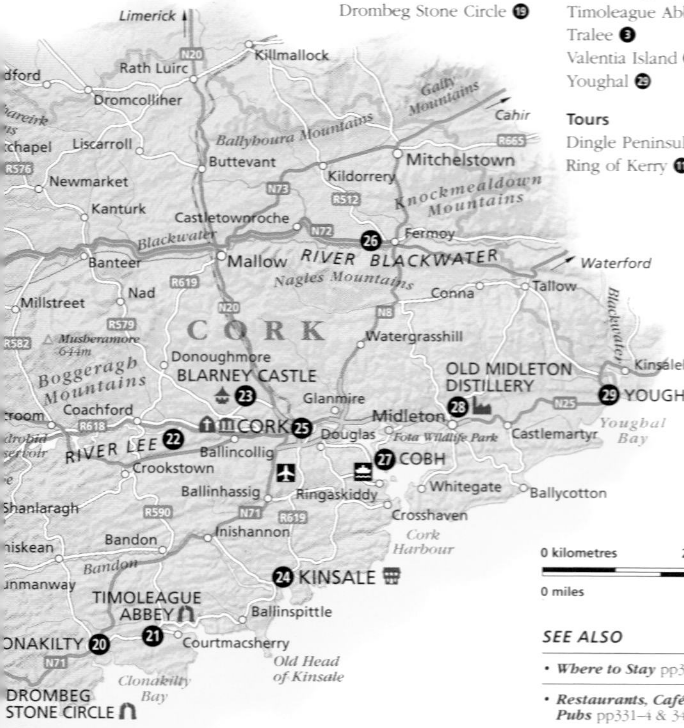

0 kilometres 20

0 miles 20

SEE ALSO

- *Where to Stay* pp302–306

- *Restaurants, Cafés and Pubs* pp331–4 & 347–8

KEY

▬	Major road
▬	Secondary road
▭	Minor road
▬	Scenic route
⊷	Main railway
	Minor railway
▬	County border
△	Summit

Newman's Mall in the quaint village of Kinsale

Ardfert Cathedral and the ruins of Teampall na Hoe and Teampall na Griffin

Carrigafoyle Castle ❶

Road Map B5. Co Kerry.
🚌 to Listowel.

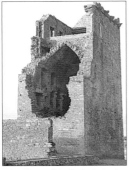

Ruined keep of Carrigafoyle Castle

High above the Shannon estuary, just west of Ballylongford, this 15th-century castle belonged to the O'Connor clan, who ruled much of northern Kerry. The English besieged or sacked it repeatedly but the body blow was delivered in 1649 by Cromwellian forces *(see p39)*. The ruins include a keep and walled bawn, with romantic views of the estuary from the top of the tower.

Ardfert Cathedral ❷

Road map A5. Co Kerry. 🚌 to Ardfert. **Tel** 066 713 4711. ☐ Easter–Sep: daily; rest of year on request. 🌀 ♿

This complex of churches is linked to the cult of St. Brendan the Navigator *(see p213)*, who was born nearby

in 484 and founded a monastery here. The ruined cathedral dates back to the 12th century and retains a delicate Romanesque doorway and blind arcading. The south transept is now restored and houses an exhibition of the history of the site. In the graveyard stand the remains of a Romanesque nave-and-chancel church, Teampall na Hoe, and a late Gothic chapel, Teampall na Griffin. The latter is named after the curious griffins carved beside an interior window.

A short walk away are the ruins of a Franciscan friary. It was founded by Thomas Fitzmaurice in 1253, but the cloisters and south chapel date from the 15th century.

Environs
Just northwest of Ardfert is **Banna Strand**. Irish patriot Roger Casement landed here in 1916 on a German U-boat, bringing in rifles for the Easter Rising *(see pp44–5)*. He was arrested as soon as he landed and a

memorial stands on the site of his capture. This beach was also used for the filming of David Lean's *Ryan's Daughter* (1970).

Tralee ❸

Road map B5. Co Kerry. 🏘 23,000.
🚌 🚆 ℹ Ashe Memorial Hall,
Denny St (066 7121288) 🛒 Thu.
www.corkkerry.ie

Host to the renowned Rose of Tralee International Festival *(see p49)*, Tralee has made great strides in promoting its cultural and leisure facilities. The town's main attraction is **Kerry County Museum**. Its theme park, "Kerry the Kingdom", offers a show on Kerry scenery and a display of archaeological finds and interactive models. The "Geraldine Experience" brings one back to medieval times.

Also based in Tralee is the **Siamsa Tíre** National Folk Theatre of Ireland, a great ambassador for Irish culture.

Steam train on the narrow gauge railway between Tralee and Blennerville, with Blennerville Windmill in the background

Traditional song and dance performances take place here throughout the summer.

Just outside Tralee is the authentic **Blennerville Windmill**. Built in 1800, it is Ireland's largest working mill and one of Tralee's most popular attractions. The **Steam Railway** connects Blennerville with Tralee along a narrow gauge track. The train also runs from Ballyard Station to the windmill.

🏛 **Kerry County Museum**
Ashe Memorial Hall, Denny St.
Tel 066 7127777. ⬤ *mid-Mar–Dec: daily.* ⬤ *25 & 26 Dec.* 🎫 ♿ ▯ ▣

🎭 **Siamsa Tíre**
Town Park. *Tel* 066 712 3055. ⬤ *for performances mid-Apr–Oct.* 🎫 ♿

🏛 **Blennerville Windmill**
Tel 066 712 1064. ⬤ *Mar–Oct: daily.* 🎫 ▯ ▯

🚂 **Steam Railway**
Ballyard Station. *Tel* 066 712 1064.
⬤ *May–Sep: daily (ring to check times).* 🎫 ♿

Dingle ❹

Road map A5. Co Kerry. 🏘 *2,100.*
🚌 *Mar–Oct.* ℹ *Main St (066 915 1188).* 🛒 *Fri.* **www**.corkkerry.ie

This once remote Irish-speaking town is today a thriving fishing port and an increasingly popular tourist

Gallarus Oratory, a dry-stone early Christian church

centre. Brightly painted craft shops and cafés abound, often with slightly hippy overtones.

Dingle Bay is attractive with a somewhat ramshackle harbour lined with fishing trawlers. Along the quayside are lively bars offering music and seafood. The harbour is home to Dingle's biggest star: Fungie, the dolphin, who has been a permanent resident since 1983 and can be visited by boat or on swimming trips.

Although Dingle has few architectural attractions, it makes an engaging base for exploring the archaeological remains on the Dingle Peninsula *(see pp158–9)*.

Gallarus Oratory ❺

Road map A5. Co Kerry.
🚌 *to Dingle. Tel* 066 915 5333.

Shaped like an upturned boat, this miniature church overlooks Smerwick harbour. Gallarus was built some time between the 6th and 9th centuries and is the best preserved early Christian church in Ireland. It represents the apogee of dry-stone corbelling, using techniques first developed by Neolithic tomb-makers. The stones were laid at a slight angle, lower on the outside than the inside, allowing water to run off.

Fishing trawlers moored alongside the quay at Dingle

A Tour of the Dingle Peninsula 6

GUINNESS
Mar is gnách

Pub sign,
Ballyferriter

The Dingle Peninsula offers some of Ireland's most beautiful scenery. To the north rises the towering Brandon Mountain, while the west coast has some spectacular seascapes. A drive around the area, which takes at least half a day, reveals fascinating antiquities ranging from Iron Age stone forts to inscribed stones, early Christian oratories and beehive huts. These are sometimes found on private land, so you may be asked for a small fee by the farmer to see them. Some parts of the peninsula – especially the more remote areas – are still Gaelic speaking, so many road signs are written only in Irish.

View from Clogher Head

Riasc (An Riasc) ⑦
This excavated monastic settlement dates from the 7th century. The enclosure contains the remains of an oratory, several crosses and an inscribed pillar stone (see p243).

**Ballyferriter
(Baile an Fheirtéaraigh) ⑥**
The attractions of this friendly village include the pastel-coloured cottages, Louis Mulcahy's pottery and a museum featuring the cultural heritage of the area.

R559

Clogher Head

**Blasket Centre
(Ionad an Bhlascaoid) ⑤**
Overlooking Blasket Sound, the centre explains the literature, language and way of life of the inhabitants of the Blasket Islands. The islanders moved to the mainland in 1953.

*Dunquin
(Dún Chaoin)*

Ve...
(Ceann...

R559

Mount
Eagle

Vent...

BLASKET ISLANDS

Blasket Sound

⑤

④

③

②

DINGLE BAY

**Dunmore Head
(Ceann an Dúin Mhoir) ④**
Mainland Ireland's most westerly point offers dramatic views of the Blaskets.

**Slea Head
(Ceann Sléibe) ③**
As you round the Slea Head promontory, the Blasket Islands come into full view. The sculpture of the Crucifixion beside the road is known locally as the Cross (An Cros).

KEY

——— Tour route
=== Other roads
⁂ Viewpoint

0 kilometres   2

0 miles   1

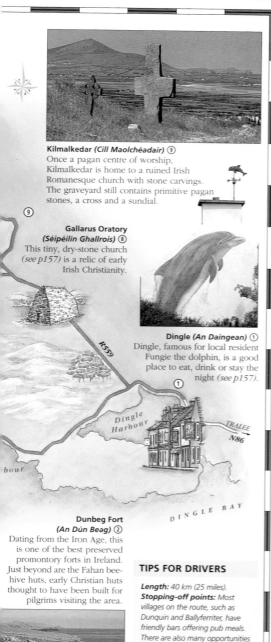

Kilmalkedar (Cill Maolchéadair) ⑨
Once a pagan centre of worship,
Kilmalkedar is home to a ruined Irish
Romanesque church with stone carvings.
The graveyard still contains primitive pagan
stones, a cross and a sundial.

**Gallarus Oratory
(Séipéilín Ghallrois)** ⑧
This tiny, dry-stone church
(see p157) is a relic of early
Irish Christianity.

Dingle (An Daingean) ①
Dingle, famous for local resident
Fungie the dolphin, is a good
place to eat, drink or stay the
night *(see p157)*.

Dingle Harbour

TRALEE N86

R559

DINGLE BAY

bour

**Dunbeg Fort
(An Dún Beag)** ②
Dating from the Iron Age, this
is one of the best preserved
promontory forts in Ireland.
Just beyond are the Fahan beehive huts, early Christian huts
thought to have been built for
pilgrims visiting the area.

TIPS FOR DRIVERS

Length: 40 km (25 miles).
Stopping-off points: Most
villages on the route, such as
Dunquin and Ballyferriter, have
friendly bars offering pub meals.
There are also many opportunities
to stop for a picnic. On the
winding coast road around Slea
Head stop only at the safe and
clearly marked coastal viewing
points. (see also pp387–9.)

Jaunting cars waiting to take
visitors to sights around Killarney

Killarney ⑦

Road map B5. Co Kerry. 🏠 9,500. 🚌
🚉 🛈 Beech Rd (064 31633). 🅿 Sat.
www.corkkerry.ie

Killarney is often derided as
"a tourist town" but this has
not dented its cheerful atmosphere. The infectious Kerry
humour is personified by the
wise-cracking jarveys whose
families have run jaunting cars
(pony and trap rides) here for
generations. The town gets
busy in summer but has much
to offer, with shops open until
10pm in summer, several
excellent restaurants, and a
few prestigious hotels around
the lake and the heights.
From the town visitors can
explore the sights around
the Lakes of Killarney *(see
pp162–3)* and the surrounding heather-covered hills.

Environs
Overlooking the lakes and a
short drive from Killarney is
Muckross House. This imposing
mansion was built in 1843 in
Elizabethan style. Inside, the
elegant rooms are decorated
with period furnishings. There
is also a museum of Kerry Life,
with displays on the history of
southwest Ireland, and a craft
centre. The landscaped gardens
are very beautiful in spring
when the rhododendrons and
azaleas are in bloom. A short
walk away is Muckross Farm,
which still uses traditional
farming techniques.

🏛 **Muckross House**
4 km (2.5 miles) S of Killarney. *Tel*
064 31440. ◯ July–Aug: 9am–6pm
daily; Sep–Jun: 9am–5:30pm daily.
● 7 days at Christmas. 🎟 🚻 🛗
🅿 📷 www.muckross-house.ie

Lakes of Killarney ❽

Fruit of the strawberry tree

Renowned for its splendid scenery, the area is one of Ireland's most popular tourist attractions. The three lakes are contained within Killarney National Park. Although the landscape is dotted with ruined castles and abbeys, the lakes are the focus of attention: the moody watery scenery is subject to subtle shifts of light and colour. The area has entranced many artists and writers including Thackeray, who praised "a precipice covered with a thousand trees … and other mountains rising as far as we could see". In autumn, the bright red fruits of the strawberry tree colour the shores of the lakes.

Meeting of the Waters
This beauty spot, best seen from Dinis Island, is where the waters from the Upper Lake meet Muckross Lake and Lough Leane. At the Old Weir Bridge, boats shoot the rapids.

Torc Waterfall
The Owengarriff River cascades through the wooded Friars' Glen into Muckross Lake. A pretty path winds up to the top of this 18-m (60-ft) high waterfall, revealing views of Torc Mountain.

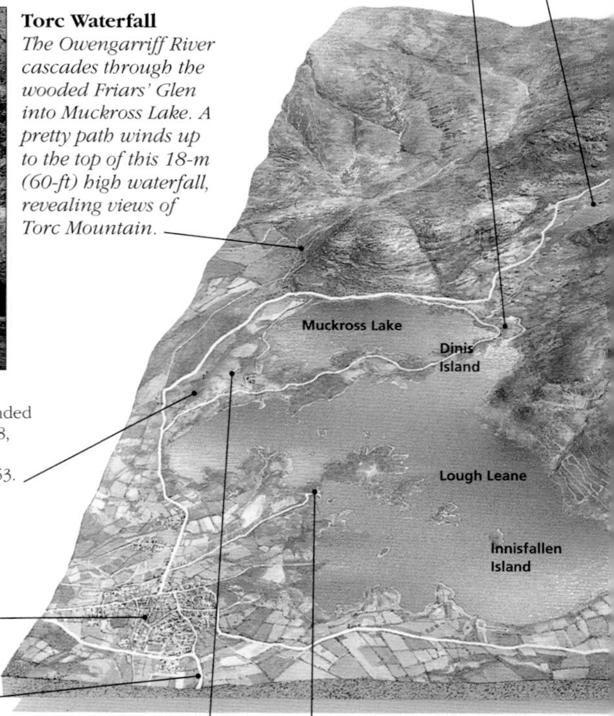
Long Range River
Muckross Lake
Dinis Island
Lough Leane
Innisfallen Island

Muckross Abbey was founded by the Franciscans in 1448, but was burnt down by Cromwellian forces in 1653.

Killarney *(see p159)* is the main town from which tourists visit the sights around the lakes.

N22 to Tralee ***(see pp156–7)***

Ross Castle, built around 1420, was the last stronghold under Irish control to be taken by Cromwellian forces in 1653.

★ Muckross House
The 19th-century manor (see p159) *enjoys a lovely location overlooking the lakes. Visit the wildlife centre for an introduction to the flora and fauna of the National Park.*

Upper Lake
This narrow lake is the smallest of the three lakes. It flows into the Long Range River to the Meeting of the Waters.

VISITORS' CHECKLIST

Road map B5. Killarney, Co Kerry.
✕ Kerry (066 976 4644). 🚌 🚉
National Park ⬜ 9am–6pm
(6:30pm Jun–Aug) daily (for access
by car). 🛈 Killarney (064 31633).
Muckross House Tel 064 31440.
⬜ Jul–Aug: 9am–6pm daily;
Sep–Jun: 9am–5:30pm daily (last
tour 4:45pm). ● 7 days over
Christmas. 🚻 🛍 ♿ 🍴 📷
Ross Castle Tel 064 35851.⬜
mid-Mar–mid-Nov: daily. 🚻📷
obligatory. 🚤 from Ross Castle:
Pride of the Lakes (064 32638):
daily (weather permitting); **The
Lily of Killarney** (064 31068):
Mar–Oct. **Kate Kearney's
Cottage Tel** 064 44146. ⬜
Easter–Sep: 9am–midnight daily;
Oct–Easter: 9:30am–6pm. 🍴 🛍

Ladies' View gets its name from the delight it gave Queen Victoria's ladies-in-waiting when they visited the spot in 1861.

N71 to
Moll's Gap
and Kenmare
(see pp164–6)

Upper Lake

Purple
Mountain,
832 m
(2,730 ft)

★ Gap of Dunloe
Glaciers carved this dramatic mountain pass which is popular with walkers, cyclists and horse riders. The route through the gap offers fabulous views of the boulder-strewn gorge and three small lakes.

Tomies
Mountain,
735 m
(2,411 ft)

Kate Kearney's Cottage was home to a local beauty who ran an illegal drinking house for passing travellers in the mid-19th century.

R562 to Killorglin
(see pp164–5)

0 kilometres   2

0 miles   1

Lough Leane
The largest lake is dotted with un-inhabited islands and fringed with wooded slopes. Boat trips run between Ross Castle and Innisfallen.

STAR SIGHTS

★ Gap of Dunloe

★ Muckross House

Valentia Island ❾

Road map A5. Co Kerry. 🚌 to
Caherciveen. 🚃 *Caherciveen (066 947
2589/064 31633).* **www**.corkkerry.ie

Although it feels like the
mainland, Valentia is an
island, albeit linked by a causeway to Portmagee. It
is 11 km (7 miles)
long and noted
for its water
sports,

Stairway leading to Skellig Michael monastery

seascapes and views from
Geokaun Mountain. Valentia
is also popular for its proximity
to the Skellig Islands which lie
around 15 km (10 miles) southwest of the Iveragh Peninsula.

The **Skellig Experience
Centre**, near the causeway
linking Valentia to the mainland, houses an audiovisual
display about the construction
and history of the monastery
on Skellig Michael, the largest
of the Skellig Islands. Other
subjects covered include sea
birds and the marine
life around the islands,
a reminder that
the Skellig cliffs
lie underwater for
a depth of 50 m
(165 ft), providing
a habitat for giant
basking sharks,
dolphins and
turtles. The centre
also operates
cruises around
the islands.

The main village on Valentia
is **Knightstown**, which offers
accommodation and lively
pubs with music and dancing.

The first transatlantic cable
was laid from the southwest
point of the island to New-
foundland, Canada, in 1866.

🏛 **Skellig Experience Centre**
Valentia Island. **Tel** 066 947 6306.
🕐 *late-Mar–Sep: daily.* 🎫 🚻

The Skelligs ❿

Road map A6. Co Kerry. 🚢 *mid-
Mar–Oct: from Valentia Island.* **Tel**
066 947 6214 (ring a few days ahead).

Skellig Michael, also known
as Great Skellig, is an
inhospitable pinnacle of rock
rising out of the Atlantic and
covering an area of 17 ha
(44 acres). Perched on a ledge
almost 218 m (714 ft) above
sea level and reached by an
amazing 1,000-year-old

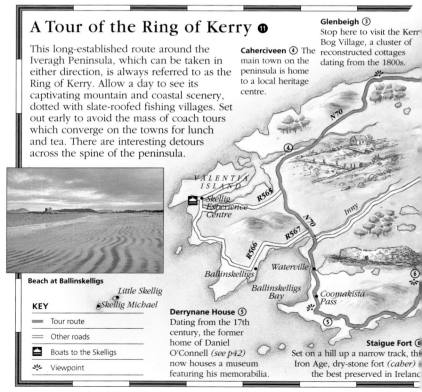

A Tour of the Ring of Kerry ⓫

This long-established route around the
Iveragh Peninsula, which can be taken in
either direction, is always referred to as the
Ring of Kerry. Allow a day to see its
captivating mountain and coastal scenery,
dotted with slate-roofed fishing villages. Set
out early to avoid the mass of coach tours
which converge on the towns for lunch
and tea. There are interesting detours
across the spine of the peninsula.

Glenbeigh ③
Stop here to visit the Kerr
Bog Village, a cluster of
reconstructed cottages
dating from the 1800s.

Caherciveen ④ The
main town on the
peninsula is home
to a local heritage
centre.

*VALENTIA
ISLAND*

Skellig
Experience
Centre

Beach at Ballinskelligs

Little Skellig
Skellig Michael

KEY

━━━ Tour route

═══ Other roads

🚢 Boats to the Skelligs

⚬ Viewpoint

Ballinskelligs

Waterville

*Ballinskelligs
Bay*

*Coomakista
Pass*

Derrynane House ⑤
Dating from the 17th
century, the former
home of Daniel
O'Connell *(see p42)*
now houses a museum
featuring his memorabilia.

Staigue Fort ⑥
Set on a hill up a narrow track, thi
Iron Age, dry-stone fort *(caher)* i
the best preserved in Irelanc

Inny

stairway is an isolated early Christian monastery. Monks settled for solitude on Skellig Michael during the 6th century, building a cluster of six corbelled beehive cells and two boat-shaped oratories. These dry-stone structures are still standing, despite being raked by storms over the centuries. The monks were totally self-sufficient, trading eggs, feathers and seal meat with passing boats in return for cereals, tools and animal skins. The skins were needed to produce the vellum on which the monks copied their religious manuscripts. They remained on this bleak island until the 12th century, when they retreated to the Augustinian priory at Ballinskelligs on the mainland.

Today the only residents on Skellig Michael are the thousands of sea birds which nest

Gannets flying around the precipitous cliffs of Little Skellig

and breed on the high cliffs, including storm petrels, puffins and Manx shearwaters. The huge breeding colonies are protected from predators by the sea and rocky shores.

Slightly closer to the mainland is Little Skellig. Covering an area of 7 ha (17 acres), the island has steep cliffs. Home to a variety of sea birds, it has one of the largest colonies of gannets (about 22,000 breeding pairs) in the British Isles.

A cruiser from Valentia Island circles the Skelligs but does not dock. Except for a pier on Skellig Michael, there are no proper landing stages on the islands. This is to discourage visitors from disturbing the birdlife, fragile plant cover and archaeological remains.

Atlantic gales permitting, local fishermen may run unofficial trips around the islands from Portmagee or Ballinskelligs, during the summer.

Killorglin ② This pretty village, sitting on the slopes above a river, is famous for its Puck Fair *(see p49)*.

Killarney ①
Visitors touring the Ring of Kerry usually start and finish here. The route passes lovely views of the Lakes of Killarney *(see pp162–3)*.

Moll's Gap ⑧
Cutting through bleak bogland and high mountainous terrain, Moll's Gap offers some stunning views.

Sneem ⑦
Brightly painted cottages line the streets of this charming town which also has a quaint village green.

TRALEE
N72
Laune
Lakes of Killarney
CORK
N22
MACGILLICUDDY'S REEKS
Caragh Lake
N71
Kenmare
R568
N71
BANTRY
N70

0 kilometres 10
0 miles 5

TIPS FOR DRIVERS

Length: 180 km (112 miles).
Stopping off points: Many towns such as Killorglin and Caherciveen offer pub snacks. Finish the day in one of the excellent gourmet restaurants in Kenmare (see also pp387–9).

Lace making at Kenmare

Kenmare ⓬

Road map B5. Co Kerry. 🏃 *1,400.*
🚌 ℹ️ *May–Sep: Main St (064 41233).* 🛒 *Wed.* **www**.corkkerry.ie

This town, on the mouth of the River Sheen, was founded in 1670 by William Petty, Cromwell's surveyor general. However, Kenmare's appearance owes more to his descendant, the first Marquess of Lansdowne who, in 1775, made it a model landlord's town of neat stone façades with decorative plasterwork.

Today Kenmare is renowned for its traditional lace. During the famine years, nuns from the local convent, St Clare's, introduced lace making to create work for the women and girls. Other attractions include the fine hotels *(see pp304–305)* and gourmet restaurants *(p333)*. The town is also an excellent base for exploring the Beara Peninsula and the Ring of Kerry *(see pp164–5)*.

Set in a riverside glade off Market Street is the **Druid's Circle**, a prehistoric ring of 15 stones associated with human sacrifice.

Beara Peninsula ⓭

Road map A6. Co Cork & Co Kerry.
🚌 *to Glengarriff (daily) & Castletownbere (Mon, Wed, Fri &Sun).*
ℹ️ *Glengarriff (027 63084).*

Dotted with sparsely populated fishing villages surrounded by bleak moorland, this peninsula is remote. It used to be a refuge for smugglers, with the Irish getting the better deal in their exchange of pilchards for contraband French brandy.

The peninsula offers some spectacular scenery and wonderful walking country. From the **Healy Pass**, which cuts a jagged path across the spine of the Caha Mountains, there are some fine views of Bantry Bay and the rugged landscape of West Cork. To the west of the pass is **Hungry Hill**, the highest mountain in the Caha range and popular with hill walkers.

Encircled by the Caha and Slieve Miskish Mountains is **Castletownbere**, the main town on the peninsula. This sheltered port was once a haven for smugglers, but is now awash with foreign fishing trawlers. McCarthey's Bar on Town Square features an authentic matchmaking booth, where Cork families used to agree marriage terms until a generation ago.

West of Castletownbere stands the shell of **Puxley Mansion**, home of the Puxley family who owned the mines at nearby **Allihies**. Centre of the copper-mining district until the 1930s, it is now a desolate place, with tall Cornish-style chimneys and piles of ochre-coloured spoil; beware of unguarded mine shafts.

From the tip of the peninsula a cable car travels across to **Dursey Island**, with its ruined castle and colonies of sea birds. Licensed to carry three passengers and one cow, the cable car swings across the strait, offering views of Bull, Cow and Calf islands.

From the headland the R757 road back to Kenmare passes through the pretty villages of **Eyeries**, noted for its brightly painted cottages and crafts, and **Ardgroom**, a centre for mussel farming and a base for exploring the scenic glacial valley around **Glenbeg Lough**.

Garinish Island ⓮

Road map B6. Co Cork. 🚤 *from Glengarriff (027 63116).* **Gardens Tel** *027 63040.* ☐ *Mar–Oct: daily.* 🎫 🅿️
♿ *limited.*

Also known as Ilnacullin, this small island was turned into an exotic garden in 1910 by Harold Peto for Annan Bryce,

View of Caha Mountains from the Healy Pass, Beara Peninsula

Italianate garden with lily pool and folly on Garinish Island

a Belfast businessman. Framed by views of Bantry Bay, the gardens are landscaped with Neo-Classical follies and planted with rich subtropical flora. The microclimate and peaty soil provide the damp, warm conditions needed for these ornamental plants to flourish.

Exotic shrubberies abound especially during the summer. In May and June, there are beautiful displays of camellias, azaleas and rhododendrons. There is also a New Zealand fernery and a Japanese rockery, as well as a rare collection of Bonsai trees. A Martello tower crowns the island and among the follies are a clock tower and a Grecian temple.

The centrepiece is a colonnaded Italianate garden, with a Classical folly and ornamental lily pool. Much of its charm resides in the contrast between the cultivated lushness of the garden and the glimpses of wild seascape and barren mountains beyond. An added attraction of the boat trip across to this Gulf Stream paradise is the chance to see cavorting seals in Bantry Bay.

Bantry House 🅖

See pp168–9.

Bantry Bay 🅖

Road map A6. Co Cork. 🚌 *to Bantry and Glengarriff.* 🛈 *Mar–Oct: The Square, Bantry (027 50229).* **www.**bantry.ie **Bamboo Park** *Tel 027 63570.* **www.**bamboo-park.com

Bantry Bay encompasses the resorts of **Bantry** and **Glengarriff**. It is also a springboard for trips to Mizen Head and the Beara Peninsula.

Bantry nestles beneath the hills which run down to the bay. Just offshore you can see **Whiddy Island**, the original home of the White family, who moved to Bantry House in the early 18th century. Further along is **Bere Island**, a British base until World War II.

Glengarriff at the head the bay, exudes an air of Victorian gentility with its neatly painted shopfronts and craft shops. On the coast is the Eccles Hotel, a haunt of Queen Victoria and where George Bernard Shaw supposedly wrote *Saint Joan*.

Bamboo Park in Glengarriff is a unique, exotic garden containing 30 different species of bamboo as well as palms and other tropical plants.

Mizen Head 🅗

Road map A6. Co Cork. 🚌 *to Goleen.* 🛈 *Town Hall, North St, Skibbereen (028 21766).*

Mizen Head, the most southwesterly tip of Ireland, has steep cliffs, often lashed by storms. In a lighthouse, **Mizen Head Visitors' Centre** is reached by a bridge. From the car park, a headland walk takes in views of cliffs and Atlantic breakers. The sandy beaches of nearby **Barley Cove** attract bathers and walkers; to the east is **Crookhaven**, a pretty yachting harbour. From here, a walk to Brow Head offers views of the lighthouse.

Mizen Head can be reached either from Bantry via Durrus or from the market town of **Skibbereen**, on the R592, via the charming crafts centre of **Ballydehob** and the village of **Schull**. Trips to Clear Island *(see p170)* leave from Schull.

🏛 **Visitors' Centre**
Mizen Head. *Tel 028 35115.*
⏺ *Mar–Oct: daily; Nov–mid-Mar: Sat & Sun.* 🎫 🅿 ♿ *limited.* ⛺
📷 www.mizenhead.ie

Rocky cliffs at Mizen Head

Bantry House ⑮

Bantry House has been the
home of the White family,
formerly Earls of Bantry,
since 1739. The original
Queen Anne house was
built around 1700, but the
north façade overlooking the bay
was a later addition. Inside there is an
eclectic collection of art and
furnishings brought from all over
Europe by the 2nd Earl of Bantry.
In the carriage house and stable
block is the French Armada
Centre, which explains the events surrounding Wolfe Tone's attempted invasion in 1796.

**William and
Mary clock in
anteroom**

North façade

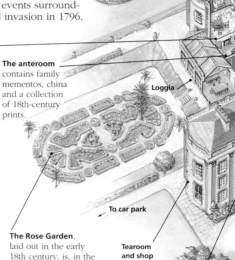

The anteroom
contains family
mementos, china
and a collection
of 18th-century
prints.

Loggia

To car park

Gobelin Room
*The subject of this 18th-
century Gobelin tapestry is*
The Bath of Cupid and
Psyche. *The room also
contains an early 19th-
century piano.*

The Rose Garden,
laid out in the early
18th century, is, in the
words of the 1st Earl
of Bantry, "a parterre
after the English
manner".

**Tearoom
and shop**

1ST EARL OF BANTRY (1767–1851)

Richard White, 1st Earl of Bantry, played a leading role in
defending Ireland against an attempted invasion by Wolfe
Tone and the United Irishmen *(see pp40–41)*. On 16 December 1796, Tone sailed from Brest in Brittany with a fleet
of 43 French ships bound for
Ireland. White chose strategic
spots around Bantry Bay and
mustered volunteers to fight.
His efforts proved unnecessary
as the French fleet was forced
back by bad weather. Nonetheless, White was rewarded
with a peerage by George III
for his "spirited conduct and
important services". In 1801 he
was made Viscount Bantry, be
coming Earl of Bantry in 1816.

★ Dining Room
*This room is dominated by
portraits of King George III and
Queen Charlotte by court
painter Allan Ramsay. The
Spanish chandelier is decorated
with Meissen china flowers.*

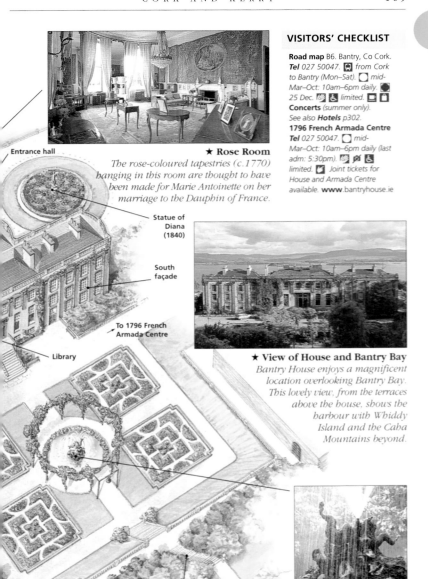

Entrance hall

★ **Rose Room**
The rose-coloured tapestries (c.1770) hanging in this room are thought to have been made for Marie Antoinette on her marriage to the Dauphin of France.

Statue of Diana (1840)

South façade

To 1796 French Armada Centre

Library

★ **View of House and Bantry Bay**
Bantry House enjoys a magnificent location overlooking Bantry Bay. This lovely view, from the terraces above the house, shows the harbour with Whiddy Island and the Caha Mountains beyond.

VISITORS' CHECKLIST

Road map B6. Bantry, Co Cork. **Tel** 027 50047. ☐ from Cork to Bantry (Mon–Sat). ☐ mid-Mar–Oct: 10am–6pm daily. ● 25 Dec. ☒ ☒ limited. ☐ ☐ **Concerts** (summer only). See also **Hotels** p302.
1796 French Armada Centre Tel 027 50047. ☐ mid-Mar–Oct: 10am–6pm daily (last adm: 5:30pm). ☒ ☒ ☒ limited. ☒ Joint tickets for House and Armada Centre available. www.bantryhouse.ie

STAR FEATURES

★ Dining Room

★ Rose Room

★ View of House and Bantry Bay

The steps, known as the "Staircase to the Sky", lead to a series of terraces with fabulous views over the house and across the bay.

Italian Garden
Inspired by the Boboli Gardens in Florence, this garden encircles a pool decorated in Classical Grotesque style. It was designed in the early 1850s by the 2nd Earl.

Baltimore ⑱

Road map B6. Co Cork. 🏘 *220.*
🚗 ⛴ *to Sherkin Island (028 20218);
to Cape Clear Island (028 39159).*

Baltimore's most bizarre claim
to fame dates back to 1631
when more than 100 citizens
were carried off as slaves by
Algerian pirates. Now that the
threat of being kidnapped has
gone, this village appeals to
the yachting fraternity and
island-hoppers. Like neighbouring Schull and
Castletownshend, the town
bustles with summer festivals.

Overlooking the harbour is
a ruined 15th-century castle,
once the stronghold of the
O'Driscoll clan. Also worth a
visit are the seafood pubs,
including Bushe's Bar, an
atmospheric inn hung with
nautical memorabilia. Behind
the village, cliff walks lead to
splendid views of Carbery's
Hundred Isles – mere specks
on Roaringwater Bay. Baltimore
Beacon is an important marker
for boats in the bay

A short ferry ride away is
Sherkin Island with its sandy
beaches in the west, ruined
15th-century abbey, marine
station and pubs. The ferry
ride to **Cape Clear Island** is
more dramatic, as the boat
weaves between sharp black
rocks to this remote, Irish-
speaking island, noted for its
bird observatory in the North
Harbour. There are some
spectacular views of the
mainland from the island.

**Distinctive white beacon for boats
approaching Baltimore**

Drombeg Stone Circle, erected around the 2nd century BC

Drombeg Stone Circle ⑲

Road map B6. Co Cork. 🚗 *to
Skibbereen or Clonakilty.*

Situated on the Glandore road
16 km (10 miles) west of
Clonakilty, Drombeg is
the finest of the many
stone circles in
County Cork. Dating
back to about 150
BC, this circle of 17
standing stones is 9
m (30 ft) in diameter.
At the winter solstice,
the rays of the setting
sun fall on the flat
altar stone which
faces the entrance to
the circle, marked by two
upright stones

Nearby is a small stream
with a Stone Age cooking pit
(*fulacht fiadh*), similar to one
at Craggaunowen (*see p190*).
A fire was made in the hearth
and hot stones from the fire
were dropped into the cooking pit to heat the water. Once
the water boiled, the meat,
usually venison, was added.

Clonakilty ⑳

Road map B6. Co Cork. 🏘 *3,000.*
🚗 ℹ *25 Ashe Street (023 33226).*

Founded as an English outpost
around 1588, this market town
has a typically hearty West
Cork atmosphere. The **West
Cork Regional Museum**, housed
in an old schoolhouse,
remembers the town's industrial heritage. A number of
quayside buildings, linked to
the town's industrial past, have

**Sign for Clonakilty
black pudding**

been restored. Particularly
pleasant is the Georgian
nucleus of Emmet Square.

Until the 19th century
Clonakilty was a noted linen
producer. Today, it is renowned for its rich black puddings, handpainted Irish signs
and traditional music pubs.

Near the town centre
is a model village,
depicting the town
as it was in the
1940s. Just east of
town is the recon-
structed **Lios-na-
gCon Ring Fort**,
with earthworks,
huts and souterrains
(*see p20*). A cause-
way links Clonakilty
to **Inchydoney** beach.

🏛 **West Cork Regional
Museum**
Western Rd. ⭘ *Jun–Sep: daily
(except Mon & Wed).* 📷 ♿

♙ **Lios-na-gCon Ring Fort**
Tel *023 32565 (after 6pm).* ⭘ *Apr–
Oct: daily.* **www**.liosnagcon.com

Timoleague Abbey ㉑

Road map B6. Co Cork. 🚗 *to
Clonakilty or Courtmacsherry.* ⭘ *daily.*

Timoleague Abbey enjoys a
waterside setting overlooking
an inlet where the Argideen
estuary opens into
Courtmacsherry Bay. Founded
around the late 13th century,
the abbey is a ruined
Franciscan friary. The buildings have been extended at
various times. The earliest
section is the chancel of the
Gothic church. The most
recent addition, the 16th-

century tower, was added by the Franciscan Bishop of Ross. The friary was ransacked by the English in 1642 but much of significance remains, including the church, infirmary, fine lancet windows, refectory and a walled court-yard in the west. There are also sections of cloisters and wine cellars. In keeping with Franciscan tradition, the complex is plain to the point of austerity. Yet such restraint

Lancet window in ruined church at Timoleague Abbey

belied the friars' penchant for high living: the friary prospered on trade in Spanish wines, easily delivered thanks to its position on the then navigable creek.

River Lee ❷

Road Map B6. Co Cork 🚆 🚌 to Cork. 🛈 Cork (021 425 5100).

Carving a course through farm- and woodland to Cork city *(see pp174–7)*, the River Lee begins its journey in the lake of the enchanting **Gougane Barra Park**. The shores of the lake are linked by a causeway to **Holy Island,** where St Finbarr, the patron saint of Cork, founded a monastery. The Feast of St Finbarr, on 25 September,

signals celebrations that climax in a pilgrimage to the island on the following Sunday.

The Lee flows through several Irish-speaking market towns and villages. Some, such as **Ballingeary**, with its fine lakeside views, have good angling. The town is also noted for its Irish language college. Further east, near the town of Inchigeela, stand the ruins of **Carrignacurra Castle**. Further downstream lies the Gearagh, an alluvial stretch of marsh and woods which has been designated a wildlife sanctuary

The river then passes through the Sullane valley, home of the thriving market town of **Macroom**. The hulk of a medieval castle, with its restored entrance, lies just off the main square. In 1654, Cromwell granted the castle to Sir William Penn. His son, who was to found the American state of Pennsylvania, also lived here for a time

Between Macroom and Cork, the Lee Valley passes through a hydroelectric power scheme surrounded by artificial lakes, water meadows and wooded banks. Just outside Cork, on the south bank of the river is **Ballincollig**, home to the fascinating Royal Gunpowder Mills museum *(see p177)*.

Blarney Castle ❷

Road Map B5. Blarney, Co Cork. **Tel** 021 438 5252. 🚌 to Cork. 🚌 to Blarney. ⬜ daily. ⬤ 24 & 25 Dec. 🖼 ♿ grounds only, no charge. 🛈 www.blarneycastle.ie

Visitors from all over the world flock to this ruined castle to see the legendary Blarney Stone. Kissing the stone is a long-standing tradition, intended to confer a magical eloquence. It is set in the wall below the castle battlements and, in order to kiss it, the visitor is grasped by the feet and suspended backwards under the parapet.

Little remains of the castle today except the keep, built in 1446 by Dermot McCarthy. Its design is typical of a 15th-century tower house *(see p20)*. The vaulted first floor was once the Great Hall. To reach the battlements you need to climb the 127 steps to the top of the keep.

The castle grounds offer some attractive walks, including a grove of ancient yew trees and limestone rock formations at Rock Close. **Blarney House**, a Scottish baronial mansion and the residence of the Colthurst family since the 18th century, is not open to the public

A short walk from the castle, Blarney has a pretty village green with welcoming pubs and a number of craft shops. The **Blarney Woollen Mills,** selling quality garments and souvenirs, is well worth a visit.

Battlemented keep and ruined towers of Blarney Castle

Street-by-Street: Kinsale ㉔

Old office sign in Kinsale

For many visitors to Ireland, Kinsale heads the list of places to see. One of the prettiest small towns in Ireland, it has had a long and chequered history. The defeat of the Irish forces and their Spanish allies in the Battle of Kinsale in 1601 signified the end of the old Gaelic order. An important naval base in the 17th and 18th centuries, Kinsale today is a popular yachting centre. It is also famous for the quality of its cuisine – the town's annual Festival of Fine Food attracts food lovers from far and wide. As well as its many wonderful restaurants, the town has pubs and wine bars to cater for all tastes.

Desmond Castle was built around 1500. It is known locally as the "French Prison".

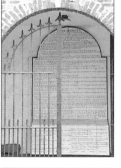

★ **Old Market House**
Incorporating the old courthouse, this museum includes a toll board listing local taxes for 1788.

Market Square

Kieran's Fo House Inn

CHARLES FORT

The star-shaped fort is 3 km (2 miles) east of town in Summercove, but can be reached by taking the signposted coastal walk from the quayside, past the village of Scilly. The fort was built in the 1670s by the English to protect Kinsale harbour against foreign naval forces but, because of its vulnerability to land attack, was taken during the siege of 1690 by William of Orange's army. Nonetheless, it remained in service until 1922 when the British forces left the town and handed it over to the Irish Government. Charles Fort remains one of the finest remaining examples of a star-shaped bastion fort in Europe.

Walls and bastions of Charles Fort

★ **St Multose Church**
This much-altered Norman church is named after an obscure 6th-century saint and marks the centre of the medieval town.

| 0 metres | | 50 |
| 0 yards | | 50 |

KEY

P	Parking
i	Tourist information
– – –	Suggested route

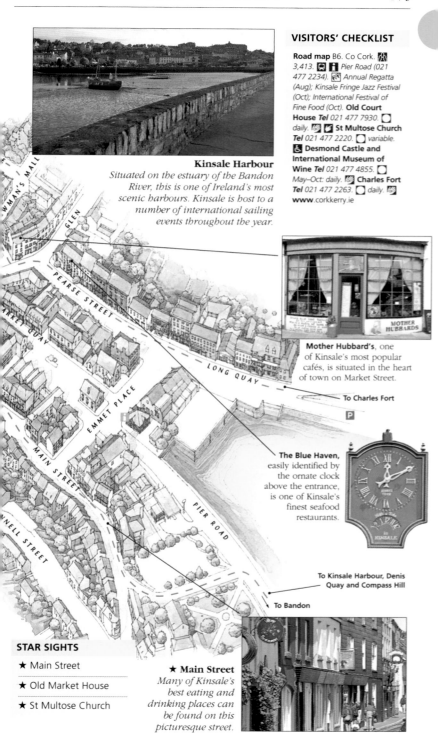

Kinsale Harbour
Situated on the estuary of the Bandon River, this is one of Ireland's most scenic harbours. Kinsale is host to a number of international sailing events throughout the year.

VISITORS' CHECKLIST

Road map B6. Co Cork. 🚌 3,413. 🚉 ℹ️ *Pier Road (021 477 2234).* 🎭 *Annual Regatta (Aug); Kinsale Fringe Jazz Festival (Oct); International Festival of Fine Food (Oct).* **Old Court House** *Tel 021 477 7930.* ⭕ *daily.* 📷 🚻 **St Multose Church** *Tel 021 477 2220.* ⭕ *variable.* ♿ **Desmond Castle and International Museum of Wine** *Tel 021 477 4855.* ⭕ *May–Oct: daily.* 📷 **Charles Fort** *Tel 021 477 2263.* ⭕ *daily.* 📷 **www.**corkkerry.ie

Mother Hubbard's, one of Kinsale's most popular cafés, is situated in the heart of town on Market Street.

To Charles Fort

The Blue Haven, easily identified by the ornate clock above the entrance, is one of Kinsale's finest seafood restaurants.

To Kinsale Harbour, Denis Quay and Compass Hill

To Bandon

STAR SIGHTS

★ Main Street

★ Old Market House

★ St Multose Church

★ Main Street
Many of Kinsale's best eating and drinking places can be found on this picturesque street.

Cork ㉕

Sign outside a Cork pub

Cork city derives its name from the marshy land on the banks of the River Lee – its Irish name *Corcaigh* means marsh – on which St Finbarr founded a monastery around AD 650. The narrow alleys, waterways and Georgian architecture give the city a Continental feel. Since the 19th century, when Cork was a base for the National Fenian movement *(see p43)*, the city has had a reputation for political rebelliousness. Today this mood is reflected in the city's attitude to the arts and its bohemian spirit, much in evidence at the lively October jazz festival.

🔒 St Ann's Shandon

Church St. **Tel** 021 450 5906.
⬜ daily. ● 25 Dec. 📷 ♿ limited.
This famous Cork landmark stands on the hilly slopes of the city, north of the River Lee. Built in 1722, the church has a façade made of limestone on two sides, and of red sandstone on the other two. The steeple is topped by a weather vane in the shape of a salmon. The clock face is known by the locals as the "four-faced liar" because, up until 1986 when it was repaired, each face showed slightly different times. Visitors can climb the tower and, for a small fee, ring the famous Shandon bells.

🦋 The Butter Exchange

O'Connell Square, Shandon. **Tel** 021 430 0600. ⬜ Mar–Oct: 10am–5pm daily. 📷 📺
This museum tells the story of Ireland's most important food export and the world's largest butter market. The exchange opened in 1770 and was where butter was graded before it was exported to the rest of the world. By 1892 it was exporting around 500,000 casks of butter a year.

The exchange shut in 1924. Part of the building was re-opened in the 1980s to house the Shandon Craft Centre. Here visitors can watch craft workers, such as crystal cutters and weavers, at work.

🏛 Crawford Municipal Art Gallery

Emmet Place. **Tel** 021 427 3377.
⬜ 10am–5pm Mon–Sat. 📷 public hols. ♿ 🍴 📺 🛍
www.crawfordartgallery.com
The red brick and limestone building that houses Cork's major art gallery dates back to 1724. Built as the city's original custom house, it became a school of design in 1850. In 1884, a well-known art patron, William Horatio Crawford, extended the building to accommodate studios and sculpture and picture galleries.

The gallery houses some fine examples of late

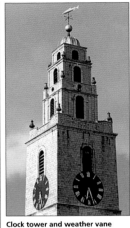

Clock tower and weather vane of St Ann's Shandon

Detail of stained-glass window *The Meeting of St Brendan and the Unhappy Judas* (1911) by Harry Clarke, Crawford Art Gallery

SIGHTS AT A GLANCE

19th- and early 20th-century Irish art including paintings by Jack Yeats. There are also three fine windows by Ireland's foremost stained-glass artist, Harry Clarke (1889–1931).

Another attraction is the small collection by British artists and international works by artists such as Joán Miró and Georges Rouault.

The gallery is well known for its excellent restaurant which is run by the Ballymaloe cookery school *(see p361)*, the exponents of authentic Irish cooking with a modern twist.

Richly decorated apse ceiling of St Finbarr's Cathedral

🔒 St Finbarr's Cathedral

Bishop Street. **Tel** 021 496 3387. ☐ daily. 📷 ♿
www.cathedral.cork.anglican.org
Situated in a quiet part of town, this cathedral is dedicated to the founder and patron saint of the city. Completed in 1870 to the design of William

VISITORS' CHECKLIST

Road map C5. Co Cork.
🏠 136,000. ✈ 6 km (4 miles) S of Cork (021 431 3131).
🚉 Kent Station (021 450 6766).
🚌 Parnell Place (021 450 8188).
ℹ Tourist House, Grand Parade (021 425 5100). 🎷 Cork Jazz Festival (Oct); Cork Film Festival (Oct). **www**.corkkerry.ie

Burges, it is an exuberant triple-spired edifice built in Gothic Revival style, and decorated with stone tracery. Inside, the painted and gilded apse ceiling shows Christ in Glory surrounded by angels. The stained-glass windows below tell the story of Christ's life.

🏛 Cork City Gaol

Convent Avenue, Sunday's Well. **Tel** 021 430 5022. ☐ daily. 📷 📹 ♿
📶 💻 🎧 www.corkcitygaol.com
A pretty, 20-minute walk west of the city centre leads to the restored City Gaol, complete with its furnished cells. An exhibition traces the lives of individual inmates imprisoned here during the 19th and 20th centuries. Conditions were miserable and, for punishment, prisoners were made to run on a human treadmill that would normally be used to grind grain.

The Radio Museum Experience is also housed in this building and chronicles the development of radio in Ireland and across the world.

South Channel of the River Lee, looking towards Parliament Bridge

Exploring Cork

One of Cork's great attractions is that it is a city built on water. Its heart lies on an island between two arms of the River Lee, and many of today's streets were in fact once waterways lined with warehouses and merchants' residences. Although the Dutch canalside appearance has faded, picturesque quays and bridges remain. Steep lanes rise to the north and south of the central island to the city's 19th-century suburbs, offering wonderful views of the city and its fine buildings.

Fitzpatrick's second-hand shop on George's Quay

The Quays

Although the river now plays only a minor part in the city's economy, much of Cork's commercial activity still takes place around the Quays (pronounced "kays" in the Cork accent). The South Mall, which covers an arm of the River Lee, was a waterway until the late 18th century. Boats were once moored at the foot of a series of stone steps, some of which are still intact today. These led to merchants' domestic quarters above. The arches below led to warehouses where goods were unloaded.

Near South Mall is **Parliament Bridge**, built in 1806 to commemorate the Act of Union *(see p42)*. It is an elegant, single-arched bridge which is made mainly from limestone. Designed by William Hargrave, it replaced a bridge on the same site which was damaged by a flood in 1804. A short walk away, on Sullivan's Quay, is the Quay Co-Op, a popular vegetarian restaurant and meeting place.

From Sullivan's Quay an elegant footbridge, built in 1985, crosses the river to the south end of Grand Parade.

Grand Parade and St Patrick's Street

On Grand Parade, also once a waterway, stands the grandiose **National Monument**, recalling the Irish patriots who died between 1798 and 1867. Bishop Lucey Park, off Grand Parade, has a section of city walls and a fine gateway from the old cornmarket. Between St Patrick's Street and Grand Parade is the **English Market**, a covered fruit and vegetable market established in 1610. Bustling St Patrick's Street, the backbone of the city, was a waterway until 1800 when boats were moored under the steps of gracious houses such as the Chateau Bar *(see p347)*. At the top of the street, near Patrick Bridge, is the **Father Mathew Statue**, a monument to the founder of the Temperance Movement.

National Monument, Grand Parade

Paul Street

Noted for its ethnic restaurants, chic bars, bookshops and trendy boutiques, Paul Street is the hub of the liveliest district in town. Just off Paul Street are the busy backstreets of Carey's Lane and French Church Street. In the early 18th century, Huguenots (French Protestants) settled in these streets and set themselves up as butter exporters, brewers and wholesale merchants. This area is Cork's equivalent to Dublin's Temple Bar *(see p78)*.

Shandon Quarter

Crossing the Christy Ring Bridge to Pope's Quay, you will see on your left **St Mary's Dominican Church**, with its portico of Ionic columns topped by a huge pediment. John Redmond Street leads to the northern slopes of Cork, dominated by the spire of St Ann's Shandon *(see p174)* with its fine views of the city. To the northeast lies the lofty Montenotte district, once the epitome of Victorian gentility.

St Finbarr's Quarter

South of the river, rising above the city, this area's distinctive landmark is St Finbarr's Cathedral *(see p175)*. Nearby is the ivy-clad **Elizabeth Fort**, a 16th-century structure which was converted into a prison in 1835 and later a *Garda* (police) station. A short walk to the east lies the **Red Abbey**, a 13th-century relic from an Augustinian abbey – the oldest building in Cork.

Selling fruit and vegetables at the English Market

Environs

Some beautiful countryside surrounds the city of Cork, especially along the lush valley of the River Lee *(see p171)*. The landscape of East Cork is much gentler than the wild, rocky coastline of West Cork and County Kerry, and the land is much more fertile. Many local attractions make good day trips and there are also plenty of opportunities for outdoor activities such as walking, riding and fishing.

♣ Blackrock Castle
Blackrock. ● *to the public.*
On the banks of the River Lee 1.5 km (1 mile) downstream from the city centre stands Blackrock Castle. Originally built in 1582 by Lord Mountjoy as a harbour fortification, the castle was destroyed by fire in 1827. It was rebuilt in 1830 to the design of architects J and GR Pain. The castle was recently bought by a private company and is no longer open to the public. A little further south at Carrigtwohill, near Fota Wildlife Park *(see pp178–9)*, is the 13th-century Barryscourt Castle, with its two intact towers.

Blackrock Castle standing on the banks of the River Lee

♦ Barryscourt Castle
Carrigtwohill, Co Cork. **Tel** *021 488 2218.* ○ *Jun–Sept: 10am–6pm daily.* 📷 ♿
This castle was the seat of the Barry family from the 12th to 17th centuries. The present building has been extensively restored by the office of public works and period fittings and furniture are gradually being reinstated. It is a fine example of a 15th century tower house

The 15th century tower house of Barryscourt Castle

with 16th century additions and alterations. It is roughly rectangular with a four-storey tower house occupying the south-west corner. What makes Barryscourt stand out from most other tower house complexes is the 50m long hall, which occupies the western section of the castle. Both the Great Hall and the Main Hall are open to the public and the keep houses an exhibition on the arts in Ireland from 1100 to 1600. The orchard has also been restored to an original 16th century design.

♣ Desmond Castle
Kinsale. **Tel** *021 477855.* ○ *Easter–Oct: 10am–6pm daily.* 📷 🌐 www.desmondcastle.ie
Situated some 16 km (10 miles) south of Cork City, Desmond Castle was built by Maurice Bacach Fitzgerald, the ninth Earl of Desmond, in around 1500. A good example of an urban tower house, the castle consists of a keep with storehouses to the rear. It has spent time as an ordnance store, workhouse, customs house and prison. In 1938 it was declared a national monument.
In 1997 a joint project between the Irish government's Heritage Service and a number of local historians and restau-ranteurs saw the **International Museum of Wine** being set up in the castle.

River Blackwater ㉖

Road Map B5. Co Cork. 🚌 *to Mallow.* 🚌 *to Fermoy, Mallow or Kanturk.*

The second longest river in Ireland after the Shannon *(see p185)*, the Blackwater rises in high bogland in County Kerry. It then flows eastwards through County Cork until it reaches Cappoquin, County Waterford, where it changes course south through wooded sandstone gorges to the sea at Youghal *(see p179)*. Much of the valley is wooded, a reminder that the entire area was forested until the 17th century. The river passes some magnificent country houses and pastoral views. However, the region is best known for its fishing – the Blackwater's tributaries are filled with fine brown trout.
The best way to see the valley is to take the scenic Blackwater Valley Drive from Youghal to Mallow. The route passes through **Fermoy**, a town founded by Scottish merchant John Anderson in 1789. Angling is the town's main appeal, especially for roach, rudd, perch and pike. Further west is **Mallow**, a prosperous town noted for its fishing, golf and horse racing, and a good base for tours of the area. Detours along the tributaries include **Kanturk**, a pleasant market town with a castle, on the River Allow.

Weirs and bridge at Fermoy on the River Blackwater

Cobh ㉗

Road map C6. Co Cork. 🚇 *12,000.*
🚉 ℹ️ *Old Yacht Club (021 4813612).*
www.cobhharbourchamber.ie

Cobh (pronounced "cove")
lies on Great Island, one of
the three islands in Cork
harbour which are now linked
by causeways. The Victorian
seafront has rows of steeply
terraced houses overlooked
by **St Colman's**, an imposing
Gothic Revival cathedral.

Following a visit by Queen
Victoria in 1849, Cobh was
renamed Queenstown but
reverted to its original name
in 1921. The town has one of
the world's largest natural harbours, hence its rise to prominence as a naval base in the
18th century. It was also a
major port for merchant ships
and the main port from which
Irish emigrants left for America.

Cobh was also a port of call
for luxury passenger liners. In
1838, the *Sirius* made the first
transatlantic crossing under
steam power from here. Cobh
was also the last stop for the
Titanic, before its doomed
Atlantic crossing in 1912.
Three years later,
the *Lusitania* was
torpedoed and
sunk by a German
submarine just
off Kinsale *(see
pp172–3)*, south-
west of Cobh. A
memorial on the
promenade is
dedicated to all
those who died
in the attack.

IRISH EMIGRATION

Between 1848 and 1950 almost six million people
emigrated from Ireland – two and a half million of them
leaving from Cobh. The famine years of 1844–8 *(see p219)*
triggered mass emigration as the impoverished made
horrific transatlantic journeys in cramped, insanitary
conditions. Many headed for the United States and Canada,
and a few risked the long journey to Australia. Up until the
early 20th century, emigrants waiting to board the ships
were a familiar sight in Cobh. However, by the 1930s world
recession and immigration restrictions in the United States
and Canada led to a fall in the numbers leaving Ireland.

19th-century engraving of emigrants gathering in Cobh harbour

🏛 The Queenstown Story
Cobh Heritage Centre. **Tel** *021 481
3591.* 🕐 *daily.* ⬤ *22 Dec–1 Jan.*
📷 🚻 ♿ 🏪
Housed in a Victorian railway
station, *The Queenstown Story*
is an exhibition detailing the
town's marine history. Exhibits
and audiovisual displays recall
the part Cobh played in Irish
emigration and the transportation of convicts. Between 1791
and 1853, 40,000 convicts
were sent to Australian penal
colonies in notorious "coffin
ships"; many prisoners
were also kept

in floating jails in Cork Harbour.
The exhibition also documents
Cobh's role as a port of call for
transatlantic liners.

Environs
North of Cobh is Fota Island,
with **Fota House and Gardens**.
This glorious Regency mansion,
surrounded by landscaped
gardens, has a 19th-century
arboretum with rare trees and
shrubs from Asia, South
America, and North America.

Also on the island, the **Fota
Wildlife Park** concentrates on
breeding and reintroducing

Cobh harbour with the steeple of St Colman's rising above the town

animals to their natural habitat. The white-tailed sea eagle is one native species that has been saved from extinction in Ireland. The park boasts over 70 species, including giraffe, flamingo, and zebra. A train links the sections of the park.

🏛 **Fota House and Gardens**
Carrigtwohill. **Tel** 021 481 5543.
⬜ daily. 🖼 🔲 🔲

🦒 **Fota Wildlife Park**
Carrigtwohill. **Tel** 021 481 2678.
⬜ daily. 🖼 ♿ 🍽 🔲

Old Midleton Distillery ㉘

Road map C5. Distillery Walk, Midleton, Co Cork.
Tel 021 461 3594. 🚌 to Midleton.
⬜ daily. ⬤ 24 Dec–2 Jan. 🖼 ♿
🔲 🛍 🍽 in summer only.
www.whiskeytours.ie

A sensitively restored 18th-century distillery, Old Midleton Distillery is part of the vast Irish Distillers group at Midleton. Bushmills *(see p266)* is the oldest distillery in Ireland but Midleton is the largest, with a series of distilleries each producing a different whiskey, including Jameson.

The story of Irish whiskey is presented through audiovisual displays, working models and authentic machinery. A tour of the old distillery takes in the mills, maltings, still-houses, kilns, granaries and warehouses. Visitors can take part in whiskey tasting and try to distinguish between various brands of Irish, Scotch and bourbon whiskies. Highlights of the visit include the world's largest pot still, with a capacity of over 30,000 gallons, and the working water wheel.

Clock tower on the main street of Youghal

Youghal ㉙

Road map C5. Co Cork. 🏘 7,500.
🚌 🚉 🛈 *Market House, Market Square (024 20170).* **www**.corkkerry.ie

Youghal (pronounced "yawl") is a historic walled town and thriving fishing port. The town was granted to Sir Walter Raleigh by Queen Elizabeth I but later sold to the Earl of Cork. In Cromwellian times, Youghal became a closed borough – an English Protestant garrison town.

The picturesque, four-storey **Clock tower** was originally the city gate, but was recast as a prison. Steep steps beside the tower lead up to a well-preserved section of the medieval town wall and fine views across the Blackwater estuary. Through the tower, in the sombre North Main Street, is the **Red House**, a Dutch mansion built in 1710. Virtually next door are some grim Elizabethan almshouses and, on the far side of the road, a 15th-century tower, known as **Tynte's Castle**.

Nestling in the town walls opposite is **Myrtle Grove** (closed to the public), one of the few unfortified Tudor manor houses to survive in Ireland. It has a triple-gabled façade and exquisite interior oak panelling. Just uphill is the Gothic **Church of St Mary**. Inside are tomb effigies and stained-glass windows depicting the coats of arms of local families.

Grain truck (c.1940) at the Jameson Heritage Centre

THE LOWER SHANNON

CLARE · LIMERICK · TIPPERARY

*I*n the three counties which flank the lower reaches of the Shannon, Ireland's longest river, the scenery ranges from the rolling farmland of Tipperary to the eerie limestone plateau of the Burren. The Shannon's bustling riverside resorts draw many visitors, and there are medieval strongholds and atmospheric towns of great historic interest. The region also boasts a vibrant music scene.

The River Shannon has long made this area an attractive prospect for settlers. There are several important Stone Age sites, including a major settlement by Lough Gur. From the 5th century, the region lay at the heart of Munster, one of Ireland's four Celtic provinces. The Rock of Cashel, a remarkable fortified abbey in county Tipperary, was the seat of the Kings of Munster for more than 700 years.

The Vikings penetrated the Shannon in the 10th century, but Gaelic clans put up stern resistance. During the Norman period, the chieftains of these clans built Bunratty Castle and other fortresses that were impressive enough to rival the strongholds erected by the Anglo-Irish dynasties. Foremost among the latter families were the Butlers, the Earls of Ormonde, who held much land in Tipperary, and the Fitzgeralds, the main landowners in the Limerick area. From the Middle Ages, Limerick was often at the centre of events in the Lower Shannon. In 1691, the army of William of Orange laid siege to the town, heralding the Treaty of Limerick that triggered the Catholic nobility's departure for Europe – the so-called "Flight of the Wild Geese".

Lush grassland, which has turned the Lower Shannon into prime dairy country, is typical of the region. In places this gives way to picturesque glens and mountains, such as the Galty range in southern Tipperary. The region's most dramatic scenery, however, is found along the coast of Clare, a county otherwise best known for its thriving traditional music scene.

Ruins of Dysert O'Dea monastery in County Clare with an outstanding 12th-century High Cross

◁ Traditional musicians playing at Feakle in County Clare

Exploring the Lower Shannon

The central location of Limerick city makes it a natural focus for visitors to the region. However, there are many charming towns that make pleasanter bases, such as Adare, Cashel and also Killaloe, which is well placed for exploring the River Shannon. Most places of interest in Tipperary lie in the southern part of the county, where historic towns such as Clonmel and Cahir overlook the River Suir. By contrast, County Clare has few towns of any size, though it boasts the major attraction of Bunratty Castle. Beyond Ennis, the landscape becomes steadily bleaker until you reach the Burren.

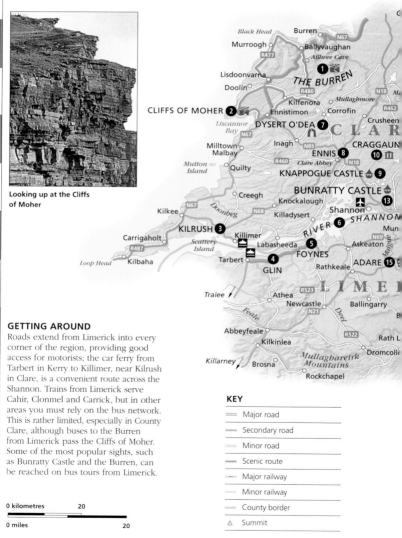

Looking up at the Cliffs of Moher

GETTING AROUND

Roads extend from Limerick into every corner of the region, providing good access for motorists; the car ferry from Tarbert in Kerry to Killimer, near Kilrush in Clare, is a convenient route across the Shannon. Trains from Limerick serve Cahir, Clonmel and Carrick, but in other areas you must rely on the bus network. This is rather limited, especially in County Clare, although buses to the Burren from Limerick pass the Cliffs of Moher. Some of the most popular sights, such as Bunratty Castle and the Burren, can be reached on bus tours from Limerick.

0 kilometres   20

0 miles   20

KEY

═══	Major road
═══	Secondary road
⋯⋯	Minor road
───	Scenic route
⤳	Major railway
───	Minor railway
───	County border
△	Summit

Boats sailing on Lough Derg near Mountshannon

Painted pub sign in Cashel

Looking south along the Cliffs of Moher, one of the most dramatic stretches of Ireland's west coast

The Burren ❶

See pp186–8.

Cliffs of Moher ❷

Road map B4. Co Clare 🚗 *from Ennis & Limerick.* **Visitors' Centre** *Tel 061 360788.* ⬤ *daily.* ⬤ *21–27 Dec.* 📷 🏛 **O'Brien's Tower** *Tel 061 360788.* ⬤ *Mar–Oct: daily.* 📷 **www**.shannonheritage.com

Even when shrouded in mist or buffeted by Atlantic gales, the Cliffs of Moher are breathtaking, rising to a height of 200 m (650 ft) out of the sea and extending for 8 km (5 miles). The sheer rock face, with its layers of black shale and sandstone, provides sheltered ledges where guillemots and other sea birds nest.

Well-worn paths lead along the cliffs. From the **Visitors' Centre**, 5 km (3 miles) northwest of Liscannor, you can walk south to **Hag's Head** in an hour. To the north, there is a three-hour coastal walk between **O'Brien's Tower** – a viewing point built for Victorian tourists – and Fisherstreet near **Doolin** *(see p188).*

Kilrush ❸

Road map B4. Co Clare. 👥 *2,800.* 🚌 ℹ *Heritage Centre, Market House (065 905 1577).* ⬤ *May–Sep.*

With a new marina and the promotion of Kilrush as a heritage town, the fortunes of this 18th-century estate town have been greatly revived. It now has a **Heritage Centre**, where an exhibition covers the Great Famine *(see p219)* and the landlord evictions of 1888

(see pp42–3). A well-marked walking trail around the town's historic sights also starts here.

Environs
From Kilrush, boats take visitors dolphin-spotting or to nearby **Scattery Island**, site of a medieval monastery. The ruins include five churches and one of the tallest round towers in the country.

The **Loop Head Drive** is a 27-km (17-mile) route which begins at the resort of Kilkee, west of Kilrush. It winds south past dramatic coastal scenery to Loop Head, from where you can enjoy superb views.

Glin ❹

Road map B5. Co Limerick. 👥 *600.* 🚌 *from Limerick.*

This charming village on the banks of the Shannon is the seat of the Knights of Glin, a branch of the Fitzgeralds who have lived in the district for seven centuries. Their first medieval castle is a ruin, but west of the village stands their

Rare 18th-century double "flying" staircase in Glin Castle

newer home, **Glin Castle**. Built in 1780, the manor succumbed to the vogue for Gothic romance in the 1820s, when it acquired battlements and gingerbread lodges. There is fine stuccowork and 18th-century furniture inside. It is now run as a hotel *(see p308).*

♣ **Glin Castle**
Tel 068 34173. ⬤ *by appt.* 📷 🏛 *obligatory.* **www**.glincastle.com

Foynes ❺

Road map B5. Co Limerick. 👥 *650.* 🚌 *from Limerick.*

Foynes enjoyed short-lived fame in the 1930s and 1940s as the eastern terminus of the first airline passenger route across the Atlantic. **Foynes Flying Boat Museum** presents a detailed history of the seaplane service. The original Radio and Weather Room and a 1940s-style tea room are particularly evocative of the era.

🏛 **Foynes Flying Boat Museum**
Aras Ide, Foynes. *Tel 069 65416.* ⬤ *Apr–Oct: daily.* 📷 📷 🏛 ♿

Environs
The historic town of **Askeaton**, 11 km (7 miles) east of Foynes, has a castle and Franciscan friary founded by the Fitzgeralds. The friary is particularly interesting, with a 15th-century cloister of black marble. In Rathkeale, 8 km (5 miles) south, **Castle Matrix** is a restored 15th-century tower house renowned for the fine library in the Great Hall.

♣ **Castle Matrix**
Rathkeale. *Tel 069 64284.* ⬤ *May–Sep: Sat–Thu.* 📷

Fishing on Lough Derg, the largest of the lakes on the Shannon

River Shannon ❻

Road map B4, C4, C3. 🚆 to Limerick or Athlone. 🚌 to Carrick-on-Shannon, Athlone or Limerick. ℹ️ Arthur's Quay, Limerick (061 317522). **www**.shannonregiontourism.ie

The Shannon is the longest river in Ireland, rising in County Cavan and meandering down to the Atlantic. Flowing through the heart of the island, it has traditionally marked the border between the provinces of Leinster and Connaught. In medieval times, castles guarded the major fords from Limerick to Portumna, and numerous monasteries were built along the riverbanks, including the celebrated Clonmacnoise (see pp250–51). Work began on the Shannon navigation system in the 1750s, but it fell into disuse with the advent of the railways. It has since been revived with the Shannon–Erne Waterway the latest stretch to be restored (see p235).

There are subtle changes of landscape along the length of the river. South of **Lough Allen**, the countryside is covered with the drumlins or low hills typical of the northern Midlands. Towards **Lough Ree**, islands stud the river in an area of ecological importance which is home to otters, geese, grey herons and whooper swans. Continuing south beyond **Athlone** (see p249), the river flows through flood plains and bog before reaching **Lough**

EXPLORING THE SHANNON

Carrick-on-Shannon is the main centre for boating on the upper reaches of the river, while Portumna and the atmospheric ports of Mountshannon and Killaloe are the principal bases for exploring Lough Derg.

Cruiser on the Shannon

KEY

ℹ️ Tourist information

🚢 Cruiser hire

🚤 Water-bus tour

Grey heron on the Shannon

Derg, the biggest of the lakes on the Shannon. The scenery is more dramatic here, with the lough's southern end edged by wooded mountains. From **Killaloe** (see p190), the river gains speed on its rush towards **Limerick** (see p191) and the sea. The mudflats of the Shannon estuary attract a great variety of birdlife. The port of **Carrick-on-Shannon** (see p235) is the cruising centre of Ireland, but there are bases all along the river – especially around Lough Derg, which is the lake most geared to boating. Water-buses connect most ports south of Athlone. If you hire a cruiser, enquire about the weather conditions before setting out, particularly on Loughs Ree and Derg, which are very exposed. The calm stretch from **Portumna** (see p213) to Athlone is easier for inexperienced sailors.

Walkers can enjoy the Lough Derg Way, a signposted route around the lake. The woods by **Lough Key** (see p219) also provide good walking territory.

Athlone and the southern reaches of Lough Ree

The Burren **❶**

The word Burren derives from *boireann*, which means "rocky land" in Gaelic – an apt name for this vast limestone plateau in northwest County Clare. In the 1640s, Cromwell's surveyor described it as "a savage land, yielding neither water enough to drown a man, nor tree to hang him, nor soil enough to bury". Few trees manage to grow in this desolate place, yet other plants thrive.

Dark red helleborine

The Burren is a unique botanical environment in which Mediterranean and alpine plants rare to Ireland grow side by side. From May to August, an astonishing array of flowers adds splashes of colour to the austere landscape. These plants grow most abundantly around the region's shallow lakes and pastures, but they also take root in the crevices of the limestone pavements which are the most striking geological feature of the rocky plateau. In the southern part of the Burren, limestone gives way to the black shale and sandstone that form the dramatic Cliffs of Moher *(see p184).*

Grazing in the Burren
A quirk in the local climate means that, in winter, the hills are warmer than the valleys – hence the unusual practice in the Burren of letting cattle graze on high ground in winter.

FAUNA OF THE BURREN

The Burren is one of the best places in Ireland for butterflies, with 28 species found in the area. The birdlife is also varied. Sky-larks and cuckoos are common on the hills and in the meadows, while the coast is a good place for razorbills, guillemots, puffins and other sea birds. Mammals are harder to spot. Badgers, foxes and stoats live here, but you are much more likely to see a herd of shaggy-coated wild goats or an Irish hare.

The pearl-bordered fritillary, *one of a number of fritillaries found in the Burren, can be seen in no other part of Ireland.*

An Irish hare's *white and brown winter coat turns to reddish-brown in the summer.*

Whooper swans *from Iceland flock to the wetlands of the Burren in winter.*

The hooded crow *is easily identified by its grey and black plumage.*

Turloughs are shallow lakes which are dry in summer but flood in winter, when they attract wildfowl and waders.

Spring gentian

Bloody Cranesbill
This striking plant, common in the Burren, is a member of the geranium family. It flowers in June.

Limestone Pavement
Glaciation and wind and rain erosion have formed limestone pavements with deep crevices known as "grykes". The porous rock is easily penetrated by rainwater, which has gouged out an extensive cave system beneath the rocky plateau.

Hawthorn is one of the few trees which manages to grow in the Burren, although the plants are usually twisted and stunted.

Exposed layers of limestone

Stone-built Burren cottage

Dry-stone wall

Limestone slabs, or "clints"

The hoary rock rose is one of several rare plants to grow abundantly in the Burren.

Holly trees can gain a foothold in the pavement, but grazing and wind restrict their growth.

Maidenhair fern thrives in the damp crevices of the Burren.

Mountain Avens
Normally a mountain plant, this flower grows here at sea level.

Exploring the Burren

If you are interested in the unique geology and natural history of the Burren, head for **Mullaghmore**, to the south-east of the area. This is one of the wildest parts of the plateau and reaches a height of 191 m (626 ft), with some of the best limestone pave-ments in the area.

A good place to begin a tour of the more accessible parts of the Burren is at the **Cliffs of Moher** *(see p184)*. From here it is a short drive north to **Doolin**, near the port for the Aran Islands *(see pp214–15)*. This rather spread-out village is renowned for its traditional music; Gus O'Connor's pub *(see p348)* acts as a focus for music-lovers in the area. The coastal road runs north from Doolin to a desolate limestone outcrop at **Black Head**, while turning inland you will reach **Lisdoonvarna**. The Victorians developed the town as a spa, but it is now most renowned for its colourful pubs and its matchmaking festival *(see p50)*.

Music shop in Doolin

To the north along the N67 lies **Ballyvaughan**, a fishing village dotted with slate-roofed cottages and busy with tourists in summer. It is well placed for reaching a number of sights. Nearby **Bishop's Quarter** has a sheltered beach with glorious views across a lagoon to-wards Galway Bay. **Aillwee Cave**, to the south, is just one of thousands of caves in the Burren, but is the only one open to the public. It consists of a tunnel which opens into a series of caverns. In the first, known as Bear Haven, the remains of hibernation pits used by bears are still visible.

Ruined forts and castles and numerous prehistoric sites dot the landscape. Just west of Aillwee Cave is **Cahermore Stone Fort**, with a lintelled doorway, and to the south

Gleninsheen Wedge Tomb, a style of grave which marks the transition between Stone and Bronze Age cultures. The more famous **Poulnabrone Dolmen** nearby is a striking portal tomb dating back to 2500–2000 BC. Continuing south you reach the ghostly shell of **Leamaneagh Castle**, a 17th-century mansion that incorporates an earlier tower house built by the O'Briens.

On the southern fringe of the Burren lies **Kilfenora**, a Catholic diocese which, by a historical quirk, has the Pope for its bishop. The village's modest cathedral, one of many 12th-century churches in the Burren, has a roofless chancel with finely sculpted capitals. Kilfenora, however, is more famous for its High Crosses: there are several in the graveyard. Best preserved is the Doorty Cross, with a carving of a bishop and two other clerics on the east face. Next door, the refurbished **Burren Centre** offers an excellent multi-dimensional exhibition giving information on the geology and fauna of the area and man's impact on the landscape.

Carved capital in Kilfenora Cathedral

🏕 **Aillwee Cave**
Ballyvaughan. **Tel** *06570 77036.*
⏱ *daily.* 🅿 ✔ 🚻 🏠

🏛 **Burren Centre**
Kilfenora. **Tel** *06570 88030.*
⏱ *Mar–Oct: daily.* 🅿 ♿ 🚻 🏠
www.theburrencentre.ie

Poulnabrone Dolmen in the heart of the Burren's limestone plateau

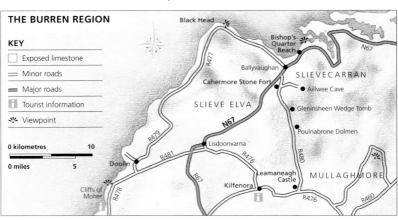

THE BURREN REGION

KEY

☐ Exposed limestone
═ Minor roads
▬ Major roads
ℹ Tourist information
🔆 Viewpoint

| 0 kilometres | 10 |
| 0 miles | 5 |

Black Head
Bishop's Quarter Beach
N67
R477
Ballyvaughan
SLIEVECARRAN
Cahermore Stone Fort
Aillwee Cave
SLIEVE ELVA
Gleninsheen Wedge Tomb
R479
N67
Poulnabrone Dolmen
R481
Lisdoonvarna
R476
R480
Doolin
R67
Leamaneagh Castle
MULLAGHMORE
Cliffs of Moher
R478
Kilfenora
R476
R460

Dysert O'Dea ❼

Road map 4 B. Corrofin, Co Clare. 🚌 *from Ennis.* **Tel** *06568 37401.* ⬜ *May–Sep: daily.* 🖳

Dysert O'Dea castle stands on a rocky outcrop 9 km (6 miles) north of Ennis. This tower house, erected in the 15th century, is home to the **Archaeology Centre**, which includes a small museum and also marks the start of a trail around nearby historic sights. A map of the path, designed for both walkers and cyclists, is available from the tea room.

Across a field from the castle is a monastic site said to have been founded by the obscure St Tola in the 8th century. The ruins are overgrown and rather worn, but the Romanesque carving above one doorway is still clear, and there is also an impressive 12th-century High Cross, with a bishop sculpted on the east side *(see p243)*.

Further south, the trail leads past the remains of two stone forts, a ruined castle and the site of a 14th-century battle.

Ennis ❽

Road map 4B. Co Clare. 🏘 *25,000.* 🚌 ❶ *Clare Rd (06568 28366).* **www.**shannonregiontourism.ie

Clare's county town, on the banks of the River Fergus, is a charming place with winding lanes that recall Ennis's medieval beginnings. The town is also renowned for its painted shopfronts and folk music festivals (known as *fleadh* in Gaelic). It abounds in "singing" pubs and traditional music shops.

Colourful exterior of Michael Kerins pub in Ennis

Ennis can trace its origins to the 13th century and to the O'Briens, Kings of Thomond, who were the area's feudal overlords in the Middle Ages. The Franciscan friary that they founded here in the 1240s is now the town's main attraction. Dating from the 14th and 15th centuries, the ruined **Ennis Friary** is famous for its rich carvings and decorated tombs in the chancel – above all the 15th-century MacMahon tomb with its finely carved alabaster panels. Extensive conservation work is ongoing here.

Next door to the friary is a delightful 17th-century house, now Cruise's restaurant, and on the corner of nearby Francis Street stands the Queen's Hotel – featured in James Joyce's *Ulysses*. To the south, O'Connell Square has a *monument* to Daniel O'Connell *(see p42)*, who was elected MP for Clare in 1828. He also gave his name to the town's main street, where, among the pubs and shops, you can spot a medieval tower, a Jacobean chimney stack and an 18th-century arch.

🏰 **Ennis Friary**
Abbey St. **Tel** *06568 29100.* ⬜ *May–Oct: daily.* 🖾 ♿

Environs
The area around Ennis is rich in monastic ruins. Just 3 km (2 miles) south of the town is **Clare Abbey**, an Augustinian foundation set up by the O'Briens in 1189 but dating mainly from the 1400s.

Quin Franciscan Friary, set in meadows 13 km (8 miles) southeast of Ennis, was also built in the 15th century, and incorporates the romantic ruins of a Norman castle. The well-preserved cloister is one of the finest of its kind in Ireland.

Knappogue Castle ❾

Road map 4B. Quin, Co Clare. **Tel** *061 360788.* 🚌 *to Ennis.* ⬜ *May– Sep; 9:30am–5pm (last adm 4:15pm).* 🖾 ❶ ♿ *limited.* **www.**shannonheritage.com

A powerful local clan called the MacNamaras erected Knappogue Castle in 1467. Apart from a ten-year spell in Cromwellian times, it stayed in their hands until 1815. During the War of Independence *(see pp44–5)*, the castle was used by the revolutionary forces.

Knappogue has been well restored and is one of Ireland's most charmingly furnished castles. The central tower house is original, but the rest is Neo-Gothic. Inside are fine Elizabethan fireplaces and linenfold wood panelling.

Medieval banquets are staged in the castle *(see p360)*, with storytelling and singing.

Finely carved Romanesque doorway at Dysert O'Dea

Craggaunowen ❿

Road map B4. Kilmurry, Co Clare. 🚗 🚌 to Ennis. **Tel** 061 360788. ⏰ mid Apr–mid Oct: 10am–6pm daily. 🍴 ♿ 📷 🏪 www.shannonheritage.com

The Craggaunowen Project, known as "Craggaunowen: the Living Past" and designed to bring Bronze Age and Celtic culture to life, is a shining example of a recreated pre-historic site. The centre was created in the grounds of Craggaunowen Castle in the 1960s by John Hunt, a noted archaeologist who had been inspired by his excavations at Lough Gur (see p194). The castle's tower house contains bronzes and other objects from Hunt's archaeological collection, the rest of which can be seen in Limerick.

In summer, people in costume act out particular trades, such as spinning or potting, or serve as guides. There is a description of how communities lived in the ring fort, a typical early Christian homestead. You can also see meat being prepared in the *fulacht fiadh*, a traditional hunter's cooking hole.

The complex includes part of a *togher*, an original Iron Age timber road that was discovered in Longford. The most eye-catching sight, however, is the crannog (see p33), a man-made island enclosing wattle and daub houses – a style of defensive homestead that survived to the early 1600s.

Another exhibit is a leather-hulled boat built in the 1970s by Tim Severin. He used it to

A woman in peasant costume spinning wool at Craggaunowen

retrace the route which legend says St Brendan took in a similar vessel across the Atlantic in the 6th century (see p27).

Mountshannon ⓫

Road map C4. Co Clare. 👥 240. 🚤 to Holy Island. **Tel** 061 921351.

This pretty village on the banks of Lough Derg (see p185) seems to have its back turned to the lake but is nevertheless a major angling centre. Solid 18th-century stone houses and churches cluster around the harbour, together with some good pubs.

Mountshannon is well placed for exploring the lake's western shores, with plenty of scope for walks and bicycle rides. Fishing boats are available for hire, and in summer you can go by boat to **Holy Island**, the site of a monastery founded in the 7th century. The ruins include four chapels and a graveyard of medieval tombs.

Killaloe ⓬

Road map C4. Co Clare. 👥 950. 🚗 ℹ️ May–Sep: Brian Ború Heritage Centre, The Bridge (061 376866). www.killaloe.ie

Killaloe, birthplace of Brian Ború (940–1014), High King of Ireland (see p34), lies close to where the Shannon emerges from Lough Derg, and is the lake's most prosperous pleasure port. A 17th-century bridge separates Killaloe from its twin town of Ballina on the opposite bank. Ballina has better pubs, such as Goosers on the waterfront (see p349), but Killaloe is the main boating centre (see p365) and offers more of historical interest.

Killaloe's grandest building is **St Flannan's Cathedral**, built around 1182. Its richly carved Romanesque doorway was once part of an earlier chapel. The church also has an ancient Ogham Stone (see p34), unusual because the inscription is carved in both Nordic runes and Ogham. Outside stands St Flannan's Oratory, built around the same time as the cathedral.

The **Brian Ború Heritage Centre**, in a converted boat-house on the bridge, has an exhibition about the Shannon and Lough Derg, and is the starting point for a marked walk along sections of the old Killaloe Canal. You can also arrange for local fishermen to take you out on the lake.

Bicycle hire and boat trips at Mountshannon

Bunratty Castle ⓭

See pp192–3.

Limerick ⑭

Road map B4. Co Limerick. 🎿
90,000. 🚆 *Shannon.* 🚌 📧 ℹ️
Arthur's Quay (061 317522). 🚐 *Sat.*
www.shannonregiontourism.ie

The third largest city in the
Republic, Limerick was
founded by the Vikings. Given
its strategic point on the River
Shannon, it thrived under the
Normans, but later bore the
brunt of English oppression.
After the Battle of the Boyne
(see p244), the rump of the
defeated Jacobite army with-
drew here. The siege which
followed has entered Irish
folklore as a heroic
defeat, sealed by
the Treaty of
Limerick in 1691.
English treachery
in reneging on
most of the terms
of the treaty still
rankles. It is no
coincidence that
Catholicism and
nationalism are
strong in the city.
Limerick has a
reputation for high
unemployment, crime and
general neglect. However, it is
fast acquiring a new image as
a commercial city, revitalized
by new industries and
restoration projects. Even so,
visitors may still have to dig a
little to appreciate its charm.

The city centre consists of
three historic districts. King's
Island was the first area to be
settled by the Vikings and was
later the heart of the medieval
city, when it was known as
Englishtown. It boasts
Limerick's two main landmarks,
King John's Castle and St Mary's
Cathedral. The old Irishtown,
south of the Abbey River, has
its fair share of drab houses
and shops, but also has its own

historic buildings and a pocket
of Georgian elegance in St
John's Square. Near here is
Limerick's most conspicuous
sight, St John's Cathedral, built
in 1861. Its 85-m (280-ft) spire
is the tallest in the country.

The most pleasant part of
Limerick in which to stroll is
Newtown Pery – a grid of
gracious Georgian terraces
focused on O'Connell Street.

♟ King John's Castle
Nicholas St. *Tel* 061 411201. ⬜
daily. ⬤ *Good Fri, Dec 24–26.* 🎫 ♿
www.shannonheritage.com
Founded by King John in 1200,
not long after the Normans
arrived, this
imposing castle
has five drum
towers and solid
curtain walls.
Inside, the
castle is less
interesting
architecturally,
but it houses a
good audio-
visual exhibition
on the history of
the city. Ongoing
excavations have
unearthed pots and jewellery,
and you can also see Viking
houses and later fortifications.
One of the most dramatic artifacts is a soldier's diary recording the Siege of Limerick.

Across the nearby Thomond
Bridge, the Treaty Stone marks
the spot where the Treaty of
Limerick was signed in 1691.

🛡 St Mary's Cathedral
Bridge Street. *Tel* 061 310293.
⬜ *9:30am–4:30pm Mon–Fri, for
services only Sun.*
Built in 1172, this is the oldest
structure in the city. Except for
a fine Romanesque doorway
and the nave, however, little
remains of the early church.
The 15th-century misericords

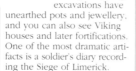

**Carved misericord in
St Mary's Cathedral**

**Characteristic Georgian doorway in
St John's Square**

in the choir stalls are the pride
of St Mary's, with superb
carvings in black oak of angels,
griffins and other creatures
both real and imaginary.

Nearby, George's Quay is a
pleasant street with restaurants
and outdoor cafés and good
views across the river.

🏛 Hunt Museum
Rutland St. *Tel* 061 312833. ⬜ *10am–
5pm Mon–Sat, 2pm–5pm Sun.* 🎫 🍴
📷 ♿ **www**.huntmuseum.com
Located in the Old Customs
House, this fine museum has
one of the greatest collections
of antiquities in Ireland,
gathered by the archaeologist
John Hunt. The best exhibits,
dating from the Bronze Age,
include gold jewellery and
a magnificent shield. Among
the other artifacts are Celtic
brooches and the 9th-century
Antrim Cross.

🏛 Limerick Museum
Nicholas St. *Tel* 061 417826. ⬜
10am–7pm Tue–Sat. ⬤ *for lunch,
public hols & 7 days at Christmas.* ♿
www.limerickcity.ie
The city museum is in a fine
19th-century granary building.
Limerick's history and traditions from lace-making to
rugby are on display.

View of Limerick showing Thomond Bridge across the Shannon and King John's Castle

Bunratty Castle & Folk Park ⓭

This formidable castle, built in the 15th century, is one of Ireland's major tourist attractions. Its most important residents were the O'Briens, Earls of Thomond, who lived here from around 1500 until the 1640s. The present interior looks much as it did under the so-called "Great Earl", who died in 1624. Abandoned in the 19th century, the castle was derelict when Lord Gort bought it in the 1950s, but it has been beautifully restored to its original state. The adjacent Folk Park reflects 19th century rural and village life. Bunratty is also famous for its splendid medieval banquets.

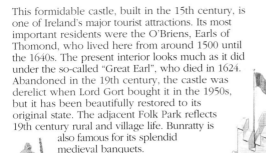

The chimney is a replica in wood of the stone original. It provided a vent for the smoke given off by the fire in the centre of the Great Hall.

★ **North Solar**
This 17th-century German chandelier is the most curious feature in the Great Earl's private apartments. The term "solar" was used during the Middle Ages to describe an upper chamber.

The Murder Hole was designed for pouring boiling water or pitch on to the heads of attackers.

North Front
Bunratty Castle is unusual for the high arches on both the north and south sides of the keep. However, the first-floor entrance, designed to deter invaders, was typical of castles of the period.

Entrance

The basement, with walls 3 m (10 ft) thick, was probably used for storage or as a stable.

STAR FEATURES

★ Great Hall

★ Main Guard

★ North Solar

For hotels and restaurants in this region see pp306–9 and pp335–6

★ **Main Guard**
Now used for medieval-style banquets, this was the room where Bunratty's soldiers ate, slept and relaxed. Music was played to them from the Minstrels' Gallery, and a gate in one corner gave instant access to the dungeons.

VISITORS' CHECKLIST

Road map B4. Bunratty, Co Clare. *Tel* 061 360788. ▲ Shannon. ◼ from Ennis, Limerick, Shannon. Castle & Folk Park. ☐ Jul & Aug: 9am–6pm daily; Jun & Sep: 9:30am–5:30pm daily. ● Good Friday, 24–26 Dec. 🅿 🍴 ♿ to Folk Park. Banquets see p360. **www**.shannonheritage.com

Anteroom

The Robing Room was where the earls put on their gowns before an audience in the Great Hall. They also used it for private interviews.

South Solar
These guest apartments have fine linenfold wood panelling, a form of decoration popular during the Tudor period. The elaborate fan-vaulted ceiling is partly a reconstruction.

BUNRATTY FOLK PARK

A meticulous recreation of rural life in Ireland at the end of the 19th century, this Folk Park began with the reconstruction of a farmhouse which was saved during the building of nearby Shannon Airport. It now consists of a complete village, incorporating shops and a whole range of domestic architecture from a labourer's cottage to an elegant Georgian house. Other buildings in the park include a farmhouse typical of the Moher region in the Burren *(see p184)* and a working corn mill. During the main summer season, people in authentic costume wander through the streets and traditional crafts are demonstrated.

A spiral staircase is found in each of the four towers.

★ **Great Hall**
This Tudor standard was among the many furnishings that Lord Gort brought to the castle. It stands in the Great Hall, once the banqueting hall and audience chamber, and still Bunratty's grandest room.

Main street of Bunratty Folk Park village

Typical thatched cottage in the village of Adare

Adare ⓯

Road map B5. Co Limerick. 🚶 *1,000.*
🚌 ℹ *Heritage Centre, Main St
(061 396255).* ⭘ *Feb–Dec: daily.*
www.shannonregiontourism.ie

Adare is billed as Ireland's
prettiest village. Cynics call it
the prettiest "English" village
since its manicured perfection
is at odds with normal notions
of national beauty. Originally a
fief of the Fitzgeralds, the
Earls of Kildare, Adare owes
its present appearance more
to the Earls of Dunraven,
who restored the village in
the 1820s and 1830s. The
village is a picture of neat
stonework and thatched roofs
punctuated by pretty ruins,
all in a woodland setting.

The tourist office is at the
new Heritage Centre, which
includes a good exhibition on
Adare's monastic history. Next
door is the **Trinitarian Priory**,
founded by the Fitzgeralds in
1230 and over-restored by the
first Earl of Dunraven; it is now
a Catholic church and convent.
Opposite, by a stone-arched
bridge, is the Washing Pool, a
restored wash-house site.

By the main bridge, on the
Limerick road, is the **Augustinian Priory** which was
founded by the Fitzgeralds in
1315. Also known as Black
Abbey, this well-restored priory
has a central tower, subtle carvings, delightful cloisters and
a graceful sedilia – a carved
triple seat. Just over the bridge,
from where it is best viewed,
is **Desmond Castle**, a 13th-
century feudal castle set on
the banks of the River Maigue.

Nearby stands the main gate
to **Adare Manor**, a luxury hotel
and golf course *(see p307).*
Within its 900 ha (2,220 acres)
of parkland lie two evocative
ruins. The **St Nicholas Church**
and **Chantry Chapel** date back
to the 12th century; both are
accessible by path. The graceful 15th-century **Franciscan
Friary**, however, is surrounded by the golf course, though
it can be seen clearly from
the pathway.

In the heart of the village is
the elegant Dunraven Arms
Hotel *(see p306)* from where
the local hunt rides to
hounds. Some of the nearby
cottages, originally built by
the Earl of Dunraven in 1828
for his estate workers, have
been converted into pleasant
cafés and restaurants.

Lough Gur ⓰

Road map B5. Co Limerick. 🚌
Visitors' Centre *Tel 061 360788.*
⭘ *May–Sep: daily.* 🎦 ♿ *limited.* 💻
www.heritageireland.com

This stone age settlement,
26 km (16 miles) south of
Limerick, was extensively inhabited in 3000 BC. Today the
horseshoe-shaped lough and
surrounding hills enclose an
archaeological park. All around
Lough Gur are standing stones
and burial mounds, including
megalithic tombs. One of the
most impressive sights is the
4,000-year-old **Great Stone
Circle**, just outside the park,
by the Limerick–Kilmallock
road. Excavations in the 1970s
unearthed rectangular, oval
and rounded Stone Age huts
with stone foundations. The

Colourfully painted shopfronts on Main Street in Adare

For hotels and restaurants in this region see pp306–9 and pp335–6

Façade of Cashel Palace Hotel

interpretive centre, which is housed in mock Stone Age huts on the site of the original settlement, offers a range of audiovisual displays, models of stone circles, burial chambers and tools and weapons.

As well as the various prehistoric sites scattered all over the Knockadoon Peninsula, there are two castle ruins from more recent times beside the lough – the 15th-century **Bourchier's Castle** and **Black Castle**, a 13th-century seat of the Earls of Desmond.

Roscrea ⑰

Road map C4. Co Tipperary. 5,500. 🚉 🚌 ℹ️ *Heritage Centre, Castle St (0505 21850)* ◯ *mid-Apr–Oct: daily.* **www**.heritageireland.com

This monastic town on the banks of the River Bunnow has an interesting historic centre. The 13th-century Anglo-Norman **Roscrea Castle**, consists of a gate tower, curtain walls and two corner towers. In the courtyard stands **Damer House**, a Queen Anne-style residence with a magnificent staircase and Georgian garden. Just over the river lies **St Cronan's Monastery** with a High Cross, Romanesque church gable and a truncated round tower. There are remains of a 15th-century **Franciscan Friary** on Abbey Street and the renovated Blackmills now houses the St Cronan's High Cross and the **Roscrea Pillar**.

🏛️ **Roscrea Castle & Gardens** Castle Street. **Tel** 0505 21850. ◯ *mid-Mar–Oct: daily; Nov & Dec: Sat & Sun.* 🎟️ 🚻 *limited.* 🎫

Holy Cross Abbey ⑱

Road map C5. Thurles, Co Tipperary. **Tel** 0504 43241. 🚉 🚌 *to Thurles.* ◯ *9am–8pm daily.* 🎟️ 🎫 🚻

Founded in 1169 by the Benedictines, Holy Cross was supposedly endowed with a splinter from the True Cross, hence its name. Now it has been completely restored, and the church is once again a popular place of worship and pilgrimage. Most of the present structure dates from the 15th century. It was built by the Cistercians, who took over the abbey in 1180. This gracious cruciform church, embellished with mullioned windows and sculpted pillars, is one of the finest examples of late Gothic architecture in Ireland.

Crucifixion carving at Holy Cross Abbey

Nearby, Farney Castle is the only round tower in Ireland that is occupied as a family home. It was built in 1495 and is currently the design studio and retail outlet of Irish international designer Cyril Cullen.

Cashel ⑲

Road map C5. Co Tipperary. 2,500. 🚌 ℹ️ *Heritage Centre, Main St (062 62511).*

The great attraction of the town is the magnificent medieval **Rock of Cashel** *(see pp196–7)*. Many people stay overnight to enjoy eerie floodlit views of the Rock. A private path leads to it from **Cashel Palace Hotel** *(see p307)*, an opulent Queen Anne residence that was once the Bishop's Palace. Nearby, the remnant of a 12th-century castle has been turned into Kearney Castle Hotel. In the evening you can sample traditional Irish culture at the **Brú Ború Heritage Centre**. Named after Brian Ború, the 10th-century king of Munster *(see pp34–5)*, the centre offers folk theatre, traditional music, banquets, and a craft shop. At the foot of the Rock is the 13th-century **Dominican Friary**. This austere sandstone church has a fine west door, a 15th-century tower and lancet windows. On farmland outside Cashel lie the scant remains of **Hore Abbey**, a 13th-century Cistercian foundation. The abbey was largely remodelled and a tower added in the 15th century, but the barrel-vaulted sacristy, the nave and chapter house are all original.

🏛️ **Brú Ború Heritage Centre** Cashel. **Tel** 062 61122. ◯ *Jun–Sep: daily; Oct–May: Mon–Fri.* 🚻 🅿️ **www**.comhaltas.com

🏛️ **Dominican Friary** Dominic Street. 🚻 *limited.*

Ruins of Hore Abbey (1272) with the Rock of Cashel in the background

Rock of Cashel

This rocky stronghold, which rises dramatically out of the Tipperary plain, was a symbol of royal and priestly power for more than a millennium. From the 4th or 5th century it was the seat of the Kings of Munster, whose kingdom extended over much of southern Ireland. In 1101, they handed Cashel over to the Church, and it flourished as a religious centre until a siege by a Cromwellian army in 1647 culminated in the massacre of its 3,000 occupants. The cathedral was finally abandoned in the late 18th century. Two hundred years on, the Rock of Cashel is besieged by visitors. A good proportion of the medieval complex is still standing, and Cormac's Chapel is one of the most outstanding examples of Romanesque architecture in the country.

★ St Patrick's Cross
The carving on the east face of this cross is said to be of St Patrick, who visited Cashel in 450. The cross is a copy of the original which stood here until 1982 and is now in the museum.

Hall of the Vicars' Choral
This hall was built in the 15th century for Cashel's most privileged choristers. The ceiling, a modern reconstruction based on medieval designs, features several decorative corbels including this painted angel.

Dormitory block

Entrance

The Museum
in the undercroft contains a display of stone carvings, including the original St Patrick's Cross.

Outer wall

Limestone rock

★ Cormac's Chapel
Superb Romanesque carving adorns this chapel – the jewel of Cashel. The tympanum over the north door shows a centaur in a helmet aiming his bow and arrow at a lion.

STAR FEATURES

★ Cathedral

★ Cormac's Chapel

★ St Patrick's Cross

For hotels and restaurants in this region see pp306–9 and pp335–6

KEY

12TH CENTURY
4 St Patrick's Cross (replica)
12 Cormac's Chapel
13 Round tower

13TH CENTURY
6 Cathedral porch
7 Nave
8 Crossing
9 South transept
10 Choir
11 North transept

15TH CENTURY
1 Ticket office
2 Hall of the Vicars' Choral (museum)
3 Dormitory
5 Castle

0 metres   50

0 yards   50

VISITORS' CHECKLIST

Road map C5. Cashel. *Tel* 062 61437. 🚌 to Thurles. 🚌 to Cashel. ◯ daily. Early Jun–mid-Sep: 9am–7pm; mid-Mar–early Jun & mid-Sep–mid-Oct: 9am–5:30pm; mid-Oct–mid-Mar: 9am–4:30pm. ● 24–26 Dec. 🗝 ⚐ ✔

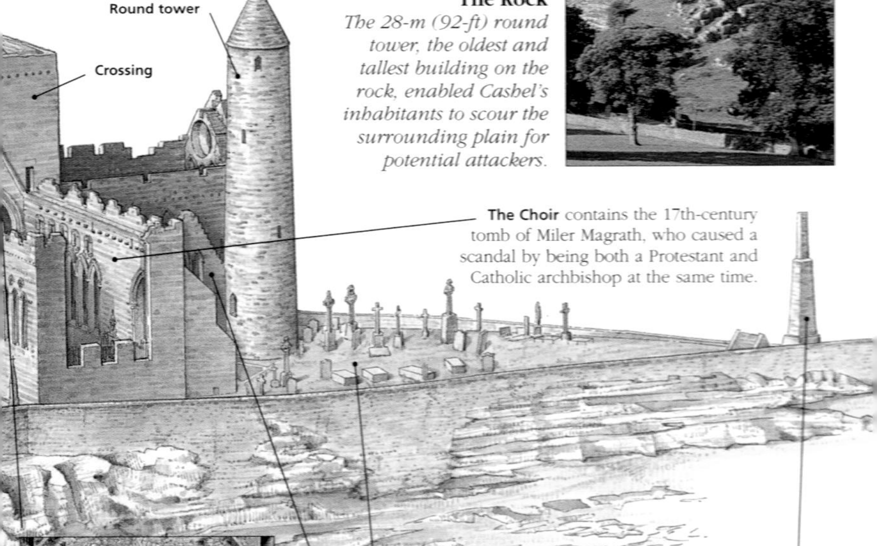

The Rock
The 28-m (92-ft) round tower, the oldest and tallest building on the rock, enabled Cashel's inhabitants to scour the surrounding plain for potential attackers.

Round tower

Crossing

The Choir contains the 17th-century tomb of Miler Magrath, who caused a scandal by being both a Protestant and Catholic archbishop at the same time.

Graveyard

The O'Scully Monument, an ornate memorial erected in 1870 by a local landowning family, was damaged during a storm in 1976.

North Transept
Panels from three 16th-century tombs in the north transept are decorated with remarkably fresh and intricate carvings. This one, against the north wall, features a vine-leaf design and strange stylized beasts.

★ Cathedral
The roofless Gothic cathedral has thick walls riddled with hidden passages; in the north transept these are seen emerging at the base of the windows.

Athassel Priory 🄴

Road map C5. 8 km (5 miles) W of
Cashel, Co Tipperary. 🚌 *to Tipperary.*
🕐 *daily.*

This ruined Augustinian priory
is situated on the west bank of
the River Suir. The tomb of
William de Burgh, the Norman
founder of the priory, lies in
the church. Established in 1192,
Athassel is believed to have
been the largest medieval priory
in Ireland until it burned down
in 1447. The scattered monastic
site conveys a tranquil atmosphere, from the gatehouse
and church to the remains of
the cloisters and chapter
house. The church has a fine
west doorway, nave and
chancel walls, as well as a
15th-century central tower.

The ruins of Athassel Priory, on the banks of the River Suir

Glen of Aherlow 🄴

Road map C5. Co Tipperary. 🚌 *to
Bansha or Tipperary.* 🏨 *Coach Rd Inn,
on R663 8 km (5 miles) E of Galbally
(062 56331).* **www.**aherlow.com

The lush valley of the River
Aherlow runs between the
Galty Mountains and the
wooded ridge of Slievenamuck.
Bounded by the villages of
Galbally and **Bansha**, the glen
was historically an important
pass between Limerick and
Tipperary and a notorious
hideout for outlaws.
  Today there are opportunities
for riding, cycling, rambling
and fishing. Lowland walks

follow the trout-filled river along
the valley floor. More adventurous walkers will be tempted
by the Galty range, which
offers more rugged hill-walking,
past wooded foothills, mountain streams, tiny corrie lakes
and splendid sandstone peaks.

Cahir 🄴

Road map C5. Co Tipperary.
🏨 *2,100.* 🚌 🚌 ℹ️ *May–Sep:
Castle Street (052 41453).*
www.tipperarycounty.ie

Once a garrison and mill
town, Cahir is today a busy
market town. The pub-lined
Castle Street is the most
appealing area. It leads to the
Suir River, Cahir Castle and the
walk to the Swiss Cottage.
  On the edge of town lies
the ruined **Cahir Abbey**, a
13th-century Augustinian
priory. Its fine windows are
decorated with carved heads.

♣ Cahir Castle
Castle Street. ***Tel*** *052 41011.*
🕐 *daily.* ⬤ *24–30 Dec.* 🅿️ 🚻
🛗 *limited.* **www.**heritageireland.ie

Built on a rocky island in the
River Suir, Cahir is one of the
most formidable castles in
Ireland and a popular film set.
This well-preserved fortress
dates from the 13th century
but is inextricably linked to its
later owners, the Butlers. A
powerful family in Ireland since
the Anglo-Norman invasion,
they were considered trusty
lieges of the English crown and
were granted the Cahir barony
in 1375. Under their command,
the castle was renovated and
extended throughout the 15th
and 16th centuries. It remained
in the Butler family until 1964.
  The castle is divided into
outer, middle and inner wards,
with a barbican at the outer
entrance. The inner ward is on
the site of the original Norman
castle; the foundations are
13th-century, as are the curtain
walls and keep. The restored
interior includes the striking
great hall, which dates largely
from the 1840s, though two of
the walls are original and the
windows are 15th-century.
From the ramparts there are
views of the river and millrace.

🏠 Swiss Cottage
Ardfinnan Road, Cahir. ***Tel*** *052
41144.* 🕐 *May–Sep: daily; Mar–Apr
& Oct–Nov: Tue–Sun.* 🅿️ *obligatory.*
The Swiss Cottage is a superb
example of a *cottage orné,* a
rustic folly. It was designed
for the Butlers by the Regency
architect John Nash in 1810.
Here, Lord and Lady Cahir
played at bucolic bliss, enjoying
picnics dressed as peasants.
Fashion dictated a *cottage*

View across the unspoilt Glen of Aherlow

orné should blend in with the countryside and all designs should be drawn from nature with nothing matching, so the windows and sloping eaves are all of different sizes and design. The beautifully restored cottage contains a tea room, gracious music room and two bedrooms.

Clonmel ㉓

Road map C5. Co Tipperary.
🏙 17,000. 🚌 🚆 ℹ 8 sarsfield St
(052 22960). **www**.clonmel.ie

Set on the River Suir and framed by the Comeragh Mountains, Clonmel is Tipperary's main town. This Anglo-Norman stronghold was a fief of the Desmonds and eventually of the Butlers. Its prosperity was founded on milling and brewing. Today, Clonmel is a bustling, brash town with quirky architecture and lively nightlife.

The **Franciscan Friary** by the quays was remodelled in Early English style in Victorian times but retains a 15th-century tower and houses 16th-century Butler tomb effigies. Nearby is O'Connell Street, Clonmel's main shopping street, which is straddled by the West Gate, built in 1831. Visitors to **Hearn's Hotel** on Parnell Street can see

The Swiss Cottage at Cahir, beautifully restored to its original state

memorabilia of Charles Bianconi (1786 –1875), including pictures of the horse-drawn coach service he established between Clonmel and Cahir. Eventually this developed into a nationwide passenger service.

Carrick-on-Suir ㉔

Road map C5. Co Tipperary. 🏙
5,500. 🚌 ℹ Heritage Centre (051 640200). **www**.tipperarycounty.ie

This sleepy market town has a distinctly old-fashioned air. In the 15th century, it was a strategic site commanding access west to Clonmel and southeast to Waterford, but after Tudor times the town sank into oblivion. Apart from Ormond Castle, there are few specific sights. However, you can stroll by the old waterside warehouses or shop for Tipperary Crystal *(see p353)* .

⚜ Ormond Castle
Castle Park. **Tel** 051 640787. ⬜ mid-Jun–Oct: daily. 🎫 📷 🚫 ♿ limited.
Although once a fortress, Ormond Castle is the finest surviving Tudor manor house in Ireland. It was built by the powerful Butler family, the Earls of Ormonde, who were given their title by the English crown in 1328. The castle has a gracious Elizabethan façade overlaying the medieval original; the battlemented towers on the south side sit oddly with the gabled façade and its mullioned and oriel windows.

The finest room is the Long Gallery, which has a stuccoed ceiling studded with heraldic crests, and two ornately carved fireplaces. The Elizabethan section was added by Black

Tom Butler, the 10th Earl of Ormonde, a loyal subject to Elizabeth Tudor. On his death, the Ormondes abandoned Carrick for Kilkenny *(see pp142 –3)*.

Intricate wood carving on a four-poster bed at Ormond Castle

Environs
In the churchyard at **Ahenny**, about 10 km (6 miles) north of Carrick, stand two magnificent High Crosses *(see p243)*. Both are crowned by "caps" or "bishops' mitres" and have intricate cable, spiral and fret patterns.

At **Kilkieran**, 5 km (3 miles) north of Carrick, are three other interesting High Crosses, dating from the 9th century. The Plain Cross is unadorned but capped; the West Cross is profusely ornamented though weathered; the Long Shaft Cross has an odd design of stumpy arms on a long shaft.

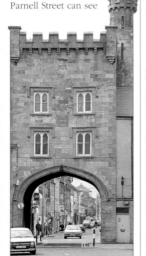
Clonmel's mock Tudor West Gate, spanning O'Connell Street

THE WEST OF IRELAND

MAYO · GALWAY · ROSCOMMON

T*his is the heart of Connaught, Ireland's historic western province. The West lives up to its image as a traditional, rural, sparsely populated land, with windswept mountains and countryside speckled with low stone walls and peat bogs. Yet it also encompasses Galway, a fast-growing university town whose youthful population brings life to the medieval streets and snug pubs.*

The rugged Atlantic coastline of the West has been occupied for over 5,000 years. It is rich in prehistoric sites such as the land enclosures of Céide Fields and the ring forts on the Aran Islands. Evidence of the monastic period can be seen in the mysterious and beautiful remains at Kilmacduagh and Clonfert; and the region's religious associations still exert an influence, apparent in the pilgrimages to Knock and Croagh Patrick in County Mayo.

In medieval times, the city of Galway was an Anglo-Norman stronghold, surrounded by warring Gaelic clans. After the Cromwellian victories of the 1640s, many Irish were dispossessed of their fertile lands and dispatched "to hell or Connacht". Landlords made their mark in the 17th and 18th centuries, building impressive country houses at Clonalis, Strokestown Park and Westport. During the Great Famine, the West – especially County Mayo – suffered most from emigration, a trend that continues to this day. In spite of this, strong Gaelic traditions have survived in County Galway, the country's largest Gaeltacht (see p229), where almost half the population speaks Irish as a first language.

The bracken browns and soft violets of Connemara in the west of Galway and the fertile farmland, extensive bogs and placid lakes of County Roscommon are in striking contrast to the magnificent cliff scenery of the remote islands off the coast. This region is often shrouded in a misty drizzle or else battered by Atlantic winds and accompanying heavy downpours.

Summer is a time for festivities: the Galway Races in July, traditional sailing ship races off Kinvarra in August and the Galway Oyster Festival in September are all lively events that attract a stream of visitors.

Swans by the quayside of the Claddagh area of Galway

◁ Typical Connemara landscape dominated by the peaks of the Twelve Bens

Exploring the West of Ireland

Galway city, Clifden and Westport make the best bases for exploring the region, with cosy pubs, good walks and access to the scenic islands. Connemara and the wilds of County Mayo attract nature lovers, while the islands of Achill, Aran, Clare and Inishbofin appeal to water-sports enthusiasts and ramblers. The lakes of County Roscommon are popular with anglers, and Lough Corrib and Lough Key offer relaxing cruises.

Decorative stuccowork in Westport House

SEE ALSO

- *Where to Stay* pp309–12

- *Restaurants, Cafés and Pubs* pp337–9 & 349–50

GETTING AROUND

The tiny airport near Rossaveal runs flights to the Aran Islands, which can also be reached by ferry from Rossaveal, Galway and Doolin (Co. Clare). Ferries run from Cleggan to Inishbofin and Roonah near Louisburgh to Clare Island. There is no rail service between Galway and Westport but the towns are linked by buses. Bus Éireann runs services to Connemara from Galway and Clifden (via Oughterard or Cong) or the area can be explored on day-long coach tours from Galway or Clifden.

0 kilometres   20

0 miles   20

For additional map symbols *see back flap*

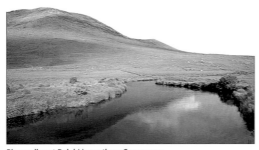

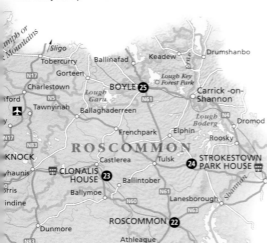

River valley at Delphi in northern Connemara

SIGHTS AT A GLANCE

Achill Island 2
Aran Islands pp214–15 15
Boyle 25
Céide Fields 1
Clare Island 7
Clifden 9
Clonalis House 23
Clonfert Cathedral 20
Cong 12
Connemara National Park 11
Croagh Patrick 6
Foxford 4
Galway pp210–11 14
Inishbofin 8
Kilmacduagh 17
Kinvarra 16
Knock 5
Kylemore Abbey 10
Lough Corrib 13
Portumna 19
Roscommon 22
Strokestown Park House 24
Thoor Ballylee 18
Turoe Stone 21
Westport 3

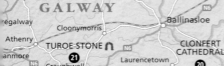

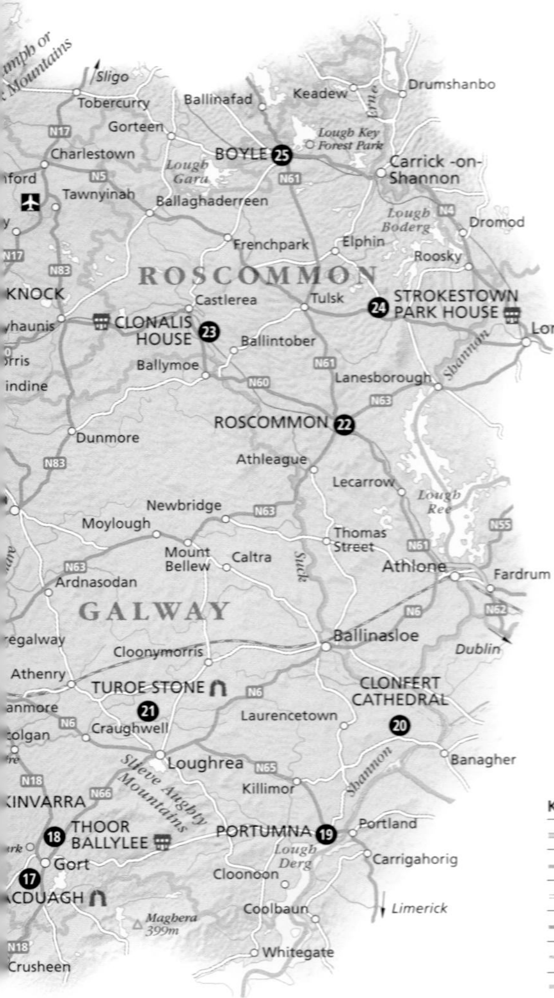

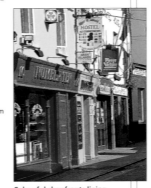

Colourful shopfronts lining Quay Street, Galway

KEY

- Major road
- Secondary road
- Minor road
- Scenic route
- Minor railway
- County border
- △ Summit

Bogwood centrepiece in Céide Fields interpretative centre

Céide Fields ❶

Road map B2. 8 km (5 miles) W of Ballycastle, Co Mayo. *Tel 096 43325.* 🚌 *from Ballycastle.* ⬜ *mid-Mar–Nov: daily.* 📷 🚫 ⬜ ♿ *ground floor.* **www**.heritageireland.ie

Surrounded by heather-clad moorlands and mountains along a bleak, dramatic stretch of north Mayo coastline is Europe's largest Stone Age land enclosure. Over 10 sq km (4 sq miles) were enclosed by walls to make fields suitable for growing wheat and barley, and grazing cattle. Remains of farm buildings indicate that it was an extensive community. The fields were slowly buried below the creeping bog formation, where they have been preserved for 5,000 years.

Part of the bog has been cut away to reveal the collapsed stone walls of the ancient fields. The remains are simple but guides help visitors to find and recognize key features.

Stone Age pottery and a primitive plough have been found in recent excavations. The striking, pyramid-shaped interpretative centre has a viewing platform overlooking the site, audiovisual presentations and displays on local geology and botany.

Environs
Scattered around the wilderness of the spectacular north Mayo coast from Ballina to the end of the Mullet peninsula is a series of sculptures forming the **North Mayo Sculpture Trail**. Created by 12 sculptors from three continents, the 15 works, often on a huge scale, are made from earth, stone and other natural materials; additional sculptures are planned. They aim to highlight the coast's grandeur and enduring nature.

Achill Island ❷

Road map A3. Co Mayo. 🚌 *from Westport.* ℹ️ *098 47353.* ⬜ *Jul & Aug.* **www**.achilltourism.com

Ireland's largest island, 22 km (13.5 miles) long and 19 km (12 miles) wide, is reached by a road bridge that can be raised for boats to pass through. Achill offers moorland, mountains, rugged cliffs and long beaches, and is a popular spot for angling and water sports.

For motorists, the best introduction is the **Atlantic Coast Drive**, a circular, signposted route from Achill Sound, by the bridge. The road goes to the island's southern tip, then north around the rest of Achill. Between Doeega and Keel in the southwest run the dramatic

Minaun Cliffs and Cathedral Rocks. In the north is Slievemore, a mountain overlooking the village of Slievemore, which was abandoned during the Great Famine *(see p219)*. Sharks can be spotted off Keem Bay in the west.

Westport ❸

Road map B3. Co Mayo. 🏔 *4,700.* 🚌 🚌 ℹ️ *James Street (098 25711).* 🏠 *Thu.* **www**.irelandwest.ie

The Angel of Welcome above the marble staircase at Westport House

Westport is a neat town and has a bustling, prosperous air. In the 1770s, architect James Wyatt laid out the wide, tree-lined streets, including the North and South Mall on either side of Carrowbeg River. The town originally traded in yarn, cloth, beer and slate, but industrialization and the Great Famine *(see p219)* brought a dramatic decline until the 1950s when new industry and visitors were attracted to the area.

Beyond the South Mall is Bridge Street, lined with cafés and pubs; the most appealing is Matt Molloy's *(see p350)*, named after and owned by the flautist from The Chieftains.

🏛 **Westport House**
Off Louisburgh Rd.
Tel 098 27766. ⬜ *Mar–Nov: Sun–Fri.* 📷 🚫 🚫
www.westporthouse.ie

Just west of the town is the Carrowbeg estuary and Clew

The deserted village of Slievemore on Achill Island

Statue of St Patrick at the foot of Croagh Patrick, looking out to Clew Bay

Bay. At the head of the bay stands Westport House, the seat of the Earls of Altamont, descendants of the Browne family, who were Tudor settlers. The town of Westport itself was started in the 1750s by John Browne, first Lord Altamont, to complement the house. Designed in 1732 by Richard Castle, and completed by James Wyatt in 1778, the limestone mansion stands on the site of an O'Malley castle. Its imposing interior includes a sweeping marble staircase and an elegant dining room and is adorned with family portraits, antique Waterford chandeliers and 18th-century Chinese wallpaper. The estate has a boating lake, miniature railway, small zoo, museum, amusement arcade and several shops.

Bog oak and silver bowl from Westport House

Foxford ❹

Road map B3. Co Mayo. 🏠 1,000. 🚌 from Galway. 🛈 Westport (098 25711).

This tranquil market town is known for good angling in nearby Lough Conn and for its woven rugs and tweeds. In the town centre is **Foxford Woollen Mills**, founded in 1892 by an Irish nun, Mother Arsenius (originally named Agnes). The thriving mill now supplies top fashion houses. An audiovisual tour traces the mill's history, and visitors can see craftspeople at work.

🏭 **Foxford Woollen Mills and Visitor Centre**
St Joseph's Place. **Tel** 094 925 6756. 🕐 daily. ● Good Fri, 24–26 Dec. 🛗🅿🏠🍴♿ Exhibition Centre

Knock ❺

Road map B3. Co Mayo. 🏠 575. 🚶 15 km (9 miles) N of Knock. 🚌 🛈 May–Sep: Knock (094 938 8193). **www**.irelandwest.ie

In 1879, two local women saw an apparition of the Virgin, St Joseph and St John the Evangelist by the gable of the Church of St John the Baptist. It was witnessed by 13 more onlookers and validated by the Catholic Church amid claims of miracle cures. Every year, over a million believers make the pilgrimage to the shrine, including Pope John Paul II in 1979 and Mother Teresa in 1993. Its focal point is the gable where the apparition was seen, which is now covered over to form a chapel. Nearby is the Basilica of Our Lady, a modern

Bottles of holy water for sale at the shrine in Knock

basilica and Marian shrine. **Knock Museum**, beside the basilica, portrays life in 19th-century rural Ireland. An Apparition section covers the background to the miracle.

🏛 **Knock Shrine and Museum**
Tel 094 938 8100. 🕐 May–Oct: daily; Nov–Apr: by appt. 📷🅿♿ **www**.knock-shrine.ie

Croagh Patrick ❻

Road map B3. Murrisk, Co Mayo. 🚌 from Westport. 🛈 Murrisk (098 45384), Westport (098 64114). 🍴 **www**.croagh-patrick.com

Ireland's holy mountain, named after the national saint *(see p281)*, is one of Mayo's best-known landmarks. From the bottom it seems cone-shaped, an impression dispelled by climbing to its flat peak. This quartzite, scree-clad mountain has a history of pagan worship from 3000 BC. However, in AD 441, St Patrick is said to have spent 40 days on the mountain fasting and praying for the Irish.

Since then, penitents, often barefoot, have made the pilgrimage to the summit in his honour, especially on Garland Friday and Reek Sunday in July. From the start of the trail at Campbell's Pub in Murrisk, where there is huge statue of the saint, it is a two-hour climb to the top, at 765 m (2,510 ft). On Reek Sunday mass is celebrated on the peak in a modern chapel. A visitor centre has amenities for exhausted hikers.

Clare Island ❼

Road map A3. Co Mayo. 🚌 165.
⛴ from Roonagh Quay, 6.5 km
(4 miles) W of Louisburgh **Tel** 098
25045 (ferry services). ℹ Westport
(098 25711).

Clare Island, set in Clew Bay, is
dominated by two hills, and a
square 15th-century castle commands the headland and harbour. In the 16th century the
island was the stronghold of
Grace O'Malley, pirate queen
and patriot, who held sway
over the western coast.
Although, according to Tudor
state papers, she was received
at Queen Elizabeth I's court,
she stood out against English
rule until her death in her
seventies in 1603. She is buried
here in a tiny Cistercian abbey
decorated with medieval murals
and inscribed with her motto:
"Invincible on land and sea".

The island is dotted with Iron
Age huts and field systems as
well as promontory forts and
Bronze Age cooking sites (see
p170). Clare is rich in bog flora
and fauna, making it popular
with walkers. Animal lovers
come to see the seals, dolphins,
falcons and otters.

Environs
The mainland coastal village
of **Louisburgh** offers rugged

The ferry to Inishbofin leaving Cleggan Harbour

Atlantic landscape, sheltered
coves and sea angling. The
Granuaile Centre tells the story
of Grace O'Malley (*Granuaile*
in Gaelic) and has displays on
Mayo folklore and archaeology.

🏛 **Granuaile Centre**
St Catherine's Church, Louisburgh.
Tel 098 66341. ◯ May–Sep: daily.
🎞 ♿

Inishbofin ❽

Road map A3. Co Galway. 🚌 200.
⛴ from Cleggan. ℹ Clifden.

The name Inishbofin means
"island of the white cow".
This mysterious, often mist-
swathed island was chosen
for its remoteness by the
exiled 7th-century St Colman,
English Abbot of Lindisfarne.
On the site of his original
monastery is a late medieval
church, graveyard and holy
well. At the sheltered harbour

entrance lies a ruined castle,
occupied in the 16th century
by Spanish pirate Don Bosco
in alliance with Grace O'Malley.
In 1653 it was captured by
Cromwellian forces and used
as a prison for Catholic priests.
Inishbofin was later owned
by a succession of absentee
landlords and now survives
on farming and lobster-fishing.

Surrounded by reefs and
islets, the island's landscape is
characterized by stone walls,
small abandoned cottages,
reed-fringed lakes and hay
meadows, where the corn-
crake (see p18) can be seen,
or heard. Inishbofin's beaches
offer bracing walks.

Clifden ❾

Road map A3. Co Galway.
🚌 920. 🚂 ℹ Mar–Nov: Galway
Road (095 21163). 🚌 Tue & Fri.
www.irelandwest.ie

Framed by the grandeur of
the Twelve Bens mountain
range and with a striking
skyline dominated by two
church spires, this early
19th-century market town
passes for the capital of the
Connemara region and is a
good base for exploring.
Clifden was founded in
1812 by John d'Arcy, a local
landowner and High Sheriff
of Galway, to create a pocket
of respectability within the
lawlessness of Connemara.
The family eventually went
bankrupt trying to bring
prosperity and order to the
town. The Protestant church
contains a copy of the Cross
of Cong (see p67).

Today craft shops have
taken over much of the town.
In the centre is the Square,
a place for lively pubs such
as EJ Kings (see p349).
Connemara is noted for its
sean-nos (unaccompanied

Clifden against a backdrop of the Twelve Bens mountains

CONNEMARA

This wild region in the west of Galway encompasses bogs, mountains and a rugged coastline. Major sights include the Connemara National Park and Kylemore Abbey *(see p208)*. For those without a car, coach tours are available from Galway and Clifden *(see p392)*.

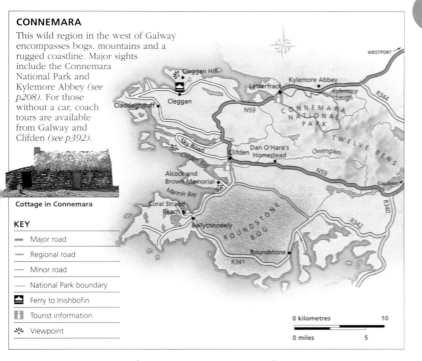

Cottage in Connemara

KEY

— Major road

— Regional road

— Minor road

— National Park boundary

⛴ Ferry to Inishbofin

ℹ Tourist information

☼ Viewpoint

0 kilometres 10

0 miles 5

---

singing), but in Clifden, general traditional music is more common.

Jutting out into **Clifden Bay** is a sand spit and beach, sign-posted from Clifden Square. South of Clifden, at the start of the Roundstone Road, is Owenglen Cascade where, in May, salmon leap on their way to spawn upstream.

Environs

The **Sky Road** is an 11-km (7-mile) circular route with stunning ocean views. The road goes northwest from Clifden

and passes desolate scenery and the narrow inlet of Clifden Bay. Clifden Castle, John d'Arcy's Gothic Revival ruin, lies just off the Sky Road, as do several inlets.

The coastal road north from Clifden to **Cleggan**, via Claddaghduff, is spectacular, passing former smuggling coves. Cleggan, a pretty fishing village, nestles into the head of Cleggan Bay. From here boats leave for Inishbofin and Inish-turk. **Cleggan Hill** has a ruined Napoleonic Martello tower and a megalithic tomb.

To the south of Clifden, the coastal route to Roundstone skirts a mass of bogland pitted with tiny lakes. The **Alcock and Brown Memorial** overlooks the bog landing site of the first transatlantic flight made by Alcock and Brown in 1919. Nearby is Marconi's wireless station, which exchanged the first transatlantic radio messages with Nova Scotia in 1907. The **Ballyconneely** area has craggy islands and the beautiful **Coral Strand Beach**. The village of **Roundstone** is best seen during the summer regatta of traditional Galway hookers *(see p211)*.

A short drive to the east of Clifden is **Dan O'Hara's Homestead**. In a wild, rocky setting, this organic farm recreates the tough conditions of life in Connemara before the 1840s. There is an audio-visual display on the history of Connemara.

🏛 **Dan O'Hara's Homestead**
Heritage Centre, Lettershea, off N59. **Tel** 095 21808. ⬤ Apr–end Oct: daily. 🅿 ♿ 🚻 🏪 ♿
www.connemaraheritage.com

View of the coast from the Sky Road

The imposing Kylemore Abbey on the shores of Kylemore Lough

Kylemore Abbey ⑩

Road map A3. Connemara, Co Galway. *Tel* 095 41146. 🚌 *from Galway and Clifden.* ⬜ *daily.* ⚫ *Christmas & Good Fri.* 🎟 *groups call to book.* **Walled garden** ⬜ *Mar–Nov.* 🏛 🍴 🅿 ♿ *ltd.* www.kylemoreabbey.com

Sheltered by the slopes of the Twelve Bens, this lakeside castle is a romantic, battlemented Gothic Revival fantasy. It was built as a present for his wife by Mitchell Henry (1826–1911), who was a Manchester tycoon and later Galway MP. The Henrys also purchased a huge area of moorland, drained the boggy hillside and planted thousands of trees as a windbreak for their new orchards and exotic walled gardens. After the sudden deaths of his wife and daughter, Henry left Kylemore and the castle was sold.

It became an abbey when Benedictine nuns, fleeing from Ypres in Belgium during World War I, sought refuge here. The nuns now run the abbey as a girls' boarding and day school.

Visitors are restricted to partial access to the abbey, the grounds, restaurant and craft shop. The earthenware pottery is painted with a fuchsia motif.

There is also a restored Victorian walled garden in the grounds, featuring the longest double herbaceous borders in Ireland, a nuttery and a meandering stream-side walk.

Connemara National Park ⑪

Road map A3. Letterfrack, Connemara, Co Galway. *Tel* 095 41054. **Visitors' Centre** ⬜ *Apr–mid-Oct: daily.* 🏛 ♿ 🅿 www.heritageireland.ie

A combination of bogland, lakes and mountains makes up this National Park in the heart of Connemara. Within its more than 2,000 ha (5,000 acres) are four of the Twelve Bens, including Benbaun, the highest mountain in the range at 730 m (2,400 ft), and the peak of Diamond Hill. At the centre is the valley of Glanmore and the Polladirk

River. Visitors come for the spectacular landscape and to glimpse the famous Connemara ponies.

Part of the land originally belonged to the Kylemore Abbey estate. In 1980 it became a National Park. There are traces of the land's previous uses all over the park: megalithic tombs, up to 4,000 years old, can be seen as well as old ridges marking former grazing areas and arable fields.

The park is open all year, while the Visitors' Centre near the entrance, just outside Letterfrack, is open only from April to mid-October. It features displays on how the landscape developed and was used and on local flora and fauna. There is also an audiovisual theatre and an indoor picnic area. Three signposted walks start from the Visitors' Centre. In summer there are guided walks, some led by botanists, and various children's activities. Climbing the Twelve Bens should be attempted only by experienced walkers equipped for all weather conditions.

CONNEMARA WILDLIFE

The blanket bogs and moorlands of Connemara are a botanist's paradise, especially for unusual bog and heathland plants. Birdlife is also varied with hooded crows, which can be recognized by their grey and black plumage, stonechats, peregrines and merlins – the smallest falcons in the British Isles. Red deer have been successfully reintroduced into the area and a herd can be seen in the National Park. Badgers, foxes, stoats and otters may also be spotted, as well as grey seals along the rocky coast.

The merlin *nests in old clumps of heather and feeds mainly on small birds.*

St Dabeoc's heath, *a pretty heather, grows nowhere else in Ireland or Great Britain.*

For hotels and restaurants in this region see pp309–12 and pp337–9

Cong @

Road map B3. Co Mayo. 350.
Mar–Nov (094 954 6089).
www.irelandwest.ie

This picturesque village lies on the shores of Lough Corrib, just within County Mayo. Cong means isthmus – the village lies on the strip of land between Lough Corrib and Lough Mask. During the 1840s, as a famine relief project, a canal was built linking the two lakes, but the water drained through the porous limestone bed. Stone bridges and stone-clad locks are still in place along the dry canal.

Cong Abbey lies close to the main street. The Augustinian abbey was founded in the early 12th century by Turlough O'Connor, King of Connaught and High King of Ireland, on the site of a 6th-century monastery established by St Fechin. The abbey has doorways in a style transitional between Romanesque and Gothic, stone carvings and restored cloisters. The Cross of Cong, an ornate processional cross intended for the abbey, is now in Dublin's National Museum *(see pp66–7)*. The most fascinating remains are the Gothic chapter house, stone bridges and the monks' fishing-house overhanging the river – the monks had a system where a bell rang in the kitchen when a fish took the bait.

Carved 12th-century doorway of Cong Abbey

Just south of Cong is **Ashford Castle**, rebuilt in Gothic Revival style in 1870 by Lord Ardilaun of the Guinness family. One of Ireland's best hotels *(see p292)*, its grounds can be visited by boat from Galway and Oughterard. Cong was the setting for *The Quiet Man*, the 1950s' film starring John Wayne. "Quiet Man" tours cover locations near the castle.

Lough Corrib ®

Road map B3. Co Galway. from Galway and Cong. from Oughterard and Wood Quay, Galway. Oughterard (091 552808).

An angler's paradise, Lough Corrib offers the chance to fish with local fishermen for brown trout, salmon, pike, perch and eels. Despite its proximity to Galway, the lake is a haven of tranquillity, dotted with uninhabited islands and framed by meadows, reed-beds and wooded shores. The waterside is home to swans and coots. On **Inchagoill**, one of the largest islands, stand the ruins of an early Christian monastic settlement and a Romanesque church.

The lake's atmosphere is best appreciated on a cruise. From Galway, the standard short cruise winds through the marshes to the site of an Iron Age fort, limestone quarries

View over Lough Corrib from the shore northwest of Oughterard

and the battlemented Menlo Castle. Longer cruises continue to Cong or include picnics on the islands.

Environs
On the banks of Lough Corrib, **Oughterard** is known as "the gateway to Connemara". The village has craft shops, thatched cottages and friendly pubs. It is also an important centre for golf, angling, hiking and pony trekking. Towards Galway City, **Brigit's Garden** in Roscahill has 4.45 ha (11 acres) of themed gardens.

About 4 km (2.5 miles) southeast of Oughterard (off the N59) is **Aughnanure Castle**. This well-restored six-storey tower house clings to a rocky island on the River Drimneen. The present castle, built by the O'Flaherty clan, is on the site of one dating from 1256. The clan controlled West Connaught from Lough Corrib to Galway and the coast in the 13th to 16th centuries. From this castle the feuding O'Flaherty chieftains held out against the British in the 16th century. In 1545 Donal O'Flaherty married the pirate Grace O'Malley *(see p206)*. The tower house has an unusual double bawn *(see p20)* and a murder hole from which missiles could be dropped on invaders.

Aughnanure Castle
Oughterard. **Tel** 091 552214.
Mar 25–Oct: daily.
limited. **www**.heritageireland.ie

Connemara ponies *roam semi-wild and are fabled to be from Arab stock that came ashore from Spanish Armada wrecks.*

Fuchsias *grow profusely in the hedgerows of Connemara, thriving in the mild climate.*

Galway ⑭

Sign with Claddagh ring design

Galway is both the centre for the Irish-speaking regions in the West and a lively university city. Under the Anglo-Normans, it flourished as a trading post. In 1396 it gained a Royal Charter and, for the next two centuries, was controlled by 14 merchant families, or "tribes". The city prospered under English influence, but this allegiance to the Crown cost Galway dear when, in 1652, Cromwell's forces wreaked havoc. After the Battle of the Boyne *(see p244)*, Galway fell into decline, unable to compete with east-coast trade. In recent years, as a developing centre for high-tech industry, the city's profile has been revived.

Inside The Quays seafood restaurant and pub

Houses on the banks of the Corrib

Exploring Galway

The centre of the city lies on the banks of the River Corrib, which flows down from Lough Corrib *(see p209)* widening out as it reaches Galway Bay. Urban renewal since the 1970s has led to extensive restoration of the narrow, winding streets of this once-walled city. Due to its compact size, Galway is easy to explore on foot, and a leisurely pace provides plenty of opportunity to stop off at its shops, pubs and historic sights.

Eyre Square

The redeveloped square encloses a pleasant plaza and park lined with imposing, mainly 19th-century, buildings. On the northwest of the square is the **Browne Doorway**, a 17th-century entrance from a mansion in Abbeygate Street Lower. Beside it is a fountain adorned with a sculpture of a Galway hooker boat. The **Eyre Square Centre**, overlooking the park, is a modern shopping mall built to incorporate sections of the historic city walls. Walkways link Shoemakers and Penrice towers, two of the 14 wall towers that used to ring the city in the 17th century.

Lynch family crest on Lynch's Castle

Latin Quarter

From Eyre Square, William Street and Shop Street are the main routes into the bustling "Latin Quarter". On the corner of Abbeygate Street Upper and Shop Street stands **Lynch's Castle**, now a bank, but still the grandest 16th-century town house in Galway. It was owned by the Lynch family, one of the 14 "tribes".

A side street leads to the **Collegiate Church of St Nicholas**, Galway's finest medieval building. The church, founded in 1320, was extended in the 15th and 16th centuries, but then damaged by the Cromwellians, who used it to stable horses. The west porch is from the 15th century and there are some finely carved gargoyles under the parapet.

Quay Street is lined with restaurants and pubs, including **The Quays** *(see p349)*. Tí Neachtain is a town house which belonged to "Humanity Dick", an 18th-century MP who promoted laws against cruelty to animals. Today, it too is a restaurant and pub *(see p349)*. Nearby are the Taibhdhearc and Druid theatres *(see p358)*.

North Galway

The **Cathedral of St Nicholas** (1965), built of local limestone and Connemara marble, stands on the west bank. From here you can see Wood Quay, where Lough Corrib cruises start *(see p209)*. **National University of Ireland Galway**,

Outside dining at one of the cosmopolitan cafés in Shop Street

GALWAY HOOKERS

Galway's traditional wooden sailing boats, featured on the city's coat of arms, were known as *pucans* and *gleotogs* – hookers in English. They have broad black hulls, thick masts and white or rust-coloured sails. Once common in the Claddagh district, they were also used along the Atlantic coast to ferry peat, cattle and beer. Hookers can be seen in action at the Cruinniú na mBád festival in Kinvarra *(see p212)*.

Small Galway hooker sailing by the old quays and Spanish Arch

further west, is a large campus with a 1849 Gothic Revival quad. Salmon Weir Bridge links the two banks. Shoals of salmon rest under the bridge on their way upstream to spawn.

The Old Quays

The **Spanish Arch**, where the river opens out, was built in 1584 to protect the harbour, which was then outside the city walls. Here, Spanish traders unloaded their ships. The old quays are a tranquil spot for a stroll down the Long Walk to the docks.

The Claddagh

Beyond the Spanish Arch, on the west bank of the Corrib, lies the Claddagh. The name comes from *An Cladach*, meaning "flat, stony shore". From medieval times, this fiercely independent fishing community beyond the city walls was governed by a "king", the last of whom died in 1954. The only remnants of this once close-knit, Gaelic-speaking community are Claddagh rings,

VISITORS' CHECKLIST

Road map B4. Co Galway.
🏠 56,000. ✈ Carnmore, 11 km (7 miles) NE of Galway. 🚉 Ceannt Station (091 561444). 🚌 Ceannt Station (091 562000). 🛈 The Fairgreen, Foster St (091 537700). 🏴 Sat. 🎭 Galway Arts Festival (mid-Jul); Galway Races (late Jul–Aug); Oyster Festival (late Sep).

betrothal rings traditionally handed down from mother to daughter *(see p356)*.

Environs

Just west of the city is Salthill, Galway's seaside resort. The beaches at Palmer's Rock and Grattan Road are particularly popular with families in summer. A bracing walk along the promenade is still a Galway tradition.

Spanish Arch on the site of the former docks

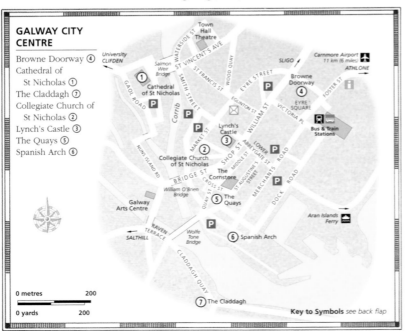

GALWAY CITY CENTRE

Browne Doorway ④
Cathedral of St Nicholas ①
The Claddagh ⑦
Collegiate Church of St Nicholas ②
Lynch's Castle ③
The Quays ⑤
Spanish Arch ⑥

0 metres 200
0 yards 200

Key to Symbols *see back flap*

Mural in the centre of Kinvarra depicting a shopfront

Aran Islands ⓯

See pp214–15.

Kinvarra ⓰

Road map B4. Co Galway. 🚶 *550.*
🚌 ℹ️ *Galway (091 537700).*

One of the most charming
fishing villages on Galway
Bay, Kinvarra's appeal lies in
its sheltered, seaweed-clad
harbour and traditional seafaring atmosphere. From
medieval times, its fortunes
were closely linked to
Kilmacduagh, the powerful
monastery and bishopric upon
which the village depended.

The pier is bordered by a
row of fishermen's cottages.
Kinvarra remains a popular
port of call for sailors
of traditional Galway
hookers *(see p211)*
and is known for
the Cruinniú na
mBád (gathering
of the boats)
festival in August.
Rambles include
historical and
nature trails.
Bird-watchers
may spot teal,
curlews and
oystercatchers
by the shore.

Environs
North of Kinvarra, on a
promontory on the shore of
Galway Bay, lies **Dunguaire
Castle**. It is perched just beyond
some quaint thatched cottages
and a stone bridge. The castle
is named after the 7th-century
King Guaire of Connaught,
whose court here was
renowned as the haunt of bards
and balladeers. Although the
medieval earthworks survive,
the present castle was built in
the 16th century, a quintessential
tower house *(see p20)* with
sophisticated machicolations.
The banqueting hall is still
used for "medieval banquets"
with Celtic harp music and
the recital of Irish poetry.

♣ **Dunguaire Castle**
Tel *091 637108.* ☐ *mid-
Apr–Sep: daily.* 📷 🏠 🛍️
www.shannonheritage.com

Kilmacduagh ⓱

Road map B4. Outside Gort on Corofin
Rd, Co Galway. 🚌 *to Gort.* ☐ *daily.*

This monastic settlement is in a
remote location on the borders
of Counties Clare and Galway,
roughly 5 km (3 miles) southwest of Gort. The sense of
isolation is accentuated by the
stony moonscape of the Burren

to the west *(see pp186–8)*.
Reputedly founded by St
Colman MacDuagh in the early
7th century, Kilmacduagh owes
more to the monastic revival
which led to rebuilding from
the 11th century onwards.

The centrepiece of the extensive site is a large, slightly
leaning 11th- or 12th-century
round tower and a roofless
church, known as the cathedral
or Teampall. The cathedral is
a pre-Norman structure, which
was later remodelled in Gothic
style, with flamboyant tracery
and fine tomb carvings. In the
surrounding fields lie the
remains of several other
churches that once depended
on the monastery. To the
northeast of the Teampall is
the late medieval Glebe or
Abbot's House, a variant of a
14th- or 15th-century tower
house *(see p20)*.

Thoor Ballylee ⓲

Road map B4. Gort, Co Galway.
Ballylee Castle Tel *091 631436.* 🚌
to Gort. ☐ *May–Sep: daily. Call to
check times.* 📷 🏠 ♿ *limited.*

For much of the 1920s, this
beguiling tower house was a
summer home to the poet WB
Yeats *(see pp22–3)*. Yeats was a
regular visitor to nearby Coole
Park, the home of his friend
Lady Gregory (1852–1932),
who was a cofounder of the
Abbey Theatre *(see p88)*.

On one visit Yeats came
upon Ballylee Castle, a 14th-
century de Burgo tower adjoining a cosy cottage with a
walled garden and stream. In
1902, both the tower and the
cottage became part of the
Gregory estate and Yeats
bought them in 1916. From
1919 onwards, his family
divided their time between

Round tower and cathedral, the most impressive monastic remains at Kilmacduagh

Dublin and their Galway tower. Yeats used the name Thoor Ballylee as the address, using the Irish word for tower to "keep people from suspecting us of modern gothic and a deer park". His collection, *The Tower* (1928), includes several poems inspired by the house.

Today, the audiovisual tour includes readings from Yeats's poetry, but the charm of a visit lies in the tower itself, with its spiral stone steps and views from the battlements over forest and farmland.

Environs

Just to the north of Gort is **Coole Park**, once the home of Lady Gregory. Although the house was demolished in the 1950s, the estate farm has been restored and the fine gardens survive. In particular, there is the "autograph tree", a spreading copper beech carved with the initials of George Bernard Shaw, JM Synge (see pp22–3), Jack Yeats (see p70) and other famous visitors. In the farm buildings is an audiovisual display. The emphasis of the visitors' centre is on natural history: it is the start of two signposted walks, one around the gardens and the other through beech, hazel, birch and ash woodland to Coole Lake.

🦌 **Coole Park**
3 km (2 miles) NE of Gort. **Tel** 091 631804. Visitors' centre ⚪ Easter–mid-Jun: Tue–Sun; mid-Jun–Sep: daily; park open all year. 🅿 🖵 🚹 limited.

Gentle hills and woodland by Coole Lake in Coole Park

Portumna ⑲

Road map C4. Co Galway. 👥 1,200.
🚌 🛈 Galway (091 537700). 🚃 Fri.

Portumna is a historic market town with scattered sights, many of which are newly restored. Situated on Lough Derg, it is a convenient base for cruising the River Shannon (see p185) and has a modern marina. **Portumna Castle**, built in the early 17th century, was the main seat of the de Burgo family. Now partially restored, it has a symmetrical façade and some elaborate interior stonework. The façade surveys formal gardens. Near the castle is **Portumna Priory**. Most of the remains date from around 1414 when the priory was founded by the Dominicans, but traces can also be found of the Cistercian abbey that was previously on the site. The large de Burgo estate to the west of the town now forms **Portumna Forest Park**, with picnic sites and signposted woodland trails leading to Lough Derg.

Human heads carved on the tympanum at Clonfert Cathedral

Clonfert Cathedral ⑳

Road map C4. Clonfert, Co Galway.
⚪ daily. 🚹

Situated near a bleak stretch of the Shannon bordering the boglands of the Midlands, Clonfert is one of the jewels of Irish-Romanesque architecture.

The tiny cathedral occupies the site of a monastery, which was founded by St Brendan in AD 563, and is believed to be the burial place of the saint.

Although a great scholar and enthusiastic founder of monasteries, St Brendan is best known as the "great navigator". His journeys are recounted in *Navigatio Sancti Brendani*, written in about 1050, which survives in medieval manuscripts including Flemish, Norse and French. The account seems to describe a voyage to Wales, the Orkneys, Iceland and conceivably the east coast of North America. His voyage and his boat (see p190), have been recreated by modern explorers in an attempt to prove that St Brendan may have preceded Columbus by about 900 years.

The highlight of Clonfert is its intricately sculpted sandstone doorway. The round arch above the door is decorated with animal and human heads, geometrical shapes, foliage and symbolic motifs. The carvings on the triangular tympanum above the arch are of strange human heads. In the chancel, the 13th-century east windows are fine examples of late Irish-Romanesque art. The 15th-century chancel arch is adorned with sculptures of angels and a mermaid. Although Clonfert was built over several centuries and altered in the 17th century, the church has a profound sense of unity.

Thoor Ballylee tower house, the summer home of WB Yeats

Aran Islands ⓯

Inishmore, Inishmaan and Inisheer, the three Aran Islands, are formed from a limestone ridge. The largest, Inishmore, is 13 km (8 miles) long and 3 km (2 miles) wide. The attractions of these islands include the austere landscape crisscrossed with dry-stone walls, stunning coastal views and several large prehistoric stone forts. In the 5th

Jaunting car on Inishmore

century, St Enda brought Christianity to the islands, starting a long monastic tradition. Protected for centuries by their isolated position, the islands today are a bastion of traditional Irish culture. Farming, fishing and tourism are the main occupations of the islanders.

Looking over the cliff edge at Dún Aonghasa

Clochán na Carraige is a large, well-preserved beehive hut (*see p21*), probably built by early Christian settlers on the islands.

The Seven Churches
(Na Seacht dTeampaill)

• Clochán na Carraige

Dún Eoghanachta •

Dún Eoghanachta is a 1st-century BC circular stone fort with a single wall terraced on the inside.

Dún Aengus
(Dún Aonghasa)

KILMURVY
(Cill Mhuirbhi)

INISHMORE

Na Seacht dTeampaill
The so-called Seven Churches make up a monastic settlement dedicated to St Brecan. Built between the 9th and 15th centuries, some are probably domestic buildings.

★ **Dún Aonghasa**
This Iron or Bronze Age promontory fort (see p20), has four concentric stone walls. It is also protected by a chevaux de frise, a ring of razor-sharp, pointed stone stakes.

ARAN TRADITIONS

The islands are famous for their distinctive knitwear (*see p354*) and for the traditional Aran costume that is still worn: for women this consists of a red flannel skirt and crocheted shawl; for men it includes a sleeveless tweed jacket and a colourful knitted belt. From

Colourful Aran costume

time to time you also see a *currach* or low rowing boat, the principal form of transport for centuries. Land-making, the ancient and arduous process of creating soil by covering bare rock with sand and seaweed, continues to this day.

Currach made from canvas coated in tar

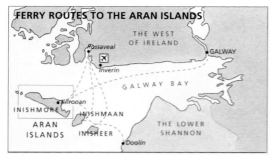

FERRY ROUTES TO THE ARAN ISLANDS

THE WEST OF IRELAND

GALWAY

Rossaveal

Inverin

GALWAY BAY

Kilronan

INISHMORE

INISHMAAN

ARAN ISLANDS

INISHEER

THE LOWER SHANNON

Doolin

VISITORS' CHECKLIST

Road map A4, B4. Co Galway.
🏠 900. ✈ *from Connemara Airport, Inverin (091 593034).*
⛴ *from Rossaveal:* **Island Ferries** (www.aranislandferries.com, 091 568903), **Doolin Ferry Company** *(Easter–Oct only; 065 707 4189). Ferries sail throughout the year; some go to all three main islands. Phone for details. Cars cannot be taken to the islands. From Kilronan, you can hire bicycles and jaunting cars, or go on minibus tours (099 61169).*
🛈 *Kilronan, Inishmore (099 61263).*
Aran Heritage Centre Kilronan.
Tel 099 61355. ◷ *Apr–May, Sep–Oct: 11am–5pm daily; Jun–Aug: 10am–7pm daily.*
📷 ♿ 🎁 🛈
www.irelandwest.ie

Kilmurvey Beach
The attractive sandy beach east of Kilmurvy offers safe swimming in a sheltered cove. The town itself is a quiet place to stay near a number of the island's most important sights.

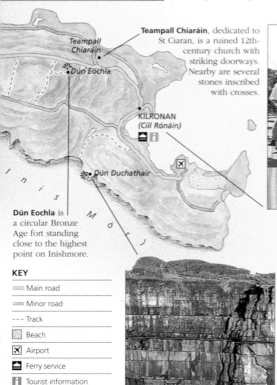

Teampall Chiaráin, dedicated to St Ciaran, is a ruined 12th-century church with striking doorways. Nearby are several stones inscribed with crosses.

Teampall Chiaráin

Dún Eochla

KILRONAN
(Cill Rónáin)

Dún Duchathair

Dún Eochla is a circular Bronze Age fort standing close to the highest point on Inishmore.

KEY

▬	Main road
▬	Minor road
---	Track
▦	Beach
✕	Airport
⛴	Ferry service
🛈	Tourist information
☀	Viewpoint

0 kilometres   2

0 miles   1

★ Kilronan
The Aran Islands' main port is a busy place, with jaunting cars (ponies and traps) and minibuses waiting by the pier to give island tours; bicycles can also be hired. Nearby, the fascinating Aran Heritage Centre is dedicated to the disappearing Aran way of life.

★ Dún Duchathair
Built on a headland, this Iron Age construction is known as the Black Fort. It has dry-stone ramparts.

STAR SIGHTS

★ Dún Aonghasa

★ Dún Duchathair

★ Kilronan

Farmer on Inishmore, largest of the Aran Islands ▷

East wall and gatehouse at Roscommon Castle

Turoe Stone ㉑

Road map B4. Turoe, Bullaun,
Loughrea, Co Galway. **Tel** 091 841580.
◯ May–Sep: daily; Oct–Apr:
weekends and public hols.

The Turoe Stone stands at the
centre of a large area of
parkland, the Turoe Pet Farm
and Leisure Park, near the
village of Bullaun (on the
R350). The white granite
boulder, which stands about
1 m (3 ft) high, dates back to
the 3rd or 2nd century BC. Its
top half is carved with curvilinear designs in a graceful
Celtic style, known as La Tène,
also found in Celtic parts of
Europe, particularly Brittany.
The lower half has a smooth
section and a band of step-
pattern carving. The stone was
originally found at an Iron
Age ring fort nearby, and is
thought to have been used
there in fertility rituals.
    The park around the Turoe
Stone is designed mainly for
children. The Pet Farm has
some small fields containing
farm animals and a pond with
several varieties of ducks and
geese. There is also a wooded

The Celtic Turoe Stone carved
with graceful swirling patterns

riverside walk, a picnic area,
tea rooms, a playground and
a 6,000 sq ft (558 sq m)
"inflatable city" bouncy castle.

Roscommon ㉒

Road map C3. Co Roscommon.
🏠 3,500. 🚌 🚆 ❓ Jun-Sep:
Harrison Hall (090 662 6342). ◒ Fri.
www.visitroscommon.com

The county capital is a busy
market town. In Main Street is
the former gaol, which had a
woman as its last executioner.
"Lady Betty", as she was
known, was sentenced to
death for the murder of her
son in 1780, but negotiated a
pardon by agreeing to
become a hangwoman. She
continued for 30 years.
    South of the town centre,
just off Abbey Street, is the
Dominican Friary, founded in
1253 by Felim O'Conor, King
of Connaught. Set in the north
wall of the choir is a late 13th-
century effigy of the founder.
    Roscommon Castle, an
Anglo-Norman fortress north
of the town, was built in 1269
by Robert d'Ufford, Lord
Justice of Ireland, and rebuilt
11 years later after being destroyed by the Irish led by Hugh
O'Conor, King of Connaught.
The rectangular castle has 16th-
century mullioned windows.

Clonalis House ㉓

Road map B3. Castlerea,
Co Roscommon. **Tel** 094 962 0014.
◯ Jun–mid-Sep: Mon–Sat.
🌐 **www**.clonalis.com

This Victorian manor just
outside Castlerea is the ancestral home of the O'Conors,
the last High Kings of Ireland

and Kings of Connaught. This
old Gaelic family can trace its
heritage back 1,500 years. The
ruins of their gabled 17th-
century home are visible in
the grounds. On the lawn lies
the O'Conor inauguration
stone, dating from 90 BC.
    The interior includes a
Venetian hallway, a library of
many books and documents
recording Irish history, a tiny
private chapel and a gallery
of family portraits spanning
500 years. In the billiard room
is the harp once played by
Turlough O'Carolan (1670–
1738), blind harpist and last
of the Gaelic bards (see p24).

Strokestown Park House ㉔

Road map C3. Strokestown, Co
Roscommon. 🏠 House, Pleasure
Gardens and Museum Tel 071 963
3013. ◯ Apr–Oct: daily; pre-booked
tours all year.
www.strokestownpark.ie

Strokestown Park House, the
greatest Palladian mansion in
County Roscommon, was
built in the 1730s for Thomas
Mahon, an MP whose family
was granted the lands by
Charles II after the Restoration.
It incorporates an earlier 17th-
century tower house (see p20).
The design of the new house
owes much to Richard Cassels,
architect of Russborough (see
p132). The galleried kitchen,
panelled stairwell and groin-
vaulted stables are undoubtedly
his work, tailoring Palladian
principles to the requirements
of the Anglo-Irish gentry.
    The house stayed in the fam-
ily's hands until 1979, when
major restoration began. In its
heyday, the estate included
ornamental parkland, a deer

park, folly, mausoleum and the village of Strokestown itself. By 1979, the estate's original 12,000 ha (30,000 acres) had dwindled to 120 ha (300 acres), but recent re-creation of the Pleasure Gardens and the Fruit and Vegetable Garden have greatly increased the area.

Set in the stable yards, the **Famine Museum** uses the Strokestown archives to tell the story of tenants and land-lords during the 1840s Famine. During the crisis, landlords divided into two camps: the charitable, some of whom started up Famine Relief schemes, and the callous, like the Mahons of Strokestown. Major Denis Mahon was murdered after forcing two-thirds of the starving peasantry off his land by a combination of eviction and passages in "coffin ships" to North America. A section of the exhibition deals with continuing famine and malnutrition worldwide.

Boyle ㉕

Road map C3. Co Roscommon. 🏛 *2,200.* 🚌 🚉 *Apr–Oct: King House (071 966 3242).* 🚩 *Fri.*

County Roscommon's most charming town, Boyle is blessed with fine Georgian and medieval architecture. **Boyle Abbey** is a well-preserved Cistercian abbey founded in 1161 as a sister house to Mellifont in County Louth *(see p245)*. It survived raids by Anglo-Norman barons and Irish chieftains, as well as the 1539 suppression of the monasteries. In 1659 it was

THE GREAT FAMINE

The failure of the Irish potato crop in 1845, 1846 and 1848, due to potato blight, had disastrous consequences for the people of Ireland, many of whom relied on this staple crop. More than a million died of starvation and disease, and by 1856 over two and a half million had been forced to emigrate. The crisis was worsened by unsympathetic landlords who often continued collecting rents. The Famine had far-reaching effects: mass emigration became a way of life *(see pp42–3)* and many rural communities, particularly in the far west, were decimated.

Peasants queuing for soup during the Famine (1847)

turned into a castle. The abbey is still remarkably intact, with a church, cloisters, cellars, sacristy and even kitchens. The nave of the church has both Romanesque and Gothic arches and there are well-preserved 12th-century capitals. The visitors' centre in the old gatehouse has exhibits on the abbey's history.

King House, a Palladian mansion near the centre of town, is the ances-tral home of the Anglo-Irish King family, later Earls of Kingston. Inside is a contemporary art gallery, and displays on various subjects, such as Georgian architecture and the mansion's restoration, the his-tory of the surrounding area and the Connaught chieftains.

Carved capital in the nave at Boyle Abbey

🏠 **Boyle Abbey**
Tel 071 966 2604. ⬜ *Easter–Oct.*

🏛 **King House**
Main St. *Tel 071 966 3242.* ⬜ *Apr–Sep: daily; rest of year on request.* 🖼 🍴 📷 ♿ 🎁 *on request.*

Environs
Lough Key is often called the loveliest lake in Ireland. The island-studded lake and surrounding woodland make a glorious setting for the **Lough Key Forest Park**. The 320-ha (790-acre) park formed part of the Rocking-ham estate until 1957, when Rockingham House, a John Nash design, burned down. The extensive woods were added by 18th-century landlords. Other features of the park include nature trails, an observation tower, a 17th-century ice house, a deer enclosure and, by the lake, a 17th-century gazebo known as the Temple. The park also has several ring forts *(see p20)*. From the jetty, cruisers ply the Boyle River. A river bus visits Church and Trinity Islands, which both contain medieval ruins, and Castle Island, which has a 19th-century folly.

🏕 **Lough Key Forest Park**
N4 8 km (5 miles) E of Boyle.
⬜ *daily.* 🖼 *Easter–Sep.* ♿

The gatehouse and remains of the nave at Boyle Abbey

NORTHWEST IRELAND

DONEGAL · SLIGO · LEITRIM

T owering cliffs, deserted golden beaches and rocky headlands abound along the rugged coast of Donegal, which incorporates some of Ireland's wildest scenery. To the south, Sligo is steeped in prehistory and Celtic myth, with its legacy of ancient monuments and natural beauty enriched by associations with the poet, WB Yeats. By contrast, Leitrim is a quiet county of unruffled lakes and waterways.

In Celtic mythology Sligo was the power base of the warrior Queen Maeve of Connaught *(see p26)*, and the county's legacy of prehistoric sites shows that the area was heavily populated in Celtic times. Later, however, both County Sligo and neighbouring County Leitrim often seemed to be little affected by events taking place in the rest of Ireland. The Normans, for example, barely disturbed the rule of local Gaelic clans.

Donegal, on the other hand, was part of Ulster until 1921 and played an active role in that province's history. The O'Donnells held sway over most of Donegal in the Middle Ages, but they fled to Europe in 1607 following their ill-fated stand against the English alongside the O'Neills *(see p255)*. Protestant settlers moved on to land confiscated from the two clans, but they left much of Donegal and its poor soil to the native Irish, who lived there in isolation from the rest of Ulster. This remote corner of the province remained largely Catholic and, at the time of Partition in 1921, Donegal was excluded from the new Protestant Northern Ireland.

County Donegal has little in common with its neighbours in the Republic, either geographically or historically. It is one of the most remote parts of Ireland, and it is no coincidence that Donegal boasts the country's largest number of Gaelic speakers.

While the beauty of Donegal lies mainly along the coast, Sligo's finest landscapes are found inland, around Lough Gill and among the sparsely populated Bricklieve Mountains.

The 19th-century interior of Hargadon's bar in Sligo town, with its original counter and stout jars

◁ View across to Falcarragh from Bloody Foreland in County Donegal

Exploring Northwest Ireland

The supreme appeal of Donegal lies in the natural beauty of its coast, with windswept peninsulas, precipitous cliffs and a host of golden beaches. There is a scattering of small seaside resorts which make good bases, and Donegal town is well placed for exploring the southern part of the county. The cultural heartland of the Northwest lies in and around Sligo, the only sizeable town in the region, from where you can reach several prehistoric remains and other historic sights. Further south, lovely scenery surrounds Lough Gill and the more remote Lough Arrow. In Leitrim, a county of lakes and rivers, the main centre of activity is the lively boating resort of Carrick-on-Shannon.

Procession during the Mary of Dungloe beauty contest in July

SEE ALSO

• *Where to Stay* pp312–14

• *Restaurants, Cafés and Pubs* pp339–41 & p350

KEY

═══	Major road
───	Secondary road
┈┈┈	Minor road
───	Scenic route
┅┅┅	Main railway
───	Minor railway
▬▬▬	National border
───	County border
△	Summit

1 TORY IS
Tory Sound   HOR
HEA
Dunfana

2 BLOODY
FORELAND   Brinlack   Gorta
Gola Island   R257   Bunbeg
Owey Island   Errigal
752m
Rosses
Bay   **3**
Burtonport **10** THE
ROSSES
Aran
Island   Dungloe   DERRYVE
MOUNT
Croby Head
Gweebarra
Bay   Fintown   N56   DO
Narin   Maas
R261   Glenties
Loughbros Pt   Labagh More
672m
Glengesh Pass   **11** ARDARA   R262
GLENCOLUMBKILLE **12**   Blue Sta
Moun
Malin More
Malin Beg **13**   Carrick   Inver   DONE
SLIEVE LEAGUE   R263   **14**   N56   **15**
KILLYBEGS   Donegal
Bay
ROSSNOWLAGH **17**
Assaroe Abbey
BALLYSHANNON **18**
Mullaghmore   Bundoran   B
Er
Inishmurray   Lough
Melvin   **25**
Grange   YEATS   THE OR
20 COUNTRY   CENTRE
LISSADELL HOUSE **19**   R280
Rosses Point   Drumcliff   Manorha
Sligo Bay   N1
Killala   Dromore   SLIGO **22** R286 PARKE'S
Bay   West   N59   Lough **21** CASTLE
Inniscrone   Ballysadare   Gill   Dromahair
R287   Dow
Colloony   R284   Drumkeeran
Lo
Ballina   Slieve Gamph or   S L I G O   Al
The Ox Mountains   N17   **23** LOUGH
Tobercurry   Ballymote   N4   ARROW   Drum
Ballinafad   Keadew   shan
Gorteen   Lough
Key
Charlestown   Lough   Boyle   **24**
Gara
N5   CARRICK
Ballaghaderreen   SHANN(
Roscommon

0 kilometres	20	
0 miles	20	

For additional map symbols *see back flap*

GETTING AROUND

The N56, linking Letterkenny and Donegal, provides access to much of the Northwest's best scenery, with minor roads branching off it around the coast's rocky peninsulas. A few buses serve this route, but travelling around without a car is easier further south, with buses running daily from Donegal along the N15 to Sligo via Ballyshannon. The rail network barely reaches the Northwest, though there are daily trains between Sligo and Carrick-on-Shannon.

Thatched cottage near Malin Head on Inishowen Peninsula

SIGHTS AT A GLANCE

View from Carrowkeel Bronze Age cemetery above Lough Arrow

Quartzite cone of Errigal, the highest of the Derryveagh Mountains

Tory Island ➊

Road map C1. Co Donegal. 🚶 175.
🚤 from Magheraroarty Pier near
Gortahork (074 913 5061) and
Bunbeg (074 953 1340): daily in
summer, weather permitting in winter.

The turbulent Tory Sound
separates this windswept
island from the northwestern
corner of mainland Donegal.
Given that rough weather can
cut off the tiny island for days,
it is not surprising that Tory's
inhabitants have developed a
strong sense of independence.
Most of the islanders speak
Gaelic and they even have
their own monarch: the powers
of this non-hereditary position
are minimal, but the current
incumbent is heavily involved
in promoting the interests of
his "subjects" and in attracting
visitors to the island.
　During the 1970s, the Irish
government tried to resettle
most of the islanders on the
mainland, but they refused to
move. Their campaign of
resistance was led by Tory's
school of Primitive artists. This
emerged after 1968, inspired
by a local man called James
Dixon who claimed he could
do better than a visiting
English painter, Derek Hill.
Since then, the school of artists
has drawn a growing number
of tourists; the **Dixon Gallery**
opened in 1992 in the main
village of West Town. There

are ruins of a monastery
founded by St Columba *(see
p34)* nearby, or else you can
explore the island's dramatic
cliffs and seabird rookeries.

🏛 **Dixon Gallery**
West Town. **Tel** 074 913 5011.
⬜ Easter–Sep: daily.

Bloody Foreland ➋

Road map C1. Co Donegal. 🚌 to
Bunbeg from Letterkenny or Dungloe.

Bloody Foreland, which gets
its name from the rubescent
glow of the rocks at sunset,
boasts magnificent scenery.
The R257 road skirts the coast
around the headland, providing lovely views. The most
scenic viewpoint is on the

north coast and looks across
to the cliffs of nearby offshore
islands, including Tory. A short
distance further south, the tiny
village of **Bunbeg** has a pretty
harbour, but elsewhere the
rocky landscape is spoiled by a
blanket of holiday bungalows.

Derryveagh Mountains ➌

Road map C1. Co Donegal.

The wild beauty of these
mountains provides one of
the high spots of a visit to
Donegal. Errigal Mountain, the
range's tallest peak at 751 m
(2,466 ft), attracts keen hikers,
but the cream of the mountain
scenery lies within **Glenveagh
National Park**. Covering
nearly 16,500 ha (40,000 acres),
this takes in the beautiful
valley occupied by Lough
Veagh, and Poisoned Glen, a
marshy valley enclosed by
dramatic cliffs. The park also
protects the largest herd of
red deer in the country.
　Glenveagh Castle stands on
the southern shores of Lough
Veagh, near the visitors' centre.
This splendid granite building
was constructed in 1870 by
John Adair, notorious for his
eviction of many families from
the area after the Famine *(see
p219)*. The castle was given
to the nation in the 1970s by
its last owner, a wealthy art
dealer from Pennsylvania.
　Minibuses whisk you up the
private road to the castle from
the visitors' centre. You can
go on a guided tour of the
sumptuous interior or just stroll

Glenveagh Castle overlooking Lough Veagh

Looking across to Dunfanaghy, gateway to the Horn Head peninsula

through the formal gardens and rhododendron woods. Trails weave all around the castle grounds; one path climbs steeply to reward you with a lovely view over Lough Veagh.

Glebe House and Gallery overlooks Lough Gartan 6 km (4 miles) south of the visitors' centre. This modest Regency mansion was the home of the painter, Derek Hill, who was also a keen collector. The house reveals his varied tastes, with William Morris wallpapers, Islamic ceramics and paintings by Tory Island artists. The gallery contains works by Picasso, Renoir and Jack B Yeats among others.

Fountain at Glenveagh

The **Colmcille Heritage Centre**, less than a kilometre south, uses stained glass and illuminated manuscripts to trace the life of St Columba (Colmcille in Gaelic), who was born in nearby Church Hill in AD 521 *(see p34)*. A flagstone in Lacknacoo is said to mark the site of the saint's birthplace.

🍀 **Glenveagh National Park and Castle**
Off R251, 16 km (10 miles) N of Churchill. **Tel** 074 913 7090. **Park & Castle** ⬜ *mid-Mar–Nov: daily.* 🈺 🈲 🈳 🈴 🈵 *ltd.* www.heritageireland.ie
🏛 **Glebe House and Gallery**
Tel 074 913 7071. ⬜ *Easter & May–Sep: Sat–Thu.* 🈺 🈳 *limited.* 🈴 🈵
🏛 **Colmcille Heritage Centre**
Tel 074 913 7306. ⬜ *Easter & Apr–Sep: daily.* 🈺

Horn Head ❹

Road map C1. Co Donegal. 🚌 *to Dunfanaghy from Letterkenny.* 🛈 *The Workhouse, Dunfanaghy (074 913 6540) mid-Mar–mid-Oct.*

Carpeted in heather and rich in birdlife, Horn Head is the most scenic of the northern Donegal headlands. It rises 180 m (600 ft) straight out of the Atlantic and gives lovely views out to sea and inland towards the mountains. The appeal of the area is enhanced by **Dunfanaghy**, a delightful town with an air of affluence and Presbyterianism unusual in this area. The local beach, **Killahoey Strand**, offers excellent swimming.

Rosguill Peninsula ❺

Road map C1. Co Donegal.

Rosguill Peninsula juts out into the Atlantic Ocean between Sheephaven and Mulroy bays. The simplest way to see it is to follow the 11-km (7-mile) Atlantic Drive, a circular route which skirts the clifftops at the tip of the headland.

Doe Castle, 5 km (3 miles) north of Creeslough village, is worth a visit as much for its setting on a pro-montory overlooking Sheephaven Bay as for its architectural or historical interest. It has been restored from the remains of a castle erected in the 16th century by the MacSweeneys, a family of Scottish mercenaries.

Fanad Peninsula ❻

Road map C1. Co Donegal. 🚌 *to Rathmelton & Portsalon from Letterkenny.*

A panoramic route winds between the hilly spine and rugged coast of this tranquil peninsula. The eastern side is by far the most enjoyable and begins at **Rathmelton**, a charming Plantation town founded in the 17th century. Elegant Georgian homes and handsome old warehouses flank its tree-lined Main Street.

Further north, **Portsalon** offers safe bathing and great views from nearby Saldanha Head. Near **Doaghbeg**, on the way to Fanad Head in the far north, the cliffs have been eroded into arches and other dramatic shapes.

Doe Castle on Rosguill Peninsula, with its 16th-century battlements

A Tour of the Inishowen Peninsula **7**

Inishowen, the largest of Donegal's northern peninsulas, is an area laden with history, from early Christian relics to strategically positioned castles and forts. The most rugged scenery lies in the west and north, around the the steep rock-strewn landscape of the Gap of Mamore and the spectacular cape of Malin Head, the northern-most point in Ireland. Numerous beaches dot the coastline and cater for all tastes, from the remote Isle of Doagh to the busy family resort of Buncrana. From the shores, there are views to Donegal's Derryveagh Mountains to the west and the Northern Ireland coast in the east. The Inishowen Peninsula can be explored by car as a leisurely day trip.

Tower on Banba's Crown, Malin Head

Carndonagh Cross ④
This 7th-century early Christian cross is carved with human figures and inter-lacing lines.

Gap of Mamore ③
The road between Mamore Hill and the Urris Hills is 250 m (820 ft) above sea level and offers panoramic views.

Dunree Head ②
On the headland, Dunree Fort overlooks Lough Swilly. It was built in 1798 to counter the threat of French invasion. Since 1986, it has been a military museum.

Buncrana ①
Buncrana has 5 km (3 miles) of sandy beaches and two castles. Buncrana Castle was rebuilt in 1718 and the intact keep of O'Doherty Castle dates from Norman times.

Shores of Lough Swilly near Dunree Fort

KEY

⎯	Tour route
═	Other roads
⅍	Viewpoint

Grianán Ailigh ⑦
At the neck of the Inishowen Peninsula, perched on a hilltop, stands this formidable circular stone fort. The solid structure that can be seen today is the result of extensive restoration in the 1870s.

TIPS FOR DRIVERS

Tour length: *157 km (98 miles).*
Stopping-off points: *Malin, Greencastle and Carndonagh all have pubs and eating places; picnic sites are dotted around the coast. The Guns of Dunree Military Museum has a café. There is a 3 km (1.8 mile) scenic walk between Moville and Greencastle. (see also pp387–9.)*

Malin Head ⑤
This traditional cottage makes a good stop for tea after enjoying the superb Atlantic views from Malin Head. At the highest point, Banba's Crown, stands a tower built in 1805 to monitor shipping.

Greencastle ⑥
A resort and fishing port, Greencastle is named after the overgrown castle ruins just outside town. Built in 1305 by Richard de Burgo, Earl of Ulster, the castle guarded the entrance to Lough Foyle.

0 kilometres   5

0 miles   5

Enjoying the views from the ramparts of the Grianán of Ailigh

Grianán Ailigh ❽

Road map C1. Co Donegal. 🚌
from Letterkenny or Londonderry.
ℹ️ *Burt (074 936 8512).*

Donegal's most impressive and intriguing ancient monument stands just 10 km (6 miles) west of the city of Londonderry *(see pp258–9)* at the entrance to the lovely Inishowen Peninsula.

Overlooking Lough Swilly and Lough Foyle, the circular stone structure, measuring 23 m (77 ft) in diameter, is believed to have been built as a pagan temple around the 5th century BC, although the site was probably a place of worship before this date. Later, Christians adopted the fort: St Patrick is said to have baptized Owen, founder of the O'Neill dynasty, here in AD 450. It became the royal residence of the O'Neills, but was damaged in the 12th century by the army of Murtagh O'Brien, King of Munster.

The fort was restored in the 1870s. Two doorways lead from the outside through 4-m (13-ft) thick defences into a grassy arena ringed by three terraces. The most memorable feature of the fort, however, is its magnificent vantage point, which affords stunning views in every direction.

At the foot of the hill stands an attractive church, dedicated to St Aengus and built in 1967. Its circular design echoes that of the Grianán.

Letterkenny ❾

Road map C1. Co Donegal.
👥 *12,000.* 🚌 ℹ️ *Blaney Rd (074 912 1160).* **www**.irelandnorthwest.ie

Straddling the River Swilly, with the Sperrin Mountains to the east and the Derryveagh Mountains *(see pp224–5)*

to the west, Letterkenny is Donegal's largest town. It is also the region's main business centre, a role it took over from Londonderry after partition in 1921. The likeable town makes a good base from which to explore the northern coast of Donegal and, for anglers, is well placed for access to the waters of Lough Swilly.

Letterkenny has one of the longest main streets in Ireland, which is dominated by the 65-m (215-ft) steeple of **St Eunan's Cathedral**. A Neo-Gothic creation built in the late 19th century, it looks particularly impressive when floodlit at night. It contains Celtic-style stonework, a rich marble altar and vivid stained-glass windows. The **County Museum** has increased in size over the last couple of years and offers informative displays on local history from the Stone Age to the 20th century. It also has a collection of archaeological artifacts found in Donegal, some of them dating from the Iron Age.

🏛 **County Museum**
High Rd. **Tel** *074 912 4613.*
⬜ *Mon–Sat.* ⬛ *10 days at Christmas and public hols.* ♿

The imposing spire of St Eunan's Cathedral in Letterkenny

Isolated cottage near Burtonport in the Rosses

The Rosses ⑩

Road map C1. Co Donegal. 🚌 to Dungloe or Burtonport from Letterkenny. 🛈 Jun–Sep: Main St, Dungloe (074 952 1297). ⛴ to Aranmore from Burtonport (074 952 0532).

A rocky headland dotted with more than 100 lakes, the Rosses is one of the most picturesque and unspoilt corners of Donegal. It is also a strong Gaeltacht area, with many people speaking Gaelic.

The hub of the Rosses, at the southern end of the headland, is **Dungloe**, a bustling market town and major angling centre.

Environs
There is a glorious sheltered beach 8 km (5 miles) west of Dungloe at **Maghery Bay**. From here you can also walk to nearby **Crohy Head**, known for its caves, arches and unusual cliff formations. From

Burtonport, 8 km (5 miles) north of Dungloe, car ferries sail daily to Donegal's largest island, **Aranmore**. The rugged northwest coast is ideal for clifftop walks, and from the south coast you can enjoy fine views across to the Rosses. Most of Aranmore's population of 700 lives in Leabgarrow. The village's thriving pub culture is due partly to the granting of 24-hour licences, for the benefit of fishermen returning from sea.

Ardara ⑪

Road map C2. Co Donegal. 🏠 700. 🚌 from Killybegs or Donegal. 🛈 Triona Design Visitors' Centre (074 954 1422). www.trionadesign.com

Ardara, the weaving capital of Donegal, proliferates in shops selling locally made tweeds and hand-knitted sweaters.

Some larger stores put on displays of hand-loom weaving. Ardara is also worth a stop for its pubs, much loved for their fiddle sessions.

Environs
A drive along the narrow peninsula to **Loughros Point**, 10 km (6 miles) west of town, provides dramatic coastal views. Another picturesque route runs southwest from Ardara to Glencolumbkille, going over **Glengesh Pass**, a series of bends through a wild, deserted landscape.

Hand-loom worker in Ardara

Glencolumbkille ⑫

Road map B2. Co Donegal. 🏠 260. 🚌 from Killybegs. 🛈 Donegal (074 972 1148). www.irelandnorthwest.ie

Glencolumbkille, a quiet, grassy valley scattered with brightly coloured cottages, feels very much like a backwater, in spite of the sizeable number of visitors who come here.

The "Glen of St Colmcille" is a popular place of pilgrimage due to its associations with the saint more commonly known as St Columba. Just north of the village of Cashel, on the way to Glen Head, is the church where St Columba worshipped: it is said that between prayers the saint slept on the two stone slabs still visible in one corner.

Another attraction here is the **Folk Village Museum**, which depicts rural Donegal lifestyles through the ages. It was started in the 1950s by a local priest called Father James

Old irons at the Folk Village Museum in Glencolumbkille

Slieve League, the highest sea cliffs in Europe

MacDyer. Concerned about the high rate of emigration from this poor region, he sought to provide jobs and a sense of regional pride, partly by encouraging people to set up craft cooperatives. The Folk Village shop sells local wares, and has a good stock of wine – made of anything from seaweed to fuchsias.

There is plenty to explore in the valley, which is littered with cairns, dolmens and other ancient monuments. The nearby coast is lovely too, the best walks taking you west across the grassy foreland of **Malinbeg**. Beyond the small resort of Malin More, steps drop down to an idyllic sandy cove hemmed in by cliffs.

🏛 **Folk Village Museum**
Cashel. **Tel** 074 973 0017. ◯ Easter–Sep: daily. 🖼 🗓 ☐ 🏠 ₰

Slieve League ⓭

Road map B2. Co Donegal. 🚌 to Carrick from Glencolumbkille or Killybegs.

The highest cliff face in Europe, Slieve League is spectacular not just for its sheer elevation but also for its colour: at sunset the rock is streaked with changing shades of red, amber and ochre. The 8-km (5-mile) drive to the eastern end of Slieve League from **Carrick** is bumpy but well worth enduring. Beyond Teelin, the road becomes a

series of alarming switchbacks before reaching **Bunglass Point** and Amharc Mor, the "good view". From here, you can see the whole of Slieve League, its sheer cliffs rising dramatically out of the ocean.

Only experienced hikers should attempt the treacherous ledges of **One Man's Pass**. This is part of a trail which climbs westwards out of Teelin and up to the highest point of Slieve League – from where you can admire the Atlantic Ocean shimmering 598 m (1,962 ft) below. The path then continues on to Malinbeg, 16 km (10 miles) west. During the summer, for a less strenuous but safer and equally rewarding excursion, pay a boat-owner from Teelin to take you out to see Slieve League from the sea.

Killybegs ⓮

Road map C2. Co Donegal. 🚹 1,700. 🚌 from Donegal. 🚹 Donegal (074 972 1148). **www**.irelandnorthwest.ie

Narrow winding streets give Killybegs a timeless feel, which contrasts sharply with the industriousness of this small town. The sense of prosperity stems in part from the manufacture of the Donegal carpets for which the town is famous, and which adorn Dublin Castle (see pp76–7) and other palaces around the world.

Killybegs is one of Ireland's busiest fishing ports and the quays are well worth seeing when the trawlers arrive to off-load their catch: gulls squawk overhead and the smell of fish fills the air. Trawlermen come from far and wide – so do not be surprised if you hear Eastern European voices as you wander around the town.

Trawler crew in Killybegs relaxing after unloading their catch

THE IRISH GAELTACHTS

The term "Gaeltacht" refers to Gaelic-speaking areas of Ireland. Up to the 16th century, virtually the entire population spoke the native tongue. British rule, however, undermined Irish culture, and the Famine (see p219) drained the country of many of its Gaelic-speakers. The use of the local language has fallen steadily since. Even so, in the Gaeltachts 75 per cent of the people still speak it, and road signs are exclusively in Irish – unlike in most other parts of Ireland.

The Donegal Gaeltacht stretches almost unbroken along the coast from Fanad Head to Slieve League and boasts the largest number of Irish-speakers in the country. Ireland's other principal Gaeltachts are in Galway and Kerry.

Gaelic pub sign in Gaeltacht region

Donegal town, overlooked by the ruins of its 15th-century castle

Donegal ⑮

Road map C2. Co Donegal. 🚶 2,300.
🚌 ℹ Quay St (074 972 1148).

Donegal means "Fort of the Foreigners", after the Vikings who built a garrison here. However, it was under the O'Donnells that the town began to take shape. The restored **Donegal Castle** in the town centre incorporates the gabled tower of a fortified house built by the family in the 15th century. The adjoining house and most other features are Jacobean – added by Sir Basil Brooke, who moved in after the O'Donnells were ousted by the English in 1607 (see pp38–9).

Brooke was also responsible for laying out the market square, which is known as the **Diamond**. An obelisk in the centre commemorates four Franciscan monks who wrote the *Annals of the Four Masters* in the 1630s, tracing the history of the Gaelic people from 40 days before the Great Flood up until the end of the 16th century. Part of it was written at **Donegal Abbey**, south of the market square along the River Eske. Built in 1474, little now remains of the abbey but a

few Gothic windows and cloister arches. About 1.5 km (1 mile) further on is **Donegal Craft Village**, a showcase for the work of local craftspeople.

Donegal town has some pleasant hotels (see p313) and makes a good base for exploring the southern part of the county.

♣ **Donegal Castle**
Tirchonaill St. **Tel** 074 972 2405.
◻ Mar–Oct: daily; Nov–Feb: Fri, Sat & Sun. 🗓 ◻ ☒ limited.

◻ **Donegal Craft Village**
Ballyshannon Rd. **Tel** 074 972 2105.
◻ May–Sep: Mon–Sat; Jun–Aug: daily. ◻ ☒ limited.

Lough Derg ⑯

Road map C2. Co Donegal. 🚢 Jun–mid-Aug (pilgrims only). 🚌 to Pettigo from Donegal.

Pilgrims have made their way to Lough Derg ever since St Patrick spent 40 days praying on one of the lake's islands in an attempt to rid Ireland of all evil spirits. The Pilgrimage of St Patrick's Purgatory began in around 1150 and still attracts thousands of Catholics every summer. Their destination is the tiny **Station Island**, close to Lough Derg's southern shore and reached by boat from a jetty

8 km (5 miles) north of the border village of Pettigo. The island is completely covered by a religious complex, which includes a basilica, built in 1921, and hostels for pilgrims.

The pilgrimage season runs from June to mid-August. People spend three days on the island, eating just one meal of dry bread and black tea per day. Although only pilgrims can visit Station Island, it is interesting to go to the jetty to savour the atmosphere and get a good view of the basilica near the shore.

Rossnowlagh ⑰

Road map C2. Co Donegal. 🚶 55.
🚌 from Bundoran & Donegal.
ℹ Apr–Oct: Main St, Bundoran (071 984 1350). **www**.irelandnorthwest.ie

Holiday-makers enjoying the fine sandy beach at Rossnowlagh

At Rossnowlagh, Atlantic waves break on to one of Ireland's finest beaches, drawing crowds of both bathers and surfers to this tiny place. Even so, the village remains far more peaceful than the resort of Bundoran, 14 km (9 miles) south. In addition, the cliffs at Rossnowlagh provide scope for exhilarating coastal walks. Away from the sea, you can visit the **Donegal Historical Society Museum**, housed in a striking Franciscan friary

Basilica on Station Island viewed from the shores of Lough Derg

For hotels and restaurants in this region see pp312–14 and pp339–41

Lissadell House dining room with Gore-Booth family portraits

Lissadell House ⑲

Road map B2. Carney, Co Sligo. **Tel** 071 916 3150. 🚌 or 🚂 to Sligo. ⏰ Mar 16–Sep: 11am–6pm daily. 🎫🌐 www.lissadellhouse.com

A Greek Revival mansion built in the 1830s, Lissadell is famous more for its occupants than its architecture. It used to be the home of the Gore-Booths who, unlike some of the Anglo-Irish gentry, have contributed much to the region over the four centuries they have been in County Sligo. During the Famine (see p219), Sir Robert mortgaged the house to help feed his employees.

The most famous member of the Gore-Booth family is Sir Robert's granddaughter, Constance Marvicz (1868–1927), a leading nationalist who took part in the 1916 Rising (see pp44–5). She was the first woman to be elected to the British House of Commons and later became Minister for Labour in the first Dáil. WB Yeats, who first visited the house in 1894, immortalized Constance and her sister, Eva, in one of his poems, describing them as "Two girls in silk kimonos, both beautiful, one a gazelle".

Built in grey limestone, the exterior of Lissadell House is rather austere. The interior, on the other hand, has an appealing atmosphere of faded grandeur, with copious memorabilia of the building's former occupants. The finest rooms are the gallery and the dining room, decorated with extraordinary full-length murals of the Gore-Booth family, their famous butler Thomas Kilgallon, the gamekeeper, head woodman and a dog. Painted directly on to the wall, they were the work of Constance's husband, adventurer and self-styled "Count" Casimir Markievicz.

Both the house and the estate are slowly being restored. You can already explore along paths skirting the seashore, and there is also a wildlife reserve which is a popular winter refuge for barnacle geese.

built in the 1950s. The tiny but fascinating collection includes displays of Stone Age flints, Irish musical instruments and other local artifacts.

Rossnowlagh never fails to make the news in July, when it hosts the only parade to take place in the Republic by the Protestant organization, the Orange Order (see p49).

🏛 **Donegal Historical Society Museum**
Tel 071 985 1267. ⏺ 25 Dec.

Ballyshannon ⑱

Road map C2. Co Donegal. 🏠 2,600. 🚌 from Bundoran & Donegal.

In Ballyshannon, well-kept Georgian homes jostle for space along hilly streets on the banks of the River Erne, near where it flows into Donegal Bay. This is a bustling town, full of character and off the main tourist track – though it gets packed during August's festival of traditional music, which is one of the best of its kind in the country.

The festival apart, Ballyshannon is most famous as the birthplace of poet William Allingham (1824–89), who recalled his home town in the lines "Adieu to Ballyshanny and the winding banks of the Erne". He lies buried in the graveyard of St Anne's Church, off Main Street. There is a fine view over the river from here: you can see the small island of **Inis Saimer** where, according to legend, Greeks founded the first colony in Ireland after the Great Flood. Beyond, you can glimpse a large Irish Army base: Ballyshannon's position on a steeply rising bluff overlooking the River Erne has always made the town a strategic military site.

Mural of the family dog in Lissadell's dining room

About 1.5 km (1 mile) northwest of town lie the scant ruins of **Assaroe Abbey**, founded by Cistercians in 1184. A graveyard with some ancient burial slabs and head-stones is all that remains. Nearby, two water wheels installed by the monks have been restored. **Water Wheels** has a small heritage centre as well as a café.

🏛 **Water Wheels**
Assaroe Abbey. **Tel** 071 985 1580. ⏰ Mar–Sep: daily. 🖥 🚻 ♿ **Heritage centre** ⏰ May–Oct: daily; Mar–Apr: Sun.

A Tour of Yeats Country ⑳

Yeats tour sign

Even for people unfamiliar with the poetry of WB Yeats, Sligo's engaging landscapes are reason enough to make a pilgrimage. This tour follows a varied route, taking you past sandy bays and dramatic limestone ridges, through forest and alongside rivers and lakes. Lough Gill lies at the heart of Yeats country, enclosed by wooded hills crisscrossed by walking trails. In summer, boats ply the length of the lough, or you can head to one of the northwest's best beaches, at Rosses Point.

Ben Bulben ⑤
The eerie silhouette of Ben Bulben rises abruptly out of the plain. You can climb to the top, but go with great care.

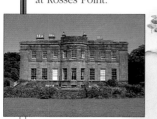

Lissadell House ④
Yeats was a close friend of the Gore-Booth sisters who lived at Lissadell. You can see the room where the poet slept as a guest *(see p231)*.

Drumcliff ③
Although he died in France, in 1948 Yeats's body was laid to rest in Drumcliff churchyard. The ruins of an old monastic site include a fine High Cross.

TIPS FOR DRIVERS

Length: 88 km (55 miles).
Stopping-off points: Outside Sligo, the best choice of eating places is at Rosses Point, although there are good pubs in Drumcliff and Dromahair, and Parke's Castle has a café. Lough Gill provides most choice in terms of picnic spots.
Boat trips: Wild Rose Water Bus (071 916 4266 or 087 259 8869). (See also pp387–9.)

KEY

━━━ Tour route

═══ Other roads

⛴ Boat trips

☼ Viewpoint

Rosses Point ②
Yeats and his brother used to spend their summers at this pretty resort. It stands at the entrance to Sligo Bay, and a steady flow of boats passes by.

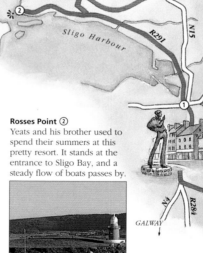

Sligo ①
This town is a good place to begin a tour of Yeats country. It has many connections with the poet and his family, whose literary and artistic legacy has helped to inspire Sligo's thriving arts scene *(see p234)*.

WB YEATS AND SLIGO

As a schoolboy in London, Yeats *(see p23)* longed for his native Sligo, and as an adult he often returned here. He lovingly describes the county in his *Reveries over Childhood and Youth*, and the lake-studded landscape haunts his poetry. "In a sense", Yeats said, "Sligo has always been my home", and it is here that he wished to be buried. His gravestone in Drumcliff bears an epitaph he penned himself: "Cast a cold eye on life, on death. Horseman pass by."

WB Yeats (1865–1939)

Parke's Castle viewed from across the calm waters of Lough Gill

Parke's Castle ㉑

Road map C2. 6 km (4 miles) N of Dromahair, Co Leitrim. **Tel** 071 916 4149. 🚌 or 🚗 to Sligo. ☐ mid-Mar–Oct: 10am–6pm daily (last adm 5:15pm). 🎫 ♿ ground floor only. 📷 🖥 www.irelandnorthwest.ie

This fortified manor house dominates the eastern end of Lough Gill. It was built in 1609 by Captain Robert Parke, an English settler who later became MP for Leitrim. It has been beautifully restored by the Office of Public Works using 17th-century building methods and native Irish oak.

Parke's Castle was erected on the site of a 16th-century tower house belonging to the O'Rourkes, a powerful local clan, and stones from this earlier structure were used in the new building. The original foundations and part of the moat were incorporated, but otherwise Parke's Castle is the epitome of a Plantation manor house *(see p39)*. It is protected by a large enclosure or bawn, whose sturdy wall includes a gatehouse and two turrets as well as the house itself.

Among the most distinctive architectural features of Parke's Castle are the diamond-shaped chimneys, mullioned windows and the parapets. There is also a curious stone hut, known as the "sweathouse", which was an early Irish sauna. Inside, an exhibition and audiovisual display cover Parke's Castle and various historic and prehistoric sites in the area. There is also a working forge.

Boat trips around sights on Lough Gill that are associated with the poet, WB Yeats, leave from outside the castle walls.

Glencar Lough ⑥

"There is a waterfall … that all my childhood counted dear", wrote Yeats of the cataract which tumbles into Glencar Lough. A path leads down to it from the road.

N16
ENNISKILLEN

Parke's Castle ⑦

This 17th-century fortified manor house commands a splendid view over the tranquil waters of Lough Gill. It is a starting point for boat trips around the lough.

LOUGH GILL

Isle of Innisfree ⑧

"There midnight's all a glimmer, and noon a purple glow", is how Yeats once described Innisfree. There is not much to see on this tiny island but it is a romantic spot. In summer, a boatman ferries visitors here.

R288

Dromahair

R289

CARRICK-ON-SHANNON

R287

Dooney Rock ⑨

A steep path leads from the road to Dooney Rock, from where glorious views extend over the lough to Ben Bulben. Trails weave through the surrounding woods and by the lake.

| 0 kilometres | 3 |
| 0 miles | 2 |

Hargadon's bar *(see p350)*, one of Sligo town's most famous watering holes

Sligo ②

Road map C2. Co Sligo. 🏘 *20,000.*
🚉 *071 916 8280.* 🚌 🚌 🛈 *Aras Reddan, Temple St (071 916 1201).*
🚢 *Fri.* **www**.irelandnorthwest.ie

The port of Sligo sits at the mouth of the River Gara-vogue, sandwiched between the Atlantic and Lough Gill. The largest town in the north-west, it rose to prominence under the Normans, being well placed as a gateway between the provinces of Ulster and Connaught. The appearance of Sligo today is mainly the result of growth during the late 18th and 19th centuries.

Sligo is perfectly situated for touring the ravishing countryside nearby, and it is also a good centre for traditional music. While at first sight it can seem a bit sombre, the town is thriving as the arts capital of northwest Ireland.

Sligo's link with the Yeats family is the main source of the town's appeal. WB Yeats *(see pp232–3)*, Ireland's best-known poet, was born into a prominent local family. The Pollexfen warehouse, at the western end of Wine Street, has a rooftop turret from which the poet's grandfather would observe his merchant fleet moored in the docks.

The town's sole surviving medieval building is **Sligo Abbey**, founded in 1253. Some original features remain, such as the delicate lancet windows in the choir, but this ruined Dominican friary dates mainly from the 15th century. The best features are a beautifully carved altar and the cloisters. A short distance west from

the abbey is O'Connell Street, with the town's main shops and Hargadon's bar – an old Sligo institution complete with a dark, wooden interior, snugs and a grocery counter. Near the junction with Wine Street, overlooking Hyde Bridge, is the Yeats Memorial Building. This houses the Yeats Society and the **Sligo Art Gallery**, which puts on shows by foreign and Irish artists. The Yeats International Summer School is held here too: a renowned annual festival of readings and lectures on the poet's life and work.

Just the other side of Hyde Bridge is a statue of the poet, engraved with lines from his own verse. **Sligo County Museum** has a collection of Yeatsian memorabilia and local artifacts but the entire Niland Collection including the paintings by Jack B Yeats have been moved to the **Model Arts &Niland Gallery** in The Mall. This outstanding new centre also puts on temporary exhibitions of major Irish and international contemporary art.

Bronze statue of WB Yeats

🏛 **Sligo Abbey**
Abbey St. **Tel** *071 914 6406.* 🕐 *mid-Mar–Oct: daily; Nov–Jan: Fri–Sun.* 🔲 *Easter–Oct.*

🏛 **Sligo Art Gallery**
Hyde Bridge. **Tel** *071 914 5847.*
🕐 *10am–5:30pm Mon–Sat.*

🏛 **Sligo County Museum**
Stephen St. **Tel** *071 914 7190.*
🕐 *Tue–Sat daily (Oct–May: pm only).*

🏛 **Model Arts & Niland Gallery** The Mall. **Tel** *071 9141405.*
🕐 *Tue–Sun.* **www**.modelart.ie

Environs

Improbably set in the suburbs of Sligo, **Carrowmore Mega-lithic Cemetery** once held the country's largest collection of Stone Age tombs. Quarrying destroyed much, but about 40 passage tombs *(see pp246–7)* and dolmens *(see p32)* survive among the abandoned gravel pits, with some in private gardens and cottages.

The huge unexcavated cairn atop **Knocknarea** mountain dates back 5,000 years and is said to contain the tomb of the legendary Queen Maeve of Connaught *(see p26)*. It is an hour's climb starting 4 km (2.5 miles) west of Carrowmore.

Tobernalt, by Lough Gill 5 km (3 miles) south of Sligo, means "cliff well", after a nearby spring with alleged curative powers. It was a holy site in Celtic times and later became a Christian shrine. Priests came here in secret to celebrate Mass during the 18th century, when Catholic worship was illegal. The Mass rock, next to an altar erected around 1900, remains a place of pilgrimage.

🏛 **Carrowmore Cemetery**
Tel *071 916 1534.* 🕐 *Easter–Oct.* 🔲

Altar by the holy well at Tobernalt, overlooking Lough Gill in Sligo

Lough Arrow

Road map C3. Co Sligo. 🚗 *to Ballinafad*. 🚉 *May–Oct: Boyle (071 966 2145)*. **www**.irelandwest.ie

People go to Lough Arrow to sail and fish for the local trout, and also simply to enjoy the glorious countryside. You can explore the lake by boat, but the views from the shore are the real joy of Lough Arrow. A full circuit of the lake is recommended, but for the most breathtaking views head for the southern end around **Ballinafad**. This small town lies in a gorgeous spot, enclosed to the north and south by the Bricklieve and Curlew Mountains.

The **Carrowkeel Passage Tomb Cemetery** occupies a remote and eerie spot in the Bricklieve Mountains to the north of Ballinafad. The best approach is up the single track road from Castlebaldwin, 5 km (3 miles) northeast of the site.

The 14 Neolithic passage graves, which are scattered around a hilltop overlooking Lough Arrow, are elaborate corbelled structures. One is comparable with Newgrange (*see pp246–7*), except that the burial chamber inside this cairn is lit by the sun on the day of the summer solstice (21 June) as opposed to the winter solstice. On a nearby ridge are the remains of Stone Age huts, presumably those occupied by the farmers who buried their dead in the Carrowkeel passage graves.

Passage tomb in Carrowkeel cemetery above Lough Arrow

Carrick-on-Shannon ⓩ

Road map C3. Co Leitrim. 🏠 *2,500*. 🚗 🚉 🛈 *Apr–Sep: The Marina (071 962 0170)*. **www**.leitrimtourism.com

The tiny capital of Leitrim, one of the least populated counties in Ireland (although this is changing), stands in a lovely spot on a tight bend of the River Shannon.

The town's location by the river and its proximity to the Grand Canal were crucial to Carrick's development. They are also the main reasons for its thriving tourist industry. There is a colourful, modern marina, which in summer fills up with private launches and boats available for hire.

Already a major boating centre, Carrick has benefited from the reopening of the Shannon-Erne Waterway, one end of which begins 6 km

(4 miles) north at Leitrim. The channel was restored in a cross-border joint venture billed as a symbol of peaceful cooperation between Northern Ireland and the Republic.

Away from the bustle of the marina, Carrick is an old-fashioned place, with 19th-century churches and convents, refined Georgian houses and shopfronts. The town's most curious building is the quaint **Costello Chapel** on Bridge Street, one of the smallest in the world. It was built in 1877 by local businessman Edward Costello, to house the tombs of himself and his wife.

The Organic Centre ⓨ

Road map C3. Rossinver, Co Leitrim. **Tel** 071 985 4338. **www**.theorganiccentre.ie

Situated about 3.2 kilometres (2 miles) from Rossinver on the Kinlough Road, The Organic Centre was established in 1995 as a non-profit making company with the aim of providing training, information and demonstrations of organic gardening, cultivation and farming.

The centre is located on a 7.7 ha (19-acre) site at Rossinver in the unspoilt countryside of the sparsely populated North Leitrim. There are display gardens for visitors including a children's garden, a taste garden and a heritage garden, as well as other unusual attractions. A café is open at weekends in the summer.

SHANNON-ERNE WATERWAY

This labyrinthine system of rivers and lakes passes through unspoiled border country, linking Leitrim on the Shannon and Upper Lough Erne in Fermanagh. It follows the course of a canal which was completed and then abandoned in the 1860s. The channel was reopened in 1993, enabling the public to enjoy both the Victorian stonework (including 34 bridges) and the state-of-the-art technology used to operate the 16 locks.

Cruiser negotiating a lock on the Shannon-Erne Waterway

THE MIDLANDS

CAVAN · MONAGHAN · LOUTH · LONGFORD
WESTMEATH · MEATH · OFFALY · LAOIS

The cradle of Irish civilization and the Celts' spiritual home, the Midlands encompass some of Ireland's most sacred and symbolic sites. Much of the region is ignored, but the ragged landscapes of lush pastures, lakes and bogland reveal ancient Celtic crosses, gracious Norman abbeys and Gothic Revival castles.

The fertile Boyne Valley in County Meath was settled during the Stone Age and became the most important centre of habitation in the country. The remains of ancient sites from this early civilization fill the area and include Newgrange, the finest Neolithic tomb in the country. In Celtic times, the focus shifted south to the Hill of Tara, the seat of the High Kings of Ireland and the Celts' spiritual and political capital. Tara's heyday came in the 3rd century AD, but it retained its importance until the Normans invaded in the 1100s.

Norman castles, such as the immense fortress at Trim in County Meath, attest to the shifting frontiers around the region of English influence known as the Pale *(see p132)*. By the end of the 16th century, this area incorporated nearly all the counties in the Midlands.

The Boyne Valley returned to prominence in 1690, when the Battle of the Boyne ended in a landmark Protestant victory over the Catholics *(see pp38–9)*.

Although part of the Republic since 1921, historically Monaghan and Cavan belong to Ulster, and the former retains strong links with the province. The rounded hills called drumlins, found in both counties, are typical of the border region between the Republic and Northern Ireland.

Grassland and bog dotted with lakes are most characteristic of the Midlands, but the Slieve Bloom Mountains and the Cooley Peninsula provide good walking country. In addition to Meath's ancient sites, the historical highlights of the region are monasteries like Fore Abbey and Clonmacnoise, this last ranking among Europe's greatest early Christian centres.

Carlingford village and harbour, with the hills of the Cooley Peninsula rising behind

◁ Temple Finghin round tower at Clonmacnoise monastery on the banks of the River Shannon

Exploring the Midlands

Drogheda is the obvious base from which to
explore the Boyne Valley and neighbouring
monastic sites, such as Monasterboice. Trim
and Mullingar, to the southwest, are less
convenient but make pleasanter places in
which to stay. The northern counties of
Monaghan, Cavan and Longford are quiet
backwaters with a patchwork of lakes that
attract many anglers.To the south, Offaly and
Laois are dominated by dark expanses of bog,
though there is a cluster of sights around the
attractive Georgian town of Birr. For a break by
the sea, head for the picturesque village of
Carlingford on the Cooley Peninsula.

West doorway of Nuns' Church at Clonmacnoise

KEY

══	Motorway
══	Major road
──	Secondary road
⋯⋯	Minor road
──	Scenic route
⚊	Main railway
──	Minor railway
══	National border
══	County border
△	Summit

GETTING AROUND

In the Midlands, there is an extensive network
of roads and rail lines fanning out across the
country from Dublin. As a result, getting around
on public transport is easier than in most other
areas. The Dublin–Belfast railway serves
Dundalk and Drogheda, while Mullingar and
Longford town lie on the Dublin–Sligo route.
The railway and N7 road between Dublin and
Limerick give good access to Laois and Offaly.
For motorists, roads in the Midlands are often
flat and straight but also potholed.

SEE ALSO

• *Where to Stay* p314–16

• *Restaurants, Cafés and Pubs*
pp341–2 & p350

Statue in Birr Castle's
formal gardens

SIGHTS AT A GLANCE

Athlone ⑱
Birr ㉑
Carlingford ⑧
Carrigglas Manor ③
Clonmacnoise pp250–51 ⑲
Drogheda ⑩
Drumlane ②
Dundalk ⑦
Emo Court ㉓
Fore Abbey ⑤
Hill of Tara ⑭
Kells ⑥
Kilbeggan ⑰
Mellifont Abbey ⑫
Monaghan ①
Monasterboice ⑨
Mullingar ⑯
*Newgrange and the Boyne
  Valley pp244–7* ⑪
Rock of Dunamase ㉔
Shannonbridge Bog Railway ⑳
Slane ⑬
Slieve Bloom Mountains ㉒
Trim ⑮
Tullynally Castle ④

| 0 kilometres | 20 |
| 0 miles | 20 |

View of Trim across the River Boyne

Rossmore Memorial drinking fountain in Monaghan

Monaghan ❶

Road map D2. Co Monaghan.
🏠 6,000. 🚌
ℹ️ Knockaconny (047 71818).
www.monaghantourism.com

The spruce and thriving town of Monaghan is the urban highlight of the northern Midlands. Planted by James I in 1613 *(see p39)*, it developed into a prosperous industrial centre, thanks mainly to the local manufacture of linen. A crannog *(see p33)* off Glen Road is the sole trace of the town's Celtic beginnings.

Monaghan centres on three almost contiguous squares. The main attraction in Market Square is the 18th-century **Market House**, a squat but charming building with the original oak beams still visible. To the east lies Church Square, very much the heart of modern Monaghan and lined with dignified 19th-century buildings, such as the Classical-style courthouse. The third square, which is known as the Diamond, was the original marketplace. It contains the **Rossmore Memorial**, a large Victorian drinking fountain with an ornate stone canopy supported by marble columns.

Do not miss the excellent **County Museum**, just off Market Square, which tells the story of Monaghan's linen and lace-making industries. The pride of its historical collection is the Cross of Clogher, an ornate bronze altar cross which dates from around 1400.

The Gothic Revival Cathedral of St Macartan perches on a hilltop south of the town, from where you can enjoy a fine view over Monaghan.

🏛 **County Museum**
Hill St. **Tel** 047 82928. ⏰ Tue–Sat.
🔴 public hols. ♿ limited.

Drumlane ❷

Road map C3. 1 km (0.5 miles) S of Milltown, Co Cavan. c to Belturbet.

Standing alone by the River Erne, the medieval church and round tower of Drumlane merit a visit as much for their delightful setting as for the ruins themselves. The abbey church, founded in the early 13th century but significantly altered about 200 years later, features fine Romanesque carvings. The nearby round tower has lost its cap but is unusual for the well-finished stonework, with carvings of birds on the north side.

Carrigglas Manor ❸

*Road map C3. Co Longford. **Tel** 043 45165. 🚌 to Longford. ⏰ 1 Jun–12 Aug: 11am–5pm Sun–Fri. 📷 🎥 📹 ♿ limited. **www**.carrigglas.com*

Carrigglas Manor has been the seat of the Lefroys, a family of Huguenot descent, ever since its construction in 1837. It has changed little in the intervening years and is a fine example of the Tudor Revival style. The Victorian atmosphere is still very much alive inside, where the rooms are decorated with pseudo-Gothic panelling

Drawing room in Carrigglas Manor with original 19th-century features

Authentic Victorian kitchen in Tullynally Castle

and ornate plasterwork ceilings. The stable block, by contrast, is a grand Neo-Classical building by James Gandon, the architect of Dublin's Custom House *(see p88)*. The manor grounds are primarily woodland but include a wild flower garden.

Environs
Just 14 km (9 miles) south of Carrigglas Manor, **Ardagh** is considered the most attractive village in Longford, with pretty stone cottages gathered around a green.

Tullynally Castle **❹**

Road map C3. Castle Pollard, Co Westmeath. **Tel** 044 61159. 🚌 to Mullingar. **Castle** 🕐 to pre-booked groups only. 🎥 📷 obligatory. 🚫 **Tea rooms and gardens** 🕐 May–Aug: daily (pm only). 🎥 🚫 ltd. 🚫 📶 www.tullynallycastle.com

This huge structure, adorned with numerous turrets and battlements, is one of Ireland's largest castles. The original 17th-century tower house was given a Georgian gloss, but this was all but submerged under later Gothic Revival changes. The Pakenham family have lived at Tullynally since 1655. Thomas Pakenham now manages the estate.

The imposing great hall leads to a fine panelled dining room hung with family portraits. Of equal interest are the Victorian kitchen, laundry room and the adjacent drying room.

The 8,000-volume library looks out on to rolling wooded parkland, much of which was landscaped in the 1760s. The grounds include Victorian terraces, walled kitchen and flower gardens, and two small lakes where black swans have recently been introduced.

Fore Abbey **❺**

Road map C3. Fore, Castle Pollard, Co Westmeath. **Tel** 044 61780. 🚌 to Castle Pollard. 🕐 daily.

The ruins of Fore Abbey lie in glorious rolling countryside about 8 km (5 miles) east of Tullynally Castle. St Fechin set up a monastery here in 630, but what you see now are the remains of a large Benedictine priory founded around 1200. Located on the northern border of the Pale *(see p132)*, Fore Abbey was heavily fortified in the 15th century as protection against the native Irish.

The ruined church was part of the original Norman priory, but the cloister and refectory date from the 1400s. On the hill opposite lies St Fechin's

Church, a Norman building said to mark the site of the first monastery. The tiny church nearby incorporates a 15th-century anchorite's cell.

Kells **❻**

Road map D3. Co Meath. 🏘 5,500. 🚌 🛈 *Kells Heritage Centre, Navan Road (046 924 9336).* ● Dec–Jan. www.meathtourism.ie

Signposted by its Irish name, Ceanannus Mór, this modest town provides an unlikely backdrop to the monastery for which it is so famous.

Kells Monastery was set up by St Columba in the 6th century, but its heyday came after 806, when monks fled here from Iona. They may have been the scribes who illuminated the superb *Book of Kells*, now kept at Trinity College, Dublin *(see p64)*.

The monastery centres on a rather gloomy 18th-century church beside which stands a decapitated round tower. There are several 9th-century High Crosses; the South Cross is in the best condition.

Just north of the enclosure is **St Columba's House**, a tiny steep-roofed stone oratory, similar to St Kevin's Kitchen at Glendalough *(see p140)*.

The Market Cross, a High Cross that once marked the entrance to the monastery, now stands outside the Heritage Centre in the Old Courthouse. It was used as a gallows during the uprising in 1798 *(see p41)*. The battle scene on the base is a subject rarely used in High Cross art.

Ruins of Fore Abbey, a medieval Benedictine priory

Thatched cottage in Carlingford on the mountainous Cooley Peninsula

Dundalk ❼

Road map D3. Co Louth. 🚶 32,000.
🚌 🚉 ℹ️ Jocelyn St (042 933 5484).
🚢 Fri. **www**.eastcoastmidlands.ie

Dundalk once marked the northernmost point of the Pale, the area controlled by the English during the Middle Ages *(see p132)*. Now it is the last major town before the Northern Irish border.

Dundalk is also a gateway to the magnificent countryside of the Cooley Peninsula. The **County Museum**, which is housed in an 18th-century distillery in the town, gives an imaginative history of the county, including a section on some of Louth's traditional industries such as beer-making.

🏛 **County Museum**
Jocelyn St. **Tel** 042 932 7056.
⬤ daily. ⬤ 25 & 26 Dec, 1 Jan.
📷 ♿

Carlingford ❽

Road map D3. Co Louth. 🚶 950.
🚌 ℹ️ **Holy Trinity Heritage Centre** Churchyard Rd (042 937 3454). **Carlingford Adventure Centre** Tholsel St (042 937 3100).
⬤ 2 weeks at Christmas.
www.carlingfordadventure.com

This is a picturesque fishing village, located between the mountains of the Cooley Peninsula and Carlingford Lough. The border with Northern Ireland runs through the centre of this drowned river valley, and from the village you can look across to the Mountains of Mourne on the Ulster side *(see pp284–5)*. Carlingford is an interesting

place to explore, with its pretty whitewashed cottages and ancient buildings clustered along medieval alleyways. The ruins of **King John's Castle**, built by the Normans to protect the entrance to the lough, still dominate the village, and there are other impressive fortified buildings, including the Mint. The **Holy Trinity Heritage Centre**, which is housed in a medieval church, traces the history of the port from Anglo-Norman times.

Carlingford is the country's oyster capital, and often holds an oyster festival in August, which draws a large crowd.The lough is a popular watersports centre too, and in summer you can go on cruises around the lough from the quayside where there is a new marina.

The **Carlingford Adventure Centre** organizes walking tours, plus sailing, kayaking, canoeing and windsurfing.

Environs
A scenic route weaves around the **Cooley Peninsula**, skirting the coast and then cutting right through the mountains. The section along the north coast is the most dramatic: just 3 km (1.8 miles) northwest of Carlingford, in the **Slieve Foye Forest Park**, a corkscrew road climbs to give a gorgeous panoramic view over the hills and lough.

The Tain Trail, which you can join at Carlingford, is a 30-km (19-mile) circuit through some of the peninsula's most rugged scenery, with cairns and other prehistoric sites scattered over the moorland. Keen hikers will be able to walk it in a day.

Monasterboice ❾

Road map D3. Co Louth. 🚌 to Drogheda. ⬤ daily.

Founded in the 5th century by an obscure disciple of St Patrick called St Buite, this monastic settlement is one of the most famous religious sites in the country. The ruins of the medieval monastery are enclosed within a graveyard in a lovely secluded spot north of Drogheda. The site includes a roofless round tower and two churches, but Monasterboice's greatest treasures are its 10th-century High Crosses.

Muiredach's High Cross is the finest of its kind in Ireland, and its sculpted biblical scenes are still remarkably fresh. They depict the life of Christ on the west face, while the east face, described in detail opposite, features mainly Old Testament scenes. The cross is named after an inscription on the base – "A prayer for Muiredach by whom this cross was made" – which is perhaps a reference to the abbot of Monasterboice.

The 6.5-m (21ft) West Cross, also known as the Tall Cross, is one of the largest in Ireland. The carving has not lasted as well as on Muiredach's Cross, but you can make out scenes from the Death of Christ. The North Cross, which is the least notable of the three, features a Crucifixion and a carved spiral pattern.

Detail from a tomb in Monasterboice graveyard

Round tower and West High Cross at Monasterboice

Ireland's High Crosses

High crosses exist in Celtic parts of both Britain and Ireland. Yet in their profusion and craftsmanship, Irish High Crosses are exceptional. The distinctive ringed cross has become a symbol of Irish Christianity and is still imitated today. The beautiful High Crosses associated with medieval monasteries were carved between the 8th and 12th centuries. The early crosses bore only geometric motifs, but in the 9th to 10th centuries a new style emerged when sculpted scenes from the Bible were introduced. Referred to as "sermons in stone", these later versions may have been used to educate the masses. In essence, though, the High Cross was a status symbol for the monastery or a local patron.

Pillar stones *inscribed with crosses, like this 6th-century example at Riasc (see p158), were precursors of the High Cross.*

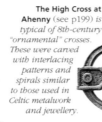

Capstone, showing St Anthony and St Paul meeting in the desert

The High Cross at Ahenny (see p199) *is typical of 8th-century "ornamental" crosses. These were carved with interlacing patterns and spirals similar to those used in Celtic metalwork and jewellery.*

MUIREDACH'S CROSS

Each face of this 10th-century cross at Monasterboice features scenes from the Bible, including the east face seen here. The 5.5-m (18-ft) cross consists of three blocks of sandstone fitted together by means of tenons and sockets.

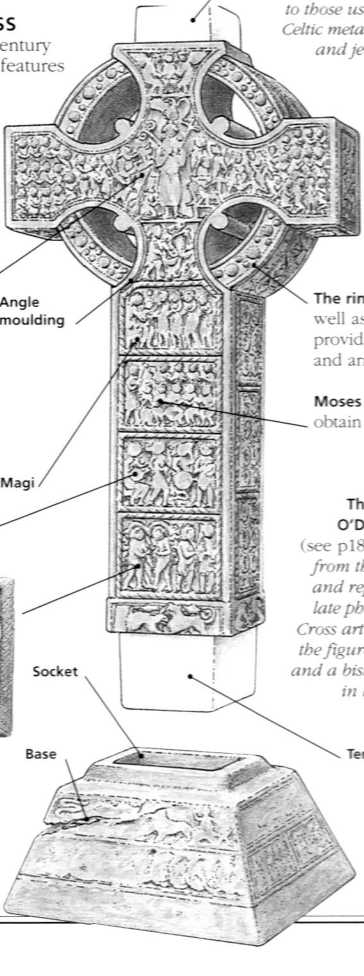

Tenon

The Last Judgment shows Christ in Glory surrounded by a crowd of resurrected souls. The devil stands on his right clutching a pitchfork, ready to chase the damned souls into Hell.

Angle moulding

The ring served a functional as well as a decorative purpose, providing support for the head and arms of the stone cross.

Moses smites the rock to obtain water for the Israelites.

Adoration of the Magi

David struggling with Goliath

The Dysert O'Dea Cross (see p189) *dates from the 1100s and represents the late phase of High Cross art. It features the figures of Christ and a bishop carved in high relief.*

The Fall of Man *shows Adam and Eve beneath an apple-laden tree, with Cain slaying Abel alongside. Both scenes are frequently depicted on Irish High Crosses.*

Socket

Base

Tenon

Drogheda

Road map D3. Co Louth. 🏠 *30,000.*
🚆 🚌 ℹ️ *Donore Rd (041 983 7070).*
Hillmount (041 984 5684). 🚢 *Sat.*
www.eastcoastmidlands.ie

In the 12th century, this
Norman port near the mouth
of the River Boyne was one of
Ireland's most important towns.
However, the place seems
never to have recovered from
the trauma of a vicious attack
by Cromwell in 1649 *(see p39)*,
in which 2,000 citizens were
killed. Although it is now a bit
dilapidated, the town still has
its original street plan and has
a rich medieval heritage.

Little remains of Drogheda's
medieval defences but **St
Lawrence Gate**, a fine 13th-
century barbican, has survived.
Nearby, there are two churches
called **St Peter's**. The one
belonging to the Church of
Ireland, built in 1753, is the
more striking and has some
splendid grave slabs. The
Catholic church is worth
visiting to see the embalmed
head of Oliver Plunkett, an
archbishop martyred in 1681.

South of the river you can
climb Millmount, a Norman
motte topped by a Martello
tower. As well as providing a
good view, this is the site of
the **Millmount Museum**,

Drogheda viewed from Millmount across the River Boyne

which contains an interesting
display of historical artifacts.

🏛 Millmount Museum
Millmount Square. **Tel** 041 983
3097. ◯ *daily (Sun pm only).* ● *7
days at Christmas.* 🎫 ✔️ ♿ *limited.*
www.millmount.net

Newgrange and
the Boyne Valley ⑪

Road map D3. Co Meath. 🚌 *to
Drogheda.* 🚌 *to Slane or Drogheda.*
ℹ️ *Brú na Bóinne Interpretative
Centre (041 988 0300).* ◯ *daily.*

Known as Brú na Bóinne,
the "Palace of the Boyne", this
river valley was the cradle of
Irish civilization. The fertile
soil supported a sophisticated
society in Neolithic times.
Much evidence survives, in
the form of ring forts, passage
graves and sacred enclosures.
The most important Neolithic
monuments in the valley are
three passage graves: supreme
among these is **Newgrange**
(see pp246–7), but **Dowth** and
Knowth are significant too.
The Boyne Valley also
encompasses the Hill of Slane
and the Hill of Tara *(see p248)*,
both of which are major sites
in Celtic mythology. Indeed,
this whole region is rich in

River Boyne near the site of the
Battle of the Boyne

THE BATTLE OF THE BOYNE

In 1688, the Catholic King of England, James
II, was deposed from his throne, to be replaced by his Protestant daughter, Mary, and
her husband, William of Orange.
Determined to win back the
crown, James sought the
support of
Irish Catholics, and challenged William at
Oldbridge by the River Boyne west of
Drogheda. The Battle of the Boyne took
place on 1 July 1690, with James's poorly
trained force of 25,000 French and Irish
Catholics facing William's hardened army of
36,000 French Huguenots, Dutch, English
and Scots. The Protestants triumphed and
James fled to France, after a battle that
signalled the beginning of total Protestant
power over Ireland. It ushered in the
confiscation of Catholic lands and the
suppression of Catholic interests,
sealing the country's fate for the
next 300 years.

William of Orange leading his troops at the Battle of the Boyne, 1 July 1690

associations with Ireland's prehistory. With monuments predating Egypt's pyramids, the Boyne Valley is marketed as the Irish "Valley of the Kings".

Newgrange and Knowth can only be seen on a tour run by **Brú na Bóinne Interpretative Centre** near Newgrange. The centre also has displays on the area's Stone Age heritage and a reconstruction of Newgrange.

⋔ Dowth
Off N51, 3 km (2 miles) E of Newgrange. ● *to the public.*

The passage grave at Dowth was plundered by Victorian souvenir hunters and has not been fully excavated. You cannot approach the tomb, but it can be seen from the road.

⋔ Knowth
1.5 km (1 mile) NW of Newgrange. ◻ *as Newgrange (see pp246–7)*.

Knowth outdoes Newgrange in several respects, above all in the quantity of its treasures, which form the greatest concentration of megalithic art in Europe. Also, the site was occupied for a much longer period – from Neolithic times right up until about 1400.

Unusually, Knowth has two passage tombs rather than one. The excavations begun in 1962 are now complete and the site is open. The tombs can only be viewed externally to prevent further decay. Keep a look out for the finely carved kerbstones. Visitors sign up for tours via Brú na Bóinne.

Ruined lavabo at Mellifont Abbey

Slane Castle in grounds landscaped by Capability Brown

Mellifont Abbey ⓬

Road map D3. Cullen, Co Louth. **Tel** 041 982 6459. 🚍 *to Drogheda.* 🚍 *to Drogheda or Slane.* ◻ *May–Oct: daily; Nov–Apr: by appt.* 📷

On the banks of the River Mattock, 10 km (6 miles) west of Drogheda, lies the first Cistercian monastery to have been built in Ireland. Mellifont was founded in 1142 on the orders of St Malachy, the Archbishop of Armagh. He was greatly influenced by St Bernard who, based at his monastery at Clairvaux in France, was behind the success of the Cistercian Order in Europe. The archbishop introduced not only Cistercian rigour to Mellifont, but also the formal style of monastic architecture used on the continent. His new monastery became a model for other Cistercian centres built in Ireland, retaining its supremacy over them until 1539, when the abbey was closed and turned into a fortified house. William of Orange used Mellifont as his headquarters during the Battle of the Boyne in 1690. The abbey is now a ruin, but it is still possible to appreciate the scale and

Glazed medieval tiles at Mellifont Abbey

ground plan of the original complex. Not much survives of the abbey church, but to the south of it, enclosed by what remains of the Romanesque cloister, is the most interesting building at Mellifont: a unique 13th-century lavabo where monks came to wash their hands in a fountain before meals. Four of the building's original eight sides survive, each with a Romanesque arch. On the eastern side of the cloister stands the 14th-century chapter house. It has an impressive vaulted ceiling and a floor laid with glazed medieval tiles taken from the abbey church.

Slane ⓭

Road map D3. Co Meath. **Tel** 041 988 0305. 🚍 950. 🚍

Slane is an attractive estate village, centred on a quartet of Georgian houses. The Boyne flows through it and skirts **Slane Castle Demesne**, set in glorious grounds laid out in the 18th century by Capability Brown. The castle was damaged by fire in 1991 but reopened in 2001.

Just to the north rises the **Hill of Slane** where, in 433, St Patrick is said to have lit a Paschal (Easter) fire as a challenge to the pagan High King of Tara *(see p248)*. The event symbolised the triumph of Christianity over paganism.

Newgrange

Tri-spiral carving on stone in chamber

The origins of Newgrange, one of the most important passage graves in Europe, are steeped in mystery. According to Celtic lore, the legendary kings of Tara *(see p248)* were buried here, but Newgrange predates them. Built in around 3200 BC, the grave was left untouched by all invaders until it was rediscovered in 1699. When it was excavated in the 1960s, archaeologists discovered that on the winter solstice (21 December), rays of sun enter the tomb and light up the burial chamber – making it the world's oldest solar observatory. All visitors to Newgrange and Knowth *(see pp244–5)* are admitted through the visitors' centre from where tours of the historic site are taken. Early arrival is advised in summer to avoid long queues.

Basin Stone
The chiselled stones, found in each recess, would have once contained funerary offerings and the bones of the dead.

The chamber has three recesses or side chambers: the north recess is the one struck by sunlight on the winter solstice.

Chamber Ceiling
The burial chamber's intricate corbelled ceiling, which reaches a height of 6 m (20 ft) above the floor, has survived intact. The overlapping slabs form a conical hollow, topped by a single capstone.

CONSTRUCTION OF NEWGRANGE

The tomb at Newgrange was designed by people with clearly exceptional artistic and engineering skills, who had use of neither the wheel nor metal tools. About 200,000 tonnes of loose stones were transported to build the mound, or cairn, which protects the passage grave. Larger slabs were used to make the circle around the cairn (12 out of a probable 35 stones have survived), the kerb and the tomb itself. Many of the kerbstones and the slabs lining the passage, the chamber and its recesses are decorated with zigzags, spirals and other geometric motifs. The grave's corbelled ceiling consists of smaller, unadorned slabs and has proved completely waterproof for the last 5,000 years.

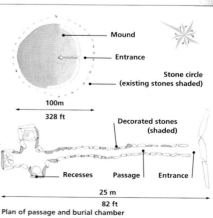

- Mound
- Entrance
- Stone circle (existing stones shaded)

100m
328 ft

Decorated stones (shaded)

Recesses   Passage   Entrance

25 m
82 ft
Plan of passage and burial chamber

VISITORS' CHECKLIST

Road map D3. 8 km (5 miles) E of Slane, Co Meath. **Tel** 041 988 0300. 🚌 to Drogheda. 🚌 to Drogheda & Drogheda to Brú na Boinne visitors' centre. ☐ May–Sep: 9am– 6:30pm (Jun–mid Sep: 7pm) daily; Oct–Apr: 9:30am–5:30pm (Nov– Feb: 5pm) daily; last tour: 1 hr 45 mins before close. ⬤ 24–27 Dec. 📷 🚫 inside tomb. ♿ Brú na Boinne visitors' centre only. ✅ obligatory. 🍴 🛍

Restoration of Newgrange
Located on a low ridge north of the Boyne, Newgrange took more than 70 years to build. Between 1962 and 1975 the passage grave and mound were restored as closely as possible to their original state.

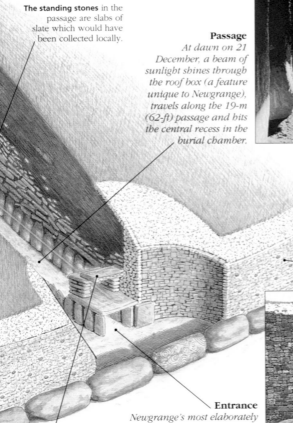

The standing stones in the passage are slabs of slate which would have been collected locally.

Passage
At dawn on 21 December, a beam of sunlight shines through the roof box (a feature unique to Newgrange), travels along the 19-m (62-ft) passage and hits the central recess in the burial chamber.

The retaining wall around the front of the cairn was rebuilt using the white quartz and granite stones found scattered around the site during excavations.

Roof box

Entrance
Newgrange's most elaborately carved kerbstone stands just in front of the entrance, forming part of the kerb of huge slabs around the cairn.

Trim Castle set in water meadows beside the River Boyne

Hill of Tara ⓮

Road map D3. Nr Killmessan Village, Co Meath. **Tel** 046 902 5903 🚌 to Navan. ☐ mid-May–mid-Sept:10am–6pm daily, (last adm 45mins before closing). 🎞 Interpretative Centre. 📷 www.heritageireland.ie

A site of mythical importance, Tara was the political and spiritual centre of Celtic Ireland and the seat of the High Kings until the 11th century. The spread of Christianity, which eroded the importance of Tara, is marked by a statue of St Patrick. The symbolism of the site was not lost on Daniel O'Connell (see p42), who chose Tara for a rally in 1843, attended by over one million people.

Tours from the Interpretative Centre take in a Stone Age passage grave and Iron Age hill forts, which, to the untutored eye, look like mere hollows and grassy mounds. Clearest is the Royal Enclosure, an oval fort, in the centre of which is Cormac's House containing the "stone of destiny" (Liath Fáil), fertility symbol and inauguration stone of the High Kings. Most moving, however, is the poignant atmosphere and views over the Boyne Valley.

Trim ⓯

Road map D3. Co Meath. 🏠 6,500. 🚌 ℹ️ Mill St (046 943 0413). 🛒 Fri. www.eastcoastmidlandsireland.com

Trim is one of the most pleasing Midlands market towns. A Norman stronghold on the River Boyne, it marked a boundary of the Pale (see

p132). Trim runs efficient heritage and genealogy centres while the **Irish Heritage Trim Folk Theatre** provides rousing summer entertainment. (This popular company is at present in search of new premises.)

The dramatic **Trim Castle** was founded in the 12th century by Hugh de Lacy, a Norman knight, and is one of the largest medieval castles in Europe. It makes a spectacular backdrop for films and was used in Mel Gibson's film Braveheart in 1995.

Over the river is **Talbot Castle**, an Augustinian abbey converted to a manor house in the 15th century. Just north of the abbey is **St Patrick's Cathedral**, which incorporates part of a medieval church with a 15th-century tower and sections of the original chancel.

Butterstream Gardens, on the edge of town, are the best in the county. A luxuriant herbaceous bed is the centrepiece, but also pleasing are the exotic woodland, rose and white gardens. The design is enhanced by pergolas, pools and bridges.

🏰 **Trim Castle**
Tel 046 943 8619. ☐ Easter–Oct: daily; Nov–Easter: weekends. ℹ️ Mill St (046 943 7227). 📷 obligatory.

Mullingar ⓰

Road map C3. Co Westmeath. 🏠 25,000. 🚌 🚌 ℹ️ Market Square (046 934 7227).

The county town of Westmeath is a prosperous but unremarkable market town encircled by the Royal Canal

Aerial view of Iron Age forts on the Hill of Tara

(see p101), which with its 46 locks links Dublin with the River Shannon. The cost of building the canal bankrupted its investors and it was never profitable. Although Mullingar's main appeal is as a base to explore the surrounding area, pubs such as Con's and the cheery Canton Casey's can make a pleasant interlude.

Environs
The Dublin to Mullingar stretch of the Royal Canal has attractive towpaths for walkers, and fishing.

Just off the Kilbeggan road from Mullingar stands **Belvedere House**, a romantic Palladian villa overlooking Lough Ennel. The house, built in 1740 by Richard Castle, is decorated with Rococo plasterwork and set in beautiful grounds.

Shortly after the house was built, the first Earl of Belvedere accused his wife of having an affair with his brother, and imprisoned her for 31 years in a nearby house. In 1760, the Earl built a Gothic folly – the Jealous Wall – to block the view of his second brother's more opulent mansion across the way. The Jealous Wall remains as does an octagonal gazebo and follies.

Charming terraces descend to the lake. On the other side of the house is a picturesque walled garden, enclosed by an arboretum and parkland.

⚙ Belvedere House
6.5 km (4 miles) S of Mullingar.
Tel 044 49060. ⬜ May–Aug:
9:30am–9pm Mon–Fri,
10:30am–7pm Sat & Sun; Sep–Oct:
10:30am–6pm daily; Nov–Apr:
10:30am–4:30pm daily. 🖼 🔲 🔲
♿ theatre & interpretative centre.
www.belvedere-house.ie

The Jealous Wall at Belvedere House, near Mullingar

Athlone Castle below the towers of the church of St Peter and St Paul

Kilbeggan ⓱

Road map C4. Co Westmeath.
🏠 1,000. 🚉

Situated between Mullingar and Tullamore, this pleasant village has a small harbour on the Grand Canal. However the main point of interest is **Locke's Distillery**. Founded in 1757, it claims to be the oldest licensed pot still distillery in the world. Unable to compete with Scotch whisky manufacturers, the company went bankrupt in 1954, but the aroma hung in the warehouses for years and was known as "the angel's share". The distillery was reopened as a museum in 1987. The building is authentic, a solid structure complete with water wheel and inside steam engine. A tour traces the process of Irish whiskey-making, from the mash tuns to the vast fermentation vats and creation of wash (rough beer) to the distillation and maturation stages. At the tasting stage, workers would sample the whiskey in the can pit room. Visitors can still taste whiskeys in the bar but, unlike the original workers, cannot bathe in the whiskey vats.

Miniature whiskey bottles at Locke's Distillery in Kilbeggan

🏛 Locke's Distillery
Main Street. **Tel** 0506 32134.
⬜ daily. 🖼 ♿ 🔲 🔲 🔲
www.lockesdistillerymuseum.com

Athlone ⓲

Road map C3. Co Westmeath.
🏠 16,000. 🚉 🚌 🛈 Market
Square (090 649 4630). 🚌 Fri.

The town owes its historical importance to its position by a natural ford on the River Shannon. **Athlone Castle** is a much altered 13th-century fortress, which was badly damaged in the Jacobite Wars *(see pp38–9)*. It lies in the shadow of the 19th-century church of St Peter and St Paul. The neighbouring streets offer several good pubs. Across the river from the castle, boats depart for Clonmacnoise *(see pp250–51)* or Lough Ree.

⚓ Athlone Castle
Visitors' Centre **Tel** 090 649 2912.
⬜ May–Sep: daily; Oct–Apr: by appt. 🖼 ♿ limited.

Environs
The **Lough Ree Trail** starts 8 km (5 miles) northeast of Athlone, at Glasson. The route passes picturesque views and unspoilt countryside. The trail is a popular cycling tour.

Clonmacnoise ⑲

This medieval monastery, in a remote spot by the River Shannon, was founded by St Ciaran in 545–548. Clonmacnoise lay at a crossroads of medieval routes, linking all parts of Ireland. Known for its scholarship and piety, it thrived from the 7th to the 12th century. Many kings of Tara and of Connaught were buried here. Plundered by the Vikings and Anglo-Normans, it fell to the English in 1552. Today, a group of stone churches (temples), a cathedral, two round towers and three High Crosses remain.

Detail on a grave slab

Last Circuit of Pilgrims at Clonmacnoise
This painting (1838), by George Petrie, shows pilgrims walking the traditional route three times around the site. Pilgrims still do this every year on 9 September, St Ciaran's Day.

The Pope's Shelter was where John Paul II conducted Mass during his visit in 1979.

Cross of the Scriptures
This copy of the original 9th-century cross (now in the museum) is decorated with biblical scenes, but the identity of most of the figures is uncertain.

VISITING CLONMACNOISE

The Visitors' Centre is housed in three buildings modelled on beehive huts *(see p21)*. The museum section contains early grave slabs and the three remaining High Crosses, replicas of which now stand in their original locations. The Nuns' Church, northeast of the main site, has a Romanesque doorway and chancel arch.

Pilgrim path to Nuns' Church

Entrance

KEY

1 South Cross	**7** Cathedral
2 Temple Dowling	**8** North Cross
3 Temple Hurpan	**9** Cross of the Scriptures
4 Temple Melaghlin	**10** Round Tower
5 Temple Ciaran	**11** Temple Connor
6 Temple Kelly	**12** Temple Finghin

0 metres   50

0 yards   50

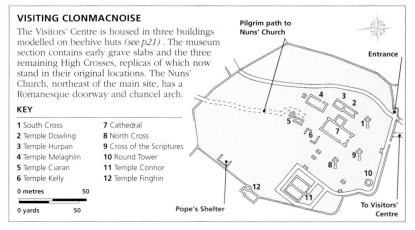

Pope's Shelter

To Visitors' Centre

VISITORS' CHECKLIST

Road map C4. 7 km (4 miles) N
of Shannonbridge, Co Offaly. **Tel**
090 967 4195. 🚂 🚌 to Athlone,
then minibus (090 647 4839/
087 240 7706). 🚌 from Athlone.
◻ daily. Groups pre-book.
● 25 Dec. 📷 📹 in summer.
🚻 💻 www.heritageireland.ie

Whispering Door

*Above the cathedral's 15th-
century north doorway are
carvings of saints Francis,
Patrick and Dominic. The
acoustics of the doorway are
such that even a whisper is
carried inside the building.*

The Shannonbridge Bog Railway
passing an area of cut bog

Shannonbridge
Bog Railway ㉖

Road map C4. 5 km (3 miles) E of
Shannonbridge, Co Offaly. **Tel** 090
967 4450. 🚌 to Athlone. ◻
Apr–Oct: daily; Nov–Mar: groups by
appt. 📷 💻 🚻 🚻 www.bnm.ie

Starting near Shannonbridge,
this guided tour by train is
run by the Irish Peat Board
(Bord na Móna). The 45-minute
tour covers 9 km (6 miles) of
bogland and gives a fascinating
insight into the history and
development of the Blackwater
raised bogs – an area of great
ecological importance, parts
of which are protected.

Tour guides describe the
transformation from lake to
marshy fen and thence to bog
(see p252), and explain that
in several hundred years the
bog will become fields and
woodland. They also point out
the area's distinctive flora and
fauna, from dragonflies to bog
cotton, bog asphodel and
sphagnum moss. The small
lakes and pools that punctuate
the bog provide excellent
habitats for wetland birds.

Bog oaks – old trees which
have been preserved in the
bog – are visible in the places
where the peat has been harvested. For centuries, peat has
been the main source of fuel
in rural Ireland, and visitors
can watch peat being cut by
hand using the traditional tool
known as a "slane". Modern
peat-harvesting machines in
use nearby supply the power
station at Shannonbridge.
There is a craft shop and also a
machinery museum here.

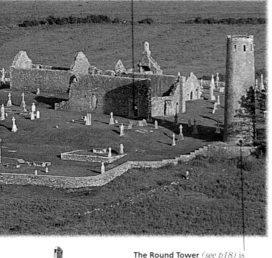

The Round Tower *(see p18)* is
over 19 m (62 ft) high with its
doorway above ground level.

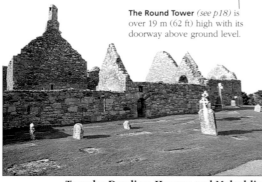

Temples Dowling, Hurpan and Melaghlin
*Built as a family crypt, Temple Hurpan was a 17th-century
addition to the early Romanesque Temple Dowling. The 13th-
century Temple Melaghlin has two fine round-headed windows.*

The Raised Bogs of the Midlands

Peatland or bog, which covers about 15 per cent of the Irish landscape, exists in two principal forms. Most extensive is the thin blanket bog found chiefly in the west, while the dome-shaped raised bogs are more characteristic of the Midlands – notably in an area known as the Bog of Allen.

Four-spotted chaser dragonfly

Although Irish boglands are some of the largest in Europe, the use of peat for fuel and fertilizer has greatly reduced their extent, threatening not only the shape of the Irish landscape but also the survival of a unique habitat and the unusual plants and insects it supports.

Unspoiled expanse of the Bog of Allen

Peat cutters *still gather turf (as peat is known locally) by hand in parts of Ireland. It is then set in stacks to dry. Peat makes a good fuel, because it is rich in partially decayed vegetation, laid down over thousands of years.*

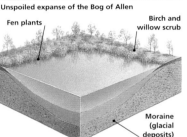

Fen plants — Birch and willow scrub — Moraine (glacial deposits)

8000 BC : *Shallow meltwater lakes that formed after the Ice Age gradually filled with mud. Reeds, sedges and other fen plants began to dominate in the marshy conditions which resulted.*

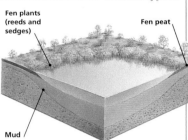

Fen plants (reeds and sedges) — Fen peat — Mud

6000 BC : *As the fen vegetation died, it sank to the lake bed but did not decompose fully in the waterlogged conditions, forming a layer of peat. This slowly built up and also spread outwards.*

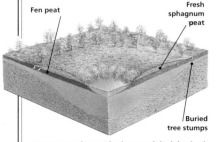

Fen peat — Fresh sphagnum peat — Buried tree stumps

3000 BC : *As the peat built up and the lake slowly disappeared, plant life in the developing bog had to rely almost exclusively on rainwater, which is acid. Fen plants could not survive in these acidic conditions and gave way to bog mosses, mainly species of sphagnum. As these mosses died, they formed a layer of sphagnum peat on the surface of the bog which, over the centuries, attained a distinctive domed shape.*

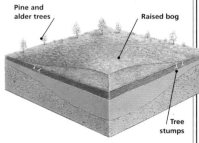

Pine and alder trees — Raised bog — Tree stumps

Present day: *Few raised bogs are actively growing today. Those that remain contain a fascinating historical record of the landscape. The survival of ancient tree stumps shows how well plants are preserved in peat.*

Sphagnum moss

Birr ㉑

Road map 4C. Co Offaly. 🏚 *4,100.*
🚌 ℹ️ *May–Sep: Rosse Row (0509 20110).*

Birr, a gentrified estate town, grew up in the shadow of the castle where the Earls of Rosse have resided for almost four centuries. It is famous for its authentic Georgian layout, with houses displaying original fanlights, door panelling and iron railings. Two particularly elegant streets are Oxmantown Mall, designed by the 2nd Earl of Rosse, and John's Mall. Emmet Square may have sold its Georgian soul to commerce, but Dooley's Hotel is still a fine example of an old coaching inn. Foster's bar, in nearby Connaught Street, is one of many traditional shopfronts to have been restored in Birr.

🏛 Birr Castle Demesne

Rosse Row. **Tel** *0509 20336.*
Gardens ⭘ *daily.* 🅿️ ♿ 🖥 🎁
www.birrcastle.com

Birr Castle was founded in 1620 by the Parsons, later Earls of Rosse, and is still the family seat. They are most noted for their contribution to astronomy – a telescope, built by the 3rd Earl in 1845, was the largest in the world at the time. The 17-m (56-ft) wooden tube, supported by two walls, can be seen in the grounds, fully restored. The Historic Science Centre traces the family's pioneering work.

The castle is closed to the public, but the glory of Birr lies in its grounds, which are open. First landscaped in the 18th century, these are famous for their 9-m (30-ft) box hedges and for the exotic trees and shrubs from foreign expeditions sponsored by the 6th Earl. The magnolias and maples are particularly striking. The gardens overlook the meeting of two rivers.

Slieve Bloom Mountains ㉒

Road map D4. Co Offaly and Co Laois.
🚌 *to Mountmellick.* ℹ️ *May–Sep: Rosse Row, Birr (0509 20110).*

This low range of mountains rises unexpectedly from the bogs and plains of Offaly and Laois, providing a welcome change in the predominantly flat Midlands. You can walk along the **Slieve Bloom Way**, a 30-km (19-mile) circular trail through an unspoiled area of open vistas, deep wooded glens and mountain streams. There are other marked paths too. Good starting points are **Cadamstown**, with an attractive old mill, and the pretty village of **Kinnitty** – both in the northern foothills.

An alcove in the front hall of Emo Court with a trompe l'oeil ceilling

Emo Court ㉓

Road map D4. 13 km (8 miles) NE of Portlaoise, Co Laois. **Tel** *056 7721450.* 🚌 *to Monasterevin or Portlaoise.* **House** ⭘ *mid-Jun–mid-Sep: 10:30am–5pm daily.* **Gardens** ⭘ *daily.* 📷 ♿ *limited.*

Emo Court, commissioned by the Earl of Portarlington in 1790, represents the only foray into domestic architecture by James Gandon, designer of the Custom House in Dublin *(see p88)*. The monumental Neo-Classical mansion has a splendid façade featuring an Ionic portico. Inside are a magnificent gilded rotunda and fine stuccowork ceilings.

Emo Court became the property of the Office of Public Works in 1994 but the previous owner is still resident on the grounds. These are adorned with fine statuary and include a lakeside walk.

Rock of Dunamase ㉔

Road map D4. 5 km (3 miles) E of Portlaoise, Co Laois. 🚌 *to Portlaoise.*

The Rock of Dunamase, which looms dramatically above the plains east of Portlaoise, has long been a military site. Originally crowned by an Iron Age ring fort, the 13th-century castle which succeeded it is now more prominent – though it was virtually destroyed by Cromwellian forces in 1650. You can reach the battered keep by climbing up banks and ditches through two gateways and a fortified courtyard.

Rock of Dunamase viewed from Stradbally to the east

For hotels and restaurants in this region see pp314–16 and pp341–2

NORTHERN IRELAND

LONDONDERRY · ANTRIM · TYRONE
FERMANAGH · ARMAGH · DOWN

*N*orthern Ireland has sights from every era of Ireland's history as well as magnificently varied coastal and lakeland scenery. In the past, it has received fewer visitors than the Republic as a result of the "Troubles". Following recent moves towards peace, there seems every chance that it will at last attract the attention it deserves.

The province of Northern Ireland was created after partition of the island in 1921. Its six counties (plus Donegal, Monaghan and Cavan) were part of Ulster, one of Ireland's four traditional kingdoms. It was most probably in Ulster that Christianity first ousted the old Celtic pagan beliefs. In 432 St Patrick landed at Saul in County Down, later founding a church at Armagh, which is still the spiritual capital of Ireland.

The dominant political force in early Christian times was the Uí Néill clan. Their descendants, the O'Neills, put up fierce resistance to English conquest in the late 16th century. Hugh O'Neill, Earl of Tyrone, had some notable successes against the armies of Elizabeth I, but was defeated and in 1607 fled to Europe with other Irish lords from Ulster, in what became known as the "Flight of the Earls". Vacant estates were granted to individuals and companies, who planted them with English and Scottish Protestants *(see p39)*. Many Plantation towns, such as Londonderry, preserve their 17th-century layout around a central square or "diamond". The arrival of new settlers meant that Irish Catholics were increasingly marginalized, thereby sowing the seeds of 400 years of conflict.

In the relative tranquillity of the 18th century, the Anglo-Irish nobility built stately homes, such as Mount Stewart House on the Ards Peninsula and Castle Coole near Enniskillen. Ulster also enjoyed prosperity in the 19th century through its ship-building, linen and rope-making industries.

Though densely populated and industrialized around Belfast, away from the capital the region is primarily agricultural. It also has areas of outstanding natural beauty, notably the rugged Antrim coastline around the Giant's Causeway, the Mountains of Mourne in County Down and the Erne lakeland in the west of the region.

Belfast's City Hall (1906), symbol of the city's civic pride

◁ Carrick-a-rede Rope Bridge, an unusual tourist attraction on the Causeway Coast

Exploring Northern Ireland

The starting point for most visitors to the province is Belfast, with its grand Victorian buildings, good pubs and the excellent Ulster Museum. However, Northern Ireland's greatest attractions lie along its coast. These range from the extraordinary volcanic landscape of the Giant's Causeway to Carrickfergus, Ireland's best preserved Norman castle. There are also Victorian resorts, like Portstewart, tiny fishing villages and unspoiled sandy beaches, such as Benone Strand. Ramblers are drawn to the Mountains of Mourne, while anglers and boating enthusiasts can enjoy the lakeland of Lower Lough Erne.

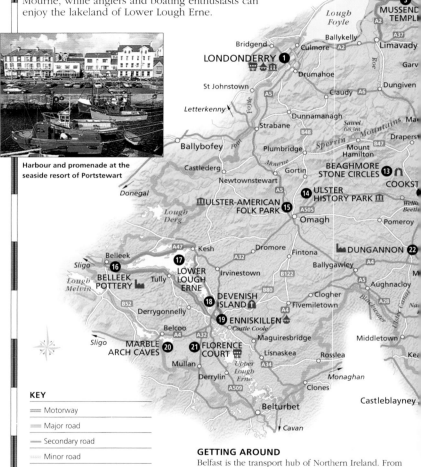

Harbour and promenade at the seaside resort of Portstewart

KEY

═══	Motorway
═══	Major road
──	Secondary road
┄┄┄	Minor road
──	Scenic route
⌐⌐⌐	Main railway
──	Minor railway
▬▬▬	National border
──	County border
△	Summit

GETTING AROUND

Belfast is the transport hub of Northern Ireland. From here the very limited train network runs northwest to Londonderry and south to Dublin. In most parts of the province you have to rely on buses, but fortunately, even in rural areas, these are fairly frequent and punctual. However, a car is essential if you want to go off the beaten track to ancient monuments or tour the coast at leisure. Depending on the security situation, you may still encounter temporary checkpoints set up by the army and police *(see p374).*

SIGHTS AT A GLANCE

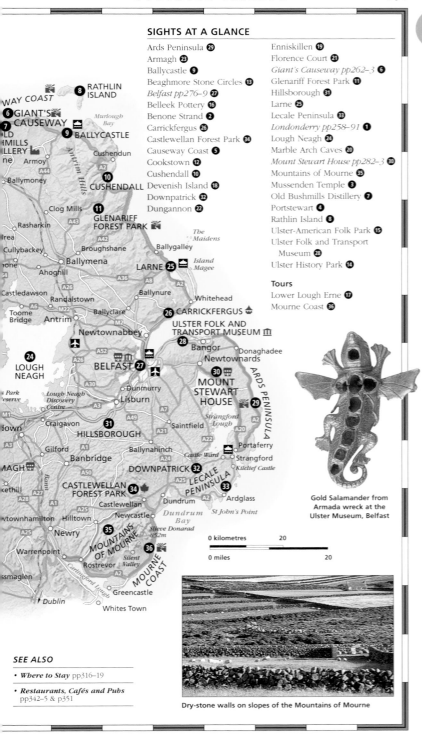

Ards Peninsula ㉙
Armagh ㉓
Ballycastle ❾
Beaghmore Stone Circles ⓭
Belfast pp276–9 ㉗
Belleek Pottery ⓰
Benone Strand ❷
Carrickfergus ㉖
Castlewellan Forest Park ㉞
Causeway Coast ❺
Cookstown ⓬
Cushendall ❿
Devenish Island ⓲
Downpatrick ㉜
Dungannon ㉒

Enniskillen ⓳
Florence Court ㉑
Giant's Causeway pp262–3 ❻
Glenariff Forest Park ⓫
Hillsborough ㉛
Larne ㉕
Londonderry pp258–91 ❶
Lough Neagh ㉔
Marble Arch Caves ⓴
Mount Stewart House pp282–3 ㉚
Mountains of Mourne ㉟
Mussenden Temple ❸
Old Bushmills Distillery ❼
Portstewart ❹
Rathlin Island ❽
Ulster-American Folk Park ⓯
Ulster Folk and Transport Museum ㉘
Ulster History Park ⓮

Tours
Lower Lough Erne ⓱
Mourne Coast ㊱

Gold Salamander from Armada wreck at the Ulster Museum, Belfast

Dry-stone walls on slopes of the Mountains of Mourne

SEE ALSO

- *Where to Stay* pp316–19
- *Restaurants, Cafés and Pubs* pp342–5 & p351

Londonderry ●

Carving on Shipquay Gate

St Columba founded a monastery here beside the River Foyle in 546. He called the place Doire or "oak grove", later anglicized as Derry. In 1613, the city was selected as a major Plantation project *(see pp38–9)*, organized by London livery companies. As a result, it acquired the prefix London, though most people still call it Derry. When British troops shot dead 13 demonstrators in 1972, Derry hit the world's headlines. Today, with an end to the Troubles in sight, the city council has undertaken several admirable heritage projects.

★ Tower Museum
The excellent displays on local history in this new museum include one on the mapping of the area during the reign of Elizabeth I.

Shipquay Gate

The Craft Village was opened in 1992 as part of the city's plans to bring the centre back to life.

Butcher's Gate

MAGAZINE ST

SHIPQUAY STREET

The Diamond
The war memorial in the Diamond or main square was erected in 1927. It was originally made for the city of Sheffield in England.

Court House

BISHOP STREET WITHIN

FERRYQUAY STREET

LINENHALL

PUMP STREET

LONDON ST

ARTILLERY STR

The Playhouse

New Gate

Bishop's Gate

★ St Columb's Cathedral
The nave's wooden ceiling dates from 1862. The corbels are carved with the heads of former bishops and deans.

KEY

P Parking

— Suggested route

VISITORS' CHECKLIST

Road map C1. Co Londonderry.
106,000. 11 km (7 miles)
E. Waterside, Duke St (028
7134 2228). c Foyle St (028 7126
2261). 44 Foyle St (028 7126
7284). Walled City Cultural Trail
(Jul–Aug); Hallowe'en Festival (Oct).
Sat. **www**.derryvisitor.com

★ **Guildhall**
*This stained-glass
window shows
St Columba.
Others feature
incidents from
the siege of Derry,
including the
apprentice boys
shutting the city
gates in 1688.*

Ferryquay
Gate

To Craigavon Bridge
and River Foyle

0 metres   100
0 yards   100

STAR SIGHTS

★ Guildhall

★ St Columb's Cathedral

★ Tower Museum

St Columb's Cathedral
St Columb's Court. **Tel** 028 7126 7313.
Mon–Sat. on request.
www.stcolumbscathedral.org
Built between 1628 and 1633,
in "Planters' Gothic" style, St
Columb's was the first
cathedral to be found-
ed in the British Isles
after the Reformation.
The interior was
extensively restored
in the 19th century.
A small museum in
the Chapter House has
relics from the
siege of 1689 *(see
pp38–9)*, including
the 17th-century locks and
keys of the city. In the
vestibule is a hollow mortar
cannonball that was fired into
the city by James II's army. It
carried terms for capitulation,
but the reply of the Protestants
within the walls was a defiant
"No surrender", a phrase used
by Loyalists to this day.

**Lock of city gate in
St Columb's Cathedral**

Tower Museum
Union Hall Place. **Tel** 028 7137
2411. 10am–4:30pm Mon–Sat.
Housed in O'Doherty Tower
(a replica of the original 16th-
century building on this site),
the museum traces the history
of the city from its foundation
to the recent Troubles using
multimedia displays. Upstairs,
an exhibition about the 1688
Spanish Armada includes
artifacts from ships wrecked
in nearby Kinnagoe Bay.

Walls of Derry
Access from Magazine Street.
Among the best preserved city
fortifications in Europe, the city
walls rise to a height of
8 m (26 ft) and in places are
9 m (30 ft) wide. Completed in
1618 to defend the new

merchant city from Gaelic
chieftains in Donegal, the walls
have never been breached, not
even during the siege of 1689,
when 7,000 out of a population
of 20,000 perished from
disease or starvation.
Restoration work
means that it should
soon be possible to
walk right around
the walls for the first
time in decades. Just
outside the old fortifications, beyond Butcher's
Gate, is the Bogside,
a Catholic area with
a famous mural that
announces "You are now
entering Free Derry".

Guildhall
Guildhall Square. **Tel** 028 7137 7335.
9am–5pm Mon–Fri.
Standing between the walled
city and the River Foyle, this
Neo-Gothic building was constructed in 1890, but a fire in
1908 and a bomb in 1972 both
necessitated substantial repairs.
Stained-glass windows – copies
of the originals – recount the
history of Derry. To the rear of
the Guildhall is Derry Quay,
from where Irish emigrants
sailed to America in the 18th
and 19th centuries.

Environs
Just off the B194, on the way
to Muff, is the **Earhart Museum**
containing a small exhibition on
American aviator Amelia Earhart,
the first woman to complete a
transatlantic solo flight. She
had intended to fly to Paris,
but in May 1932 landed in a
field outside Derry. The nearby
park is lovely for picnics.

Earhart Museum
Ballyarnet. **Tel** 028 7135 4040.
9am–4pm Mon–Thu, 9am–1pm Fri.

The old walled city viewed across the River Foyle

Terraced houses behind the promenade at Portrush

Benone Strand ❷

Road map. D1 Co Londonderry.
🛈 *Benone Tourist Complex, 53
Benone Ave, Seacoast Rd, Magilligan
(028 7775 0555).* ⭘ *daily.*
www.caravancampingsites.co.uk

The wide, golden sands of
Ireland's longest beach, also
known as Magilligan Strand,
sweep along the Londonderry
coastline for more than 10 km
(6 miles). The magnificent
beach has been granted EU
Blue Flag status for its
cleanliness. At the western
extremity of the beach is
Magilligan Point where a
Martello tower, built during
the Napoleonic wars, stands
guard over the entrance to
Lough Foyle. To get to the
point, renowned for its rare
shellfish and sea birds, you
have to drive below the
watchtowers and listening
devices of an army base. The
experience is rather unsettling,
but well worth the trouble.

Mussenden Temple ❸

Road map. D1. Co Londonderry.
Tel *028 7084 8728.* ⭘ *Jun–Aug:
11am–7:30pm daily; Mar–May &
Sep–Oct: 11am–6pm Sat, Sun & public
hols.* ♿ *ltd.* **www.**ntni.org.uk

The oddest sight along the
Londonderry coast is this
small, domed rotunda perched
precariously on a windswept
headland outside the family resort of Castlerock. The temple

was built in 1785 by Frederick
Augustus Hervey, the eccentric
Earl of Bristol and Protestant
Bishop of Derry, as a memorial
to his cousin Mrs Frideswide
Mussenden. The design was
based on the Temple of Vesta
at Tivoli outside Rome.

The walls, made of basalt
faced with sandstone, open
out at the four points of the
compass to three windows
and an entrance. Originally
designed for use as a library
(or, as some stories go, an
elaborate boudoir for the
bishop's mistress), the structure is now maintained by the
National Trust and remains in
excellent condition.

The bishop allowed the local
priest to say Mass for his
Roman Catholic tenants in the
basement. The bishop's
former residence, the nearby
Downhill Castle, was gutted
by fire and is now little more
than an impressive shell.

The surrounding area offers
some good glen and cliff walks
and there are some magnificent views of the Londonderry
and Antrim coastline. Below
the temple is Downhill
Strand, where the
bishop sponsored
horseback
races be-
tween his
clergy.

Portstewart ❹

Road map D1. Co Londonderry.
🚶 *6,000.* 🚌 *to Coleraine or
Portrush.* 🚌 🛈 *Jul & Aug: Town
Hall, The Crescent (028 7034 4723).*

A popular holiday destination
for Victorian middle-class
families, Portstewart is still a
family favourite today. Its
long, crescent-shaped seafront
promenade is sheltered by
rocky headlands. Just west of
town, and accessible by road
or by a cliffside walk, stretches
Portstewart Strand, a magnificent, long, sandy beach,
protected by the National Trust.

On Ramore Head, just to the
east, lies **Portrush**, a brasher
resort with an abundance of
souvenir shops and amusement
arcades. The East Strand is
backed by sand dunes and runs
parallel with the world-class
Royal Portrush Golf Links.
You can stroll along the beach
to White Rocks – limestone
cliffs carved by the wind and
waves into caves and arches.

To the south is the university
town of **Coleraine**. The North
West 200 (*see p28*), the world's
fastest motorcycle road race, is
run between Portstewart,
Coleraine and Portrush. The
race is held in May in front of
100,000
people.

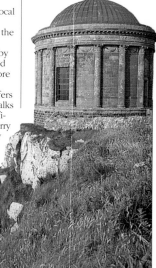

Mussenden Temple set on a cliff top on the Londonderry coast

Causeway Coast ❺

Road map D1. Co Antrim. 🛈 *Giant's Causeway (028 2073 1855).* **Carrick-a-rede Rope Bridge** *Tel 028 2073 1582.* ⬜ *13 Mar–Sep: daily, weather permitting.* 🅿 *for car park.* 🔲 ♿ **www.**nationaltrust.org.uk

The renown of the **Giant's Causeway** *(see pp262–3),* Ireland's only World Heritage Site, overshadows the other attractions of this stretch of North Antrim coast. When visiting the Causeway, it is well worth investigating the sandy bays, craggy headlands and dramatic ruins that punctuate the rest of this inspirational coastline.

Approaching the Causeway from the west, you pass the eerie ruins of **Dunluce Castle** perched vulnerably on a steep crag. Dating back to the 13th century, it was the main fortress of the MacDonnells, chiefs of Antrim. Although the roof has gone, it is still well preserved, with its twin towers, gateway and some original cobbling intact.

Dunseverick Castle can be reached by road or a lengthy hike from the Causeway. It is a much earlier fortification than Dunluce and only one massive

The roofless ruins of 13th-century Dunluce Castle

wall remains. Once the capital of the kingdom of Dalriada, it was linked to Tara *(see p248)* by a great road and was the departure point for 5th-century Irish raids on Scotland.

Just past the attractive, sandy **White Park Bay,** a tight switchback road leads down to the picturesque harbour of **Ballintoy**, reminiscent – on a good day – of an Aegean fishing village. **Sheep Island**, a rocky outcrop just offshore, is a cormorant colony. Boat trips run past it in the summer.

Just east of Ballintoy is one of the most unusual and scary tourist attractions in Ireland, the **Carrick-a-rede Rope Bridge**. The bridge hangs 25 m (80 ft) above the sea and wobbles and twists as soon as you stand on it. Made of planks strung between wires, it provides access to the salmon fishery on the tiny

island across the 20-m (65-ft) chasm. There are strong handrails and safety nets, but it's definitely not for those with vertigo. Further east along the coast lies **Kinbane Castle**, a 16th-century ruin with spectacular views.

🏰 **Dunluce Castle**
Tel 028 2073 1938. ⬜ *daily.* 🅿
🎟 *in summer and by appt.*
www.ehsni.gov.uk

Fishing boats moored in the shelter of Ballintoy harbour

Carrick-a-rede Rope Bridge

THE NORTH ANTRIM COASTLINE

KEY

═ Minor road	🅿 Parking
▬ Major road	🛈 Tourist information

[Map showing the North Antrim coastline with locations including Giant's Causeway, Dunseverick Castle, White Park Bay, Sheep Island, Carrick-a-rede Rope Bridge, Ballintoy, Kinbane Castle, Dunluce Castle, Portballintrae, Bushmills, Portrush, Portstewart, Ballycastle, and roads B146, A2, B17, B62, B66, B15, B147, B67]

0 kilometres 5
0 miles 3

Giant's Causeway ❻

The sheer strangeness of this place and the bizarre regularity of its basalt columns have made the Giant's Causeway the subject of numerous legends. The most popular tells how the giant, Finn MacCool *(see pp26–7)*, laid the causeway to provide a path across the sea to his lady love, who lived on the island of Staffa in Scotland – where similar columns are found. The Giant's Causeway attracts many tourists, who are taken by the busload from the visitors' centre down to the shore. Nothing, however, can destroy the magic of this place, with its looming grey cliffs and shrieking gulls; paths along the coast allow you to escape the crowds.

Chimney stacks

Aird's Snout
This nose-shaped promontory juts out from the 120-m (395-ft) basalt cliffs that soar above the Giant's Causeway.

THE FORMATION OF THE CAUSEWAY

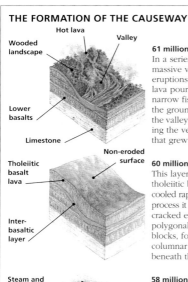

Hot lava
Valley
Wooded landscape
Lower basalts
Limestone

61 million years ago: In a series of massive volcanic eruptions molten lava poured from narrow fissures in the ground, filling in the valleys and burning the vegetation that grew there.

Tholeiitic basalt lava
Non-eroded surface
Inter-basaltic layer

60 million years ago: This layer of tholeiitic basalt lava cooled rapidly. In the process it shrank and cracked evenly into polygonal-shaped blocks, forming columnar jointing beneath the surface.

Steam and gas clouds
New lava flows

58 million years ago: New volcanic eruptions produced further lava flows. These had a slightly different chemical composition from earlier flows and, once cool, did not form such well defined columns.

Snow
Scree
Ice
Sea water

15,000 years ago: At the end of the Ice Age, when the land was still frozen, sea ice ground its way slowly past the high basalt cliffs, eroding the foreshore and helping to form the Giant's Causeway.

Inter-basaltic layer

Shape of the Columns
Most columns are hexagonal, but some have four, five, eight or even ten sides. They generally measure about 30 cm (12 in) across.

Giant's Causeway and the North Antrim Coast
Millions of years of geological activity can be witnessed in the eroded cliffs flanking the Causeway. The striking band of reddish rock is the inter-basaltic layer, which formed during a long period of temperate climatic conditions. The high iron content explains the rock's rich ochre colour.

VISITORS' CHECKLIST

Road map D1. Co Antrim. ☒ to Portrush. ☒ from Portrush, Bushmills or Coleraine. **Visitors' Centre** Causeway Head (028 2073 1855). ○ daily. ☒ limited. ☒ on request. ☒ **Giant's Causeway Bushmills Railway** heritage steam trains. **Tel** 028 2073 2844; talking timetable 028 2073 2594. ○ call for times. ☒ ☒ ☒ www.giantscausewaycentre.com

Middle Causeway
This section of the Middle Causeway is known as the Honeycomb. Like other unusual rock formations along the coast, it was christened by local guides during Victorian times.

Road

Little Causeway

GIANT'S CAUSEWAY TODAY
It has been estimated that 37,000 basalt columns extend from the cliffs down into the sea. Close to the shore, they have been eroded to form the Grand, Middle and Little Causeways.

Plant debris
is trapped between the lava flows.

Lower basalts

Grand Causeway

Wishing Chair
Myth has it that this rocky seat was made for Finn MacCool when he was a boy, and that wishes made here will come true.

Visitors exploring the Giant's Causeway at low tide ▷

Old Bushmills Distillery ❼

Road map D1. Bushmills, Co Antrim. **Tel** 028 2073 3218. 🚌 from Giant's Causeway & Coleraine. ◻ daily. ● 2 weeks at Christmas. Oct–Apr: Sat & Sun am. 🎫 🅿 obligatory. 🏠 🍴 ♿ limited. **www**.emeraldtiger.com

The small town of Bushmills has an attractive square and a great river for salmon and trout fishing, but its main claim to fame is whiskey. The Old Bushmills plant on the edge of town prides itself on being the world's oldest distillery. Its Grant to Distil dates from 1608, but the spirit was probably made here at least 200 years before that.

In 1974 Bushmills joined the Irish Distillers Group based at the Jameson plant (see p179) in Midleton, but its products have retained their own character. Most are a blend of different whiskeys; Old Bushmills, in contrast, is made from a blend of a single malt and a single grain.

The tour of the distillery ends with a whiskey sampling session in the 1608 Bar in the former malt kilns, which are also home to a small museum with old distilling equipment on display.

Whiskey barrel at Bushmills Distillery

Murlough Bay, on the coast facing Scotland to the east of Ballycastle

Rathlin Island ❽

Road map D1. Co Antrim. 🚶 75. ⛴ daily from Ballycastle (028 2076 9299). 🛈 Ballycastle (028 2076 2024).

Rathlin is shaped rather like a boomerang – 11 km (7 miles) in length and at no point more than 1.6 km (1 mile) wide. The island is just a 50-minute boat ride from Ballycastle. About 30 families remain on Rathlin Island, making a living from fishing, farming and a little tourism. Facilities are limited to a café, a pub, a guesthouse, a hostel and a campground. The fierce, salty Atlantic winds ensure that the landscape on Rathlin is virtually treeless.

High white cliffs encircle much of the island, and at craggy **Bull Point** on the westerly tip, tens of thousands of seabirds, including kittiwakes, puffins and razorbills, make their home. A local minibus service will take visitors to view the birds. At the opposite end of the island is **Bruce's Cave**, where, in 1306, Robert Bruce, King of Scotland, supposedly watched a spider climbing a thread. The spider's perseverance inspired the dejected Bruce to return and win back his kingdom.

Ballycastle ❾

Road map D1. Co Antrim. 🚶 4,800. 🚌 ⛴ to Campbeltown (Scotland). 🛈 Sheskburn House, 7 Mary St (028 2076 2225). 🎪 Lammas Fair (end Aug), Apple Fair (end Oct). **www**.moyle-council.org

A medium-sized resort town, Ballycastle boasts a pretty harbour and a sandy beach. Near the harbour is a memorial to Guglielmo Marconi, whose assistant sent the first wireless message across water from here to Rathlin Island in 1898.

Ballycastle's Oul' Lammas Fair, held in late August, is one of the oldest traditional fairs in Ireland, featuring stalls selling dulce (dried, salted seaweed) and yellowman (honeycomb toffee).

On the outskirts of town, the ruined 15th-century **Bonamargy Friary** houses the remains of Sorley Boy MacDonnell, former chieftain of this part of Antrim. Sections of the church, gatehouse and cloisters are well preserved.

IRISH WHISKEY

The word whiskey comes from the Gaelic *uisce beatha*, meaning water of life. Distillation was probably introduced to Ireland by monks from Asia over 1,000 years ago. Small-scale production became part of the Irish way of life, but in the 17th century, the English introduced a licensing system and started to close down stills. In the 19th century, post-famine poverty and the Temperance movement combined to lower demand. The result was that Scotch whisky (with no "e") stole an export march on the Irish, but in recent years, thanks to lower production costs, improved marketing and the rise in popularity of Irish coffee, sales have been increasing.

Poster showing the Old Bushmills Distillery beside the River Bush

Environs

Off the A2, 5 km (3 miles) east of town, a narrow scenic road starts to wind its way along the coast to Cushendall. First stop is **Fair Head**, where a poorly marked path meanders across heathery marshland to towering cliffs 200 m (650 ft) above the sea. From here there are stunning views of Rathlin and the islands off the Scottish coast.

To the lee side of the headland lies **Murlough Bay**, the prettiest inlet along the coast. This can be reached by road. Further to the southeast stands **Torr Head**, a peninsula that reaches to within 21 km (13 miles) of the Mull of Kintyre making it the closest point in Ireland to Scotland.

Cushendall ❿

Road map D1. Co Antrim. 🏚 *2,400.*
🚌 🛈 *24 Mill St (028 2177 1180).*
◯ *all year; Oct–June: mornings only.*
www.moyle-council.org

Three of the nine Glens of Antrim converge towards Cushendall, earning it the unofficial title of "Capital of the Glens". This attractive village has brightly painted houses and an edifice known

Carnlough harbour, a popular stop south of Cushendall

as Curfew Tower, built in the early 19th century as a lock-up for thieves and idlers.

Environs

About 1.5 km (1 mile) north of the village stands **Layde Old** Church. It can be reached by a pretty walk along the cliffs. Founded by the Franciscans, it was a parish church from 1306 to 1790 and contains many monuments to the local chieftains, the MacDonnells.

Just over 3 km (2 miles) west of Cushendall, on the slopes of Tievebulliagh mountain, lies **Ossian's Grave**, named after the legendary warrior-poet and son of the giant Finn MacCool *(see pp26–7)*. It is in fact a

Neolithic court tomb: the area was a major centre of Stone Age toolmaking and axeheads made of Tievebulliagh's hard porcellanite rock have been found at a wide range of sites all over the British Isles.

Other attractive villages further south along the coast road include **Carnlough**, which has a fine sandy beach and a delightful harbour, and **Ballygally**, whose supposedly haunted 1625 castle is now a hotel *(see p317)*.

Glenariff Forest Park ⓫

Road map D1. Co Antrim. **Tel** *028 9052 4480.* ◯ *daily.* 🅿 *for car park.* ♿ *ltd.* **www**.forestserviceni.gov.uk

Nine rivers have carved deep valleys through the Antrim Mountains to the sea. Celebrated in song and verse, the Glens of Antrim used to be the wildest and most remote part of Ulster. This region was not "planted" with English and Scots settlers in the 17th century and was the last place in Northern Ireland where Gaelic was spoken.

Today the Antrim coast road brings all the glens within easy reach of the tourist. Glenariff Forest Park contains some of the most spectacular scenery. The main scenic path runs through thick woodland and wildflower meadows and round the sheer sides of a gorge, past three waterfalls. There are also optional trails to distant mountain viewpoints. William Makepeace Thackeray, the 19th-century English novelist, called the landscape "Switzerland in miniature".

Glenariff Forest Park

Stone circle and stone rows at Beaghmore

🏛 **Ardboe Cross**
Off B73, 16 km (10 miles) E of Cookstown.

⚙ **Wellbrook Beetling Mill**
Off A505, 6.5 km (4 miles) W of Cookstown. **Tel** 028 8674 8210. ○ Mar 17–Oct: 1–6pm (closed on some days). 📷 www.nationaltrust.org.uk

Beaghmore Stone Circles ⑬

Road map D2. Co Tyrone. Off A505, 14 km (9 miles) NW of Cookstown.

On a stretch of open moorland in the foothills of the Sperrin Mountains lies a vast collection of stone monuments, dating from between 2000 and 1200 BC. There are seven stone circles, several stone rows and a number of less prominent features, possibly collapsed field walls of an earlier period. Their exact purpose remains unknown, though in some cases their alignment correlates with movements of the sun, moon and stars. Three of the rows, for example, are clearly aligned with the point where the sun rises at the summer solstice.

The individual circle stones are small – none is more than 1.20 m (4 ft) in height – but their sheer numbers make them a truly impressive sight. As well as the circles and rows, there are a dozen round cairns (burial mounds). Up until 1945, the whole complex, one of Ulster's major archaeological finds, had lain buried beneath a thick layer of peat.

Cookstown ⑫

Road map D2. Co Tyrone. 🏘 12,000. 🚌 🚉 Burnavon, Burn Road (028 8676 2205). 🛒 Sat. www.cookstown.gov.uk

Cookstown sticks in the memory for its grand central thoroughfare – 2 km (1.25 miles) long and perfectly straight. The road is about 40 m (130 ft) wide and, as you look to the north, it frames the bulky outline of Slieve Gallion, the highest of the Sperrin Mountains. A 17th-century Plantation town (see pp38–9), Cookstown takes its name from its founder Alan Cook.

Environs
The countryside around Cookstown is rich in Neolithic and early Christian monuments. To the east, on a desolate stretch of Lough Neagh shore-line, the **Ardboe Cross** stands on the site of a 6th-century monastery. Although eroded, the 10th-century cross is one of the best examples of a High Cross (see p243) in Ulster: its 22 sculpted panels depict Old Testament scenes on the east side and New Testament ones on the west. The **Wellbrook Beetling Mill**, west of Cookstown, is a relic of Ulster's old linen industry. "Beetling" was the process of hammering the cloth to give it a sheen. Set amid trees beside the Ballinderry River, the mill dates from 1768 and is now a popular tourist attraction. The National Trust has restored the whitewashed two-storey building and its water wheel. Inside, working displays demonstrate just how loud "beetling" could be. From the mill, there are pleasant walks along the river banks.

Ardboe Cross

ULSTER'S HISTORIC LINEN INDUSTRY

The rise in Ulster's importance as a linen producer was spurred on by the arrival from France of refugee Huguenot weavers at the end of the 17th century. Linen remained a flourishing industry for a further two centuries, but today it is produced only in small quantities for the luxury goods market. Hundreds of abandoned mills dot the former "Linen Triangle" bounded by Belfast, Armagh and Dungannon. One of the reasons why the material diminished in popularity was the expensive production process: after cutting, the flax had to be retted, or soaked, in large artificial ponds so that scutching – the separation of the fibres – could begin. After combing, the linen was spun and woven before being bleached in the sun, typically in fields along river banks. The final stage was "beetling", the process whereby the cloth was hammered to give it a sheen.

18th-century print, showing flax being prepared for spinning

Copy of Iron Age Celtic stone head at the Ulster History Park

Ulster History Park ⑭

Road map C2. Co Tyrone. *Tel* 028 8164 8188. 🚌 from Omagh. ⬜ Apr–Sep: daily; Oct & Mar: Mon–Fri. ⬤ 23–29 Dec, Jan–Feb. 📷 🅿 ♿ 🏪 🚻

Nestling at the edge of the Sperrin Mountains, the Ulster History Park is filled with full-scale models of structures built by successive waves of settlers in Ireland. They range from a Mesolithic hunter/gatherer's hut covered with animal pelts, dating from 7000 BC, to a 17th-century Plantation village (*see pp38–9*). There are also megalithic burial tombs, a crannog (*see p33*) from the early Christian period and a Norman motte and bailey (a wooden fortress built on a high mound). An exhibition centre helps put the exhibits in perspective.

Ulster-American Folk Park ⑮

Road map C2. Co Tyrone. *Tel* 028 8224 3292. 🚌 from Omagh. ⬜ Apr–Sep: daily; Oct–Mar: Mon–Fri. ⬤ 24–28 Dec, 1–3 Jan. 📷 🏪 🚻 ♿ www.folkpark.com

One of the best open-air museums of its kind, the Folk Park grew up around the restored boyhood home of Judge Thomas Mellon (founder of the Pittsburgh banking dynasty). The Park's permanent exhibition, called "Emigrants", examines why two million people left Ulster for America during the 18th and 19th centuries. It also shows what became of them, with stories of both fortune and failure, including the grim lives of indentured servants and the 15,000 Irish vagrants and convicts sent to North America in the mid-18th century.

The park has more than 30 historic buildings, some of them original, some replicas. There are settler homesteads (including that of John Joseph Hughes, the first Catholic Archbishop of New York), churches, a schoolhouse and a forge, some with craft displays, all with costumed interpretative guides. There's also an Ulster streetscape, a reconstructed emigrant ship and a Pennsylvania farmstead,

complete with log barn, corn crib and smokehouse. The six-roomed farmhouse is based on one built by Thomas Mellon and his father in the early years of their new life in America.

A fully stocked library and database allow visitors to trace their family roots. Popular American festivals such as Independence Day and Hallowe'en are celebrated at the park and there is an Appalachian-Bluegrass music festival in early September.

Belleek Pottery ⑯

Road map C2. Belleek, Co Fermanagh. *Tel* 028 6865 9300. 🚌 ⬜ Apr–Oct: daily; Nov–Mar: Mon–Fri. ⬤ 17 Mar & 10 days at Christmas. 📷 ♿ 🏪 🚻 www.belleek.ie

Worker at the Belleek factory making a Parian ware figurine

The little border village of Belleek would attract few visitors other than anglers were it not for the world-famous Belleek Pottery, founded in 1857. The company's pearly coloured china is known as Parian ware. Developed in the 19th century, it was supposed to resemble the famous Parian marble of Ancient Greece.

Belleek is now best known for its ornamental pieces of fragile lattice work decorated with pastel-coloured flowers. These are especially popular in the USA. Several elaborate showpieces stand on display in the visitors' centre and small museum. There's also a 20-minute video presentation on the company's history, a gift shop and ample parking space for tour buses.

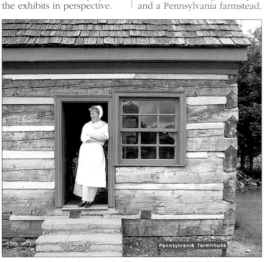

Pennsylvania log farmhouse at the Ulster-American Folk Park

A Tour of Lower Lough Erne ⑰

Kingfisher

The area around Lower Lough Erne boasts a rich combination of both natural and historic sights. From pre-Christian times, settlers sought the security offered by the lough's forests and inlets. Monasteries were founded on several of its many islands in the Middle Ages, and a ring of castles recalls the Plantation era *(see p39)*. The lake is a haven for water birds such as ducks, grebes and kingfishers, and the trout-rich waters attract many anglers. Lough Erne is a delight to explore by land or by boat. In summer, ferries serve several islands, and cruisers are available for hire.

View across Lower Lough Erne

Belleek ⑦
Northern Ireland's most westerly village, Belleek is famous for its pottery *(see p269)*. There is also a museum, ExplorErne, which covers most aspects of the region.

Castle Caldwell Forest Park ⑥
The park's wooded peninsulas are a sanctuary for birds, and you can watch waterfowl from hides on the shore. You may see great crested grebes, the common scoter duck and perhaps even otters.

Boa Island ⑤
Two curious double-faced figures stand in Caldragh cemetery, a Christian graveyard on Boa Island. While little is known about the stone idols, they are certainly pre-Christian.

Lough Navar Forest Drive ⑧
An 11-km (7-mile) drive through pine forest leads to a viewpoint atop the Cliffs of Magho, with a magnificent panorama over Lough Erne and beyond. Trails weave through the woods.

TIPS FOR WALKERS

Length: 110 km (68 miles).
Stopping-off points: Outside Enniskillen, the best places to eat are the pubs in Kesh and Belleek; in summer, a café opens in Castle Archdale Country Park. There are good picnic places all along the route of this tour, including at the Cliffs of Magho viewpoint.
(see also pp387–9.)

KEY

▬ Tour route
═ Other roads
⛴ Boats to islands
☆ Viewpoint

Tully Castle ⑨
A delightful 17th-century-sty herb garden has recently been planted and is maturing well alongside thi fortified Plantation house.

White Island ④

The Romanesque church on White Island has bizarre pagan-looking figures set into one wall. Of uncertain origin, they probably adorned an earlier monastery on this site. Ferries to the island leave from Castle Archdale Marina in summer.

Beautifully constructed round tower on Devenish Island

Devenish Island ⓫

Road map C2. Co Fermanagh.
🚤 *Devenish Ferry (028 6862 1588) from Trory Point, 5 km (3 miles) N of Enniskillen: Easter–Sep: daily.* 🎫 *for museum and tower.* **www**.ehsni.gov.uk

St Molaise, who had 1,500 scholars under his tutelage, founded a monastery on this tiny windswept island in the 6th century. Though raided by Vikings in the 9th century and burned in 1157, it remained an important religious centre up to the early 17th century.

Several fine buildings have survived, including **Teampall Mor** near the jetty. Built in 1225, this church displays the transition between Romanesque and Gothic styles. On the highest ground stands **St Mary's Priory**, an Augustinian church that was erected in the 15th century. An intricately carved stone cross close by dates from the same period.

The most spectacular sight on Devenish Island, however, is the 12th-century round tower, which stands some 25 m (82 ft) tall. From the high windows the monks could spot approaching strangers. It is perfectly preserved, and the five floors can be reached by internal ladders. Supporting the roof is an elaborate cornice with a human face carved above each of the four windows; this is a unique feature in an Irish round tower. A small museum covers both the history and architecture of the island, and contains a collection of antiquities discovered at the site.

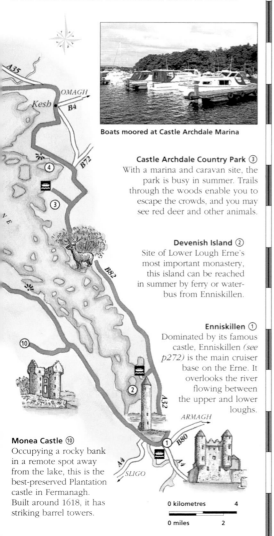

Boats moored at Castle Archdale Marina

Castle Archdale Country Park ③
With a marina and caravan site, the park is busy in summer. Trails through the woods enable you to escape the crowds, and you may see red deer and other animals.

Devenish Island ②
Site of Lower Lough Erne's most important monastery, this island can be reached in summer by ferry or waterbus from Enniskillen.

Enniskillen ①
Dominated by its famous castle, Enniskillen *(see p272)* is the main cruiser base on the Erne. It overlooks the river flowing between the upper and lower loughs.

Monea Castle ⑩
Occupying a rocky bank in a remote spot away from the lake, this is the best-preserved Plantation castle in Fermanagh. Built around 1618, it has striking barrel towers.

0 kilometres   4

0 miles   2

For hotels and restaurants in this region see pp316–19 and pp342–5

Enniskillen ⑲

Road map C2. Co Fermanagh.
🏚 *14,000.* 🚌 ℹ️ *Wellington Road
(028 6632 3110).* 🔄 *Thu.*

The busy tourist centre of
Enniskillen occupies an island
between Upper and Lower
Lough Erne. The town gained
fame for the wrong reason in
1987, when 11 people died in
an IRA bomb attack, but it
deserves a visit for its setting
and sights.

At the west end of town
stands **Enniskillen Castle**,
dating from the 15th century.
It houses **Fermanagh County
Museum** and the Inniskilling
Regimental Museum. Its most
stunning feature, however, is
the Watergate, a fairy-tale twin-
turreted tower, best admired
from the far bank of the river.
Further west, **Portora Royal
School**, founded in 1618,
counts among its old boys the
playwrights Oscar Wilde and
Samuel Beckett *(see pp22–3).*

The **Cole Monument** stands
on a little hill in a pretty
Victorian park on the east
side of town. It is a tall Doric
column with a spiral staircase

Enniskillen Castle seen from across the River Erne

that can be climbed for views
of the lake country.

⛪ Enniskillen Castle
Tel 028 6632 5000. ☐ Jul & Aug:
10am–5pm Tue–Fri, 2–5pm Sat–Mon;
May–Jun & Sep: 10am–5pm Tue–Fri,
2–5pm Mon & Sat; Oct–Apr: 10am–
5pm Tue–Fri, 2–5pm Mon. 🚫 1
Jan, 25 & 26 Dec. ☐ ♿ *limited.*
www.enniskillencastle.co.uk

Environs
Just outside town, set in a
park with mature oak
woodland overlooking a lake,
is **Castle Coole**, one of the
finest Neo-Classical homes in
Ireland. It has a long Portland
stone façade, with a central
portico and small pavilions at
each end. The stone was
shipped from Dorset to
Ballyshannon in Co Donegal.
The first Earl of Belmore, who
commissioned the house in
the 1790s, was almost bankrupted by the cost of it. The
original design was by Irish
architect Richard Johnston, but
the Earl then commissioned a
second set of drawings by the
fashionable English architect
James Wyatt. The extravagant
Earl died, deep in debt, in 1802
and it was left to his son to
complete the decorating and
furnishing during the 1820s.

The glory of Castle Coole is
that almost all the house's
original furniture is still in
place. Family portraits from
the 18th century line the walls
of the dining room. In the
lavish State Bedroom there is
a bed made specially for King
George IV on the occasion of
his visit to Ireland in 1821,
though in the end he never
came here to sleep in it. One
of the finest rooms is the oval
saloon (or ballroom) at the
back of the house. The heavy
curtains and richly gilded
Regency furniture may not be
to everyone's taste, but the
spacious oak-floored room
produces a magnificent effect
of unostentatious luxury.

🏛 Castle Coole
Off A4, 1.6 km (1 mile) SE of Enniskillen.
Tel 028 6632 2690. **House** ☐ 13
Mar–10 Oct: noon–6pm (closed on
some dates). 🚫 ♿ ☐ ☐ **Park**
☐ daily. www.nationaltrust.org.uk

The saloon at Castle Coole, with original Regency furnishings

For hotels and restaurants in this region see pp316–19 and pp342–5

Marble Arch Caves 20

Road map C2. Marlbank Scenic Loop, Florence Court, Co Fermanagh. *Tel* 028 6634 8855. ☐ Mar–Sep: daily (phone first as bad weather can cause closure). 🖼 🎫 obligatory. 🍴 🚻 www.marblearchcaves.net

The marble arch caves are cut by three streams which flow down the slopes of Cuilcagh Mountain, unite underground and emerge as the Cladagh River. Tours lasting 75 minutes consist of a boat ride into the depths of the cave complex and a guided walk that leads past stalagmites, calcite cascades and other curious limestone formations. The 9-m (30-ft) "Marble Arch" itself stands outside the cave system in the glen where the river gushes out from below ground.

The caves are very popular, so it's best to book ahead. It is also advisable to ring to check the local weather conditions before setting out; the caves may be closed because of rain. Whatever the weather, bring a sweater and sensible walking shoes.

Boat trip through Marble Arch Caves

Florence Court 21

Road map C2. Co Fermanagh. *Tel* 028 6634 8249. 🚌 from Enniskillen (Jul & Aug). **House** ☐ Jun–Aug: daily (pm only); 15 Mar–May & Sep: Sat & Sun (pm only). 🖼 🚻 ♿ 🍴 🚻 **Grounds** ☐ daily. 🖼 for car park. www.enniskillen.com

This three-storey Palladian mansion was built for the Cole family in the mid-18th century. The arcades and pavilions, which are of a later date than the main house, were added around 1770 by William Cole, first Earl of Enniskillen. The house features flamboyant Rococo plasterwork said to be by the Dublin stuccodore Robert West. Sadly, however, not much of what you see today is original as most of the central block was seriously damaged by fire in 1955. Much of the furniture was lost, but the plasterwork was painstakingly recreated from photographs. The finest examples are in the dining room, the staircase and the small Venetian room.

Perhaps more spectacular are the grounds, which occupy a natural mountain-ringed amphitheatre. The area is fairly wild and there are many enjoyable walks around the house. One woodland trail leads to the famous Florence Court yew tree, whose descendants are to be found all over Ireland. Closer to the house is a walled garden where pink and white roses make an attractive sight in summer.

Dungannon 22

Road map D2. Co Tyrone. 🚗 10,000. 🚌 🚆 Killymaddy Tourist Centre, Ballygawly Rd, 8 km (5 miles) W of town (028 8776 7259). 🚌 Thu.

Dungannon's hilly location made an ideal site for the seat of government of the O'Neill dynasty from the 14th century until Plantation (*see pp38–9*), when their castle was razed. The town's **Royal School** is the oldest school in Northern Ireland. Opened in 1614, it moved to its present site in 1789.

Once a major linen centre, this busy market town's best-known factory is now **Tyrone Crystal**, the largest concern of its kind in Northern Ireland. Tours of its modern complex cover all stages of production, including glass-blowing.

🏭 Tyrone Crystal
Coalisland Road. *Tel* 028 8772 5335. ☐ 9am–6pm Mon–Sat; 1–5 pm Sun. ● 10 days Christmas. 🎫 fee. ♿ 🍴 www.tyronecrystal.com

Florence Court, the former seat of the Earls of Enniskillen

View of Armagh dominated by St Patrick's Roman Catholic Cathedral

Armagh ㉓

Road map D2. Co Armagh.
🏘 17,000. 🚌 🚉 40 English St
(028 3752 1800). 🛍 Tue & Fri.
www.discovernorthernireland.com

One of Ireland's oldest cities,
Armagh dates back to the age
of St Patrick (see p281) and the
advent of Christianity. The
narrow streets in the city centre
follow the ditches that once
ringed the church, founded by
the saint in 455. Two cathedrals, both called **St Patrick's**,
sit on opposing hills. The
huge Roman Catholic
one is a twin-spired
Neo-Gothic building
with seemingly
every inch of
wall covered in
mosaic. The older
Protestant Cathedral
dates back to med-
ieval times. It
boasts the bones of
Brian Ború, the King of Ireland
who defeated the Vikings in
1014 (see pp34–5), and an
11th-century High Cross.
    Armagh's gorgeous oval, tree-
lined Mall, where cricket is
played in summer, is surrounded by dignified Georgian
buildings. One of these houses
the small **Armagh County
Museum**, which has a good
exhibition on local history. Off
the Mall, **St Patrick's Trian** is a
heritage centre telling the
story of the city. It also has a
"Land of Lilliput" fantasy
centre for children, based on
Gulliver's Travels by Jonathan
Swift (see p82). Ireland's only
planetarium is on College Hill
in the **Observatory Grounds**,
from where there are splendid
views over the city.

🏛 **Armagh County Museum**
The Mall East. **Tel** 028 3752 3070.
⭘ Mon–Sat. ⬤ some public hols.
📷 by arrangement.
www.armaghcountymuseum.org.uk

🏛 **St Patrick's Trian**
40 English St. **Tel** 028 3752 1801.
⭘ daily. ⬤ 25, 26 Dec. 📷 🍴 ♿ 📷
www.nitowns.com

♣ **Observatory Grounds**
College Hill. **Tel** 028 3752 2928. ⭘
daily, pm only. **Planetarium Tel** 028
3752 3689. 📷 for shows. 📷 ♿

Environs

Skull of Barbary ape
from Navan Fort

To the west of
Armagh stands
Navan Fort, a
large earthwork
on the summit of
a hill. In legend,
Navan was Emain
Macha, ceremonial and
spiritual capital of
ancient Ulster,
associated with tales
of the warrior
Cúchulainn (see p26). The site
may have been in use as
much as 4,000 years ago, but
seems to have been most
active around 100 BC when a
huge timber building, 40 m
(130 ft) across, was erected
over a giant cairn. The whole
thing was then burned and the
remains covered with soil.
Archaeological evidence indicates that this was not an act of
war, but a solemn ritual
performed by the inhabitants
of Emain Macha themselves.
    Below the fort, the grass-
roofed **Navan Centre** interprets
the site, but is now only open
for groups of 25 or more. One
unexpected exhibit is the skull
of a Barbary ape, found in the
remains of a Bronze Age
house. The animal must come
from Spain or North Africa,
evidence that by 500 BC Emain
Macha was already a place
with far-flung trading links.

🏛 **Navan Centre**
On A28 4 km (2.5 miles) W of Armagh.
Tel 028 3752 5550. ⭘ large groups
only. Call. 📷 ♿

Lough Neagh ㉔

Road map D2. Co Armagh, Co
Tyrone, Co Londonderry, Co Antrim.

Legend has it that the giant
Finn MacCool (see pp26–7)
created Lough Neagh by
picking up a piece of turf and
hurling it into the Irish Sea, thus
forming the Isle of Man in the
process. At 400 sq km (153 sq
miles), the lake is the largest
in Britain. Bordered by sedgy
marshland, it has few roads
along its shore. The best rec-
reational areas lie in the
south: Oxford Island, actually
a peninsula, has walking
trails, bird lookouts and the
informative **Lough Neagh
Discovery Centre**. In the
southwest corner, a narrow-
gauge railway runs through
the bogs of **Peatlands Park**.
Salmon and trout swim in the

Navan Fort, the site of Emain Macha, legendary capital of Ulster

Hide for birdwatchers at Oxford Island on the southern shore of Lough Neagh

rivers that flow from Lough Neagh. The lake is famous for its eels, with one of the world's largest eel fisheries at **Toome** on the north shore.

🏛 Lough Neagh Discovery Centre
Oxford Island. Exit 10 off M1. *Tel* 028 3832 2205. ◯ daily. ● 25, 26 Dec. 🎦 ♿ 🍴 🛍
www.craigavon.gov.uk

🌿 Peatlands Park
Exit 13 off M1. *Tel* 028 3885 1102. Park ◯ daily. ● 25 Dec. **Visitors' centre** ◯ Jun–Aug: daily (pm only); Easter–end May & Sep: Sat, Sun & public hols (pm only). ♿ 🛍 🛍
www.peatlandsni.gov.uk

Larne ㉕

Road map D1. Co Antrim. 🏚 20,000. 🚌 🚆 🚹 Narrow Gauge Rd (028 2826 0088). www.larne.gov.uk

Industrial Larne is the arrival point for ferries from Scotland *(see pp384–6)*. The town is not the finest introduction to Ulster scenery, but it lies on the threshold of the magnificent Antrim coastline *(see p267)*.

The sheltered waters of Larne Lough have been a landing point since Mesolithic times – flint flakes found here provide some of the earliest evidence of human presence on the island – nearly 9,000 years ago. Since then, Norsemen used the lough as a base in the 10th century, Edward Bruce landed his Scottish troops in the area in 1315, and in 1914 the Ulster Volunteer Force landed a huge cache of German arms here during its campaign against Home Rule *(see pp44–5)*.

Carrickfergus ㉖

Road map E2. Co Antrim. 🏚 38,500. 🚌 🚆 🚹 Antrim St (028 9335 8000). ◯ 9am–5pm Mon–Fri. 🖥 Thu. www.carrickfergus.org

Carrickfergus grew up around the massive castle begun in 1180 by John de Courcy to guard the entrance to Belfast Lough. De Courcy was the leader of the Anglo-Norman force which invaded Ulster following Strongbow's conquest of Leinster in the south *(see pp36–7)*.

Carrickfergus Castle was shaped to fit the crag on which it stands overlooking the harbour. The finest and best-preserved Norman castle in Ireland, it even has its original portcullis *(see pp36–7)*. Many changes have been made since the 12th century, including wide ramparts to accommodate the castle's cannons. Arms and armour are on display in the large keep, while life-size model soldiers are posed along the ramparts. In continuous use up to 1928, the castle has changed hands several times over the years. Under Edward Bruce, the Scots took it in 1315, holding it for three years. James II's army was in control of the castle from 1688 until General Schomberg took it for William III in 1690. William himself stayed here before the Battle of the Boyne *(see p244)* in 1690.

De Courcy also founded the pretty **St Nicholas' Church**. Inside are rare stained-glass work and a "leper window", through which the afflicted received the sacraments. Other attractions include the **Andrew Jackson Centre**, which celebrates the town's link to the seventh president of the USA, and **Flame**, a museum based around a Victorian coal gasworks.

♟ Carrickfergus Castle
Tel 028 9335 1273. ◯ daily. ● Sun am, 25 Dec. 🎦 ♿ 🍴 🛍 🛍

🏛 Flame
44 Irish Quarter West. *Tel* 028 9336 9575. www.gasworksflame.com

The massive Norman keep of Carrickfergus Castle

Belfast ㉗

Belfast was the only city in Ireland to experience the full force of the Industrial Revolution. Its ship-building, linen, rope-making and tobacco industries caused the population to rise to almost 400,000 by the end of World War I. The Troubles and the decline of traditional industries have since damaged economic life, but regeneration projects, such as the Odyssey complex at Queen's Quay, are breathing new life into run-down areas. Belfast remains a handsome city and visitors are agreeably surprised by the friendliness of the "Big Smoke".

Red Hand of Ulster, Linen Hall Library

Mosaic in St Anne's Cathedral, showing St Patrick's journey to Ireland

Interior of the Grand Opera House

🏛 City Hall

Donegall Square. **Tel** 028 9027 0456 ext 2346. ▪ 11am and 2:30pm daily; all other times by appointment.

Most of Belfast's main streets (and many major bus routes) radiate out from the hub of Donegall Square. In the centre of the square stands the vast rectangular Portland stone bulk of the 1906 City Hall. It has an elaborate tower at each corner and a central copper dome that rises to a height of 53 m (173 ft). Highlight of the tour of the interior is the sumptuous oak-panelled council chamber.

Statues around the building include a glum-looking Queen Victoria outside the main entrance and, on the east side, Sir Edward Harland, founder of the Harland and Wolff shipyard, which built the *Titanic*. A memorial to those who died when the *Titanic* sank in 1912 stands close by.

Detail of *Titanic* Memorial outside City Hall

🎭 Grand Opera House

Great Victoria St. **Tel** 028 9024 1919. **www**.goh.co.uk

Designed by Frank Matcham, the renowned theatre-architect, this exuberant late-Victorian building opened its doors in 1894. The sumptuous interior, with its gilt, red plush and intricate plasterwork, was restored to its full glory in 1980. On occasions, bombings of the adjacent Europa Hotel disrupted business at the theatre, but it survives as a major venue for plays and concerts.

⛪ Belfast Cathedral

Donegall St. **Tel** 028 9032 8332. **www**.belfastcathedral.org

The Neo-Romanesque façade of this Protestant cathedral, consecrated in 1904, is not particularly impressive. The interior is far more attractive, especially the colourful mosaics executed by the two Misses Martin in the 1920s. The one covering the baptistry ceiling contains over 150,000 pieces. The wide nave is paved with Canadian maple and the aisles with Irish marble. Lord Carson (1854–1935), implacable leader of the campaign against Home Rule (*see p44*), is buried in the south aisle.

Key to Symbos see back flap

SIGHTS AT A GLANCE

Albert Memorial Clock Tower ⑩
Belfast Cathedral ⑥
Botanical Gardens ⑨
City Hall ③
Crown Liquor Saloon ②
The Entries ⑤
Grand Opera House ①
Lagan Weir Lookout ⑪
Linen Hall Library ④
Queen's University ⑦
Ulster Museum ⑧
W5 ⑫

```
0 metres        500
0 yards         500
```

VISITORS' CHECKLIST

Road map D2. Co Antrim. 🏛
500,000. ✈ *Belfast City, 6.5 km
(4 miles) E; Belfast International,
29 km (18 miles) NW.* 🚉 *Central
Station, East Bridge St (028 9089
9400); Great Victoria St Station
(028 9066 6630).* 🚌 *Europa Bus
Centre, Great Victoria St; Laganside Bus Centre, Victoria Sq (028
9066 6630).* ℹ *47 Donegall Pl
(028 9024 6609).* **www**.goto
belfast.com 🎪 *Royal Agricultural
Show & Lord Mayor's Show (May).*

determination to win, one cut off his own hand and threw it to the shore.

🚪 The Entries
The Entries are a series of narrow alleys between Ann Street and High Street. They feature some of the best pubs in the city, including White's Tavern *(see p351)*, reputedly the oldest bar in Belfast. The Globe in Joy's Entry and the Morning Star on Pottinger's Entry both serve excellent lunches. In 1791, the United Irishmen, a radical movement inspired by the new ideas of the French Revolution, was founded in a tavern on Crown Entry. Its most famous member was Wolfe Tone *(see pp40–41)*.

🍺 Crown Liquor Saloon
Great Victoria St. **Tel** *028 9027 9901.*
⏰ *daily.* **www**.nationaltrust.org.uk
Even teetotallers should make a detour to the tiled façade of this flamboyant Victorian drinking palace. The Crown, which dates back to the 1880s, is one of only two pubs owned by the National Trust. The lovingly restored interior features stained glass, marbling, mosaics and a splendid ceiling with scrolled plasterwork. The wooden snugs facing the long bar have their original gas lamps: the perfect place for a pint of Guinness or Bass and some Strangford Lough oysters.

🚪 Linen Hall Library
17 Donegall Square North.
Tel *028 9032 1707.* ⏰ *Mon–Sat.*
💻 **www**.linenhall.com
Founded as the Belfast Society for Promoting Knowledge in 1788, the library has thousands of rare, old books. There is also extensive documentation of political events in Ireland since 1968 and a vast database of genea-logical information. Even if you have no special reason for visiting the library, it is still worth going inside, if only for the delightful coffee shop and the vast selection of news-papers and periodicals. Above the library door you will see the Red Hand of Ulster, the emblem of the province. It is the subject of a gory legend about two Celtic heroes racing to see who would touch the land of Ulster first. In his

The ornate Victorian interior of the Crown Liquor Saloon

Exploring Belfast

Away from the city centre, Belfast has many pleasant suburbs unaffected by the civil strife of recent times. The area around Queen's University to the south of the city has two major attractions in the Ulster Museum and the Botanic Gardens. To the north, there are splendid views to be enjoyed from the heights of Cave Hill, while visitors interested in Belfast's industrial heritage will be keen to see both the old docks and the Harland and Wolff working shipyards.

Interior of the Victorian Palm House at the Botanic Gardens

🏛 Ulster Museum

Botanic Gardens. **Tel** 028 9038 3000. ◯ daily (Sat & Sun: pm only). ⬤ public hols. ♿ ▢ ▢ ▢
www.ulstermuseum.org.uk
This four-floor bunker of a museum covers all aspects of Ulster, from local history, archaeology, antiquities and art to geology, natural history and technology. Especially prized treasures include gold and silver jewellery recovered from the *Girona*, a Spanish Armada ship that sank off the Giant's Causeway in 1588 *(see p257).*

One of the most interesting exhibits is of Belfast industry, featuring some crude turn-of-the-century textile machinery.

In the top-floor gallery is a collection of paintings mostly by British and Irish artists, including many by Belfast-born Sir John Lavery (1856–1941).

In addition to the Irish collections, there are exhibits ranging from ancient Egyptian mummies to dinosaurs. The museum also mounts frequent temporary exhibitions on a wide variety of themes.

🌷 Botanic Gardens

Stranmills Rd. **Tel** 028 9032 4902. ◯ daily.
Backing on to the university, the Botanic Gardens provide a quiet refuge from the bustle of campus. The 1839 Palm House is a superb example of curvilinear glass and cast-iron work. The Tropical Ravine, or Fernery, is another fine piece of Victorian garden architecture. Visitors can look down from the balcony to a sunken glen of exotic plants.

🏫 Queen's University

University Rd. **Tel** 028 9033 5252. A 15-minute stroll south from Donegall Square, through the lively entertainment district known as the Golden Mile, leads to Northern Ireland's most prestigious university. The main building, designed in Tudor-style red and yellow brick by Charles Lanyon in 1849, bears similarities to Magdalene College, Oxford. A towered gateway leads to a colonnaded quadrangle.

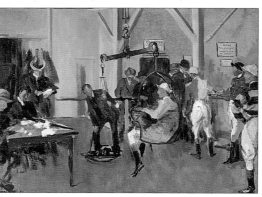
Weighing Room, Hurst Park (1924) by Sir John Lavery, Ulster Museum

THE POLITICAL MURALS OF WEST BELFAST

Republican mural in the Falls Road

Ever since the onset of the "Troubles" in 1968, popular art has played a conspicuous role in proclaiming the loyalties of Belfast's two most intransigent working-class communities, on the Protestant Shankill Road and the Catholic Falls Road. The gable walls of dozens of houses in these areas have been decorated with vivid murals expressing local political and paramilitary affiliations. Likewise, kerbstones on certain streets are painted either in the red, white and blue of the United Kingdom or the green, white and gold of Ireland. Even with the successes of the current peace process, many are likely to remain. Some tourists make the journey out to West Belfast just to see the murals. The simplest way to do this is to pre-book a "Black Cab Tour" through the Belfast Welcome Centre. Call 028 9024 6609.

Protestant Loyalist mural

🏛 W5

Odyssey, 2 Queen's Quay. **Tel** 028 9046 7700. ⬭ daily (Sun: pm only) (last adm: 5pm). **www**.w5online.co.uk

W5, short for "whowhatwhere whenwhy", is an award-winning interactive museum, which presents science as an exciting process of discovery.

There are sections on the elements (including the Fire Tornado, a huge column of twisting fire), perception experiments, and problem solving. Visitors can try working a replica of a Port of Belfast crane, designing and building a boat, forensically examining replica bones, or composing music.

Belfast cityscape showing the giant cranes, Samson and Goliath

🏰 Albert Memorial Clock Tower

Queen's Square.

One of Belfast's best-known monuments, today the clock tower leans slightly as a result of subsidence. Beyond it, facing the river, stands the Custom House (1854) by Charles Lanyon, architect of Queen's University.

🏛 Lagan Weir Lookout

Donegall Quay. **Tel** 028 9031 5444. ⬭ daily (Sat & Sun: pm only). 📷 ♿ 🚻 📷 **www**.laganside.com

Belfast's once thriving harbour area can best be viewed from the footbridge alongside the Lagan Weir development. Five computer-controlled steel gates maintain a fixed water level, getting rid of the mudbanks produced by varying tide levels and allowing for angling and watersports along the river. The visitors' centre, on the footbridge, explains how it all works and tells some good tales of modern Belfast folklore. At night, the weir is

The unmistakable profile of Cave Hill above the roofs of Belfast

lit by gas-filter blue light that shimmers across the water.

There is a partly obscured view across to the giant yellow cranes – appropriately named Samson and Goliath – of the once-mighty Harland and Wolff shipyards.

🏰 Cave Hill

Antrim Rd, 6.5 km (4 miles) N of city. **Belfast Castle visitors' centre** *Tel* 028 9077 6925. ⬭ daily. ● 25 Dec. ♿ 🚻 📷 **www**.belfastcastle.co.uk **Zoo** *Tel* 028 9077 6277. ⬭ daily. ● 25 Dec. 📷 ♿ 🚻 📷 **www**.belfastzoo.co.uk

It was on Cave Hill, next to MacArt's Fort (named after an Iron Age chieftain), that Wolfe Tone *(see p41)* and the northern leaders of the United Irishmen met in 1795 to pledge themselves to rebellion. The five artificial caves near the fort were carved out during the Neolithic period.

On the wooded eastern slopes of the hill stands the baronial pile of Belfast Castle, built in 1870. Previously home to the Earl of Shaftesbury, the castle now belongs to the city and houses a restaurant and a visitors' centre that interprets the area's history. A little further along the road past the castle is Belfast Zoo.

⌂ Giant's Ring

Off B23, 5 km (3 miles) S of city centre.

Little is known about this awe-inspiring prehistoric enclosure almost 200 m (660 ft) in diameter. It is surrounded by a grassy bank averaging almost 6 m (20 ft) in width and 4.5 m (15 ft) in height. Bones from a Stone Age burial were found under the dolmen in the centre. During the 18th century the ring was a popular venue for horse races.

🏛 Stormont

Newtownards Rd, 8 km (5 miles) SE of city centre. ● to the public. 📷 by arrangement only.

Built between 1928 and 1932, at a cost of £1,250,000, Stormont was designed to house the Northern Ireland Parliament. The huge Anglo-Palladian mass of Portland stone and Mourne granite stands at the end of a majestic avenue, 1.6 km (1 mile) long, bordered by parkland. A statue of Lord Carson *(see p44)* stands near the front entrance.

Since the parliament was disbanded in 1972, the building has been used as government offices. Its future depends very much on the outcome of the ongoing peace process. The debating chamber was badly damaged in a fire in 1994.

Stormont in its parkland setting outside Belfast

Ulster Folk and Transport Museum ㉘

Road map E2. Cultra, near Holywood, Co Down. *Tel* 028 9042 8428. 🔲
🔲 🔲 *daily.* ● *24–25 Dec.* 📷
(free for the disabled). 🔲 🔲 📷
www.uftm.org.uk

Dozens of old buildings, including flax-, corn- and sawmills, have been plucked from the Ulster countryside and re-erected in this folk park. Demonstrations of traditional crafts, industries and farming methods are given.

The A2 road splits the folk museum from the transport section. This is dominated by a hangar that houses the Irish Railway Collection. The smaller Transport Gallery exhibits machinery made in Ulster, including a saloon carriage from the tram service that ran from Portrush to Giant's Causeway *(see pp262–3)*. Of particular note is a test model of the spectacularly unsuccessful De Lorean car, made in the early 1980s with a huge government subsidy. There's also a popular exhibit on another ill-fated construction – the *Titanic*. It's best to allow half a day to take in most of the attractions.

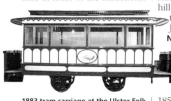

1883 tram carriage at the Ulster Folk and Transport Museum

Ards Peninsula ㉙

Road map E2. Co Down. 🔲 🔲 *to Bangor.* ℹ️ *Newtownards (028 9182 6846).* Heritage Centre *Tel 028 9127 1200.* www.ards-council.gov.uk

The peninsula – and some of Northern Ireland's finest scenery – begins east of Belfast at **Bangor**. This resort town has a modern marina and some well-known yacht clubs. A little way south is **Donaghadee**, from where boats sail to the three **Copeland Islands**,

Scrabo Tower, a prominent landmark of the Ards Peninsula

inhabited only by seabirds since the departure of the last human residents in the 1940s. The **Ballycopeland Windmill** (1784) is Northern Ireland's only working windmill and stands on the top of a small hill a little further south, near the town of Millisle.

Just across the peninsula is **Newtownards**. On a hill above the town is the pleasant and shady **Scrabo Country Park**. In the park stands the **Scrabo Tower**, built in 1857 as a memorial to the third Marquess of Londonderry.

Past the grounds of **Mount Stewart House** *(see pp282–3)* is the hamlet of Greyabbey, with its antique shops and Cistercian abbey ruins. Founded in 1193, **Grey Abbey** was used as a parish church until the 17th century. It is idyllically set in lush meadows by a stream and some of its features, particularly the finely carved west doorway, are well preserved.

On the tip of the peninsula, **Portaferry** overlooks the Strangford Narrows across from the Lecale Peninsula *(see p284)*. Portaferry's large aquarium, **Exploris**, displays

the diversity of life in the Irish Sea and Strangford Lough.

🎡 Ballycopeland Windmill
On B172 1.6 km (1 mile) W of Millisle. *Tel* 028 9054 3037. ◯ *Jul–Aug: Tue–Sun; winter on request.* 📷

🎡 Scrabo Country Park
Near Newtownards. *Tel* 028 9181 1491. ◯ *daily.* Tower ◯ *Easter–Sep: Sat–Thu or by appt.*

🏠 Grey Abbey
Greyabbey *Tel summer: 028 4278 8585; winter: 028 9054 3037.* ◯ *Apr–Sep: Tue–Sun; Oct–Mar: Sat and Sun only or on request.* 🔲

🛥 Exploris
Castle Street, Portaferry. *Tel* 028 4272 8062. ◯ *daily.* ● *25 Dec.* 📷 🔲 🔲

Ballycopeland Windmill, which dates back to 1784

Mount Stewart House ㉚

See pp282–3.

Hillsborough ㉛

Road map D2. Co Down. 2,600. *The Square (028 9268 9717).* www.discovernorthernireland.com

Dotted with craft shops and restaurants, this Georgian town lies less than 16 km (10 miles) from Belfast. **Hillsborough Castle**, with its elaborate wrought-iron gates and coat of arms, is where visiting dignitaries to Northern Ireland normally stay.

Across from the 18th-century Market House in the town square is **Hillsborough Fort**. An artillery fort dating from 1650, it was remodelled in the 18th century for feasts held by the descendants of Arthur Hill, founder of the town.

⚓ **Hillsborough Castle**
Tel 028 9268 1308. Easter–Sep: Sat only (call to check times).

⚓ **Hillsborough Fort**
Access from town square or car park at Forest Park. *Tel 028 9268 3285.* daily.

Downpatrick ㉜

Road map E2. Co Down. 10,300. *53a Market St (028 4461 2233).* Jul–Aug: daily; Jun & Sep: Mon–Sat. Sat.

Were it not for its strong links with St Patrick, Downpatrick would attract few visitors. The Protestant **Down Cathedral**, high on the Hill of Down, dates in its present form from the early 19th century – previous incarnations have been razed. In the churchyard is a well-worn 10th-century cross and the reputed burial place of St Patrick, marked by a 20th-century granite slab with the inscription "Patric".

Down County Museum, which is housed in the 18th-century Old County Gaol, features refurbished cells and exhibits relating to St Patrick, while close by is the **Mound of Down**, a large Norman motte and bailey.

Terraced houses in the town of Hillsborough

🏛 **Down County Museum**
English Street, The Mall. *Tel 028 4461 5218.* daily. 25–26 Dec; Sat & Sun am ltd. www.downcountymuseum.com

Environs
There are several sights linked to St Patrick on the outskirts of Downpatrick. **Struell Wells**, believed to be a former pagan place of worship that the saint blessed, has a ruined church, 17th-century bath houses and good potential for a picnic. Further out and to the north at **Saul**, where St Patrick landed and began his Irish mission in 432, is a small memorial church.

The nearby hill of **Slieve Patrick** is an important place of pilgrimage and has a granite figure of the saint at its summit. An open-air mass is celebrated here every June.

Not far from the banks of the River Quoile is the Cistercian **Inch Abbey**, founded by John de Courcy in about 1180. Its attractive marshland setting is more memorable than its remains, but it's worth a visit.

🔒 **Inch Abbey**
5 km (3 miles) NW of Downpatrick. daily. www.ehsni.gov.uk

THE LIFE OF ST PATRICK

Little hard information is known about St Patrick, the patron saint of Ireland, but he was probably not the first missionary to visit the country – a certain Palladius was sent by Pope Celestine in 431. Most stories tell that Patrick was kidnapped from Britain by pirates and brought to Ireland to tend sheep. From here he escaped to France to study Christianity. In 432, he sailed to Saul in County Down, where he quickly converted the local chieftain. He then travelled throughout the island convincing many other Celtic tribes of the truth of the new religion. The fact that Ireland has no snakes is explained by a legend that St Patrick drove them all into the sea.

19th-century engraving showing St Patrick banishing all snakes from Ireland

Mount Stewart House ⑳

**Lord Castlereagh
(1769–1822)**

This grand 19th-century house has a splendid interior, but it is the magnificent gardens which are the main attraction. These were planted only in the 1920s, but the exotic plants and trees have thrived in the area's subtropical microclimate. Now owned by the National Trust, Mount Stewart used to belong to the London-derry family, the most famous of whom was Lord Castlereagh, British Foreign Secretary from 1812 until his death in 1822.

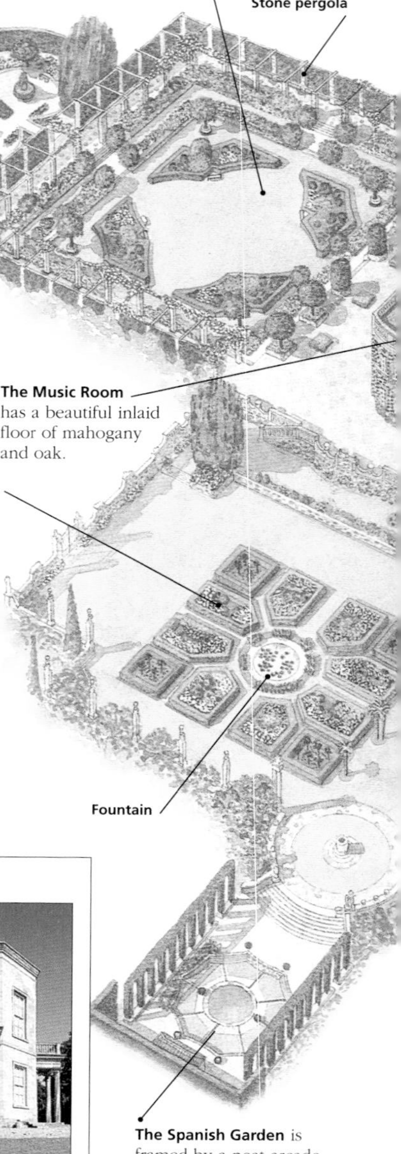

The Sunk Garden
comprises symmetrical beds which in summer are full of rich blue, yellow and orange flowers, complemented by purple foliage.

Stone pergola

★ **Shamrock Garden**
*A yew hedge in the shape
of a shamrock encloses
this topiary Irish harp
and a striking flower-
bed designed in the
form of a red hand,
emblem of Ulster.*

The Music Room
has a beautiful inlaid floor of mahogany and oak.

Italian Garden
The flowers in the Italian Garden, the largest of the formal gardens, are planted so that strong oranges and reds on the east side contrast with the softer pinks, whites and blues on the west.

Fountain

THE TEMPLE OF THE WINDS

This banqueting pavilion looks over Strangford Lough to the east of the house. It was built in 1785 by James "Athenian" Stuart, a renowned pioneer of Neo-Classical architecture, who took his inspiration from the Tower of the Winds in Athens. Restored in the 1960s and now being worked on once more, the building's finest features are the spiral staircase and the upper room's plasterwork ceiling and exquisite inlaid floor.

The Spanish Garden is framed by a neat arcade of clipped cypress trees.

★ **Hambletonian by George Stubbs**
This picture of the celebrated racehorse at Newmarket, painted in 1799, hangs halfway up the main staircase.

VISITORS' CHECKLIST

Road map E2. 3 km (2 miles) N of Greyabbey, Co Down. *Tel* 028 4278 8387. 🚌 from Belfast. **House** ☐ May–Sep: daily (not Tue in May & Jun); Easter, Apr & Oct: noon–6pm Sat, Sun & public hols. **Temple** ☐ Apr–Oct: 2–5pm Sun & public hols. **Gardens** ☐ Apr–Oct: daily; Mar: Sat, Sun & public hols. **Lake** ☐ all year. 📷 🚫 in house. ♿ 🅿 🍴 🛍

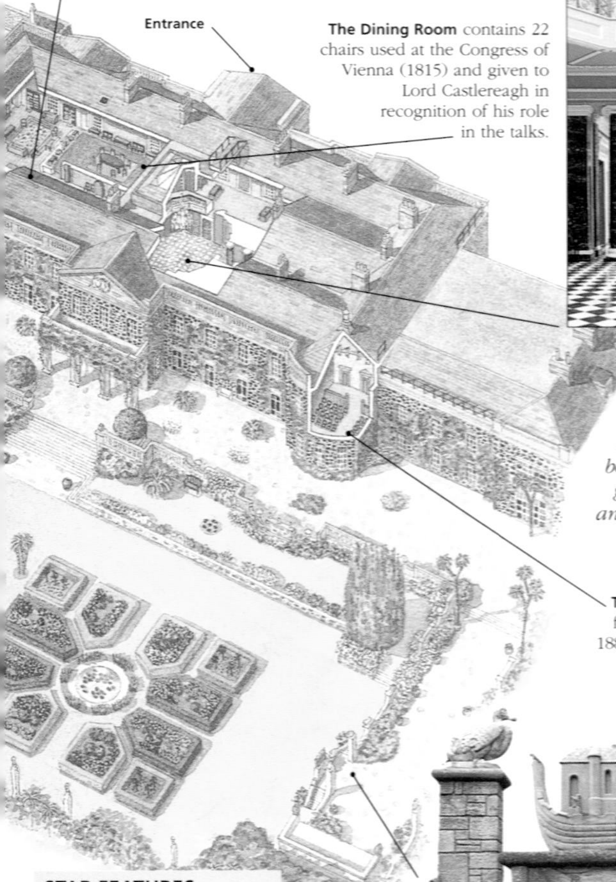

Entrance

The Dining Room contains 22 chairs used at the Congress of Vienna (1815) and given to Lord Castlereagh in recognition of his role in the talks.

Entrance Hall
The most austere room in the house, this hall features Ionic stone pillars which have been painted to resemble green marble. It is lit by an impressive glass dome.

The Chapel, converted from a sitting room in 1884, is still used by the Londonderry family.

STAR FEATURES

★ Dodo Terrace

★ Hambletonian by George Stubbs

★ Shamrock Garden

★ **Dodo Terrace**
The stone dodos and ark on this terrace relate to the Ark Club, a social circle set up by Lady Londonderry in London during World War I. Each member was given an animal nickname.

Lady Bangor's Gothic boudoir in Castle Ward on the Lecale Peninsula

Lecale Peninsula ㉝

Road map E2 Co Down. 🚌 to *Ardglass.* ℹ️ *Downpatrick (028 4461 2233).* 🎭 *Castle Ward Opera Festival (Jun; 028 9066 1090).*
www.discovernorthernisland.com

A good way. to get to this part of County Down is to take the car ferry from Portaferry on the Ards Peninsula to Strangford. Just outside this tiny port is **Castle Ward**, the estate of Lord and Lady Bangor, who seemed to argue about everything – including the design of their 18th-century mansion. His choice, Palladian, can be seen at the front, while her favourite Gothic style influences the garden façade. Likewise, the interior is a mix of Classical and Gothic fantasy. Look out for Lady Bangor's cluttered boudoir, with its extravagant fan-vaulted ceiling based on Henry VIII's chapel in Westminster Abbey. Around the grounds are trails, gardens, play areas and a farm-yard with a working corn mill.

About 4 km (2.5 miles) south of Strangford, the A2 passes **Kilclief Castle**, dating from the 15th century, one of the oldest tower houses *(see p20)* in Ireland. The road continues to **Ardglass**, now a small fishing village but once Ulster's busiest harbour. A cluster of castles was erected between the 14th and 16th centuries to protect the port, of which six remain. Only one of these is open to the public, **Jordan's Castle**. **St John's Point**, 6 km (3.5 miles)

southwest of Ardglass, offering a sweeping panorama over Dundrum Bay.

🏰 Castle Ward
On A25, 2.5 km (1.5 miles) W of Strangford. **Tel** *028 4488 1204.*
House ⬜ *mid-Mar–Apr: Sat, Sun, & public hols (pm only); May: Wed–Mon (pm only); Jun–Aug: daily (pm only); Sep–Oct: Sat–Sun (pm only).* 🚫🚻🅿️🛍️
Grounds ⬜ *daily.* 🛍️ *car park.*
www.nationaltrust.org.uk

⚓ Jordan's Castle
Ardglass. ⬜ *Jul–Aug: Tue–Sun.* 🛍️

Castlewellan Forest Park ㉞

Road map D2. Main St, Castlewellan, Co Down. **Tel** *028 4377 8664.*
⬜ *daily.* 🛍️ *for car park.*

The outstanding feature of Castlewellan Forest Park, in the foothills of the Mourne Mountains, is its magnificent arboretum. This has grown far beyond the

original walled garden, begun in 1740, and now comprises hothouses, dwarf conifer beds and a rhododendron wood.

Elsewhere in the park are a 19th-century Scottish baronial-style castle (now a conference centre), a lake and pleasant woodlands; these are at their most colourful in autumn.

Mountains of Mourne ㉟

Road map D2. Co Down. 🚌 to Newry. 🚌 to Newcastle. ℹ️ *10–14 Central Promenade, Newcastle (028 4372 2222).*
www.kingdomsofdown.com

These mountains occupy just a small corner of County Down, with no more than a dozen peaks surpassing 600 m (2,000 ft), and yet they attract thousands of visitors each year.

Only one road of any size, the B27 between Kilkeel and Hilltown, crosses the Mournes, making this ideal territory for walkers. A popular but tough trail runs from **Newcastle**, the main gateway to the area, up to the peak of **Slieve Donard**: at 848 m (2,781 ft), this is the highest mountain in the range. Part of the route follows the **Mourne Wall**, which was erected in 1904–22 to enclose the catchment area of the two reservoirs in the **Silent Valley**.

Over 20 short hikes are to be enjoyed in the area. These range from easy strolls around Rostrevor Forest to rather more arduous treks up Slieve Muck and other Mourne peaks. Tourist offices will have details.

Some 35 km (22 miles) north of Newcastle, the **Legananny Dolmen** *(see p32)* is one of the finest and most photo-graphed ancient sights in the country.

Rounded peaks of the Mountains of Mourne

A Tour of the Mourne Coast ㊱

Newcastle, where, in the words of the 19th-century songwriter Percy French, "the Mountains of Mourne sweep down to the sea", makes a good base from which to explore this area. Driving up and down the dipping roads of the Mournes is one of the highlights of a trip to Northern Ireland. Along the coast, the road skirts between the foothills and the Irish Sea, providing lovely views and linking a variety of fishing villages and historic castles. Heading inland, you pass through an emptier landscape of moorland, purple with heather. The Silent Valley, with a visitors' centre and well-marked paths, is the only area to have been developed especially for tourists.

Dundrum ②
The town is overlooked by the ruins of a Norman castle, and from the nearby bay you can see the mountains rising in the distance.

Tollymore Forest Park ③
This attractive park is dotted with follies like the Gothic Gate that formed part of the original 18th-century estate.

Spelga Dam ④
There are stunning views north from the Spelga Dam over the Mourne foothills.

Rostrevor with Slieve Martin behind

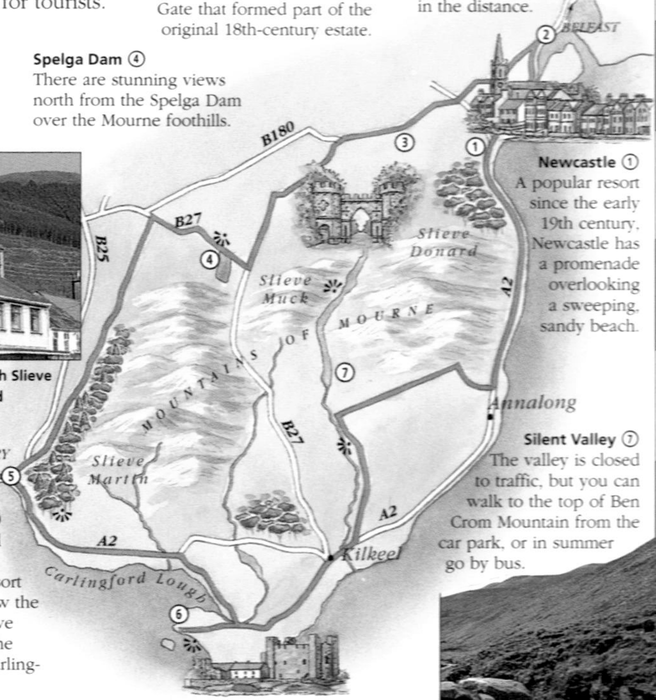

Newcastle ①
A popular resort since the early 19th century, Newcastle has a promenade overlooking a sweeping, sandy beach.

Rostrevor ⑤
This tranquil and leafy Victorian resort nestles below the peak of Slieve Martin, on the shores of Carlingford Lough.

Silent Valley ⑦
The valley is closed to traffic, but you can walk to the top of Ben Crom Mountain from the car park, or in summer go by bus.

Green Castle ⑥
Erected in the 13th century, Green Castle lies at the end of a single track road on a rocky outcrop at the entrance to Carlingford Lough.

TIPS FOR DRIVERS

Length: 85 km (53 miles).
Stopping-off points: Newcastle has the biggest choice of pubs and restaurants. Dundrum, Annalong, Kilkeel and Rostrevor all have pubs, and a café opens in the Silent Valley in summer. The Spelga Dam and Tollymore Forest Park are good picnic spots. (See also pp387–9.)

KEY

▬▬ Tour route
═══ Other roads
⁂ Viewpoint

0 kilometres   5

0 miles   3

TRAVELLERS' NEEDS

WHERE TO STAY

Whether you are staying in exclusive luxury or modest self-catering accommodation, one thing you can be certain of in Ireland is that you'll receive a warm welcome. The Irish are renowned for their friendliness. Even in big corporate hotels, where you might expect the reception to be more impersonal, the staff go out of their way to be hospitable. The choice is enormous: you can stay in an elegant 18th-century country house, a luxurious (or slightly run-down) castle, a Victorian town house, an old-fashioned commercial hotel, a cosy village inn, or on a working farm. For the hardier visitor there are good hostels, plenty of trailer and camping sites, or even your own horse-drawn caravan. We give details here of the types of accommodation available, tourist board ratings and the choices for house or apartment rental. Our listings on pages 294–319 recommend over 300 hotels around the country – all places of quality, ranging from simple bed-and-breakfast to unashamed luxury accommodation. Fáilte Ireland (the Irish Tourist Board) and the Northern Ireland Tourist Board both publish comprehensive guides.

Waterford Castle doorman

Entrance hall of the Delphi Lodge *(see p311)* in Leenane

HOTELS

At the top of the price range there are a handful of expensive, luxury hotels in castles and stately country houses. Magnificently furnished and run, they offer maximum comfort, delicious food and a wide range of sports facilities – either owned by the hotel or available close by. Salmon-fishing, fox-hunting and shooting can be arranged as well as riding, golf, sailing and cycling.

If your priority is a full range of indoor facilities, such as a gym, sauna and swimming pool, the modern hotel chains will best cater to your needs. **Jury's-Doyle** and **Great Southern Hotels** offer this standard of accommodation in the Republic, as does **Hastings Hotels** in Northern Ireland. However, these establishments can sometimes lack the charm and individuality of privately run hotels.

Coastal resort hotels usually offer a range of sports activities or can advise you on the best places to go. In smaller towns, the main hotel is often the social centre of the area with a lively public bar, popular with locals and guests alike.

The shamrock symbols of both the Northern Ireland Tourist Board and Fáilte Ireland are displayed by hotels (and other forms of accommodation) that have been inspected and officially approved.

COUNTRY HOUSE ACCOMMODATION

Visitors wishing to stay in a period country home and sample authentic Irish country life can contact a specialist organization called **Hidden Ireland**. However, this type of accommodation may not suit everybody, as the houses are not guesthouses, hotels or bed-and-breakfast establishments, but something quite different. You should therefore not expect the same facilities and service usually found in a hotel, such as a swimming pool, elevators, televisions, porters and room service. Instead, the experience is a very intimate one; guests dine together with their host and hostess as if at a private dinner party. Many of the houses have been in the same family for hundreds of years and the history attached to them can be fascinating. Prices reflect the type of house and the standard of accommodation, but all offer excellent value for money and

The entrance to the Shelbourne Hotel in Dublin

Bar at the Hunter's Hotel *(see p301)* in Rathnew, County Wicklow

a first-hand experience of an aspect of the Irish way of life.

There are many other private residences that also take paying guests. Two useful publications, *Friendly Homes of Ireland* and *Ireland's Blue Book*, provide listings and information and are available from tourist offices and bookshops. Tourist boards throughout Ireland also supply listings and make reservations.

GUESTHOUSES

Most guesthouses are found in cities and large towns. They are usually converted family homes and have an atmosphere all of their own. Most offer a good-value evening meal and all give you a delicious full Irish breakfast *(see p322)*. Top-of-the-range guesthouses can be just as good, and sometimes even better, than hotels. You will see a much more personal side of a town or city while staying at a guesthouse. If you are looking for anonymity, however, a guesthouse may not suit you – both the proprietor and your fellow guests are likely to try and draw you into conversation.

There are plenty of good guesthouses to choose from in the Dublin area and the prices are usually reasonable. The **Irish Hotels Federation** publishes a useful booklet with guesthouse listings that cover the whole of Ireland including Dublin. The Northern Ireland Tourist Board publishes its own

similar booklet, called *Where to Stay in Northern Ireland*. This includes a comprehensive list of approved guesthouses which is updated annually. However, it is hard to beat personal recommendations you might receive from fellow guests.

Bedroom at Enniscoe House *(see p310)*, Crossmolina in County Mayo

PRICES

Room rates advertised in both Northern Ireland and the Republic are inclusive of tax and service. In general, prices in the Republic are marginally cheaper than

in the North. Hotel rates can vary by as much as 40 per cent depending on the time of year; country house rates also vary a great deal according to the season. Guesthouse prices are influenced more by their location in relation to tourist sights and public transport.

For those on a tight budget, farmhouse accommodation represents excellent value for money, though the cheapest option is self-catering in a rented cottage *(see p290)* .

TIPPING

Tipping in Ireland is a matter of personal discretion but is not common practice, even at the larger hotels. Tasks performed by staff are considered part of the service. Tipping is not expected, for example, for carrying bags to your room or for serving drinks. However, it is usual to tip the waiting staff in hotel restaurants: the standard tip is around 10 per cent and anything over 15 per cent of the bill would be considered generous.

BOOKING

It is wise to reserve your accommodation during the peak season and public holidays *(see p51)*, particularly if your visit coincides with a local festival or major sporting event *(see pp28–9)*. Fáilte Ireland can offer advice and make reservations through its nationwide accommodation service; the Northern Ireland Tourist Board runs a similar service. Central reservation facilities are available at the hotel chains that have been listed here.

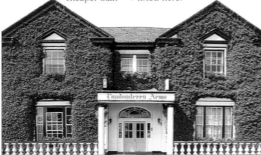

Façade of the Londonderry Arms *(see p318)* in Carnlough, County Antrim

A bed-and-breakfast on the River Corrib in Galway

BED-AND-BREAKFAST ACCOMMODATION

Ireland has the reputation for the best B&Bs in Europe. You will never be far from a place to stay, even in the remotest spots. Your welcome will always be friendly and the food and company excellent. Even if the house is no architectural beauty, the comfort and atmosphere will more than compensate. Not all bedrooms have bathrooms *en suite*. When one is available, you may have to pay a little extra, but considering the inexpensive rates, the surcharge is negligible.

The Irish swear by their B&Bs and many stay in them by choice rather than suffer the impersonality and prices of the mainstream hotels; frequent visitors to Ireland agree. The **Bed and Breakfast Association** will provide details of bed-and-breakfast accommodation in Northern Ireland, while the **Town and Country Homes Association** covers the Republic.

FARMHOUSES

Farmhouse vacations are a popular tradition in Ireland. **Irish Farmhouse Holidays Ltd** has a list of farmhouses in the Republic that take paying guests. You can stay for one night or longer and they

make an excellent base for touring the countryside. As with most things in Ireland, it is the hospitality and friendliness of the people that makes staying on a farm so memorable. You get a feel of rural Ireland with its rich agricultural heritage, and the families are determined you will enjoy every moment of your stay.

HOUSE AND APARTMENT RENTALS

Vacations spent in rental houses are an increasingly popular option in Ireland and there are properties to rent all over the country. You are likely to have more choice in the south and west as these areas have traditionally attracted the majority of tourists. Fáilte Ireland has a small section in its accommodation guide, but local tourist offices have lists

of apartments and houses to rent in their area. It is also worth looking for ads in the newspapers, both local and international. Accommodation can range from quaint, stone cottages, converted barns and stable yards to more modern, purpose-built bungalows. All will generally have adequate facilities, with simple but comfortable furnishings, modern kitchen equipment and televisions.

The properties available through the popular organization **Rent an Irish Cottage** are built in traditional style with whitewashed walls inside and out, and painted roofs and windows; the decor is also traditional – simple and attractive. Locations are generally superb; the only possible criticism is, if you wanted to be "away from it all", they are built in clusters of about ten, so there isn't a great deal of privacy.

At the other end of the scale, you could rent a castle or country house, furnished with paintings and antiques. In some cases, the properties are fully staffed. A company called **Elegant Ireland** has a selection of such properties.

CAMPING, TRAILERS AND MOTOR HOMES

A list of fully inspected camping and trailer parks is given in the Fáilte Ireland accommodation guide. Many of the camp sites and parks offer additional facilities – these might include a shop, restaurant or café/snack bar, an indoor games room, laundry, tennis court and minature golf course. The standard and con-

A farmhouse in Clonakilty, County Cork

Traditional painted horse-drawn caravan from Slattery's in Tralee

dition of these facilities will vary but you can be reliably guided by the tourist board's star ratings: four-star parks have an extensive range of facilities with a high standard of management; three-star parks have good facilities and management; two-star parks offer limited facilities and good management and the one-star parks have the minimum facilities required for registration with Fáilte Ireland. A complete list of approved camping sites in the North is produced by the Northern Ireland Tourist Board.

If you want to experience the Irish countryside at a more leisurely pace, it is possible to hire a traditional horse-drawn caravan. Two of the best companies specializing in this type of trip are **Kilvahan Caravans**, based at Portlaoise in the Midlands, and **Slattery's Travel Agency** in Tralee, County Kerry.

YOUTH HOSTELS

There are 31 youth hostels registered with **An Óige** (the Irish Youth Hostel Association), set in some wonderfully scenic areas of Ireland in buildings ranging from castles to military barracks. Accommodation is generally provided in simple dormitories with comfortable beds and basic cooking facilities. You can only use these hostels if you are a member of An Óige or

another youth organization affiliated to the International Youth Hostel Federation. Charges vary according to the standard of accommodation, location and season. Northern Ireland is covered by the **Youth Hostel Association of Northern Ireland**, which has 8 registered hostels.

Independent Holiday Hostels of Ireland publishes a guide to 151 independent hostels, and places such as universities offer similar inexpensive accommodation. Tourist boards have listings of those they recommend.

DISABLED TRAVELLERS

A fact sheet for disabled visitors can be obtained from tourist offices, Dublin Tourism, and Fáilte Ireland, and in their main accommodation guide there is a symbol for wheelchair accessibility. A similar symbol is used in the accommodation listings in this book *(see pp294–319)*. Comhairle *(see pp372–3)* is another body that offers information on accommodation for the disabled.

The annual publication *Holidays in the British Isles* caters specifically for the disabled traveller and covers Northern Ireland. There is also a guide,

Fáilte Ireland sign for approved accommodation

with comprehensive listings, available from the Northern Ireland Tourist Board entitled *Accessible Accommodation*.

Typical bed-and-breakfast sign in Pettigo, County Donegal

DIRECTORY

An Óige (Irish YHA)
61 Mountjoy St, Dublin 7.
Tel 01 830 4555.
www.irelandyha.org

Bed and Breakfast Ass'n
30 St Patrick's Rd, Downpatrick.
Tel 028 4461 5542.

Elegant Ireland
15 Harcourt St, Dublin 2.
Tel 01 475 1665. www.elegant.ie

Great Southern Hotels
6 Charlemont Terrace, Crofton Rd, Dun Laoghaire, Co Dublin.
Tel 1850 383848. www.gsh.ie

Hastings Hotels
Midland Building, Whitla St, Belfast. *Tel 028 9075 1066.*
www.hastingshotels.com

Hidden Ireland
P. O. Box 31, Westport, Co Mayo.
Tel 01 662 7166 or 098 66050
www.hidden-ireland.com

Independent Holiday Hostels of Ireland
57 Lower Gardiner St, Dublin 1. *Tel 01 836 4700.*
www.hostels-ireland.com

Irish Farmhouse Holidays Ltd
2 Michael St, Limerick.
Tel 061 400700.
www.irishfarmholidays.com

Irish Hotels Federation
13 Northbrook Rd, Dublin 6.
Tel 01 497 6459.
www.irelandhotels.com

Jury's-Doyle Hotels
Pembroke Rd, Dublin 4.
Tel 01 660 5000.
www.jurysdoyle.com

Kilvahan Caravans
Kilvahan, Portlaoise, Co Laois. *Tel 0502 35178.*
www.horsedrawncaravans.com

Rent an Irish Cottage
51 O'Connell St, Limerick.
Tel 061 411109.
www.rentacotttage.ie

Slattery's Travel Agency
1 Russell St, Tralee, Co Kerry.
Tel 066 718 6200.
www.slatterys.com

Town and Country Homes Association
Bellek Rd, Ballyshannon, Co Donegal. *Tel 071 985 1377.*

YHA Northern Ireland
22–32 Donegall Rd, Belfast.
Tel 028 9032 4733. www.hini.org.uk

Ireland's Best: Hotels

The hotels featured here are a selection from our lists of recommended places to stay on pages 294–319. They give an indication of the very best that Ireland has to offer, ranging from private establishments which are members of the Hidden Ireland group *(see p288)* to the efficiency and luxury of five-star hotels and the romance of historic castles. All are impressive places, both for their setting and the buildings themselves.

St Ernan's House
This elegant, pink Regency country house is situated on its own private island not far from Donegal.
(See p313.)

Delphi Lodge
The atmosphere at this comfortable, well-run fishing lodge is extremely relaxing. The River Delphi and nearby loughs provide plenty of sport. (See p311.)

NORTHWEST IRELAND

Ashford Castle
This huge Gothic-style edifice is set on the shores of Lough Corrib. The standard of service is impeccable and the food is excellent.
(See p310.)

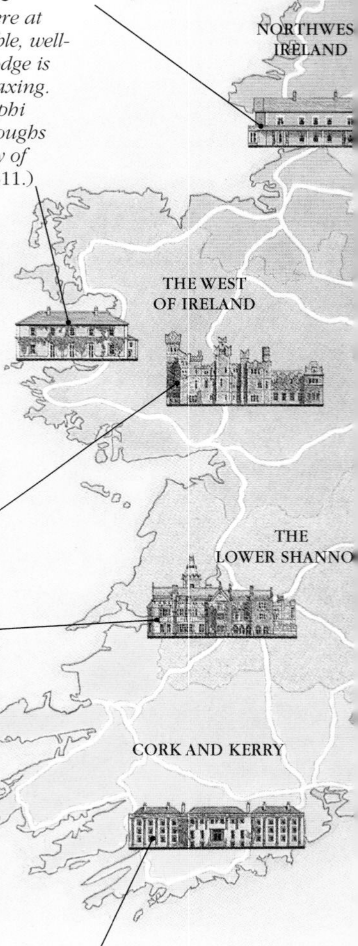

THE WEST OF IRELAND

THE LOWER SHANNON

Adare Manor
Set in a large estate beside one of the prettiest villages in the country, this luxurious hotel occupies a magnificent Victorian Gothic mansion.
(See p307.)

CORK AND KERRY

Bantry House
The spacious library in this 18th-century house looks out on to the gardens. Many of the bedrooms enjoy superb views of Bantry Bay. (See pp168–9 and p302.)

Everglades Hotel
This imposing hotel sits on the banks of the River Foyle, a short drive from the wild beaches of County Donegal and the stunning Sperrin Mountains. (See p319.)

NORTHERN
IRELAND

Hunter's Hotel
Cobbled courtyards, paddocks and a magnificent garden are only a few of the attractions of this friendly and comfortable inn. The building dates back to 1720, and is owned and run by the fourth generation of the Hunter family. (See p301.)

THE
MIDLANDS

Roundwood House
This fine, small Palladian house is set in chestnut and beech woods. The Slieve Bloom Mountains are close by and you can fish and play golf locally. The lovely rooms are filled with antiques, books and pictures and the atmosphere is one of relaxed informality. (See p316.)

SOUTHEAST
IRELAND

0 kilometres   50

0 miles   25

Waterford Castle
The ultimate in "getting away from it all", this 15th-century castle sits on a beautifully located island in the estuary of the River Suir. The hotel is reachable only by its own private ferry. (See p302.)

Choosing a Hotel

These hotels have been selected for their good value, facilities and location. They are listed by region, starting with Dublin, and then by price. Price bands for Northern Ireland are given on pages 317 and 319. Map references refer either to the Dublin Street Finder on pages 116 and 117, or the road map on the inside back cover.

PRICE CATEGORIES
For a double room per night, including tax, service charges and breakfast. These categories are for hotels in the Republic, which has adopted the euro.

€ under 65 euros
€€ 65–130 euros
€€€ 130–190 euros
€€€€ 190–260 euros
€€€€€ over 260 euros

DUBLIN

SOUTHEAST DUBLIN Kilronan House   🏃   €€
70 Adelaide Rd, Dublin 2 Tel 01 475 5266 Fax 01 478 2841 Rooms 15

Situated on a leafy street near St Stephen's Green, around the corner from the National Concert Hall, this listed town house dates from 1834. Still retaining its Georgian character, it is newly refurbished with modern comforts, including orthopaedic beds. Delicious breakfasts with home-made breads. Friendly hosts. **www.dublinn.com**

SOUTHEAST DUBLIN Leeson Hotel   🖥️🏃   €€
27 Leeson St Lower, Dublin 2 Tel 01 676 3380 Fax 01 661 8273 Rooms 20   **Map E5**

Close to St Stephen's Green, this cheerfully decorated hotel is spread across two Georgian buildings. The ambience is relaxed and informal, and service is of a high quality. Its bar, Kobra, is elegant with wood furnishings. Bedrooms are tidy and comfortable, if on the small side.

SOUTHEAST DUBLIN Georgian Hotel   🍴🏃   €€€
18–22 Baggot St Lower, Dublin 2 Tel 01 634 5000 Fax 01 634 5100 Rooms 20   **Map F5**

Warm and friendly, this three-star hotel consists of three Georgian houses with a modern extension and is well located, just a short stroll from St Stephen's Green. Comfortably done-up bedrooms are neat and well equipped. Complimentary guest parking is available. There's a traditional Irish bar, Maguires. **www.georgianhotel.ie**

SOUTHEAST DUBLIN Harcourt Hotel   🖥️🍴🏃   €€€
60 Harcourt St, Dublin 2 Tel 01 478 3677 Fax 01 475 2013 Rooms 104   **Map D5**

Just off St Stephen's Green, Harcourt Hotel boasts a central location. Though the interior is unremarkable, bedrooms are modern and well equipped. There is a popular nightclub, D-Two, situated in the basement of the hotel which is a draw for late-night revellers. **www.harcourthotel.ie**

SOUTHEAST DUBLIN Longfields   🖥️🍴🏃   €€€
10 Fitzwilliam St Lower, Dublin 2 Tel 01 676 1367 Fax 01 676 1542 Rooms 26   **Map F5**

Two interconnected Georgian buildings make up this small, stylish hotel, situated between the appealing Fitzwilliam and Merrion Squares. Furnished with antiques and reproduction pieces, it exudes the warmth of a private home. Rooms have an individual character. Good restaurant, Stephen McAllister, on site. **www.longfields.ie**

SOUTHEAST DUBLIN Molesworth Court Suites   🏃   €€€
Molesworth Court, Schoolhouse Lane, Dublin 2 Tel 01 676 4799 Fax 01 676 4982 Rooms 12   **Map E4**

Tucked away in a quiet lane off the fashionable Molesworth Street, this four-star hotel comprises 12 purpose-built, self-contained apartments and penthouses. Equipped with modern conveniences, rooms are clean and cosy. Service is friendly. Enclosed parking is provided. Good value for families. **www.molesworthcourt.ie**

SOUTHEAST DUBLIN Mont Clare   🖥️🍴🏃   €€€
Merrion Square, Dublin 2 Tel 01 607 3800 Fax 01 661 5663 Rooms 80   **Map F4**

Though not as grand as its sister hotel, the Davenport opposite, Mont Clare enjoys a good location and is traditionally furnished in mahogany and brass. Well-appointed bedrooms are air conditioned and tastefully decorated. The sizeable and popular bar serves carvery lunches. Guests may visit the gym across the road. **www.ocallaghanhotels.ie**

SOUTHEAST DUBLIN Morgan Hotel   🍴🖥️   €€€
10 Fleet St, Dublin 2 Tel 01 679 3939 Fax 01 679 3946 Rooms 106   **Map D3**

In the heart of Temple Bar, this self-styled boutique hotel is contemporary in design with clean lines and uncluttered public spaces. Minimalistic bedrooms have beech wood furnishings, cotton linen and CD systems. The ambience is relaxing, though rooms overlooking the street can be noisy. There's a fine Morgan bar. **www.themorgan.com**

SOUTHEAST DUBLIN Number 31   €€€
31 Leeson Close, Leeson St Lower, Dublin 2 Tel 01 676 5011 Fax 01 676 2929 Rooms 20   **Map E5**

Reputedly the most stylish guesthouse in the city, this elegant Georgian house is more of a boutique hotel than a B&B, with individually decorated, luxurious bedrooms. The Coach House features a collection of original art and a sunken seating area. Delicious breakfasts are served in the plant-filled conservatory. **www.number31.ie**

Key to Symbols *see back cover flap*

SOUTHEAST DUBLIN Russell Court

21–25 Harcourt St, Dublin 2 **Tel** *01 478 4066* **Fax** *01 478 4994* **Rooms** *46*   €€€   *Map D5*

Jolly and welcoming, Russell Court is a good choice for younger clientele. Bedrooms are neat and service is modest. The hotel's main attraction lies in its upbeat nightclubs – Bojangles for the 30-plus, and Ruby's for a younger crowd. At the rear, Dicey's Garden is a popular beer garden. Trams pass at the front of the hotel. **www.russellcourthotel.ie**

SOUTHEAST DUBLIN

83 St Stephen's Green, Dublin 2 **Tel** *01 478 2300* **Fax** *01 478 2263* **Rooms** *38*   €€€   *Map D5*

Beside the Ministry of Foreign Affairs, this guesthouse offers cosy and modest accommodation in three terraced Georgian houses. While all bedrooms are reasonably equipped and en suite, those to the rear are quieter, with views of the private garden and Iveagh gardens. Valet-serviced parking available. **www.dublincityrooms.com**

SOUTHEAST DUBLIN Stephen's Hall Hotel

14–17 Leeson St Lower, Dublin 2 **Tel** *01 638 1111* **Fax** *01 638 1122* **Rooms** *33*   €€€   *Map E5*

Close to St Stephen's Green, Stephen's Hall Hotel provides suites, which include an attached kitchen. Its proximity to the vibrant city centre makes it a very good-value family option. The hotel has been recently refurbished and there's a fine new restaurant. Underground parking is available. **www.stephens-hall.com**

SOUTHEAST DUBLIN Temple Bar Hotel

Fleet St, Dublin 2 **Tel** *01 677 3333* **Fax** *01 677 3088* **Rooms** *129*   €€€   *Map D3*

Its location in the heart of Temple Bar – a lively area, with several pubs and restaurants – makes this modern hotel popular for stag and hen parties. Bedrooms are clean and adequate, if a little on the small side and lacking in character. Multi-storey parking nearby. **www.tarahotelgroup.ie**

SOUTHEAST DUBLIN Trinity Lodge

12 South Frederick St, Dublin 2 **Tel** *01 617 0900* **Fax** *01 617 0999* **Rooms** *16*   €€€   *Map E4*

Close to Grafton Street and a stone's throw from Trinity College, this Georgian town house enjoys one of the best locations in town. Though traditional in style, it is furnished with modern conveniences. Warmly-coloured en suite bedrooms are well maintained. Massage and aromatherapy treatments available. **www.trinitylodge.com**

SOUTHEAST DUBLIN Browne's

22 St Stephen's Green, Dublin 2 **Tel** *01 638 3939* **Fax** *01 638 3900* **Rooms** *11*   €€€€   *Map D4*

Set in a Georgian house overlooking St Stephen's Green, this charming and intimate boutique hotel is stylishly furnished with antiques and quality reproduction pieces. Each of the bedrooms is individually designed with comfort and character in mind. The sophisticated Brasserie restaurant serves outstanding food. **www.brownesdublin.com**

SOUTHEAST DUBLIN Buswells

25 Molesworth St, Dublin 2 **Tel** *01 614 6500* **Fax** *01 676 2090* **Rooms** *69*   €€€€   *Map E4*

Comprising five Georgian town houses, this slightly old-fashioned hotel has been in operation since 1882. It has a central location beside government buildings and on a street renowned for high-level commercial art galleries. The sophisticated interior is done in warm colours. Frequented by political figures. **www.quinnhotels.com**

SOUTHEAST DUBLIN Conrad Hotel

Earlsfort Terrace, Dublin 2 **Tel** *01 602 8900* **Fax** *01 676 5424* **Rooms** *192*   €€€€€   *Map D5*

Opposite the National Concert Hall, this international-style hotel is geared towards business people. The decor is tasteful and the atmosphere airy. Bedrooms are fitted out in a contemporary style with light-wood furnishings and comfortable beds. The higher floors have good views. Professional service. **www.conraddublin.com**

SOUTHEAST DUBLIN Davenport

Merrion Square, Dublin 2 **Tel** *01 607 3500* **Fax** *01 661 5663* **Rooms** *115*   €€€€€   *Map F4*

Close to the National Gallery, this hotel lies in the heart of Georgian Dublin. The Neo-Classical façade dates from 1863. Mahogany, brass and marble furnishings give it the feel of a gentleman's club. Ample bedrooms are well appointed with warmly coloured decor. There's a fitness suite and a business centre. **www.ocallaghanhotels.ie**

SOUTHEAST DUBLIN The Merrion

Merrion St Upper, Dublin 2 **Tel** *01 603 0600* **Fax** *01 603 0700* **Rooms** *142*   €€€€€   *Map E4*

In the heart of Georgian Dublin, the Merrion is an elegant and stylish oasis with open log fires, opulent interiors and a collection of Irish art and period antiques. It's a landmark hotel, comprising four listed town houses from the 1760s, sensitively restored to their original grandeur. Guests can use the excellent Tethra Spa. **www.merrionhotel.ie**

SOUTHEAST DUBLIN Westbury Hotel

Grafton St, Dublin 2 **Tel** *01 679 1122* **Fax** *01 679 7078* **Rooms** *204*   €€€€€   *Map D4*

Enjoying possibly the most convenient location in the city, the Westbury is only seconds from Dublin's main shopping street. The first-floor lobby of this smart, ritzy, yet traditionally-styled hotel, is a popular meeting place for afternoon tea. Underground parking comes with free valet service. There's also a small gymnasium. **www.jurysdoyle.com**

SOUTHEAST DUBLIN Westin Hotel

College Green, Dublin 2 **Tel** *01 645 1000* **Fax** *01 645 1234* **Rooms** *163*   €€€€€   *Map D3*

Two 19th-century landmark buildings and part of the former Allied Irish Bank were reconstructed to create this sizeable hotel, across the street from Trinity College. Well-appointed bedrooms are furnished to a high standard. The beds are particularly comfortable. The former vaults of the bank are now a bar, the Mint. **www.westin.com**

SOUTHWEST DUBLIN Avalon House

55 Aungier St, Dublin 2 **Tel** *01 475 0001* **Fax** *01 475 0303* **Rooms** *70*   **Map** *C4*

One of the longest established hostels in the city, the centrally located Avalon House provides cheap and cheerful accommodation in a restored redbrick Victorian building. Rooms are clean, with pine and tile floors, high ceilings and an open fire. Popular with young, independent travellers. There's a café in the front. **www.avalon-house.ie**

SOUTHWEST DUBLIN Central Hotel

1–5 Exchequer St, Dublin 2 **Tel** *01 679 7302* **Fax** *01 679 7303* **Rooms** *70*   **Map** *D5*

Established in 1887, this three-star hotel is aptly named, given its convenient location, very close to Grafton Street. Recently refurbished with modern facilities, it retains a somewhat old-fashioned atmosphere, with traditional, yet cosy, decor. Bedrooms are neat, functional and reasonably priced. **www.centralhotel.ie**

SOUTHWEST DUBLIN Mercer Hotel

Lower Mercer St, Dublin 2 **Tel** *01 478 2179* **Fax** *01 672 9926* **Rooms** *41*   **Map** *C5*

Well located in the city centre, this three-star hotel combines the traditional with the contemporary, as seen in its wooden floors, subtle colours and modern furnishings. Bedrooms are clean and comfortable and include all modern conveniences. Helpful staff. There's a newly refurbished bar as well as a restaurant, Cusacks. **www.mercerhotel.ie**

SOUTHWEST DUBLIN Blooms Hotel

Anglesea St, Dublin 2 **Tel** *01 671 5622* **Fax** *01 671 5997* **Rooms** *86*   **Map** *D3*

On the fringes of bustling Temple Bar and close to Trinity College, Blooms Hotel's location is its main selling point. Unremarkable inside, it appeals with its modern exterior. Compact bedrooms are adequate, but those at the front are preferable. There's live music in the busy Vat House Bar, while Club M is a popular nighclub. **www.blooms.ie**

SOUTHWEST DUBLIN Grafton Capital Hotel

Lower Stephen's St, Dublin 2 **Tel** *01 648 1100* **Fax** *01 648 1122* **Rooms** *75*   **Map** *D4*

Located in the centre, this modern hotel with a Georgian façade offers neat and well-furnished accommodation at reasonable prices. Bedrooms provide all modern facilities. The popular bar, also a casual dining restaurant and night-club, features live music. Multi-storey parking nearby. Business facilities available. **www.graftoncapitalhotel.com**

SOUTHWEST DUBLIN Jury's Christchurch Inn

Christ Church Place, Dublin 8 **Tel** *01 454 0000* **Fax** *01 454 0012* **Rooms** *182*   **Map** *B4*

Opposite Christ Church Cathedral, in the old Viking centre of Dublin, this modern hotel lies within walking distance of Temple Bar and the city centre. Rooms are neat and well equipped. Bathrooms are adequate, if a little on the small side. Prices charged per room prove particularly good value for families. **www.jurysdoyle.com**

SOUTHWEST DUBLIN Brooks

59–62 Drury St, Dublin 2 **Tel** *01 670 4000* **Fax** *01 670 4455* **Rooms** *98*   **Map** *D4*

This immaculately maintained boutique hotel, excellently located just minutes from Grafton Street, has a club-like feel and welcoming ambience. It was built in 1997 and remodelled in 2003 with contemporary flourishes and warm colours, though the decor is tastefully traditional. Enjoys a great reputation. **www.sinnotthotels.com**

SOUTHWEST DUBLIN Clarence Hotel

6–8 Wellington Quay, Dublin 2 **Tel** *01 407 0800* **Fax** *01 407 0820* **Rooms** *49*   **Map** *C3*

Overlooking the River Liffey, this 1852 Dublin landmark was bought by the rock band U2 in 1992. Extensively refurbished, it has acquired cult status. With original wood-panelling in arts and crafts style, and luxuriously furnished rooms, this old establishment successfully combines contemporary cool and comfort. **www.theclarence.ie**

NORTH OF THE LIFFEY Clifden Guest House

32 Gardiners Place, Dublin 1 **Tel** *01 874 6364* **Fax** *01 874 6122* **Rooms** *15*

This three-star, family-run guesthouse is set in a four-storey Georgian town house, just a few minutes' walk from the centre of the city. The high-ceilinged rooms are functional, yet comfortably furnished and cheerfully decorated. They come in varying sizes; one of them can accommodate up to five people. **www.clifdenhouse.com**

NORTH OF THE LIFFEY Harvey's Hotel

11 Upper Gardiner St, Dublin 1 **Tel** *01 874 8384* **Fax** *01 874 5510* **Rooms** *16*

This very hospitable, family-run Georgian town house, north of the Liffey, is 10 minutes' walk from the top of O'Connell Street. Bedrooms are clean and pleasant. While some are a little jaded, most are nicely decorated. Those at the back are quieter. The atmosphere is friendly and relaxed. Non-smoking property. **www.harveysguesthouse.com**

NORTH OF THE LIFFEY Hotel Isaacs

Store St, Dublin 1 **Tel** *01 855 0067* **Fax** *01 836 5390* **Rooms** *90*   **Map** *E2*

Conveniently located opposite the bus station, this three-star hotel is furnished in a contemporary style. Bedrooms are relaxing, if modest. A European-style café-bar serves light lunches. There's also an Italian restaurant, Il Vignardo. Minimum stay at weekends is two nights. **www.isaacs.ie**

NORTH OF THE LIFFEY Cassidy's Hotel

Cavendish Row, Upper O'Connell St, Dublin 1 **Tel** *01 878 0555* **Fax** *01 878 0687* **Rooms** *88*   **Map** *D2*

This hotel is conveniently located at the top of O'Connell Street, opposite the Gate Theatre, in three adjoining redbrick Georgian town houses. The generously-proportioned rooms have been modernized, while retaining some period features. Spacious bedrooms are all en suite, with contemporary furnishings. **www.cassidyshotel.com**

Key to Price Guide *see p294* **Key to Symbols** *see back cover flap*

NORTH OF THE LIFFEY Gresham Hotel

23 O'Connell St Upper, Dublin 1 **Tel** *01 874 6881* **Fax** *01 878 7175* **Rooms** *288*

Map D1

One of Dublin's oldest and best-known hotels, the Gresham is a popular rendezvous spot with ever-lively public areas. It has been recently refurbished, with pleasant furnishings that combine classic and contemporary styles. Well-equipped bedrooms cheerfully decorated. A good business hotel. **www.gresham-hotels.com**

NORTH OF THE LIFFEY Royal Dublin

40–42 O'Connell St, Dublin 2 **Tel** *01 873 3666* **Fax** *01 873 3120* **Rooms** *120*

Map D1

The modern Royal Dublin is located in one of Dublin's most famous and historic streets. The street has been extensively upgraded in recent times, making it much more pleasant than in the past. This hotel may be lacking in atmosphere, but the rooms are self-sufficient. Those at the rear are quieter. Friendly staff. **www.royaldublin.com**

NORTH OF THE LIFFEY Clarion IFSC

International Financial Service Centre, North Wall Quay, Dublin 1 **Tel** *01 433 8800* **Rooms** *163*

Map F2

Overlooking the River Liffey, in the heart of the financial district, this hotel opened in 2001 and is becoming popular with tourists as much as with business travellers. Public spaces are bright, airy and minimalist in style. A short stroll from the centre, it offers well-designed and decent accommodation. **www.clarionhotelifsc.com**

NORTH OF THE LIFFEY The Morrison

Ormond Quay, Dublin 1 **Tel** *01 887 2400* **Fax** *01 878 3185* **Rooms** *138*

Map C3

Located on the quay overlooking the river, this luxurious contemporary hotel was built in 1999, with John Rocha as design consultant. The interior is a mix of high ceilings, dark woods, pale white walls, dim lighting, handcrafted Irish carpets and original art. Bedrooms have a modern design. There's a stylish restaurant, Halo. **www.morrisonhotel.ie**

FURTHER AFIELD Bewley's Hotel

Merrion Rd, Ballsbridge, Dublin 4 **Tel** *01 668 1111* **Fax** *01 668 1999* **Rooms** *304*

This magnificent redbrick building, formerly a school, is now part of the reliable Bewley's chain of hotels. Comfortably furnished in a contemporary style, it has big and well-equipped bedrooms. Price is per room, which offers good value particularly for families. O'Connell's is a popular restaurant. **www.bewleyshotels.com**

FURTHER AFIELD Clara House

23 Leinster Rd, Rathmines, Dublin 6 **Tel** *01 497 5904* **Fax** *01 497 5580* **Rooms** *13*

Built in 1840, this listed redbrick Georgian house is a favoured B&B. It's a 15-minute walk from the city centre and there's a good bus route into town. The atmosphere is relaxed and friendly. Secure private car park available at the rear of the house. Pleasant waterside walks along the canal are an added attraction. **www.clarahouse.com**

FURTHER AFIELD Druid Lodge

Killiney Hill Rd, Killiney, Co Dublin **Tel** *01 285 1632* **Fax** *01 285 1632* **Rooms** *4*

Road Map D4

Situated on picturesque Killiney Hill, overlooking the bay, Druid Lodge is 11 km (7 miles) south of Dublin city centre. It's a charming ivy-clad guesthouse, built in 1832 and named after the adjoining sacred site of Druid's Chair. Exuding a peaceful, old-world charm, it is well furnished and comfortable. **www.druidlodge.com**

FURTHER AFIELD Glenogra Guesthouse

64 Merrion Road, Ballsbridge, Dublin 4 **Tel** *01 668 3661* **Fax** *01 668 3698* **Rooms** *12*

This stylish and award-winning guesthouse provides pleasant and good-value B&B accommodation in this leafy, up-market area of Dublin. The owners create a welcoming atmosphere for their guests. Bedrooms are well appointed and the breakfast is good. **www.glenogra.com**

FURTHER AFIELD Grand Canal Hotel

Grand Canal St, Ballsbridge, Dublin 4 **Tel** *01 646 1000* **Fax** *01 646 1001* **Rooms** *142*

Winner of the "New Hotel of the Year" Award in 2005, Grand Canal Hotel was built in 2004. It is spacious and modern, with a friendly staff. The on-site pub, Kitty O'Sheas, is one of the best in town. There's also a new restaurant, Ulysses. Convenient location between Trinity College and Landsdowne Road. **www.grandcanalhotel.com**

FURTHER AFIELD Marble Hall Guest Accommodation

81 Marlborough Rd, Donnybrook, Dublin 4 **Tel** *01 497 7350* **Rooms** *3*

This much-loved house is set in a leafy residential area, a 20-minute walk from town and on an excellently serviced bus route. Victorian in style, it is meticulously maintained by Shelagh Conway, renowned for her excellent breakfasts. Bedrooms are spacious and tastefully decorated with antique furniture. **www.marblehall.net**

FURTHER AFIELD Mount Herbert Hotel

7 Herbert Rd, Ballsbridge, Dublin 4 **Tel** *01 668 4321* **Fax** *01 660 7077* **Rooms** *172*

Established as a hotel for over 50 years, Mount Herbert is located in a residential area close to the Landsdowne Road rugby and soccer stadium. It consists of a terrace of interconnecting houses decorated with modern furnishings. The en suite bedrooms are equipped with good facilities. There is free access to a nearby gym. **www.mountherberthotel.ie**

FURTHER AFIELD Tara Towers Hotel

Merrion Rd, Booterstown, Dublin 4 **Tel** *01 269 4666* **Fax** *01 269 1027* **Rooms** *111*

South of the city centre, this three-star hotel is situated on the coast road. Dun Laoghaire is a 15-minute drive away. Ambience is relaxed and service modest. Bedrooms are comfortable and spacious, if rather basic in decor. There's a traditional restaurant on site. Well-serviced bus route and near-by DART station are add-ons. **www.taratowers.com**

FURTHER AFIELD Waterloo House   €€

8–10 Waterloo Rd, Ballsbridge, Dublin 4 **Tel** *01 660 1888* **Fax** *01 667 1955* **Rooms** *17*

A short walk from St Stephen's Green, this lovely guesthouse comprises two adjoining Georgian buildings on a tree-lined road, away from the bustle of the city. The ambience is informal and the bedrooms cosy. Good breakfast is served in a cheerful dining room. Off-street parking is provided. **www.waterloohouse.ie**

FURTHER AFIELD Anglesea Town House   €€€

63 Anglesea Rd, Ballsbridge, Dublin 4 **Tel** *01 668 3877* **Fax** *01 668 3461* **Rooms** *7*

This Edwardian guesthouse, beautifully decorated and furnished, resembles a country house. Its discreet elegance and informal atmosphere is further enhanced by good housekeeping and warm hospitality. Pretty bedrooms are all en suite and very cosy. Helen Kirrane's award-winning breakfasts are superb. **www.63anglesea.com**

FURTHER AFIELD Belcamp Hutchinson   €€€

Carrs Lane, Malahide Rd, Balgriffin, Dublin 17 **Tel** *01 846 0843* **Fax** *01 848 5703* **Rooms** *8*

Only 15 minutes' drive from the airport, this secluded, creeper-clad Georgian house offers B&B accommodation. Welcoming hosts and large, high-ceilinged rooms make for a pleasant stay. Nearby, the picturesque seaside village of Malahide offers golf, tennis, sailing and horse-riding. **www.belcamphutchinson.com**

FURTHER AFIELD Butlers Town House   €€€

44 Landsdowne Rd, Ballsbridge, Dublin 4 **Tel** *01 667 4022* **Fax** *01 667 3960* **Rooms** *20*

Luxuriously furnished in a country-house style, the Georgian Butlers Town House offers four-star accommodation. There are individually designed bedrooms with Egyptian cotton sheets. Good breakfast is served in the Conservatory Restaurant, which features an all-day menu, making this more of a small hotel than B&B. **www.butlers-hotel.com**

FURTHER AFIELD Crowne Plaza Hotel   €€€

Northwood Park, Santry Demesne, Santry, Dublin 9 **Tel** *01 862 8888* **Fax** *01 862 8800* **Rooms** *204*

Set in mature parkland, just five minutes from Dublin Airport and 15 minutes from the city centre, the Crowne Plaza offers modern comfort. Rooms are well equipped and there's an on-site fitness centre. A 24-hour Courtesy Coach for the airport is available. Located close to the M1 and M50 motorways. **www.cpdublin-airport.com**

FURTHER AFIELD Herbert Park Hotel   €€€

Ballsbridge, Dublin 4 **Tel** *01 667 2200* **Fax** *01 667 2595* **Rooms** *153*

Overlooking the park from where it derived its name, this big contemporary hotel is bright and airy Materials used to furnish the interiors include polished granite, Irish abstract art, Irish furniture and glass walls. Bedrooms are well appointed and stylishly designed. **www.herbertparkhotel.ie**

FURTHER AFIELD Raglan Lodge   €€€

10 Raglan Rd, Ballsbridge, Dublin 4 **Tel** *01 660 6697* **Fax** *01 660 6781* **Rooms** *7*

This impressive redbrick Victorian house is set in the leafy residential Raglan Road, immortalized by the poet Patrick Kavanagh. Though away from the hubbub of the city, it is only 20 minutes' walk to the centre. It provides the comforts of an elegantly furnished four-star guesthouse. Superb breakfasts.

FURTHER AFIELD The Red Bank   €€€

6–7 Church St, Skerries, Co Dublin **Tel** *01 849 0439* **Fax** *01 849 1598* **Rooms** *18*   **Road Map** *D3*

On the premises of a former bank, in the heart of the village of Skerries, this guesthouse offers comfortably furnished rooms with good facilities. The award-winning Red Bank Restaurant has great character and specializes in seafood. Warm hospitality is guaranteed. Dublin Airport is a short drive from here. **www.redbank.ie**

FURTHER AFIELD Four Seasons   €€€€€

Simmonscourt Rd, Ballsbridge, Dublin 4 **Tel** *01 665 4000* **Fax** *01 665 4099* **Rooms** *259*

Luxurious Four Seasons successfully combines period-style elegance with contemporary comfort. Generously proportioned public spaces are opulently decorated with deep-pile rugs and rich furnishings. Bedrooms are large and lavish. Service is exceptional. The Ice Bar is a magnet for the fashionistas. **www.fourseasons.com**

FURTHER AFIELD The Burlington   €€€

Leeson St, Dublin 4 **Tel** *01 660 5222* **Fax** *01 660 8496* **Rooms** *506*

This four-star hotel is a genuine Dublin stitution at the heart of the city's south side. The rooms are smart and there is a choice of two restaurants, The Sussex or The Diplomat. Buck Mulligan's bar has a relaxed atmosphere for an afternoon drink. **www.jurysdoyle.com**

FURTHER AFIELD Portmarnock Hotel & Golf Links   €€€€€

Portmarnock, Co Dublin **Tel** *01 846 0611* **Fax** *01 846 2442* **Rooms** *84*   **Road Map** *D3*

Famous for their Irish whiskey, the Jameson family originally owned this house with a lovely beachside location. It is tastefully decorated, with bright public spaces. Bedrooms are excellently furnished, with views of the sea or the 18-hole championship golf course. There's also a spa. Close to Dublin Airport. **www.portmarnock.com**

FURTHER AFIELD Berkeley Court Hotel   €€€€€

Landsdowne Rd, Ballsbridge, Dublin 4 **Tel** *01 665 3200* **Fax** *01 661 7238* **Rooms** *187*

In the heart of the embassy belt, this well-located five-star hotel is convenient to the Royal Dublin Society and Landsdowne Road stadium. Beyond the unappealing exterior, the chandeliered lobby sets the tone for a plush ambience. Rooms are well appointed. There are two good restaurants. **www.jurysdoyle.com**

Key to Price Guide *see p294* **Key to Symbols** *see back cover flap*

SOUTHEAST IRELAND

ANNESTOWN Annestown House €€

Annestown, Co Waterford **Tel** *051 396 160* **Fax** *051 396 474* **Rooms** *5* **Road Map** *C5*

This 1830s country guesthouse is wonderfully located overlooking the sea, on Waterford's "Copper Coast". Well furnished, it provides B&B facilities in an old-fashioned setting. Spacious bedrooms are decorated in a simple, traditional style and have lovely views. The library is well-stocked with antiquarian books. **www.annestown.com**

ARTHURSTOWN Glendine Country House €€

Arthurstown, Co Wexford **Tel** *051 389 258* **Fax** *051 389 677* **Rooms** *8* **Road Map** *D5*

Home to the hospitable Crosbie family, this well-maintained 19th-century house is set amidst landscaped gardens and paddocks. Reasonably-priced bedrooms vary between old-fashioned and contemporary, though all have scenic views of the Barrow estuary. Good breakfasts are served by a friendly staff. **www.glendinehouse.com**

ASHFORD Ballyknocken House €€

Ashford, Glenealy, Co Wicklow **Tel** *0404 44627* **Fax** *0404 44696* **Rooms** *7* **Road Map** *D4*

A romantic 19th-century Victorian farmhouse, this long-established hotel is furnished in country-house style with period pieces. The on-site dining room features wholesome Irish cooking. Breakfasts are delicious. The location is ideal for walkers wishing to explore the Wicklow Mountains. **www.ballyknocken.com**

ATHY Coursetown House €€

Stradbally Rd, Co Kildare **Tel** *059 863 1101* **Fax** *059 863 2740* **Rooms** *4* **Road Map** *D4*

This 200-year-old farmhouse is set in the centre of a 260-acre arable farm. Attractions include a superb natural history library and beautifully maintained gardens. Bedrooms vary in size but all are thoughtfully decorated in a country-house style. Delicious breakfasts feature pancakes and seasonal fruits.

AUGHRIM Clone House €€€

Aughrim, Co Wicklow **Tel** *0402 36121* **Fax** *0402 36029* **Rooms** *7* **Road Map** *D4*

Dating from the early 19th century, this large house is set deep in the Wicklow Mountains. It's a tranquil retreat, surrounded by landscaped gardens, a stream and waterfall. The stylish bedrooms are a fusion of eclectic design and modern comfort. Owner and chef Carla is Italian and prepares traditional Tuscan dinners. **www.clonehouse.com**

BAGENALSTOWN Lorum Old Rectory €€

Bagenalstown, Co Carlow **Tel** *059 977 5282* **Fax** *059 977 5455* **Rooms** *5* **Road Map** *D4*

Built in 1863 of local cut granite, the old rectory lies at the foot of the Blackstairs Mountains. It's elegant and full of character, with wood fires and marble fireplaces. Imaginative home cooking, using home-grown and local organic produce. There's a croquet lawn here. Ideal for walks and cycle rides. Open February to November. **www.lorum.com**

BALLON Sherwood Park House €€

Kilbride, Co Carlow **Tel** *059 915 9117* **Fax** *059 915 9355* **Rooms** *5* **Road Map** *D4*

This imposing Georgian residence, set amid rolling parklands on its own estate, is close to the celebrated Altamount Gardens. It's a good country retreat with log fires, romantic bedrooms with brass and canopy beds and candlelit dinners. Delicious home cooking and delightful hosts make for a great experience. **www.sherwoodparkhouse.ie**

BALLYMACARBERRY Clonanav Farm Guesthouse €€

Ballymacarbry, Co Waterford **Tel** *052 36141* **Fax** *052 36294* **Rooms** *10* **Road Map** *C5*

Traditionally furnished, this three-star bungalow farmhouse and dry fly-fishing centre is situated on a working farm in the Nire valley. Rooms are en suite and there are log and peat fires. Savour the excellent Irish breakfast. Attractions include an on-site hard tennis court and wild brown trout fishing on river and stream. **www.flyfishingireland.com**

CALLAN Ballaghtobin House €€

Callan, Co Kilkenny **Tel** *056 772 5227* **Fax** *056 772 5712* **Rooms** *3* **Road Map** *C5*

Home to the Gabbett family for 350 years, this ivy-clad period-style house is set on a sprawling working farm that produces wheat, blackcurrants and Christmas trees. The furnishings are tasteful and the large rooms appealing. On-site facilities feature hard tennis court as well as croquet lawn and clock golf. **www.ballaghtobin.com**

CAPPOQUIN Richmond House €€€

Cappoquin, Co Waterford **Tel** *058 54278* **Fax** *058 54988* **Rooms** *10* **Road Map** *C5*

This delightful Georgian house is owned by the Deevy family, celebrated for its genuine warm hospitality. Set in peaceful parkland, it is charmingly decorated with antiques. Each of the bedrooms is a blend of Georgian splendour and modern comfort. Relish the excellent award-winning, country-house cooking. **www.richmondhouse.net**

CARLOW Barrowville Town House €€

Kilkenny Rd, Co Carlow **Tel** *059 914 3324* **Fax** *059 914 1953* **Rooms** *7* **Road Map** *D4*

Standing on its own mature grounds, this three-star listed Regency house is just a few minutes' walk from the town centre. It is immaculately maintained and well furnished with antiques, with an open fire in the lovely drawing room. Bedrooms vary in size, though all have good bathrooms. Superb breakfasts. **www.barrowvillehouse.com**

CASTLEDERMOT Kilkea Lodge Farm   €€

Castledermot, Co Kildare **Tel** *059 914 5112* **Fax** *059 914 5112* **Rooms** *5*   **Road Map** *D4*

Set in 260 acres of rolling parkland, this attractive farmhouse has been in the same family since 1740. It's popular with race-goers, as the Curragh, Punchestown and Naas racecourses are all within easy reach. Warm hospitality with open fires. There's also an equestrian centre holding regular courses. Golf nearby. **www.kilkealodgefarm.com**

THE CURRAGH Martinstown House   €€€

The Curragh, Co Kildare **Tel** *045 441 269* **Fax** *045 441 208* **Rooms** *4*   **Road Map** *D4*

This charming Gothic-style cottage *orné*, idyllically set on a farm in mature woodland and gardens, offers old-fashioned hospitality and unassuming elegance. Each bedroom has its own character and fresh flowers. Hens, goats, sheep and horses create a delightful pastoral setting. **www.martinstownhouse.com**

DUNGARVAN An Bohreen   🍴   €€

Dungarvan, Co Waterford **Tel** *051 291 010* **Fax** *051 291 011* **Rooms** *4*   **Road Map** *C5*

Situated at the foothills of the Comeragh Mountains with views over Dungarvan Bay, this good-value modern guest-house offers comfort and warm hospitality. Bedrooms are neat and traditionally furnished. The delicious award-winning cooking is a real attraction. A short drive west of Waterford. Open March to October. **www.anbohreen.com**

DUNGARVAN Powersfield House   🍴 🚹   €€

Ballinamuck, Co Waterford **Tel** *058 45594* **Fax** *058 45550* **Rooms** *6*   **Road Map** *C5*

This mock-Georgian house has been stylishly decorated with antiques and rich fabrics. The Powers are ebullient hosts, with a flair for creating bright and relaxing interiors as well as imaginative cooking. Delicious breakfasts and dinner can be arranged for residents. A cooking school is on the premises. **www.powersfield.com**

DUNGARVAN Clonea Strand Hotel   🏊 🍴 ⛳ 🚹 📺   €€€

Dungarvan, Co Waterford **Tel** *058 4555* **Fax** *058 42880* **Rooms** *60*   **Road Map** *C5*

The main attraction of this large, modern three-star resort hotel is its location beside a lovely two-mile sandy beach. Bedrooms are en suite; most have sea views. Leisure facilities include a 20-metre (65-ft) indoor heated pool and bowling alley. Good facilities for children makes it ideal for families. Live Irish music in the bar. **www.clonea.com**

DUNLAVIN Rathsallagh House   🍴 🚹   €€€€

Dunlavin, Co Wicklow **Tel** *045 403 112* **Fax** *045 403 343* **Rooms** *31*   **Road Map** *D4*

Just one hour's drive from Dublin, this creeper-clad rambling country house is set in 530 acres of peaceful parkland. It is comfortably furnished with open fires and has a relaxed atmosphere. Service is professional and courteous, and the breakfast is one of the best in Ireland. Excellent restaurant and lovely gardens. **www.rathsallagh.com**

DUNMORE EAST Church Villa   🚹   €

Dunmore East, Co Waterford **Tel** *051 383 390* **Fax** *051 383 023* **Rooms** *6*   **Road Map** *D5*

This long-established, attractive Victorian town house, in the centre of the picturesque fishing village of Dunmore East, offers excellent-value B&B accommodation. Bedrooms are bright and neat, and the owners friendly. Good home baking and breakfasts can be enjoyed. Ideal for the diet-conscious. **www.churchvilla.com**

ENNISCORTHY Salville House   📺 🍴   €€

Enniscorthy, Co Wexford **Tel** *054 35252* **Fax** *054 35252* **Rooms** *5*   **Road Map** *D5*

Standing on a hilltop overlooking the River Slaney, this 19th-century house offers comfort and friendly hospitality. Ample rooms with large windows provide lovely views over the wooded countryside. Dinner available by prior arrangement in a gracious dining room. Award-winning country cooking. **www.salvillehouse.com**

ENNISCORTHY Ballinkeele House   🍴 🚹   €€€

Enniscorthy, Co Wexford **Tel** *053 38105* **Fax** *053 38468* **Rooms** *5*   **Road Map** *D5*

This elegant manor house has been the ancestral home of the Maher family since 1840. It is set in 350 acres of mature parkland, game-filled woods, ponds and lakes. Rooms are well proportioned and the original furniture very well preserved. The place is known for its good home cooking as well as painting courses. **www.ballinkeele.com**

FERRYCARRIG Ferrycarrig Hotel   🏊 🍴 ⛳ 🚹 📺   €€€

Ferrycarrig, Co Wexford **Tel** *053 20999* **Fax** *053 20982* **Rooms** *102*   **Road Map** *D5*

With sweeping vistas across the River Slaney, this modern hotel is furnished in a smart, contemporary style. A calm and airy atmosphere prevails. Staff are very friendly and competent. Well-equipped bedrooms offer lovely views. There's an excellent health and fitness club, with a 20-metre (65-ft) pool. **www.ferrycarrighotel.ie**

GLENDALOUGH Derrymore House   €€

Lake Rd, Co Wicklow **Tel** *0404 45493* **Fax** *0404 45517* **Rooms** *4*   **Road Map** *D4*

In the heart of Wicklow, this country house is set in a mountain woodland, overlooking the beautiful lakes of Glendalough. Bedrooms are en suite. Experience warm hospitality and good breakfasts in peaceful surroundings. Local activities include walks, horse-riding and fishing. Open April to October. **http://homepage.eircom.net/@derrymore/**

GOREY Marlfield House   🍴 🚹   €€€€

Gorey, Co Wexford **Tel** *055 21124* **Fax** *055 21572* **Rooms** *18*   **Road Map** *D5*

One of Ireland's leading country houses, this Regency-style mansion is luxuriously furnished with antiques, fine art, crystal chandeliers and marble fireplaces. Secluded amid woodland and beautifully maintained gardens, it is a haven of tranquility. Opulent bedrooms feature fresh flowers and marble bathrooms. **www.marlfieldhouse.com**

Key to Price Guide *see p294* **Key to Symbols** *see back cover flap*

INISTIOGE Cullintra House €€
The Rower, Co Kilkenny **Tel** *051 423 614* **Rooms** *6* **Road Map** *D5*

An attractive 200-year-old farmhouse, set in beautiful woods and farmland, this cat lovers' paradise is a cosy place with log fires. The host is an accomplished cook and offers leisurely breakfasts until noon. Tasty food, using local produce, is served for candlelit dinners. The farm is an animal and bird sanctuary. **http://indigo.ie/@cullhse**

KILKENNY Butler House €€
16 Patrick St, Co Kilkenny **Tel** *056 776 5707* **Fax** *056 776 5626* **Rooms** *13* **Road Map** *C4*

This gracious Georgian town house is an integral part of the Kilkenny Castle estate. Decor is contemporary, with period features such as marble fireplaces and plasterwork ceilings. Bedrooms are large and relatively snug. Excellent breakfasts in the refurbished stables of the castle, which now houses the Kilkenny Design Centre. **www.butler.ie**

KILKENNY Lacken House and Restaurant €€€
Dublin Rd, Co Kilkenny **Tel** *056 776 1085* **Fax** *056 776 2435* **Rooms** *11* **Road Map** *C5*

A short walk from the city centre, this Victorian house was originally built as a dower house in 1847 and has been extensively refurbished. With the warm and personal service of a guesthouse, it offers hotel facilities, including excellent breakfasts. The restaurant is highly regarded and has won several accolades. **www.lackenhouse.ie**

MACREDDIN The BrookLodge Hotel & Well Spa €€€€
Macreddin Village, Co Wicklow **Tel** *0402 36444* **Fax** *0402 36580* **Rooms** *54* **Road Map** *D4*

Built on the site of a deserted village in a Wicklow valley, this new hotel complex is decorated in a contemporary, yet elegant country-house style with open fires and large airy spaces. Actons Country Pub serves excellent pints from its own microbrewery. There's also a collection of shops on the grounds. **www.brooklodge.com**

MAYNOOTH Moyglare Manor €€€
Maynooth, Co Kildare **Tel** *01 628 6351* **Fax** *01 628 5405* **Rooms** *16* **Road Map** *D4*

Only 30 km (18 miles) from Dublin, this charming Georgian house is surrounded by beautiful pastures. Antiques and rich furnishings have been used to a lavish effect. Bedrooms are individually styled, all with views of the rolling countryside. Candlelit dining rooms offer fine dining in a great romantic setting. **www.moyglaremanor.ie**

RATHNEW Hunter's Hotel €€€
Rathnew, Co Wicklow **Tel** *0404 40106* **Fax** *0404 40338* **Rooms** *16* **Road Map** *D4*

A rambling, old coaching inn, now in the fifth generation of the Hunter family, Hunter's offers old-fashioned comfort and charm. Surrounded by picturesque gardens along the banks of the river and decorated with chintzy furnishings, it exudes a traditional and relaxing atmosphere. Simple country-house cooking. **www.hunters.ie**

RATHNEW Tinakilly Country House & Restaurant €€€
Rathnew, Co Wicklow **Tel** *0404 69274* **Fax** *0404 67806* **Rooms** *51* **Road Map** *D4*

This classical Victorian-Italianate mansion, 48 km (30 miles) south of Dublin, was built by Captain Halpin, who laid the first telegraph cable linking Europe and America. Standing on lovely Victorian gardens, the house is furnished with elegant antiques. Bedrooms decorated in period style feature modern comforts. Fine dining. **www.tinakilly.ie**

ROSSLARE Kelly's Resort Hotel €€€€
Rosslare, Co Wexford **Tel** *053 32114* **Fax** *053 32222* **Rooms** *123* **Road Map** *D5*

A reliable, family-run hotel overlooking an expansive sandy beach, Kelly's is cosy if lacking in character. It boasts an extensive collection of art. Many of the bedrooms have views; some have balconies. Its vast choice of leisure facilities, two reputed restaurants and a supervised creche make it an ideal location for families. **www.kellys.ie**

STRAFFAN Kildare Hotel & Country Club €€€€€
Straffan, Co Kildare **Tel** *01 601 7200* **Fax** *01 601 7297* **Rooms** *69* **Road Map** *D4*

Originally built in the 17th century, the Kildare has since been luxuriously renovated to become a five-star hotel, with an air of French elegance. Well-furnished rooms have been styled individually. The restaurants are excellent. Facilities include two 18-hole championship golf courses, health spa, tennis, river fishing and coarse fishing. **www.kclub.ie**

THOMASTOWN Ballyduff House €€
Thomastown, Co Kilkenny **Tel** *056 775 8488* **Rooms** *3* **Road Map** *D5*

Overlooking the River Nore, this charming 18th-century manor house is a haven of tranquility, done up in a country-house style with antiques. Bedrooms are large, with pretty views over the river or garden. Beautiful walks as well as salmon and trout fishing. Woodstock Gardens are nearby. Open March to October. **ballydhouse@eircom.net**

THOMASTOWN Mount Juliet Conrad €€€€
Thomastown, Co Kilkenny **Tel** *056 777 3000* **Fax** *056 777 3019* **Rooms** *32* **Road Map** *D5*

Set in 1,500 acres of rolling parkland, rich pastures and formal gardens, this is one of Ireland's finest Georgian houses and most luxurious hotels. Rich furnishings complement plasterwork ceilings and Adam fireplaces. Bedrooms are individually styled. Facilities include an 18-hole championship golf course, archery and spa. **www.mountjuliet.com**

WATERFORD Coast Townhouse €€
Upper Branch Rd, Co Waterford **Tel** *051 393 646* **Fax** *051 393 647* **Rooms** *4* **Road Map** *D5*

This town house offers very chic and smartly furnished accommodation, with a contemporary feel and scenic views. The antique blends with the modern, creating a romantic ambience. The bedrooms are sizeable and the glass-walled bathrooms have become quite a talking point! The Coast restaurant is excellent. **www.coast.ie**

WATERFORD Foxmount Country House

Passage East Rd, off Dunmore Rd, Co Waterford **Tel** *051 874 308* **Fax** *051 854 906* **Rooms** *5*   **Road Map** *D5*

A 15-minute drive from Waterford city, Foxmount is an imposing, yet peaceful and welcoming, 18th-century country house and working dairy farm. Appealing bedrooms overlook the valley on one side of the house, the farmyard on the other. The Kent family are warm hosts. Delicious home baking. **www.foxmountcountryhouse.com**

WATERFORD Waterford Castle

The Island, Ballinakill, Co Waterford **Tel** *051 878 203* **Fax** *051 879 316* **Rooms** *19*   **Road Map** *D5*

Dating from the 15th century, this luxury hotel lies on a private 310-acre island, 5 km (3 miles) outside Waterford city. Reached by a private car ferry, the Castle mixes old-world elegance with modern comfort. Good fine-dining choices as well as an 18-hole golf course and tennis. Non-smoking property. **www.waterfordcastle.com**

WEXFORD McMenamin's Townhouse

3 Auburn Terrace, Redmond Rd, Co Wexford **Tel** *053 46442* **Fax** *053 46442* **Rooms** *6*   **Road Map** *D5*

This late-Victorian redbrick B&B is highly rated and within walking distance of the town centre and only 15 minutes' drive from the Rosslare ferry. Nicely decorated bedrooms are equipped with modern facilities. Some rooms have four-poster beds. Seamus and Kay McMenahin are friendly and helpful hosts. **www.wexford-bedandbreakfast.com**

WEXFORD Newbay Country House

Newbay, Co Wexford **Tel** *053 42779* **Fax** *053 46318* **Rooms** *12*   **Road Map** *D5*

This beautiful late-Georgian house is set amidst gardens and parklands, only 3 km (2 miles) from Wexford town. A home-away-from-home atmosphere is created by friendly hosts, interesting antiques, open fires and warmly coloured rooms. Most bedrooms feature four-poster beds, and all have lovely views. Superb cooking. **www.newbayhouse.com**

CORK AND KERRY

BALTIMORE Baltimore Bay Guest House

The Waterfront, Co Cork **Tel** *028 20600* **Fax** *028 20495* **Rooms** *8*   **Road Map** *B6*

This guesthouse, overlooking the harbour, is run by Youen Jacob, the younger son of celebrated restauranteur Youen. Airy bedrooms provide modern facilities and some have views over the sea and Sherkin Island. Well-chosen antiques add character to this contemporary house. There's a great restaurant on site.

BALTIMORE Baltimore Harbour Hotel & Leisure Centre

Baltimore, Co Cork **Tel** *028 20361* **Fax** *028 20466* **Rooms** *64*   **Road Map** *B6*

A few minutes' walk from the village, with a location overlooking the harbour, this three-star hotel is bright with modern furnishings. Rooms are well equipped, and most of them enjoy sea views. On-site health and leisure centre as well as massage and reflexology treatments. There's a fine restaurant too. **www.baltimoreharbourhotel.ie**

BANDON Glebe Country House

Ballinadee, Co Cork **Tel** *021 477 8294* **Fax** *021 477 8456* **Rooms** *6*   **Road Map** *B6*

A 10-minute drive from Bandon, this attractive Georgian rectory is beautifully furnished. Classically proportioned rooms have a stylish decor. Four-course communal candlelit dinner available, if booked before noon. The gardens here are quite lovely. Self-catering accommodation is available in Coach House. **http://indigo.ie/~glebehse**

BANTRY Ballylickey Manor House

Bantry Bay, Co Cork **Tel** *027 50071* **Fax** *027 50124* **Rooms** *14*   **Road Map** *B6*

Built over 300 years ago by Lord Kenmare as a shooting lodge, this delightful manor stands in award-winning gardens and parkland. It has a romantic setting, surrounded by mountains and moorland. The furnishings are luxurious and bedrooms cosy. Delicious food. Outdoor heated swimming pool. **www.ballylickeymanorhouse.com**

BANTRY Bantry House

Bantry, Co Cork **Tel** *027 50047* **Fax** *027 50795* **Rooms** *8*   **Road Map** *B6*

An 18th-century stately home, Bantry House has a wonderful collection of period furniture. The current owner is the ninth generation of his family to live in this grand home. Restful bedrooms look out over the pretty gardens. Climb the monumental stone "Stairway to the Sky" for stunning views. Open March to October. **www.bantryhouse.ie**

CAHERDANIEL Iskeroon

Bunavalla, Co Kerry **Tel** *066 947 5119* **Fax** *066 947 5488* **Rooms** *3*   **Road Map** *A6*

Overlooking the stunning Derrynane harbour, this beautiful old house was originally built by the Earl of Dunraven in 1936. The design-conscious Hare family have extensively renovated it with warm colours and natural stone floors. Semitropical gardens surround the house and sweep down to the sea. Open May to September. **www.iskeroon.com**

CARAGH LAKE Carrig Country House

Caragh Lake, Co Kerry **Tel** *066 976 9100* **Fax** *066 976 9166* **Rooms** *16*   **Road Map** *A5*

Set in woodland and timeless gardens full of rare plants close to the water's edge, this extended family-run Victorian house exudes a relaxed atmosphere. There are open fires and antiques, and bedrooms are large and snug. Lakeside restaurant features trout and Kerry lamb. Boats are available for fishing. **www.carrighouse.com**

CARAGH LAKE Caragh Lodge
€€€€

Caragh Lake, Co Kerry **Tel** *066 976 9115* **Fax** *066 976 9316* **Rooms** *15*   **Road Map** *A5*

Originally a fishing lodge, this mid-Victorian house is set in a beautiful award-winning garden. It borders the lake and looks out towards Ireland's highest mountains. All rooms are furnished with antique furniture. Enjoy the delicious cooking. Boating, swimming, salmon and trout fishing offered. Open mid-April to mid-October. **www.caraghlodge.com**

CASTLELYONS Ballyvolane House
€€

Castlelyons, Co Cork **Tel** *025 36349* **Fax** *025 36781* **Rooms** *6*   **Road Map** *C5*

Surrounded by extensive gardens and parkland, this 1728 house was remodelled in the Italianate style in the 1800s, as seen in the classical pillared hall, with a baby grand piano. There are open fires and elegant furnishings. Large bedrooms feature period furniture. Trout lake and salmon fishing are arranged. **www.ballyvolanehouse.ie**

CASTLETOWNSHEND Bow Hall
€€

Main St, Co Cork **Tel** *028 36114* **Rooms** *3*   **Road Map** *B6*

In the heart of the picturesque village of Castletownshend stands Bow Hall, a 17th-century house offering stylish accommodation and warm service. Overlooking well-maintained gardens, it is decorated in Shaker style, with interesting collectables. Dinner is served on request for residents. **dvickbowhall@eircom.net**

CLONAKILTY O'Donovan's Hotel
€€

Clonakilty, Co Cork **Tel** *023 33250* **Fax** *023 33883* **Rooms** *26*   **Road Map** *B6*

This traditional hotel, in the centre of the vibrant market town, is owned by the fifth generation of the O'Donovan family. Though old-fashioned, with a modest decor, it has a friendly ambience. There's a fully licensed restaurant as well as a bar featuring live music. Sheltered coves and sandy beaches are close by. **www.odonovanshotel.com**

CLOYNE Ballymaloe House
€€€€

Shanagarrry, Co Cork **Tel** *021 465 2531* **Fax** *021 465 2021* **Rooms** *34*   **Road Map** *C6*

Perhaps Ireland's best-known country house, restaurant and cookery school, the elegantly furnished Ballymaloe House is surrounded by 400 acres of farmland and gardens. Bedrooms are tastefully decorated. The restaurant is nationally renowned. Professional and courteous staff. There's a good craft shop on site. **www.ballymaloe.ie**

CORK Garnish House
€€

Western Rd, Co Cork **Tel** *021 427 5111* **Fax** *021 427 3872* **Rooms** *14*   **Road Map** *C5*

Five minutes' walk from the city centre, Garnish House is a comfortable guesthouse, furnished in warm colours. Hot home-baked scones with tea and coffee on arrival reflects the gracious hospitality of the Lucey family. Bedrooms, all en suite, some with Jacuzzis, include modern facilities. B&B only. **www.garnish.ie**

CORK Jury's Cork Inn
€€

Anderson's Quay, Co Cork **Tel** *021 427 6444* **Fax** *021 427 6144* **Rooms** *133*   **Road Map** *C5*

This three-star hotel, with a fixed-price room rate, is located in the heart of Cork city and overlooking the River Lee. Reasonably priced bedrooms are en suite with regular modern facilities and can accommodate up to two adults and two children. Room service is not available. Breakfast is an extra charge. **www.jurysdoyle.com**

CORK Lancaster Lodge
€€

Lancaster Quay, Western Rd, Co Cork **Tel** *021 425 1125* **Fax** *021 425 1126* **Rooms** *39*   **Road Map** *C5*

This modern, purpose-built four-storey guesthouse is located within five minutes' walk of the city centre. The interior is contemporary in design, with light wood furnishings. Bedrooms are spacious and well appointed. Bathrooms are intelligently designed. Excellent breakfasts provided. **www.lancasterlodge.com**

CORK Great Southern Hotel
€€€

Cork Airport, Co Cork **Tel** *021 494 7500* **Fax** *021 494 7501* **Rooms** *81*   **Road Map** *C5*

Conveniently located within walking distance of the terminal, this very successful four-star hotel is particularly peaceful, given its location. Bedrooms are well designed in a contemporary style. There's a 24-hour complimentary transfer coach as well as a small fitness suite. Courteous and helpful staff. **www.gshotels.com**

CORK Maryborough House Hotel
€€€€

Maryborough Hill, Douglas, Co Cork **Tel** *021 436 5555* **Fax** *021 436 5662* **Rooms** *79*   **Road Map** *C5*

The 18th-century core building stands at the heart of this hotel, which has been extended significantly. There are 24 acres of ornate gardens and woodland. Bedrooms are large and contemporary, with well-designed bathrooms. Only 10 minutes' drive from the airport and the city centre. Very good leisure facilities. **www.maryborough.com**

CORK Hayfield Manor Hotel
€€€€€

Perrott Ave, College Rd, Co Cork **Tel** *021 484 5900* **Fax** *021 431 6839* **Rooms** *88*   **Road Map** *C5*

A member of the Small Luxury Hotels of the World, this delightful place is set amid gardens. Though opened in 1996, it has the feel of a fine period house. Elegant furnishings are of a high standard. Generously proportioned and thoughtfully designed bedrooms come with good bathrooms. Excellent leisure facilities. **www.hayfieldmanor.ie**

COURTMACSHERRY Travara Lodge
€€

Courtmacsherry, Co Cork **Tel** *023 46493* **Rooms** *6*   **Road Map** *C5*

This early-Victorian terraced building, in a cheerful seaside village, overlooks Courtmacsherry Bay. A former captain's house, then a gentleman's residence, it is now a guesthouse with attractive, cosy furnishings. Simple and tasty food uses fresh local produce. Staff are friendly and helpful.

DINGLE The Captain's House   €€
The Mall, Co Kerry **Tel** *066 915 1531* **Fax** *066 915 1079* **Rooms** *8*   **Road Map** *A5*

So called because the host was a former captain in the merchant navy, this hotel is approached via a small footbridge over the River Mall and a pretty garden. The interior comprises antiques and nauticalia, collected by Captain Jim Milhench on his travels. Open turf fire and a warren of cosy rooms create a warm ambience. **www.captainsdingle.com**

DINGLE Emlagh House   €€
Dingle, Co Kerry **Tel** *066 915 2345* **Fax** *066 915 2369* **Rooms** *10*   **Road Map** *A5*

A few minutes' walk from the heart of Dingle, this luxurious guesthouse is set in peaceful landscaped gardens. It is furnished in a tasteful country-house style with Irish art, though a contemporary feel prevails. Bedrooms are cosy, ample and decorated with flowers. Most of them have harbour views. **www.emlaghhouse.com**

DINGLE Greenmount House   €€
Upper John St, Co Kerry **Tel** *066 915 1414* **Fax** *066 915 1974* **Rooms** *12*   **Road Map** *A5*

Five minutes' walk from the centre of Dingle, this modern B&B offers lovely accommodation and wonderful views of the town and harbour. Many of the well-equipped bedrooms are junior suites with sitting rooms and balconies. Decor features floral furnishings and wooden floors. Award-winning breakfasts. **www.greenmount-house.com**

DINGLE Dingle Skellig Hotel   €€€
Dingle, Co Kerry **Tel** *066 915 0200* **Fax** *066 915 1501* **Rooms** *110*   **Road Map** *A5*

With a modest exterior, this four-star hotel enjoys a wonderful seaside location on the fringes of Dingle. It is particularly ideal for families, with neat and adequately furnished bedrooms. The airy interiors make the most of the sea views. Excellent leisure facilities are available along with the Peninsula Spa. **www.dingleskellig.com**

DINGLE PENINSULA Gorman's Clifftop House & Restaurant   €€€
Glaise Bheag, Ballydavid, Co Kerry **Tel** *066 915 5162* **Fax** *066 915 5003* **Rooms** *9*   **Road Map** *A5*

This guesthouse is beautifully located in the Gaeltacht area of Slea Head drive, overlooking the Atlantic. Open log fires, pottery lamps and locally handmade tapestries create a relaxed feel. Bedrooms are furnished in handmade waxed pine and natural fabrics. Friendly hosts. Superb breakfasts. **www.gormans-clifftophouse.com**

FARRAN Farran House   €€
Farran, Co Cork **Tel** *021 733 1215* **Fax** *021 733 1450* **Rooms** *4*   **Road Map** *B6*

This elegant 18th-century manor house is set in the rolling hills of the Lee Valley, only 16 km (10 miles) from Cork city and airport. Surrounded by mature beech woodland and landscaped gardens, it has been sensitively restored with a contemporary touch, yet retains its original charm. Open April to October. **www.farranhouse.com**

GOLEEN Fortview House   €€
Gurtyowen, Toormore, Co Cork **Tel & Fax** *028 35324* **Rooms** *5*   **Road Map** *B6*

Situated on a working farm, this farmhouse is elegantly furnished with country pine. Bedrooms feature antiques and cast-iron and brass beds. Help with milking the cows, or stroll across the grounds. Generous breakfasts. Dinner for guests is by arrangement. Convenient self-catering cottages available for hire. **www.fortviewhousegoleen.com**

INNISHANNON Innishannon House Hotel   €€€
Co Cork **Tel** *021 477 5121* **Fax** *021 477 5121* **Rooms** *25*   **Road Map** *B6*

This 1720 house, set in four acres of parkland and riverside gardens, has been completely refurbished in country-house style. Romantically positioned, overlooking the River Bandon, the rooms have an old-world atmosphere. Bedrooms are spacious and nicely decorated. The restaurant has views of the gardens. **www.innishannon-hotel.ie**

KANTURK Assolas Country House   €€€
Kanturk, Co Cork **Tel** *029 50015* **Fax** *029 50795* **Rooms** *9*   **Road Map** *B5*

This elegant creeper-clad 17th-century manor house is an oasis of calm, surrounded by mature prize-winning gardens and parkland that sweep down to the river. Award-winning cuisine is served in a gracious dining room with white linen, antiques and deep-red walls. Activities feature lawn tennis, croquet, boating and fishing. **www.assolas.com**

KENMARE Hawthorn House   €€
Shelbourne St, Co Kerry **Tel** *064 41035* **Fax** *064 41932* **Rooms** *8*   **Road Map** *B5*

Modestly decorated, yet immaculately kept, this family-run B&B is welcoming and restful. Generous hospitality can be expected. En suite bedrooms are cheerfully painted and furnished in pine. Mary O'Brien, the lively and warm-hearted host, prepares a lovely breakfast. **www.hawthornhousekenmare.com**

KENMARE Park Hotel Kenmare   €€€€€
Kenmare, Co Kerry **Tel** *064 41200* **Fax** *064 41402* **Rooms** *46*   **Road Map** *B5*

In a stunning setting overlooking the gardens to Kenmare Bay, this 1897 hotel is one of Ireland's finest. The luxurious style and antique furnishings add to the plush ambience. Bedrooms are individually decorated. There's a new world-class destination spa and an 18-hole golf course on site. Exceptional service. **www.parkkenmare.com**

KENMARE Sheen Falls Lodge   €€€€€
Kenmare, Co Kerry **Tel** *064 41600* **Fax** *064 41386* **Rooms** *66*   **Road Map** *B5*

Across the river from town, this five-star waterside hotel set in 300 acres, has garnered a reputation as one of the best in the country, since it opened in 1991. Lavishly decorated, the classic and modern furnishings create a grand yet restful ambience. There's an equestrian centre as well as salmon fishing on site. **www.sheenfallslodge.ie**

Key to Price Guide *see p 294* **Key to Symbols** *see back cover flap*

KILLARNEY Earls Court House

Woodlawn Junction, Muckross Rd, Co Kerry **Tel** *064 34009* **Fax** *064 34366* **Rooms** *24*   **Road Map** *B5*

A five-minute walk from the heart of Killarney, this purpose-built award-winning guesthouse is superbly maintained. Open fire, antiques, tasteful furnishings and fresh flowers create a relaxed atmosphere. Neat bedrooms are generously proportioned. Excellent breakfast is served. **www.killarney-earlscourt.ie**

KILLARNEY Hotel Dunloe Castle

Killarney, Co Kerry **Tel** *064 71350* **Fax** *964 44583* **Rooms** *110*   **Road Map** *B5*

This modern hotel stands in lovely subtropical gardens, with its award-winning collection of rare plants and flowers, by the ruins of the 13th-century castle. Rooms are large and well appointed. Facilities feature an on-site equestrian centre, indoor tennis courts and fishing on the River Luane. **www.killarneyhotels.ie**

KILLARNEY Hotel Europe

Killarney, Co Kerry **Tel** *064 71350* **Fax** *064 32118* **Rooms** *206*   **Road Map** *B5*

A huge five-star resort hotel with stunning views of the Lakes of Killarney and the nearby mountains, Hotel Europe is excellently maintained. It has large open rooms and elegant furnishings. Bedrooms, too, are well-proportioned and those on the lakeside enjoy wonderful views. Several golf clubs adjacent to the hotel. **www.killarneyhotels.ie**

KILLARNEY Killarney Royal Hotel

College St, Co Kerry **Tel** *064 31853* **Fax** *064 34001* **Rooms** *29*   **Road Map** *B5*

Beautifully furnished in a period style, this family-run hotel is a short stroll from the centre of Killarney. Bedrooms are individually decorated to the highest standard, each boasting marble bathrooms and sitting areas. Welcoming and restful atmosphere. Staff are personable and most helpful. **www.killarneyroyal.ie**

KINSALE Blindgate House

Blindgate, Co Cork **Tel** *021 477 7858* **Fax** *021 477 7868* **Rooms** *11*   **Road Map** *B6*

Set in its own gardens, this purpose-built house boasts inspiring interiors and a bright and airy atmosphere. Excellent breakfasts include fresh juices, farmhouse yogurts, cheeses and fresh fish as well as the full Irish. Contemporary in style, the en suite bedrooms are uncluttered and well equipped. B&B only. **www.blindgatehouse.com**

KINSALE Longquay House

Kinsale, Co Cork **Tel** *021 477 4563* **Fax** *021 477 3201* **Rooms** *7*   **Road Map** *B6*

This three-storey Georgian town house, overlooking the inner harbour and marina, is just a minute's walk to the town centre. Airy en suite bedrooms are neatly decorated. Breakfast includes poached smoked haddock and home-made brown bread. Sea angling trips with local skippers can be arranged. **www.longquayhousekinsale.com**

KINSALE Old Presbytery

43 Cork St, Co Cork **Tel** *021 477 2027* **Fax** *021 477 2166* **Rooms** *6*   **Road Map** *B6*

High-quality accommodation is provided at this charming Georgian guesthouse. The atmosphere is restful and oozes character. Pretty bedrooms have antique brass beds and simple pine country furniture. Some rooms have a Jacuzzi or balcony. Breakfasts are a treat. The penthouse suite sleeps up to five guests. **www.oldpres.com**

KINSALE Old Bank House

11 Pearse St, Co Cork **Tel** *021 477 4075* **Fax** *021 477 4296* **Rooms** *17*   **Road Map** *B6*

Situated right in the centre of town, this used to be a working branch of the Munster and Leinster Bank. Now it is a well-run guesthouse, offering excellent accommodation. Bedrooms are spacious and decorated in a country-house style with good bathrooms. Some enjoy picturesque views of the town. **www.oldbankhousekinsale.com**

KINSALE Sovereign House

Newman's Mall, Co Cork **Tel** *021 477 2850* **Fax** *021 477 4723* **Rooms** *6*   **Road Map** *B6*

This charming Queen Anne stone house, dating from 1706, retains its old-world character, while offering modern comforts. The interior is furnished with Jacobean furniture, paintings and richly coloured walls. There's a full games room. Bedrooms come with four-poster beds and en suite Victorian bathrooms. **www.sovereignhouse.com**

KINSALE The Harbour Lodge

Scilly, Co Cork **Tel** *021 477 2376* **Fax** *021 477 2675* **Rooms** *9*   **Road Map** *B6*

This four-star waterfront guesthouse provides well-maintained accommodation. Bedrooms are large and well furnished with quality bedding. Some have balconies with views of the harbour. Service is friendly and attentive. Very good breakfasts are served. There's a relaxing conservatory on the grounds. **www.harbourlodge.com**

LISTOWEL Allo's Town House and Restaurant

41–43 Church St, Co Kerry **Tel** *068 22880* **Fax** *068 22803* **Rooms** *3*   **Road Map** *B5*

Just off the main square of the market town, this hotel combines modern comforts with old-world charm. Stylishly decorated bedrooms feature period furniture. Bathrooms are furnished in distinct Connemara marble. Friendly hosts. No breakfast is served, but there is a lovely on-site bar and bistro.

LISTOWEL Listowel Arms Hotel

Listowel, Co Kerry **Tel** *068 21500* **Fax** *068 22524* **Rooms** *42*   **Road Map** *B5*

Situated in a quiet corner of the main square, this historic three-star hotel is renowned as the venue for the annual Listowel Writers' Week, held in June. Refurbished recently, it has added modern comforts, without losing any of its character. On-site restaurant serves traditional cuisine. **www.listowelarms.com**

MALLOW Longueville House

Co Cork **Tel** *022 47156* **Fax** *022 47459* **Rooms** *20*   **Road Map** *B5*

Set in 500 acres of wooded estate in the heart of the Blackwater Valley, this historic Georgian mansion has classically proportioned rooms with plasterwork ceilings and sumptuous family antiques. The President's is an award-winning restaurant and there is a period conservatory. Beautiful walks. **www.longuevillehouse.ie**

MIDLETON Barnabrow House

Barnabrow, Cloyne, Co Cork **Tel** *021 465 2534* **Fax** *021 465 2534* **Rooms** *21*   **Road Map** *C6*

Barnabrow is romantically set in rolling parkland, enjoying beautiful views over nearby Ballycotton Bay. A tranquil house, it is stylishly decorated and features African furniture. Bedrooms are generously proportioned; some are in restored buildings to the rear of the house. There's an on-site crafts shop. **www.barnabrowhouse.ie**

PARKNASILLA Great Southern Hotel

Parknasilla, Co Kerry **Tel** *064 45122* **Fax** *064 45323* **Rooms** *83*   **Road Map** *A6*

Surrounded by 300 acres of subtropical parkland, this Victorian hotel commands a stunning position overlooking Kenmare Bay. Elegant antiques, fine art and fresh flowers create a relaxed ambience. En suite bedrooms vary in size, though all are well equipped. There's a good seafood restaurant. **www.greatsouthernhotels.com**

SCHULL Rock Cottage

Barnatonicane, Co Cork **Tel** *028 35538* **Fax** *028 35538* **Rooms** *3*   **Road Map** *B6*

This Georgian hunting lodge is set amongst lightly wooded paddocks, fields and heather-covered hills. A walk into the hills reveals scenic views of the nearby Dunmanus Bay. Stylish interiors are contemporary in design, with wonderful attention to detail. Immaculately maintained. Delicious breakfast and dinners. **www.rockcottage.ie**

SKIBBEREEN West Cork Hotel

Ilen St, Co Cork **Tel** *028 21277* **Fax** *028 22333* **Rooms** *30*   **Road Map** *B6*

Built in 1900, West Cork Hotel has a wonderful location on the banks of the river. It was recently refurbished in a tasteful contemporary style. Self-sufficient bedrooms are equipped with modern facilities. Those at the back overlook the river. On-site restaurant and bar. **www.westcorkhotel.com**

SNEEM Tahilla Cove Country House

Sneem, Co Kerry **Tel** *064 45204* **Fax** *064 45104* **Rooms** *9*   **Road Map** *A6*

A friendly guesthouse spread over two houses and surrounded by mature oak forest and garden, which sweep down to the water's edge. Neatly furnished bedrooms vary, but all are en suite and most enjoy views of the mountains or the sea. The Waterhouse family is hospitable. Good country cooking. **www.tahillacove.com**

VALENTIA ISLAND Glanleam House

Glanleam, Co Kerry **Tel** *066 947 6176* **Fax** *066 947 6108* **Rooms** *6*   **Road Map** *A5*

Originally built in 1775 as a linen mill, this elegant house is today a gardener's dream, set on a beautiful estate, surrounded by spectacular subtropical gardens and woodland. A mixture of antiques and modern comforts, it has an extensive library and slate fireplaces. Dinner is by advance arrangement.

YOUGHAL Ballymakeigh House

Killeagh, Co Cork **Tel** *024 95184* **Fax** *024 95370* **Rooms** *7*   **Road Map** *C5*

Set in rich farmlands, this 18th-century creeper-clad farmhouse has won numerous awards for its warm hospitality and meticulously maintained accommodation. It is well-furnished inside with elegant antique pieces. Bedrooms are tastefully decorated. Its delightful host, Margaret Browne, is a cookbook writer. **www.ballymakeighhouse.com**

YOUGHAL Glenally House

Copperalley, Co Cork **Tel** *024 91623* **Rooms** *4*   **Road Map** *C5*

Located just outside the town, Glenally House wonderfully combines contemporary cool with classical period features. Each vibrantly coloured bedroom is large and uniquely furnished. Fresh flowers from the garden feature throughout. Dinner is by prior arrangement. Members of Slow Food Movement. **www.glenally.com**

THE LOWER SHANNON

ABBEYFEALE Fitzgerald's Farmhouse & Equestrian Centre

Mount Marian, Co Limerick **Tel** *068 31217* **Fax** *068 31558* **Rooms** *6*   **Road Map** *B4*

Situated on the Kerry/Limerick border, this is an ideal retreat for children. There's an animal sanctuary and riding centre, with sheep, goats, guinea fowl, hens and over 30 horses. Ride cross-country on the beach or enjoy a more leisurely trek. Delightful nature-trail. Friendly and very hospitable, with open fire. **www.fitzgeraldsfarmhouse.com**

ADARE Dunraven Arms

Adare, Co Limerick **Tel** *061 396 633* **Fax** *061 396 541* **Rooms** *86*   **Road Map** *B5*

Established in 1792, in one of Ireland's most picturesque villages, this inn has retained its atmosphere and character and grown into a luxurious country-house hotel. With its open fires, antique furniture and friendly staff, it is renowned for its exemplary Irish hospitality. Bedrooms are beautifully furnished. **www.dunravenhotel.com**

Key to Price Guide *see p 294* **Key to Symbols** *see back cover flap*

ADARE Adare Manor Hotel & Golf Resort €€€€€

Adare, Co Limerick **Tel** *061 396 566* **Fax** *061 396 124* **Rooms** *63* **Road Map** *B5*

Set in 900 acres, on the banks of the River Maigue, this Neo-Gothic mansion dates from 1720 and was the former home of the Earls of Dunraven. High-ceilinged rooms with period features are luxuriously furnished and overlook formal gardens and an impressive golf-course. Elegant bedrooms and health spa. **www.adaremanor.com**

ARDFINNAN Kilmaneen Farmhouse €€

Newcastle, Co Tipperary **Tel** *052 36231* **Fax** *052 36231* **Rooms** *3* **Road Map** *C5*

This 200-year-old award-winning farmhouse is situated on a working dairy farm in a garden setting. The hosts are pleasant and the ambience is relaxed. Good home cooking. Dinner by arrangement. Surrounded by the mountains and close to the River Suir, it makes an ideal base for a walking or fishing holiday. **www.kilmaneen.com**

BALLINDERRY Kylenoe House €€

Ballinderry, Nenagh, Co Tipperary **Tel** *067 22015* **Fax** *067 22275* **Rooms** *3* **Road Map** *C4*

Close to Lough Derg, this 200-year-old stone house stands on farm and woodland. It is furnished in a country-house style with antiques and open fires, creating the ambience of a welcoming home and a peaceful retreat. Award-winning breakfasts. Dinner available if requested.

BALLYVAUGHAN Hylands Burren Hotel €€€

Ballyvaughan, Co Clare **Tel** *065 707 7037* **Fax** *065 707 7131* **Rooms** *29* **Road Map** *B4*

In the heart of Ballyvaughan village, this traditionally-styled family-run hotel dates from the 18th century. Bedrooms are neat and simple. Informal and cheerful atmosphere with turf fires and live Irish music in the bar. Food available all day. Its location, on the edge of the Burren, makes it a popular spot. **www.hylandsburren.com**

BANSHA Lismacue House €€€

Bansha, Co Tipperary **Tel** *062 54106* **Fax** *062 54055* **Rooms** *5* **Road Map** *C5*

A member of the Hidden Ireland group, this classically proportioned Irish country house dates back to 1813. Set in 200 acres, it is approached by an avenue of lime trees. Ornate interiors with period furniture make it an elegant and peaceful retreat, within view of the Galtee Mountains. Trout fishing on the estate. **www.lismacue.com**

BORRISOKANE Ballycormac House €€

Aglish, Co Tipperary **Tel** *067 21129* **Fax** *067 21200* **Rooms** *11* **Road Map** *C4*

This farmhouse has been converted into a restful hostelry, offering cosy accommodation with cottage-style bedrooms. Dining is informal and by reservation only. Good country cooking includes produce from the organic garden. Trail and cross country horse-riding is offered. **www.ballyc.com**

BUNRATTY Bunratty Castle Hotel €€€

Bunratty, Co Clare **Tel** *061 478 700* **Fax** *061 364 891* **Rooms** *80* **Road Map** *B4*

Just 8 km (5 miles) from Shannon Airport, this Georgian hotel is situated in its own grounds, opposite the historic Bunratty Castle and folk-park. Good-sized, modern bedrooms. Kathleen's Irish Pub & Restaurant, which serves lunch and dinner, frequently hosts traditional Irish music sessions. **www.bunrattycastlehotel.com**

CASHEL Legends Townhouse & Restaurant €€

Cashel, Co Tipperary **Tel** *062 61292* **Rooms** *7* **Road Map** *C5*

Situated at the foot of the great Rock of Cashel, this town house has fine views from both the bedrooms and the dining room. Bedrooms are simply furnished with good bathrooms. Open fires add to the pleasing ambience. It provides a convenient base for exploring the surrounding sites. **www.legendsguesthouse.com**

CASHEL Cashel Palace Hotel €€€€

Main St, Co Tipperary **Tel** *062 62707* **Fax** *062 61521* **Rooms** *23* **Road Map** *C5*

Originally a bishop's palace, this beautiful Queen Anne-style house, dating from 1730, is set in its own grounds in the centre of Cashel town. The large, elegant rooms overlook tranquil gardens to the rear and the famed Rock of Cashel. The Bishop's Buttery restaurant serves lunch and dinner. A peaceful retreat. **www.cashel-palace.ie**

CLONMEL Clonmel Arms Hotel €€

Sarsfield St, Co Tipperary **Tel** *052 21233* **Fax** *052 21526* **Rooms** *31* **Road Map** *C5*

Predictable but convenient, this family-run three-star country town hotel is centrally located. All bedrooms are en suite and neatly decorated. The restaurant and bars are popular with local clientele. The Paddock Bar hosts lively music sessions several evenings a week. **www.clonmelarmshotel.com**

CLONMEL Minella Hotel €€€

Clonmel, Co Tipperary **Tel** *052 22388* **Fax** *052 24381* **Rooms** *70* **Road Map** *C5*

Overlooking the River Suir, Minella Hotel has been gradually expanded from the original 1863 house. Great racing enthusiasts, the Nallens have carried this equine theme throughout the hotel, with stables nearby. Traditional Irish food is served. Leisure centre with swimming pool and outdoor hot tub. **www.hotelminella.ie**

COROFIN Fergus View €€

Kilnaboy, Co Clare **Tel** *065 683 7606* **Fax** *065 683 7192* **Rooms** *6* **Road Map** *B4*

This good-value guesthouse has small but nice bedrooms, furnished with information packs on the surrounding areas. Locally sourced and home-grown produce feature in Mary Kelleher's cooking. Prior booking required for dinner. Well-maintained garden stretches down to the River Fergus. Open Easter to October. **www.fergusview.com**

ENNIS The Old Ground €€

Ennis, Co Clare **Tel** *065 682 8127* **Fax** *065 688 8112* **Rooms** *85*   **Road Map** *B4*

This ivy clad hotel dates back to the 18th century. It is located centrally in one of Ireland's most energetic towns. The Poets Corner is a traditional bar with Irish music from Wednesday to Friday night. The O'Brien Room is a quality restaurant, drawing in a good m ix of locals and tourists. **www.oldgroundhotel.com**

ENNIS Newpark House €€

Ennis, Co Clare **Tel** *065 682 1233* **Fax** *065 682 1233* **Rooms** *6*   **Road Map** *B4*

Within walking distance of the town, this historic house is surrounded by lovely old lime, beech and oak trees. Peaceful and nicely decorated bedrooms vary in size, but are all convenient and en suite. The Barron family can give genealogical advice on tracing your family roots. **www.newparkhouse.com**

GLEN OF AHERLOW Aherlow House €€€

Glen of Aherlow, Co Tipperary **Tel** *062 56153* **Fax** *062 56212* **Rooms** *29*   **Road Map** *C5*

Situated in the middle of a pine forest in the Glen of Aherlow Nature Park, this hotel offers good accommodation with views of the Galty Mountains. Forest walks and fishing are popular pursuits, while cycling and horse-riding are available close by. Well-equipped self-catering lodges with open fires are also available. **www.aherlowhouse.ie**

GLIN Glin Castle €€€€€

Glin, Co Limerick **Tel** *068 34173* **Fax** *068 34364* **Rooms** *15*   **Road Map** *B5*

The Fitzgerald family, the hereditary knights of Glin, have resided in this magnificent castle since the 1780s. Its present owners, the 29th knight, Desmond, and his wife, have lavishly done up the interior of the castle. There's a superb collection of Irish antiques and fine art. Stunning formal and woodland gardens. **www.glincastle.com**

KILKEE Stella Maris Hotel €€

Kilkee, Co Clare **Tel** *065 905 6455* **Fax** *065 906 0006* **Rooms** *20*   **Road Map** *B4*

Situated in the centre of the vibrant town of Kilkee, this family-run hotel is both relaxed and friendly. With open log fires, it provides a warm welcome on a winter's day and its coastal position makes it popular with summer visitors. Bedrooms are bright and airy. There is a restaurant on the premises. **www.stellamarishotel.com**

KILMALLOCK Flemingstown House €€

Kilmallock, Co Limerick **Tel** *063 98093* **Fax** *063 98546* **Rooms** *5*   **Road Map** *B5*

This 250-year-old farmhouse is set on a working farm. The original house has been extended and now offers well-maintained accommodation, warm hospitality and laid-back atmosphere. Breakfasts are a treat and include home-made bread and creamy butter from the farm. Dinner can also be arranged. **www.flemingstown.com**

LAHINCH Moy House €€€€

Lahinch, Co Clare **Tel** *065 708 2800* **Fax** *065 708 2500* **Rooms** *9*   **Road Map** *B4*

With its breathtaking sea views across Liscannor Bay, towards the Cliffs of Moher, this 1820s house is the area's most luxurious hotel, furnished with rugs, antiques and elegant fabrics. Well-appointed bedrooms overlook the sea. The 15 acres of grounds include a fruit orchard and an organic vegetable garden. **www.moyhouse.com**

LIMERICK Woodfield House €€

Ennis Rd, Co Limerick **Tel** *061 453 022* **Fax** *061 326 755* **Rooms** *25*   **Road Map** *B4*

This pleasant, three-star family run house is traditional in style. Bedrooms are smartly coordinated and well-equipped with modern facilities. Located just outside Limerick en route to Ennis. The city centre and major sights are easily accessible. Woodies Steakhouse is a good restaurant on the premises. **www.woodfieldhousehotel.com**

LIMERICK The Clarion Hotel €€€

Steamboat Quay, Dock Rd, Co Limerick **Tel** *061 444 113* **Fax** *061 444 103* **Rooms** *93*   **Road Map** *B4*

Overlooking the River Shannon, this modern 17-storey hotel is reputedly the tallest in Ireland. Clean-lined and contemporary in style, it uses modern colours and walnut panelling. Well-appointed bedrooms. The Sinergie restaurant has an excellent waterfront location. On-site health and fitness club. **www.clarionhotellimerick.com**

LOOP HEAD Anvil Farm Guesthouse €

Kilbaha, Co Clare **Tel** *065 905 8018* **Fax** *065 905 8331* **Rooms** *5*   **Road Map** *B4*

This tastefully decorated cliff-top farmhouse is located on the beautifully unspoilt Loop Head. En suite bedrooms are cosy. It's an ideal base to explore the remote area, with dolphin-watching, walking, angling, diving, pony-trekking and bird-watching. Good home cooking. Open March to October.

NENAGH Ashley Park House €€

Ardcroney, Co Tipperary **Tel** *067 38223* **Fax** *067 38013* **Rooms** *5*   **Road Map** *C4*

This lovely 18th-century country house is set in beech woodland and gardens, on the shores of Lough Ourna. Elegantly furnished, it exudes an air of old-fashioned charm and comfort. Bedrooms invariably have views of the lake and beyond to the Slieve Bloom Mountains, and boast period pieces and brass beds. **www.ashleypark.com**

NEWMARKET-ON-FERGUS Carrygerry House €€

Newmarket-on-Fergus, Co Clare **Tel** *061 360 500* **Fax** *061 360 700* **Rooms** *11*   **Road Map** *B4*

Only 10 minutes from Shannon Airport, this late-18th-century house is set in a peaceful rural setting and overlooks the Shannon and Fergus estuaries. It is furnished in a relaxed country-house style, with open fires. Tasty farm breakfasts are served. There's a pleasant restaurant serving home cooking. **www.carrygerryhouse.com**

Key to Price Guide *see p294* **Key to Symbols** *see back cover flap*

NEWMARKET-ON-FERGUS Dromoland Castle

Newmarket-on-Fergus, Co Clare **Tel** *061 368 144* **Fax** *061 363 355* **Rooms** *100*   **Road Map** *B4*

A magnificent sister castle of Ashford in Mayo, this is one of Ireland's finest hotels. Its grand elegance, with lush furnishings, antiques and crystal chandeliers, is enhanced by the picture-postcard scenery of the surrounding estate. Bedrooms are luxurious. Just 13 km (8 miles) from Shannon Airport. **www.dromoland.ie**

SHANNON Great Southern Hotel

Shannon Airport, Co Clare **Tel** *061 471 122* **Fax** *061 471 982* **Rooms** *114*   **Road Map** *B4*

This three-star hotel is within walking distance of the airport terminal building and offers decent accommodation. Bedrooms are pleasant and well equipped, some with views of the estuary. There's a small fitness suite as well as a restaurant serving Irish and Continental cuisine. Good business facilities provided. **www.gshotels.com**

THURLES Inch House

Bouladuff, Co Tipperary **Tel** *0504 51348* **Fax** *0504 51754* **Rooms** *5*   **Road Map** *C4*

This stately Georgian house is set in 250 acres of rich farmland. Large, high-ceilinged rooms are nicely furnished. The William Morris-style drawing room has a beautiful plasterwork ceiling and stained-glass windows. There's an award-winning restaurant on site. **www.inchhouse.ie**

THE WEST OF IRELAND

ACHILL ISLAND Bervie

Keel, Co Mayo **Tel** *098 43114* **Fax** *098 43407* **Rooms** *15*   **Road Map** *A3*

Formerly a coastguard station, this low-lying beachside house has a wicker gate opening onto the sand. Warm hospitality and a turf fire await. Bedrooms are compact and en suite. Afternoon tea with freshly baked scones are a treat. Evening meals are served primarily for residents. **www.bervieachill.com**

ACHILL ISLAND Gray's Guest House

Dugort, Co Mayo **Tel** *098 43244* **Rooms** *14*   **Road Map** *A3*

Comprising several houses in the small village of Dugort, this long-established guesthouse has been known for its warm hospitality since 1970. It is somewhat rambling, with different areas varying in decor. Bedrooms offer old-fashioned comfort. Lunch, afternoon tea and dinner served.

ARAN ISLANDS An Dún Guest House

Inis Meain, Co Galway **Tel** *099 73047* **Fax** *099 73047* **Rooms** *4*   **Road Map** *B4*

This welcoming guesthouse is located at the foot of Connor's Fort on Inismeain, the most traditional of the three Aran Islands. It is run by the Faherty family. En suite bedrooms have great views. There's a mini-spa offering aroma-therapy massage. Activities include cliff walking and fishing. **www.inismeainaccommodation.com**

ARAN ISLANDS Kilmurvey House

Kilronan, Co Galway **Tel** *099 61218* **Fax** *099 61397* **Rooms** *12*   **Road Map** *B4*

On the west side of the island, at the foot of Dun Aonghasa, this 150-year-old stone house is close to the glorious beach of Kilmurvey Bay. En suite bedrooms have great views. The affable Mrs Joyce picks vegetables from the walled garden for residents' dinners, served during summer. Ideal base for cycling or walking. **www.kilmurveyhouse.com**

ARAN ISLANDS Man of Aran Cottage

Kilmurvey, Inishmore, Co Galway **Tel** *099 61301* **Fax** *099 61324* **Rooms** *3*   **Road Map** *B4*

Renowned for its starring role in the film of the same name, this delightful cottage offers limited but good accommodation. Situated beside Kilmurvey beach, it is surrounded by wildflowers and a vegetable garden. Only one room is en suite. Open March to October. **www.manofarancottage.com**

BALLINA Teach Iorrais

Geesala, Co Mayo **Tel** *097 86888* **Fax** *097 86855* **Rooms** *30*   **Road Map** *B2*

This functional but good-value hotel in the Gaeltacht area provides friendly service. Bedrooms are neat and pleasant with en suite bathrooms. The bar has some character, a welcoming fire in the hearth and serves light food during the day. Good fishing, cycling, golf and walking possibilities nearby. **www.teachiorrais.com**

BALLYCONNEELY Emlaghmore Lodge

Ballyconneely, Co Galway **Tel** *095 23529* **Fax** *095 23860* **Rooms** *4*   **Road Map** *A3*

This small, secluded period fishing lodge, situated halfway between Roundstone and Ballyconneely, is furnished with antiques and family portraits. Uncluttered bedrooms enjoy beautiful views. Sail in the family's Galway Hooker or go fly-fishing for brown trout or salmon in the river running through the garden. **www.emlaghmore.com**

BOYLE Forest Park House

Rockingham, Co Roscommon **Tel & Fax** *071 966 2227* **Rooms** *7*   **Road Map** *C3*

This newly renovated guesthouse is nestled amongst the trees at the entrance to Lough Key Forest Park. Cosy bedrooms and friendly hosts. Full Irish breakfast with home-made brown bread served late. Dietary needs accommodated. Light snacks available. Drying room and bait fridges make it ideal for fisherfolk. **www.bed-and-breakfast-boyle.com**

CARRICK-ON-SHANNON Glencarne Country House   €€

Ardcarne, Co Roscommon **Tel** *071 966 7013* **Fax** *071 966 7013* **Rooms** *5*   **Road Map** *C3*

Situated on the Leitrim-Roscommon border, this award-winning Georgian guesthouse has a garden to the front and the farm to the rear. The interior is tastefully furnished with antiques. Bedrooms are en suite and spacious. Some have brass beds. Good home cooking using farm produce. Open March to October.

CASHEL BAY Zetland House   €€€€

Cashel Bay, Co Galway **Tel** *095 31111* **Fax** *095 31117* **Rooms** *22*   **Road Map** *A3*

Originally built in the 19th century as a sporting lodge, this stylish country-house hotel is a quiet retreat. It commands an enviable position overlooking Cashel Bay and is surrounded by woodland gardens and flowering shrubs. Inside, peaceful rooms are furnished with antiques and exude an easy-going atmosphere. Superb cooking. **www.zetland.com**

CASHEL BAY Cashel House   €€€€€

Cashel Bay, Co Galway **Tel** *095 31001* **Fax** *095 31077* **Rooms** *32*   **Road Map** *A3*

This renowned country house, set in sprawling gardens and woodland, enjoys excellent views of Cashel Bay. Previous guests included Charles de Gaulle and his wife. Patrons are attracted by the quiet comfort of the antique-furnished rooms, with their log fires and fresh flowers, and the excellent cooking. **www.cashel-house-hotel.com**

CASTLEBAR Lynch Breaffy House Hotel & Spa   €€€

Castlebar, Co Mayo **Tel** *094 902 2033* **Fax** *094 902 2276* **Rooms** *125*   **Road Map** *B3*

Situated on the outskirts of Castlebar town, this hotel dates back to 1890. Having undergone significant renovations in recent years, it has been substantially modernized, while retaining a flavour of an old country house. Bedrooms are neat and well appointed. Very good leisure facilities as well as health spa available. **www.lynchhotels.com**

CASTLECOOTE Castlecoote House   €€€

Castlecoote, Co Roscommon **Tel** *0906 663 794* **Fax** *0183 30666* **Rooms** *5*   **Road Map** *C3*

Surrounded by pastoral countryside and overlooking the River Suck, this fine Georgian house stands on the grounds of a medieval castle. Lavish interior comprises stucco ceilings, marble fireplaces and portraits by Sir Joshua Reynolds. Delightful bedrooms. Games room, tennis courts and croquet on site. **www.castlecootehouse.com**

CASTLEREA Clonalis House   €€€

Castlerea, Co Roscommon **Tel** *094 962 0014* **Fax** *094 962 0014* **Rooms** *4*   **Road Map** *C3*

Set in a 700-acre wooded estate, this impressive Victorian-Italianate mansion is the ancestral home of the O'Connors of Connacht, descendants of Ireland's last high kings. Rich in history, with a wonderful library, heirlooms include the famous Carolan's harp. Rooms are vast and well furnished. Country home cooking. **www.clonalis.com**

CLIFDEN Sea Mist House   €€

Clifden, Co Galway **Tel** *095 21441* **Rooms** *4*   **Road Map** *A3*

This stone house, carefully renovated to include modern facilities, is a charming guesthouse in the heart of Clifden. Stylish decor reflects the host's refined tastes. Bedrooms are well appointed and the conservatory overlooks a serene cottage garden, which provides fruit for the tasty breakfasts. **www.connemara.net/seamist**

CLIFDEN Dolphin Beach Country House   €€€

Lower Sky Rd, Co Galway **Tel** *095 21204* **Fax** *095 22935* **Rooms** *9*   **Road Map** *A3*

This charming beachside house, with its own private cove, is bright and stylish, with a friendly atmosphere. Bedrooms are spacious, with antique furniture and crisp bed linen and there is delicious home cooking in the dining room overlooking the bay. **www.connemara.net/DolphinBeachHouse/**

CLIFDEN The Quay House   €€€

Beach Rd, Co Galway **Tel** *095 21369* **Fax** *095 21608* **Rooms** *12*   **Road Map** *A3*

Built on the quayside in 1820 for the harbour master, The Quay House is now the oldest building in Clifden. Seasoned hosts Paddy and Julia Foyle have an innate sense of wordly style, evident in the sumptuous and quirky rooms. Delicious breakfasts are served in the conservatory. **www.thequayhouse.com**

CONG Ashford Castle   €€€€€

Cong, Co Mayo **Tel** *094 954 6003* **Fax** *094 954 6260* **Rooms** *83*   **Road Map** *B3*

Ireland's most luxuriously grand castle hotel is romantically set in 350 acres of beautiful parkland, lakes and landscaped gardens. Dating back to the 13th century, its lavish interiors feature dark wood panelling, an armoury, fine art, antiques and beautiful fireplaces. Formal yet very peaceful atmosphere. **www.ashford.ie**

CROSSMOLINA Enniscoe House   €€€€

Castlehill, near Crossmolina, Co Mayo **Tel** *096 31112* **Fax** *096 31773* **Rooms** *6*   **Road Map** *B2*

This fine Georgian house, set in magnificent grounds leading down to Lough Conn, is full of beautiful antiques and fine art. It has a relaxed, lived-in feel. Susan Kellet, the charming owner, is a direct descendant of the original family who arrived here in the 1660s. A gracious host, she provides simply delicious country cooking. **www.enniscoe.com**

GALWAY Devondell   €€

47 Devon Park, Lower Salthill, Co Galway **Tel** *091 528 306* **Rooms** *4*   **Road Map** *B4*

Located in a residential area, this small, modern guesthouse is unremarkable from the outside but promises genuine hospitality and very good accommodation. Berna Kelly is a warm host and an excellent housekeeper. Pretty bedrooms are thoughtfully furnished, with cast-iron and brass beds. Superb breakfasts. **www.devondell.com**

GALWAY Jurys Inn Galway

€€€

Quay St, Co Galway **Tel** *091 566 444* **Fax** *091 568 415* **Rooms** *130* · **Road Map** *B4*

Situated beside the historic Spanish Arch, this centrally located three-star hotel is convenient for exploring the bustling heart of Galway. Geared towards the cost-conscious traveller, reasonably priced rooms are convenient, if basically decorated with functional, pine-coloured furniture. Breakfast is an extra. **www.jurysdoyle.com**

GALWAY Killeen House

€€€

Bushy Park, Co Galway **Tel** *091 524 179* **Fax** *091 528 065* **Rooms** *6* · **Road Map** *B4*

Set amidst gardens sweeping down to Lough Corrib, this charming 1840 house reflects the host's love for antiques and flair for design. Each bedroom is decorated in a different style – Victorian, Edwardian, Regency and Art Nouveau – and furnished impressively with well-appointed bathrooms. Delicious breakfasts. **www.killeenhousegalway.com**

GALWAY Great Southern Hotel

€€€€

Eyre Square, Co Galway **Tel** *091 564 041* **Fax** *091 566 704* **Rooms** *99* · **Road Map** *B4*

In the heart of Galway, this railway hotel was built in 1845 and has been sensitively modernized, without losing its sense of historic grandeur. The tasteful interior consists of mahogany and brass features and the rooms are as elegant. There is a new health spa, with interesting views of the city. **www.gshotels.com**

GALWAY Radisson SAS Hotel & Spa Galway

€€€€

Lough Atalia Rd, Co Galway **Tel** *091 538 300* **Fax** *091 538 380* **Rooms** *217* · **Road Map** *B4*

This contemporary hotel, overlooking Lough Atalia, is a five-minute walk to the city centre. The decor is appealing and the ambience restful. Bedrooms are designed in three distinct styles: Scandinavian, maritime or classic. All are equipped with good facilities. Marinas restaurant serves international cuisine. **www.galway.radissonsas.com**

INISHBOFIN ISLAND Murray's Doonmore Hotel

€€

Inishbofin Island, Co Galway **Tel** *095 45804* **Fax** *095 45814* **Rooms** *20* · **Road Map** *A3*

Situated overlooking the entrance to the island's peaceful harbour, this traditional family-run hotel is an ideal base for exploring the Inishbofin Island. The restaurant serves breakfast, lunch and dinner and specializes in locally-caught seafood. The welcoming bar with open fire is popular with traditional musicians. **www.doonmorehotel.com**

KNOCKRANNY Knockranny House Hotel

€€€€

Knockranny, Co Mayo **Tel** *098 28600* **Fax** *098 28611* **Rooms** *53* · **Road Map** *B3*

Opened in 1997, this four-star hotel is approached through secluded and rapidly maturing gardens. It is built in a Victorian style and overlooks the town of Westport. Log fires, warm colour schemes and antique furniture enhance the inviting ambience. Contemporary Irish cuisine served. A health spa is on site. **www.khh.ie**

LEENANE Delphi Lodge

€€€€

Leenane, Co Galway **Tel** *095 42222* **Fax** *095 42296* **Rooms** *12* · **Road Map** *B3*

One of Ireland's most famous sporting lodges, Delphi Lodge was built by the Marquis of Sligo in the 1830s. The 600-acre estate is set in a valley surrounded by majestic mountains. Inside, there's a wonderful selection of books, antiques and fishing gear. Communal dining. Activities include fly-fishing and hiking. **www.delphilodge.ie**

LETTERFRACK Renvyle House Hotel

€€€

Renvyle, Co Galway **Tel** *095 43511* **Fax** *095 43515* **Rooms** *68* · **Road Map** *A3*

This historic and romantic house, on the edge of the Atlantic, is among Ireland's best-loved hotels. Wooden beams, polished floors and turf fires create a stylish yet relaxed atmosphere. Good food. Former guests include WB Yeats and Winston Churchill. Ideal for families. Attractions include tennis, golf, croquet and trout fishing. **www.renvyle.com**

LETTERFRACK Rosleague Manor House Hotel

€€€

Letterfrack, Co Galway **Tel** *095 41101* **Fax** *095 41168* **Rooms** *20* · **Road Map** *A3*

This wonderful, 200-year-old Regency Manor is a tranquil retreat appealing to all sensibilities. Gardens planted with exotic plants and shrubs sweep down to Ballinakill Bay. Elegantly furnished, it holds great charm and character and provides relaxed luxury and panoramic views. Country house cuisine is superbly executed. **www.rosleague.com**

MULRANY Rosturk Woods

€€

Mulrany, Co Mayo **Tel** *098 36264* **Fax** *098 36264* **Rooms** *3* · **Road Map** *B3*

Set in secluded woodland and close to the sea, this stylishly furnished house is family-run and informal. Service is friendly and the en suite bedrooms are pretty. Delightful veranda overlooking Clew Bay. The host is a qualified sailing instructor and leads boating and fishing outings. There's tennis on the grounds. **www.rosturk-woods.com**

NEWPORT Newport House

€€€€

Newport, Co Mayo **Tel** *098 41222* **Fax** *098 41613* **Rooms** *18* · **Road Map** *B3*

This magnificent historic Georgian mansion, clad in Virginia creeper, is set in gardens that sweep down to the River Newport. Ideal for guests seeking refined comfort and gracious hospitality. The restaurant is greatly celebrated for its fresh seafood and exceptional wine list. Salmon and sea trout fishing nearby. **www.newporthouse.ie**

OUGHTERARD Currarevagh House

€€€

Oughterard, Co Galway **Tel** *091 552 312* **Fax** *091 552 731* **Rooms** *15* · **Road Map** *B3*

In a tranquil spot on the shores of Lough Corrib and surrounded by woods, parkland and gardens, this romantic Victorian country house is traditionally run. Good home cooking using fresh local produce. Fishing is a popular pursuit in these parts: salmon, brown trout, pike and perch. Great country walks. **www.currarevagh.com**

OUGHTERARD Ross Lake House
€€€

Rosscahill, Co Galway **Tel** *091 550 109* **Fax** *091 550 184* **Rooms** *13*   **Road Map** *B3*

Situated in delightful gardens, this 1850 country house provides comfortably furnished accommodation. Antiques and four-poster beds may be found in the generously proportioned bedrooms. Charming hosts. Fishing is possible on the nearby loughs and tennis on the grounds. **www.rosslakehotel.com**

PONTOON Healy's Restaurant & Country House Hotel
€€

Pontoon, Foxford, Co Mayo **Tel** *094 925 6443* **Fax** *094 925 6572* **Rooms** *14*   **Road Map** *B3*

In a stunning position on the shores of Lough Conn and Lough Cullen, this traditional old stone building has been refurbished, yet retains its old-world feel. Simple, neat bedrooms are reasonably priced. There's a pleasant garden on the grounds. Popular with bird-watchers and fishing afficionados. Good Irish cooking. **www.healyspontoon.com**

RECESS Ballynahinch Castle Hotel
€€€€

Recess, Co Galway **Tel** *095 31006* **Fax** *095 31085* **Rooms** *40*   **Road Map** *A3*

This Victorian castle, once the home of an Indian maharajah, Ranjit Singh, is known as a fishing destination. Set in 450 acres of beautiful woodland and gardens on the banks of the River Ballynahinch. The elegant Owenmore restaurant, overlooking the winding river, features Connemara lamb and fresh fish. **www.ballynahinch-castle.com**

ROSCAHILL Knockferry Lodge
€€

Roscahill, Co Galway **Tel** *091 550 122* **Fax** *091 550 0328* **Rooms** *10*   **Road Map** *B3*

Situated in a tranquil spot on the western shores of Lough Corrib, it provides reasonably-priced B&B accommodation with plain decor and furnishings. The atmosphere is very friendly and peaceful and the food good. Outside the front door is a quay with fishing boats moored. A good base for fishing and cycling. **www.knockferrylodge.com**

ROSCOMMON Abbey Hotel Conference & Leisure
€€€

Galway Rd, Co Roscommon **Tel** *090 662 6240* **Fax** *090 662 6021* **Rooms** *50*   **Road Map** *C3*

Set on its own grounds and gardens, this three-star hotel takes its name from a 13th-century Dominican abbey, whose ruins may still be seen. Recently refurbished, it provides decent accommodation and a friendly atmosphere. En suite bedrooms are reasonably furnished and are equipped with modern facilities. **www.abbeyhotel.ie**

ROUNDSTONE The Anglers Return
€€

Toombeola, Co Galway **Tel & Fax** *095 31091* **Rooms** *5*   **Road Map** *A3*

This 18th-century sporting lodge is now a charming guesthouse. It has an uncluttered interior, furnished by occasional antique pieces, whitewashed walls and wooden floors. Open fires and fresh flowers add to the quiet ambience. Rooms are tastefully done. Lynn Hill is an attentive and friendly host. **www.anglersreturn.com**

SPIDDAL Iverna Cottage
€€

Salahoona, Co Galway **Tel** *091 553 762* **Rooms** *4*   **Road Map** *B4*

Overlooking Galway Bay, this immaculate, recently built stone guesthouse is the most architecturally appealing structure in the area. Pretty bedrooms with cast-iron beds and attractive handmade quilts are inviting. Cosy, informal atmosphere created by welcoming hosts and turf fires. Open May to September. **www.ivernacottage.8m.com**

TUAM Waterslade House
€€

Waterslade Place, Co Galway **Tel** *093 60888* **Fax** *093 60838* **Rooms** *4*   **Road Map** *B3*

Just 20 minutes from Galway, this historic 18th-century house is now a well-rated B&B and restaurant, located in the centre of Tuam. The charming hosts have an innate flair for design, which is reflected in the romantic interiors and carefully chosen furnishings. Individually designed bedrooms. Tasty breakfasts. **www.watersladehouse.com**

WESTPORT Olde Railway Hotel
€€€

The Mall, Co Mayo **Tel** *098 25166* **Fax** *098 25090* **Rooms** *26*   **Road Map** *B3*

Built in 1780 as a coaching inn for the guests of Lord Sligo, this traditional hotel retains its character and charm. It is an ideal base for exploring Westport town. Antique furnishings and pleasant staff enhance the warm ambience. Organic garden at the rear supplies the kitchen. **www.theolderailwayhotel.com**

NORTHWEST IRELAND

ARDARA The Green Gate
€€€

Ardvally, Co Donegal **Tel** *074 954 1546* **Rooms** *4*   **Road Map** *C2*

Efficiently run by its French owner, Paul Chatenoud, this is one of the best B&Bs around. The beautiful landscape adds to its fantastic reputation. The accommodation is spread over three low thatched-roof cottages. The rooms are primitive but pleasant, with tweed coverlets on the simple beds. **www.thegreengate-ireland.com**

BUNDORAN Gillaroo Lodge
€

West End, Bundoran, Co Donegal **Tel** *071 984 2357* **Rooms** *5*   **Road Map** *C2*

Located in the pretty seaside town of Bundoran, Gillaroo Lodge is ideal for anglers, with excellent fishing locally. All rooms are en suite and Tourist Board approved. Fishing guides can be arranged on request. The scenic landscape around is ideal for walks. There are reputed golf courses nearby. **http://ireland.iol.ie/~gillaroo/**

BUNDORAN Fitzgerald's Hotel and Bistro

Bundoran, Co Donegal **Tel** *071 984 1336* **Fax** *071 984 2121* **Rooms** *16*   **Road Map** *C2*

Situated on the main street west of the town centre, this hotel overlooks stunning Donegal Bay. Though unspectacular, the rooms are spacious and comfortable, while the service is efficient and warm. The bistro has a good reputation for standard Irish fare. Turf fires warm the reception rooms. **www.fitzgeraldshotel.com**

DONEGAL Atlantic Guest House

Main St, Donegal Town, Co Donegal **Tel & Fax** *074 972 1187* **Rooms** *16*   **Road Map** *C2*

This family-run guesthouse provides friendly accommodation in the heart of Donegal Town. Well-priced rooms are spacious, if a little sparse, and each one has a colour TV and coffee-maker. Some rooms share a bathroom. Staff are courteous. Only a minute's walk from the bus stop. **www.atlanticguesthouse.ie**

DONEGAL St. Ernan's House

Country Inn Lodgings, Co Donegal **Tel** *074 972 1065* **Fax** *074 972 2098* **Rooms** *10*   **Road Map** *C2*

Built by the Duke of Wellington's nephew in 1826, this pink-painted house is set on a small island, linked to the mainland by a causeway. Inside, it is elegantly furnished, while maintaining an informal atmosphere. Each room is individually decorated and most have breathtaking views. Open mid-April to late October. **www.sainternans.com**

DRUMCLIFF Urlar House

Co Sligo **Tel** *071 916 3110* **Rooms** *4*   **Road Map** *C2*

Enjoying a quiet location in the shadow of Ben Bulben, this attractive farmhouse makes a perfect base for exploring Yeats country. Simple en suite accommodation is provided. The superb house cooking is highly recommended in the Galtee Breakfast Awards. Book in advance.

DUNFANAGHY The Mill

Figart, Co Donegal **Tel** *074 913 6985* **Fax** *074 913 6985* **Rooms** *6*   **Road Map** *C1*

With a beautiful location on the New Lake shore, The Mill was once home to the current owner's grandfather. The rooms have some nice touches, with good new beds and antique furnishings. Relax in the conservatory overlooking the lake. The guesthouse is attached to the excellent Mill Restaurant. **www.themillrestaurant.com**

DUNKINEELY Castle Murray House

St John's Point, Co Donegal **Tel** *074 973 7022* **Fax** *074 973 7330* **Rooms** *10*   **Road Map** *C2*

Stunningly located with views of McSweeney Bay, this is a wonderful place to stay. The decor is simple, but each room is individually themed, such as Hunting Room, Oriental Room, Golf Room. The restaurant offers a delicious menu, with head chef Remy Dupuy specializing in seafood with a French flair. **www.castlemurray.com**

LETTERKENNY Croaghross

Portsalon, Co Donegal **Tel** *074 915 9548* **Fax** *074 915 9548* **Rooms** *5*   **Road Map** *C1*

A modern guesthouse set high on the hill overlooking Lough Swilly, Croaghross is owned by marvellous hosts, John and Kay Deane. There's a shared living room with a large open fire and a newly landscaped rock garden. Excellent breakfasts feature fresh juices, fruit and yogurt, as well as porridge and muesli. **www.croaghross.com**

LETTERKENNY Castle Grove Country House Hotel

Ballymaleel, Co Donegal **Tel** *074 915 1118* **Fax** *074 915 1384* **Rooms** *15*   **Road Map** *C1*

Approached down a long avenue through lovely parkland, this 17th-century house looks out on to Lough Swilly and is a peaceful and relaxing place to stay. Rooms are spacious and attractive with luxurious in-house services available. Complete with an elegant library and drawing rooms. **www.castlegrove.com**

LETTERKENNY Radisson SAS Hotel Letterkenny

Loop Road, Letterkenny, Co Donegal **Tel** *074 919 4444* **Fax** *074 919 4455* **Rooms** *114*   **Road Map** *C1*

Only a five-minute walk from the town centre, this four-star establishment is a relatively new branch of the highly-rated Radisson group. The atrium-style lobby creates a contemporary ambience that exists throughout the hotel. Disabled bedroom facilities as well as ample parking are provided. **www.radissonsas.com**

LOUGH ESKE Harvey's Point

Donegal Town, Co Donegal **Tel** *074 972 2208* **Fax** *074 972 2352* **Rooms** *33*   **Road Map** *C2*

A Swiss-style hotel on the banks of Lough Eske, Harvey's Point has neat, modern furnishings, an excellent restaurant and many sports facilities. Most rooms overlook the lough and are airy and comfortable. The Executive Suites have four-poster beds and are located slightly away from the main hotel complex. **www.harveyspoint.com**

MOHILL Glebe House

Ballinamore Rd, Co Leitrim **Tel** *071 963 1086* **Fax** *071 963 1886* **Rooms** *8*   **Road Map** *C3*

B&B accommodation on a grand scale is available in this early 19th-century former rectory, set in 20 ha (50 acres) of parkland, woods and farmland. It's peaceful and attractive with extensive gardens to wander in. There is special pricing for senior citizens and children. **www.glebehouse.com**

RIVERSTOWN Coopershill House

Riverstown, Co Sligo **Tel** *071 916 5108* **Fax** *071 916 5466* **Rooms** *8*   **Road Map** *C2*

This is a very civilized, elegant 17th-century house surrounded by a vast estate. Rooms are decorated with tasteful antiques. Elegantly furnished bedrooms are huge, with four-poster or canopy beds. Open log fires and personal attention combine with the historic atmosphere to make it a real joy. Excellent food. **www.coopershill.com**

ROSSES POINT Yeats Country Hotel €€

Rosses Point, Co Sligo **Tel** *071 917 7211* **Fax** *071 917 7203* **Rooms** *100*   **Road Map** *B2*

At the foot of Ben Bulben and looking out to the Atlantic, this hotel is an ideal base for exploring Yeats country. En suite rooms, though ordinary in decor, are equipped with a multi-channel TV, direct dial telinfo, hairdryer and coffee-maker. Look out for a wide range of events held here. **www.yeatscountryhotel.com**

ROSSNOWLAGH Smuggler's Creek €€

Rossnowlagh, Co Donegal **Tel** *071 985 2366* **Fax** *071 982 2000* **Rooms** *5*   **Road Map** *C2*

In an area where the smuggling trade once flourished and pirates roamed the seas, Smuggler's Creek is a very cosy place in a wonderful location on top of a cliff overlooking Rossnowlagh beach. There's a choice of bar food, with oysters and mussels harvested from local beds, and a restaurant.

ROSSNOWLAGH Sand House Hotel €€€

Rossnowlagh, Donegal Bay, Co Donegal **Tel** *071 985 1777* **Fax** *071 985 2100* **Rooms** *60*   **Road Map** *C2*

An imposing, white castellated building, right on a sandy beach at Donegal Bay, this long-established hotel is very comfortable and well decorated and has a relaxed atmosphere. Originally a fishing lodge, it now has many beautiful rooms, some with four-poster beds. **www.sandhouse-hotel.ie**

STRANORLAR Kee's Hotel and Leisure Club €€€

Ballybofey, Co Donegal **Tel** *074 913 1018* **Fax** *074 913 1917* **Rooms** *53*   **Road Map** *C2*

A coaching inn and mail staging post in the 19th century, the hotel has been in the Kee family for four generations and still maintains a tradition of generous hospitality. Excellent modern cuisine is served in the restaurant, which has earned two AA Rosettes. There's an excellent leisure centre. **www.keeshotel.ie**

THE MIDLANDS

ATHLONE Hodson Bay Hotel €€€€

Hodson Bay, Co Westmeath **Tel** *090 644 2000* **Fax** *090 644 2020* **Rooms** *133*   **Road Map** *C3*

In the centre of Ireland, on the shores of Lough Ree, this cheerfully decorated hotel is adjacent to Athlone Golf Club. Spacious bedrooms have been recently refurbished and many of them enjoy great views of the lake. Located 90 minutes from Dublin and Galway. Acitivities include cruising on the River Shannon. **www.hodsonbayhotel.com**

BALLYCONNELL Slieve Russell Hotel, Golf & Country Club €€€€

Ballyconnell, Co Cavan **Tel** *049 952 6444* **Fax** *049 952 6046* **Rooms** *159*   **Road Map** *C3*

Taking its name from the nearby mountain, this hotel is set in 300 acres of landscaped gardens and lakes. It is very much a focus for business and social activity in the area. Bedrooms are spacious, with good bathrooms. The excellent leisure facilities include an 18-hole golf course, spa and treatment centre. **www.quinnhotels.com**

BELTURBET International Fishing Centre €€

Loughdooley, Co Cavan **Tel** *049 952 2616* **Fax** *049 952 2616* **Rooms** *14*   **Road Map** *C3*

Frenchman Michael Neuville offers residential fishing holidays at this delightfully tranquil waterside place. Individual wooden chalets, on the edge of the River Erne, can accommodate up to five people, making it ideal for a family holiday, whether fishing or not. For enthusiasts, coarse and pike fishing await. **www.angling-holidays.com**

BIRR The Stables Town House & Restaurant €€

6 Oxmantown Mall, Co Offaly **Tel** *0509 20263* **Fax** *0509 21677* **Rooms** *6*   **Road Map** *C4*

On a tree-lined mall in the centre of the town, this Georgian house is a long-established B&B with a popular restaurant. The comfortable, old-world bedrooms are en suite and either overlook the mall or the courtyard. Pets are allowed. Its central location makes it an ideal base to explore this heritage town. **www.thestablesrestaurant.com**

CARLINGFORD Grove House €€

Grove Rd, Co Louth **Tel** *042 937 3494* **Fax** *042 938 3851* **Rooms** *6*   **Road Map** *D3*

Offering views of the Mourne Mountains, Grove House is just a short walk form Carlingford Lough. Decent B&B accommodation is available in a friendly atmosphere. Bedrooms are brightly decorated, reasonably priced and all en suite. Breakfast is served in the dining room overlooking the mountains. **www.grovehousecarlingford.com**

CARLINGFORD Viewpoint €€

Omeath Rd, Co Louth **Tel** *042 937 3149* **Rooms** *6*   **Road Map** *D3*

This motel-style B&B provides modern accommodation. Well-equipped bedrooms, each with its own private entrance, have views across picturesque Carlingford Lough to the majestic Mourne Mountains. The atmosphere is informal and easy-going. Caters for individuals and groups. **www.viewpointcarlingford.com**

CARLINGFORD McKevitt's Village Hotel €€€

Market Square, Co Louth **Tel** *042 937 3116* **Fax** *042 937 3144* **Rooms** *17*   **Road Map** *D3*

This popular family-run country village inn is located in the town centre. Bedrooms are bright, clean and pretty, with adequate bathrooms. The bar, lounge and dining room combine old-world charm with modern comfort. Rooms have real fires and a lively atmosphere. Occasional special offers are available. **www.mckevittshotel.com**

CLONES Hilton Park
⚐ €€€€

Clones, Co Monaghan **Tel** *047 56007* **Fax** *047 56033* **Rooms** *6*   **Road Map** *C2*

One of Ireland's greatest country houses, this magnificent mansion overlooks 200 acres of woodland and green pastures. A romantic and cinematic setting with lakes, a lover's walk and formal gardens. In the charming Madden family since 1734, the house is beautifully furnished and exudes a relaxed grandeur. **www.hiltonpark.ie**

CLOVERHILL Olde Post Inn
▦▥ €€

Cloverhill, Co Cavan **Tel** *047 55555* **Fax** *047 55111* **Rooms** *6*   **Road Map** *C3*

Originally a post office, this pretty stone building has been a popular inn since 1974. The ambience is rustic, with wooden beams and exposed walls. En suite rooms are modest but cosy. The superb restaurant uses regional produce. Service is efficient. Hiking, horse-riding and fishing nearby. **www.theoldepostinn.com**

COLLINSTOWN Lough Bishop House
▤▥ €€

Derrynagara, Co Westmeath **Tel** *044 61313* **Rooms** *3*   **Road Map** *C3*

This attractive Georgian house is nestled into a south-facing slope overlooking Bishop's Lough and rolling countryside. Extensively renovated, it now offers appealing rooms in peaceful surroundings. Bedrooms have lovely views. Good country cooking using seasonal farm produce. Dinner by advance notice. **www.derrynagarra.com**

CROSSDONEY Lisnamandra Country House
⚐ €

Lisnamandra, Co Cavan **Tel** *049 433 7196* **Fax** *049 433 7196* **Rooms** *5*   **Road Map** *C3*

This restored and modernized 17th-century farmhouse is ideal for those looking for simple but good accommodation at a reasonable price. The pastoral setting is relaxing. Bedrooms have en suite facilities. It is run by the Neill family, who are welcoming hosts. Open May to October. **lisnamandra@eircom.net**

DROGHEDA Boyne Valley Hotel & Country Club
▧▥▦▨▩ €€€

Drogheda, Co Louth **Tel** *041 983 7737* **Fax** *041 983 9188* **Rooms** *72*   **Road Map** *D3*

Surrounded by gardens and woodland, this much-extended 18th-century manor house, though refurbished with modern furnishings, preserves its traditional feel. It offers good leisure facilities and capable service. Bedrooms in the old building have more character, while the newer ones provide better facilities. **www.boyne-valley-hotel.ie**

DULEEK Annesbrook
⚐ €€

Duleek, Co Meath **Tel** *041 982 3293* **Fax** *041 982 3024* **Rooms** *5*   **Road Map** *D3*

This classically proportioned Georgian house, set in rich parkland, is a tranquil retreat. Contemporary Irish art lines the walls and open fires create an atmosphere of laid-back elegance. Bedrooms are spacious, quiet and thoughtfully decorated. George IV and William Thackeray were among its illustrious visitors. **www.annesbrook.com**

KILMESSAN Station House Hotel & Restaurant
▥⚐ €€€€

Kilmessan, Co Meath **Tel** *046 902 5239* **Fax** *046 902 5588* **Rooms** *20*   **Road Map** *D3*

The last passenger train made its final stop in Kilmessan in 1947. A nostalgic reminder of a bygone era, this Victorian station building is now a cosy hotel with upgraded bedrooms featuring modern facilities. The bar overlooks very pleasant landscaped gardens, whose fresh flowers feature within the hotel. **www.thestationhousehotel.com**

KINNITY Ardmore House
▤⚐ €€

The Walk, Co Offaly **Tel** *0509 37009* **Rooms** *5*   **Road Map** *C4*

This sensitively restored Victorian house, set in its own garden, is located in the picturesque village of Kinnitty, at the foot of the Slieve Bloom Mountains. The turf fire, home cooking and relaxed atmosphere add to the old-fashioned feel of the house. Bedrooms are tastefully decorated, if free of many modern amenities. **www.kinnitty.net**

LONGFORD Viewmount House
▥ €€

Dublin Rd, Co Longford **Tel** *043 41919* **Fax** *043 42906* **Rooms** *5*   **Road Map** *C3*

This 1750s Georgian house, on the outskirts of Longford town, was originally owned by the Earl of Longford and has been recently restored with flair and sensitivity. The wooded gardens create an elegant and welcoming atmosphere. Lovely bedrooms with period furniture and rug-covered wooden floors. **www.viewmounthouse.com**

LONGFORD The Longford Arms Hotel
▥▦▨▩ €€€

Main St, Co Longford **Tel** *043 46296* **Fax** *043 46244* **Rooms** *60*   **Road Map** *C3*

Located in the heart of Longford town, this is a popular family-run hotel, furnished in traditional style. All bedrooms are en suite and comfortable. Food is served all day in the coffee shop until 8pm. The restaurant serves evening meals. Health and leisure centre on site. **www.longfordarms.ie**

MOATE Temple Country House & Spa
▥▩ €€€€

Horseleap, Co Westmeath **Tel** *0506 35118* **Fax** *0506 35008* **Rooms** *23*   **Road Map** *C4*

Set in rolling parkland, this beautiful 250-year-old country house is a haven of relaxation and well-being. Meticulously maintained bedrooms are bright, airy and stylishly decorated. Delicious home cooking. Variety of spa treatments available. Attractions include nature walks, horse-riding and cycling. **www.templespa.ie**

MOUNTNUGENT Ross House Equestrian Centre
⚐ €€

Mountnugent, Co Cavan **Tel** *049 854 0218* **Fax** *049 854 0218* **Rooms** *6*   **Road Map** *C3*

On the shores of Lough Sheelin, this old manor house enjoys a peaceful location amidst gardens. Reasonably priced accommodation comes with a range of outdoor pursuits. Bedrooms are comfortable, some with their own conservatories or fireplaces. Good home cooking for each meal. Packed lunches available. **www.ross-house.com**

MOUNTRATH Roundwood House

Mountrath, Co Laois **Tel** *0502 32120* **Fax** *0502 32711* **Rooms** *10*

Road Map *C4*

This impressive 18th-century Palladian house, set in mature parkland, is surrounded by beech, lime and horse chestnut trees. Rooms are comfortable and well-proportioned. The Kennan family are delightful hosts. Enjoy good home cooking and delicious breakfasts. Communal dining. **www.roundwoodhouse.com**

MULLINGAR Greville Arms

Pearse St, Co Westmeath **Tel** *044 48563* **Fax** *044 48052* **Rooms** *40*

Road Map *C3*

In the heart of Mullingar, this three-star traditional country town hotel caters for local clientele and tourists. Bedrooms are comfortable and neat. There's a large and welcoming bar, Ulysses, and a nightclub, Le Louvre. Former patrons include James Joyce who immortalized the bar in his book *Stephen Hero*. Food served all day. **www.grevillearmshotel.com**

MULLINGAR Bloomfield House

Mullingar, Co Westmeath **Tel** *044 40894* **Fax** *044 43767* **Rooms** *111*

Road Map *C3*

Situated 5 km (3 miles) outside the town of Mullingar, this recently refurbished hotel overlooks the peaceful waters of Lough Ennell. Lovely parkland surrounds this former dower house, with a comfortably furnished interior and well-equipped bedrooms. Staff are helpful. Leisure centre on site. **www.bloomfieldhouse.com**

MULTYFARNHAM Mornington House

Mornington, Co Westmeath **Tel** *044 72191* **Fax** *044 72338* **Rooms** *5*

Road Map *C3*

Home to the O'Hara family since 1858, this charming Victorian house lies close to Lough Derravarragh. Warm colours, open fires, period furniture and paintings create a classic Irish country house. The gardens are a delight. Canoes, boats and bicycles for hire. A variety of horse-based activities are available. **www.mornington.ie**

OLDCASTLE Lough Crew House

Oldcastle, Co Meath **Tel** *049 854 1356* **Fax** *049 854 1921* **Rooms** *3*

Road Map *D3*

Lying in the heart of this archeologically rich area, this B&B is set in 100 acres of woodland and lakes. Fine furniture, paintings and log fires exude elegance. The creative Naper family, when not graciously hosting guests, are busy organizing the summertime garden opera or running the school of gilding. **www.loughcrew.com**

PORTLAOISE Ivyleigh House

Bank Place, Church St, Co Laois **Tel** *0502 22081* **Fax** *0502 63343* **Rooms** *6*

Road Map *C4*

This lovingly restored 1850 house is probably the best B&B in town. Thoughtfully furnished with comfort and grace in mind, it combines the ancient with the modern. Bedrooms are large and very comfortable. Breakfasts are excellent and cooked using the finest of local and seasonal produce. **www.ivyleigh.com**

SLANE Conyngham Arms

Slane, Co Meath **Tel** *041 988 4444* **Fax** *041 982 4205* **Rooms** *15*

Road Map *D3*

This family-run, three-star hotel is situated in the heart of a charming estate village, originally developed by the Conyngham family of Slane Castle. Possessing an attractive stone façade, it is inviting and restful. En suite bedrooms are neat. Well located for visiting the rich Boyne Valley area. **www.conynghamarms.com**

TULLAMORE Annaharvey Farm

Tullamore, Co Offaly **Tel** *0506 43544* **Fax** *0506 43766* **Rooms** *7*

Road Map *C4*

Equestrian activities are the main attraction at this restored grain barn with pitch-pine floors and beams and open fires. En suite bedrooms are provided. Horseriding tuition is available in indoor and outdoor arenas. Cross-country riding and trekking can be organized. Cycling, walking and golf close by. **www.annaharveyfarm.ie**

NORTHERN IRELAND

ANNALONG Glassdrumman Lodge

Mill Rd, Co Down, BT34 4RH **Tel** *028 4376 8451* **Fax** *028 437 67041* **Rooms** *10*

Road Map *D2*

Set deep in the "Kingdom of Mourne", the hotel looks out on the region's famous dry-stone walls. All the rooms are bright and tastefully decorated with satellite television, hairdryers, 24-hour room service and direct dial telephones. A valet service is also available, as are ironing and laundry facilities. **www.glassdrummanlodge.com**

ARMAGH Charlemont Arms

57–65 English St, Armagh, BT61 7LB **Tel** *028 3752 2028* **Fax** *028 3752 6979* **Rooms** *30*

Road Map *D2*

This country-style hotel is perfectly located for the major attractions. What it lacks in luxury it makes up for in the warmth of its welcome. The recently refurbished rooms are all en suite and finished in designer fabrics. A TV, hospitality tray and temperature control are provided in each room. **www.charlemontarmshotel.com**

ARMAGH Desart Guest House

99 Cathedral Rd, Co Armagh, BT61 8AE **Tel & Fax** *028 3752 2387* **Rooms** *3*

Road Map *D2*

Although this formidable mansion may have a sort of Hitchcockian appearance to it, the traveller can be assured of a comfortable stay here. Character seeps from this place, whether it's the building's extraordinary appearance or the stuffed bird in the hallway. Rooms are large and comfortable. **lucymcroberts@yahoo.co.uk**

Key to Symbols *see back cover flap*

BALLYCASTLE Fragrens' B&B

34 Quay Rd, Co Antrim, BT54 6BH **Tel** *028 2076 2168* **Rooms** *7*   **Road Map** *D1*

This fully-modernized 17th-century house is situated at the harbour end of Quay Road in the centre of Ballycastle. All rooms are centrally heated, with a coffee-maker and colour TV. There are panoramic views and helpful service is provided by the family. All rooms are en-suite. **www.members.aol.com/jgreene710**

BALLYGALLY Hastings Ballygally Castle

274 Coast Rd, Co Antrim, BT40 2QZ **Tel** *028 2858 1066* **Fax** *028 2858 3681* **Rooms** *44*   **Road Map** *D1*

Reputedly haunted, the castle showpiece is the Ghost Room, a tiny old tower bedroom with a macabre legend. Original beamed ceilings and antique pine furniture make these rooms extremely appealing, though they are suitably equipped with all modern conveniences. **www.hastingshotels.com**

BALLYMENA Galgorm Manor

136 Fenaghy Rd, Co Antrim, BT42 1EA **Tel** *028 2588 1001* **Fax** *028 2588 0080* **Rooms** *24*   **Road Map** *D1*

The River Maine sweeps past this converted gentleman's residence, enhancing the view from many of the rooms. All rooms are en suite and luxurious, and service is excellent. There are also six self-catering cottages for families. Fishing and other pursuits are available on the magnificent 85-acre estate. **www.galgorm.com**

BANGOR Cairn Bay Lodge

278 Seacliff Rd, Co Down, BT20 5HS **Tel** *028 91 467636* **Rooms** *5*   **Road Map** *E2*

This turn-of-the-19th-century B&B, situated on the shores of Ballyholme Bay, is a rare treasure set in its own mature gardens. Inside, there are elegant lounges decorated with a Victorian touch. Meals are served in the oak-panelled lounge overlooking the gardens and the proprietress offers beauty and natural therapies. **www.cairnbaylodge.com**

BELFAST Maranatha Guesthouse

254 Ravenhill Rd, Co Antrim, BT6 8GJ **Tel** *028 9046 0200* **Fax** *028 9059 8740* **Rooms** *11*   **Road Map** *D2*

This carefully restored, 18th-century redbrick town house looks over one of Belfast's largest and most beautiful parks, Ormeau Park. Rooms are spacious with modern facilities that belie the building's age. A cosy place located in a pretty area, slightly removed from the city centre. Entirely non-smoking property. **www.maranatha-guesthouse.com**

BELFAST Marine House

30 Eglantine Ave, Co Antrim, BT9 6DZ **Tel & Fax** *028 9066 2828* **Rooms** *10*   **Road Map** *D2*

This large Victorian villa stands adjacent to a tree-lined avenue. The airy interior is graceful with towering ceilings. A good-value option given the high standards of housekeeping, large rooms, and front gardens. Rooms have en suite bathrooms and an oil-fired central heating at night. **www.marineguesthouse3star.com**

BELFAST Avenue Guesthouse

23 Eglantine Ave, Co Antrim, BT9 6DW **Tel** *028 9066 5904* **Rooms** *4*   **Road Map** *D2*

This refurbished Victorian town house is located in the leafy suburbs of the University area. Old and new meld well, and while all the original features have been retained, wireless Internet is available, as are Internet facilities in the lounge. Bedrooms are large and elegant, with shower, TV and direct-dial phones. **www.avenueguesthouse.com**

BELFAST Duke's Hotel

65 University St, Co Antrim, BT7 1HL **Tel** *028 9023 6666* **Fax** *028 9023 7177* **Rooms** *12*   **Road Map** *D2*

In the heart of the city, this recently-refurbished modern hotel provides comfort, style and international cuisine. Each room comes complete with TV, direct-dial telephones and tea and coffee facilities. There's a lively public bar, frequented by students from nearby Queen's University. **www.welcome-group.co.uk**

BELFAST Ash Rowan

12 Windsor Ave, Co Antrim, BT9 6EE **Tel** *028 9066 1758* **Fax** *028 9066 3227* **Rooms** *5*   **Road Map** *D2*

In the leafy southside of the city, Ash Rowan is a luxury guesthouse providing elegant rooms, furnished with luxurious Irish linen sheets and complimentary snacks. The tasteful decor features beautiful antiques. Nine different gourmet breakfasts are served here, all excellent.

BELFAST Hastings Stormont Hotel

587 Upper Newtonards Rd, Co Antrim, BT4 3LP **Tel** *028 9065 1066* **Fax** *028 9048 0240* **Rooms** *105* **Road Map** *D2*

Close to the airport and overlooking the gardens of Stormont Castle, this modern and functional hotel is excellent for business people. The lounge area has been recently refurbished. Rooms are luxurious and tastefully decorated in muted tones, with spacious desk areas and en suite facilities. **www.hastingshotels.com**

BELFAST Belfast Hilton

4 Lanyon Place, Co Antrim, BT1 3LP **Tel** *028 9027 7000* **Fax** *028 9027 7277* **Rooms** *197*   **Road Map** *D2*

This gigantic, sumptuous hotel in the docklands adds immeasurably to the Belfast skyline. The luxury and high rates befit a Hilton hotel. The Executive Rooms on the top three levels provide spectacular views of the city. Wireless broadband is available in the lobby. The superb Sonoma restaurant is worth visiting. **www.hilton.co.uk/Belfast**

BELFAST Europa Hotel

Great Victoria St, Co Antrim, BT2 7AP **Tel** *028 9027 1066* **Fax** *028 9032 7800* **Rooms** *240*   **Road Map** *D2*

An imposing building in the heart of the Golden Mile, Europa is one of Belfast's best hotels, ideal for business people and tourists. Bill Clinton stayed here during his visits to the city. Standard rooms offer en suite facilities and all other expected amenities. The Grand Opera House and Waterfront Hall are nearby. **www.hastingshotels.com**

CARNLOUGH Londonderry Arms Hotel

20 Harbour Rd, Co Antrim, BT44 0EU **Tel** *028 2888 5255* **Fax** *028 2888 5263* **Rooms** *35* **Road Map** *D1*

Winston Churchill once owned this ivy-covered inn next to the harbour of Carnlough, a breathtaking setting at the foot of Glencloy. It is now owned and managed by the O'Neill family, one of the longest-established hotelier families in the country, giving the residence a genuine warmth of welcome. **www.glensofantrim.com**

COLERAINE Camus House

27 Curragh Rd, Castleroe, Co Londonderry, BT51 3RY **Tel** *028 7034 2982* **Rooms** *3* **Road Map** *D1*

This listed country house was built in 1685 and overlooks the River Bann. An elegant pebble driveway is offset by an ivy-covered façade. Tastefully decorated rooms are non-smoking and furnished with TV and coffee-maker. Regional Galtee Irish Breakfast award winner.

CRAWFORDSBURN The Old Inn at Crawfordsburn

Crawfordsburn, Co Down, BT19 1JH **Tel** *028 9185 3255* **Fax** *028 9185 2775* **Rooms** *31* **Road Map** *E2*

One of Ireland's oldest hostelries, this thatched 16th-century inn offers quality and comfort with roaring log fires and four-poster beds in some rooms. Each en suite room is individually decorated in a tasteful fashion and named after local landmarks, historic houses and wildflowers. **www.theoldinn.com**

CUSHENDALL Glendale

46 Coast Rd, Co Antrim, BT44 0RX **Tel** *028 2177 1495* **Rooms** *6* **Road Map** *D1*

Generously proportioned rooms and a warm welcome make Glendale a cut above the other B&Bs in Cushendall. Coffee-maker, biscuits and TV are provided in each colourfully decorated bedroom. Bathrooms are en suite and there's also a TV lounge. The rates are reasonable and offer good value for money.

DOWNHILL Downhill Hostel

12 Mussenden Rd, Coleraine, Co Londonderry, BT51 4RP **Tel** *028 7084 9077* **Rooms** *9* **Road Map** *D1*

This beautiful backpackers' hostel has a beach in front, cliffs at the rear and a rocky stream flowing just past it. There are laundry facilities, a guest kitchen, and a barbecue area, as well as a working pottery studio. Private rooms are available as well as dormitories with high bunks, hand-sewn quilts and full-sized beds. **www.downhillhostel.com**

DOWNPATRICK Denvir's Hotel

14–16 English St, Co Down, BT30 6AB **Tel** *028 4461 2012* **Fax** *028 4461 7002* **Rooms** *6* **Road Map** *E2*

Built in 1642 by Thomas McGreevy, this is a listed building. Recent restoration revealed a number of interesting features, and the hotel has been well converted for modern purposes. En suite bedrooms are spacious. An atmospheric restaurant serves local specialities such as wild mushrooms and sloke (seaweed). **www.denvirshotel.co.uk**

DOWNPATRICK Pheasants' Hill Country House

37 Killyleagh Rd, County Down, BT30 9BL **Tel & Fax** *028 4461 7246* **Rooms** *5* **Road Map** *E2*

Right in the middle of the wild Down countryside and lapped by Strangford Lough, this luxurious country house has its own grounds and is surrounded by the Quoile Pondage National Nature Reserve. The on-site farm provides the breakfast ingredients. Each room is decorated in a different style. **www.pheasantshill.com**

DUNGANNON Grange Lodge

7 Grange Rd, Co Tyrone, BT71 7EJ **Tel** *028 8778 4212* **Fax** *028 8778 4313* **Rooms** *5* **Road Map** *D2*

This lovely, old Georgian house, set in pleasant surroundings, is known for its Ulster home-style cooking and warm hospitality. The proprietress, Norah Brown, has been creating award-winning culinary delights on her Aga stove for over 20 years. There's a spacious drawing room as well as a TV lounge. **www.grangelodgecountryhouse.com**

ENNISKILLEN Railway Hotel

32–34 Forthill St, Co Fermanagh, BT74 6AJ **Tel** *028 6632 2084* **Fax** *028 6632 7480* **Rooms** *19* **Road Map** *C2*

This convenient family-run hotel should appeal to more than just trainspotters. Across the road from the old Great Northern Railway station, this cheery yellow hostelry has a number of nicely decorated rooms, all en suite with TV and coffee-maker. The big rooms come with private baths. **www.railwayhotelenniskillen.com**

ENNISKILLEN Killyhevlin Hotel

Killyhevlin, Co Fermanagh, BT74 6RW **Tel** *028 6632 3481* **Fax** *028 6632 4726* **Rooms** *70* **Road Map** *C2*

The grounds of the hotel sweep down to Lower Lough Erne and many bedrooms look out on the lake, but you will need to pay extra for the view. Outstanding natural beauty in a terrific location makes this an attractive place to stay. Great hospitality. Chalets are also available. **www.killyhevlin.com**

ENNISKILLEN Manor House Country Hotel

Killadeas, Co Fermanagh, BT94 1NY **Tel** *028 6862 2200* **Fax** *028 6862 1545* **Rooms** *81* **Road Map** *C2*

On the shores of Lough Erne, this country hotel has a rich interior, with antiques and paintings as well as a friendly staff. Rooms are tastefully decorated and there's a wide range of choice from deluxe doubles to interconnecting family suites. Some rooms have canopied four-poster beds. **www.manor-house-hotel.com**

HOLYWOOD Hastings Culloden Hotel

Bangor Rd, Co Antrim, BT18 0EX **Tel** *028 9042 1066* **Fax** *028 9042 6777* **Rooms** *79* **Road Map** *E2*

A superb hotel, set in gardens and woodland by Belfast Lough, this was originally the palace of the Bishops of Down. It retains its opulence, visible in the fine antiques and valuable paintings. Many of the rooms have exquisite views of the lough and beautifully tended gardens. All of them are pleasantly decorated. **www.hastingshotels.com**

Key to Symbols *see back cover flap*

KILKEEL The Kilmorey Arms Hotel

41–43 Greencastle St, Co Down, BT34 4BH **Tel** *028 4176 2220* **Fax** *028 4176 5399* **Rooms** *25* **Road Map** *D3*

An excellent base for the Mourne area, this hotel has well-furnished and simple rooms, with full en suite facilities that include coffee-maker and direct-dial phones. Service is friendly and efficient. Golf, tennis, pony trekking and a host of other leisure activities are all locally available. **www.kilmoreyarmshotel.co.uk**

LONDONDERRY Everglades Hotel

Prehen Rd, Co Londonderry **Tel** *028 7132 1066* **Fax** *028 7134 9200* **Rooms** *64* **Road Map** *C1*

This magnificent imposing hotel, set on the banks of the River Foyle is the perfect base to explore 17th century Derry City. The bedrooms are beautifully decorated, luxurious and spacious. Satchmo's Restaurant concentrates on fresh local ingredients and the Bibrary Bar provides a more informal setting for light snacks. **www.hastingshotels.com**

LONDONDERRY Saddlers House

36 Great James St, Co Londonderry, BT48 7DB **Tel** *028 7126 9691* **Fax** *028 7126 6913* **Rooms** *7* **Road Map** *C1*

An elegantly restored Victorian town house, this B&B is located near the city centre in a conservation area. Due to the soothing interior design and the staff's friendly demeanour, a cosy atmosphere prevails. All rooms are equipped with TV and books, and there's freshly brewed coffee and home-made jams. **www.thesaddlershouse.com**

LONDONDERRY Travelodge Hotel

22–24 Strand Rd, Co Londonderry, BT48 7AB **Tel** *028 7127 1271* **Fax** *028 7127 1277* **Rooms** *39* **Road Map** *C1*

Situated right in the city centre, adjacent to the river and famous city walls, the Travelodge is one of Derry's better hotels. The large, clean rooms are all en suite and comfortably equipped with all modern conveniences. Family rooms offer good value. **www.travelodge.ie**

LONDONDERRY Beech Hill Country House

32 Ardmore Rd, Co Londonderry, BT47 3QP **Tel** *028 7134 9279* **Fax** *028 7134 5366* **Rooms** *27* **Road Map** *C1*

Good service and food and a real "home from home" atmosphere. Some of the bedrooms have beautiful pieces of Victorian furniture, giving the feel of a grand old country house. Guests can walk through the hotel's 32-acre woodland and gardens. Massage, reflexology and reiki treatment are available. **www.beech-hill.com**

NEWCASTLE Burrendale Hotel and Country House

51 Castlewellan Rd, Co Down, BT33 0JY **Tel** *028 4372 2599* **Fax** *028 4372 2328* **Rooms** *69* **Road Map** *E2*

This hotel is an excellent base for climbing, horse-riding and golf. All bedrooms are very well equipped, while some have spectacular views of the Mourne mountains. Some of the Ambassador rooms have Jacuzzi baths. There's a cosy bar and the excellent restaurant, Vine. Also on-site is the Impressions day health spa. **www.burrendale.com**

NEWCASTLE Hastings Slieve Donard

Downs Rd, Co Down, BT33 0AH **Tel** *028 4372 1066* **Fax** *028 4372 4830* **Rooms** *126* **Road Map** *E2*

This stunning Victorian redbrick building overlooks the beach and the Royal County Down Golf Course. A central tower rises from the hotel, complementing the magnificent eponymous mountain behind it. Most rooms have spectacular views and 24-hour room service is available. **www.hastingshotels.com**

NEWTOWNARDS Strangford Arms Hotel

92 Church St, Co Down, BT23 4AL **Tel** *028 9181 4141* **Fax** *028 9181 1010* **Rooms** *38* **Road Map** *E2*

The town's only hotel, this family-run, three-star Victorian building has been home to the famous rose-growing Dicksons of Hawlmark and the headquarters of the North Down Militia. A friendly atmosphere prevails, particularly in the Horseshoe Lounge Bar. All rooms come with private bathrooms. **www.strangfordhotel.co.uk**

OMAGH Four Winds

63 Dromore Rd, Co Tyrone, BT78 1RB **Tel & Fax** *028 8224 3554* **Rooms** *4* **Road Map** *C2*

Just on the outskirts of the town, this pleasant B&B is owned by a former chef, who will provide filling Irish breakfasts and packed lunches on request. Rooms are slightly small, but all have hair dryers and coffee-makers. The guest's lounge has a TV and VCR. **www.fourwinds.org.uk**

PORTADOWN Cherryville Luxury House

180 Dungannon Rd, Co Armagh, BT62 1UR **Tel** *028 3885 2323* **Fax** *028 3885 2526* **Rooms** *3* **Road Map** *D2*

Warm hospitality is assured at this large two-storey house, standing in its own grounds. Modem lines, fax and photocopier facilities are available. Bright, airy rooms are en suite, with TV and coffee-maker. Excellent and varied breakfasts brighten up the morning. **www.cherryvillehouse.com**

PORTAFERRY Portaferry Hotel

The Strand, Co Down, BT22 1PE **Tel** *028 4272 8231* **Fax** *028 4272 8999* **Rooms** *14* **Road Map** *E2*

This waterside inn on the Ards Peninsula overlooks Strangford Lough, in a designated conservation area. Many of the rooms have lovely water views and all are peaceful and pleasantly decorated. A wide range of activities are available locally. **www.portaferryhotel.com**

PORTRUSH Clarmont House

10 Landsdowne Crescent, Co Antrim, BT56 8AY **Tel** *028 7082 2397* **Rooms** *10* **Road Map** *D1*

A spacious period town house, with a beautiful white exterior, Clarmont House is located on the seafront. Panoramic views of the Skerries Islands and the Causeway coastline are the biggest draw. En suite bedrooms come with TV and fluffy blankets. Booking early is recommended in this family-run place. **www.clarmont.com**

RESTAURANTS, CAFÉS AND PUBS

A lthough the highest concentration of top gourmet restaurants is in Ireland's main cities, equally fine cuisine can be found in some very unlikely, remote locations around the country. Good, plain cooking is on offer at moderately priced, family-style restaurants all over Ireland. The restaurants listed on pages 324–45 are recommended for their high standards of service, quality of food and value

Restaurant sign in Kinsale

for money. To supplement these listings, look out for the *Dining in Ireland* booklet published by Fáilte Ireland, the Irish Tourist Board. Pub lunches are one of Ireland's top travel bargains, offering generous portions of fresh vegetables and prime meats, and can often serve as the main meal of the day for a very reasonable price. Light meals, bar food and a variety of takeout dishes are also widely available.

IRISH EATING PATTERNS

Traditionally, the Irish have started the day with a huge breakfast: bacon, sausages, black pudding, eggs, tomatoes and brown bread. In Northern Ireland this, plus potato cakes and soda farls *(see p322)*, is known as an "Ulster Fry". The main meal, dinner, was served at midday, with a lighter "tea" in the early evening.

Although continental breakfasts are now available, you will be hard-pressed to escape the traditional breakfast, which is included in most hotel and bed-and-breakfast rates. Increasingly, however, even the Irish settle for a light salad or soup and sandwiches at midday and save their main meal for the evening. Vestiges of the old eating patterns remain in the huge midday platefuls still served in pubs.

Enjoying breakfast at Adare Manor Hotel *(see p307)*

Arriving at a café in Kinvarra *(see p212)*

TIPS ON EATING OUT

Elegant dining becomes considerably more affordable when you make lunch your main meal of the day. In many of the top restaurants, the fixed-price lunch and dinner menus offer much the same, but lunch will usually come to about half the price. House wines are quite drinkable in most restaurants and can reduce the total cost of your meal. If you are travelling with children, shop around for one of the many restaurants that provide a less expensive children's menu.

Lunch is usually served between noon and 2:30pm, with dinner between 6:30 and 10pm, although many ethnic and city-centre restaurants stay open later, particularly in Temple Bar. Bed-and-breakfast hosts will often provide an ample home-cooked evening meal, and many will serve tea and scones in the late evening at no extra charge.

In top restaurants, men are expected to wear a jacket, though not necessarily a tie, and women to wear a dress or suit. Elsewhere, the dress code is pretty informal, stopping short of bare chests and very short shorts.

Visa and MasterCard are the most commonly accepted credit cards. Fewer restaurants accept American Express and Diners Club, although many now accept debit cards. In rural areas, especially in small cafés and pubs, be prepared to pay with cash.

GOURMET AND ETHNIC DINING

This once gourmet-poor land now sports restaurants that rank among Europe's very best, with chefs trained in outstanding domestic and continental institutions. There is a choice of Irish, French, Italian, Chinese, Indonesian and even Russian and Cuban cuisines, with styles ranging from traditional to regional to *nouvelle cuisine*. Locations vary as widely as the cuisine, from hotel dining rooms, town house basements and city mansions to castle hotels and tiny village cafés. The small County Cork town of Kinsale has established itself as the "Gourmet Capital of Ireland". Outstanding chefs also reign over the gracious houses listed in *Ireland's Blue Book of Country Houses and Restaurants*, available from tourist offices.

Selection of cakes served at Bantry House café *(see pp168–9)*

BUDGET DINING

It is quite possible to eat well on a small budget wherever you are in Ireland. In both city and rural locations, there are small cafés, tea rooms and family-style restaurants with inexpensive meals. Even if a café or tea room is at a main tourist attraction, such as Bantry House, you can still expect good, home-made food and freshly baked bread and cakes. Sandwiches are usually made with thick, tasty slices of cheese or meat (not processed); salad plates feature smoked salmon, chicken, ham, pork and beef; and hot meals usually come with large helpings of vegetables, with the beloved potato often showing up roast, boiled and mashed, all on one plate.

PUB FOOD

Ireland's pubs have moved into the food field with a vengeance. In addition to bar snacks (soup, sandwiches and

so on), available from noon until late, salads and hot meals are served from midday to 2:30pm. At rock-bottom prices, hot plates all come heaped with mounds of fresh vegetables, potatoes in one or more versions, and good portions of local fish or meat. Particularly good bargains are the pub carveries that offer a choice of joints, sliced to your preference. In recent years, the international staples of spaghetti, lasagne and quiche have also appeared on pub menus. For a list of recommended pubs, see pages 346–51.

Café sign at Baltimore

FISH AND CHIPS AND OTHER FAST FOODS

The Irish, from peasant to parliamentarian, love their "chippers", immortalized in Roddy Doyle's novel *The Van*, and any good pub night will end with a visit to the nearest

fish-and-chip shop. At virtually any time of day, however, if you pass by Leo Burdock's in Dublin, there will be a long queue for this international institution *(see p326)*. With Ireland's long coastline, wherever you choose, the fish will usually be the freshest catch of the day – plaice, cod, haddock, whiting or ray (a delicacy). The many other fast-food outlets include a host of familiar international names, such as McDonald's and Kentucky Fried Chicken, as well as a wide variety of burger and kebab shops. Relatively new arrivals on the scene are several quite good pasta and pizza chains, such as Pizza Express and Milano.

PICNICS

Ireland is glorious picnic country. Farmhouse cheeses and flavoursome tomatoes are picnic treats, or stop by one of the many small shops that offer sandwiches made with fresh local ingredients. As for where to picnic, the long, indented coast is ringed with sandy beaches and over 400 forest areas, many with picnic tables; great views add to the pleasure of mountainside picnics; and there are often places to pull off the road in scenic spots. Turn off a main road onto almost any lane and you will find a picnic spot by a lakeside, riverbank or the shady edge of a field.

Empty kegs outside a pub in Kinsale

The Flavours of Ireland

Boxty, barm brack, champ, coddle, cruibins, colcannon – the basic dishes that have nourished Ireland are spiced with fancy names. But the secret of their success is their ingredients, which are nurtured in a warm, damp climate on lush hills that brings them flavour. Beef and dairy cattle can stay out all year and they make abundant butter, cheese and cream. Pork and pork products, such as ham and bacon, are a mainstay, though lamb is traditional, too. Potatoes, the king of vegetables, turn up in soup, pies, cakes, bread and scones that are piled on breakfast and tea tables. And the rivers, lakes and shores are rich in seafood.

Oysters

A chef in Connemara displays traditional Irish cuisine

THE BASIC DISHES

Irish stews are thick and tasty, traditionally featuring lamb or mutton, onion and potatoes, while beef and Guinness make a darker casserole, sometimes with addition of oysters. Carrots and turnips are the first choice of vegetables for the pot. Pork is the basis of many dishes. Trotters, called cruibins or crubeens, are sometimes pickled, while bacon can be especially meaty. Dublin coddle, a fill-me-up after the pub on a Saturday night, relies on sausages and potatoes as well as bacon. Ham is sometimes smoked over peat and, for special occasions, it is baked with cloves and brown sugar and served with buttered cabbage. Cabbage is the basis of colcannon, cooked and chopped with mashed potato and onions, sometimes with the addition of butter and milk. Boxty is a bake of raw and cooked potato mashed with butter, buttermilk and flour; champ is potatoes mashed with milk, butter and onions.

FISH AND SEAFOOD

The Atlantic Ocean and Irish Sea have a rich variety of shellfish, from lobsters and Dublin Bay prawns to mussels and oysters,

Barm brack   **White soda bread**   **Brown soda bread**   **Potato bread**

Potato farls   **Wheaten bread**

Selection of the many traditional Irish breads

IRISH TRADITIONAL FOOD

Gubbeen cheese

If your heart is up to it, start the day with an Ulster Fry. This breakfast fry-up includes thick, tasty bacon, plus black pudding, soda farls and potato cake. A "lady's breakfast" will have one egg, a "gentleman's" two. Gooseberry jam will be spread on fried bread, and mugs of tea will wash it down. Irish stews traditionally use mutton, not so common today, while Spiced Beef uses up brisket, which is covered in a various spices then left for a week before being cooked slowly with Guiness and vegetables. A high tea in the early evening is the major meal in many homes; a main course will be followed by a succession of breads and cakes.

Irish Stew *Traditionally, neck of mutton, potatoes, carrots and onions are slowly cooked together for hours.*

Delivery in time-honoured style at Moore Street Market, Dublin

scallops, clams and razor-shells. Herring, mackerel, plaice and skate are brought in from the sea, while the rivers and lakes offer up salmon, trout and eels, which are often smoked. Galway salmon has the best reputation and its oyster festival is famous. Salmon is usually smoked in oak wood kilns. Along the shore, a red seaweed called dulse is collected and mixed with potatoes mashed in their skins to make dulse champ.

BAKED GOODS

Bread and cakes make up a large percentage of the Irish diet. Unleaven soda bread is ubiquitous (it's great with Irish cheeses). In Northern Ireland, brown soda bread is called wheaten bread. Potato bread is fried or eaten cold, as cake.

Farls ("quarters") are made with wheat flour or oats, bicarbonate of soda and buttermilk, which goes into many recipes. Fruit breads include barm brack, traditionally eaten at Hallowe'en and on All Saint's Day, while rich

Sea trout, plucked fresh from the Atlantic Ocean

porter cake is made with Guinness or other stout. White, brown and fruit scones will never be far from tea and breakfast tables.

DAIRY PRODUCTS

Butter, usually salted, is used generously, on vegetables and in sauces as well as in puddings and on bread. Cream, too, is used in cooking, stirred into soups and whipped for puddings. The variety and quality of Irish farmhouse cheeses is impressive, although a medium Cheddar produced by a large manufacturer was hailed "Best Irish Cheese" at the 2005 World Cheese Awards.

IRISH CHEESES

Carrigaline Nutty-tasting, Gouda-like cheese from Cork.

Cashel Blue The only Irish blue cheese. Soft and creamy. Unpasteurized; from Tipperary.

Cooleeny Small, Camembert-style unpasteurized cheese from Tipperary.

Durrus Creamy, natural-rind unpasteurized cheese from West Cork. May be smoked.

Gubbeen Semi-soft washed rind cheese. Rich, milky taste.

Milleens Soft, rich rind-washed cheese. Unpasteurized; from the Beara peninsula, Cork.

St Killian Hexagonal Brie-like creamy cheese from Wexford.

Dublin Coddle *This is a comforting mixture of sausages, bacon, potatoes and onions, stewed in ham stock.*

Galway Salmon *Top quality fish can be simply served with an Irish butter sauce, watercress and colcannon.*

Irish Coffee Pudding *This is a chilled soufflé of coffee, cream and Irish whiskey, topped with crushed walnuts.*

Choosing a Restaurant

These restaurants have been selected for their good value, food and location. They are listed by region, starting with Dublin, and then by price. Price bands for Northern Ireland are given on pages 343 and 345. Map references refer either to the Dublin Street Finder on *pp116–17*, or the road map on the inside back cover.

PRICE CATEGORIES
For a three-course meal for one, half a bottle of wine, and all extra charges. These categories are for the Republic, where the euro is accepted.

€ under 25 euros
€€ 25–35 euros
€€€ 35–50 euros
€€€€ 50–70 euros
€€€€€ over 70 euros

DUBLIN

SOUTHEAST DUBLIN Cornucopia
€

19 Wicklow St, Dublin 2 **Tel** *01 677 7583*
Map *D3*

Small and often crowded, Cornucopia is one of the few exclusively vegetarian restaurants in the city, serving breakfast, lunch and dinner. This melting pot of bookworm bachelors and earthy students serves delicious, cheap, wholesome food. The menu includes salads, soups, pastas, casseroles and quiches.

SOUTHEAST DUBLIN Kilkenny Restaurant & Café
€

6–10 Nassau St, Dublin 2 **Tel** *01 677 7075*
Map *E4*

Situated on the first floor of a high-quality craft shop, the Kilkenny overlooks the grounds of Trinity College. Wholesome, freshly-prepared soups, sandwiches, panini, salads, quiches, hot casseroles and pies are available in this self-service restaurant. Lovely desserts include baked cheesecake, carrot cake and fruit tarts. Prices are reasonable.

SOUTHEAST DUBLIN Nude
€

21 Suffolk St, Dublin 2 **Tel** *01 672 5577*
Map *D3*

Bono's brother, Paul Hewson, has created a very successful hip and intimate restaurant, which serves freshly prepared food, organic where possible. Soups, panini, wraps, salads and freshly-squeezed juices are ordered at the counter. Take a seat at the long wooden tables and enjoy these colourful snacks in an upbeat atmosphere.

SOUTHEAST DUBLIN Steps of Rome
€

1 Chatham St, Dublin 2 **Tel** *01 670 5630*
Map *D4*

This tiny Italian café, selling great coffee, is invariably abuzz with people coming and going to collect tasty slices of pizza. The reasonably priced menu includes pastas and bruschetta. Service is brisk, if a little brusque. Popular with students and fast-moving shoppers pausing for breath. Open all day and into the evening.

SOUTHEAST DUBLIN Avoca Café
€€

11–13 Avoca Café, Dublin 2 **Tel** *01 672 6019*
Map *D3*

Climb to the top floor of the renowned Irish craft shop, Avoca, and be rewarded with creative, wholesome and colourful cooking in a bright and airy room. The queues get lengthier during peak lunch hour. Such popularity is testament to the delicious salads, panini, hot dishes and wonderful desserts. Open daytime only.

SOUTHEAST DUBLIN Café Bar Deli
€€

18 South Great George's St, Dublin 2 **Tel** *01 677 1646*
Map *C4*

Vibrant and modestly priced, Café Bar Deli is decorated in a European café style, with bentwood chairs and a mahogany and brass interior. Imaginative and colourful menus feature pizzas, pastas, salads. Service is prompt and enthusiastic. Particularly popular with 20- and 30-somethings. Wines, beer and stout are served.

SOUTHEAST DUBLIN Dunne & Cresenzi
€€

14 South Frederick St, Dublin 2 **Tel** *01 677 3815*
Map *E4*

This delightful Italian wine bar or *enoteca* serves authentic food and wine in a stylishly rustic atmosphere. Enjoy the excellent minestrone, antipasti platters, bruschetta, panini, pasta, delicious fruit tartlets and excellent coffee. There's a superb collection of wines, also served by the glass. Open all day and into the evening.

SOUTHEAST DUBLIN Gotham Café
€€

8 South Anne St, Dublin 2 **Tel** *01 679 5266*
Map *D4*

This lively and colourful spot is always abuzz. Offering bistro-style food at affordable prices, and with covers of *Rolling Stone* lining the walls, it is popular with the young and young-at-heart. Known for tasty and imaginative pizzas, it also serves pastas and salads.

SOUTHEAST DUBLIN La Maison des Gourmets
€€

15 Castle Market, Dublin 2 **Tel** *01 672 7258*
Map *D4*

This smart *boulangerie* has a stylish and intimate room upstairs, where high-quality snacks are served. French onion soup, home-baked breads, *tartines* (open gourmet sandwiches), salads, a hot special and delicious pastries are on the menu. Takeaway is available from the downstairs shop. In fine weather, sit outside and watch the world go by.

Key to Symbols *see back cover flap*

SOUTHEAST DUBLIN Bang Café

€€€

11 Merrion Row, Dublin 2 **Tel** *01 676 0898*

Map E5

Across the road from the Shelbourne Hotel, this hip restaurant is the essence of stylish minimalism, reflected in its food as well as the decor of natural tones and dark wood furnishings. Contemporary cuisine includes good fish dishes, mouthwatering scallops and excellent bangers and mash. Service is professional.

SOUTHEAST DUBLIN Ely Winebar & Café

€€€

22 Ely Place, Dublin 2 **Tel** *01 676 8986*

Map E5

The basement of a Georgian house, just off St Stephen's Green, has been stylishly converted into an excellent wine bar. Choose exceptional wines from the imaginative menu. The menu features cheese dishes, fish cakes, Kilkee oysters, lamb stew and home-made sausages. The atmosphere is cosy and lively.

SOUTHEAST DUBLIN Good World Chinese Restaurant

€€€

18 South Great George's St, Dublin 2 **Tel** *01 677 5373*

Map C4

This restaurant's popularity with the Chinese community attests to the good quality of food on offer. The dim sum selection is a popular choice. Authentic beef, chicken and fish dishes are served, along with the standard Westernized dishes. Friendly and efficient service.

SOUTHEAST DUBLIN Pearl Brasserie

€€€

20 Merrion St Upper, Dublin 2 **Tel** *01 661 3572*

Map D4

This basement brasserie exudes a cool, contemporary French ethos. It combines charming service with good food at affordable prices. Seafood features prominently. The separate Oyster Bar offers lighter fare, including a fish platter. The impressive wine list is heavy on French wines. Lunch is particularly good value.

SOUTHEAST DUBLIN Peploe's Wine Bistro

€€€

16 St Stephen's Green, Dublin 2 **Tel** *01 676 3144*

Map D4

Located in the basement of a Georgian building, this is a glamorous, cosy and immensely popular restaurant. Always rushed, due to the high-quality and consistently good food. It provides an extensive wine list – over 30 are served by the glass. Book in advance.

SOUTHEAST DUBLIN Trocadero

€€€

3–4 Andrew St, Dublin 2 **Tel** *01 677 5545*

Map D3

This much-loved restaurant has been in operation since 1956. A haunt of actors and the literati, it has deep-red walls lined with black-and-white images of the notables who have passed through its doors. Traditional classics include rack of lamb, steak, Dublin Bay prawns and tempting desserts. Service is intimate and welcoming.

SOUTHEAST DUBLIN Unicorn

€€€

12B Merrion Court, Dublin 2 **Tel** *01 676 2182*

Map E4

Situated around St Stephen's Green, Unicorn has maintained an excellent standard since it opened in 1938. Its casual atmosphere is unparalleled and is enhanced by the friendly staff. The Italian-Mediterranean food served here is delicious and the veal is particularly appetizing.

SOUTHEAST DUBLIN Yamamori Noodles

€€€

71 South Great George's St, Dublin 2 **Tel** *01 475 5001*

Map C4

Very popular with the young crowd, this lively and informal Japanese restaurant specializes in Yamamori ramen (a noodle dish with meat and vegetables), sushi and sashimi. Try the interesting bento box for variety. Dishes are good value, service is prompt and the atmosphere is friendly. Evenings are very busy. Open for lunch and dinner.

SOUTHEAST DUBLIN Browne's Brasserie

€€€€

22 St Stephen's Green, Dublin 2 **Tel** *01 638 3939*

Map D4

The award-winning restaurant of the stylish Browne's Hotel *(see p295)* has a wonderfully romantic atmosphere. Elegantly furnished with antiques, it is warm and welcoming with a friendly staff. Good international cooking is backed up by delicious desserts.

SOUTHEAST DUBLIN Dobbins Wine Bistro

€€€€

15 Stephen's Lane, Dublin 2 **Tel** *01 661 3321*

Map F5

Popular since 1978, this cheerful bistro has a warm and pleasing ambience, with red-and-white checkered table-cloths and the floor scattered with sawdust. Given the good wine list, it is a popular spot for a leisurely liquid lunch. Menu includes smoked fish cakes and prime sirloin of beef.

SOUTHEAST DUBLIN Jaipur

€€€€

41–46 South Great George's St, Dublin 2 **Tel** *01 677 0999*

Map C4

Often acclaimed as the best Indian restaurant in the city, Jaipur offers high-quality, innovative dishes. The decor, stylish with a contemporary feel, is done up in warm, tasteful colours. It is superbly managed by a well-informed and charming staff. Vegetarians are well catered for. Branches have now opened in Malahide and Dalkey.

SOUTHEAST DUBLIN La Stampa

€€€€

35 Dawson St, Dublin 2 **Tel** *01 677 8611*

Map D4

The brasserie-style La Stampa's main attraction is its dining room, perhaps the most romantic in the city, set in a charming 19th-century mirrored ballroom. Given its modest quality, the food is rather pricey. However, the pleasing ambience and cordial staff more than make up for any mediocrity.

SOUTHEAST DUBLIN L'Ecrivain
109a Lower Baggot St, Dublin 2 **Tel** *01 661 1919*

Map *F5*

One of the best restaurants in the city, L'Ecrivain combines classic formality with contemporary cool. Authentic French cuisine with an Irish flavour includes delicacies such as Galway Bay oysters with vanilla-champagne *sabayon* and caviar. Seasonal game and seafood as well as tasty desserts and cheeses also figure on the menu. Service is great.

SOUTHEAST DUBLIN Shanahan's on the Green
119 St Stephen's Green, Dublin 2 **Tel** *01 407 0939*

Map *D5*

The most succulent steaks in Dublin are to be found in this renowned steakhouse, set in an elegantly furnished Georgian house. Though steeply priced, the food is consistently of the highest quality and the portions gargantuan. Skip starters, if you hope to finish your main. Seafood, too, is available at this superbly managed establishment.

SOUTHWEST DUBLIN Leo Burdock's
2 Werburgh St, Dublin 8 **Tel** *01 454 0306*

Map *B4*

The patrons of Leo Burdock's, the oldest fish-and-chip takeaway in Dublin, include the ordinary folk of Dublin and the stars. Fresh fish and chips made from top-grade Irish potatoes. There's a wide choice of fish including scampi, smoked cod, haddock and lemon sole goujon. Service is efficient. There's another branch on Liffey Street.

SOUTHWEST DUBLIN Queen of Tarts
4 Cork Hill, Dame St, Dublin 2 **Tel** *01 670 7499*

Map *C3*

Opposite Dublin Castle and Dublin City Hall, this charming little café is cosy and welcoming. Apart from freshly prepared soups, sandwiches and hot savoury tarts, there's a dazzling array of mouthwatering desserts such as chocolate fudge cake, fruit tarts and home-made biscuits. Ideal for a quick and reasonably priced snack.

SOUTHWEST DUBLIN Gruel
68a Dame St, Dublin 2 **Tel** *01 670 7119*

Map *C3*

This tiny, quirky café blends the rustic with the innovative in its light snacks, soups and hot specials. The roast in the roll is delicious and a firm favourite among the colourful patrons. Good pizzas and tasty sweet dishes make it an ideal spot for a quick bite at affordable prices. Eat in or take away.

SOUTHWEST DUBLIN Eden
Meeting House Square, Temple Bar, Dublin 2 **Tel** *01 670 5372*

Map *C3*

With an outside terrace on the Square, this split-level restaurant is bright and modern in design, with cool-blue tiled walls and an open kitchen. It is known for its sirloin steaks, cleverly-contrived fish dishes and imaginative use of seasonal vegetables. Weekend brunch menu features smoked fish for starters. The early-evening menu is good value.

SOUTHWEST DUBLIN Elephant & Castle
18 Temple Bar, Dublin 2 **Tel** *01 679 3121*

Map *D3*

Very lively and ever popular, this American-style brasserie, in the heart of Temple Bar, is invariably busy. Have the mouthwatering chicken wings to start. Good omelettes, steaks, hamburgers and salads are available at affordable prices. Weekend brunches are also popular. Telephone bookings are not accepted.

SOUTHWEST DUBLIN Lord Edward
23 Christchurch Place, Dublin 8 **Tel** *01 454 2158*

Map *B4*

The oldest seafood restaurant in the city, Lord Edward is located above a cosy and traditional pub, which serves lunch downstairs. It has changed little over the years and maintains an old-fashioned feel. Long-established waiters are known for their charming service.

SOUTHWEST DUBLIN The Mermaid Café
69–70 Dame St, Dublin 2 **Tel** *01 670 8236*

Map *C3*

A bright contemporary restaurant, with large windows, wooden furniture and floors, The Mermaid Café is a firm favourite for weekend brunches. There's an ambience of the American East Coast, which is also evident in specialities such as New England crab cakes. There's a creative use of high-quality Irish artisan produce. Lively in the evenings.

SOUTHWEST DUBLIN Monty's of Kathmandu
28 Eustace St, Dublin 2 **Tel** *01 670 4911*

Map *C3*

This friendly Nepalese restaurant serves tasty and interesting fish, chicken and lamb dishes at affordable prices. Vegetarians are well catered for. Try the dumplings or the tandoori butter chicken in a deliciously creamy sauce. Upstairs is more cheerful than the basement dining room. Service is good and the atmosphere relaxed.

SOUTHWEST DUBLIN Les Frères Jacques
74 Dame St, Dublin 2 **Tel** *01 679 4555*

Map *C3*

This elegant restaurant is French in style, cuisine, atmosphere and service. Seafood and game feature prominently on the well-balanced seasonal menus. Try the grilled lobster fresh from the tank or the roast lamb *tian* (casserole) with courgette, aubergine and thyme. Classic desserts are on the menu. Good wine list favours French bottles.

SOUTHWEST DUBLIN The Tea Room
The Clarence Hotel, 6–8 Wellington Quay, Dublin 2 **Tel** *01 407 0800*

Map *C3*

Come in by the Essex Street entrance, opposite the Project Theatre, and savour excellent cuisine served in this stylish dining room. High ceilings and large windows create a bright and airy atmosphere. Menus are innovative and seasonal. Lunch menu is particularly good value. Food is of a very high standard and service attentive.

Key to Price Guide *see p324* **Key to Symbols** *see back cover flap*

NORTH OF THE LIFFEY Epicurean Food Hall   €

Lower Liffey St, Dublin 1   **Map** D2

This food hall comprises a number of outlets serving a range of international light meals and snacks. There's a bustling communal dining area in the centre, or take away and enjoy on a seat on the boardwalk overlooking the Liffey. Itsabagel's snacks, Burdock's fish and chips, as well as Turkish, Italian and Mexican cuisines are on offer.

NORTH OF THE LIFFEY Kingfisher Grill   €

166 Parnell St, Dublin 1 **Tel** *01 872 8732*   **Map** C2

Modestly decorated but immaculately maintained, Kingfisher Grill is a no-frills diner. Prompt service and cheap prices make it a good spot for the simple dishes many of us miss. Potato wedges and prawn cocktail are popular starters. Finish with jelly or ice cream.

NORTH OF THE LIFFEY Panem   €

Ha'penny Bridge House, 21 Lower Ormond Quay, Dublin 1 **Tel** *01 872 8510*   **Map** C3

This tiny café and bakery offers freshly prepared Italian and French food, using high-quality ingredients. The menu includes delicious croissants and *focaccia* with savoury fillings, sweet brioches with chocolate, home-baked biscuits and good coffee. The mouthwatering hot chocolate is made from dark Belgian chocolate. Nice staff.

NORTH OF THE LIFFEY The Cobalt Café   €

16 North Great Georges St, Dublin 1 **Tel** *01 873 0313*   **Map** D3

This daytime café offers a range of homemade soups, sandwiches and cakes, as well as the signature 'chicken cobalt'. The café doubles as a gallery exhibiting the work of up-and-coming Irish artists and consequently is a popular venue for art lovers.

NORTH OF THE LIFFEY 101 Talbot   €€

100–102 Talbot St, Dublin 1 **Tel** *01 874 5011*   **Map** E2

Mediterranean style is reflected in the decor as much as the cuisine at 101 Talbot, livening up the rather drab street on which it is located. The early-bird menu is good value and attracts many theatre-goers. Vegetarians are spoilt for choice. Dietary needs may be met.

NORTH OF THE LIFFEY Stillroom Restaurant   €€

Old Jameson Distillery, Bow St, Dublin 1 **Tel** *01 807 2248*   **Map** A2

This restaurant is a part of the Old Jameson Distillery, which lies on the site of the original 18th-century distillery. At lunch time the legal eagles from the nearby Courts swoop in here, to savour the comfort food on offer. Traditional dishes include a daily roast as well as delicious sandwiches and soups.

NORTH OF THE LIFFEY Bar Italia   €€€

Quartier Bloom, Lower Ormond Quay, Dublin 1 **Tel** *01 874 1000*   **Map** C3

The popular Bar Italia, specializing in Italian fare, is a hive of activity around lunch time, when patrons stream in for freshly prepared antipasti, risotto, grilled vegetables or the pasta specials. Desserts are also an attraction, as is the excellent espresso.

NORTH OF THE LIFFEY D.One Restaurant   €€€

IFSC, North Wall Quay, Dublin 1 **Tel** *01 856 1622*   **Map** F2

Built at the very edge of the River Liffey, D.One Restaurant has a lovely waterside location. It is decorated in a clean, contemporary style with large views to take advantage of its position. Traditional dishes are given a modern twist. Try the fish and chips. The early dinner is good value.

NORTH OF THE LIFFEY Chapter One   €€€€

18–19 Parnell Sq, Dublin 1 **Tel** *01 873 2266*   **Map** C1

In the cellar of the Dublin Writers' Museum, Chapter One is often cited by critics as the best restaurant north of the Liffey. Relish the imaginative European cuisine, with an Irish twist, in a dining room of character and comfort. The pre-theatre menu is a favourite among regulars who frequent the nearby Gate theatre. There's a good Oyster Bar.

FURTHER AFIELD Abbey Tavern   €€€

Abbey St, Howth, Co Dublin **Tel** *01 839 0307*

Open fires, linen-clad tables, fresh flowers and a slightly old-fashioned atmosphere define this restaurant on the first floor of a characteristic pub. Good, uncomplicated fish and meat dishes are served. The traditional cabaret evening downstairs, featuring set dinners, is popular with visitors.

FURTHER AFIELD Beaufield Mews Restaurant, Gardens & Antiques   €€€

Woodlands Ave, Stillorgan, Co Dublin **Tel** *01 288 0375*   **Road Map** D4

One of County Dublin's oldest restaurant, Beaufield Mews is beautifully set in an 18th-century cobbled courtyard with a rose garden to the rear. Good modern European food is served in an elegant dining room decorated with Irish art and antiques. An inviting atmosphere prevails throughout.

FURTHER AFIELD Aqua Restaurant   €€€

1 West Pier, Howth, Co Dublin **Tel** *01 832 0690*

This first-floor restaurant, with lovely views over the sea and harbour, was formerly a yacht club, now converted into a bright contemporary space. Prominent on the menu are steaks as well as fresh fish and chicken dishes. The cuisine betrays a Californian-Italian influence. Set menus are good value. Sunday brunch is accompanied by live jazz.

FURTHER AFIELD Bon Appetit

9 St James Terrace, Malahide, Co Dublin **Tel** *01 845 0314*

Situated in the basement of a Georgian terrace, this well-respected restaurant is inviting, with its warm colours, art collection and excellent seafood. Try the fresh prawn bisque with cognac, the Sole Creation McGuirk and the roast crispy duckling in Grand Marnier sauce. Desserts are equally tempting. Book in advance.

FURTHER AFIELD Brasserie Na Mara

1 Harbour Road, Dun Laoghaire, Co Dublin **Tel** *01 280 6767*

Conveniently located beside the harbour, ferry terminal and DART station, the welcoming Brasserie Na Mara is housed in a graceful period building. Stylish contemporary decor features large windows, linen-clad tables and fresh flowers. Seafood is a speciality. Home-made desserts are lovely.

FURTHER AFIELD Caviston's Seafood Restaurant

59 Glasthule Road, Dun Laoghaire, Sandycove, Co Dublin **Tel** *01 280 9120*

Stunning seafood, prepared with simple flair. Sadly, this culinary cult address is only open for lunch. Book early and reserve the last sitting so that you can enjoy a leisurely afternoon lingering over coffee and dessert. The adjoining delicatessen sells delicious fare great for a picnic.

FURTHER AFIELD Expresso Bar Café

1 St Mary's Road, Ballsbridge, Dublin 4 **Tel** *01 660 0585*

This small restaurant is decorated in a contemporary, minimalist style. Open from breakfast time, it is popular for lunch and weekend brunches. The Californian-Italian fare, featuring chicken and fish dishes, salads and pastas, uses high-quality ingredients. The delicious bread-and-butter pudding makes a perfect dessert. Service could be friendlier.

FURTHER AFIELD The Forty Foot

Pavilion Centre, Dun Laoghaire, Co Dublin **Tel** *01 284 2982*

After a walk on the pier, relax in this very modern upstairs restaurant to watch the day fade over Dublin Bay. The views are the main attraction, but the food is also appealing. Try the *tian* of crab and salmon with crème fraîche. Pleasant and competent staff.

FURTHER AFIELD Johnnie Fox's Pub

Glencullen, Co Dublin **Tel** *01 295 5647*

About 30 minutes' drive south of the city, on the way up to the Dublin mountains, this friendly pub has traditional Irish food, open fires, traditional music and dancing. Pan-seared scallops, dressed crab salad, smoked salmon, sirloin steak are on the menu. The "Hooley Night", featuring dinner and a traditional show, attracts overseas visitors.

FURTHER AFIELD Nosh

111 Coliemore Rd, Dalkey, Co Dublin **Tel** *01 284 0666*

In the heart of Dalkey village, Nosh is contemporary in style, with light wood furniture. Well-balanced menus feature good fish and vegetarian dishes as well as succulent steaks. Cod and chips, pea and asparagus risotto, seared scallops are also on the menu. Home-made desserts are good. The weekend brunch menu is very popular.

FURTHER AFIELD Roly's Bistro

7 Ballsbridge Terrace, Ballsbridge, Dublin 4 **Tel** *01 668 2611*

In the heart of Ballsbridge, this lively, bustling bistro offers reliable, colourful and delicious food. Try the Kerry lamb pie or the Dublin Bay prawns Provençal. Other specialities include fish and game dishes and succulent steaks. Sit upstairs if possible. Take home the delicious home-made breads which are on sale. Reservations are advised.

FURTHER AFIELD King Sitric Fish Restaurant & Accommodation

East Pier, Howth, Co Dublin **Tel** *01 832 5235*

Named after the medieval Norse king of Dublin, this restaurant is acclaimed for good seafood and game. The dining room is stylishly modern, with scenic views. Specialities are crab bisque, Balscadden Bay lobster, black sole meunière and fillet steak with forest mushrooms. Excellent wine cellar.

FURTHER AFIELD The Lobster Pot

9 Ballsbridge Terrace, Ballsbridge, Dublin 4 **Tel** *01 668 0025*

This long-established upstairs restaurant deservedly commands a loyal following. High-quality food is well presented by professional, charming waiters. Specialities feature dressed Kilmore crab, Dublin Bay prawns in Provençal sauce, generously-sized sole on the bone, delicious steaks, chicken and game dishes.

SOUTHEAST IRELAND

BALLYMACARBRY Hanora's Cottage

Nire Valley, Co Waterford **Tel** *052 36134*   **Road Map** *C5*

Hanora's Cottage is a celebrated family-run riverside restaurant, drawing patrons across long distances. The Walls are charming hosts and excellent cooks. The cosy dining room, overlooking lovely gardens, has won many awards and showcases local artisan produce where possible. Try the delicious roast rack of lamb. Reservations advised.

Key to Price Guide *see p 324* **Key to Symbols** *see back cover flap*

BALLYMORE EUSTACE The Ballymore Inn
Ballymore Eustace, Co Kildare **Tel** *045 864 585*   **Road Map** *D4*

Run by the O'Sullivan family, The Ballymore Inn has garnered a wonderful reputation for producing consistently good food. Ingredients, organic as much as possible, are carefully sourced. Home-made soups are served with home-baked breads. Regulars on the menu are sirloin steak with Béarnaise sauce, pastas and fish.

BLESSINGTON Grangecon Café
The Old Schoolhouse, Kilbride Rd, Co Wicklow **Tel** *045 857 892*   **Road Map** *D4*

Set in a lovingly restored building in the centre of Blessington, this tastefully decorated café is a delightful spot to visit. Good, honest and wholesome cooking features salads, quiches, savoury tarts, sandwiches on home-made bread, delicious farmhouse cheese and chutneys. Organic juices as well as home-baked desserts are available.

CAMPILE The Georgian Tea Rooms
Great Island, Co Wexford **Tel** *051 388 109*   **Road Map** *D5*

Located in Kilmokea Country Manor & Gardens, a charming Georgian house set in its own magnificent gardens, the Georgian Tea Rooms offer delicious home-made fare and light lunches in the bright and spacious conservatory. Views over the walled garden and on to the River Barrow and beyond. Open 10am–5pm, February to November.

CARLOW Lennon's Café Bar
121 Tullow St, Co Carlow **Tel** *059 913 1575*   **Road Map** *D4*

Contemporary in design, this daytime café bar is expertly run by the Byrnes who offer keenly-priced wholesome food. Try the delicious home-made soups such as the Cashel Blue and bacon and courgette, open sandwiches on home-baked breads, gorgeous salads and a selection of hot dishes. Don't miss the lovely home-made desserts.

CARLOW Reddy's
67 Tullow St, Co Carlow **Tel** *059 914 2224*   **Road Map** *D4*

This restaurant and bar has been in the Reddy family since 1768. Traditional Irish food is prepared with an international flair, using day-fresh ingredients. The Reddy family and their staff are warm and friendly. A wide range of steak and fish dishes feature on the menu.

CARNE The Lobster Pot Seafood Bar
Carne, Near Rosslare, Co Wexford **Tel** *053 31110*   **Road Map** *D5*

The Lobster Pot, an award-winning seafood bar, is housed in a well-maintained 19th-century building. Home cooking and warm rural hospitality create a relaxing atmosphere. The restaurant is famed for its ultra-fresh fish, including a delicious chowder, crab-meat salad and smoked salmon platter.

CASTLEDERMOT De Lacy's Restaurant
Castledermot, Co Kildare **Tel** *059 914 5156*   **Road Map** *D4*

De Lacy's is housed in Kilkea Castle Hotel, a sensitively modernized 12th-century building that still maintains its grandeur. Inside, it is elegantly furnished with linen-draped tables, candles and fresh flowers, with fabulous views over the surrounding countryside. Try the pan-fried fillet of pork. Food is available in the bar all day and evening.

DUNGARVAN The Tannery Restaurant
10 Quay St, Co Waterford **Tel** *058 45420*   **Road Map** *C5*

The superbly designed, award-winning Tannery Restaurant is located in an old leather warehouse, which has been ingeniously converted with great flair and imagination. High-quality furnishings, artwork and fresh flowers complement the outstanding and highly innovative contemporary cuisine, creating a memorable meal.

ENNISKERRY Poppies Restaurant
The Square, Co Wicklow **Tel** *01 282 8869*   **Road Map** *D4*

This small café restaurant is a cosy and vibrant place, serving good country cooking at reasonable prices. Try the leek and blue cheese tart or the beef and Guinness pie. Other dishes include, soups, sandwiches, salads and baked potatoes. Desserts are worth savouring. Vegetarians are well catered for. Open daily until 6pm.

GOREY Marlfield House
Courtown Rd, Co Wexford **Tel** *055 21124*   **Road Map** *D4*

Possibly the best in the region, this wonderfully romantic dining room is elegantly furnished and runs into a stunning conservatory. Enjoy the excellent cooking in a warm and welcoming ambience. Organically grown vegetables come from the garden. There's an extensive wine list. Staff are well-informed and personable. Reservations advised.

GREYSTONES The Hungry Monk
Church Rd, Co Wicklow **Tel** *01 287 5759*   **Road Map** *D4*

This delightful first-floor restaurant is well-established and regarded as a sure-bet for food, wine and good fun. The theme of cheerful robed monks is apparent throughout. It has possibly the best wine list in the country. Favourite dishes include lamb's kidneys in mustard sauce as well as locally-caught seafood specials.

KILDARE The Silken Thomas
The Square, Co Kildare **Tel** *045 522 232*   **Road Map** *D4*

Named after an extravagantly dressed Lord of Kildare who led an uprising against Henry VIII, this purpose-built establishment houses three bars, a restaurant and a nightclub. The main lounge bar serves food from 11am to 9pm. The restaurant offers a carvery lunch and evening meals.

KILKENNY Kilkenny Design Centre

Castle Yard, Co Kilkenny **Tel** *056 772 2118*   **Road Map** *C4*

This bright, self-service restaurant overlooks the cobbled courtyard of Kilkenny Castle. Freshly prepared wholesome soups, salads, sandwiches, quiches, hot dishes and casseroles are offered at reasonable prices. Tasty desserts include apple crumble, carrot cake and banana bread. Wine and locally brewed ale is also served. Open 10am–7pm.

KILKENNY Marble City Bar

66 High St, Co Kilkenny **Tel** *056 776 1143*   **Road Map** *C4*

Stylishly refurbished in recent years, this historic bar retains great character and a lively atmosphere. European-style bar food, including breakfast, is served all day from 10am, when the good breakfast menu is on offer. Cod in a beer batter with chips, Thai fish cakes and home-made burgers with cheese, bacon and relish are on the menu.

KILKENNY Zuni

26 Patrick St, Co Kilkenny **Tel** *056 772 3999*   **Road Map** *C4*

Also offering stylish accommodation, Zuni has become a by-word for contemporary chic and superb food in this delightful medieval town. The cuisine is worldly in style, with influences from Morocco to Southeast Asia. A well-designed restaurant, it has great atmosphere and tasteful furnishings. Try the tasty risottos, salads and pastas.

KILMACANOGUE Avoca Café

Kilmacanogue, Co Wicklow **Tel** *01 286 7466*   **Road Map** *D4*

Set in the grounds of the old Jameson (of whiskey fame) estate and surrounded by lovely gardens, this award-winning restaurant is in the headquarters of the renowned craft shop, Avoca. Wholesome country cooking, with a Mediterranean twist, includes casseroles, salads, vegetarian lasagne, freshly baked breads and home-baked desserts.

KILMACOW The Thatch

Grannagh Castle, Co Waterford **Tel** *051 872 876*   **Road Map** *D5*

This cosy thatched pub is located opposite the lovely Grannagh Castle. Owner David Ryan offers good freshly prepared bar food. Soups, open sandwiches, salads, panini, omelettes are on offer. Hot dishes include a hearty Irish mixed grill, featuring bacon, egg, sausage, black pudding, potato cake and French fries.

LEIGHLINBRIDGE Lord Bagenal Inn

Leighlinbridge, Co Carlow **Tel** *059 972 1668*   **Road Map** *D4*

Housed in a well-established family-run hotel, on the banks of the River Barrow, this bright riverside restaurant offers classical and traditional dishes with a contemporary twist. There's an award-winning wine list. Popular carvery lunch is served in the bar.

LISMORE Barça Wine Bar & Restaurant

Main St, Co Waterford **Tel** *058 53810*   **Road Map** *C5*

This smart tapas bar, in the heart of Lismore, is truly a delight. A stylish contemporary stamp has been put on the interior of the bar, which retains many of its charming traditional features. Tapas dishes include chorizo croquettes with caramelized onions.

ROUNDWOOD The Roundwood Inn

Roundwood, Co Wicklow **Tel** *01 281 8107*   **Road Map** *D4*

In Roundwood, supposedly Ireland's highest village, this 17th-century inn is a good stopping-off point after a walk in the Wicklow Hills. Its slightly formal restaurant, with a welcoming open fire and traditional furnishings, serves excellent bar food all day. Menu includes crab bisque, smoked salmon, Irish stew and smoked trout.

THOMASTOWN Hudson's

Station Rd, Co Kilkenny **Tel** *056 779 3900*   **Road Map** *D5*

Hip Hudson's has become a huge hit on the culinary scene, serving wonderful contemporary cooking in a smart and comfortable dining room. Specialities include crab spring rolls with a soya butter sauce; Barbary duck with figs and balsamic dressing. Service is attentive. The daytime "branch" is Carroll's, a traditional pub offering lunch daily.

THOMASTOWN The Lady Helen

Mount Juliet Conrad Hotel, Co Kilkenny **Tel** *056 777 3000*   **Road Map** *D5*

Enjoy classic cuisine in a very elegant, high-ceilinged room with beautiful views over the gardens, which provide fresh vegetables and herbs. Wild salmon from the nearby River Nore and chicken breast with fennel stuffing in a tomato and red pepper sauce are real treats. Reservations advised. The adjacent Kendal's restaurant is less formal.

TRAMORE Coast

Upper Branch Rd, Co Waterford **Tel** *051 393 646*   **Road Map** *D5*

The smart, contemporary Coast is one of the most talked-about restaurants in the region. Chic and stylish, with classy furnishings, it exudes an upbeat atmosphere, complemented by excellent food. The main course, served with seasonal vegetables, features fish and meat dishes. The wine list is somewhat pricey.

WATERFORD The Gingerman

6–7 Arundel Lane, Co Waterford **Tel** *051 879 522*   **Road Map** *D5*

Located in the Norman part of the city, this pub is to be found in a pedestrianized lane, just off Broad Street. Welcoming fires and friendly staff make this an enjoyable spot for daytime food. Reasonably priced menu features home-made soup, sandwiches, panini and baked potatoes. Tasty hot dishes and daily specials are also on the menu.

Key to Price Guide *see p324* **Key to Symbols** *see back cover flap*

WATERFORD Bodega!

54 John St, Co Waterford **Tel** *051 844 177*

€€€
Road Map *D5*

The exclamation mark in the title hints at the vibrant atmosphere of this popular eatery. Inside, it is cheerfully decorated in heart-warming colours, with wooden tables and ever-changing artwork. Sunday brunch is available, while the dinner menu features fresh *foie gras*, steaks and sea bass.

WATERFORD The Wine Vault

High St, Co Waterford **Tel** *051 853 444*

€€€
Road Map *D5*

Over a decade in business, this intimate wine bar and restaurant is set in an 18th-century bonded warehouse and wine vault. There's a superb selection of wines. Open for lunch and dinner, it serves appetizing and keenly priced fare including fresh oysters, linguini, risotto of fresh asparagus, chicken curry, steaks and pizzas. Service is efficient.

WATERFORD Fitzpatrick's Restaurant

Manor Court Lodge, Cork Rd, Co Waterford **Tel** *051 378 851*

€€€€
Road Map *D5*

In a listed stone building on the outskirts of the city, this bright and colourful fine-dining restaurant is reputed for its classical cuisine with a French influence. Linen-clad tables with fresh flowers and candles create a welcoming atmosphere. Try the roasted sea bass. Staff are courteous and attentive. Reservations are recommended.

WEXFORD Westgate Design

22a North Main St, Co Wexford **Tel** *053 23787*

€
Road Map *D5*

Located at the back of the design and craft shop, Westgate Design is a daytime restaurant, well managed and very popular. It serves good home cooking at keen prices, in a cosy room simply decorated in a rustic style. Quiches, salads, sandwiches and soups are on offer as well as a selection of hot dishes. Service is prompt and friendly.

CORK AND KERRY

BALLYCOTTON Grapefruit Moon

Main St, Co Cork **Tel** *021 464 6646*

€€€
Road Map *C6*

This wonderful little restaurant boasts an impressive minimalism, blending neutral tones, fresh flowers, contemporary paintings and comfortable leather chairs. Innovative cooking is refreshingly original and seasonal, showcasing locally caught fish from Ballycotton Bay, and carefully sourced meats and poultry.

BALLYDEHOB Annie's Restaurant

Main St, Co Cork **Tel** *028 37292*

€€€
Road Map *B6*

The ever-popular Annie's Restaurant has been extended to accommodate demand. Have an apéritif in Levi's Bar nearby. Wholesome home cooking uses fresh seafood, local meats and duck. Choose from the West Cork farmhouse cheeses, home-made breads, desserts and ice creams. Annie is a charming host, Dano a conscientious chef.

BALTIMORE Chez Youen

The Waterfront, Co Cork **Tel** *028 20441*

€€€€
Road Map *B6*

Established since 1979, Youen Jacob's restaurant has quite a following of regulars and visitors following warm recommendations. Seafood is the star attraction and the dishes are beautifully presented. The Shellfish Platter is a delight and a work of art in itself. Try the turbot in a black butter sauce. There's an excellent wine list.

BANDON Otto's Creative Catering

Dunworley, Butlerstown, Co Cork **Tel** *023 40461*

€€€
Road Map *B6*

Overlooking the Atlantic Ocean, this incredible enterprise is gaining a formidable reputation. Otto and Hilda Kunze oversee the grassland and gardens where they rear hens and pigs and grow organic crops. The farmhouse is delightful. Menu features salad with roasted pheasant, barbecued pork chops and local seafood. Reservations only.

BANTRY O'Connor's Seafood Restaurant

The Square, Co Cork **Tel** *027 50221*

€€€
Road Map *B6*

Situated in the heart of the town, this long-running restaurant serves lunch and dinner and specializes in seafood. Also on the menu are fine fillet steaks, local mountain lamb, chicken and game. Mussels are a particular speciality. Live lobsters and oysters in a fresh seawater tank are indicative of the freshness of the produce.

BANTRY Blair's Cove House & Restaurant

Durrus, near Bantry, Co Cork **Tel** *027 61127*

€€€€
Road Map *B6*

This waterside restaurant enjoys a stunningly romantic setting, overlooking Dunmanus Bay. The main candlelit dining room has great character with its stone walls and black-beamed ceilings, chandelier and grand piano. The superb hors d'oeuvre buffet is a star feature.

BANTRY Sea View House Hotel

Ballylickey, Co Cork **Tel** *027 50462*

€€€€
Road Map *B6*

The elegant restaurant of the four-star country-house hotel, which overlooks Bantry Bay, is furnished with antiques and fresh flowers. It specializes in country-house cooking, with a particular focus on seafood. Try the Bantry Bay crab salad or roast rack of lamb with rosemary. Classic desserts include summer berries, mousses and tiramisù.

BLARNEY Blair's Inn

Cloghroe, Co Cork **Tel** *021 438 1470*

€€€

Road Map B5

Immaculately maintained and very inviting, this pretty whitewashed riverside pub has hanging flower baskets and a lovely garden outside. Inside, open fires and a charming interior are complemented by reliably good food. Traditional dishes include casserole of beef and stout; baked lemon sole stuffed with crab meat in a white butter sauce.

CASTLETOWNSHEND Mary Ann's Bar

Castletownshend, Skibbereen, Co Cork **Tel** *028 36146*

€€

Road Map B6

A landmark restaurant in the heart of a picturesque village, the bar dates back to 1846 and retains a cosy and unique character. The welcoming charm is most appealing. Consistently superb food is the real draw. Seafood specialities include exquisite platters, chowders, crab claws, pan-fried brill. There's also an excellent cheeseboard.

CORK Crawford Gallery Café

Emmet Place, Co Cork **Tel** *021 427 4415*

€€

Road Map C5

Located in the old Customs House, the Crawford Municipal Art Gallery is home to one of the city's best daytime eateries. Crawford Gallery Café is a bright and delightful spot to enjoy freshly prepared country house cooking and excellent home-baked desserts.

CORK Farmgate Café

The English Market, Co Cork **Tel** *021 427 8134*

€€

Road Map C5

Farmgate Café is located upstairs in the gallery over the bustling English Market, from where many of the ingredients are sourced. It's a lively restaurant, split between a self-service section and the restaurant proper. Wooden tables and black-and-white tiles create a down-to-earth yet stylish ambience. Honest home cooking is the main draw.

CORK Isaacs Restaurant

48 MacCurtain St, Co Cork **Tel** *021 450 3805*

€€€

Road Map C5

Housed in an 18th-century red-bricked warehouse, this informal, yet stylish, restaurant provides reliably good bistro-style cooking. The fairly-priced menu features baked cod, bruschetta with wild mushrooms and roast peppers. Wine list is extensive and descriptive. Friendly and efficient service.

CORK The Ivory Tower

The Exchange Buildings, 35 Prince's St, Co Cork **Tel** *021 427 4665*

€€€

Road Map C5

One of Ireland's most creative chefs, Seamus O'Connell, sources the best-quality ingredients, all organic, creating unusual and delicious combinations of flavours and produce. The Crozier cheese soufflé served in an artichoke is a favourite signature dish, as is the aphrodisiac of tropical fruits.

CORK The Pembroke

Imperial Hotel, South Mall, Co Cork **Tel** *021 427 4040*

€€€

Road Map C5

The Pembroke is a modern restaurant located in the Imperial Hotel. Traditional Irish food is served in the recently refurbished dining room. A comprehensive wine list supports the à la carte menu. Try the jumbo prawns and crispy duck. Open for breakfast, lunch and dinner.

CORK Jacobs on the Mall

30a South Mall, Co Cork **Tel** *021 425 1530*

€€€€

Road Map C5

This highly acclaimed restaurant, with one of the country's leading chefs, is set in the former Turkish baths. Decorated in a charming contemporary style, it has a unique ambience. Creative and colourful dishes include scallops and crab cakes with mango salad and a hot-and-sour dressing. Home-made ice creams are irresistible.

CORK Café Paradiso

16 Lancaster Quay, Western Rd, Co Cork **Tel** *021 427 7939*

€€€€€

Road Map C5

Undoubtedly the best vegetarian restaurant in Ireland, Café Paradiso attracts even the most committed carnivores. The ever-changing seasonal menus are radically imaginative and consistently good. Cheerfully decorated in a contemporary and eclectic style, its intimate atmosphere is lively and welcoming. Desserts are exquisite.

DINGLE The Chart House

The Mall, Co Kerry **Tel** *066 915 2255*

€€€

Road Map A5

This award-winning restaurant is informal in style with exposed stone walls, warm colours and wooden floors. Ebullient and attentive hosts create a welcoming atmosphere. High-quality ingredients are used to outstanding effect. Classic dishes include roast fillet of cod with fennel risotto; and Kerry lamb with red onion and feta.

DINGLE The Half Door

John St, Co Kerry **Tel** *066 915 1600*

€€€

Road Map A5

Decorated in a pretty cottage style, this charming little restaurant is well known for a good, seasonal seafood menu. Try the seafood platter which is available either hot or cold and features crab claws, lobster, oysters, mussels, scallops and prawns. There are tasty desserts and a good selection of farmhouse cheeses. Portions are generous.

DINGLE Lord Baker's Restaurant & Bar

Main St, Co Kerry **Tel** *066 915 1277*

€€€

Road Map A5

Believed to be the oldest bar in Dingle, this welcoming hostelry, with an open fire, serves delicious bar food such as home-made soups, crab claws in garlic butter and smoked salmon and capers. The restaurant is more formal. Specialities include excellent roast duckling, poached wild Atlantic salmon and grilled lobster.

DINGLE Out of the Blue
Waterside, Co Kerry **Tel** *066 915 0811* €€€ **Road Map** *A5*

Interestingly named, this restaurant and deli serves the freshest of fish. The decor is uncluttered and the food excellent. Try the John Dory with garlic eggplant, sole on the bone with almond cream or langoustines in a sweet chilli sauce. The lobster is well priced. There's a well-assembled wine list.

DURRUS Good Things Café
Ahakista Rd, Co Cork **Tel** *027 61426* €€€ **Road Map** *B6*

This intimate café-restaurant has created a real stir among Irish foodies since it opened in 2003. Its menu has been described as reading like a roadmap of the region's acclaimed artisan producers. Specialities include West Cork fish soup and smoked haddock with Desmond cheese. Open April to September, but it's worth calling to check.

KENMARE The Purple Heather
Henry St, Co Kerry **Tel** *064 41016* € **Road Map** *B5*

A traditional bar and restaurant, The Purple Heather was one of the first to establish Kenmare as a culinary town. Consistently good home-cooked food features soups, pâtés, breads and desserts. Also on the menu are lovely seafood salads, smoked salmon and open sandwiches with crab meat.

KENMARE The Lime Tree Restaurant
Shelburne St, Co Kerry **Tel** *064 41225* €€€ **Road Map** *B5*

Though this charming stone building dates from the 1830s, its unique character is retained throughout. With an open fire and upstairs contemporary art gallery, it enjoys a special atmosphere. Excellent local seafood, roast Kerry lamb and delicious desserts are served by a friendly and competent staff. Open Easter to October.

KENMARE Mulcahy's
36 Henry St, Co Kerry **Tel** *064 42383* €€€ **Road Map** *B5*

Bruce Mulcahy is one of Ireland's leading young chefs, whose experience and imagination attract not only locals and visitors, but other chefs and restauranteurs as well. The room is decorated in a tasteful contemporary style and exudes a friendly and intimate ambience. The selections of pasta, fish and meat dishes use organic ingredients.

KENMARE Packie's
Henry St, Co Kerry **Tel** *064 41508* €€€ **Road Map** *B5*

This well-established and highly regarded restaurant enjoys a devoted following of regulars and return visitors. The emphasis is on local seafood and organic produce, yet Mediterranean and contemporary flavours also find their way into the imaginative cooking. Welcoming ambience.

KILLARNEY Panis Angelicus
15 New St, Co Kerry **Tel** *064 39648* € **Road Map** *B5*

An inviting little café, Panis Angelicus promises delicious home cooking, in a stylish contemporary setting. Don't miss the tasty gourmet sandwiches, home-made soup or hot Irish potato cake with garlic butter. Home-baked breads and biscuits are also available. Ideal for a lunch-time pit stop, it serves dinner on the weekend in summer.

KILLARNEY The Cooperage
Old Market Lane, Co Kerry **Tel** *064 37716* €€€ **Road Map** *B5*

This very appealing contemporary restaurant is furnished in a well-designed minimalist style, creating a warm and welcoming ambience. It promises reliably good food, which has been carefully sourced and prepared with great flair. Try the crispy duck with sweet fruit sauce topped with onions and fried leeks.

KILLARNEY Old Presbytery
Cathedral Place, Co Kerry **Tel** *064 30555* €€€ **Road Map** *B5*

Set in a beautifully restored Georgian house, Old Presbytery is the leading fine-dining restaurant in the area. Dining rooms exude contemporary elegance and the ambience is welcoming. Dishes include sole meunière, braised Kerry lamb shank, warm and melting chocolate cake. Service is charming.

KILLARNEY Gaby's Seafood Restaurant
27 High St, Co Kerry **Tel** *064 32519* €€€€ **Road Map** *B5*

A member of the World Master Chefs Society and one of Ireland's longest established seafood restaurants, Gaby's reputedly offers the best seafood in town. Cooking is imaginative and of a high standard with a carefully chosen wine list. A real treat is the lobster "Gaby" with cognac and cream. Desserts are exquisite.

KILLORGLIN Nick's Seafood Restaurant & Piano Bar
Lower Bridge St, Co Kerry **Tel** *066 976 1219* €€€€ **Road Map** *A5*

Renowned for its succulent meats as much as its seafood, this is one of Ireland's much-loved restaurants. Intimate ambience prevails, with open fires and an accompanying pianist. Try the Lobster Thermidor or the peppered steak in a brandy cream sauce.

KINSALE Fishy Fishy Café
Guardwell, Co Cork **Tel** *021 477 4453* €€ **Road Map** *B6*

This outstanding delicatessen, fishmonger and café is renowned for the freshness of its fare and the ingeniously simple manner of preparation. Informal in atmosphere, it is immensely popular and queues can be long, as there is a no-reservations policy. The scampi with potato wedges, tartare sauce and pesto is tempting.

KINSALE Man Friday
Scilly, Co Cork **Tel** *021 477 2260*

Road Map *B6*

The oldest restaurant in Kinsale, Man Friday is nationally regarded for its excellent cuisine, unique atmosphere and friendly service. A recipient of numerous awards, it comprises a number of adjoining rooms of character and a garden terrace, lovely on a summer's evening. There's a great choice of comfort food and a superb seafood platter.

KINSALE Max's Wine Bar
48 Main St, Co Cork **Tel** *021 477 2443*

Road Map *B6*

For three decades, this bustling wine bar and eatery has been in the forefront of Kinsale's gourmet restaurants. Offering light lunches, early-evening meals and full dinner menus, it is a charming little spot, with great character. Wooden tables, exposed stone walls and a small conservatory add to its charm.

KINSALE Casino House
Coolmain Bay, Kilbrittain, Co Cork **Tel** *023 49944*

Road Map *B6*

Set in a lovely, welcoming old building, Casino House is considered to be one of the region's best restaurants. Fresh local seafood and Ballydehob duck feature prominently in an extensive and original menu. Try the lobster risotto or the roast breast of duck served on a lentil potato cake with a honey and port sauce. Desserts are superb.

LEAP All Things Nice
Main St, Co Cork **Tel** *028 34772*

Road Map *B6*

A pretty café and delicatessen in the centre of the village, All Things Nice is worth a stop for its excellent home baking. Plate of Irish and international cheeses, such as Gubeen and Durrus, olive salami and freshly baked bread are on the menu. Try the delicious sandwiches and home-made ice cream and organic milk shakes.

LISTOWEL Allo's Restaurant, Bar & Bistro
41–43 Church St, Co Kerry **Tel** *068 22880*

Road Map *B5*

This charming bar successfully combines traditional with modern Irish cooking. Dating back to 1859 it is traditionally furnished and has a wonderful character and welcoming atmosphere. Try the Dover sole with caper and herb butter or the fillet of Irish beef in puff pastry.

MALLOW Presidents' Restaurant
Longueville House, Co Cork **Tel** *022 47156*

Road Map *B5*

Portraits of Irish presidents line the walls of this elegant dining room, which opens into a beautiful Victorian Turner conservatory, making it one of the most romantic restaurants in the country. Much of the fresh produce, which is expertly prepared and presented, comes from the farm on the estate.

MITCHELSTOWN O'Callaghan's Café & Delicatessen
19–20 Lower Cork St, Co Cork **Tel** *025 24657*

Road Map *C5*

In the heart of the busy market town, this café offers delicious quiches, panini, sandwiches, soups, tasty *focaccia* bread with melted cheese and char-grilled vegetables. Fish kebabs and garlic mussels are good. Home-baked breads, house preserves and chutneys are also available for sale. Eat in or take away. Service is warm.

MOLL'S GAP Avoca Handweavers
Moll's Gap, Co Kerry **Tel** *064 34720*

Road Map *B5*

Spectacularly located on a high rocky ridge overlooking the mountain lakes of Killarney, the restaurant within the high-quality craft shop, is a good stop-over point. Wholesome home cooking is on offer, from soups and freshly prepared salads to hot dishes and appetizing home-baked desserts. Open daytime, from March to October.

MONKSTOWN The Bosun
The Pier, Co Cork **Tel** *021 484 2172*

Road Map *B5*

On the banks of the River Lee, this well-known bar and restaurant serves tempting seafood. Main attractions include baked garlic mussels, stuffed fillet of trout, medallions of monkfish and wild smoked salmon. For meat-eaters, the menu offers fillet steaks, lamb cutlets and venison sausages. Tasty desserts are well worth trying.

SHANAGARRY Ballymaloe House
Shanagarry, Midleton, Co Cork **Tel** *021 465 2531*

Road Map *C6*

This nationally renowned culinary institution is acclaimed for excellent country-house cooking, served in elegant interconnecting dining rooms. Much of the produce is organically grown in the walled garden. Five-course dinner menu is imaginatively conceived and expertly realized. There's a well-known cookery school nearby.

TRALEE Restaurant David Norris
Ivy House, Ivy Terrace, Co Kerry **Tel** *066 718 5654*

Road Map *B5*

Located on the first floor of a modern building, this highly acclaimed fine-dining restaurant is tastefully furnished with Art Nouveau-style chairs and linen-clad tables set with fresh flowers. Great attention has been paid to detail. There's a well-chosen wine list. The menu of perfectly executed classic dishes, such as Kerry beef, changes every so often.

YOUGHAL Ahernes Seafood Restaurant & Townhouse
163 North Main St, Co Cork **Tel** *024 92424*

Road Map *C5*

This award-winning seafood restaurant, now in the hands of the third generation of the Fitzgibbon family, spells warm hospitality and relaxing atmosphere. Savour the finest fish from the day's catch in Youghal harbour, locally reared beef and lamb, seasonal vegetables as well as home-baked breads and delicious desserts.

Key to Price Guide *see p324* **Key to Symbols** *see back cover flap*

THE LOWER SHANNON

ADARE The Wild Geese Restaurant   €€€
Rose Cottage, Main St, Co Limerick **Tel** *061 396451*   **Road Map** *B5*

Housed in a beautiful cottage in the picture-postcard village of Adare, this seafood restaurant has garnered an award-winning reputation for its fine dining, extensive wine list and friendly service. All products are sourced locally and where possible, organically grown. Mains include ravioli of lobster and pan-fried scallops. Superb desserts.

BALLINDERRY Brocka-on-the-Water Restaurant   €€€€
Kilgarvan Quay, Co Tipperary **Tel** *067 22038*   **Road Map** *C4*

A long-standing family affair, the highly respected Brocka-on-the-Water is particularly gorgeous on a fine day. Its open fires, tasteful furnishings, imaginative cuisine and warm hospitality make this immaculately maintained restaurant a perennial favourite. Seasonal menus are exceptionally good. Book in advance.

BALLINGARRY The Mustard Seed at Echo Lodge   €€€€
Ballingarry, Co Limerick **Tel** *069 68508*   **Road Map** *B5*

Set in a Victorian residence, The Mustard Seed is one of the prettiest restaurants in the country. It is renowned for impressive service and excellent cooking. The menu, a mix of classical and modern Irish cuisine, prominently features local fillet of beef and pan-fried sea bass. The charming hosts create a warm atmosphere.

BALLYVAUGHAN Monks   €€
Ballyvaghan, Co Clare **Tel** *065 90 51977*   **Road Map** *B4*

This well regarded pub-restaurant is widely known for its seafood chowder and fishcakes with salad. The mussels steamed in garlic, crab claws and seafood platter are also a sheer delight, especially taken outdoors in the summer sunshine.

BIRDHILL Matt the Thresher Pub & Restaurant   €€
Birdhill, Co Tipperary **Tel** *061 379 227*   **Road Map** *C4*

This traditional country pub, on the main Dublin-Limerick road, is a frequent stopping-off point for travellers. Food is served through the day into the evening. Fresh scampi, chicken and mushroom pie, fillet steaks and monkfish goujons are a good step up from regular bar food.

BUNRATTY Durty Nelly's   €€
Bunratty, Co Clare **Tel** *061 364861*   **Road Map** *B4*

Beside Bunratty Castle, this long-standing pub is always busy and often over-crowded with tourists during the summer. Nevertheless, it retains some character with its traditional decor. The bar serves informal food all day, while the Oyster Restaurant offers lunch and dinner. The Loft Restaurant upstairs serves evening meals.

CAHIR Cahir House Hotel   €€€
Cahir House Hotel, The Square, Co Tipperary **Tel** *052 42727*   **Road Map** *C5*

Cahir House Hotel is a hub of social and economic activity in the area. The Butler's Pantry, a cheerfully decorated restaurant, specializes in traditional Irish cooking, using fresh local produce. The sirloin steak and baked fillet of salmon are particularly good. Open for dinner.

CAHIR Gannon's above the Bell   €€€
Pearse St, Co Tipperary **Tel** *052 45911*   **Road Map** *C5*

Regarded as the best restaurant in town, this split-level dining room has plenty of character, evident in its exposed stone walls and white linen tablecloths. The cooking is imaginative modern and Irish, and meat is sourced from nearby Ballybrado organic farm. Excellent freshly baked breads. Informal bar food is available downstairs.

CARRON Burren Perfumery Tea Rooms   €
Carron, Co Clare **Tel** *065 708 9102*   **Road Map** *B4*

Ireland's first perfumery, set up over 30 years ago, is a family-run enterprise with an organic herb garden, distillation room and shop. The simple and pretty tearooms offer excellent home-made soups, quiches, sandwiches. Fresh juices as well as traditional home-baked cakes and scones are also available. Open Easter to October.

CASHEL Café Hans   €€
Moore Lane, Co Tipperary **Tel** *062 63660*   **Road Map** *C5*

A sister of the celebrated Chez Hans restaurant, this tiny contemporary café is one of the best in the county. For those travelling from Dublin to Cork, it provides an ideal break point on a road with a dearth of good eateries. Choose from a variety of delicious salads, open sandwiches, hot dishes and celebrated home-made French fries.

CASHEL Chez Hans Restaurant   €€€€
Moore Lane, Co Tipperary **Tel** *062 61177*   **Road Map** *C5*

Since 1968, patrons have been travelling from all over the county to savour the excellent cooking here. Housed in a converted church, it has become a veritable temple for food-lovers. Dishes showcase succulent Tipperary beef and lamb. Sole on the bone is particularly good. The early-bird dinner is good value. Reservations advised.

CLONMEL Angela's Restaurant   €€

14 Abbey St, Co Tipperary **Tel** *052 26899*   **Road Map** *C5*

This centrally located daytime restaurant is ideal for tasty and wholesome food. Baking is a speciality. Home-made desserts include plum tart and bread-and-butter pudding. Sample the delicious quiches, grilled bruschetta, or heart-warming casseroles. Vegetarians are well catered for. Service is efficient and friendly.

CLONMEL Clifford's Restaurant   €€€

29 Thomas St, Co Tipperary **Tel** *052 70677*   **Road Map** *C5*

Housed in a well-preserved stone building, this is probably the best restaurant in town. Tastefully decorated, with fine art and awards lining the walls. Family-grown organic produce and carefully sourced meats. Gâteau of Clonakilty black pudding, meat casseroles and fish dishes are on the menu. Marvellous desserts and cheeses.

CROOM Croom Mills   €

Croom, Co Limerick **Tel** *061 397130*   **Road Map** *B4*

This sensitively restored stone mill house comprises a craft shop, pub and bistro. Overlooking a giant cast-iron millwheel, the bistro is open for lunch and serves traditional Irish fare. Daily roasts are on the menu. Chicken in mustard sauce is a speciality.

DOOLIN Cullinan's Seafood Restaurant and Guest House   €€€

Doolin, Co Clare **Tel** *065 707 4183*   **Road Map** *B4*

Overlooking the River Aille, this cheerfully decorated and popular restaurant specializes in locally caught seafood and is reasonably priced. Mains include pan-seared scallops, roast loin of Burren lamb, pan-fried John Dory and Doolin crabmeat. Lovely desserts include cardamon brulée. Friendly and efficient team.

ENNIS Town Hall Café   €€€

O'Connell St, Co Clare **Tel** *065 682 8127*   **Road Map** *B4*

Situated in the well-restored town hall, adjacent to the Old Ground Hotel, this elegant café offers informal, bistro-style cooking. Open for lunch and dinner, it serves fillet of beef with grain mustard, sea bass with couscous and roast rack of lamb. Desserts include Bailey's parfait and hazelnut brownies. Service is efficient.

KILLALOE Cherry Tree Restaurant   €€€

Lakeside, Ballina, Co Clare **Tel** *061 375688*   **Road Map** *C4*

This delightful waterside purpose-built restaurant, with an impressive and colourful interior, has a reputation for outstanding contemporary cooking. One of the best in the region, it uses carefully sourced local ingredients. Specialities include wild sea bass with lobster tortellini and butter roasted fillet of beef. Desserts are luscious.

LAHINCH Barrtra Seafood Restaurant   €€€

Lahinch, Co Clare **Tel** *065 708 1280*   **Road Map** *B4*

A few miles south of Lahinch, this whitewashed house overlooking Liscannor Bay boasts a superb and long-established award-winning restaurant. It is decorated in a simple cottage style, with lovely sea views from the window tables. Food is of a consistently good standard. Try the delicious lobster. Wonderful hospitality.

LIMERICK Copper and Spice   €€

2 Cornmarket Row, Co Limerick **Tel** *061 338791*   **Road Map** *B4*

The stylish Copper and Spice is decorated in a bright contemporary style and offers an interesting and extensive menu, featuring Indian and Thai cuisine, with the former being more authentic. Combination platters are popular, with an opportunity to taste meat samosa, dim sum and chicken satay. Vegetarians are well catered for.

LIMERICK Green Onion Restaurant   €€

Old Town Hall, Rutland Street, Co Limerick **Tel** *061 400710* **Road Map** *B4*

This lively split-level eatery is contemporary and eclectic in style, with bistro style table settings and friendly, competent staff. The good-value menu offers sandwiches made to order, salads, soups and some pasta dishes. Specialities include baked goat's cheese with walnut topping, chargrilled lamb noisette and tasty desserts.

LIMERICK Brûlées Restaurant   €€€

Corner of Henry St & Mallow St, Co Limerick **Tel** *061 319931* **Road Map** *B4*

Though the exterior is somewhat unremarkable, this intimate restaurant is tastefully furnished inside. Imaginative menu, using locally sourced ingredients, including fresh seafood. Freshly baked bread and home-made desserts are also worth trying. Lunch menus are particularly good value. Friendly and efficient service.

NEWMARKET-ON-FERGUS Earl of Thomond Restaurant   €€€€€

Dromoland Castle, Co Clare **Tel** *061 368144*   **Road Map** *B4*

Excellent for fine dining, this elegant room is opulently decorated with rich fabrics and chandeliers and enjoys views over the nearby lake. A traditional Irish harpist accompanies evening meals, which are either six courses or à la carte. Try the pan-fried fillet of sea-bass with mussel risotto. Full lunch is available on Sundays.

TERRYGLASS The Derg Inn   €€€

Terryglass, Co Tipperary **Tel** *067 22037*   **Road Map** *C4*

A short stroll from the harbour, this superb gastro-pub is a favourite among boating enthusiasts and locals. The menu offers traditional Irish fare such as beef and Guinness pie, home-made patés and Tipperary rack of lamb. Try the succulent fresh fish, caught on nearby Lough Derg. In summer, enjoy live music on weekends.

Key to Price Guide *see p 324* **Key to Symbols** *see back cover flap*

THE WEST OF IRELAND

ACHILL ISLAND The Beehive Coffee & Craft Shop
Keel, Co Mayo **Tel** *098 43018*   **Road Map** *A3*

Overlooking Keel Beach, this informal, self-service daytime restaurant and craft shop offers high-quality home-made food such as heart-warming soups, seafood chowder and home-baked brown scones. Sandwiches, farmhouse cheese plate, as well as a lovely selection of traditional cakes, tea-bracks and fruit tarts, are also made in-house.

ACHILL ISLAND Ferndale Restaurant & Guest Accommodation
Crumpaun, Keel, Co Mayo **Tel** *098 43908*   **Road Map** *A3*

Ferndale Restaurant and Guest Accommodation enjoys a lovely location on an elevated site above the village. The restaurant commands sweeping views of the sea and island. The menu exhibits a range of international influences, from the Mongolian barbecue to more traditional dishes.

BALLINA Gaughan's
O'Rahilly St, Co Mayo **Tel** *096 70096*   **Road Map** *B2*

In the same family since 1936, this immaculately maintained traditional pub has a charming character and an old-world feel. Old-fashioned cooking includes hot roasts, such as baked ham and roast chicken, as well as fish pies, meat loaves, wild salmon and fresh crab meat. Lighter snacks available include open sandwiches and soups.

BALLYCASTLE Mary's Cottage Kitchen
Main St, Co Mayo **Tel** *096 43361*   **Road Map** *B2*

In the centre of the village, this charming restaurant offers domestic cooking in a warm atmosphere, with an open fire. On the menu are home-made soups, sandwiches and fresh salads as well as a selection of hot dishes. Try the delicious quiches, particularly the traditional bacon and cheese flavour. Good home-baked bread and desserts.

BARNA O'Grady's on the Pier
Seapoint, Barna, Co Galway **Tel** *091 592223*   **Road Map** *B4*

Commanding wonderful views across the sea to the distant mountains, O'Grady's is renowned for simply prepared, high-quality seafood. Tastefully blending the contemporary with charming traditional features of the house, it enjoys a cosy atmosphere. The superb seafood platter is immensely popular.

CLEGGAN Oliver's Bar
Cleggan, Co Galway **Tel** *095 44640*   **Road Map** *A3*

Situated overlooking the working pier and the harbour where boats leave for Inishbofin, Oliver's Bar is very popular with locals and island day-trippers for its ultra-fresh seafood – served all day and into the evening. The menu offers squid, wild smoked salmon, chowder, open crab-meat sandwiches, oysters, steaks, as well as the day's catch.

CLIFDEN Ardagh Hotel & Restaurant
Ballyconneely Rd, Co Galway **Tel** *095 21384*   **Road Map** *A3*

This award-winning restaurant, situated on the first floor of the hotel, has lovely views of the sea, particularly at sunset. The modern dining room is pleasantly furnished and welcoming, with linen tablecloths, candles, fresh flowers and an open fire. On the menu are lobsters from the on-site sea tank, locally caught seafood and prime meats.

CLIFDEN Mitchell's Restaurant
Market St, Co Galway **Tel** *095 21867*   **Road Map** *A3*

The delightful family-run Mitchell's Restaurant offers consistently good food in a very warm and friendly atmosphere. Exposed stone walls and a fireplace give it a lovely, welcoming character. Keenly priced menus offer tasty home cooking, such as seafood chowder, excellent crab-meat salad, home-made brown bread and Irish stew.

CONG The Connaught Room
Ashford Castle, Co Mayo **Tel** *094 954 6003*   **Road Map** *B3*

One of Ireland's most beautiful dining rooms, with woodcarvings and magnificent fireplaces, the Connaught Room serves excellent classic French cuisine with an Irish twist, such as Cleggan lobster and Connemara lamb. Exquisite desserts include hot lemon soufflé. The surprise seven-course tasting menu is a real treat. Open May to September.

GALWAY Goya's Coffee Shop
2–3 Kirwan's Lane, Co Galway **Tel** *091 567010*   **Road Map** *B4*

This contemporary corner café and bakery is open during the day and is a lively spot. Elegantly decorated, it offers home-made soups, pâtés, salads, toasted sandwiches, as well as hot speciality dishes such as chicken, leek and mushroom pie. It is known for its wonderful home baking. Don't miss the traditional porter cake.

GALWAY McDonagh's Seafood Bar
22 Quay St, Co Galway **Tel** *091 565001*   **Road Map** *B4*

This renowned Galway institution is a must for anyone seeking delicious high-quality traditional fish and chips and super-fresh seafood. Situated on the most lively and atmospheric streets of the city, it comprises a takeaway section with wooden benches and tables on one side and an intimate and colourful restaurant on the other.

GALWAY Kirwan's Lane Restaurant 🚶 🚻 €€€
Kirwan's Lane, Co Galway **Tel** *091 568266* **Road Map** *B4*

Located in an appealing stone building, the restaurant is contemporary in decor and cuisine. The tasteful furnishings exude a warm and friendly ambience. Menus display clear Asian influences and offer bistro-style dishes. The Oriental crispy duck salad is a popular favourite, as are the seared scallops.

GALWAY The Park Room Restaurant 🚶 ♿ €€€
Park House Hotel, Co Galway **Tel** *091 564924* **Road Map** *B4*

Located within the pleasant Park House hotel, this restaurant offers Irish and international cuisine of a very good standard. Linen-clad tablecloths and fresh flowers create a relaxed, welcoming atmosphere. Sample dishes include pan-fried fillet of John Dory and ostrich fillet with garlic potato grilled shallot. Just off Eyre Square.

GALWAY Homeplate 🗐 €
Mary St, Co Galway **Tel** *091 561475* **Road Map** *B4*

Homeplate boasts one of the best breakfasts in town. The cramped interior somehow lends itself to the relaxed ambiance and the fried potatoes are just the job the morning after a long night out in Ireland's party town.

INISHMORE Aran Fisherman Restaurant 🚶 🎵 🚻 €€
Kilronan, Co Galway **Tel** *099 61104* **Road Map** *B4*

In the heart of Kilronan village, the family-run Aran Fisherman Restaurant is a short walk from the pier. It specializes in locally caught seafood, organic vegetables, meat and poultry dishes and home baking. There's also a children's menu. Enjoy traditional Irish music and the song and dance show during the summer months. Very warm hospitality.

INISHMORE Dun Aonghasa 🚶 ♿ 🚻 €€€
Kilronan, Co Galway **Tel** *099 61104* **Road Map** *B4*

Set high above Kileaney Bay, Dun Aonghasa is a new restaurant with an impeccable interior. The food served here is imaginatively prepared, using traditional island recipes. Besides fish, the menu also includes meat and poultry creations. The spectacular view of the bay is an add-on.

KILCOLGAN Moran's Oyster Cottage 🚶 ♿ 🚻 €€€
The Weir, Kilcolgan, near Clarinbridge, Co Galway **Tel** *091 796113* **Road Map** *B4*

Now in the seventh generation of the Moran family, this seafood restaurant specializes in oysters. The original picturesque thatched cottage, with a simple decor, has been extended to accommodate a larger clientele. Menu features crab, lobster, dressed prawns, wild smoked salmon, garlic crab claws and mussels.

KINVARRA The Pier Head Bar & Restaurant 🚶 🚻 €€
The Quay, Co Galway **Tel** *091 638188* **Road Map** *B4*

Located in the harbour of this scenic fishing village, The Pier looks out over Kinvara Bay and Dunguaire Castle. It is the best restaurant in the area where seafood is the main attraction. Warm colours exude a friendly atmosphere. Lobster is a speciality and so is prime fillet steak. Live music is often played here.

LEENANE Blackberry Café 🚶 €€
Leenane, Co Galway **Tel** *095 42240* **Road Map** *B3*

Situated at Killary Harbour, this charming little café and restaurant offers lovely home cooking during the summer months from noon until 9pm. Home-made soups, sandwiches, panini, fresh oysters, smoked salmon, traditional Irish stew, seafood salads. Finish with a delicious dessert such as the rhubarb tart.

LETTERFRACK Kylemore Abbey Restaurant 🚶 ♿ 🚻 €€
Kylemore, Co Galway **Tel** *095 41455* **Road Map** *A3*

This self-service restaurant is set in the grounds of Kylemore Abbey, which enjoy a stunning mountainside setting, overlooking a peaceful lake. The industrious Benedictine nuns run a girls' boarding school, garden, craft shop as well as this popular self-service eatery. Good wholesome cooking includes soups, sandwiches, casseroles and quiches.

LETTERFRACK Pangur Bán Restaurant 🚶 ♿ €€€
Letterfrack, Co Galway **Tel** *095 41243* **Road Map** *A3*

The elegant Pangur Bán is housed in a beautifully restored 300-year-old stone cottage. Good home cooking with influences from the Orient make for an interesting and imaginative menu. Try the char-grilled breast of chicken with black pudding on garlic and *wasabi* mash with tomato *jus*. Advanced booking advised.

MOYCULLEN Moycullen House ♿ 🎵 €€€
Moycullen, Co Galway **Tel** *091 555566* **Road Map** *B4*

Only 10 minutes from Galway city, this 1890s house overlooks Lough Corrib. The restaurant is simply furnished with dark-wood tables and exposed stone walls. Specialities include pan-fried venison with caramelized onions in a light *jus*; vegetarian tartlet with smoked cheese and sweet pepper sauce. Warm hospitality and good service.

OUGHTERARD The Yew Tree 🗐 🚶 €
Main St, Oughterard, Co Galway **Tel** *091 866986* **Road Map** *B3*

Delicious home-baked treats are the hallmark of this wonderful bakery and small restaurant, in the heart of the village. Open gourmet sandwiches, soups, quiches, wraps are available. Superb breads include Norwegian rye, Swiss, Irish soda and *focaccia*. Try the lemon sponge cake, chocolate muffins and ginger cake. A great stopping-off point.

Key to Price Guide *see p324* **Key to Symbols** *see back cover flap*

PORTUMNA Castlegates Restaurant
Shannon Oaks Hotel, Co Galway **Tel** *090 974 1777*   **Road Map** *C4*

The bright Castlegates Restaurant serves evening meals in its warmly coloured dining hall. Its menu comprises classic and fusion dishes using finest local produce, fish and meats. The bar serves a carvery lunch and informal food during the day. In summer, the nearby River Shannon keeps the place pleasantly breezy.

ROSCOMMON Gleeson's Restaurant & Townhouse
Market Sq, Co Roscommon **Tel** *090 662 6954*   **Road Map** *C3*

This well-restored 19th-century house overlooks the historic town square. The café and restaurant offer delicious home cooking in a warm and welcoming atmosphere. Try the roast cod with Welsh rarebit topping on a bed of tomato and basil served with *sauce vierge* or a succulent steak.

ROUNDSTONE O'Dowd's Seafood Bar & Restaurant
Roundstone, Co Galway **Tel** *095 35923*   **Road Map** *A3*

In business since 1906, O'Dowd's has a warm and welcoming atmosphere, with its wood panelled walls and open fires. Bar food is served until 9:30pm. The slightly more formal restaurant is traditionally furnished and serves good seafood – chowder, fresh oysters, hot buttered lobster, mussels, home-made chicken and mushroom pie.

WESTPORT McCormack's at The Andrew Stone Gallery
Bridge St, Co Mayo **Tel** *098 25619*   **Road Map** *B3*

McCormack's butcher shop has been in operation since 1847 and is now in the sixth generation of the family. Upstairs lies this daytime, simply decorated restaurant. Family recipes are used for the home-made dishes such as seafood chowder, savoury tarts and meat casseroles. Sample the mouthwatering home-baked desserts.

WESTPORT The Lemon Peel
The Octagon, Co Mayo **Tel** *098 26929*   **Road Map** *B3*

This lively, modern bistro-style restaurant serves popular contemporary dishes. The no-frills decor creates a warm atmosphere, complemented by a pleasant staff. Start with baked crab, Cajun blackened shrimp or Caesar salad. Follow with traditional roast duck in Grand Marnier. Great desserts. The early-bird menu is very good value.

NORTHWEST IRELAND

ANNAGRY Danny Minnie's Restaurant
Teach Killindarragh, Co Donegal **Tel** *074 954 8201*   **Road Map** *C1*

A romantic candlelit dinner can be had in this elegant restaurant, housed in a luxurious family-owned B&B in the heart of the Gaelic-speaking Gaeltacht. Danny Minnie's is beautifully decorated with hanging prints, tapestries and paintings, and there are two fireplaces. Seafood and Irish meats figure heavily on the menu.

BALLYSHANNON Smuggler's Creek
Rosnowlagh, Co Donegal **Tel** *071 985 2366*   **Road Map** *C2*

Situated on a clifftop overlooking Rosnowlagh Beach, Smuggler's Creek is a prestigious seafood restaurant. The maritime theme is also reflected in the decor. The fresh oyster and lobster dishes are particularly tempting.

CARRICK-ON-SHANNON Oarsman Bar & Boathouse Restaurant
Bridge St, Co Leitrim **Tel** *071 962 1733*   **Road Map** *C3*

This attractive pub is owned by Conor and Ronan Maher, who are the seventh generation of their family in the hospitality industry. The brothers' legacy is reflected in the bar's easy-going ambience and the restaurant's superb food, prepared by a strong kitchen staff led by head chef Shaun Hanna.

CASTLEBALDWIN Cromleach Lodge Country House
Castlebaldwin, Co Sligo **Tel** *071 916 5155*   **Road Map** *C3*

Fabulous views of Lough Arrow and the Bricklieve Mountains form a backdrop for gourmet dining in this hilltop country house. Moira Tighe is an innovative chef who carefully sources local ingredients. Specialities include loin of rabbit in crisp *pancetta* (cured Italian bacon) on vanilla risotto.

DUNKINEELY Castle Murray House
St John's Point, Co Donegal **Tel** *074 973 7022*   **Road Map** *C2*

With wonderful views across the bay and spectacular surroundings, this relaxed restaurant makes a perfect setting for enjoying classic French dishes. The house speciality is prawns and monkfish in garlic butter, but the menu is seasonal with more of an emphasis on red meats in winter.

GLENTIES Highlands Hotel
Main St, Co Donegal **Tel** *074 955 1111*   **Road Map** *C1*

Considered by many to be the centre of town life, this upbeat restaurant and bar has great steak. Other attractions include vegetarian curry and stir-fry. Local seafood is also available. The gigantic lunches are great value. The friendly staff extend great hospitality. There's also a small gallery here.

GREENCASTLE Kealy's Seafood Bar

The Harbour, Co Donegal **Tel** *074 938 1010*   **Road Map** *C1*

Right by the harbour, Kealy's uses fresh seafood and organic farm produce to create its award-winning cuisine. House specialities include baked Atlantic salmon with a wholegrain mustard crust and baked fillet of hake on braised fennel with a tomato and saffron buttered sauce. All dishes are healthy, yet delicious.

INISHOWEN PENINSULA Nancy's

Malin Head, Co Donegal **Tel** *074 954 1187*   **Road Map** *C1*

Owned by the seventh generation of the same family, Nancy's is well-known for its good-value bar meals and snacks that are simple, yet very satisfying. Star attractions include the chowder as well as Charlie's Supper – prawns and smoked salmon warmed in garlic and chilli sauce. The atmosphere is exhilarating.

KILCAR Teach Barnai

Main St, Co Donegal **Tel** *074 973 8160*   **Road Map** *B2*

Exuding a rustic feel, with old furniture and antiques, this family-run restaurant offers gourmet cuisine at affordable prices. Though the menu shows a French influence, dishes such as the *colcannon* (potatoes and cabbage, boiled and mashed together) are typically Irish. There's a wide range of local seafood and a very popular Sunday lunch.

KINCASSLAGH Iggy's Bar

Kincasslagh, Co Donegal **Tel** *074 954 3112*   **Road Map** *C2*

Also known as the Atlantic Bar, this great little pub is a popular haunt for locals and visitors alike. Ann and Iggy Murray serve simple pub food with the emphasis on seafood. The sandwiches and soups are particularly appetizing. The crab sandwich goes very well with a pint of their excellent Guinness.

LETTERKENNY Yellow Pepper

Lower Main St, Co Donegal **Tel** *074 912 4133*   **Road Map** *C1*

Enjoying a central location, Yellow Pepper is housed in a Victorian shirt factory dominated by a cast-iron beam that runs through the converted dining room. The menu offers a wide selection of modern Irish dishes. The fish specialities are certainly worth considering. The carefully chosen wine list is equally extensive.

LETTERKENNY Castle Grove Country House Hotel

Ballymaleel, Co Donegal **Tel** *074 915 1118*   **Road Map** *C1*

This recent addition to the Castle Grove group is in keeping with the style of the rest of the house. Head chef Joe Cannon combines ingredients from the hotel garden with Gallic flair to create beautiful dishes. A particular favourite is pan-fried fillet of beef with grilled horseradish polenta and caramelized chicory.

RATHMULLAN Weeping Elm

Rathmullan Country House, Co Donegal **Tel** *074 915 8188*   **Road Map** *C1*

Liam McCormick, known for his imaginative Donegal churches, designed the tented ceiling of this lovely gourmet restaurant. Sample the unusual seaweed-based dessert of carrageen moss with stewed fruits. Yogurt and carrageen pudding is also on offer at the excellent buffet-style breakfasts.

ROSSES POINT The Austies

Rosses Point Rd, Co Donegal **Tel** *071 917 7111*   **Road Map** *B2*

A 200-year-old pub high above Sligo Bay, The Austies offers fresh seafood dishes such as crab au gratin, garlic mussels and seafood chowder. The menu is not restricted to the sea, however, and there are steaks and home-made burgers available to those who prefer meat.

ROSSES POINT Waterfront Bar and Restaurant

Rosses Point, Co Sligo **Tel** *071 917 7122*   **Road Map** *B2*

The brightly coloured pub exterior belies the quality of the cuisine in this excellent restaurant. Chef Alan FitzMaurice offers simple delicious bar food alongside an innovative à la carte menu, featuring slow roast duck, fresh lobster and king scallops. There's also a wide selection of wines and Irish cheeses as well as a pizza menu.

SLIGO Atrium Restaurant

The Niland Model Arts Centre, The Mall, Co Sligo **Tel** *071 914 1418*   **Road Map** *C2*

An award-winning gourmet café housed in Sligo's Model Arts Centre, Atrium Restaurant is bright and modern in design, with chairs spilling out into the gallery's atrium. Tasty light foods, such as sandwiches, omelettes and soups, are skilfully prepared by expert hands. Try the lovely compote.

SLIGO Garavogue

Rear 15–16 Stephen's St, Co Sligo **Tel** *071 914 0100*   **Road Map** *C2*

Drawing mainly a young clientele, the excitingly designed Garavogue is named after the river flowing past it. It's certainly impressive with tall windows, an old mill wheel and a riverside terrace. Dishes include Thai and Spanish specialities, with bar food portions downstairs and a full menu available in the restaurant.

SLIGO Yeats Tavern Restaurant

Drumcliff Bridge, Co Sligo **Tel** *071 916 3117*   **Road Map** *C2*

With the refurbishment of its interior, Yeats Tavern Restaurant has evolved into an award-winning bar and eaterie. It is a popular stop-off point for locals and tourists in the Northwest. The menu features traditional and international dishes, including irresistible garlic mussels and sweet chilli prawns.

Key to Price Guide *see p 324* **Key to Symbols** *see back cover flap*

TOBERCURRY Killoran's Traditional Restaurant   🅗🅐🎵�   €€€
Teeling St, Co Sligo **Tel** *071 918 5679*   **Road Map** *B3*

As the name suggests, this restaurant is ideal for authentic Irish fare. Boxty (potato pancakes), crubeens (pig's trotters) and Irish stew are on the menu on Irish music nights in July and August. There's also fresh salmon caught from the River Moy. Snacks and full meals are served all day. A great place for traditional music and food.

THE MIDLANDS

ATHLONE The Left Bank Bistro   🅗🅐🎵�   €€€
Fry Place, Co Westmeath **Tel** *090 649 4446*   **Road Map** *C3*

Situated in the heart of Old Athlone, this stylishly designed restaurant is the essence of soulful minimalism. Creative and delicious food is served in a relaxed, informal atmosphere. Lunches feature soup, chicken fajitas, vegetable tartlets and *focaccia* sandwiches. Extensive dinner menu includes steaks and seafood.

BETTYSTOWN Bacchus at the Coastguard   🅗�   €€€
Bayview, Co Meath **Tel** *041 982 8251*   **Road Map** *D3*

A beachside restaurant overlooking Bettystown Bay, the Bacchus is one of the most popular in the area and has a pleasing ambience. The well-balanced menu features a number of seafood dishes as well as Duleek lamb with rosemary and redcurrant sauce. Don't miss the delicious desserts. The early-dinner menu is very good value.

BIRR The Thatch Bar & Restaurant   🅗🎵�   €€€
Crinkill, Co Offaly **Tel** *0509 20682*   **Road Map** *C4*

This beautiful traditional thatched pub, with whitewashed walls, cobblestones and fresh flowers, is situated just outside the town. In the same family for the last 200 years, it offers genuine, warm hospitality and good, imaginative food. Try the delicious roast pheasant with fresh herbs and fruit stuffing.

BLACKLION MacNean House & Bistro   🅗🅐   €€€€
Main St, Co Cavan **Tel** *071 985 3404*   **Road Map** *D2*

Neven Maguire, one of Ireland's leading chefs, has drawn huge national attention with his excellent cooking. His family-run guesthouse has earned him numerous awards. Local artisan produce features in well-balanced and imaginative menus. Sea scallops with crab and saffron risotto is a winning recipe. The game dishes are excellent.

CARLINGFORD Georgina's Bakehouse Tearooms   🍽🅗�   €
Castle Hill, Co Louth **Tel** *042 937 3346*   **Road Map** *D3*

Georgina's intimate little tearooms are tucked away, somewhat difficult to find, but worth discovering. There is a genuine friendliness about the place. Elegantly decorated in a modern style, it serves wholesome soups, sandwiches and salads. Desserts feature home-baked cakes, tarts and biscuits.

CARLINGFORD Kingfisher Bistro   🅐�   €€€
Darcy McGee Court, Dundalk St, Co Louth **Tel** *042 937 3716*   **Road Map** *D3*

This cosy little restaurant at the heritage centre is perhaps the best in the area. It offers reliably good food at reasonable prices. Set in a stone building, with warmly coloured walls, it offers Continental cuisine with an occasional Southeast Asian flavour. Tasty steaks and fish dishes. Vegetarians are well catered for.

CARRICKMACROSS Nuremore Hotel & Country Club   🅗🅐🎵�   €€
Carrickmacross, Co Monaghan **Tel** *042 966 1438*   **Road Map** *D3*

The restaurant at the scenic Nuremore Hotel is regarded as one of the best in the area. Elegantly furnished, it boasts an immensely talented chef who is attracting patrons from around the country. Try the signature *tian* of crab and Annagassan lobster, with fine cucumber, caviar and sauce gazpacho. Worth a detour.

COLLON Forge Gallery Restaurant   🅗🅐�   €€€
Collon, Co Louth **Tel** *041 982 6272* **Fax** *041 9826584*   **Road Map** *D3*

The leading restaurant in the area, this is an immaculately-maintained place of great character. In operation for over two decades, it is adept at combining French and Irish cooking to good effect. Local seafood and game feature prominently on the seasonal menus.

DUNDALK Quaglino's   🅗   €€€
The Century Bar, 19 Roden Place, Co Louth **Tel** *042 933 8567*   **Road Map** *D3*

Housed on the first floor of an attractive listed building dating to 1902, the award-winning Quaglino's offers high-quality meals. Baked Carlingford oysters in an herb and garlic butter is a house speciality. The Century Bar has great character and retains many of its period and historic features. There's a good early dinner menu.

KELLS The Vanilla Pod   🅗🅐🎵   €€€
Headfort Arms Hotel, Co Meath **Tel** *046 924 0084*   **Road Map** *D3*

Part of the hotel, this hip bistro-style restaurant is contemporary in design, with oak tables, dim lighting and stylish table settings. The food is modern, with a variety of global influences. Try the grilled goat's cheese *crostini* (thin slices of toasted bread) with plum chutney, followed by black sole with prawns and garlic. The chocolate fondue is a treat.

KINNEGAD The Cottage Restaurant
Kinnegad, Co Westmeath **Tel** *044 75284*   €€
Road Map *D3*

This small, traditional restaurant is a popular stop-off point for those travelling to and from the West. Savour comfort food in a cosy atmosphere. Tasty soups, salads, sandwiches and hot dishes, such as home-made omelettes and quiches, are on the menu. Home-baked delicacies include lovely cakes, biscuits and scones. Open weekdays only.

LONGFORD Aubergine Gallery Café
The White House, 17 Ballymahon St, Co Longford **Tel** *043 48633*   €€
Road Map *C3*

This bright and stylish first-floor restaurant, with interesting artwork, serves international fare with a Mediterranean and modern Irish slant. Succulent steaks, good seafood, poultry and tasty vegetarian dishes are served, all at a reasonable price. Try the sirloin steak with whiskey and pepper cream.

MONAGHAN Andy's Restaurant
12 Market St, Co Monaghan **Tel** *047 82277*   €€
Road Map *D2*

The immaculately maintained, family-run Andy's Restaurant is located in the heart of town and has been the recipient of many awards. The cheerful old-fashioned atmosphere draws a regular clientele. Quality ingredients are used in its good cooking. Informal food is available downstairs in the lovely traditionally-styled bar.

MULLINGAR Ilia A Coffee Experience
28 Oliver Plunkett St, Co Westmeath **Tel** *044 40300*   €
Road Map *C3*

Vibrant and colourful, this contemporary café and daytime restaurant is immensely popular for its wholesome and freshly prepared food. Delicious breakfasts, soups, bruschetta, panini and salads are served during the day. There's also a wide variety of fresh juices, smoothies, lovely pastries and other desserts to choose from.

MULLINGAR The Belfry Restaurant
Ballinagall, Co Westmeath **Tel** *044 42488*   €€€€
Road Map *C3*

Formerly a church, now a wonderfully designed restaurant, the Belfry is tastefully furnished, well-lit and has a welcoming atmosphere. The expertly cooked and appealingly presented food is a blend of modern Irish and traditional French cuisine. Open from Wednesday to Sunday.

NAVAN Ryan's Bar
22 Trimgate St, Co Meath **Tel** *046 902 1154*   €
Road Map *D3*

Cosy and impeccably run, Ryan's Bar enjoys a central location and an enviable popularity. The reasonably priced bar food is above average. Modern snacks are served at lunch time: soups, delicious seafood chowder, open prawn and salmon sandwiches, wraps, panini, toasted sandwiches, daily specials and tasty desserts.

PORTLAOISE The Kitchen & Foodhall
Hynds Sq, Co Laois **Tel** *0502 62061*   €
Road Map *C4*

This delightful self-service bistro and delicatessen is a landmark establishment in the centre of town. With its open fire and relaxed atmosphere, it has earned a reputation for delicious home cooking. Terrines, quiches, home-baked breads, freshly prepared salads, wholesome hot dishes and wonderful desserts are on the menu. Open daytime only.

SLANE Franzini O'Brien's
French's Lane, Co Meath **Tel** *046 943 1002*   €€€
Road Map *D3*

Set in a lovely location, overlooking Trim Castle, this smart and spacious eaterie is well designed with easy parking. It offers well-informed, friendly service and international cuisine at affordable prices. The atmosphere is informal and lively. Menu features delicious fajitas and soups. There's a very good wine list. Open evenings only.

NORTHERN IRELAND

ARDGLASS Aldo's
7 Castle Place, Ardglass, Downpatrick, Co Down BT30 7TP **Tel** *028 4484 1315*   €€€
Road Map *E2*

This Italian restaurant has been owned and managed by the Vinaccia family for over two decades. The service is very good and friendly, with a menu of antipasti, pasta, fresh fish and meats. Vegetarians are well catered for and, with prior notice, an extensive selection can be provided. Open for Sunday lunch and dinner.

ARMAGH Pilgrim's Table
38–40 English St, Co Armagh BT61 7LJ **Tel** *028 3752 1814*   €€
Road Map *D2*

Expect fine home cooking with fresh local produce at Pilgrim's Table. The self-service menu offers a wide variety of salads, casseroles, sandwiches and delicious pastries. Unfussy dishes, especially the soups, are tasty, filling and of superb value. Though the restaurant doesn't serve wine, it's a great choice for a hearty meal.

ARMAGH The Famous Grouse Country Inn
16 Ballyhagan Road, Loughgall, Co Armagh BT61 8PX **Tel** *028 3889 1778*   €€
Road Map *D2*

This meat-eater's paradise is housed in a recently refurbished building. The combination of quality local produce and good cooking produces tasty steaks, king prawns and Oriental kebabs. The menu is very reasonably priced and the quiet country setting is an add-on.

Key to Symbols *see back cover flap*

BALLYCASTLE Wysner's Restaurant

16 Anne St, Co Antrim, BT54 6AD **Tel** *028 2076 2372*   **Road Map** *D1*

Downstairs at Wysner's is an elegant French-style café, while upstairs is a small family-run restaurant. The Bushmills Malt cheesecake is a must. Adventurous savoury combinations, such as seared scallops with guacamole and chilli, are also available alongside more traditional fare such as champ with onion gravy.

BANGOR Seasalt

51 Central Promenade, Newcastle, Co Down, BT33 0AA **Tel** *028 4372 5027*   **Road Map** *D2*

Situated on a seafront terrace facing the water, Seasalt has a stunning range of dishes. Unsurprisingly, the local shellfish is top-notch, especially the Ardglass crab and Dundrum Bay mussels. The views are great and there's a casual, friendly atmosphere here. The restaurant is not licensed to sell alcohol, but allows you to bring your own.

BELFAST Belfast Castle Restaurant

Antrim Rd, Belfast, Co Antrim BT15 5GR **Tel** *028 9077 6925*   **Road Map** *D2*

With a strikingly romantic setting, Belfast Castle Restaurant offers one of the best views in Belfast. The decor is in keeping with the grandeur of the castle's design. The star attractions include peppered fillet of venison and cured salmon. Open for lunch and dinner everyday except Sunday.

BELFAST Café Paul Rankin

27–29 Fountain St, Co Antrim, BT1 6ET **Tel** *028 9031 5090*   **Road Map** *D2*

Part of a chain conceived by Northern Ireland's food saviour, Paul Rankin, this neighbourhood café has a Continental style tempered by a delightful selection of home-made goodies, including a wide choice of breads, soups and chutneys. This is an excellent, good value alternative to Rankin's other creation, Cayenne *(see p344).*

BELFAST Crown Liquor Saloon

46 Great Victoria St, Belfast, Co Antrim BT2 7BA **Tel** *028 9027 9901*   **Road Map** *D2*

Crown Liquor Saloon is a real Belfast landmark with swing doors and a Wild West feel. The bar's snug-like booths include table space for a bowl of Irish stew and champ – a local speciality of potatoes, spring onions and butter. It's well worth a visit if only for a pint and a look around at the fascinating Victoriana.

BELFAST Duke of York

11 Commercial Court, Co Antrim, BT1 2NB **Tel** *028 9024 1062*   **Road Map** *D2*

In a long narrow bar, this very reasonably priced restaurant offers typical pub grub. Near St Anne's Cathedral and tucked down a cobbled alleyway, one of the city's oldest streets, the Duke of York is Irish in style and cluttered with Belfast memorabilia, particularly printer's trade paraphernalia.

BELFAST Raj Put

461 Lisburn Rd, Co Antrim, BT9 7EY **Tel** *028 9066 2168*   **Road Map** *D2*

A good-value Indian restaurant with sophisticated and mildly-spiced fare. There's excellent *saag aloo* (a potato and spinach dish) and *saag paneer* (spinach with cottage cheese) for those with vegetarian tastes, and tasty chicken tikka masala for the carnivores. Though located very far south, the place is convenient to local B&Bs.

BELFAST The Barnett Room

Malone House, Barnett Demesne, Co Antrim, BT9 5LH **Tel** *028 9068 1246*   **Road Map** *D2*

Housed in a graceful late-Georgian mansion, the Barnett Room is renowned for its excellent cuisine. Only the best-quality Ulster produce is used in the brasserie-style menu served at this local favourite. Vegetarian dishes are often the house special.

BELFAST Archana Balti House

53 Dublin Rd, Co Antrim, BT2 7HE **Tel** *028 9032 3713*   **Road Map** *D2*

One of the best Indian restaurants in Belfast and one of the first on the island, Archana serves up a mouthwatering selection of curries and Balti dishes. It's particularly noted for its vegetarian options, even catering widely for vegans. The Thali lunch is particularly good value. Fully licensed to serve alcohol.

BELFAST Bourbon

60 Great Victoria St, Belfast BT2 7BB **Tel** *028 9033 2121*   **Road Map** *D2*

The plush red and burgundy interior is matched by an elegant menu, which has clearly been designed to entice the customers. The venison and crispy duck are tempting in a restaurant with enough variety to suit most palattes

BELFAST Metro Brasserie

13 Lower Crescent, Co Antrim, BT7 1NR **Tel** *028 9032 3349*   **Road Map** *D2*

This is a trendy modern version of the traditional brasserie housed in the beautiful Crescent Townhouse. The interior design is striking and unusual and gives the place a sophisticated but relaxed atmosphere. There's a separate vegetarian menu as well as an extensive selection of cocktails.

BELFAST The Potthouse

1 Hill Street, Co Antrim, BT1 2LB **Tel** *028 9024 4044*   **Road Map** *D2*

Built on the site of a 17th-century pottery, this restaurant is part of a three-storey complex which also includes a nightclub and guestroom. Despite its glass floors, young crowd and general exuberance, it offers a wide-ranging yet simple gastro-pub menu based on traditional Irish fare.

BELFAST Zen

55–59 Adelaide St, Co Antrim, BT2 8FE **Tel** 028 9023 2244   **Road Map** D2

As the name suggests, Zen is a restaurant with the calmness and serenity of a rock garden. The beautiful elegant surroundings are matched only by the presentation of the food. Extensive menu of sashimi, sushi, tempura, maki rolls and other Japanese specialities. Try the dinner set.

BELFAST Alden's

229 Upper Newtownards Rd, Co Antrim, BT4 3JF **Tel** 028 9065 0079   **Road Map** D2

A welcome modern addition to Belfast's burgeoning restaurant scene, Alden's has a warmth and casualness that is at odds with the sophistication of the menu and decor. Though the menu of this critically-acclaimed place changes regularly, the fish and seafood are consistently good.

BELFAST Cayenne

7 Lesley House, Shaftesbury Sq, Co Antrim, BT2 7DB **Tel** 028 9033 1532   **Road Map** D2

Celebrity chefs Paul and Jeanne Rankin opened this restaurant in 1999, and serve a delicious mix of Thai, Japanese and other Asian-influenced dishes. Exotic and innovative mains, such as spiced breast of duck with Shanghai noodles, sprouting broccoli, oyster mushrooms and black bean sauce are typical.

BELFAST Nick's Warehouse

35–39 Hill St, Co Antrim, BT1 2LB **Tel** 028 9043 9690   **Road Map** D2

Nick and Kathy Price's converted warehouse, tucked away in the cobbled backstreets of central Belfast, gets top marks for atmosphere. The menu includes Nick's latest culinary innovations made from produce sourced from the best suppliers, including "the organic lettuce man and the wild boar and rare pig lady".

BELFAST Restaurant Michael Deane

36–40 Howard St, Co Antrim, BT1 6PF **Tel** 028 9033 1134   **Road Map** D2

You have a choice here of smart and elegant formal dining on the first floor, or the more informal brasserie on the ground floor. Chef Michael Deane has a superb reputation so it is hardly surprising that you will find excellent food, whichever of the two you choose.

BUSHMILLS Bushmills Inn

9 Dunluce Rd, Co Antrim, BT57 8QG **Tel** 028 2073 2339   **Road Map** D1

Originally an old coaching inn, this popular hostelry is only a few miles from the Giant's Causeway and close to the Bushmills Distillery. It overlooks the garden courtyard making for a lovely view and wonderful atmosphere. Food is a combination of classical and new Irish, presided over by Chef Donna Thompson.

DUNDRUM The Buck's Head

77 Main St, Co Down, BT33 0LU **Tel** 028 4375 1868   **Road Map** E2

Open fires and hospitable, friendly service make this a preferred stop for lunch, high tea or dinner. The cuisine is a mix of traditional and modern, made from local produce. Seafood particularly features fresh catch, such as oysters from Dundrum Bay. The atmosphere is pleasant and the large attractive dining room overlooks a walled garden.

DUNGANNON Viscount's Restaurant

10 Northland Row, Co Tyrone, BT71 6AP **Tel** 028 8775 3800   **Road Map** D2

A Victorian church has been converted into a medieval-style banqueting hall with the emphasis on fun as much as food. The decor is almost Arthurian with maroon drapes, heraldic banners and beautiful stained-glass windows. The large menu caters to all appetites and is popular with families in the daytime. There's a good carvery.

ENNISKILLEN Oscar's

29 Belmore St, Co Fermanagh, BT74 6AA **Tel** 028 6632 7037   **Road Map** C2

As a testament to Oscar Wilde, who attended the nearby Portora Royal school, this unique pub and restaurant boasts book-lined walls, portraits of the writer and even a re-creation of his cell in Reading Gaol. The menu is impressive with Mediterranean influences and even some East Asian dishes.

ENNISKILLEN The Sheelin

Bellanaleck, Co Fermanagh, BT92 2BA **Tel** 028 6634 8232   **Road Map** C2

On the shores of Lower Lough Erne, the Sheelin is a thatched cottage restaurant that promises a true gourmet experience. The traditional Irish menu features T-bone steak and Guinness beef pie as specialities. The wine list is comprehensive and well priced.

FLORENCE COURT Arch Tullyhona House Restaurant

59 Marble Arch Rd, Co Fermanagh, BT92 1DE **Tel** 028 6634 8452   **Road Map** C2

Beside Marble Arch caves, this farm restaurant offers great food and service. Produce fresh from the farm is used, with wild salmon and Lough Erne trout on offer too. Desserts such as lemon soufflé and fresh fruit pavlova are a speciality. If you're in the mood for some home cooking, this is a good bet.

HILLSBOROUGH Hillside Restaurant & Bar

21 Main St, Co Down, BT26 6AE **Tel** 028 9268 2765   **Road Map** D2

This attractive country-style pub and restaurant has an excellent seasonal menu. Patrons can choose between the Edwardian Restaurant with its starched tablecloths, or the more informal Refectory. The bar serves a good selection of real ales, while mulled wine is available on cold winter nights.

Key to Symbols see back cover flap

HOLYWOD Bay Tree Coffee House
118 High St, Co Down, BT18 9HW **Tel** *028 9042 1419* **Road Map** *E2*

This café is part of a wonderful craft shop that sells characteristic Irish wares, mainly pottery. Lunch is served daily, with an emphasis on fresh fish, vegetarian food and organic salads. Dinner is served only on Fridays, when booking is advised. The dinner menu includes interesting options such as *gumbo* and *quesadilla*.

LIMAVADY The Lime Tree
60 Catherine St, Co Londonderry, BT49 9DB **Tel** *028 7776 4300* **Road Map** *D1*

Right on the main street of the attractive town, The Lime Tree is small and quite simply decorated. The impressive menu offers unusual and subtle tasting dishes put together with local ingredients. There are excellent options for carnivores such as Sperrin lamb with Moroccan spiced sauce and roasted stuffed saddle of rabbit.

LONDONDERRY The Sandwich Company
The Diamond, Co Londonderry, BT48 6HP **Tel** *028 7137 2500* **Road Map** *C1*

A good source for sandwiches served in a black-and-white interior, The Sandwich Company has a wide choice of fillings and breads, both hot and cold. It's a perfect place to have delicious pastries and great coffee, served by a pleasant staff. Smoked salmon and prawn baguette is a nice alternative to your typical ham and cheese sandwich.

LONDONDERRY Badger's Bar & Restaurant
16–18 Orchard St, Co Londonderry, BT48 6EG **Tel** *028 7136 3306* **Road Map** *C1*

Attracting an older type of clientele for chat, pints and conviviality, Badger's Bar & Restaurant is a charming pub specializing in steaks, salad and afternoon tea. Guinness casserole is particularly recommended, although its liquid form doesn't appeal to everyone's taste.

LONDONDERRY The Metro
3–4 Bank Pl, Co Londonderry, BT48 6EA **Tel** *028 7126 7401* **Road Map** *C1*

Shadowed by Derry's city walls, the Metro is a local favourite. Although it only dates back to the 1980s, it has a formidable presence in the area. The food, from soup and sandwiches to Guinness beef stew, is first-rate. Service is very good with friendly staff. The lovely views can be enjoyed over a pint. Open for lunch only.

LONDONDERRY Brown's Bar & Brasserie
1 Bonds Hill, Co Londonderry, BT 47 6DW **Tel** *028 7134 5180* **Road Map** *C1*

Look past the rather unremarkable façade of the building and you'll discover some of the best-value food in the city. A modern European menu, relying on fresh and often organic ingredients, is complemented by minimalist yet warm decor. Dress is casual as is the environment. Lunch Tuesday to Saturday, dinner Wednesday to Saturday

OMAGH Grant's Restaurant
29 George's St, Co Tyrone, BT78 2EY **Tel** *028 8225 0900* **Road Map** *C2*

Named after Ulysses S Grant, this restaurant offers a bistro menu or bar snack food in comfortable pub surroundings. Evening meals comprise seafood, pasta and steak and although some of the dishes are quite pricey, the lunch and set dinner options are extremely good value.

PORTAFERRY The Narrows
8 Shore Rd, Co Down, BT22 1JY **Tel** *028 4272 8148* **Road Map** *E2*

A bright, light restaurant housed in an 18th-century courtyard development, with delicious, locally sourced ingredients, the Narrows specializes in seafood. Options include Portaferry mussels with garlic and white wine cream and whole grilled lobster. A tapas menu is on offer in the Ruffian Bar and there's an extensive wine list.

PORTBALLINTRAE Sweeney's Wine Bar
6b Seaport Ave, Co Antrim, BT57 8SB **Tel** *028 2073 2405* **Road Map** *D1*

Modestly priced and cheerful, Sweeny's Wine Bar offers creatively prepared food. Seafood specialities include lobster, wild salmon and locally caught white fish. Situated on the Causeway Coast, the restaurant occupies a converted stable block overlooking Portballintrae Harbour. Evenings can get busy.

PORTRUSH The Harbour Bistro
The Harbour, Co Antrim, BT56 8DF **Tel** *028 7082 2430* **Road Map** *D1*

The Harbour is probably the nicest place in town. The traditional pub area on the ground floor has roaring fires and a great atmosphere. The restaurant is also informal and offers a good selection of à la carte dishes. Food is traditional Irish with a twist and there is a good wine selection.

PORTSTEWART Morellis Ninos
53 The Promenade, Portstewart, Co Londonderry, BT55 7AF **Tel** *028 7083 2150* **Road Map** *D1*

Opened in 1911 as an ice cream parlour, Morellis Ninos recently is now an Italian-style café. It has expanded to include hot food such as authentic Italian pasta, sandwiches and paninis as well as a long coffee list. Home-made pastries and desserts are a delight. Lovely location on the Promenade with a view of the bay.

STRANGFORD The Lobster Pot Bar & Restaurant
The Square, Co Down, BT30 7ND **Tel** *028 4488 1288* **Road Map** *E2*

Only the finest local catches are served in this predominantly fish restaurant overlooking Strangford Lough. Unsurprisingly, lobster is a speciality but the seafood on offer is diverse: Dundrum Bay oysters, dressed crab and mussels. There's a lovely beer garden where you can dine in summer. Dinner is well priced.

Pubs in Ireland

The archetypal Irish pub is celebrated for its convivial atmosphere, friendly locals, genial bar staff and the "crack" – the Irish expression for fun. Wit is washed down with whiskey or Guinness, the national drinks. Irish pubs date back to medieval taverns, coaching inns and she-beens, illegal drinking dens which flourished under colonial rule. In Victorian times, brewing and distilling were major industries. The sumptuous Edwardian or Victorian interiors of some city pubs are a testament to these times, furnished with mahogany and marble bar counters. Snugs, partitioned-off booths, are another typical feature of Irish pubs. Traditional pubs can be boldly painted, thatched or "black-and-white" – beamed with a white façade and black trim. Some rural pubs double as grocers' shops. All pubs in the Republic are now smoke-free.

Good pubs are not evenly distributed throughout the country: in the Southeast, Kilkenny is paradise for pub-lovers, while Cork and Kerry possess some of the most picturesque pubs. The Lower Shannon region is noted for its boisterous pubs, especially in County Clare where spontaneous music sessions are common. The West has an abundance of typical Irish pubs, and the many tourists and students guarantee a profusion of good pubs in Galway. The listings below cover a selection of pubs throughout Ireland; for Dublin pubs, see pages 110–11.

SOUTHEAST IRELAND

Brittas Bay: *Jack White's Inn*
Jack White's Cross, Co Wicklow.
Road map D4. **Tel** 0404 47106.
A typical Irish country pub perfectly situated off the N11, which runs from Dublin to the Southeast. Simple but tasty pub fare is served until 9pm. A real local legend, this pub is mired in controversy, due to a murder committed here in 1996. 🍴 🔊 🎵

Carlow: *Teach Dolmain*
Tullow St, Co Carlow.
Road map D4. **Tel** 059 913 0911.
This multi-award winning pub, win Carlow's town centre, has a curious collection of unique pottery and ancient artifacts from the town's and Ireland's history. This pub has an excellent menu and is ideally suited for large groups. 🍴 🖼 🔊 🎵

Dunmore East: *The Ship Inn*
Co Waterford. **Road map** D5.
Tel 051 383141.
This old, ivy-clad pub lies above the harbour, away from the crowds on the beach. It is noted both for its Michelin-rated seafood and its seafaring links. Inside, nautical memorabilia and half-barrel seats abound in the front bar. There is a large, pleasant deck perfect for drinking and eating on long summer days. 🍴 🖼

Enniscorthy: *The Antique Tavern*
14 Slaney St, Co Wexford.
Road map D5. **Tel** 054 33428.
This traditional, timbered, black-and-white pub is charming. The dark, intimate bar contains relics such as pikestaffs from Vinegar Hill, the decisive battle in the 1798 uprising that was fought outside town. Pub lunches and local chat are on offer. In good weather, you can sit on the balcony and enjoy the pleasant views of the River Slaney. 🍴 🖼

Enniscorthy: *Holohan*
Slaney Place, Co Wexford.
Road map D5. **Tel** 054 33179.
At the back of the Castle Museum, this is essentially a workaday pub with few pretensions. Its unusual location makes it worth a visit for a pint or two – it is built right into the base of an old quarry and a vertical cliff forms part of the back wall of the bar.

Kilkenny: *Bollard's Pub*
St Kieran's St, Co Kilkenny.
Road map C4. **Tel** 056 772 1353.
Located 200 m (656 ft) from the ever popular Saint Francis's Abbey Brewery, this pub has been in the Bollard family since 1904. It has a fine sporting tradition, often attracting large crowds for hurling and football fixtures. Enjoy a pint and watch the Sunday game. 🍴 🖼

Kilkenny: *Hibernian*
1, Armonde St, Co Kilkenny.
Road map C4. **Tel** 056 777 1888.
Sited in an old bank and part of the Hibernian Hotel, this rather formal pub, popular with a fairly young crowd, still has its original decor. Tall wooden partitions create nice private spaces. Modern Irish food is available. 🍴 🖼 🔊

Kilkenny: *Kyteler's Inn*
27 St Kieran's St, Co Kilkenny.
Road map C4. **Tel** 056 772 1064.
In good weather you can sit in the courtyard of this historic coaching inn and cellar bar. Food is available all day, and meals are served daily until 9:45pm (last orders). An effigy of a witch sits in the window frame, a reminder of the story of a former resident, Dame Alice Kyteler. In 1324, Alice and her maid were pronounced guilty of witchcraft after four of Alice's husbands had died in mysterious circumstances; although pardoned, Alice was again accused but escaped, leaving her maid to burn at the stake. 🍴 🖼 🔊 🎵

Kilkenny: *Langton's*
69 John St, Co Kilkenny.
Road map C4. **Tel** 056 776 5133.
Langton's is noted for its black-and-white exterior, Edwardian ambience and the stylish glass interior at the back. The front bar is cosy with a low ceiling. Pub food is on offer, and there's music and dancing three or four nights a week; Tuesday, Thursday and Saturday are disco nights. 🍴 🖼 🔊

Kilkenny: *Marble City Bar*
66 High St, Co Kilkenny.
Road map C4. **Tel** 056 776 1143.
Marble City Bar, the most famous pub in town, is named after the local limestone, which becomes black when polished. This four-storey building has an Art Deco façade. A busy café-bar with no reservations. Bar food till 9pm. 🍴 🖼

Kilkenny: *Tynan's Bridge House Bar*
2 John's Bridge, Co Kilkenny.
Road map C4. **Tel** 056 772 1291.
This is the most genuine old-world pub in town, with an intimate interior lit by charming lamps. Quaint relics of the former grocery store and pharmacy are on display, from a set of old scales to the drawers labelled with names of nuts and spices. No music, no TV; as the publican puts it, this is "a chat bar". Friendly service with fine views of Kilkenny Castle.

Kilmore Quay: *The Wooden House Lodge*
Co Wexford. **Road map** D5.
Tel 053 29804.

This traditional – if over-restored – thatched pub is full of nautical memorabilia and quirky sayings while the small terrace is decorated with anchors. Hearty pub fare is served. 🍴 🚭 🎵

Leighlinbridge: *The Lord Bagenal*
Co Carlow. **Road map** D5.
Tel 059 972 1668.

This pub is a well-known stop-off point for those travelling south from Dublin. Set in a small, peaceful village in County Carlow, the Lord Bagenal overlooks a picturesque marina on the River Barrow. It boasts award-winning food and also has a children's crèche. 🚭 🍴 🎵

New Ross: *Corcoran's Pub*
Irishtown, Co Wexford.
Road map D5. *Tel 051 425920.*

Head here if you crave fresh, home-made food. Having had five generations of continuous ownership, Corcoran's is one of the oldest pubs in town and has a friendly atmosphere. Card games are played every Monday with music sessions on weekends, including Irish music, singing and dancing. 🎵 🍴

Waterford: *Axis Mundi*
The Mall, Co Waterford.
Road map D5. *Tel 051 855087.*

Set beside Reginald's Tower, Axis Mundi incorporates part of the Viking city walls and the medieval sallyports (attack exits), which are still visible. The service is rather brusque. There is an adjoining nightclub. 🍴 🚭 🚻 🎵

Waterford: *Jack Meade's Pub*
Cheekpoint Rd, Co Waterford.
Road map D5. *Tel 051 850950.*

Situated under an old stone bridge 7 km (4 miles) south of town, Jack Meade's provides a quiet and quaint atmosphere. In the summer, musicians play outdoors and children can amuse themselves in the playground. Drop by for the setting and some lunch. 🍴 🎵

Waterford: *T and H Doolin*
George's St, Co Waterford.
Road map D5. *Tel 051 841504.*

Set in the city's most charming pedestrianized street, this traditional, 18th-century black-and-white pub offers an intimate atmosphere and good "crack". Traditional folk music sessions are held every night. 🎵

Wexford: *Centenary Stores*
Charlotte St, Co Wexford.
Road map D5. *Tel 053 24424.*

Tucked away in a converted warehouse, this dimly lit pub is the most charming in Wexford. The friendly bar staff and a mixed local and bohemian crowd chat in the wood-panelled bar. Drinkers are entertained with sessions of traditional music every Sunday morning, and on Monday and Wednesday evenings in summer. 🍴 🚭 🎵

Wexford: *Westgate Tavern*
Westgate, Co Wexford.
Road map D5. *Tel 053 22086.*

Licensed since 1761, this distinctive tavern faces the path leading to the famous Selskar Abbey and Westgate Heritage Centre. Lunch menu and bar snacks are available in the welcoming bar and there are music sessions on Sunday evenings. 🎵 🍴 🚻

CORK AND KERRY

Baltimore: *Bushe's*
Co Cork. **Road map** B6.
Tel 028 20119.

Famous in County Cork, this pub serves the best ales and pints in the village and is well used to visitors dropping by. Sit outside in the summer and gaze out onto the islands or watch the beautiful sunset. 🍴 🚭 🚻

Cahirciveen: *The Point Bar*
Valentia Harbour, Co Kerry.
Road map A5. *Tel 066 947 2165.*

Best to save this one for the summer months. Ultra-fresh seafood, spontaneous musical sessions and a stunning view of Valentia Island, the Point Bar is considered by many to be one of Kerry's greatest. 🍴 🚭 🚻 🎵

Castletownshend: *Mary Ann's*
Co Cork. **Road map** B6.
Tel 028 36146.

Since opening in 1846, Mary Ann's has maintained excellent service and a great reputation for quality home-made food. Full of interesting antiques, this is one of the best examples of a traditional pub in Ireland. 🍴 🚭 🚻

Clonakilty: *De Barra's*
Co Cork. **Road map** B6.
Tel 023 33381.

This is one of the best-known pubs in West Cork, with a traditional folk club open most nights; many musicians come from the Gaeltacht (*see p229*). The bar is lovingly restored, with hand-painted signs and traditional whiskey jars. Simple snacks and full lunches are served from noon to 3pm. 🍴 🚭 🎵

Cork: *Bodega*
46–49 Cornmarket St, Co Cork.
Road map C5. *Tel 021 427 2878.*

This bright, modern pub and restaurant was once a warehouse. The high ceilings create a feeling of openness; the huge wall-spaces are taken up by art, much of it for sale. Soup and sandwiches in the afternoon give way to an international menu in the evening. On Saturdays, the open air market outside adds to the hustle and bustle. 🍴 🚭 🚻 🚻

Cork: *Chateau Bar*
St Patrick's St, Co Cork.
Road map C5. *Tel 021 427 0370.*

This bar in the heart of the city occupies a striking building that was once on the quayside. Founded in 1793, this elegant pub has a stylish Victorian interior and offers good quality bar fare. 🍴 🚭 🚻

Cork: *Chimes*
27 Church St, Co Cork.
Road map C5. *Tel 021 430 4136.*

Set in the hilly, old-world Shandon district, this convivial working-class pub attracts a mixed, friendly crowd, from local pensioners to sports fans and students. On Saturday and Sunday nights there's music, usually in the form of accordion or keyboard soloists. 🎵 🚻

Cork: *The Gables*
31/32 Douglas St, Co Cork.
Road map C5. *Tel 021 431 3076.*

This traditional Irish pub combines good food and live music. The menus, both food and wine, are an alternative to typical pub food and are well worth sampling. Food is served from 12:30 to 3pm and 5 to 9pm. Traditional live music on Wednesday, Thursday and Sunday complements this already atmospheric pub. 🍴 🎵

Cork: *Henchy's*
40 St Luke's Cross, Co Cork.
Road map C5. *Tel 021 450 7833.*

This traditional pub dates from 1884 and has retained much of its Victorian ambience, enhanced by the mahogany bar and stained glass. It has long been associated with poets and is where young hopefuls come to recite their work to a largely sympathetic audience. 🚻

Cork: *The Long Valley*
Winthrop St, Co Cork. **Road map** C5.
Tel 021 427 2144.

Located just off Patrick Street, this pub has a sense of the unexpected. It attracts all sorts of characters from chancers to professionals. It is well known for its smooth pints of Murphy's, which any self-respecting local will choose over Guinness. 🍴 🚭 🎵

348 TRAVELLERS' NEEDS

Dingle: *Dick Mack's*
Green St, Co Kerry.
Road map A5.

This individualistic spot is part shoe shop, part pub, and retains the original shop and drinking counters. The pub is a haunt of local artists, eccentrics and extroverts. In the evening, regulars often congregate around the piano.

Dingle: *Doyle's Townhouse*
John St, Co Kerry. **Road map** A5.
Tel 066 915 1174.

This bar and restaurant is celebrated for its delicious freshly caught seafood, and the bar's rustic, yet cosy, stone interior is an appealing place for dinner. Don't miss the house speciality, lobsters. Doyle's is open mid-February to December. 🍴

Dunquin: *Krugers*
Co Kerry. **Road map** A5.
Tel 066 915 6127.

Situated close to the quays for the Blasket Islands, this well-known family pub is also a guesthouse from March to September. The pub is decorated with family memorabilia and stills from the famous films made in the area, such as *Ryan's Daughter* and *Far and Away.* 🍴 🛏 🎵

Glencar: *The Climber's Inn*
Co Kerry. **Road map** B5.
Tel 066 976 0101.

This family run pub is a famous landmark on the way to the Kerry highlands. It boasts an open fire and live Irish music and serves up great home-cooked meals with interesting vegetarian options. Chat with other hikers and climbers after a day's trekking. 🍴 🛏 🎵

Killarney: *Buckley's Bar*
College St, Co Kerry.
Road map B5. **Tel** 064 31037.

This oak-panelled bar is noted for its regular traditional music sessions and its filling meals. The pub was opened in 1926 when Tom Buckley, a homesick emigrant, returned from New York. Bar food is served until 4pm. 🍴 🛏 👶 🎵

Killarney: *The Laurels*
Main St, Co Kerry. **Road map** B5.
Tel 064 31149.

This claims to be Killarney's liveliest pub and is popular with young locals and tourists. It provides excellent bar snacks and good meals (steak, mussels, oysters, fish) in a separate restaurant area. Ballads are performed occasionally from 9:15pm between February and November, and more sporadically in winter.
🍴 🛏 👶 🎵

Killorglin: *The Old Forge*
Co Kerry. **Road map** A5.
Tel 066 976 1231.

Set on the popular Ring of Kerry, this thatched pub is delightfully old fashioned and authentic. Expect it to be packed during the Puck Fair in August (*see p49*). Music is played in summer. 🎵

Kinsale: *Kieran's Folk House Inn*
Guardwell, Co Cork. **Road map** B6.
Tel 021 477 2382.

This convivial corner of old Kinsale draws locals and visitors alike. The interior is snug and welcoming, with live music every night during the season. The inn also houses a pleasant guesthouse and a noted restaurant – the Shrimps Seafood Bistro, open for lunch and dinner all year. 🍴 👶 🎵

Kinsale: *The Lord Kingsale*
Main St, Co Cork. **Road map** B6.
Tel 021 477 2371.

This beamed, old-fashioned pub attracts a quiet, genteel crowd. It is several hundred years old but the interior is, in part, a clever fake. In summer, live music is performed at weekends and on Mondays. Bar food is served from noon to 3pm. 🎵 🍴

Scilly: *The Spaniard Inn*
Kinsale, Co Cork. **Road map** B6.
Tel 021 477 2436.

Set on a hairpin bend in the village of Scilly, this popular fishermen's pub has the air of a smugglers' inn. There is often live traditional music in one of the bars most nights during the summer and it is particularly popular at weekends. The restaurant (open in the summer season) and bar offer simple, but excellent fare. 🍴 🛏 🎵

Sherkin Island: *The Jolly Roger*
Co Cork. **Road map** B6.
Tel 028 20379.

Island atmosphere pervades this cosy pub, which serves outstandingly good-value lunches. In summer you can sit outside and admire the view of Baltimore Harbour and the bay. 🛏 🎵

THE LOWER SHANNON

Annacotty: *Finnegan's*
Co Limerick. **Road map** B5.
Tel 061 337338.

Originally a 17th-century coach stop, history and folklore permeate this renowned establishment in County Limerick. Finnegan's specializes in steaks and freshly caught seafood. Cosy and extremely friendly. 🍴 👶

Ballyvaughan: *Monk's Pub*
The Pier, Co Clare. **Road map** B4.
Tel 065 707 7059.

This quaint pub is situated on the quay. Inside, country furniture and peat fires are matched by local seafood including chowder, served until 9pm. There's live music every Saturday and traditional music on Thursdays in summer. Ring for details. 🍴 🛏 🎵

Bunratty: *Durty Nelly's*
Co Clare. **Road map** B4.
Tel 061 364072.

Set beside Bunratty Castle, this extremely commercialized pub appeals to locals as well as tourists. The 17th-century atmosphere is sustained by the warren of rooms, inglenook fireplaces and historical portraits. Traditional music is performed most evenings, and wholesome food is available both from the bar and from the two restaurants. 🍴 🛏 🎵

Doolin: *McDermott's*
Roadford, Co Clare. **Road map** B4.
Tel 065 707 4328.

No Clare pub is complete without a traditional music session and McDermott's does not disappoint. It has live music every night from St Patrick's Day until late October. A warm welcome and a cold pint are guaranteed by the staff. The original 1867 tiled floor is still in place. 🍴 🛏 🎵

Doolin: *O'Connor's*
Co Clare. **Road map** B4.
Tel 065 707 4168.

This famous pub is known to lovers of traditional music the world over. The pub has been in the O'Connor family for over 150 years and combines an authentic grocery store with a lively pub. This is the place for spontaneous music, simple bar food, young company and great "crack". 🍴 🛏 👶

Ennis: *The Cloister*
Abbey St, Co Clare. **Road map** B4.
Tel 065 682 9521.

This recently-refurbished historic pub is situated by the famous Ennis Friary (*see p189*). The pub's cosy, atmospheric interior is complemented by a patio in summer, and by traditional music on some nights. 🎵

Ennis: *Queen's Front Bar*
Abbey St, Co Clare. **Road map** B4.
Tel 065 682 8963.

This historical pub lies beside the impressive ruins of Ennis Friary (*see p189*). It serves superb, traditional Irish food. Good for families, the Queen's welcomes all ages. 🍴 🛏 👶 🎵

Key to Symbols *see back cover flap*

Killaloe: *Goosers*
Ballina, Co Clare. **Road map** C4.
Tel 061 376791.
This delightfully picturesque waterfront pub on the Ballina side of the river has a thatched roof, traditional interior and a welcoming atmosphere. Noted for its cuisine, Goosers serves fairly pricey seafood in the restaurant and more reasonably priced but satisfying "pub grub" in the rustic bar. 🍴 📶 ♿ 🎵

Kilrush: *Crotty's Pub*
Market Square, Co Clare.
Road map B4. **Tel** 065 905 2470.
This popular pub was once run by one of the foremost exponents of the concertina, Lizzie Crotty (1885–1960). Today it hosts live traditional music four nights of the week in summer. Tasty bar food is available from 9:30am to 5pm on weekdays. 🍴 📶 ♿ 🎵

Limerick: *The Locke*
3 George's Quay, Co Limerick.
Road map B4. **Tel** 061 413733.
Set on a quay on the Shannon, this is a typical black-and-white pub. In summer, it is a favourite port of call for riverside strollers. In winter, blazing fires and snugs make it a cosy spot. Traditional music is played on Thursday and Sunday nights. The restaurant is open all day. 🍴 📶 ♿ 🎵

Limerick: *Nancy Blake's*
Upper Denmark St, Co Limerick.
Road map B4. **Tel** 061 416443.
Limerick's best-known bar, Nancy Blake's has much to offer in the way of good "crack" and traditional music. If you prefer rhythm and blues, try the adjoining Outback Bar. The cosy main bar serves soup and sandwiches at lunchtime. Music is played on Monday, Wednesday, and Saturday. 📶 🎵

THE WEST OF IRELAND

Aran Islands: *Ti Joe Macs*
Kilronan, Inishmore, Co Galway.
Road map B2. **Tel** 099 61248.
This pub stands straight in front of visitors as they leave the boat. It serves soup and sandwiches. 🍴 📶 🎵

Clarinbridge: *Moran's Oyster Cottage*
The Weir, Kilcolgan, Co Galway.
Road map B4. **Tel** 091 796113.
Set in a thatched cottage, this bar was a regular port of call for crews from passing "hookers" (traditional ships). Nowadays, you can sample all kinds of seafood here, though Moran's *(see p338)* is best known as an oyster bar – the owner holds the local speed record for shelling oysters. You can watch fishermen at work from the terrace tables. 🍴 📶 ♿

Clarinbridge: *Paddy Burke's Oyster Inn*
Co Galway. **Road map** B4.
Tel 091 796226.
Founded in 1835, this authentic thatched pub has leaded window-panes and a charming beamed interior. Apart from the renowned Clarinbridge oysters and buffet lunches, gourmet menus are also available at lunch and dinner. 🍴 📶 ♿

Clifden: *EJ Kings*
The Square, Co Galway.
Road map A3. **Tel** 095 21330.
This spacious, bustling pub is situated on several floors, with the ground floor the most appealing. Seafood platters or varied pub fare can be enjoyed by the peat fire. In summer, live music is often on offer, especially folk and ballads. The staff are exceptionally friendly. 🍴 📶 🎵

Galway: *Busker Brownes*
Cross St Upper, Co Galway.
Road map B4. **Tel** 091 563377.
This barn-like city pub occupies several storeys, including the shell of a 16th-century convent on the top floor. The Slate House, the pub next door, is under the same management, and both are popular with local students. There are jazz sessions on Sundays. 🍴 📶 ♿ 🎵

Galway: *Cooke's Thatch Bar*
Cooke's Corner, 2 Newcastle Rd, Co Galway. **Road map** B4.
Tel 091 521749.
Situated on the outskirts of Galway, this traditional thatched inn has passed into new owner-ship after seven generations in the same family, but is still renowned for its friendliness. The pub includes an off-licence with over 20 wines on sale as well as beer and spirits. 📶

Galway: *Dew Drop Inn*
Mainguard St, Co Galway.
Road map B4. **Tel** 091 561070.
Locally known as Myles Lee, this is an intimate, vintage pub that encapsulates Galway's Bohemian traditions. The authentic low level lighting makes this pub a comfy place, especially on cold nights when the log fire is crackling. The Dew Drop serves one of the best pints of Guinness in town.

Galway: *The King's Head*
15 High St, Co Galway.
Road map B4. **Tel** 091 566630.
Founded in 1649, this historic pub is adorned with a bow-fronted façade. The homely interior contains 17th-century fireplaces. Simple lunch snacks are served in the main bar. In the back bar, various live bands playing in the evenings attract a youthful crowd. 📶 ♿ 🎵

Galway: *McSwiggan's*
Eyre St, Wood Quay, Co Galway.
Road map B4. **Tel** 091 568917.
In the centre of the city, this snug, relaxing bar has terracotta floors and comfortable seats. It features music on Thursday and Friday. 🍴 ♿

Galway: *O'Flaherty's*
Great Southern Hotel, 15 Eyre Sq, Co Galway. **Road map** B4.
Tel 091 564041.
This solid cellar bar began as wine cellars but now offers cosy snugs and railway memorabilia. The popular pub provides a contrast to the more sophisticated hotel cocktail bar on the floor above. A carvery lunch is on offer daily in the bar, while at weekends live popular music sessions draw locals and visitors alike. 🍴 🎵

Galway: *The Quays*
Quay St, Co Galway. **Road map** B4.
Tel 091 568347.
The Quays was originally a small thatched cottage but the building was knocked down to make way for this three-storyed bar. The top floor is a circular mezzanine that overlooks the rest of the bar. A good venue for music, the traditional music nights are Friday to Sunday evenings between 6 and 8pm. Hearty lunches are served daily. Outside seating during the summer months. 🍴 📶 ♿ 🎵

Galway: *Ti Neachtain*
Quay St, Co Galway.
Road map B4. **Tel** 091 568820.
Set in the "Latin Quarter", this 18th-century town house boasts a distinctive oriel window. Inside, a musty wood interior is home to old-world snugs and friendly service. Traditional music can often be heard here, and upstairs is Ard Bia restaurant. 🍴 📶 ♿ 🎵

Killala: *Golden Acres* Co Mayo.
Road map B2. **Tel** 096 32183.
This comfortable pub is located near the major activity centres of the area. Deep-sea fishing, golf and boat trips are all within walking distance of this homely country bar. It features good pub food. 🍴 ♿ 🎵

Maam Cross: *Peacocks Hotel*
Connemara, Co Galway.
Road map B3. **Tel** 091 552306.

Next to a replica of the traditional cottage used in the 1950s John Wayne film *The Quiet Man* is a hotel complex with a modern pub. It is highly popular with locals and a good choice of pub food is available daily. Music every weekend. 🍴 �"' 🎵

Westport: *The Asgard Tavern*
The Quay, Co Mayo. **Road map** B3.
Tel 098 25319.

This old inn facing the pier and Clew Bay is decorated with a nautical theme. Both the main downstairs back bar and the up-stairs restaurant provide excellent seafood and salads. The small downstairs front bar is the most atmospheric. 🍴 🚻 🎵

Westport: *Matt Molloy's*
Bridge St, Co Mayo. **Road map** B3.
Tel 098 26655.

Founded by the flautist from the traditional Irish folk band The Chieftains, this deceptively spacious pub is designed along equally traditional lines. There is live music in the back room every evening, when the pub is packed. No children after 9pm. 🚻 🎵

NORTHWEST IRELAND

Burtonport: *The Lobster Pot*
Co Donegal. **Road map** C1.
Tel 074 954 2012.

This cosy pub lies near the pier. The old timber surrounds of the interior are used as a backdrop to an incredible selection of Gaelic sporting memorabilia. The seafood is renowned as the best, but other good dishes are served as well. 🍴 �"' 🚻 🎵

Crolly: *Leo's Tavern*
Menaleck, Co Donegal.
Road map C1. **Tel** 074 954 8143.

Owned by the father of modern folk musicians Clannad and of the singer Enya, this friendly pub attracts locals and tourists for its sing-songs round the accordion, and traditional music nights. 🍴 �"' 🚻 🎵

Culdaff: *McGrory's*
Co Donegal. **Road map** C1.
Tel 074 937 9104.

On the idyllic Inishowen Peninsula *(see pp226–7)*, this is a place of quality food and drink. McGrory's restaurant caters for up to 60 diners in a comfortable yet stylish setting. The Backroom Bar, also located in the pub, is a top music venue, featuring live music of all kinds. 🍴 �"' 🚻 🎵

Donegal: *O'Donnell's*
The Diamond, Co Donegal.
Road map C2. **Tel** 074 972 1049.

Regularly winning awards for food and service, this cheerfully decorated pub showcases some of the finest food in Donegal. Local musicians entertain during the Saturday night traditional music sessions. 🍴 🚻 🎵

Dromahair: *Stanford's Inn*
Main St, Co Leitrim.
Road map C2.
Tel 071 916 4140.

Set in a picturesque village, this traditional pub has been in the same family for generations. The tiny, quaint Biddy's Bar remains unchanged, adorned with family portraits and old grocery jars. The main bar has mellow brick-work and flagstones from a ruined castle. Delicious food is on offer all day in the restaurant, and in summer there are often impromptu evening music sessions. 🚻 🎵

Rossnowlagh: *Smugglers' Creek Inn*
Co Donegal. **Road map** C2.
Tel 071 985 2366.

On a clifftop overlooking Donegal Bay, this pub is popular with surfers and other water sports enthusiasts. Bar food is served in the beer garden, which offers panoramic views. 🍴 🚻 🎵

Sligo: *The Blue Lagoon*
Riverside, Co Sligo. **Road map** C2.
Tel 071 914 2530.

Enjoy drinks, lunch, teas, coffees and snacks in one of Sligo's most original settings on the Garavouge River just five-minutes' walk from the town centre. There is occa-sionally live music on weekends. 🍴 🚻 🚻 🎵

Sligo: *Hargadon's*
O'Connell St, Co Sligo.
Road map C2. **Tel** 071 917 0933.

This legendary pub has a beau-tifully unspoilt interior. It offers delicious bar food, cosy snugs and great pints. A separate dining room is also available for a slightly more formal experience. In the summer the beer garden is a cool place to relax, attracting great crowds. 🍴 🚻 🎵

Sligo: *McGraths*
Tobbergal Lane, Co Sligo.
Road map C2. **Tel** 071 914 3031.

This pub's owner has created a friendly ambience for Sligo Rovers Football Club supporters. There is a live acoustic session on Thursdays or Sundays. 🍴 🚻 🚻 🎵

THE MIDLANDS

Abbeyleix: *Morrissey's*
Main St, Co Laois. **Road map** C4.
Tel 0502 31233.

If driving through County Laois, it is worth stopping at this genuinely traditional pub. The 18th-century inn was remodelled in the Victorian era and has stayed the same ever since. The grocery section survives while the plain and unpretentious bar serves simple bar snacks.

Carlingford: *PJ O'Hare's Anchor Bar*
Tholsel St, Co Louth. **Road map** D3.
Tel 042 937 3106.

Known locally as PJ's, this atmos-pheric pub and grocery store is popular with sailors and locals alike. A friendly and often eccentric welcome is matched by bar food such as oysters and sandwiches. Music is played in the summer. 🍴 🚻 🚻 🎵

Crinkill: *The Thatch*
Birr, Co Offaly. **Road map** C4.
Tel 0509 20682.

Mooted as *the* traditional pub, the Thatch is one of the oldest pubs in South Offaly and, as its name suggests, has always been thatched. It has won All Ireland Pub of the Year five times and certainly lives up to its reputation. Children are welcome. 🍴 🚻

Dundalk: *The Jockeys*
Anne St, Co Louth. **Road map** D3.
Tel 042 933 4621.

This friendly pub offers home-cooked lunches daily at very reasonable prices. The walls are covered in Gaelic Athletic Association mementos *(see p29)*, portraying its proud Gaelic sports' tradition. This pub has been in existence, in one guise or another, since 1799 and is an ideal stop for refreshment on the way north. 🍴 🚻 🎵

Kilbeggan: *Locke's Distillery Museum*
Mullingar, Co Westmeath.
Road map C3. **Tel** 0506 32307.

As well as being the oldest licensed pot still distillery in the world (established in 1757), this historic complex has a whiskey bar – the ideal place to sample a few brands before buying *(see p249)*. There is an adjoining restaurant. 🍴 🚻

Kilnaleck: *The Copper Kettle*
Co Cavan. **Road map** C3.
Tel 0494 336223.

This lively family-run pub has a wonderful atmosphere. It is well known for its wholesome, home-cooked meals, served all day. There's entertainment every Saturday night during the summer months. 🍴 🎵

Kinnitty: *The Dungeon Bar*
Birr, Co Offaly.
Road map C4. *Tel 0509 37318.*
Sited in the basement of medieval Kinnitty Castle, less than a mile from Kinnitty village, this candle-lit bar is not quite as spooky as it sounds. Historic Irish memorabilia covers the walls and the food and drinks are well presented. There's traditional Irish music to stir the atmosphere on Thursday, Friday and Saturday nights. 🍴 ♿ 🎵

Longford: *Edward Valentine's* Main St, Co Longford.
Road map C3. *Tel 043 45509.*
Relax in Edward Valentine's wonderful, warm, old-world atmosphere. A carvery lunch is served daily and there is also a bar menu, which is served throughout the day. 🍴

Portlaoise: *The Village Inn*
Co Laois. **Road map** C4.
Tel 0502 35958.
Located at the foot of the Slieve Bloom Mountains, this is a homely little place, offering warmth and good food after a day of hiking or cycling. This charming pub has a thatched roof and a traditional interior, largely unchanged since it opened. Traditional music and set dancing are enjoyed throughout the year.

Portlaoise: *Tracey's Pub and Restaurant*
The Heath, Co Laois.
Road map C4. *Tel 0502 46539.*
This charming thatched cottage pub and restaurant is 5 km (3 miles) outside of the town, but is well worth the journey. It is the oldest family-run pub in these parts, and there is a good range of pub grub (roasts, fish, salads) as well as prime steak at amazingly reasonable prices. 🍴 🍽

NORTHERN IRELAND

Ardglass: *The Lighthouse Bar*
Bath St, Co Down.
Road map E2.
Tel 028 4484 1443.
Come to the Lighthouse in the typical fishing town of Ardglass to talk net mending, baiting and sailing over a pint with locals. A unique experience in a beautiful rural setting. 🎵

Bangor: *Jenny Watt's*
41 High St, Co Down. **Road map** E2.
Tel 028 9146 0682.
Likable and very popular, this bar with Victoriana trimmings is found in the centre of town. The walls are adorned with local photos and memorabilia. There's live jazz at Sunday lunch times, traditional on Tuesday and folk music on Thursday nights. Bar food is served until 7pm, and there's a beer garden. 🍽 🎵

Belfast: *Crown Liquor Saloon*
46 Great Victoria St, Co Antrim.
Road map D2. *Tel 028 9027 9901.*
This Victorian gin palace ranks as one of the most gorgeous bars in Ireland *(see p277)*. Lunch includes several local specialities, such as Irish stew and champ, but the Strangford Lough oysters really do stand out. Robinson's, the pub next door, is particularly lively in the evening. 🍴

Belfast: *Irene and Nans*
12 Brunswick St, Co Antrim.
Road map D2. *Tel 028 9023 9123.*
Conveniently located next to the Grand Opera House, this stylish bar echoes with the spirit of the 1950s. The superb cocktail list and great menu make this the perfect place to be seen, with evening entertainment from Monday to Thursday. The staff are well-trained and courteous. 🍴

Belfast: *Lavery's Gin Palace*
12–14 Bradbury Place, Co Antrim.
Road map D2. *Tel 028 9087 1106.*
Yet another of Belfast's fine old gin palaces. Bar food served at lunch and discos in the evenings. It is popular with students from Queen's University. 🍴 ♿ 🎵

Belfast: *White's Tavern*
Winecellar Entry, Co Antrim.
Road map D2. *Tel 028 9024 3080.*
Just one of several daylight-free pubs tucked away in the Entries *(see p277)* sector of Belfast city that are best at lunch time when decent, reasonably priced pub food is served. White's lays claim to be the oldest bar in the city. Other pubs in this series of alleys that are worth a look include the Morning Star and the Globe. 🍴 ♿ 🎵

Broughshane: *The Thatch Inn*
57 Main St, Co Antrim.
Road map D2.
Tel 028 2586 2727.
This old-thatched pub in the ancient village of Broughshane exudes charm, character and warmth. The Thatch Inn is well known for great food, warm welcomes and live music. 🍴 🎵

Bushmills: *Bushmills Inn*
9 Dunluce Rd, Co Antrim.
Road map D1.
Tel 028 2073 2339.
Set in an old coaching inn, this cosy bar is lit by gaslights. There is also an excellent restaurant on the premises. 🍴 🍽 ♿

Enniskillen: *Blake's of the Hollow*
6 Church St, Co Fermanagh.
Road map C2.
Tel 028 6632 2143.
One of a number of popular town-centre pubs, Blake's dates back to Victorian days and has many of its original fittings. 🍴 ♿ 🎵

Hillsborough: *Plough Inn*
The Square, Co Down.
Road map D2.
Tel 028 9268 2985.
This typical village pub, dating from the 1750s, has wooden ceiling beams and a selection of crockery, china and other ornaments on the walls. There's a bistro upstairs open during the day, serving oysters, and a nice beer garden. The Hillside, just down the main street, is also worth a visit. 🍴 🍽

Londonderry: *The Park Bar*
35 Francis St, Co Londonderry.
Road map C1. *Tel 028 7126 4674.*
A warm, welcoming, family-run bar close to the city centre and adjacent to St Eugene's Cathedral. The usual choices of European lagers and Guinness are on tap. During term time, students play traditional Irish music on Monday nights. 🎵

Omagh: *Molly Sweeney's*
Gortin Rd, Co Tyrone.
Road map C2.
Tel 028 8225 2595.
Molly Sweeney's is practically a museum to Irish drinking life. An eccentric mix of decorations furnish its many rooms – the Library Lounge, the Snug Bar, the Celtic Room and the Gothic Tower. Along with good food and drink, this place is very welcoming to visitors. It also has a nightclub with DJs. 🍴 ♿ 🎵

Portadown: *Jameson's*
Thomas St, Co Armagh.
Road map D2.
Tel 028 3833 4644.
In Jameson's beautiful lounge bar, guests are entertained with disco and dance music every night, and bar snacks are available all day. Upstairs at Toddy's Steakhouse, enjoy good food including sandwiches and traditional pub grub.

SHOPPING IN IRELAND

Ireland offers a wide range of handmade goods, usually regionally based and highly individual. Its most renowned products include chunky Aran sweaters, Waterford crystal, Irish linen, handloomed Donegal tweed and tasty farmhouse cheeses. The thriving crafts industry is based on traditional products with an innovative twist. Typical of contemporary Irish crafts are good design, quality craftsmanship and a range spanning

Linen shirt and tweed waistcoat

Celtic brooches, bone china, knitwear and designer fashion, carved bogwood and books of Irish poetry. Kitsch souvenirs also abound, from leprechauns and shamrock emblems to Guinness tankards and garish religious memorabilia. In the directory on page 355, a map reference is given for each address. Dublin shopping is covered in detail on pages 104–107. Road map references are to the towns and cities on the inside back cover.

Fruit and vegetable market in Moore Street, Dublin

WHERE TO SHOP

The choice of places to shop in Ireland ranges from tiny workshops to large factory outlets, and from elegant boutiques to high-street chain stores. Bargains can often be had at bric-à-brac shops and local markets, although the banter is sometimes the best thing on offer. This guide lists market days for every town featured. Sometimes the best produce or products are to be found off the beaten track; locals are always happy to let you know where.

WHEN TO SHOP

Most shops are open from Monday to Saturday, 9am to 5:30 or 6pm. In shopping centres and large towns, shops tend to have at least one late-night opening, usually on Thursday or Friday (Thursday in Dublin). In tourist areas, craft shops are generally open on Sundays too. Shops are closed at Easter and Christmas and on St Patrick's Day but are open on most other public holidays. In Killarney, Ireland's tourist capital, most shops are open until 10pm in summer.

HOW TO PAY

Major credit cards are generally accepted in department stores and larger retail outlets, but smaller shops prefer cash. Most traveller's cheques are accepted in major stores with a passport as identification.

SALES TAX AND REFUNDS

Most purchases are subject to VAT (sales tax) at 21 per cent, included in the sales price. However, visitors from outside the European Union (EU) can reclaim VAT prior to departure. When shipping goods overseas, refunds can be claimed at the point of purchase. If taking your goods with you, look for the CashBack logo in shops, fill in the special voucher, then visit CashBack offices at Dublin or Shannon Airport.

BOOKS

Reading is a national passion in Ireland, so bookshops are generally very good. In bigger shops expect solid sections on Irish archaeology and architecture, folklore, history, politics and cuisine. **Eason and Son** is one of the most widespread bookstore chains in the country with a large collection of Irish literature and newspapers. Seek out the smaller, "Irish Interest" shops too. In Galway, **Kenny's Bookshop and Art Gallery** is packed with both new and second-hand books.

MUSIC

Traditional musical instruments (see pp24–5) are made in many regions, especially County Clare, also known as the "singing county". Hand-made harps are a speciality in Mayo and Dublin. Instruments such as handcrafted *bodhráns*, uillean pipes, tin whistles

A traditional fiddle maker in his workshop in Dingle

Colourful bric-à-brac shop in Kilkenny

and fiddles are on sale throughout Ireland. There are several specialist record shops that sell traditional Irish recordings. **Golden Discs** is a chain of music stores, and stocks a good selection of traditional Irish music.

FOOD AND DRINK

In recent years, markets have become a popular way to shop for food in Irish cities. Most of what's on offer is produced locally under organic conditions. Smoked salmon, home-cured bacon, farmhouse cheeses, soda bread, preserves and handmade chocolates make perfect last-minute gifts.

Kylemore Abbey teapot

Guinness travels less well and is best drunk in Ireland. Irish whiskey is hard to beat as a gift or souvenir. Apart from the cheaper Power's and Paddy brands, the big names are Bushmills *(see p266)* and Jameson *(see p179)* . Rich Irish liqueurs include Irish Mist and Baileys Irish Cream.

CRAFTS

Crafts are a flourishing way of life in rural Ireland, and the distinctive products can be purchased from either city department stores or workshops and individual vendors. The **Crafts Council of Ireland** has branches in Dublin and Kilkenny, and can recommend good small-scale outlets in the country. Tourist offices also provide lists of local workshops, where you can watch the production

process. Craft shops, such as the **Kilkenny Design Centre** and **Bricin**, sell good examples of different crafts. In Cork and Kerry there is an abundance of workshops, mainly in Kinsale and Dingle. The *Guide to Craft Outlets* is available at local tourist offices. Distinctive products from this area are traditional tiles based on designs found in Kilkenny Cathedral and nearby medieval abbeys. Further west, green Connemara marble is made into "worry stones", small charms traditionally exchanged between families as marks of long-lasting friendship. Also in Connemara, **Roundhouse Music** makes "bodhrans" in front of interested tourists.

Other crafts include metalwork, leatherwork and carpentry. Local woods are used for ash or beech furniture, blackthorn walking sticks and sculptures made of 1,000-year-old bogwood – petrified wood salvaged from Ireland's unique boglands during turf cutting.

CRYSTAL AND GLASSWARE

In the wake of **Waterford Crystal** *(see p147)*, the brand leader, come countless followers. The price depends on reputation, the quantity of lead used in the glass and the labour-intensiveness of the design. **Tyrone Crystal** rates almost as highly as Waterford and is less expensive. Like Waterford, the factory runs an illuminating tour. **Tipperary Crystal** offers a range of lines, including trophies and lamps. **Galway Irish Crystal** is another elegant brand.

In Kilkenny, the famous Jerpoint Abbey inspires local designs by **Jerpoint Glass**. Decorated with simple yet stylish motifs, the small vases, candlesticks, jugs and bowls make pleasing gifts. Most stores will pack and send glassware overseas for you.

CERAMICS AND CHINA

Although more renowned for crystal, Ireland also has many reputable producers of ceramics and china. Established in 19th-century Ulster, Belleek Pottery *(see p269)* produces creamy china with a lustrous sheen and subtle decorative motifs, including shamrocks and flowers. In Galway, **Royal Tara China** is Ireland's leading fine bone china manufacturer, with Celtic-influenced designs, while Kylemore Abbey *(see p208)* specializes in exquisite handpainted pottery. **Louis Mulcahy's Pottery**, in Ballyferriter, is noted for fine decorative glazes, while in Bennettsbridge, **Nicholas Mosse Pottery** produces hand-painted designs. Enniscorthy in Wexford is another centre for ceramics.

Pottery display in Kilkenny Design Centre

Sign for the linen department at Brown Thomas store

LINEN

Damask linen was brought to Armagh by Huguenot refugees fleeing French persecution during the late 17th century. As a result, Belfast became the world's linen capital. Ulster is still the place for linen, with sheets and double-damask table linen on sale in Belfast – at **Smyth's Irish Linen**, for example – and in other towns. Linen, embroidered by hand, is made in Donegal. Linen-making can be seen at **Wellbrook Beetling Mill** *(see p268)*.

KNITWEAR AND TWEED

Aran sweaters are sold all over Ireland, particularly in County Galway and on the Aran Islands themselves. One of Ireland's best buys, these oiled, off-white sweaters used to be handed down through generations of Aran fishermen. Legend has it that each family used its own motifs. If a fisherman died at sea and his body

was unidentifiable, his family could recognize him by his sweater.

Given the Irish experience of wet weather, warm and waterproof clothes are generally of good quality, from waxed jackets and duffel coats to sheepskin jackets. Knitwear is on sale all over Ireland. **Avoca Handweavers** and **Blarney Woollen Mills** are the best-known outlets. Good buys include embroidered sweaters and waistcoats as well as hand-woven shawls, hats, caps and scarves.

Donegal tweed is a byword for quality, and is noted for its texture, tension and subtle colours (originally produced by dyes made from lichens and minerals). Tweed caps, scarves, ties and suits are sold in outlets such as **Magee and Co** in Donegal.

Façade of an antique furniture shop in Kenmare

JEWELLERY

In its golden age, Celtic metalwork was the pride of Ireland *(see pp32–5)*, and many contemporary crafts-people are still inspired by traditional Celtic designs. Handcrafted or factory-made silver, gold and ceramic jewellery is produced in a variety of designs. The Claddagh ring from Galway is the most famous Celtic design – the lovers' symbol of two hands

cradling a crowned heart. **Cahalan Jewellers** in County Galway is one of the most renowned and has a huge range of unique Irish and antique jewellery. For heraldic jewellery, try **James Murtagh Jewellers** in County Mayo.

FASHION

Inspired by a predominantly young population, Ireland is fast acquiring a name for fashion. Conservatively cut tweed and linen suits continue to be models of classic good taste, though young designers are increasingly experimental, using bold lines and mixing traditional fabrics.

A-Wear is a quality boutique that features funky, young designs for women and has branches in most cities. Here, and in other boutiques and department stores, you will find clothes designed by the best Irish designers, including Quin and Donnelly, Paul Costelloe, John Rocha, Louise Kennedy and Mariad Whisker.

Some new designers, such as Samantha Corcoran, Pauric Sweeney and Antonia Campbell Hughes, have eschewed traditional Irish textiles and forged fresh styles in new materials.

Ladies' fashion and the hottest trends can be found in **O'Donnell's** in Limerick, while up north, there are many outlets of **Clockwork Orange** and **Fosters Clothing**. For a unique boudoir-style shoe shopping experience, try **The Pink Room** near Carlingford Lough.

For budget clothing Dunnes Stores have branches throughout the Republic and Northern Ireland. Clothing and shoe sizes are identical to British fittings.

Selection of hand-knitted sweaters at a craft shop in Dingle

DIRECTORY

BOOKS

A.B. O'Connor Bookshop
Shelburne St, Kenmare,
Co Kerry. **Road map** B6.
Tel 064 41578.

Eason and Son
113 St Patrick's St, Cork,
Co Cork. **Road map** C5.
Tel 021 427 0477.

Kenny's Bookshop and Art Gallery
High St, Galway,
Co Galway.
Road map B4.
Tel 091 709 350.

McLoughlin's Books
Shop Street, Westport,
Co Mayo. **Road map** B3.
Tel 098 27777.

MUSIC

The Dingle Record Shop
Green St, Dingle, Co Kerry.
Road map A5.
Tel 087 298 4550.

Golden Discs
Eglinton St, Galway,
Co Galway.
Road map B4.
Tel 091 565688.

Mulligan Records
5 Middle St Court, Galway,
Co Galway.
Road map B4.
Tel 091 564961.

FOOD AND DRINK

McCambridges
38 / 39 Shop St, Galway,
Co Galway. **Road map** B4.
Tel 091 562259.

Spillane Seafoods
Lackabane, Killarney,
Co Kerry. **Road map** B5.
Tel 064 31320.

CRAFTS

Bricín
26 High St, Killarney,
Co Kerry. **Road map** B5.
Tel 064 34902.

Crafts Council of Ireland
Castle Yard, Kilkenny, Co
Kilkenny. **Road map** C4.
Tel 056 776 1804.

Craftworks Shop
Bedford House, Bedford
St, Belfast, Co Antrim.
Road map D2.
Tel 028 9024 4465.

Doolin Crafts Gallery
Ballyvoe, Doolin, Co Clare.
Road map B4.
Tel 065 707 4309.

Geoffrey Healy Pottery
Rocky Valley,
Kilmacanaogue, Co
Wicklow. **Road map** D4.
Tel 01 282 9270.

Kilkenny Design Centre
Castle Yard, Kilkenny, Co
Kilkenny. **Road map** C4.
Tel 056 7722118.

Keltic Knott
Main Street, Ballydehob,
Co Cork. **Road map** B6.
Tel 027 61217.

Roundstone Music
Roundstone, Connemara.
Road map B4.
Tel 095 35875.

CRYSTAL AND GLASSWARE

Connemara Marble Factory
Moycullen, Co Galway.
Road map B4.
Tel 091 555102.

Galway Irish Crystal
Merlin Park, Galway,
Co Galway. **Road map** B4.
Tel 091 757311.

Jerpoint Glass
Stoneyford, Co Kilkenny.
Road map D5.
Tel 056 772 4350.

Sligo Crystal
2 Hyde Bridge, Sligo,
Co Sligo. **Road map** C2.
Tel 071 914 3440.

Tipperary Crystal
Ballynoran, Carrick-on-
Suir, Co Tipperary.
Road map C5.
Tel 051 641 188.

Tyrone Crystal
Killybrackey, Coal Island Rd,
Dungannon, Co Tyrone.
Road map D2.
Tel 028 8772 5335.

CERAMICS AND CHINA

Louis Mulcahy's Pottery
Clogher, Ballyferriter,
Tralee, Co Kerry.
Road map A5.
Tel 066 915 6229.

Michael Kennedy Ceramics
Bolands Lane, Gort,
Co Galway.
Road map B4.
Tel 091 632245.

Nicholas Mosse Pottery
Bennettsbridge,
Co Kilkenny.
Road map D5.
Tel 056 772 7105.

Royal Tara China
Tara Hall, Mervue,
Co Galway.
Road map B4.
Tel 091 705602.

Treasure Chest
31–33 William St,
Galway, Co Galway.
Road map B4.
Tel 091 567237.

LINEN

Forgotten Cotton
Savoy Centre,
St Patrick's St, Cork,
Co Cork.
Road map C5.
Tel 021 427 6098.

Smyth's Irish Linen
65 Royal Ave, Belfast,
Co Antrim. **Road map** D2.
Tel 028 9024 2232.

KNITWEAR AND TWEED

Avoca Handweavers
Kilmacanogue, Bray,
Co Wicklow.
Road map D4.
Tel 01 286 7466.

Blarney Woollen Mills
Blarney, Co Cork.
Road map B5.
Tel 021 438 5280.

Magee and Co
The Diamond, Donegal,
Co Donegal.
Road map C2.
Tel 074 972 2660.

Quills Woollen Market
1 High St, Killarney, Co
Kerry. **Road map** B5.
Tel 064 32277.

Studio Donegal
The Glebe Mill, Kilcar,
Co Donegal.
Road map B2.
Tel 074 973 8194.

JEWELLERY

Cahalan Jewellers
Main St, Ballinasloe,
Co Galway. **Road map** B2.
Tel 09096 42513.

Cladagh Jewellers
24 Main St, Killarney,
Co Kerry. **Road map** B5.
Tel 064 32720.

Hilser Brothers
Grand Parade, Cork,
Co Cork. **Road map** C5.
Tel 021 427 0382.

James Murtagh Jewellers
14 Bridge St, Westport,
Co Mayo. **Road map** B3.
Tel 098 25322.

Faller's Jewellers
Williamsgate St, Galway,
Co Galway. **Road map** B4.
Tel 091 561226.

FASHION

A-Wear
110 Patrick St, Cork,
Co Cork. **Road map** C5.
Tel 021 427 2690.

Clockwork Orange
25/27 Wellington Place,
Belfast, Co Antrim.
Road map D2.
Tel 028 9024 9830.

Fosters Clothing
5 Strand Rd, Londonderry,
Co Londonderry.
Road map C1.
Tel 028 7136 6902.

O'Donnell's
11 Catherine St, Limerick,
Co Limerick.
Road map B4.
Tel 061 415932.

The Pink Room
Dundalk St, Carlingford
Co Louth.
Road map D3.
Tel 042 9383 6691.

What to Buy in Ireland

St Brigid's cross

Hundreds of gift and craft shops scattered throughout Ireland make it easy to find Irish specialities to suit all budgets. The best buys include linen, tweeds and crystal from factory shops which invariably offer an extensive choice of good quality products. Local crafts make unique souvenirs, from hand-made jewellery and ceramics to traditional musical instruments. Religious artifacts are also widely available. Irish food and drink are evocative reminders of your trip.

Traditional hand-held drum (*bodhrán*) and beater

Connemara marble "worry stone"

Traditional Claddagh ring

Enamel brooch

Modern jewellery and metalwork *draw on a long and varied tradition. Craftspeople continue to base their designs on sources such as the* Book of Kells *(see p64) and Celtic myths. Local plants and wildlife are also an inspiration. County Galway produces Claddagh rings – traditional betrothal rings – in gold and silver as well as "worry stones".*

Fuchsia earring from Dingle

Celtic-design enamel brooch

Bronzed resin Celtic figurine

Donegal tweed jacket and waistcoat

Tweed skirt and jacket

Clothing *made in Ireland is usually of excellent quality. Tweed-making still flourishes in Donegal where tweed can be bought ready-made as clothing and hats or as lengths of cloth. Knitwear is widely available all over the country in large factory outlets and local craft shops. The many hand-knitted items on sale, including Aran sweaters, are not cheap but should give years of wear.*

Tweed cap

Tweed fisherman's hat

Aran sweater

Irish linen *is world-famous and the range unparalleled. There is a huge choice of table and bed linen, including extravagant bedspreads and crisp, formal tablecloths. On a smaller scale, tiny, intricately embroidered hand-kerchiefs make lovely gifts as do linen table napkins. Tea towels printed with colourful designs are widely available. You can also buy linen goods trimmed with fine lace, which is still hand-made in Ireland, mainly in Limerick and Kenmare.*

Set of linen placemats and napkins

Fine linen handkerchiefs

Nicholas Mosse plate

Belleek teapot

Nicholas Mosse cup

Irish ceramics *come in traditional and modern designs. You can buy anything from a full dinner service by established factories, such as Royal Tara China or the Belleek Pottery, to a one-off contemporary piece from a local potter's studio.*

Irish crystal, *hand-blown and hand-cut, can be ordered or bought in many shops in Ireland. Visit the outlets of the principal manu-facturers, such as Waterford Crystal, Tyrone Crystal and Jerpoint Glass, to see the full range – from glasses and decanters to elaborate chandeliers.*

·IRISH· PROVERBS

ILLUSTRATED BY KAREN BAILEY

Book of Irish Proverbs

Books and stationery *are often beautifully illustrated. Museums and bookshops stock a wide range.*

Celtic-design cards

Waterford crystal tumbler and decanter

Food and drink *will keep the distinctive tastes of Ireland fresh long after you arrive home. Whiskey connoisseurs should visit the Old Bushmills Distillery (see p266) or the Jameson Heritage Centre (see p179) to sample their choice of whiskeys. Good regional food can be found at local shops all over Ireland. Try the dried seaweed, which is eaten raw or added to cooked dishes.*

Jameson whiskey

Bushmills whiskey

Fruit cake made with Guinness

Jar of Irish marmalade

Packet of dried seaweed

ENTERTAINMENT IN IRELAND

If there is one sphere in which Ireland shines, it is entertainment. For details about entertainment in Dublin, see pages 108–15. Elsewhere in Ireland, nightclubs and concerts by international entertainers tend to be concentrated in large cities, but many other events including theatre, arts festivals, traditional music and dance, cultural holidays and even medieval banquets take place all over the country. Most towns and cities also have one or two cinemas showing the latest movies on release.

Morris Minor van advertising the Clonakilty Folk Club

Not to be overlooked is the free entertainment (planned or spontaneous) provided by a night in a pub. For more active forms of entertainment, covered on pages 362–7, the list is even longer, from golf to pony trekking and cycling to scuba diving. Those who prefer their sports sitting down can go along as spectators to Ireland's famous horse race meetings, as well as Gaelic football, hurling, soccer and rugby matches. A happy mix of these activities can easily be put together with almost any itinerary.

Ulster Symphony Orchestra at the Ulster Hall in Belfast

INFORMATION SOURCES

The tourist board for the Republic, **Fáilte Ireland**, and the **Northern Ireland Tourist Board** (see p371) both publish a yearly *Calendar of Events* that lists major fixtures around the country, and all the regional tourist offices have information about happenings in each locality. To supplement these listings, check regional newspapers and inquire locally.

BOOKING TICKETS

Tickets can usually be bought at the door on the day or evening of most events. Advance booking is a must, however, for popular concerts and plays. Many cultural and arts festivals require tickets only for the key performances, but for internationally famous festivals, such as the Wexford Opera Festival, you will need to book well in advance through the festival office for all performances.

Credit-card bookings for plays, concerts and other events around Ireland can be made by telephone through **Keith Prowse Travel (IRL) Ltd** and **Ticketmaster** in Dublin.

MAJOR VENUES

In many Irish cities, the main theatres host a huge variety of events. In Cork, the **Opera House** presents predominantly Irish plays during the summer months, with musical comedy, opera and ballet at other times of year. The city's **Everyman Palace Theatre** stages plays by local and visiting companies interspersed with concerts of both classical and popular music. Sligo's **Hawks Well Theatre** and Limerick's **Belltable Arts Centre** are venues for drama and concerts. In the centre of Belfast, the **Grand Opera House**, **Waterfront Hall** and **Lyric Theatre** present a varied programme, including Irish and inter– national plays, experimental drama, pantomime and opera.

THEATRE

From international tours to amateur productions, there is excellent theatre to be seen in virtually every location in Ireland. In Galway, the **Druid Theatre** specializes in avant-garde plays, new Irish plays and Anglo-Irish classics, with frequent lunchtime and late-night performances, while Gaelic drama, Irish music, singing and dancing have all thrived at the **Taibhdhearc Theatre** since 1928. Waterford boasts its resident Red Kettle Theatre Company which performs at the **Garter Lane Theatre**, while the **Theatre Royal** brings amateur drama and musicals to the city.

Keep an eye out for small theatre groups performing in local halls around the country. Many of them are superb and they have spawned several of Ireland's leading actors.

Home of the Druid Theatre Company in Galway (see p210)

The Moscow Ballet at Belfast's Grand Opera House *(see p276)*

CLASSICAL MUSIC, OPERA AND DANCE

Major venues for classical music include the **Crawford Art Gallery**, Opera House and Everyman Palace in Cork; the Theatre Royal in Waterford; the Hawks Well Theatre in Sligo; and the Belltable Arts Centre in Limerick. Belfast's **Ulster Hall** hosts concerts from rock bands to the Ulster Symphony Orchestra.

Opera lovers from around the world come to Ireland for the **Wexford Festival of Opera** in October and November and the **Waterford Festival of Light Opera** in late September and early October. At Wexford, neglected operas are revived, while Waterford selects more mainstream operas and musicals. Elsewhere, opera is performed in Cork's Opera House and in Belfast's Grand Opera House.

Ireland has no resident ballet or avant-garde dance companies, but leading international companies perform occasionally at the major venues around the country.

ROCK, JAZZ AND COUNTRY

When international music stars tour Ireland, concerts outside Dublin are held at large outdoor sites. **Semple Stadium** in County Tipperary and Slane Castle *(see p245)* in County Meath are popular venues. Tickets and information are available from Ticketmaster.

Musical pubs *(see pp346–51)* are your best bet for good rock and jazz performed by Irish groups. Check local tourist offices and newspapers for rock and jazz nights, which usually take place midweek, with country and traditional music at weekends. For some of Ireland's "big band" jazz music, keep an eye out for Waterford's Brass and Co who play at dances around the country. Jazz lovers have a field day at the **Cork Jazz Festival** in late October, when music pours from every pub and international jazz greats play in the city's theatres.

Pub scene at Feakle Traditional Music Weekend, County Clare

TRADITIONAL MUSIC AND DANCE

The country pub has helped keep Irish music alive and provided the setting for the musical revival that began in the 1960s. Today, sessions of informal or impromptu music are still commonplace. In pubs, traditional music embraces ballads and rebel songs, as well as the older *sean-nos* – unaccompanied, understated stories, often sung in Irish.

Nights of Irish music and song are scheduled in many pubs, such as The Laurels and the Danny Mann in Killarney, the Yeats Tavern in Drumcliff, near Sligo, and An Phoenix and The Lobby in Cork. In Derry, the Gweedore Bar, Castle Bar and Dungloe Bar are among the cluster of musical pubs along Waterloo Street. Wherever you are, a query to the locals will send you off to the nearest musical pub. For more pub listings, *see pages 346–51.*

In Tralee, **Siamsa Tire**, the National Folk Theatre, stages marvellous folk drama incorporating traditional music, singing and dance. The Barn, in Bunratty Folk Park, is the setting for a traditional Irish night during the summer months.

Comhaltas Ceoltóiri Éireann, in Monkstown *(see p102)* has branches around the country and organizes traditional music and dance nights all year. Traditional Irish dancing can be stylish step dancing or joyous set dancing. Visitors are usually encouraged to join in the fun.

The **Fleadh Cheoil** (national traditional music festival) is a weekend of music, dance, song and stage shows that spill over into colourful street entertainment. It takes place at the end of August in a different town each year. Earlier in August, the **Feakle Traditional Music Weekend** in County Clare is a more intimate celebration of traditional music, song and dance.

A large audience for open-air music at the Cork Jazz Festival

Knappogue banquet at Knappogue Castle, County Clare

FESTIVALS

The Irish are experts at organizing festivals, staging a week of street entertainment, theatre, music and dance to celebrate almost everything under the sun *(see pp48–51)*.

In mid-July the lively town of Galway is host to the **Galway Arts Festival**, one of the largest festivals in Ireland. Here you will find Irish and international theatre and music, street entertainment and events for children. Taking place over one week in late July and early August is the **Boyle Arts Festival**. The events here include art exhibitions, poetry and drama performances as well as classical, traditional, folk and jazz concerts. Creative workshops are run for both adults and children.

Kilkenny Arts Festival in August, another major festival, features poetry, classical music concerts, movies and a range of crafts. The **Cork Film Festival** takes place within the first two weeks of October when international feature, documentary and short films are screened at venues all over the city. The **Belfast Festival at Queen's** is held for two weeks in October to late November. The lively and cosmopolitan programme includes a mixture of drama, ballet, comedy, cabaret, music and film. These take over the Queen's University campus plus theatres and other venues throughout Belfast.

In May, June, and July the **County Wicklow Gardens Festival** entices gardening enthusiasts to wander around

the county's most beautiful gardens. In mid-June, the **Music in Great Irish Houses** festival opens the doors to many of Ireland's historic homes to which the public seldom has access, with classical music performed by top-rate musicians. Venues include Mount Stewart House *(see pp282–3)* and University College, Cork.

Kilkenny Arts Week street theatre

TRADITIONAL BANQUETS WITH ENTERTAINMENT

Ireland's banquets have gained international fame and are great fun. Each of the banquets features costumed waiters and performers, as well as traditional food and drink of the chosen period.

Most famous are the medieval banquets – the one at Bunratty Castle *(see pp192–3)* was the first and is the liveliest, with year-round performances. From April to October, there is a medieval banquet at Knappogue Castle *(see p189)*, and at Dunguaire Castle *(see p212)* there is a quieter, more intimate programme of music and poetry. From March until November, the highly enjoyable Killarney Manor Banquet, held at the stately manor on the Loreto road just south of Killarney, creates an early 19th-century atmosphere.

CULTURAL BREAKS

A break in Ireland focused on any one of the cultural aspects of Irish life is enriching as well as fun. Choose from a variety of cultural topics and study courses: Irish music and literature, great houses and gardens, Irish language and folklore, crafts and cookery.

One of the most fascinating possibilities is the exploration of Ireland's 5,000-year history as revealed in the many relics strewn across the landscape. The **Achill Archaeological Summer School** in County Mayo, for example, runs a course that includes the active excavation of ancient sites.

To learn the secret of Irish cooking, there is no better place than the **Ballymaloe School of Cookery** in County Cork; it is run by Darina Allen, Ireland's most famous cook.

For literature enthusiasts, the **Yeats International Summer School** studies the works of Yeats and his contemporaries, while **Listowel Writers' Week** brings together leading writers for lectures and workshops.

Folk dancers in traditional Irish costume

DIRECTORY

BOOKING TICKETS

Keith Prowse Travel (IRL) Ltd
Irish Life Mall, Dublin 1.
Tel 01 878 3500.

Ticketmaster
Grafton House,
70 Grafton St, Dublin 2.
Tel 01 648 6060.

MAJOR VENUES

Belltable Arts Centre
69 O'Connell St, Limerick.
Tel 061 319866.
www.belltable.ie

Everyman Palace Theatre
MacCurtain St, Cork.
Tel 021 450 1673.
www.everymanpalace.com

Grand Opera House
Great Victoria St, Belfast.
Tel 028 9024 1919.
www.goh.co.uk

Hawks Well Theatre
Johnston Ct, Sligo.
Tel 071 916 1526.

Lyric Theatre
55 Ridgeway St, Belfast.
Tel 028 9038 1081.

Opera House
Emmet Place, Cork.
Tel 021 427 4308.
www.corkopera-house.com

Waterfront Hall
2 Lanyon Place, Belfast.
Tel 028 9033 4455.

THEATRE

Druid Theatre
Chapel Lane, Galway.
Tel 091 568660.
www.druidtheatre.com

Garter Lane Theatre
22A O'Connell St,
Waterford.
Tel 051 855038.
www.garterlane.ie

Taibhdhearc Theatre
Middle St, Galway.
Tel 091 562024.

Theatre Royal
The Mall, Waterford.
Tel 051 874402.

CLASSICAL MUSIC, OPERA AND DANCE

Crawford Art Gallery
Emmet Place, Cork.
Tel 021 427 3377.
www.crawfordart-gallery.com

Ulster Hall
Bedford St, Belfast.
Tel 028 9032 3900.
www.ulsterhall.co.uk

Waterford Festival of Light Opera
Theatre Royal, Waterford.
Tel 051 874402.

Wexford Festival of Opera
Theatre Royal, High St,
Wexford. *Tel* 053 22144.
www.wexfordopera.com

ROCK, JAZZ AND COUNTRY

Cork Jazz Festival
20 South Mall, Cork.
Tel 021 427 0463.
www.corkjazzfestival.com

Semple Stadium
Thurles, Co Tipperary.
Tel 0504 21308.

TRADITIONAL MUSIC AND DANCE

Comhaltas Ceoltóirí Éireann
32 Belgrave Sq,
Monkstown, Co Dublin.
Tel 01 280 0295.

Feakle Traditional Music Weekend
Maghera, Caher, Co Clare.
Tel 061 924322.

Siamsa Tíre
National Folk Theatre, The
Town Park, Tralee, Co
Kerry. *Tel* 066 712 3055.

The Traditional Irish Night
Bunratty Castle and Folk
Park, Bunratty, Co Clare.
Tel 061 360788.

FESTIVALS

Belfast Festival at Queen's
Festival House, 25 College
Gardens, Belfast.
Tel 028 9097 1197.
www.belfastfestival.com

Boyle Arts Festival
King House, Main St,
Boyle, Co Roscommon.
Tel 071 966 3085.
www.boylearts.com

Cork Film Festival
10 Washington St, Cork.
Tel 021 427 1711.
www.corkfilmfest.org

County Wicklow Gardens Festival
St Manntan's House,
Kilmantin Hill, Wicklow.
Tel 0404 20070.

Galway Arts Festival
Black Box Theatre, Dyke
Rd, Terryland, Galway.
Tel 091 509700.
www.galwayarts-festival.com

Kilkenny Arts Festival
9/10 Abbey Business
Centre, Kilkenny.
Tel 056 775 2175.
www.kilkennyarts.ie

Music in Great Irish Houses
29 Rose Pk, Dun
Laoghaire, Co Dublin.
Tel 01 280 9850 (1–6pm).
www.musicirishhouses.com

CULTURAL BREAKS

Archaeology
Achill Archaeological Summer School
Folk Life Centre, Dooagh,
Achill Island, Co. Mayo.
Tel 098 43564.
www.achill-field school.com

Gerard Manley-Hopkins Summer School
Drogheda Street,
Monasterevin, Co. Kildare.
Tel 045 525416.

Oideas Gael
Gleanncholmcille,
Co Donegal.
Tel 074 973 0248.

Cookery
Ballymaloe School of Cookery
Shanagarry, Midleton,
Co Cork.
Tel 021 464 6785.
www.cookingisfun.ie

Houses, Castles & Gardens of Ireland

16A Woodlands Pk,
Blackrock, Co Dublin.
Tel 01 288 9114.
www.gardensireland.com;
www.castlesireland.com

National Trust
Rowallane House,
Saintfield, Ballynahinch,
Co Down.
Tel 028 9751 0721.

Irish Language Conversation Classes
Oidhreacht Chorca
Dhuibhne, Ballyferriter,
Co Kerry.
Tel 066 915 6100.

Literary
Goldsmith Summer School
Rathmore, Ballymahon,
Co Longford.
Tel 090 643 71448.

James Joyce Summer School
University College Dublin,
Belfield, Dublin 4.
Tel 01 716 8480.

Listowel Writers' Week
24 The Square, Listowel,
Co Kerry.
Tel 068 21074.
www.writersweek.ie

William Carleton Summer School
Dungannon District
Council, Circular Rd,
Dungannon, Co Tyrone.
Tel 028 8772 5311.

Yeats International Summer School
Yeats Society, Yeats
Memorial Building,
Douglas Hyde Bridge, Sligo.
Tel 071 914 2693.
www.yeats-sligo.com

Music
South Sligo Summer School of Traditional Music, Song and Dance
Tubbercurry, Co Sligo.
Tel 071 912 0912.
www.sssschool.org

Willie Clancy Summer School
Miltown Malbay, Co Clare.
Tel 065 708 4148.

Sports and Outdoor Activities

Sign outside a fishing tackle shop in Donegal

Even in the largest Irish cities, the countryside is never far away, and it beckons alluringly to every lover of the great outdoors. Topping the list of spectator sports is Ireland's famous horse racing, followed by hurling, Gaelic football and soccer, which also make for very exciting viewing. Those who want to do more than just watch, can choose between fishing, golf, horse riding, sailing, cycling, walking and water sports. Entire vacations can be based around any of these activities. In addition to the contacts on pages 366–7, Fáilte Ireland in the Republic, the Northern Ireland Tourist Board and all local tourist offices have information on spectator and participant sports. For details of main events in the sporting calendar, see pages 28–9.

Steeplechase at Fairyhouse Racecourse

SPECTATOR SPORTS

The Irish passion for horse racing is legendary. **The Curragh** *(see p129)*, where the Irish Derby is held, is a leading racecourse. **Fairyhouse**, the venue for Ireland's Grand National, is a popular spot year round, but especially around Christmas when Dubliners descend to lay bets on the annual races. **Punchestown**, in County Kildare, has been a fixture of the racing scene for more than 150 years and has a capacity of 80,000 people. **Leopardstown** in Dublin is also a well-liked track and has year round racing.

Many smaller racecourses, with exciting, informal atmospheres, are found throughout Ireland. Galway Race Week in late July is a great social event. A racing calendar for the whole of Ireland, available from **Horse Racing Ireland**, lists National Hunt and flat race meets, which occur on 230 days of the year.

There are also 18 recognized greyhound stadia operating in the Republic. The best known are Dublin's **Shelbourne Park** and **Harold's Cross Stadium**, both of which have excellent dining facilities.

Croke Park is Ireland's most impressive sports stadium and hosts Gaelic football and hurling matches. International rugby and soccer matches are usually held at the Lansdowne Road Stadium. For soccer tickets, contact the **Football Association of Ireland**. Rugby enthusiasts should get in touch with the **Irish Rugby Football Union**.

For golfers, the annual highlight is the Irish Open Golf Championship in July. The venue varies from year to year. For tickets and information, contact the **Irish Open Office**.

FISHING

With its abundant coastline and some of the cleanest stretches of freshwater found in all of Europe, Ireland is a paradise for anglers. Coarse, game and sea fishing are all very popular. The lakes and rivers are home to bream, pike, perch and roach. Coastal rivers yield the famous Irish salmon, along with other game fish. The sea trout and brown trout also offer anglers a challenge.

Flounder, whiting, mullet, bass and coalfish tempt the sea angler, while deep-sea excursions chase abundant supplies of dogfish, shark, skate and ling. You can plan sea-angling trips from many different places – the Cork and Kerry coastline is a highly favoured starting point.

Clonanav Fly Fishing Centre near Clonmel, County Waterford, is popular with both novice and experienced anglers as it has superb accommodation, as well as a reliable, experienced staff. Regarded as the best fishing river in the east, River Slaney has many fisheries along its banks. **Ballintemple Fishery** is a good choice, and offers angling equipment for hire, and instruction if needed. **Mike's Fishing Tackle** in south Dublin also hires out fishing tackle. Live bait is available for purchase.

Information on the required permits can be obtained from

Fishing in the canal at Robertstown, County Kildare *(see p128)*

Walking in the Gap of Dunloe, Killarney (see p163)

the **Central Fisheries Board** in the Republic, and from **Inland Fisheries**, Department of Culture, Arts and Leisure, Northern Ireland. Contact the **Irish Federation of Sea Anglers** for useful tips, or in order to book sea fishing trips or courses.

Maps and other information on fishing locations can be obtained from Fáilte Ireland in the Republic, and from the Northern Ireland Tourist Board (see pp370–71). It is also worth consulting the **Irish Angling Update** website, which posts helpful and regularly updated reports on angling conditions throughout Ireland.

WALKING AND MOUNTAINEERING

A walking holiday puts you in the very middle of the glorious Irish landscape. The network of waymarked trails all over the country cut through some truly breathtaking and lovely areas. Information on long-distance walks is available from Fáilte Ireland and the Northern Ireland Tourist Board. The loveliest routes include Wicklow Way (see p139), Dingle Way, Kerry Way, Munster Way and Barrow Towpath. Each of these may be split into shorter sections for less experienced walkers or those short of time. The 800-km (500-mile) Ulster Way encircles Northern Ireland, taking in the spectacular scenery around Giant's Causeway (see pp262–3) and the peaks of the mountains of Mourne (see pp284–5).

Irish Ways offers walking holidays in the Republic. To find out about organized walks in Northern Ireland, contact the **Ulster Federation of Rambling Clubs**.

An **Óige Hill Walkers Club** organizes a hike each Sunday on the Wicklow and Dublin mountains for experienced walkers. Once a month, the club's programme includes an introductory hard hike which allows novices to try out more rigorous hiking.

The award-winning **Michael Gibbons' Walking Ireland Centre** specializes in half-day walks and full-day tours in summer that guide walkers through the landscape and heritage of Connemara.

Skibbereen Historical Walks enables visitors to learn about Ireland's past via Skibbereen, a small town largely associated with the Famine.

Contact the **Mountaineering Council of Ireland** for more details about mountaineering and rock climbing holidays. For any hike, remember to go well-equipped for the highly changeable Irish weather.

CYCLING

With the exhilarating range of countryside to be explored, and the largely traffic-free roads, cycling is a pleasure in Ireland. Several organizations such as **Celtic Cycling** offer planned itineraries as well as accommodation. **Premier Cycling Holidays** have several bicycle tours, which seem to have been designed to maximize the thrill of cycling.

Sign for the Ulster Way, the trail around Northern Ireland

The **MTB Commission of Cycling Ireland** website contains details of many trails and mountain biking events, as well as having links to other cycling websites in Northern Ireland and the Republic.

You can transport your bike fairly cheaply by train or bus. For bike rental, try **Raleigh Rent-a-Bike** depots, found in both Northern Ireland and the Republic, or the **Cycleways** outlet in Parnell Street, Dublin.

Cycling through the Muckross House estate near Killarney (see p159)

Golfers at Portstewart in Northern Ireland *(see p260)*

GOLF

Out of the 300 or more golf courses spread throughout Ireland, over 50 are championship class. Many of the most beautiful greens verge on spectacular stretches of coast, and are kept in top condition.

In County Kilkenny, the internationally acclaimed golf course, **Mount Juliet**, was designed by golfing legend Jack Nicklaus. County Kildare's **K Club** is home to two superb 18-hole championship golf courses. Arnold Palmer designed both, but each has its own characteristics and special set of challenges. Champion golfer Christy O'Connor Junior designed **Galway Bay Golf Club**. This difficult course, a must for all keen golfers, is dotted with historic ruins dating back to the 16th century.

Acknowledged as one of the truly great links courses, **Portmarnock Golf Club** is situated to the north of Dublin, about 19 kms (12 miles) from the city centre. Its quality and location have made it a splendid venue for some of the game's most celebrated events. On the Atlantic coast, **Lahinch Golf Club** in County Clare is a must for devoted golfers, and is a recognized Mackenzie course.

Northern Ireland's best-known courses are **Royal Portrush Golf Club** and **Royal County Down Golf Club**.

The **Golfing Union of Ireland**, the **Irish Ladies Golfing Union** and the tourist boards have information on courses, conditions and green fees all over the country. Equipment can be hired at most clubs, but most golfers prefer to bring their own.

HORSE RIDING AND PONY TREKKING

The Irish are rightly proud of their fine horses. Many riding centres, both residential and non-residential, offer trail riding and trekking along woodland trails, deserted beaches, country lanes and mountain routes. Dingle, Donegal, Connemara and Killarney are all renowned areas for trail riding – post-to-post and based. Post-to-post trails follow a series of routes with accommodation in a

Horse riding in Killarney

different place each night. Based trail rides follow different routes in one area, but riders return to stay at the same location each night.

Aille Cross Equestrian Centre in Connemara provides horseback trail riding for both experienced and novice riders. Riders spend four to six hours a day on Connemara ponies or hunting horses. Further south, **Killarney Riding Stables** is located just 2 km (1 mile) from the heart of Killarney town. Adventurous riders can begin the four- or six-day Killarney Reeks Trail

from here.

The **Mountpleasant Trekking and Riding Centre** can be found within 2,000 acres of forestry and rolling countryside around Castlewellan in County Down. The centre caters for new and experienced riders.

Five Counties Holidays provides vacations that include horse riding in different areas of the northwest of Ireland. Also, many riding centres such as **Equestrian Holidays Ireland** offer guidance and lessons to beginners as well more advanced riders, along with lessons in show jumping.

WATER SPORTS

With a coastline of over 4,800 km (3,000 miles), Ireland is the perfect venue for water sports. Surfing, windsurfing, scuba diving and canoeing are the most popular activities, as there are ample facilities along the entire Irish coastline.

Conditions in Sligo are the best in Ireland for surfing, but many other coastal locations offer good conditions. The **Irish Surfing Association**, the national governing body for surfing and related activities such as knee boarding and body surfing, has plenty of information about surfing in all 32 Irish counties. Windsurfing centres in Ireland are

Surfing at Bundoran, Donegal Bay *(see p230)*

SPORTS AND OUTDOOR ACTIVITIES

365

mainly found near Dublin, Cork and Westport.

Diving conditions are variable but visibility is particularly good on the west coast. The **Irish Underwater Council** will put you in touch with courses and facilities. **DV Diving** organizes scuba diving courses and offers accommodation near Belfast Lough and the Irish Sea where there are a number of historic wrecks to be explored.

Inland, Lower Lough Erne (see pp270–71) and Killaloe by Lough Derg (see p190) are popular holiday centres. The **Lakeland Canoe Centre** between Upper and Lower Lough Erne gives canoeing courses and also organizes canoeing holidays (with overnight camping), including one down the charming Shannon-Erne Waterway (see p235). From March, **Atlantic Sea Kayaking** organizes one-day outings, as well as two- to eight-day trips around Castlehaven, Baltimore and beyond.

There are several areas all around the coast that are safe for experienced swimmers. Ask locally for details. In Dublin, the popular 40 Foot in Sandycove is a favourite haunt of dedicated sea swimmers. Children are quite safe in the sandy waters inside the harbour while adults can enjoy the deeper waters on the seaward side of the harbour wall. Contact the **Dun Laoghaire-Rathdown County Council** for more details.

CRUISING AND SAILING

A tranquil cruising holiday is an ideal alternative to the stress and strain of driving, and Ireland's 14,000 km (900 mile) of rivers and some 800 lakes offer a huge variety of conditions for those who want a waterborne holiday. Stopping over at waterside towns and villages puts you in touch with the Irish on their home ground. Whether you opt for Lough Derg or elsewhere on the Shannon, or the Grand Canal (see p101) from Dublin to the Shannon, a unique view of the Irish countryside opens up all along the way.

Yachting off Rosslare, County Wexford (see p151)

Running between Carrick-on-Shannon in Country Leitrim and Upper Lough Erne in Fermanagh, is the **Shannon-Erne Waterway** (see p235), a disused canal reopened in 1993. From here it is simple to continue through Upper and Lower Lough Erne (see pp270–71) to Belleek. **Emerald Star** has a fleet of cruisers for use on the waterway.

Shannon Castle Line runs a modern and high-quality fleet of cruisers on the Shannon. **Silver Line Cruisers**, which also operates on the Shannon, is barely 2 kms (1 mile) from the grand canal, and promises relaxed, uncrowded cruises.

The coast between Cork and the Dingle Peninsula is a popular sailing area. The **International Sailing Centre** near Cork offers tuition. The **Ulster Cruising School** in Carrickfergus provides lessons at all levels. More experienced sailors can charter a yacht and sail up the dramatic Irish shore to the western coast of Scotland.

HUNTING AND SHOOTING

Ireland's hunting season runs from October to March, and although fox-hunting tends to predominate in the Republic (it is banned in Northern Ireland), stag and hare hunts also take place. Contact **The Irish Master of Foxhounds Association** in the Republic, and the **Countryside Alliance** in Northern Ireland.

Duck shooting is also available. The shooting season is from September to the end of January. Clay-pigeon (year round) and pheasant shooting (November to January) are also popular. **Mount Juliet Estate** offers guns for hire and supplies cartridges. **Colebrook Park** in County Fermanagh offers deer-stalking outings and lodging. Northern Ireland's **National Countrysports Fair**, usually held in May, is a major attraction for game enthusiasts.

The **National Association of Regional Game Councils** will provide you with details of permits required for hunting.

SPORTS FOR THE DISABLED

Sports enthusiasts with a disability can obtain details of facilities for the disabled from the **Irish Wheelchair Association**. Central and local tourist boards and many of the organizations listed in the directory also advise on available facilities. The **Share Village** provides a range of activity holidays for both disabled and able-bodied people.

Boats moored at Carnlough Harbour on the Antrim coast (see p267)

DIRECTORY

SPECTATOR SPORTS

Croke Park
Dublin 3. *Tel 01 819 2300.*
www.crokepark.ie

Curragh Racecourse
The Curragh, Co Kildaire.
Road map D4.
Tel 045 441 205.
www.curragh.ie

Fairyhouse
Rataoth, Co Meath.
Road map D3.
Tel 01 825 6167.
www.
fairyhouseracecourse.ie

Football Association of Ireland
80 Merrion Sq, Dublin 2.
Dublin map F4.
Tel 01 703 7500.
www.fai.ie

Harold's Cross Stadium
Harold's Cross Rd, Dublin 6.
Tel 01 497 9023.

Horse Racing Ireland
Thoroughbred County House, Kill, Co Kildaire.
Road map D4.
Tel 045 842 800.
www.hri.ie

Irish Open Office
Dartmouth House,
Grand Parade, Dublin 6.
Tel 01 498 0300.
www.nissan-irishopen.ie

Irish Rugby Football Union
62 Lansdowne Road,
Dublin 4.
Tel 01 647 3800.
www.irishrugby.ie

Leopardstown
Foxrock, Dublin 18.
Tel 01 289 0500.
www.leopardstown.com

Punchestown
Naas, Co Kildaire.
Road map D4.
Tel 045 897 704.
www.punchestown.com

Shelbourne Park
Pearse Street, Dublin 2.
Tel 01 202 6621.
www.
shelbournepark.com

FISHING

Ballintemple Fishery
Ardattin, Co Carlow.
Road map D4.
Tel 059 915 5037.
www.ballintemple.com

Central Fisheries Board
Swords.
Tel 01 884 2600.
www.cfb.ie

Clonanav Fly Fishing Centre
Ballymacarbry,
Co Waterford.
Road map C5.
Tel 052 36141.
www.flyfishingireland.com

Inland Fisheries
Interpoint,
20–24 York St, Belfast.
Road map D2.
Tel 028 9025 8825.
www.dcalni.gov.uk

Irish Angling Update
www.cfb.ie

Irish Federation of Sea Anglers
Mr Hugh O'Rorke,
67 Windsor Dr,
Monkstown, Co Dublin.
Tel 01 280 6873.
www.ifsa.ie

Mike's Fishing Tackle
Patrick St,
Dun Laoghaire, Co Dublin.
Road map D4.
Tel 01 280 4177.

WALKING AND MOUNTAINEERING

An Óige Hill Walkers Club
61 Mountjoy St, Dublin 7.
Dublin map C1.
Tel 01 830 4555.
http://homepage.eircom.n
et/-thehillwalker/

Irish Ways
Ballycanew, Gorey,
Co Wexford.
Road map D4.
Tel 055 27479.
www.irishways.com

Michael Gibbons' Walking Ireland Centre
Market Street, Clifden,
Co Galway.
Road map A3.
Tel 095 21492.
www.walkingireland.com

Mountaineering Council of Ireland
13 Joyce Way, Parkwest
Business Park, Dublin 12.
Tel 01 625 1115.
www.mountaineering.ie

Skibbereen Historical Walks
Skibbereen Heritage Ctr,
Skibbereen, Co Cork.
Road map B6.
Tel 028 40900.
www.skibereenheritage.
com

Ulster Federation of Rambling Clubs
12B Breda Hse, Drumart Dr,
Belfast. **Road map** D2.
Tel 028 9064 8041.
www.ufrc-online.co.uk

CYCLING

Ardclinis Activity Centre
High St, Cushendall,
Co Antrim. **Road map** D1.
Tel 028 2177 1340.
www.ardclinis.com

Celtic Cycling
Lorum Old Rectory,
Bagenalstown,
Co Carlow.
Road map D4.
Tel 059 977 5282.
www.celticcycling.com

Cycleways
185–6 Parnell St, Dublin 1.
Dublin map C3.
Tel 01 873 4748.
www.cycleways.com

MTB Commission of Cycling Ireland
www.mtbireland.com

Premier Cycling Holidays
Portland, Nenagh, Co
Tipperary. **Road map** C4.
Tel 090 974 7134.
www.premiercycling.com

Raleigh Rent-a-Bike
Long Mile Rd, Dublin 12.
Tel 01 465 9659.
www.raleigh.ie

GOLF

Galway Bay Golf Club
Renville, Oranmore,
Co Galway. **Road map** B4.
Tel 091 790 500.

Golfing Union of Ireland
Unit 8, Block G, Business
Campus, Maynooth,
Co Kildare. **Road map** D3.
Tel 01 505 4000.
www.gui.ie

Irish Ladies Golfing Union
1 Clonskeagh Sq, Dublin
14. *Tel 01 269 6244.*
www.ilgu.ie

The K Club
Straffan, Co Kildare. **Road map** D4. *Tel 01 601 7200.*
www.kclub.ie

Lahinch Golf Club
Lahinch, Co Clare.
Road map B4.
Tel 065 708 1003.
www.lahinchgolf.com

Mount Juliet
Thomastown, Co Kilkenny.
Road map D5.
Tel 056 777 3000.
www.mountjuliet.com

Portmarnock Golf Club
Portmarnock, Co Dublin.
Road map D3. *Tel 01 846
2968.* www.portmarnock
golfclub.ie

Professional Golf Association
Dundalk Golf Club,
Blackrock, Dundalk,
Co Louth. **Road map** D3.
Tel 042 932 1193.
www.pga.info

Royal County Down Golf Club
36 Golf Links Rd,
Newcastle, Co Down.
Road map E2.
Tel 028 4372 3314.
www.royalcountydown.
org

Royal Portrush Golf Club
Dunluce Rd, Portrush, Co
Antrim. **Road map** D1.
Tel 028 7082 2311.
www.royalportrush
golfclub.com

DIRECTORY

HORSE RIDING AND PONY TREKKING

Aille Cross Equestrian Centre
Loughrea,
Co Galway.
Road map B4.
Tel 091 841216.
www.aille-cross.com

Association of Irish Riding Establishments
11 Moore Park,
Newbridge,
Co Kildare.
Road map D4.
Tel 045 431584.
www.aire.ie

British Horse Society
House of Sport,
Upper Malone Rd,
Belfast.
Road map D2.
Tel 028 9268 3801.
www.bhs.org.uk

Mountpleasant Trekking and Horse Riding Centre
Bannonstown Rd,
Castlewellan, Co Down.
Road map D2.
Tel 028 4377 8651.
www.mountpleasant centre.com

Equestrian Holidays Ireland
Whispering Pines,
Crosshaven, Co Cork.
Road map C6.
Tel 021 483 1950.
www.ehi.ie

Five Counties Holidays
Ardmourne House,
Castlederg, Co Tyrone.
Road map C2.
Tel 028 8167 0291.
www.five-counties-holidays.com

Killarney Riding Stables
Ballydowney,
Killarney, Co Kerry.
Road map B5.
Tel 064 31686.
www.killarney-riding-stables.com

WATER SPORTS

Atlantic Sea Kayaking
The Abbey,
Skibbereen, Co Cork.
Road map B6.
Tel 028 21058.
www.atlanticseakayaking.com

Baltimore Diving and Watersports Centre
Baltimore, Co Cork.
Road map B6.
Tel 028 20300.
www.baltimorediving.com

Dun Laoghaire-Rathdown County Council
County Hall, Marine Rd,
Dun Laoghaire, Co Dublin.
Road map D4.
Tel 01 205 4700.

DV Diving
138 Mountstewart Rd,
Newtownards, Co Down.
Road map E2.
Tel 028 9186 1686.
www.dvdiving.co.uk

Irish Surfing Association
Easkey Surf and
Information Centre,
Easkey, Co Sligo.
Road map B2.
Tel 096 49428.
www.isasurf.ie

Irish Underwater Council
78a Patrick St,
Dun Laoghaire, Co Dublin.
Road map D4.
Tel 01 284 4601.
www.scubaireland.com

Lakeland Canoe Centre
Castle Island, Enniskillen,
Co Fermanagh.
Road map C2.
Tel 028 6632 4250.

CRUISING AND SAILING

Athlone Cruisers
Jolly Mariner, Athlone,
Co Westmeath.
Road map C3.
Tel 090 272892.
www.acl.ie

Emerald Star
The Marina,
Carrick-on-Shannon,
Co Leitrim.
Road map C3.
Tel 071 962 1433.
www.emeraldstar.ie

Erne Marine
Bellanaleck,
Enniskillen,
Co Fermanagh.
Road map C2.
Tel 028 6634 8267.
www.ernemarine.com

International Sailing Centre
East Beach,
Cobh, Co Cork.
Road map C6.
Tel 021 481 1237.
www.sailcork.com

Lough Melvin Holiday Centre
Garrison,
Co Fermanagh.
Road map C2.
Tel 028 6865 8124.
www.loughmelvincentre.com

Shannon Castle Line
Williamstown Harbour,
Whitegate, Co Clare.
Road map C4.
Tel 061 192 7042.
www.shannoncruisers.com

Silver Line Cruisers
The Marina,
Banagher, Co Offaly.
Road map C4.
Tel 0509 51112.
www.silverlinecruisers.com

Tara Cruisers
Unit 12,
Market Yard Centre,
Carrick-on-Shannon,
Co Leitrim.
Road map C3.
Tel 071 962 2266.

Ulster Cruising School
The Marina,
Carrickfergus, Co Antrim.
Road map E2.
Tel 028 9336 8818.
www.silverlinecruisers.com

HUNTING AND SHOOTING

Colebrooke Park
Brookeborough,
Co Fermanagh.
Road map C2.
Tel 028 8953 1402

Countryside Alliance
Larchfield Estate,
Bailliesmills Road,
Lisburn, Co Antrim.
Road map D2.
Tel 028 9263 9911.
www.caireland.org

The Irish Master of Foxhounds Association
Tel 086 255366.
www.imfha.com

Mount Juliet Estate
Thomastown,
Co Kilkenny.
Road map D5.
Tel 056 777 3000.
www.mountjuliet.com

National Association of Regional Game Councils
6 Sandford Road,
Ranelagh, Dublin 6.
Tel 01 497 4888.
www.nargc.ie

National Countrysports Fair
Moira Demesne,
Lisburn, Co Antrim.
Road map D2.
Tel 2892 662306.
www.irishfieldsports.com

SPORTS FOR THE DISABLED

Irish Wheelchair Association
Blackheath Dr,
Clontarf, Dublin 3.
Tel 01 818 6400.
www.iwa.ie

Share Village
Smith's Strand, Lisnaskea,
Co Fermanagh.
Road map C2.
Tel 028 6772 2122.
www.sharevillage.org

SURVIVAL
GUIDE

PRACTICAL INFORMATION

Tourist Board logo

Although Ireland is quite a small island, visitors should not expect to see everything in a short time, since many of the country's most magnificent attractions are in rural areas. In remote parts of the island the roads are narrow and winding, the pace of life is very slow, banks often open for only one or two days of the week and public transport tends to be infrequent. However, although the Republic of Ireland remains one of Europe's most unspoiled destinations, its economy is developing fast. Any decent-sized town in the Republic is likely to have a tourist information centre and offer a full range of facilities for the visitor. Northern Ireland has its own tourist board which also has offices in most towns. The standard of facilities available to those travelling in the North equals that across the border and, as with the Republic, the level of hospitality is first-rate.

TOURIST INFORMATION

In both the Republic and Northern Ireland there is an impressive network of tourist information offices. As well as providing lots of free local information, the tourist offices in large towns sell maps and guide books and can reserve accommodation for a nominal charge. There are also tourist information points in some of the smaller towns and villages. The opening hours can be somewhat erratic and many are open only during the summer season. The local museums and libraries often stock a selection of useful tourist literature.

Before leaving for Ireland you can get brochures and advice from **Tourism Ireland**, which has information on both Northern Ireland and the Republic. Their offices can be found in major cities all over the world – a reflection of the universal appeal of Ireland. **Fáilte Ireland** (the Irish Tourist Board) and the **Northern Ireland Tourist Board** (NITB) can also supply you with maps and leaflets. For more local information on sights, accommodation and car rental, it's worth contacting the regional tourist offices in Dublin, Cork, Galway and Limerick.

If you pick up a list of places to stay in a tourist office, it's worth noting that not every local hotel and guesthouse will be included – these lists recommend only those establishments that have been approved by the Tourist Board.

The Heritage Service-run Parke's Castle in County Leitrim *(see p233)*

ADMISSION CHARGES

Most of Ireland's major sights, including ancient monuments, museums and national parks, have an admission fee. For each place of interest in this guide, we specify whether or not there is a charge. The entrance fees in the Republic of Ireland are normally between 1.50 euros and 6.50 euros, with some offering discounts for students and seniors.

Heritage Card giving access to historic sites

The Irish Heritage Service manages and maintains national parks, museums, monuments and gardens. At most Heritage Service sites you can buy a Heritage Card, which allows unlimited, free admission to all sites managed by the service for a year. At 21 euros for adults, 16 euros for senior citizens, 8 euros for children and students, and 55 euros for a family ticket, the card is a good investment. Popular Heritage Service sites include Céide Fields *(see p204)*, Cahir Castle *(see p198)* and the Blasket Centre *(see p158)*. Entrance fees in Northern Ireland are about the same as in the Republic, also with discounts offered to students and senior citizens.

North of the border the **National Trust** has a scheme similar to the Heritage Card, but membership costs more (just under £35 per annum per person or under £50 for a family ticket) and there are fewer sites to see. It is only good value for money if you are also planning to visit National Trust sites across the water in Great Britain.

Interpretative centre at Connemara National Park *(see p208)*

OPENING TIMES

Opening hours are usually between 10am and 5pm, though some sights close for lunch. Few places are open on Sunday morning. Some museums shut on Monday.

From June to September all the sights are open but crowds are at their biggest. July is the marching season in the North *(see p49)* and tensions can run high in Belfast and Derry; many shops and restaurants close at this time.

Some attractions close for winter, while others keep shorter hours. Many places open for public holidays such as Easter and then close again until summer.

INTERPRETATIVE CENTRES

Many of Ireland's major sights are ruins or Stone Age archaeological sites and can be difficult to appreciate. In recent years, however, money has become available for building interpretative or visitors' centres which explain the historical significance of sites. Entry to the site may be free, but you have to pay to visit the interpretative centre.

In areas of natural beauty, such as Connemara National Park, an interpretative centre acts as a useful focal point. The centre typically provides information leaflets and has reconstructions of sights. Connemara has 3D models and displays, as well as an audiovisual presentation on the development of the local landscape over the last 10,000 years. There is also a shop for postcards, books and posters.

RELIGIOUS SERVICES

Ireland is a deeply religious country and for much of the population, churchgoing is a way of life. Because the Republic of Ireland is 95 per cent Roman Catholic, finding a non-Catholic church may sometimes be difficult. In the Republic and Northern Ireland, the tourist offices, hotels and B&Bs all keep a list of local church service times.

DIRECTORY

TOURISM IRELAND OFFICES ABROAD

United Kingdom
For the whole of Ireland:
Tourism Ireland UK, Nations House, 103 Wigmore St, London W1U 1QS. *Tel 0800 039 7000.*
www.tourismireland.com

United States
345 Park Avenue, New York, NY 10154. *Tel 1 800 223 6470.*
www.tourismireland.com

TOURIST BOARD OFFICES IN IRELAND

Fáilte Ireland
Baggot St Bridge, Dublin 2.
Tel 01 602 4000.
www.ireland.ie

Northern Ireland Tourist Board
St Anne's Court, 59 North St, Belfast BT1 1NB.
Tel 028 9023 1221.
Belfast Welcome Centre:
47 Donegall Place.
Tel 028 9024 6609.
www.discovernorthernireland.com

OTHER ADDRESSES

National Trust
Rowallane House, Saintfield, Ballynahinch, Co Down BT24 7LH. *Tel 028 9751 0721.*
www.nationaltrust.org.uk

The Heritage Service
6 Upper Ely Place, Dublin 2.
Tel 01 647 6587.
www.heritageireland.ie

LANGUAGE

The Republic of Ireland is officially bilingual – almost all road signs have place names in both English and Irish. English is the spoken language everywhere apart from a few parts of the far west, called Gaeltachts *(see p229)*, but now and then you may find signs written only in Irish. Here are some of the words you are most likely to come across.

USEFUL WORDS

an banc – **bank**
an lár – **town centre**
an trá – **beach**
ar aghaidh – **go**
bád – **boat**
bealach amach – **exit**
bealach isteach – **entrance**
bus – **bus**
dúnta – **closed**
fáilte – **welcome**
fir – **men**
gardaí – **police**
leithreas – **toilet**

Sign using old form of Gaelic

mná – **women**
oifig an phoist – **post office**
oscailte – **open**
óstán – **hotel**
siopa – **shop**
stop/stad – **stop**
ticéad – **ticket**
traein – **train**

Additional Information

European Youth Card

Ireland is divided between the state of the Republic of Ireland, and Northern Ireland – a part of the United Kingdom. Each has a separate currency, postal service and telecommunications system *(see pp376–81)*. However, there are many similarities between them: they are part of the European Union, English is their first language and, both north and south of the border, the tourist industry is well established. These two pages describe the regulations that affect the Republic and Northern Ireland, and the special facilities that are available to travellers, including students and the disabled. There is also a general guide to the media in both the North and South as well as a directory of useful names and addresses.

Students at Trinity College, Dublin

VISAS

Visitors from the EU, US, Canada, Australia and New Zealand require a valid passport but not a visa for entry into the Republic or Northern Ireland. All others, including those wanting to study or work, should check with their local Irish or British Embassy first. UK nationals born in Britain or Northern Ireland do not need a passport to enter the Republic of Ireland but should take one with them for car rental, medical services, cashing of traveller's cheques or if travelling by air.

DUTY-FREE GOODS AND CUSTOMS ALLOWANCES

In 1999 the duty-free allowances on goods bought between the Republic of Ireland and other countries were abolished. However, a wide range of items may still be purchased at airport shops

and on ferries, including goods that were previously duty-free, such as beers, wines, spirits, perfume and cigarettes. Electrical goods and camera equipment, items which were traditionally considerably cheaper in duty-free, are still on sale at the airport shops but travellers should have some idea of comparative prices for the goods and know the different exchange rates before making an expensive purchase.

STUDENT INFORMATION

Students with a valid ISIC card (International Student Identity Card) benefit from a range of travel discounts as well as reduced admission to museums and concerts. Buy a Travelsave stamp from any branch of **USIT** and affix it to your ISIC card to get a good discount on Irish Rail, NIR train services and Irish Ferries. A Travelsave stamp

will also get you discounts on various rail and bus services in the South and special rates on commuter tickets (Sep–Jun only) in Dublin, Limerick, Cork, Galway and Waterford. In the North, an ISIC card gives a 15 per cent discount on Ulsterbus services and 20 per cent on Belfast Citybus "Gold Card" commuter services. ISIC cards can be obtained from branches of USIT travel in Dublin, Belfast and other college towns.

USIT will also supply non-students under 26 with an EYC (European Youth Card) for discounts on air fares, and in restaurants, shops and theatres. Recognized in over 20 European states, the card varies from country to country but can be identified by its distinctive logo.

FACILITIES FOR THE DISABLED

Most sights in Ireland have access for wheelchairs. This book gives basic information about disabled access for each sight, but it's worth phoning to check details. **Comhairle** provides information for the Republic, publishing county guides to accommodation, restaurants and amenities. In the North, **Disability Action** can advise on accessibility, while **ADAPT** provides information and a book on disabled access to over 400 venues in the cultural sector. Both **tourist boards** also have guides to accommodation and amenities.

Shop at Shannon Airport

Relaxing with newspapers in Eyre Square, Galway

RADIO AND TELEVISION

Ireland has three state-controlled television channels, RTE 1, RTE 2, Network 2 and the Irish-language Teilifís na Gaeilge (TG4), and one privately run channel, TV3. There are six national radio stations and many local ones.

The five British TV channels can be picked up in most parts of Ireland on Cable TV, which is commonly available in hotels in the Republic.

A selection of daily newspapers from North and South

NEWSPAPERS AND MAGAZINES

The Republic of Ireland has six national daily papers and five Sunday papers. Quality dailies include the *Irish Independent*, the *Examiner* and the *Irish Times*, the latter being well known for its journalistic excellence. The broadsheets are useful for up-to-date information on theatre and concerts. Ireland's daily

tabloid is the *Star*. The North's top local paper is the *Belfast Telegraph*, on sale in the afternoon. The province's morning papers, the *News Letter* and *Irish News*, are less rewarding.

In larger towns throughout Ireland, British tabloids are on sale. Newspapers such as *The Times* are also available and cost less than the quality Irish press. Most towns have a local or regional paper, which will tell you what's on and where.

USA Today, *Newsweek* and *Time* magazine are sold in major cities but are very hard to find in rural areas.

IRISH TIME

The whole of Ireland is in the same time zone as Great Britain, i.e. five hours ahead of New York and Toronto, one hour behind Germany and France, and ten hours behind Sydney. In both the North and the South, clocks go forward one hour for summer time.

CONVERSION CHART

Imperial to Metric
1 inch = 2.5 centimetres
1 foot = 30 centimetres
1 mile = 1.6 kilometres
1 ounce = 28 grams
1 pound = 454 grams
1 pint = 0.6 litres
1 gallon = 4.6 litres

Metric to Imperial
1 millimetre = 0.04 inches
1 centimetre = 0.4 inches
1 metre = 3 feet 3 inches
1 kilometre = 0.6 miles
1 gram = 0.04 ounces
1 kilogram = 2.2 pounds
1 litre = 1.8 pints

DIRECTORY

EMBASSIES

Australia
Fitzwilton House, Wilton Terrace, Dublin 2. *Tel 01 664 5300.*

Canada
65–68 St Stephen's Green, Dublin 2. *Tel 01 417 4100.*

UK
29 Merrion Rd, Dublin 4.
Tel 01 205 3700.

US
42 Elgin Rd, Ballsbridge, Dublin 4.
Tel 01 668 7122.

USEFUL ADDRESSES

ADAPT
109–113 Royal Avenue, Belfast.
Tel 028 9023 1211.
www.adaptni.org

Comhairle
Hume House, Ballsbridge, Dublin 4.
Tel 01 605 9000.
www.comhairle.com

Disability Action
189 Airport Rd West, Belfast.
Tel 028 9029 7880.
www.disabilityaction.org

USIT
19/21 Aston Quay, Dublin 2.
Tel 01 602 1904. Fountain Centre, College St, Belfast BT1 6ET.
Tel 028 9032 7111. **www**.usit.ie

METRICATION

The change towards metrication is slow in Ireland, particularly the North, where distances are still measured in miles. In the Republic, all new road signs show distances in kilometres, but there are still many old ones left that use miles (*see p388*). However, throughout Ireland all speed limits are shown in miles. In both Northern Ireland and the Republic, fuel is sold in litres but draught beer is always sold in pints. And just to add to the confusion, food may be weighed out either in imperial or in metric measures.

km **4 Ceann Trá**
    17 Dún Chaoin

One of the new metric road signs used in the Republic of Ireland

Personal Security and Health

Ireland is probably one of the safest places to travel in Europe. Petty theft, such as pickpocketing, is seldom a problem outside certain parts of Dublin and a few other large towns. Tourist offices and hoteliers gladly point out the areas to be avoided. In the recent past, the main security risk in Northern Ireland has been the threat of bombings, though this has hardly ever affected tourists. In fact, crimes against the individual tend to be fewer than in other parts of the UK and Europe.

Pharmacy in Dublin showing old-fashioned snake and goblet symbol

Pearse Street Garda Station, Dublin

PERSONAL SECURITY

The police, should you ever need them, are called the Gardaí in the Republic of Ireland and the Police Service of Northern Ireland (PSNI) in the North. Violent street crime in Ireland – North or South – is relatively rare but it's still advisable to take suitable precautions, such as avoiding poorly lit streets in the cities and larger towns. Poverty and a degree of heroin addiction

Garda   PSNI policeman

in inner-city Dublin has been known to cause a few problems, and Limerick isn't the most inviting of places after dark. There have also been a number of racial attacks recently in Dublin. But if you take sensible precautions, avoiding back-streets at night and keeping to the popular and busy areas, there should be little cause for concern. In some of the larger southern towns you may be approached in the street by people asking for money. This rarely develops into a troublesome situation, but it is still best to avoid eye contact and leave the scene as quickly as possible.

PERSONAL SAFETY IN NORTHERN IRELAND

Even at the height of the Troubles in Northern Ireland, there was never a significant threat to the tourist, and travelling around the province was deemed to be as safe as in the Republic. As long as peace prevails, no extra precautions need to be taken here, but in the event of the Troubles resurfacing, first-time visitors should be prepared for certain unfamiliar situations. When driving, if you see a sign that indicates you are approaching a checkpoint, slow down and use dipped headlights. To keep fuss down to a minimum in these situations, it is a good idea to keep a passport or some other form of identification close at hand. If you are walking around the city centres of Belfast and Londonderry, you may notice

a strong police or military presence. This is unlikely to inconvenience you. Occasionally, you may be asked by shop security to reveal the contents of your bags – don't be alarmed, this is a routine procedure.

Try to avoid visiting in July, as tensions are higher during the Orange marches (see p49).

PERSONAL PROPERTY

Before you leave, make sure that your possessions are insured, as it might be difficult and more expensive to do this in Ireland. Travel insurance for the UK may not cover you for the Republic, so make sure you have an adequate policy. As pickpocketing and bag-snatching can be a problem in some of the larger towns in the Republic, it's best not to carry around your passport or large amounts of cash, or leave them in your room. Most hotels have a safe and it makes sense to take advantage of this facility. Those carrying large amounts of money around should use traveller's cheques (see pp378–9). When out and about, use a bag that can be held securely, and be alert in crowded places and restaurants. A money belt may be a good investment.

If travelling by car, ensure all valuables are locked in the boot and always lock the car, even when leaving it for just a few minutes. If visiting Northern Ireland, do not leave any of your bags or packages unattended, as they are likely to result in a security scare.

Garda station

PSNI badge

LOST PROPERTY AND BAGGAGE ROOMS

Report all lost or stolen items at once to the police. In order to make a claim against your insurance company you need to send in a copy of the police report. Most train and bus stations in the Republic operate a lost-property service but there is no such service in Northern Ireland.

If you wish to do a day's sightseeing unencumbered by baggage, most hotels and some main city tourist offices, both in the Republic and Northern Ireland, offer baggage storage facilities. Ensure all luggage is locked.

MEDICAL TREATMENT

Residents of countries in the European Union, the European Economic Area and Switzerland can claim free medical treatment in Ireland by getting the European Health Insurance Card. Also, be sure to let the doctor know that you want treatment under the EU's social security regulations. In Northern Ireland, British citizens need no documentation.

Non-EU travellers should either have their own travel insurance or be willing to pay for any treatment received up front.

Private health insurance policies may include a certain level of travel coverage. US visitors in particular should check before leaving home whether they are covered by their insurance companies for medical care abroad. You may have to pay first and reclaim costs; if so, be sure to get an itemized bill.

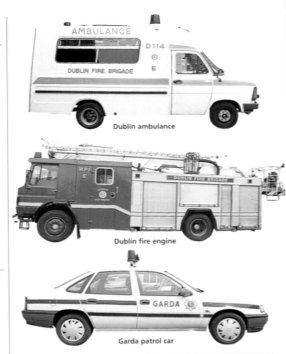
Dublin ambulance

Dublin fire engine

Garda patrol car

Small rural health centre in County Donegal

PHARMACIES

A wide range of medical supplies is available over the counter at pharmacies. However, many medicines are available only with a prescription authorized by a local doctor. If you are likely to require specialized drugs during your stay, ensure you take your own supplies along with a copy of the original prescription. You can also ask your doctor to write a letter with the generic name of the medicine you require. Always obtain a receipt for insurance claims.

Up until 1993, condoms were not freely available in the Republic. They are now easy to obtain throughout much of the country, but there are still a few rural areas where availability is limited. Consider taking your own supply.

DIRECTORY

USEFUL ADDRESSES

Police, Fire, Ambulance and Coastguard Services
Tel Dial 999 in both the Republic and Northern Ireland.

Police Exchange
For non-emergency police assistance in Northern Ireland.
Tel 028 9065 0222.

Hickey's Late Night Pharmacy
55 O'Connell Street Lower, Dublin.
Tel 01 873 0427.

Beaumont Hospital
Beaumont Road, Dublin 9.
Tel 01 809 2714.

Dublin Dental Hospital
Lincoln Place, Dublin 2.
Tel 01 612 7200.

Royal Victoria Hospital
Grosvenor Road, Belfast BT12 6BA. *Tel* 028 9024 0503.

City Hospital
Lisburn Road, Belfast BT9 7AB. (offers emergency dental treatment)
Tel 028 9032 9241.

Local Currency

The Republic and Northern Ireland have different currencies. The euro is the currency in the Republic and the pound sterling is the currency in Northern Ireland, the same as in Great Britain. When travelling between Northern Ireland and the Republic, there's no shortage of money-changers in towns on either side of the border. Look in the daily newspapers for the standard rate of exchange to give yourself a guideline. Some tourist attractions offer money changing facilities but for the best exchange rates use the banks or *bureaux de change*.

Ulster Bank sub-office in Delvin, County Westmeath

CURRENCY IN NORTHERN IRELAND

Northern Ireland uses British currency – the pound sterling (£), which is divided into 100 pence (p). As there are no exchange controls in the UK, there is no limit to the amount of cash you can take into and out of Northern Ireland. In addition to the British currency, four provincial banks issue their own banknotes (bills), worth the same as their counterparts. To tell them apart, look for the words "Bank of England" on British notes. It is best to use the provincial banknotes in Northern Ireland rather than in Britain – some shops may be reluctant to accept notes that are unfamiliar to them.

Banknotes
British banknotes are issued in the denominations £50, £20, £10 and £5. Their different colours help make them easily distinguishable.

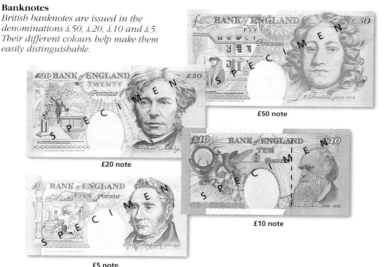

£50 note

£20 note

£10 note

£5 note

Coins
Coins come in the following denominations: £2, £1, 50p, 20p, 10p, 5p, 2p and 1p. All have the Queen's head on one side and are the same as those elsewhere in the UK, except that the pound coin has a different detail – a flax plant – on the reverse side.

£2

£1

50p

20p

10p

5p

2p

1p

THE EURO

The single European currency, the euro, has been adopted by 12 of the 25 member states of the EU. Austria, Belgium, Finland, France, Germany, Greece, Ireland, Italy, Luxembourg, Netherlands, Portugal and Spain chose to join the new currency; the UK, Denmark and Sweden stayed out, with an option to review their decision at a later date.

The euro was introduced on 1 January 1999, but only for banking purposes. Notes and coins came into circulation on 1 January 2002.

Irish euro notes and coins can be used in any of the 12 member states listed. However, with the high cost of living in Ireland, they go less far here than in some neighbouring European countries.

Banknotes

Euro banknotes have seven denominations. The 5-euro note (grey in colour) is the smallest, followed by the 10-euro (pink), 20-euro (blue), 50-euro (orange), 100-euro (green), 200-euro (yellow) and 500-euro (purple). All notes show the 12 stars of the EU and a specific style of European architecture.

5 euros

10 euros

20 euros

50 euros

100 euros

200 euros

500 euros

2 euros

1 euro

50 cents

20 cents

10 cents

Coins

The euro has eight coin denominations: 2 euros and 1 euro (gold and silver); 50 cents, 20 cents, 10 cents (gold); 5 cents, 2 cents and 1 cent (bronze). The reverse sides of all coins are the same in all euro-zone countries, while the obverse sides are different in each state.

5 cents

2 cent

1 cent

Banks in Ireland

The opening times of banks in Ireland vary depending on whether the banks are situated in the town or country, in the Republic or Northern Ireland. Both north and south of the border, banks in small towns are often sub-offices where banking services may be provided on only one or two days of the week, so it's advisable to make the most of facilities in the bigger towns whenever you can. Banks throughout Ireland generally provide a very good service and, along with many of the larger post offices, will exchange traveller's cheques, often without charging commission.

Bank of Ireland sub-office in Sneem, County Kerry

USING BANKS

The five retail banks in the Republic of Ireland are the Bank of Ireland, the Allied Irish Bank (AIB), the Ulster Bank, the National Irish Bank and the Permanent tsb. In Northern Ireland there are four retail banks: the Ulster Bank, the Bank of Ireland, the Northern Bank and the First Trust Bank.

In the Republic of Ireland the usual banking hours are Monday to Friday from 10am to 12:30pm and from 1:30 to 4pm, but most branches now stay open during lunch time. There is extended opening (till 5pm) on one day of the week. In Dublin, Cork and most other cities and towns, late opening is on

Bank machine

First Trust Bank logo

Thursdays but in rural areas banks often stay open late on market day instead. Some rural areas are visited once or twice a week by a mobile bank. Check locally for days and times. Branches of the Permanent tsb remain open at lunch time and up to 5pm on weekdays. Most banks in Northern Ireland open from 10am till 4pm, though a few close for lunch between 12:30 and 1:30pm. In both the Republic and in Northern Ireland, all banks close on public holidays, some of which differ from North to South (see p51). Banks in the cities and most towns have automated teller machines (ATMs), or cash dispensers, so if the local bank is closed, it isn't necessarily a major catastrophe.

CREDIT CARDS

Throughout Ireland you can pay by credit card in most hotels, petrol (gas) stations, large shops and supermarkets. Keep in mind that you will need your PIN. VISA and MasterCard are the most commonly accepted. Fewer businesses take American Express and Diners Club cards. Cash can be withdrawn from most ATMs using a credit card.

TRAVELLER'S CHEQUES

Traveller's cheques are the safest way to carry around large amounts of money. These are best changed at one of the main banks but, failing this, many shops and restaurants accept them – usually for a small charge.

Traveller's cheques can be bought before setting out at American Express, Travelex,

Ornate post office and *bureau de change* in Ventry, County Kerry

or your own bank. In Ireland, traveller's cheques can be purchased at banks and from *bureaux de change*, which can be found in the larger cities and at airports.

TRANSFERRING MONEY

The cheapest way to get money from home is to have your own bank wire funds to a bank in Ireland. This process is very slow, often taking several days; it's much faster, though expensive, to get money sent through a dedicated money transfer company such as Western Union (tel: 1800 395395).

Drawing money from an Allied Irish Bank ATM

BUREAUX DE CHANGE

In addition to the foreign exchange counters at the main banks, there are some private *bureaux de change* in Dublin. As with most other exchange facilities, *bureaux de change* stay open later than banks. However, it's worth checking their rates before undertaking any transactions.

BUREAUX DE CHANGE

American Express
41 Nassau Street, Dublin 2.
Tel 1 890 205511.
Branches also at Dublin Tourism Centre, Suffolk Street & Killarney.

Thomas Cook
51 & 118 Grafton Street, Dublin 2.
Tel 01 677 7422.
11 Donegall Place, Belfast.
Tel 028 9088 3900.

Travelex
Belfast International Airport.
Tel 028 9444 7500.
www.travelex.com

Sending a Letter

Northern Ireland Post Office sign

Main post offices in the Republic and Northern Ireland are usually open from 9am to 5:30pm during the week and from 9am to around 1pm on Saturdays, although times do vary. Some smaller offices close for lunch on weekdays and do not open on Saturdays. Standard letter and postcard stamps can also be bought from some corner shops. The Republic of Ireland does not have a first- and second-class system, but sending a postcard is a few cents less expensive than a letter.

Though it is improving all the time, the postal service in the Republic is still quite slow – allow three to four days when sending a letter to Great Britain and at

Republic of Ireland Post Office logo

least six days for the United States. Swiftpost guarantees delivery within two working days. In Northern Ireland, letters to other parts of the UK can be sent either first- or second-class, with most first-class letters reaching their UK destination the next day. The cost of a letter from Northern Ireland is the same to all EU countries.

POSTBOXES

Postboxes in Ireland come in two colours – green in the Republic and red in the North. Many of Ireland's postboxes are quite historic. Some of those in the Republic even carry Queen Victoria's monogram on the front, a relic from the days of British rule. Even the smallest towns in Ireland have a postbox, from which the mail is collected regularly – anything from once to four times daily.

Letter stamps used in the Republic of Ireland

First-class and second-class stamps used in the North

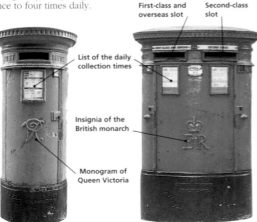

First-class and overseas slot

Second-class slot

List of the daily collection times

Insignia of the British monarch

Monogram of Queen Victoria

Postbox in the Republic   **Northern Ireland double postbox**

Using Ireland's Telephones

eircom phonebox

The Republic's national telephone company, eircom (previously Telecom Eireann), once ran all the telephone services in the country, but changes in the law have meant that other companies can now provide public phones. Eircom's service includes up-to-date coin, card and credit card telephones that provide a modern, efficient service. For those intending to spend more than 5 euros on calls during their stay, it is worth using a phonecard, as these offer discounts. Northern Ireland uses British Telecom public phones. Both BT and eircom phonecards are available from post offices, supermarkets and other retail outlets.

Coffee and computers at the Central Cyber Café in Dublin

ACCESSING THE INTERNET

The main cities in the Republic have plenty of public access to computers and the Internet. Public facilities are available free of charge from public libraries, but you may have to book in advance. The easiest and fastest way to access the Internet is at one of the ever-increasing number of Internet cafés found all over Dublin and throughout the country in major towns and cities. The cafés often charge by the half-hour for computer use, so costs can build up quickly especially when including the cost of printed pages. Internet access is often cheaper during off-peak times so check charges beforehand.

PHONING FROM THE REPUBLIC OF IRELAND

Cheap call rates within the Republic and to the UK are from 6pm to 8am on weekdays and all day at weekends. Off-peak times for international calls vary from country to country, but are generally as above.
• To call Northern Ireland: dial 048, then the area code, followed by the number.
•To call the UK: dial 00 44, the area code (minus the

leading 0), then the number.
• To call other countries: dial 00, followed by the country code (for example, 1 for the USA, 61 for Australia), the area code (minus the leading 0), then the number.
• Credit cards issued in certain countries including the USA, Australia and Canada are accepted as payment for calls to the country in which the card was issued.

USING AN EIRCOM PHONE

1 Lift the receiver and wait for the dial tone.

2 Insert your phonecard or credit card into the slot, or deposit any of the following coins: 10c, 20c, 50c, €1, €2. The minimum amount is 40c. Dial the number and wait to be connected.

3 The display indicates how much credit you have left. A rapid bleeping noise means your credit has run out. Insert more coins or another card.

4 If you want to make a further call and you have credit left, do not replace the receiver, press the follow-on-call button instead.

5 To redial the number you have just called, press the button marked "R".

6 After you have replaced the receiver, retrieve your card or collect your change. Only wholly unused coins are refunded.

Paying by credit card

Phonecards of varying amounts

1 euro

50 cents

20 cents

10 cents

PHONING FROM NORTHERN IRELAND

Cheap call rates within and from the Province are as for the Republic.

• For calls within Great Britain and Northern Ireland: dial the area code and the number required.

• For calls to the Republic of Ireland: dial 00 353, then the area code minus the first 0, then the number.

• For international calls: dial 00, then the country code (for example, 1 for Canada, 64 for New Zealand), then the area code minus the first 0, and finally the number you require.

In addition to using coins and pre-paid phonecards in the BT phone boxes as indicated below, credit card boxes are also available.

In 1999, all phone numbers in Northern Ireland changed from having a prefix of 01 and an area code, to having an area code of 028, followed by an 8-digit local number.

USING A BT PHONE

1 Lift the receiver and wait for the dial tone.

3 Dial the number and wait to be connected.

2 Insert your phonecard into the slot or deposit any of the following coins: 10p, 20p, 50p, £1, £2. The minimum amount is 20p.

4 The display indicates how much credit you have left. A rapid bleeping noise means your money has run out. Deposit more coins or insert another phonecard.

5 If you want to make another call and you have money left in credit, do not replace the receiver, press the follow-on-call button.

6 When you have finished speaking, replace the receiver and retrieve your card or collect your change. Only wholly unused coins are refunded.

£1   50p   20p   10p

PHONE BOOTHS IN NORTHERN IRELAND

Most of the phone booths in the Republic are modern. In Northern Ireland there are two different types of BT phone booths: traditional red phone booths and a newer modern style. Both are issued with the same type of telephone. In both Northern Ireland and in the Republic, the wording around the top of each booth shows whether it is a coin, phonecard or credit card phone.

Old BT phone booth

New BT phone booth

DIRECTORY

USEFUL NUMBERS REPUBLIC OF IRELAND

Emergency Calls
Tel 999.

Directory Enquiries
Tel 11811 (Republic and Northern Ireland).
Tel 11818 (all other countries).

Operator Assistance
Tel 10 (Ireland and Great Britain).
Tel 114 (international calls).

USEFUL NUMBERS NORTHERN IRELAND

Emergency Calls
Tel 999.

Directory Enquiries
Tel 118118 (UK, Republic of Ireland and all other countries).
Tel 153 (all other countries).

Operator Assistance
Tel 100 (UK).
Tel 114 (all other countries).

INTERNET CAFÉS

Armagh Computer World
43 Scotch Street, Armagh.
Tel 028 3751 0002.
www.computerworlds.co.uk

bean-there.com
20 The Diamond, Derry.
Tel 028 7128 1303.

Central Cyber Café
6 Grafton Street, Dublin.
Tel 01 677 8298.
www.centralcafe.ie

Global Internet Café
8 Lower O'Connell Street, Dublin.
Tel 01 878 0295.
www.centralcafe.ie

Planet Cyber
13 St Andrew's Street, Dublin.
Tel 01 670 5182.

Revelations Internet Café
27 Shaftesbury Square, Belfast.
Tel 028 9032 0337.
www.revelations.co.uk

Surf City Café
207 Woodstock Road, Belfast.
Tel 028 9046 1717.
www.surfcitycafe.co.uk

TRAVEL INFORMATION

Ireland's three main airports, Dublin, Shannon and Belfast, are well served by flights from Britain, the United States and an increasing number of countries around the world. If you are travelling by sea from the UK, there is a very good choice of ferry routes from ports in Britain to both the Republic and Northern Ireland. Instead of buying separate tickets, you can purchase combined coach/ferry and rail/ferry tickets from almost all of the towns in mainland Britain. The less-than-comprehensive public transport systems in both the North and South reflect the rural nature of the island. With this in mind, travelling around Ireland is probably best enjoyed if you embrace the Irish way of thinking and just take your time.

Aer Lingus Airbus in flight

The modern exterior of Dublin International Airport

FLYING TO THE REPUBLIC OF IRELAND

Flights from most of the major cities in Europe arrive at **Dublin Airport**, which is the country's busiest airport. Regular services to the Republic depart from all five of the London airports (Heathrow, City, Gatwick, Luton and Stansted) and 15 other cities in Britain, plus the Channel Islands and the Isle of Man.

The major airline operating scheduled flights between Britain and the Republic is **Aer Lingus**. However since deregulation, the rival company **Ryanair** has grown fast, with cheap fares from several airports in Britain and around Europe, including Barcelona, Brussels, Paris, Faro and Malaga.

Aer Lingus and **Continental Airlines** fly direct from the US to Dublin Airport and

Shannon Airport, ten miles outside Limerick – gone is the old ruling that all planes flying eastward to Dublin must first touch down at Shannon, but **Delta Air Lines** does serve both airports.

Cork Airport is served by flights from London (Heathrow and Stansted), Birmingham, Manchester, Bristol, Plymouth, Cardiff, Leeds, Glasgow, Paris, Amsterdam and Dublin. None of the airlines flies direct to Ireland from Australia or New Zealand, but there are plenty of connections via London and other capitals.

The Republic's other airports have fewer flights. There are many charter flights for pilgrims to **Knock International Airport** in Co Mayo, which also has flights from Dublin, London (Stansted) and Manchester. There are flights into Kerry from Dublin and Stansted airports and Waterford Airport has flights from both London and Luton. Galway is well served with five daily flights from Dublin.

GETTING TO AND FROM THE AIRPORT

The Republic's three main airports are all served by regular bus services, whereas the smaller airports depend mainly on local taxi services. Two express bus services run between Dublin Airport, the city's main rail and bus stations and the city centre every 15 to 20 minutes, from early morning to around midnight. The journey takes 30 minutes.

At Cork, the Bus Éireann service takes 15 minutes from the airport into the city. Buses run every 45 minutes on weekdays and hourly at the weekends. At Shannon Airport, Bus Éireann runs a regular service into Limerick which takes 35 minutes to the city centre. In addition, several buses a day go to the town of Ennis, about 30 km (18 miles) away. All airports in the Republic have both long- and short-stay parking facilities.

Information signs in the main concourse of Shannon Airport

One of the Airlink buses which take passengers from Dublin Airport into the city centre

Passengers checking in at Belfast International Airport

DIRECTORY

MAJOR AIRPORTS

Belfast City Airport
Tel 028 9093 9093.

Belfast International
Tel 028 9442 2888.

Cork International
Tel 021 431 3131.

Dublin Airport
Tel 01 814 1111.

Knock International
Tel 1 850 672 222.

Shannon Airport
Tel 061 712000.

AIRLINES

Aer Lingus
Tel 01 886 8844 (Ireland).
Tel 1 800 474 7424 (US).
Tel 0845 084 4444 (UK).
www.aerlingus.com

Continental Airlines
Tel 1 890 925 252 (Ireland).
Tel 1 800 523 3273 (US).
www.continental.com

British Airways
Tel 1890 626747 (Ireland).
Tel 0870 850 9850 (UK).
Tel 1 800 403 0882 (US).
www.ba.com

British Midland (bmi)
Tel 0870 607 0555 (UK).
www.flybmi.com

Cityjet
Tel 01 870 0100 (Ireland).
www.cityjet.com

Delta Air Lines
Tel 1800 768080 (Ireland).
Tel 1 800 221 1212 (US).
Tel 0800 414767 (UK).
www.delta.com

easyJet
Tel 0870 600 0000 (UK).
www.easyjet.com

KLM
Tel 01 663 6900 (Ireland).
Tel 20 474 7747 (Netherlands).
Tel 1 800 447 4747 (US).
www.klmuk.com

Qantas
Tel 01 407 3278 (Ireland).
Tel 02 9691 3636 (Aus).
Tel 1 800 227 4500 (US).
www.qantas.com.au

Ryanair
Tel 1 530 787 787 (Ireland).
Tel 0906 270 5656 (UK).
www.ryanair.com

FLYING TO NORTHERN IRELAND

There are hourly flights, operated by either **British Airways** or **British Midland**, from London Heathrow to **Belfast International Airport**, 30 km (18 miles) northwest of Belfast city centre. The airport is also served by flights from Luton and some regional airports like Stansted, Bristol, Liverpool and Glasgow. There are also **easyJet** flights from Amsterdam.

Belfast City Airport is used by smaller aircraft, but is favoured by many because of its location – it is just 6.5 km (4 miles) from the city centre. The airport also has more flights from the UK – around 15 cities plus London Gatwick, Stansted and Luton – than Belfast International. The City of Derry Airport is Northern Ireland's smallest, with flights from Stansted, Manchester and Glasgow.

AIRPORT CONNECTIONS IN NORTHERN IRELAND

The arrangements for getting to and from the airports in Northern Ireland are generally good. BIA's Airbus service will take you from the airport to the Europa Bus-centre via Oxford Street Bus Station and Central Railway Station. This runs every half hour and takes about 30 minutes from end to end. At Belfast City Airport the number 21 bus passes every half hour, taking around 10 minutes to get to the Belfast City Hall bus depot. There are trains from the airport to Central Station about every 30 minutes. Derry's airport is on a local bus route: the number 143 goes into the city centre once an hour (less frequently at weekends). All airports in Northern Ireland have taxi ranks and both long- and short-term parking facilities.

AIR FARES

Airline options between the United States and Ireland have increased in the last few years, with frequent flights now from both the East and West coasts.

It's quite easy to get a round-trip flight to Shannon from the East Coast for under US$700 (prices are so competitive now it could cost as little as US$200), but these tickets often restrict your visit to between 7 and 30 days. The best bargains are on flights with fixed dates.

Air fares from the US are at their highest in the peak season which runs from July to September.

Many UK airports serve Ireland and airlines offer a host of options on fares. It's not difficult to get a round-trip flight from mainland UK to Dublin for well under £100. The cheapest place to fly from is usually London, especially Luton and Stansted airports. Prices are fairly constant all year except at Christmas, during summer and on public holidays, when there are few discounted fares.

Many airlines offer discounts to those under 25, while USIT (*see p372*), Campus Travel and other specialist travel agents often have cheaper rates for students and under-26s.

◄ Arrivals ►
⬆ Shops ⬆ Siopaí
⬆ Bar ⬆ Beár
⬆ Snacks ✕ Sólaistí

Airport sign in English and Gaelic

Arriving by Sea

Travelling by ferry is a popular way of getting to Ireland, especially for groups or families intending to tour the country by car. Nine ports in Great Britain and two in France provide ferry crossings to Ireland's six ports. Nowadays, all ferries are of the modern drive-on/drive-off variety with lounges, restaurants and, if you're sailing to the Republic, tax-free shops. Crossing the Irish Sea is now faster than ever before, thanks to a new generation of high-speed ferries.

Logo of Irish Ferries

Stena HSS on the Dun Laoghaire to Holyhead crossing

FERRIES TO DUBLIN AND DUN LAOGHAIRE

There is a good choice of ferry services running between Wales and Ireland. **Irish Ferries**, the country's largest shipping company, operates on the Holyhead–Dublin Port route and has up to six crossings a day. The high-speed service takes 1 hour 49 minutes, while the conventional ferry takes about 3¼ hours. **Stena Line** also operates two conventional ferry crossings each day on this route. Like most ferry companies, Irish Ferries does not operate on Christmas Day or on Boxing Day.

The service from Holyhead to the Dublin suburb of Dun Laoghaire – traditionally the busiest port in Ireland – is operated by Stena Line. This route is served by the Stena HSS (High-speed Sea Service). As the largest ferry on the Irish Sea, the HSS has the same passenger and vehicle capacity as the conventional ferries but its jet-engine propulsion gives it twice the speed.

Vehicle loading and unloading times on the fast ferries are considerably shorter than with other ferries. Passengers requiring special assistance at ports or on board the ship

should contact the company they are booked with at least 24 hours before the departure time. Like most other ferry companies, Irish Ferries and Stena Line take bicycles free of charge on some routes, but mention this when booking. **P&O Irish Sea, Norse Merchant Ferries** and **Seacat Dublin Maritime** offer an eight-hour crossing from Dublin to Liverpool.

FERRIES TO ROSSLARE

Rosslare, in County Wexford, is the main port for crossings from South Wales to Ireland. Stena Line runs a service from Fishguard using both the conventional ferry and the speedier Sea Lynx catamaran-

Irish Ferries ship loading up at Rosslare Harbour

style ferries. Those intending to take a car on Sea Lynx should make sure the measurements of their vehicle, when fully loaded, are within those specified by Stena Line. The maximum dimensions allowable per vehicle are 3 m (10 ft) high by 6 m (20 ft) long and up to 3 tonnes.

Irish Ferries operates two crossings to Rosslare from Pembroke (4 hours) all year round. They also run a service from Roscoff in France (17 hours) between March and October. Irish Ferries and P&O run services to Rosslare from Cherbourg (18 hours). Cabins and berths are available on all crossings to Rosslare and should be booked in advance.

FERRIES TO CORK

The prospect of a 10-hour sea journey could be enough to deter some from taking the ferry to Cork, but for those heading for southwest Ireland, sailing to the small town of Ringaskiddy, near Cork, can help cut out a cross-Ireland car journey of up to 250 miles. During the high season, **Swansea Cork Ferries** has up to six crossings per week between the two cities but the service doesn't operate between the end of January and mid-March. The crossing takes about 10 hours.

There is also one route direct to Cork from Roscoff in France operated by **Brittany Ferries**. The ferry runs once a week leaving from Cork on a Saturday and from Roscoff on a Friday. The service is only available from mid-March to early November and the crossing time is 14 hours. Cabins and berths are available on routes to Cork but need to be

Gallery overlooking the quayside at Rosslare Harbour

DIRECTORY

FERRY COMPANIES

Brittany Ferries
Tel 021 427 7801 (Cork).
Tel 0870 366 5333 (UK).
www.brittany-ferries.com

Irish Ferries
Tel 0818 300400 (ROI).
Tel 0870 517 1717 (UK).
www.irishferries.com

Isle of Man Steam Packet and SeaCat
Tel 1800 805055 (ROI).
Tel 240 8070 (UK).
www.seacat.co.uk

Norse Merchant Ferries
Tel 01 819 2999 (ROI).
Tel 0870 600 4321 (UK).
www.norsemerchant.com

P&O Irish Sea
Tel 01 407 3434 (ROI).
Tel 0870 242 4777 (UK).
www.poirishsea.com

Stena Line
Tel 0289 0747747 (Dublin).
Tel 0870 400 6798 (UK).
www.stenaline.co.uk

Swansea Cork Ferries
Tel 021 483 6000 (Cork).
Tel 01792 456116 (UK).
www.swansea-cork.ie

BUS COMPANIES

Eurolines
Tel 01 836 6111(Dublin).
Tel 0870 514 3219 (UK).
www.eurolines.ie

National Express
Tel 0870 580 8080 (UK).
www.gobycoach.com

Ulsterbus/Translink
Tel 028 9066 6630 (Belfast).
www.translink.co.uk

booked well in advance in high season. There is a small charge for taking bicycles on Swansea Cork Ferries and it should be mentioned when booking.

PORT CONNECTIONS

All Ireland's ports have adequate bus and train connections. At Dublin Port, Bus Éireann buses meet ferry arrivals and take passengers into the city centre for a small charge. From Dun Laoghaire, DART trains run into Dublin every 10 to 15 minutes calling at Pearse Street, Tara Street and Connolly Stations. These go from the railway station near the main passenger concourse. Buses run from Dun Laoghaire to Eden Quay and Fleet Street in the city centre every 10 to 15 minutes. At all ports, taxis are there to meet arrivals. For those interested in car hire, Hertz has a desk at Dun Laoghaire. Passengers arriving at Dublin Port have to rent cars from the city centre.

Directions for ferry passengers

TRAIN AND BUS THROUGH-TICKETS

It is possible to travel from any train station in Great Britain to any specified destination in Ireland on a combined sea/rail ticket. Combined tickets can be bought from most train stations throughout Britain. **Eurolines** runs a through-bus service from about 35 towns in Britain to over 100 destinations in the Republic. **Ulsterbus/ Translink** offers the same service to destinations in Northern Ireland. Tickets for both these bus companies can be booked through **National Express**, which has over 2,000 agents in Great Britain. Travellers from North America, Australia, New Zealand and certain countries in Asia can buy a Brit Ireland pass. As well as including the return ferry crossing to Ireland, it allows unlimited rail travel through-out Great Britain and Ireland on any five or ten days during one month.

FERRY ROUTES TO THE REPUBLIC OF IRELAND	OPERATOR	LENGTH OF JOURNEY
Fishguard–Rosslare	Stena Line Stena Line	3hrs 30min (Stena Europe) 1hr 50min (Fastcraft)
Holyhead–Dublin	Irish Ferries Stena Line	1hr 49min (Jonathan Swift) 3hrs (Stena Adventurer)
Holyhead–Dun Laoghaire	Stena Line	1hr 49min (Stena HSS)
Liverpool–Dublin	Norse Merchant Ferries P&O SeaCat Dublin Maritime	8hrs 8hrs (Norbay) 3hrs 55min (Super Seacat 3)
Cherbourg–Rosslare	Irish Ferries	18hrs (Normandy)
Pembroke–Rosslare	Irish Ferries	3hrs 45min (Isle of Inishmore)
Swansea–Cork	Swansea Cork Ferries	10hrs (Superferry)

FERRIES TO BELFAST AND LARNE

The fastest crossing to Belfast is the 90-minute **SeaCat** service from Stranraer in Scotland. This catamaran-style ferry sails up to four times per day, all year round. On the same route, Stena Line has introduced the second of their new HSS Stena Voyager ferries. On these the sailing time is only 15 minutes longer than that of the SeaCat.

A Liverpool to Belfast service is run by **Norse Merchant Ferries**, leaving Liverpool (Birkenhead) every evening and six mornings a week, and taking over 8 hours to reach Belfast. Crossing the Irish Sea with the **Isle of Man Steam Packet Co** lets you visit the Isle of Man en route. Leaving from both Liverpool and Heysham, this service provides the added advantage of allowing you to disembark at Dublin and return from Belfast or vice versa.

There are now three routes to Larne (north of Belfast): from the Scottish ports of Cairnryan (1 hour 45 minutes) and Troon (4 hours); and from Fleetwood in Lancashire, (8 hours). The services are operated by **P&O Irish Sea**, who run both conventional ferries and the high-speed Superstar Express on the Larne–Cairnryan route. This service runs from mid-April to mid-September and takes only an hour. During the week in high season there are four sailings a day to Cairnryan.

Cars and lorries disembarking at Larne Port

Port of Belfast

Port of Belfast logo

PORT CONNECTIONS

Although it takes only ten minutes on foot into the city centre from Belfast Port, Flexibus shuttles are on hand to take ferry passengers into the city centre via the Europa Buscentre and Central Railway Station. A regular bus service connects Larne Harbour to the town's bus station, and from here, buses run every hour into Belfast city centre. From Larne Port, there are trains to take ferry passengers to Belfast's Yorkgate and Central train stations. Taxis are available at both ports.

FARES AND CONCESSIONS

Fares on ferry crossings to Ireland vary dramatically according to the season – prices on certain days during the peak period of mid-June to mid-September can be double those at other times of the year. Prices increase greatly during the Christmas and New Year period, too. It is advisable to book your journey both ways before setting out. Those travelling to ports without a reservation should always check availability before setting out.

Often, the cheapest way for families or groups of adults to travel is to buy a ticket that allows you to take a car plus a maximum number of passengers. At certain times of the year on particular routes, the return ticket for a car and five adults (two children count as one adult) can cost less than 70 euros. The cheapest crossings are usually those where the passenger must depart and return within a specified period. Fares are normally reduced for mid-week travel and early-morning or late-night crossings. Ferry companies offer discounts for students bearing an ISIC card (see p372) and some have cut-price deals for those with InterRail tickets (see p391).

FERRY ROUTES TO NORTHERN IRELAND	OPERATOR	LENGTH OF JOURNEY
	P&O	1hr 45min (European Causeway)
Cairnryan–Larne	P&O	1hr (Superstar Express)
	P&O	1hr 45min (European Highlander)
Fleetwood–Larne	Stena Line	8hrs (Stena Pioneer)
		8hrs (Stena Leader)
Heysham–Belfast	SeaCat Scotland	4hrs (Seacat Rapide)
Liverpool–Belfast	Norse Merchant Ferries	9hrs
Stranraer–Belfast	Stena Line	1hr 45 (Stena HSS)
		3hrs 15min (Stena Caledonia)
	SeaCat Scotland	1hr 30min (HSS Stena Voyager)
Troon–Belfast	SeaCat Scotland	2hrs 30min
Troon–Larne	P&O	1hr 50 min (Superstar Express)

On the Road

One of the best ways to see Ireland's magnificent scenery and ancient sites is by car. Driving on the narrow, twisting country roads can be a pleasure; often you don't see another vehicle for miles. It can also be frustrating, especially if you find yourself stuck behind a slow-moving tractor or a herd of cows. If you don't want to take your own vehicle, car rental in Ireland is no problem. All the international car rental firms operate in the Republic and are also well represented in the North. Touring by bicycle is another enjoyable way of seeing the best parts of the island at your own leisurely pace.

Gaelic road sign instructing motorists to yield or give way

TAKING YOUR OWN CAR

If you intend to take your own car across on the ferry *(see pp384–6)* check your car insurance to find out how well you are covered. To prevent a fully comprehensive policy being downgraded to third-party coverage, ask your insurance company for a Green Card. Carry your insurance certificate, Green Card, proof of ownership of the car and, importantly, your driver's licence. If your licence was issued in Great Britain, you should also bring your passport with you for ID.

Membership of a reputable automobile club like the **AA, RAC** or **Green Flag National Breakdown** is advisable unless you are undaunted by the prospect of breaking down in remote parts. Non-members can join up for just the duration of their trip. Depending on the type of coverage, automobile clubs may offer only limited services in Ireland.

RENTING A CAR

Car rental firms do good business in Ireland, so in summer it's wise to book ahead. Rental – particularly in the Republic – is quite expensive and the best rates are often obtained by renting in advance. Broker companies, such as **Holiday Autos**, will shop around to get you the best deal. Savings can also be made by choosing a fly-drive or even a rail-sail-drive vacation, but always check for hidden extras.

Car rental usually includes unlimited mileage plus passenger indemnity

One for the road

insurance and coverage for third party, fire and theft, but not damage to the vehicle. If you plan to cross the border in either direction, however briefly, you must tell the rental company, as there may be a small insurance premium.

To rent a car, you must show a full driver's licence, held for two years without violation. US visitors are advised to obtain an international licence through AAA before leaving the States to facilitate dealing with traffic officials should problems occur.

BUYING FUEL

Unleaded petrol (gas) and diesel fuel are available just about everywhere in Ireland. Although prices vary from station to station, fuel in the Republic is quite expensive; in Northern Ireland it costs even more. Almost all the stations accept VISA and MasterCard, although it is worth checking before filling up, particularly in rural areas.

ROAD MAPS

The road map on the inside back cover shows virtually all the towns and villages mentioned in this guide. In addition, each chapter starts with a map of the region showing all the major sights and tips on getting around. However, if you plan to do much driving or cycling, you should equip yourself with a more detailed map. Ordnance Survey Holiday Maps are among the best road maps. You can usually get town plans free from tourist offices *(see p370)*. The tourist boards of the Republic and Northern Ireland both issue free lists of suggested routes for cyclists.

A busy Hertz car rental desk at Dublin Airport

The familiar sight of a farmer and cattle on an Irish country road

RULES OF THE ROAD

Even for those unused to driving on the left, driving in Ireland is unlikely to pose any great problems. For many, the most difficult aspect of it is getting used to over-taking on the right and giving way to traffic on the right at roundabouts (traffic circles). On both sides of the border, the wearing of seat belts is compulsory for drivers and all passengers. Rear seat belts must also be worn. Children must have a suitable restraint system. Motorcyclists and passengers must wear helmets. Northern Ireland uses the same Highway Code as Great Britain. The Republic of Ireland's Highway Code is very similar – copies of both are available from bookstores.

Speed limit signs in mph on a country road in County Cork

In Northern Ireland, you will notice some cars carrying a red "R" plate. These identify "restricted" drivers who have passed their driving test within the previous 12 months and have to keep to lower speeds.

SPEED LIMITS

In the Republic and Northern Ireland the maximum speed limits, which are shown in miles per hour, are much the same as those in Britain:
• 30 mph (50 km/h) in built-up areas.
• 60 mph (100 km/h) outside built-up areas.
• 70 mph (110 km/h) on motorways.
On certain roads, which are clearly marked, the speed limits are either 40 mph (65 km/h) or 50 mph (80 km/h). Where there is no indication, the speed limit is 60 mph (95 km/h). In the Republic, vehicles towing caravans (trailers) must not exceed 55 mph (90 km/h). Speed limits are strictly enforced in both the North and the Republic.

ROAD SIGNS

Most road signs in the Republic are in both Gaelic and English. Ireland is striving toward metrication so all the new-style green and white signs are in kilometres. However, nothing's quite that simple in Ireland, so expect to come across some black-on-white signs showing distances in miles. As in Britain, road signs in the North are always

in miles. One road sign that is unique to the Republic is the "Yield" sign – in the UK this is worded "Give Way". Throughout both the Republic and Northern Ireland, brown signs with white lettering indicate places of historic, cultural or leisure interest.

SIGNS IN THE REPUBLIC

Unprotected quay or river ahead

Junction ahead

Children or school ahead

Dangerous bends ahead

SIGNS IN NORTHERN IRELAND

Motorway direction sign

Primary route sign

ROAD CONDITIONS

Northern Ireland's roads are well surfaced and generally in better condition than those in the Republic, though there are just as many winding stretches requiring extra caution. The volume of traffic, particularly in the South, is much lower than in Britain. On some of the more rural roads you may not come across another driver for miles. Even the major roads can be surprisingly quiet. There are only a few sections of motorway in the whole of Ireland, though recent years have seen extensive construction of two-lane highways in the Republic, including rural areas such as County Donegal.

PARKING

Finding parking in Ireland used to be easy, but this has changed in recent years. Due to increased congestion, the majority of towns now have paid parking on and off street. Dublin, Belfast and a few other cities have either parking meters or (fairly expensive) parking lots. Parking on the street is allowed, though a single yellow line along the edge of the road means there are some restrictions (there should be a sign nearby showing the permitted parking times). Double yellow lines indicate that no parking is allowed at any time.

Parking disc sign

Disc parking – a version of "pay & display" – operates in most large towns and cities in the Republic and the North. Discs can be purchased from fuel stations, tourist offices and many small shops. In Northern Ireland, almost all towns and villages have Control Zones, which are indicated by large yellow or pink signs. For security reasons, unattended parking in a Control Zone is not permitted at any time of the day.

Warning sign in Northern Ireland

CYCLING

The quiet roads of Ireland help to make touring by bicycle a real joy. The **Raleigh** Rent-a-Bike network of bike dealers operates a reasonably priced rental scheme throughout Ireland. Also local shops, such as **Cycle Ways** in Dublin, rent bikes to tourists and are open at least six days a week. You can often rent a bike in one town and drop it off at another for a small charge. Many dealers can also provide safety helmets, but bring your own lightweight waterproof clothing to help cope with the unpredictable weather. Buses and trains will carry bikes for a surcharge.

SECURITY ROADBLOCKS IN NORTHERN IRELAND

In the late 1960s, when the Northern Ireland troubles began, roadblocks were introduced on to the roads of the province. These days if you are travelling by road, whether in the centre of Londonderry or the remote Sperrin Mountains, you are very unlikely to come across a roadblock, depending on the political climate at the time. Checkpoints can be staffed by either the army or the police, who will ask for proof of identity. In the unlikely event of your being stopped, show your driver's licence and insurance certificate or rental agreement when asked.

DIRECTORY

CAR-RENTAL COMPANIES

Alamo
Tel 0870 599 4000 (UK).
Tel 1 800 462 5266 (US).
www.alamo.com

Argus Rent-a-Car
Tel 01 490 4444 (Dublin).
www.argusrentals.com

Avis
Tel 021 428 1111 (Dublin).
Tel 0870 60 60 100 (UK).
Tel 1 800 331 1084 (US).
www.avis.com

Budget
Tel 090 66 27 711 (Dublin).
Tel 1 800 793159 (US).
www.budget.ie

Dan Dooley
Tel 01 677 2723 (Dublin).
www.dan-dooley.ie

Hertz
Tel 01 844 5466 (Dublin).
Tel 0207 026 007 (UK).
Tel 800 654 3001 (US).
www.hertz.com

Holiday Autos
Tel 0870 400 0000 (UK).
www.holidayautos.co.uk

Irish Car Rentals
Tel 1850 206088 (ROI).
Tel 0800 4747 4227 (UK).
www.irishcarrentals.com

Murrays/Europcar
Tel 01 614 8000 (Dublin).
www.europcar.ie

National Car Rental
Tel 021 432 0755 (Cork).
www.carhire.ie

BREAKDOWN SERVICES

Automobile Association
Tel 01 617 9977 (ROI).
Tel Rescue No. 1800 667788.
www.aaireland.ie

Royal Automobile Club
Tel 01 412 5500 (ROI).
Tel Rescue No. 1800 535005.

Green Flag National Breakdown
Tel 0800 000111 (to enrol in UK).

BICYCLE-RENTAL SHOPS

Cycle Ways
Tel 01 873 4748 (Dublin).

Raleigh Rent-a-Bike
Tel 01 456 5280 (Dublin).

Galway Cycle Shop
Tel 091 561600.

Cyclists checking their directions in Ballyvaughan, County Clare

Travelling by Train

The Republic of Ireland's rail network is run by **Irish Rail** (Iarnród Éireann) and is state-controlled. The rail network is far from comprehensive and quite expensive, but the trains are generally reliable and comfortable and can be a good way of covering long distances. The service provided by **Northern Ireland Railways** (NIR) is more limited but fares are slightly cheaper. There is an excellent train service between Dublin and Belfast, with a journey time of just under two hours. Fares can be as little as 43 euros round trip.

Train at Killarney station on the southwest rail network

TRAIN SERVICES IN THE REPUBLIC OF IRELAND

Although the more rural areas in the Republic of Ireland are not served by train, Irish Rail operates a satisfactory service to most of the large cities and towns. Taking the train is probably the fastest and most convenient way of going from Dublin to places like Cork, Waterford, Limerick and Galway. However, there are glaring gaps in the network; for example, Donegal is totally devoid of train services, so if you are planning to explore the west coast of Ireland using public transport, you will have to continue westward from towns such as Galway, Sligo, Limerick and Westport using the local bus services.

The two main train stations in Dublin are Connolly Station, for trains to the north, northwest and Rosslare, and Heuston Station, which serves the west, midlands and southwest. These two stations are connected by the No. 90 bus service which runs every 10 to 15 minutes and takes a quarter of an hour – traffic permitting. All trains in the Republic of Ireland have standard and super-standard (first-class) compartments.

Bicycles can be taken on intercity trains but there is a fee of up to 10 euros.

OUTER DUBLIN RAIL SERVICES

The handy electric rail service known as DART (Dublin Area Rapid Transit) serves 30 stations between Malahide and Greystones with several stops in Dublin city centre. A Rail/Bus ticket allows three consecutive days' travel on DART trains as well as Dublin Bus services. Tickets can be purchased at any of the DART stations. The Luas light rail service connects central Dublin with the suburbs. The first lines were completed in 2004, and will eventually interconnect with the DART.

TRAIN SERVICES IN NORTHERN IRELAND

Other than an express service out to Larne Harbour and a commuter line to Bangor, there are only two main routes out of Belfast: a line westward to Londonderry via Coleraine (for the Giant's Causeway) and Ireland's only cross-border service, operating a high-speed link between Belfast and Dublin eight times a day. All trains leave from Central Station. Great Victoria Street station opened in 1995 and brings rail travellers right to the heart of the city's business and shopping district. Bear in mind that there are no baggage rooms at any of Northern Ireland's train or bus stations.

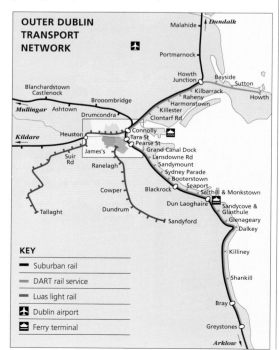

OUTER DUBLIN TRANSPORT NETWORK

Malahide · *Dundalk*

Portmarnock

Howth Junction · Bayside · Sutton

Blanchardstown Castleknock

Brooombridge

Kilbarrack · Raheny · Howth

Mullingar · Ashtown · Drumcondra

Harmonstown · Killester · Clontarf Rd

Kildare · Heuston

Connolly · Tara St · Pearse St

James's

Grand Canal Dock · Lansdowne Rd · Sandymount · Sydney Parade · Booterstown · Seaport

Suir Rd · Ranelagh

Cowper · Blackrock · Salthill & Monkstown

Tallaght · Dundrum · Sandyford

Dun Laoghaire · Sandycove & Glasthule · Glenageary · Dalkey

Killiney

Shankill

Bray

Greystones

Arklow

KEY

▬ Suburban rail
▭ DART rail service
▬ Luas light rail
✈ Dublin airport
⛴ Ferry terminal

TICKETS AND FARES

Throughout Ireland, train tickets are generally quite expensive, but there are lots of bargain incentives and concessionary passes. Most of these include bus travel, so you can get virtually anywhere in Ireland on one ticket.

The most comprehensive ticket available is the Emerald Card, which can be used on all Irish Rail, Northern Ireland Railways, and Ulsterbus services. For around 200 euros the Emerald Card gives eight days' unlimited travel in a 15-day period. An 8-day Irish Explorer ticket, which costs 194 euros, is valid on all Irish Rail and Bus Éireann services throughout the Republic; travel in Northern Ireland is not included. Both passes cover many local services, including transport in Cork, Waterford, Limerick and Galway.

The modern ticket office at Belfast's Central Station

CONCESSIONS

Students can buy a Travel-save Stamp (see p372) to affix to their student travel cards for discounts on train fares. For those under 26, Faircards give discounts on all Irish Rail single journeys, and can be bought at the train station.

Under-26 InterRail passes allow unlimited rail travel for 15 days or one month in the Republic and 25 other European countries. Older travellers can get InterRail Plus 26 cards costing slightly more. However, InterRail cards allow only a one-third discount on Northern Ireland Railways.

IRELAND'S RAIL NETWORK

Irish Rail (Iarnród Éireann)
35 Abbey St Lower, Dublin 1.
Tel 01 836 6222. www .irishrail.ie

Northern Ireland Railways
Central Station, East Bridge St,
Belfast BT1 3PB. *Tel* 028 9066 6630.
www .translink.co.uk

KEY
— Irish Rail
— NIR

Travelling by Bus and Taxi

The bus services throughout Ireland are quite good, for such a rural island. However, longer journeys often involve changing buses en route so extra travelling time should be allowed for. Touring by bus is also a good way to see Ireland – local tourist offices have details of tours as well as prices and often take bookings. Taxi services are available in all major cities and towns in Ireland. In the Republic, taxis can be four or eight-seater cars and are identified by a yellow light on the roof. In the North, cities like Belfast and Londonderry have both mini-cabs and London-style black cabs.

Boarding a bus at the Europa Buscentre in Belfast

Bus Éireann

Logo on Bus Éireann local and express buses

GETTING AROUND BY BUS

The Republic of Ireland's national bus company, **Bus Éireann**, operates a country-wide network of buses serving all the cities and most of the towns. In Dublin, the main bus station is the Busáras on Store Street, a short walk from O'Connell Street. There are a number of private bus companies which either compete with the national network or provide services on routes not covered by Bus Éireann. In rural Donegal, for example, there are several private bus services. Some are not fully licensed, so check whether you would be covered in the event of an accident. Local tourist offices should be able to point out the most reputable firms.

Ulsterbus runs an excellent service throughout Northern Ireland including express links between all the major

towns. Belfast has two main bus stations – the Europa Buscentre off Great Victoria Street and Laganside Station. Check before setting out that you are going to the right one. Note that for reasons of security, there are no baggage rooms at any of the stations in Northern Ireland.

FARES AND TICKETS

In the Republic, long-distance buses are about half the price of the equivalent train trip. If you are making the return trip on the same day, ask for a day-return ticket, which is much cheaper than the normal round-trip fare. Under 16s pay approximately half the adult fare. Students with a Travelsave stamp (see p372) get a healthy reduction. For those intending to do a lot of travelling it is cheaper to buy a "Rambler" ticket. This allows unlimited bus travel throughout the Republic for a certain

number of days in a set period, for example, 15 days' travel out of 30 consecutive days. A variety of other tickets are also available.

A "Freedom of Northern Ireland" ticket gives you unlimited travel on all Ulsterbus routes for either a day or a week. Ulsterbus also offers cheap day-return tickets. Students can get a 15 per cent discount by showing their ISIC card. There are also a number of period passes available that combine bus and rail travel (see p391).

BUS TOURS

While the bus services in Ireland are generally adequate for getting from town to town, using public transport isn't a very practical way of exploring specific areas or regions in great detail, unless you have a lot of time on your hands. If you find yourself in a remote area like Connemara (see pp206–8) but have only a very limited amount of time in which to see its main attractions, a local guided tour of the area is a good idea. For about 25 euros per adult you can do the picturesque "figure of eight" circuit by bus, starting from Galway and taking in Spiddal, Kylemore, Letterfrack, Oughterard and then returning to Galway. The bus sets out at 10am and returns at about 5:30pm, making regular stops at places of interest. The price does not include admission fees or

Express service bus in Northern Ireland

lunch. Bookings are made at Galway Tourist Information Centre and can be arranged in advance or on the day. Four-hour or one-day tours such as this are available in many of Ireland's main tourist areas. Other popular tours of rural Ireland include Glendalough *(see pp140–41)*, Donegal *(see pp224–31)*, and the Ring of Kerry *(see pp164–5)*. In Dublin and other cities in the Republic, Bus Éireann and some local companies run half- and one-day excursions. **Dublin Bus** (Bus Átha Cliath) runs a Dublin City tour, which leaves from O'Connell Street Upper. This guided tour takes in the city's most famous sights.

In Northern Ireland, Ulsterbus operates tours from the Europa Buscentre in Belfast to all the major places of interest. These tours include the Causeway Coast, the Glens of Antrim and the Ulster-American Folk Park near Omagh. Ulsterbus prefers bookings to be made in person at their Belfast office. In summer, **Belfast Citybus** operates up to two guided bus tours per day around the city; in winter there are tours on Thursday and Saturday.

LOCAL TRANSPORT

Local bus services throughout the Republic are generally well-run and reasonably priced. **Dublin Bus** runs the bus services in the Greater Dublin area. Buses in the city centre run from about 6am until 11:30pm with an

Passengers alighting from a Waterford city bus

extended "nitelink" service at weekends. One-day passes, costing 5 euros, are good value. The new on-street light rail service, **Luas**, provides an easy way to reach suburban areas previously only accessible by bus. The Luas lines connect with the DART rail service *(see p390)* at Connolly Station and eventually into a proposed Metro system. In the rest of the Republic the bus services, including city buses in Galway, Limerick, Waterford and Cork, are operated mainly by Bus Éireann; a timetable is available at tourist offices and bus stations. Some bus routes connecting towns and villages are served by private companies as well as Bus Éireann. For bus times (and stops) in more remote areas, try asking the locals.

Except for Belfast, Northern Ireland's bus network is run by **Ulsterbus/Translink**. In the province's capital the local service is operated by **Citybus**. A wide variety of travel passes are available for Citybus and Ulsterbus/Translink lines. Regional timetables are available at bus stations.

TAXIS IN THE REPUBLIC

Except in the most rural of places, there is usually a local taxi service – your hotel or B&B will provide details. In Dublin, taxis range from four-seater cars to minivans. Cruising taxis are a rarity: the best places to find taxis are at train or bus stations, hotels and taxi ranks. Prices are usually based on metered mileage; if not, always ask the fare to your destination.

TAXIS IN NORTHERN IRELAND

Taxis in Northern Ireland are reasonably priced. Journeys within the centre of Belfast usually cost no more than £5 by mini-cab or black cab. In most decent-sized towns in the North you will find at least one taxi office or rank where you can wait for a cab. Otherwise, ask for the number of a taxi firm at a local hotel or B&B.

DIRECTORY

CITY TRANSPORT

Citybus (Belfast)
Tel 028 9045 8484.

DART (Dublin)
Tel 01 836 6222. www.irishrail.ie

Dublin Bus
Tel 01 873 4222.
www.dublinbus.ie

Luas (Dublin)
Tel 1 800 300604. www.luas.ie

NATIONAL BUS COMPANIES

Bus Éireann
Tel 01 836 6111.
www.buseireann.ie

Ulsterbus/Translink
Tel 028 9066 6630.
www.translink.co.uk

BUS TOURS

Irish City Tours and Gray Line
Dublin Tourist Office, Dublin 2.
Tel 01 605 7705.

McGeehan Coaches
Fintown PO, Co Donegal.

Taxis lined up outside the arrivals building at Dublin Airport

General Index

Acknowledgments

7Dorling Kindersley would like to thank the following people whose contributions and assistance have made the preparation of this book possible.

Main Contributors
Lisa Gerard-Sharp is a writer and broadcaster who has contributed to numerous travel books, including the *Eyewitness Travel Guide to France*. She is of Irish extraction, with roots in County Sligo and County Galway, and a regular visitor to Ireland.

Tim Perry, from Dungannon, County Tyrone, writes on travel and popular music for various publishers in North America and the British Isles.

Additional Contributors
Cian Hallinan, Eoin Higgins, Douglas Palmer, Audrey Ryan, Trevor White, Roger Williams.

Additional Photography
Peter Anderson, Joe Cornish, Andy Crawford, Michael Diggin, Steve Gorton, Anthony Haughey, Mike Linley, Ian O'Leary, Stephen Oliver, Magnus Rew, Clive Streeter, Matthew Ward.

Additional Illustrations
Richard Bonson, Brian Craker, John Fox, Paul Guest, Stephan Gyapay, Ian Henderson, Claire Littlejohn, Gillie Newman, Chris Orr, Kevin Robinson, John Woodcock, Martin Woodward.

Additional Picture Research
Miriam Sharland.

Editorial and Design
MANAGING EDITORS Vivien Crump, Helen Partington
MANAGING ART EDITOR Steve Knowlden
DEPUTY EDITORIAL DIRECTOR Douglas Amrine
DEPUTY ART DIRECTOR Gaye Allen
PRODUCTION David Proffit, Hilary Stephens
PICTURE RESEARCH Sue Mennell, Christine Rista
DTP DESIGNER Adam Moore
MAPS Gary Bowes, Margaret Slowey, Richard Toomey (ERA-Maptec, Dublin, Ireland)
MAP CO-ORDINATORS Michael Ellis, David Pugh
Marion Broderick, Margaret Chang, Martin Cropper, Guy Dimond, Fay Franklin, Yael Freudmann, Sally Ann Hibbard, Annette Jacobs, Erika Lang, Michael Osborn, Polly Phillimore, Caroline Radula-Scott.

Relaunch – Editorial and Design
EDITORIAL Fay Franklin, Anna Freiberger, Bhaswati Ghosh, Kathryn Lane, Susan Millership, Alka Thakur, Asavari Singh
FACTCHECK Des Berry
DESIGN Maite Lantaron, Baishakhee Sengupta, Shruti Singhi
PICTURE RESEARCH Ellen Root
DTP Vinod Harish, Jason Little, Shailesh Sharma
CARTOGRAPHY Uma Bhattacharya, Casper Morris, Kunal Singh

Index
Hilary Bird.

Special Assistance
Dorling Kindersley would like to thank all the regional and local tourist offices in the Republic and Northern Ireland for their valuable help. Particular thanks also to: Ralph Doak and Egerton Shelswell-White at Bantry House, Bantry, Co Cork; Vera Greif at the Chester Beatty Library and Gallery of Oriental Art, Dublin; Alan Figgis at Christ Church Cathedral, Dublin; Labhras ó Murchu at Comhaltas Ceoltóirí Éireann; Catherine O'Connor at Derry City Council; Patsy O'Connell at Dublin Tourism; Tanya Cathcart at Fermanagh Tourism, Enniskillen; Peter Walsh at the Guinness Hop Store, Dublin; Gerard Collet at the Irish Shop, Covent Garden, London; Dónall P Ó Baoill at ITE, Dublin; Pat Cooke at Kilmainham Gaol, Dublin; Angela Shanahan at the Kinsale Tourist Office; Bill Maxwell, Adrian Le Harivel and Marie McFeely at the National Gallery of Ireland, Dublin; Philip McCann at the National Library of Ireland, Dublin; Willy Cumming at the National Monuments Divison, Office of Public Works, Dublin; Eileen Dunne and Sharon Fogarty at the National Museum of Ireland, Dublin; Joris Minne at the Northern Ireland Tourist Office, Belfast; Dr Tom MacNeil at Queen's University, Belfast; Sheila Crowley at St Mary's Pro-Cathedral, Dublin; Paul Brock at the Shannon Development Centre; Tom Sheedy at Shannon Heritage and Banquets, Bunratty Castle, Co Clare; Angela Sutherland at the Shannon-Erne Waterway, Co Leitrim; Máire Ní Bháin at Trinity College, Dublin; Anne-Marie Diffley at Trinity College Library, Dublin; Pat Maclean at the Ulster Museum, Belfast; Harry Hughes at the Willie Clancy School of Traditional Music, Miltown Malbay, Co Clare.

Additional Assistance
Des Berry, Kathleen Crowley, Rory Doyle, Peter Hynes, Kate Molan, David O'Grady, Mary O'Grady, Madge Perry, Poppy, Tom Prentice.

Photography Permissions
The publisher would like to thank all those who gave permission to photograph at various cathedrals, churches, museums, restaurants, hotels, shops, galleries and other sights too numerous to list individually.

Picture Credits
tl = top left; tc = top centre; tr = top right; cla = centre left above; ca = centre above; cra = centre right above; cl = centre left; c = centre; cr = centre right; clb = centre left below; cb = centre below; crb = centre right below; bl = bottom left; bc = bottom centre; br = bottom right.

Every effort has been made to trace the copyright holders and we apologize in advance for any unintentional omissions. We would be pleased to insert the appropriate acknowledgments in any subsequent edition of this publication.

Works of art have been reproduced with the permission of the following copyright holders: © DACS, London 1995 70tr, 90tr.
The publisher would like to thank the following individuals, companies and picture libraries for permission to reproduce their photographs:

Aer Lingus/Airbus Industrie: 382tc; Akg, London: National Museum, Copenhagen/Erich Lessing 26cl; Alamy Images: BL Images Ltd 10c; Robert Harding Picture Library 322cla; Barry Mason 104b; Peter Titmus 323tl; Allsport: David Rogers 28cb; Steve Powell 47tl; Appletree Press Ltd, Belfast (Irish Proverbs © illustrations Karen Bailey) 357cl.

© Bristol City Museums and Art Gallery: 32bl; © British Library: Richard II's Campaigns in Ireland Ms.Harl.1319, f.18 37tl; © British Museum: 33bl; BT Payphones: 381cl, 381cr, 381b; Bus Éireann: 392CL; © Bushmills Ltd: 266bl.

© Central Bank of Ireland: Lady Lavery as Cathleen ni Houlihan, John Lavery 15ca, 376 (all banknotes and coins except for tr), 377; Central Cyber Café, Dublin: Finbarr Clarkson 380tr; © Chester Beatty Library, Dublin: 77t; © Classic Designs/Lj Young Ltd, Blarney: 357c; Clo Iar-Chonnachta: publishers of Litríocht agus Pobal by Gearóid Denvir 47cr; Bruce Coleman Ltd: Mark Boulton 17tr; Patrick Clement 18clb, 18bl; Adrian Davies 18br; Rodney Dawson 19cl; Frances Furlong 18tl; David Green 208bl; Pekka Helo 19cr; Jan Van de Kam 186bl; Gordon Langsbury 18cl, 186cr; John Markham 252br; George McCarthy 19tl, 19bl,19br, 138tl, 209bl; MR Phicon 18crb; Eckhart Pott 19cb; Hans Reinhard 19tcb, 162tl, 270tl; Kim Taylor 19tc, 252t; R Wanscheidt 19cbr; Uwe Walz 18cr, 185cb; G Ziesler 209bl; Corbis: Jack Fields 323c; © Cork Examiner: 29tl; © Cork Public Museum: 35cla; Joe Cornish: 19cla, 212b, 270tr, 368–9; Crawford Municipal Art Gallery: The Meeting of St Brendan and the Unhappy Judas, Harry Clarke 174bl.

Davison & Associates, Ltd, Ireland: 81cra; © The Department of the Environment, Heritage and Local Government, Ireland: 172bl, 177t, 246cl, 247tl, 247cr, 248br, 250tl; Derry City Council: 258tr; Michael Diggin: 20tl, 153b, 163cr, 164cla, 165tr, 185tl, 206bl, 225t, 226tr, 226cl, 227cra, 363tl, 363b, 364c, 371br, 373b, 375cl, 378b; Bill Doyle: 214bl; The Dubliner Magazine: Jennifer Philips 104tc, 104cr, 105br; GA Duncan: 46cb, 46bl; © Dundee Art Galleries and Museums: The Children of Lir, John Duncan 27tc.

eircom: 380tl, 380bl, 380cr; Emphics Ltd: Hayden West 362cl; ET Archive: 27bl; Mary Evans Picture

Library: 9 (inset), 24tl, 26tr, 26bl, 26br, 27cla, 34bl, 37bc, 38bl; 44bl, 53 (inset), 77cl, 89bl, 121 (inset), 281br, 287 (inset), 369 (inset).
Fáilte Ireland/Irish Tourist Board: 11c; Brian Lynch 24–25, 25tl, 246tl, 246tr, Pat Odea 360c; © Stephen Faller Ltd, Galway: 356cla; © Famine Museum Co Rosscommon: 219tr; Jim Fitzpatrick: 79bl.

Gill and MacMillan Publishers, Dublin: 45bl; Ronald Grant Archive: The Commitments, Twentieth Century Fox 23br; © Guinness Ireland Ltd: 98bl, 98br, 99tl, 99tr, 99bl, 99br.
Hulton Deutsch Collection: 22clb, 23tr, 39t, 42br, 42cbl, 46br, Reuter 47c, 62bl.

Images Colour Library: 48bl, 55tl; 229bc; Inpho, Dublin: 28cla, Billy Stickland 28br, Lorraine O'Sullivan 29br; Irish Picture Library, Dublin: 38cla, 41tl, 44tl; Irish Rail (Iarnród Éireann): 390tr; © Irish Times: 134br; © Irish Traditional Music Archive, Dublin: 25bl.

Jarrold Colour Publications: Ja Brooks 62br; Michael Jenner: 243cr.

Kennedy PR: 58cla.

Timothy Kovar: 78bl; 109tl, 114bl.

© Lambeth Palace Library, London: Plan of the London Vintners' Company Township of Bellaghy, Ulster, 1622 (ms. Carew 634 f.34) (detail) 39cra; Frank Lane Picture Agency: Roger Wilmshurst 186bc; © Leeds City Art Gallery: The Irish House of Commons, Francis Wheatley 40cla; Pat Liddy: 105tl.

Hugh Mcknight Photography: 101t; Mander and Mitcheson Theatre Collection: 24cl; Mansell Collection: 40bl, 45cra, 81bl, 268bc; Archie Miles: 208br; John Murray: 51bl, 96cl, 128c; © Museum of the City of New York: Gift of Mrs Robert M Littlejohn, The Bay and Harbor of New York 1855, Samuel B Waugh 42–43.

National Concert Hall, Dublin: Frank Fennell 115bl; © National Gallery of Ireland, Dublin: WB Yeats and the Irish Theatre, Edmund Dulac 22tr, George Bernard Shaw, John Collier 22cr, Carolan the Harper, Francis Bindon 24tr, Leixlip Castle, Irish School 41cla, The Custom House, Dublin, James Malton 41bc, Queen Victoria and Prince Albert Opening the 1853 Dublin Great Exhibition, James Mahoney 43bl, The Houseless Wanderer, JH Foley 70tl, Pierrot, Juan Gris 68tr, For the Road, JB Yeats 70cla, The Taking of Christ, Caravaggio 71cra, Judith with the Head of Holofernes, Andrea Mantegna 71cra, The Sick Call, Matthew James

Lawless 71crb, *Jonathan Swift, Satirist*, Charles Jerval 82bc, *James Joyce*, Jacques Emile Blanche 90t, *Interior with Members of a Family*, P Hussey 132br, *William Butler Yeats, Poet*, JB Yeats 233tl, *The Last Circuit of Pilgrims at Clonmacnoise*, George Petrie 250tr; © National Gallery, London: *Beach Scene*, Edgar Degas 91br; © National Library of Ireland, Dublin: 23cla, 23crb, 31b, 34tl, 34clb. 36bl, 38tl, 38clb, 40clb, 42tl, 42cla, 42bl, 43crb, 43tl, 44clb, 45tl, 45crb, *St Stephen's Green*, James Malton 52–53, 141tr, 178cra, 244b; © National Museum of Ireland, Dublin: 3, 32tl, 32clb, 32cb 32crb, 32–33, 33c 33clb, 33br, 34cla, 35cb, 35br, 55bl, 59cr, all 66–7, 101b; The National Trust, Northern Ireland: *Lord Castlereagh* after Lawrence 282tl, *Hambletonian*, George Stubbs 283tl, 283cra; The National Trust Photographic Library: Mathew Antrobus 273b, John Bethell 284tl, Patrick Pendergast 272bl, Will Webster 277br, 286–7; Nature Photographers: B Burbridge 187bc, Paul Sterry 186clb; Northern Ireland Tourist Board: 28tr, 258cl, 273tr, 358cl, 359tl; Norton Associates: 74 clb.

Kyran O'Brien 115tr; Oxford Scientific Films: Frithjof Skibbe 186tl. Pacemaker Press International, Ltd: 374bc, 374br; Walter Pfeiffer Studios, Dublin: 25tr, 25cra, 25c, 25cr, 25crb, 25br; Photo Flora: Andrew N Gagg 186br; Photostage: Donald Cooper 114tr, 115tl; Popperfoto: 46cla, 46crb, 46tr, Reuter/Crispin Rodwell 47tr; Powerscourt Estate, Enniskerry: 135c.

Range Pictures: 43cra; The Reform Club, London: 42cla; Report/Derek Spiers, Dublin: 46tr, 278bl, 278br; Retna Pictures: Chris Taylor 24bl, Jay Blakesberg 24br; Retrograph Archive, London: © Martin Ranicar-Breese 65br; Rex Features: Sipa Press 47cl, 47bc.

Shannon Development Photo Library: 360tl; Shannon-Erne Waterway: 235bc; The Slide File, Dublin: 16bc, 17t, 17c, 18cla, 18cra, 22cla, 29cra, 29clb, 29bl, 32cla, 48cla, 48bl, 49cb, 50cla, 50cra, 50cb, 50bl, 51cra, 77tr, 77br, 114br, 122cla, 129br, 38cl 138br, 151br, 185br, 211tl, 213tr, 214cb, 214br,

215bc, 224br, 227tr, 230tl, 230b, 232tr, 237b, 240tl, 242tl, 248tl, 250–51, 252cra, 270clb, 359br, 360br; Sportsfile, Dublin: 29tc; Stena Line: 384cl; Don Sutton International Photo Library: 290br. © Tate Gallery Publications: *Captain Thomas Lee*, Marcus Gheeraedts 38br; Topham Picture Source: 41br, Tim Graham 96t; Translink: 392bl; © Trinity College, Dublin: Ms.1440 (Book of Burgos) f.20v 37clb; Ms.58 (Book of Kells) f.129v 4tr, *The Marriage of Princess Aoite and the Earl of Pembroke*, Daniel Maclise 36cla, Ms.57 (Book of Durrow) f.84v 55cr, Ms.57 (Book of Durrow) f.85v 63cr, Ms.58 (Book of Kells) f.129v 64cra, Ms.58 (Book of Kells) f.36r 64cl, Ms.58 (Book of Kells) f.28v 64crb, Ms.58 (Book of Kells) f.200r 64b; Trip: R Drury 17br, 140c.

© Ulster Museum, Belfast: *The Festival of St Kevin at the Seven Churches, Glendalough*, Joseph Peacock 30, *The Relief of Derry*, William Sadler II 38–9, 39crb, 44cla, 257crb, 278clb.

Viking Ship Museum, Strandengen, Denmark: watercolour by Flemming Bau 35tl.

© Waterford Corporation: 35bl, 36tl, 36clb, 37bl; © Writers Museum, Dublin: 22tl.

Peter Zöller: 14, 16tl, 48tc, 48cr, 49cra, 49bl, 146br, 200, 216–17, 219bl, 220, 236, 249tr, 364br.

Front endpaper: all commissioned photography with the exception of Peter Zöller: tl, tc, cb.

Jacket
Front – Corbis: Richard Cummins main image; DK Images: Tim Daly bl.

Back – DK Images: Joe Cornish cla, bl; Alan Williams clb, tl.
Spine – Corbis: Richard Cummins t; Walter Pfeiffer Studios, Dublin: b.

All other images © Dorling Kindersley.
For further information see www.DKimages.com

DORLING KINDERSLEY SPECIAL EDITIONS

Dorling Kindersley books can be purchased in bulk quantities at discounted prices for use in promotions or as premiums. We are also able to offer special editions and personalized jackets, corporate imprints, and excerpts from all of our books, tailored specifically to meet your own needs.

To find out more, please contact: (in the United Kingdom) **Sarah.Burgess@dk.com** or **Special Sales,** Dorling Kindersley Limited, 80 Strand, London WC2R 0RL; (in the United States) Special Markets Dept, DK Publishing, Inc., 375 Hudson Street, New York, NY 10014.

EYEWITNESS TRAVEL INSURANCE

FOR PEACE OF MIND ABROAD
we've got it covered **wherever you are**

For an **instant quote** on quality worldwide travel insurance visit **www.dk.com/travel-insurance** or call:

- **USA** 1 800 749 4922 (Toll Free)
- **UK** 0800 258 5363
- **Australia** 1300 669 999
- **New Zealand** 0800 55 99 11
- **Canada** www.dk.com/travel-insurance
- **Worldwide** +44 870 894 0001

Cover provided to residents of over 46 countries for virtually every kind of trip

Please quote our ref: Eyewitness Travel Guides

Insurance is arranged through and provided by Columbus Travel Insurance Services Ltd (trading as Columbus Direct), Advertiser House, 19 Bartlett St, Croydon, CR2 6TB . Columbus Direct is authorised and regulated by the Financial Services Authority.

COLUMBUS

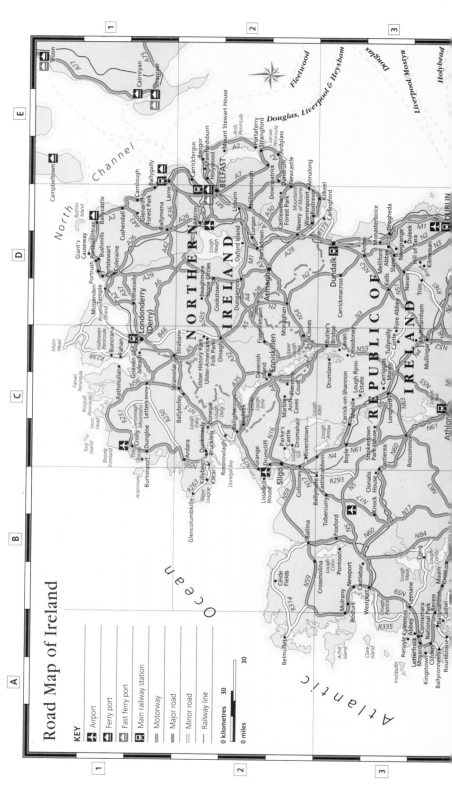